ATLANTIC STUDIES ON SOCIETY IN CHANGE

NO. 66

Editor-in Chief, Béla K. Király

Associate Editor-in-Chief, Peter Pastor

Assistant Editor, Edit Völgyesi

Sándor Bíró

THE NATIONALITIES PROBLEM IN TRANSYLVANIA 1867-1940

A SOCIAL HISTORY OF THE ROMANIAN MINORITY UNDER HUNGARIAN RULE, 1867-1918 AND OF THE HUNGARIAN MINORITY UNDER ROMANIAN RULE, 1918-1940

Translated from the Hungarian Original by

Mario D. Fenyo

Social Science Monographs, Boulder, Colorado
Atlantic Research and Publications,
Highland Lakes, New Jersey

Distributed by Columbia University Press, New York
1992

EAST EUROPEAN MONOGRAPHS, NO. CCCXXXIII

Library of Congress Catalog Card Number 91-62217
ISBN 0-88033-228-X
Printed in the United States of America

Table of Contents

Part I
The Romanian Minority Under
Hungarian Rule, 1867-1918

Part II
The Hungarian Minority Under
Romanian Rule, 1918-1940

Acknowledgments

Atlantic Research and Publications, Inc. conducts research, organizes conferences, administers scholar exchanges, and publishes books in the series "Atlantic Studies on Society in Change." The Soros Foundation has generously contributed funds in support of the various projects of ARP, including the translation of this monograph. Further financial support for the publication of this book was provided by Mr. Elemér Nyárády of Bolton, Connecticut, and by the American Transylvanian Federation under the presidency of the late Béla Teleki. The indexes were prepared by Ms. Edit Völgyesi, and copy editing was done by Ms. Jane Clancy and Ms. Jean Cornelisse. Professor Ignác Romsics had the maps prepared at the Magyarságkutató Intézet, Budapest. To all these individuals and institutions I wish to express my sincere appreciation and thanks.

Highland Lakes, NJ   Béla K. Király
October 23, 1991   Professor Emeritus of History

Preface to the Series

The present volume is a component of a series that, then completed, will constitute a comprehensive survey of the many aspects of East Central European society. These volumes deal with the peoples whose homelands lie between the Germans to the west, the Russians to the east and north, and the Mediterranean and Adriatic seas to the south. They constitute a civilization that is at once an integral part of Europe yet substantially different from the West. The area is characterized by rich variety in language, religion, and government. The study of this complex subject demands a multidisciplinary approach and, accordingly, our contributors represent several academic disciplines. They have been drawn from universities and other scholarly institutions in the United States, Canada, Western Europe, and East Central Europe.

The author of the present volume, Sándor Bíró (1907-1975), was a distinguished historian in Hungary. Because of the political atmosphere during the Kádár era, his manuscript was not considered by Hungarian publishers for publication, nor was the author offered the usual editorial advice for revising the manuscript. The work was eventually published in Switzerland under the title *Kisebbségben és többségben. Románok és magyarok 1867-1940* (Bern, 1989). When Professor Bíró's manuscript was considered for translation and publication in this series, it was decided by the Editor-in-Chief that the posthumous English language publication would follow the original text with minor corrections.

The Editor-in-Chief, of course takes full responsibility for ensuring the comprehensiveness, cohesion, internal balance, and scholarly quality of the series he has launched. I cheerfully accept this responsibility and do not intend this work to be a condemnation of the policies, attitudes, and activities of any of the persons involved. At the same time, because the contributors represent so many different disciplines, interpretations, and schools of thought, our policy, as in past and future volumes, is to present their contributions without modification.

B.K.K.

Foreword

In examining this topic the author undertakes a task which, in the past, has led only to partial or one-sided attempts at solution. Yet the topic's significance goes well beyond Eastern European historiography. The issue had an indirect impact on Europe in general, along both military and political lines. I am referring, in particular, to the Southeastern European theater in World War I and World War II, and to the uninhibited exploitation of Romanian-Hungarian tension by the great powers. Had the relationship between these two nations been characterized by mutual understanding, had the great powers been unable to pit them against one another, then the events on the Southeastern theater of operations in the world wars would have taken a different course.

To be sure, Romanian-Hungarian relations leave a lot to be desired even nowadays [1975]. Although both nations form part of a military alliance under the aegis of the same ideology, and have identical interests in a number of significant areas, the relations between the two are far from satisfactory. This relationship is deeply affected by the present condition and prospects of the approximately two million Hungarians living in Romania. The assessment of this situation and the prospects of the Hungarian ethnic group are the nodal points which reveal the tension in the relations between the two nations.

To the superficial observer, it may seem as if there were no special problems in this relationship. The official pronouncements reveal no sign of any kind of tension. The leaders of the town countries refer to the people of the other country as "fraternal people" and to the respective states as "fraternal Romania" or "fraternal Hungary". The treaty of mutual friendship and collaboration between the two countries was renewed not long ago. The Hungarian leaders have repeatedly asserted they fully recognize the territorial integrity of Romania, and have no territorial claims against that country. Hungarian historiography brands and condemns the manifestations of Hungarian nationalism, a topic on which a special monograph has been published in Hungary. The nationalist point of view has been deleted from the Hungarian educational system and from the textbooks. Hence, on the surface of it, everything is all right regarding Hungarian-Romanian relations.

However, concealed passions are boiling in Transylvania. Almost everyone in Hungary has friends or relatives living in Transylvania. They keep in touch, they visit one another often. On such occasions they become eyewitnesses to and direct observers of what the Hungarians of Transylvania are undergoing. Only rarely, after considerable effort and at the cost of overcoming immense obstacles is it possible for Hungarians living under Romanian rule to obtain a passport. Often they become victims of painful discrimination in favor of Romanians when seeking employment or promotion and when seeking admittance to a university. The administration has found special devices to squeeze the Hungarians out of the cities of Transylvania and to replace them with large masses of Romanians brought in from other areas. Members of the Hungarian intelligentsia are deliberately transferred to purely Romanian areas — usually to the provinces of the *Regat* (Old Romania) — while Romanians who cannot even understand the Hungarian language are relocated to Hungarian areas. Specialized training is offered only in Romanian. By this process, and by the administration of examinations for admission, those young Hungarians who have not perfectly mastered the Romanian language are excluded from institutions of higher learning. They are prevented from improving themselves materially and socially. Newspapers and literary works from Hungary can be obtained only with the greatest difficulty. Such developments unavoidably remind the Hungarians of Romanian chauvinism in the period between the two world wars; yet, according to the Romanian interpretation, the above phenomena derive not from nationalist sentiment, but from a justified effort to compensate for the mistakes of the past.

Indeed, it is the past, particularly the recent past, the past 120 years, which gave rise to the greatest number of disagreements and contradictions among the representatives of the scientific and political communities of the two people. In these debates historical facts intermingle with prejudice, distortions, and unlikely assertions that have become second nature for a long time now. The basic explanation of this peculiar situation is to be sought in the circumstance that, for well-nigh fifty years, both sides have recoiled from confronting historical truth. Neither Hungarian nor Romanian public opinion is willing to acknowledge that part of history which is emotionally reprehensible to it. Of course, this state of mind has historical precedents as well.

The precedents go back to the mid-nineteenth century. In 1838, at the instigation of the ambassador of the Polish Prince Adam Georg Czartoryski, the Romanian Principalities secretly formulated the political objective of the Greater Romania: the unification of all Romanians under one rule. Among those who signed the pertinent declaration was the Orthodox bishop of Buran, Cesario, who made the participants swear that this programmatic declaration would remain strictly secret. In this period the Romanians of Hungary, Transylvania, and Bukovina were under Habsburg rule, those of Bessarabia under Russian rule, and those of Wallachia and Moldavia under Ottoman domination. Their unification aimed to overthrow the domination of the three neighboring great powers, an endeavor which, of course, the latter regarded as jeopardizing their interests. Hence the secrecy was warranted. Some of the Romanian leaders of the Transylvania also agreed with the aim of unification of all Romanians, although they never referred to the matter openly in that period.

In the Hungarian War of Independence of 1848-49 the Hungarians clashed with the Romanians who supported Austria. The Romanians sided with Austria because they could expect more from the latter than from the Hungarians. But they were disappointed in their expectations. It is true that Austria did not recognize the reunion of Transylvania with Hungary that had been voted into law in 1848; moreover, between 1861 and 1865, in order to put pressure on the Hungarians, Austria employed mainly Romanian officials in the counties of Transylvania. The majority of the extremely-mixed population of the Grand Principality of Transylvania, which continued to be ruled from Vienna, was already Romanian. But Austria, having reached a compromise with the Hungarians in 1867, recognized the laws of 1848; Transylvania once again became an integral part of Hungary and Romanians there came under Hungarian rule. From then on Romanian leaders regarded Hungary and the Hungarians as the greatest obstacle to their goal of a Greater Romania. They resorted to every possible means to overcome this obstacle. Influencing public opinion within and abroad came to be one of their most effective means. Thus the attack against the Dual Monarchy was launched. "We must compromise that regime," was the watchword of the newspaper of the Romanian ethnic group in Transylvania, the *Tribuna* of Nagyszeben [Sibiu] which engaged in a struggle against the Hungarian state and the Hungarians over a period of twenty years. The state, and Hungarian rule in general, were criticized and attacked in their papers, in their pamphlets, political and otherwise (for censorship was unknown in the period of the Dual Monarchy), orally and in writing, inside and outside the country. The regime was accused of barbaric repression, of compulsory Hungarianization, of perpetrating "Asiatic" administrative abuses, of impeding the civilization and culture of the Romanians. For a long time the Hungarians did not take this campaign seriously, and the Romanian side was able to gain a number of advantages.

Public opinion in Romania, and eventually in the Entente countries, increasingly sympathized with the Romanian arguments. A special agency, the famous Romanian League of Culture, was founded in Bucharest to mastermind this propaganda. The academic propaganda work was carried out by well-known Romanian scholars through works written in French and German. Those French and British scholars who, in the interest of the foreign policy of their country, were intent on weakening the Austro-Hungarian Monarchy, allied as it was with Germany, soon sided with them. Thus the Hungarian-Romanian conflict became a function of the rivalry and struggle between the blocs of great powers and systems of military alliances.

From that time to our day great power interests played a decisive role in the evolution of Romanian-Hungarian relations. The basic causes of the contradiction, the actual facts of the living conditions of the two peoples, became increasingly hazy behind the continuously-renewed conflict between Romanian and Hungarian leaders. Since 1867 the impact of propaganda only enhanced this haze both inside and outside the country. This development strikes us as unavoidable, given the complexity and contradictory nature of the social, economic, and cultural relations of the two peoples sharing the same area. Even those directly acquainted with the situation often tended to misjudge the true situation of the Romanians and Hungarians. The principal obstacle to a realistic appraisal of the situation derived from the geographical circumstances of the Hungarian and Romanian settlements and their historical evolution. Settlement by Romanians and Hungarians resulted in an intricately-subdivided and often ethnically-mixed situation. In certain areas there were numbers of villages where Romanians, Hungarians, and Saxons intermingled. It was not unusual to find a purely Hungarian village next to a community half Romanian and half Hungarian, with a Saxon town nearby. The Romanians constituted the majority in the counties nearest the *Regat* in Southern Transylvania and in the North. To the East the border counties of Csík [Ciuc] and Háromszék [Trei Scaune] formed a Hungarian block along with the inhabitants of the counties of Udvarhely [Odorhei] and Maros-Torda [Mureş-Turda]. The inhabitants of these counties are the Székelys. Central Transylvania was inhabited by a mixed Romanian-Hungarian population, the majority varying from district to district. In the Hungarian regions to the west of historical Transylvania, the so-called *Partium*, i.e. the counties of Máramaros [Maramureş], Bihar [Bihor], Arad, and Temes [Timiş] the population was likewise mixed: Hungarians, Romanians, Slovaks, Serbians, and Germans living side by side.

The Saxons, as the descendants of German settlers were called, constituted the majority in certain towns and regions of Brassó [Braşov], Küküllő [Tîrnava], Beszterce [Bistriţa] counties. In other areas, such as the Királyföld, the original settlement area of the Saxons, they were soon outnumbered by the dynamically proliferating Romanians. An accurate geographical survey of the settlement relations was not an easy task, even for the native analysts. In order to gain accurate information it was absolutely necessary to become acquainted with the languages of the three ethnic groups living there, as well as to acquire a thorough knowledge of the evolution which determined the prevailing situation. Under the given circumstances, the authors of articles and essays written for the sake of winning-over public opinion discussed these issues in oversimplified terms. Instead of writing of a mixed population, they referred to areas with a Romanian majority, to the need for Romanian autonomy, to guaranteeing the rights of the majority while keeping silent about the relative Hungarian majority at the time of the Dual Monarchy, or about other nationalities in the area. To those who advocated irredentism, the simplest solution, of course, was to unite the areas "inhabited by Romanians" with the *Regat.* Since, however, the counties with a Hungarian majority were surrounded by areas with a Romanian majority, and the areas with a mixed population could not be sorted out on the basis of geography, union with Romania would have meant the absorption of more than one million Hungarians into an eventual Greater Romania. It was clear to those acquainted with the situation that, in the long run, this would lead to the oppression of the Hungarian and Saxon ethnic groups; even the demand for Romanian autonomy — according to the Romanian writer Ion Slavici — concealed this intention.

The attacks against the Hungarian state and the Hungarian leaders derived from a mixture of real offenses, of administrative abuses, and of distortion by deliberately overlooking certain facts. The Romanian regime had reason to be satisfied with the results obtained by these attacks. The assertion that Romanians were suffering oppression under Hungarian rule became generally accepted both within the country and abroad. It eventually turned into a slogan taken for granted and found a place even in serious historical studies down to the very present.

The centuries-old dream of the unification of all Romanians was realized through the Greater Romania created under the terms of the Trianon Peace Treaty of June 4, 1920. By the same token, however, almost two million Hungarians came under Romanian rule. The Saxons of Transylvania, the Russians of Bessarabia, and the Bulgarians of the Dobrudja suffered a similar fate. Thus, Romania became a multinational state in which every fourth inhabitant was a member of an ethnic group other than Romanian. The so-called Minority Agreement was formulated at the Paris Peace Conference for their protection. The Romanian regime in power at the time objected to this agreement, and opted to resign rather than sign it. The liberal cabinet led by Ion C. Brătianu had to be replaced by a new regime which accepted the treaty. This hesitation, however, was a bad omen regarding the future of the agreement.

Indeed, the Hungarian press of the following years resounded with protests against the oppressive Romanian policies on nationalities. The Romanian-Hungarian tension became sharper once again; politicians and associations repeatedly issued statements regarding the offenses committed against the Hungarians of Transylvania. The background of these polemics were attempts to revise the Treaty of Trianon, or to maintain it. Both sides, Hungarians and Romanians alike, sought the support of domestic and foreign public opinion. A real flood of articles, of geographical and historical monographs written in diverse languages were published to prove the validity of the Hungarian or Romanian thesis. This time the two parties struggled from different bases, from inverted roles; before World War I the Romanian side attacked while the Hungarian side was on the defensive, but after Trianon it was the Romanian side that had to assume a defensive position in the face of Hungarian criticism of the Romanian nationalities policies. The struggle was determined from the start by the fact that the Hungarian objective was the revision of the Peace Treaty, while the Romanian objective was the maintenance of the status quo. The nature, sequence, reception, and effectiveness of the arguments were all a function of this factor. The Hungarian polemicists stressed the shortcomings of the Trianon Treaty, its injustices, its disregard of the Wilsonian principles, and historical evolution, all for the sake of revision. Those who represented the Romanian point of view argued in favor of the status quo on the grounds of the absolute majority of the Romanian population in Transylvania or the oppressive nature of Hungarian rule in the period of the Dual Monarchy, and referred to Romania's patient nationalities policy. They felt far more secure than the authors of the Hungarian publications attacking them. The absolute majority of Romanians in Romania and on Transylvanian territory was an undeniable reality, and this majority could only grow as a result of the expulsion of 200,000 Hungarians and by other maneuvers to decrease the numbers of Hungarians. The Hungarian arguments brought up against the Treaty of Trianon had but little effect on Romania's former

and new allies (the Little Entente). The general diplomatic lineup that
evolved after the war favored the Romanians. The leading role in the
diplomacy of Central and Southern Europe was played by France who,
it so happened, had likewise played a leading role in the formulation of
the Treaty of Trianon. It was also French influence that dominated the
League of Nations at Geneva. The Romanians could always count on
the active support of French diplomacy. On the other hand, Hungary
remained isolated because of its right-wing domestic policies, the
scandal of the forged French francs, and other reasons. Albeit some
circles in the United Kingdom, prompted by envy of French influence,
did express certain critical opinions regarding the policies of the Little
Entente as supported by France, official British foreign policy could not
be expected to favor revisionist moves. Once Adolf Hitler came to power
in 1933, Hungary gradually joined the anti-western Axis powers,
expecting support for its territorial claims from those quarters. Thus,
once again, the Hungarian-Romanian conflict was allowed to sink to the
level of a function of great-power rivalry. The Hungarian and Romanian authors who participated in the polemics naturally conformed to the
position taken by their respective governments.

In the situation that prevails in 1975, the outcome of familiar
factors, there can no longer be an open Hungarian-Romanian conflict.
Nor is it the intention of the author of these lines to upset this
beneficial (in many ways) armistice. Hence our work differs, in its
objective, in its structure, and in its choice of sources, from the
polemical writings mentioned above. Instead of stressing historical
arguments and territorial claims, its objective is to reveal the living
conditions of the Romanians under Hungarian rule in the period before
1918 and of the Hungarians under Romanian rule from 1918 to 1940.
In their evolution and consequences these conditions offer many lessons
bearing upon Hungarian-Romanian relations in the future. It is clear
that the survival, prosperity, or destruction of every ethnic group living
under foreign rule depends on conditions affecting different aspects of
existence. What are the most important conditions for the survival of
ethnic groups? In the opinion of the author these conditions may be
grouped under the following five categories:

1. Existential conditions, i.e. economic factors.
2. Circumstances affecting the use of the language of the nationality.
3. Religious life.
4. Opportunities for preserving the culture of the nationality.
5. The conditions for validating human and citizens' rights.

In the author's opinion, it is only by examining conditions according to these categories that light can be shed on the actual life of the nationality concerned, and that it becomes possible, both for Hungarians and Romanians, to acknowledge the mistakes of the past and to carry out serious soul-searching. It is hardly possible to imagine a Romanian-Hungarian reconciliation, long overdue, on any other basis. None of the previous studies in this field have even attempted such an approach: i.e. to present the living conditions of Romanians and Hungarians on the basis of sources from the two historical periods. Our approach determines the nature of the sources to be used. Clearly, the true conditions of Romanians and Hungarians can only be unraveled through those sources which depict them in their most favorable light. In previous treatments of the subject the main sources have been laws and ordinances, official pronouncements, and historical events, as well as the often-conflicting statistical data. Neither laws nor ordinances can provide a true picture of living conditions since it is their manner of application and the activities of the executive agencies that carry the regulations into life. The author has relied, as his main primary source, on items in dailies and periodicals illustrating everyday life and comparing and contrasting these with the texts of the laws and ordinances; and also using occasional publications, pamphlets, popular calendars depicting the life of the people, etc. The picture that emerges from the sources listed above differs markedly from what the public of Hungary and Romania and the international public has been able to perceive.

What traits characterize the picture that emerges before the reader from the study of living conditions based on the categories above? The evolution of the relations of the five categories has not been straightforward during either one of the periods. This evolution depended on the nationalities policies of the prevailing regimes and on economic laws.

Both the Hungarian governments of the Dual Monarchy and the governments of Greater Romania considered and dealt with nationalities issues from a more or less nationalist point of view. But the extent of state interference in the case of the Romanians of the Dual Monarchy in the life of the nationalities and the nature of the methods of intervention and their impact differed radically from that of the Hungarians under Romanian rule. The results of the process were also different. Under the Hungarian rule of the Dual Monarchy the Romanians grew stronger economically, socially, and in their national consciousness. In contrast, the majority of the Hungarians of Romania became impoverished; their economic, social, and cultural development came to a halt. Their national consciousness, however, did become stronger and their literature began to blossom. Interestingly and encouragingly, during both periods well-intentioned understanding and even cooperation prevailed over the spirit of impatient nationalism. This explains the fact that the general picture, whether in relation to Hungarian or to Romanian rule, is not entirely negative. Under some of the categories living conditions became darker and more depressing, while they grew brighter under others. If the objective of the nationalities policy of the ruling circles in Hungary or Romania was to thwart the national consciousness of the Romanian or Hungarian ethnic groups who were regarded as the enemy, they failed to achieve this end during either one of the periods under consideration. It is true that some individuals did assimilate for the sake of advancement or as a result of administrative pressure, while others became indifferent or cosmopolitan. But the majority not only persisted in their nationality but became decidely richer and more resilient, in their national consciousness. The official nationalities policy elicited dislike, often even hatred, towards those who dominated from either ethnic group. This feeling, while understandable, resulted in further unfortunate developments and poisoned the atmosphere between the two people. This is the most dangerous heritage of the nationalities policy of Hungarian rule in the Dual Monarchy period and of the Romanian rule from 1918 to 1940.

Only by means of a sincere confrontation with the past can the poisoned atmosphere be ventilated, can hatred be dissolved. This was the consideration which prompted the author of these lines to tackle the issue. We felt we would be serving the cause of understanding between the two people if we were to contribute to revealing those actual living conditions which best describe the Romanians of Transylvania in the period of the Dual Monarchy, and the Hungarians in the period of Romanian rule between 1918 and 1940. The description of these living conditions on the basis of authentic sources can only contribute to the evolution of a more objective perspective and to — more accurate information for the general public. It would provide both sides with an opportunity for self-examination and for a sincere acknowledgement of the sins of the past. By closing down the painful chapters of the past, the confrontation of these mistakes becomes a prerequisite for advancing, with purified souls, towards a fresh start in Romanian-Hungarian relations, based on better mutual understanding and mutual good will.

Budapest, January 1975

Dr. Sándor Bíró

Part I

The Romanian Minority Under
Hungarian Rule, 1867-1918

Chapter I

The Welfare of the Romanians and Their Means of Livelihood

The economic situation of the peoples of Central and Southeastern Europe in the 19th century was determined by two decisive developments. One was the collapse of a system based on serfdom, i.e. the emancipation of the serfs; the other was the inauguration of a new economic system: modern capitalism. Of course, these two decisive developments occurred at different times, under varying circumstances, and with varying results among each people and in each country. The economic conditions of particular nations evolved according to whether the abolition of serfdom and the inauguration of a capitalist system came about under favorable or unfavorable conditions.

The emancipation of the serfs, which signified a profound change in the life of the Romanian people, occurred in 1848. The abolition of serf obligations was proclaimed first in Hungary, then in Transylvania, in response to the revolutionary demands presented by the middle ranks of the Hungarian nobility. In other words, the feudal system came to an end for the various nationalities living on Hungarian lands as a result of the Hungarian revolution much sooner than in neighboring Russia, or in the two Romanian principalities. As is commonly known, the peasants of the tsarist empire were emancipated from the burdens of serfdom in 1861, but those of the Romanian principalities only in 1884.

The Evolution of the Romanian Peasantry's Situation.

Since the great majority of Romanians* were serfs, the abolition of serfdom in 1848, fundamentally altered their material conditions. As one Romanian author noted: "The liberation of village households from the robot and the tithe, signified a rebirth for these households as

---

* The term "Romanian", as used in this study, usually refers to the Romanians living in Hungarian territory of the Dual Monarchy, that is, to all Romanians living in the countries of Hungary and of Transylvania.

1

regards their material and social well-being."[1] Before 1848 the former
serfs held serf plots ranging between 19 and 30 *holds*,* depending on
the quality of the soil. Consequently, after 1848:

> the economic condition of the Transylvanian peasantry became
> bearable, in fact in certain places the peasantry even prospered...
> the peasant class visibly enjoyed economic well-being from 1848
> to 1900. Our villages were flourishing, with well-kept farms.[2]

This favorable economic situation of the Romanian peasantry
resulted from political circumstances. And these favorable conditions
in turn were the result of the Hungarian War of Independence of 1848-
49. As we know, an armed struggle evolved between the Hungarians
and the Habsburg dynasty in 1848, under the leadership of the
Hungarian nobility. In this struggle the majority of the Romanians
participated alongside the Habsburgs, against the Hungarians. Once
the Habsburgs succeeded, with Russian help, to quench the Hungarian
fight for freedom in blood, the country was governed by an autocratic
regime from 1849 to 1867. This absolutistic regime was characterized
by anti-Hungarian measures designed to take revenge on the Hungarians for the revolution and the war of independence. Because the
Romanians had supported the Habsburgs in 1848-49, the authorities
applied the Hungarian laws aimed at the abolition of feudalism in such
a way as to protect the interests of the former Romanian serfs; in other
words, in all disputed matters, the Austrian authorities were wont to
favor the Romanian peasant against the Hungarian nobility. As a
Romanian writer observed, the Austrians "had the interest of the people
[i.e. the Romanian people] at heart," and the law regarding the abolition
of serfdom was "regarded as merely the restitution of lost rights."[3]
Thus the imperial order issued in 1853 and its execution bore the
interest of the people in mind. Through this order Francis Joseph
legalized the squatting rights emanating from the occupation of lands
which had taken place when the serfs received the news of the
emancipation in 1848. At that moment the emancipated peasants
immediately moved onto those land and meadows which until then were
used by tenant farmers and cotters. The explicit order of 1853 by the
Emperor was to the effect that the

---

* A *hold* is equal to .057 hectares of land.

Purchases of Land by the Romanian Peasantry.

The well-to-do Romanian peasants were able to purchase significant amounts of land in several areas. Taking advantage of the indebtedness of the Hungarian smallholders, they bought up lands, increasing their own holdings. Their land-purchasing activities were promoted by the loan policies of the fast-growing Romanian banks. The first Romanian bank, the Albina, was founded in 1872. Within two decades more than fifty Romanian banks were founded along the same formula. Most of these were altruistic banks striving, first of all, to strengthen the Romanians economically and help them acquire land. Practically all these banks made the objectives of the Albina their own: namely, according to one paragraph of their basic statutes, "to obtain the means necessary for maintaining and developing the farms of the Romanian peasantry; to awaken in them the spirit of thrift, improve their credit and promote national economic interests." Of course, the Romanian banks also awarded loans to the intelligentsia, including lawyers and bank officials, thus promoting the wealth of the stratum of middle-size landowners among the Romanians. It seems, however, that the peasants were adequately represented among the buyers of the land. The case of the Romanian peasants of Kristyór [Criştior] was not an isolated instance. In about 1880 four-fifths of the farms in this area were in the hands of the Hungarian nobility. Fifteen years later the ratio was exactly the reverse for, in the meantime, the Romanians had bought up four-fifths of the farms and only one-fifth remained in Hungarian hands.[23]

It is difficult, today, to determine the total amount of land purchased by the peasants prior to 1900, for the statistics mention only the numbers of Romanian purchasers without any reference to social status. Slavici, one of the foremost experts on conditions in the period of the Compromise, states that in the space of fifty years, from 1850 to 1900, "the land owned by Romanians in the kingdom of Hungary increased tenfold."[24] According to certain authors the land purchased by Romanians from the beginning of the Compromise to the turn of the century amounted to close to one million *holds.*

At the end of the century the pace of purchases of holdings by peasants slowed down temporarily; in some areas the peasant farms even suffered bankruptcy. As Slavici noted:

> Lightly-contracted loans, successive years of bad harvests, lack of cash, the decrease in the number of animals, but most of all the lack of intensive and sensible exploitation of the land

gave the already unfavorable economic situation an aspect of economic crisis.

All this led to an even greater misfortune: the sale of farms, the consequence of which was the "atomization of peasant holdings" and the growth of the large estates. "Many a well-organized farm disappeared mainly as a result of two sins: alcoholism and senseless spending. These and many other sins, especially the lack of sensible exploitation, deeply and mercilessly undermined the basis of the peasant economy."[25]

The peasant holdings were often bought up by members of the Romanian intelligentsia and by those Romanian landowners who already owned sizable holdings. Often their acquisition of land was promoted by the very banks which had placed the land of the indebted peasants under auction. This resulted in considerable backlash, not only among Romanians but even in Hungarian circles. A Hungarian daily brought up the matter, condemning the procedures employed by the Romanian banks which, in many places, resulted in a major blow to the Romanian peasantry. The *Tribuna*, the daily of the Romanian chauvinists, took up the cudgels in defense of the banks, while admitting that errors had been committed by them. The Romanian daily wrote in its reply:

> We also know that the foundations on which these banks were built were not always the healthiest. We cannot claim that those who obliged peasants to sign bills for a three-month period, while well aware that they wouldn't be able to repay in less than a year, have acted morally. We do not deny that there are Romanians here and there who take advantage of the straitened circumstances of their brothers from the village, of their lack of competence, of their naivety, and who entice them into business deals that are not appropriate to their economic condition. We are also aware of cases of inhuman exploitation, and we know of lawyers who have bought up farms auctioned off for no good reason at ridiculously low prices.[26]

Often there seemed only one way left to the indebted and bankrupt peasant: emigration to America. Indeed, this was the period when many a Romanian peasant emigrated from Hungary. True enough, emigration affected the whole country, without distinction of nationality. Though a relatively larger number of Hungarian peasants opted for emigration, the phenomenon frightened the Romanian press and public ment and enrichment of the peasant class," as the author already quoted has observed.[49] The organization of cooperatives on the Raiffeisen model started in 1893. The first of these was organized that year by an association of Nagyszeben, called the *Reuniunea Română de Argricultură* at Veresmart [Roşia Săsească]. By 1913 this association had promoted a further 24 cooperatives in the county of Szeben. By that time there were altogether 72 cooperatives on the Raiffeisen model operating in areas of the country inhabited by Romanians.

These cooperatives came into existence primarily for the purpose of promoting the purchases of land. The example of the community of Egerszeg [Cornăţel] in the county of Maros-Torda was rather typical. Here, in 1901, 103 residents united to purchase an estate of 400 *holds* belonging to a count. They bought not only the estate for 80,000 crowns, but the residence and the annexes as well. In 1907 they managed a further purchase. For the sum of 58,000 crowns, 125 peasant members of the cooperative bought a nobleman's estate of 200 *holds*, along with his manor house on the outskirts of the village. Thereby "the Romanian inhabitants of the community became lords over the estate wherein their ancestors had worked as serfs."[50]

Because of such promising results the Greater Romanian Cultural Association, Astra decided to take over the management of cooperatives. Its expert travelled throughout the central portions of Transylvania as well as to villages in the north-western part where no cooperatives had yet been formed. He presented his proposal, according to which there was a dire need for organizing cooperatives in these places, to counter the practice of usury. But there was unexpected resistance to the proposal, not on the part of the Hungarian authorities, but rather from the Romanian banks. The latter were worried lest their own financial interests suffer in the face of this unexpected rise of competing cooperatives. Therefore, with the help of the intelligentsia which had a vested interest in the banks, they attempted to hamper the organizational efforts of Astra. Nevertheless, Astra did succeed in establishing 24 new cooperatives by 1915, overcoming many internal obstacles.

While the loan cooperatives rendered good service to the Romanian peasantry in many locations, the consumer cooperatives were unable to consolidate in the villages. The first such cooperative was formed at Balázsfalva [Blaj] in 1890. Until the First World War there were no more than eight such cooperatives, and eventually all had to close.

Unlike these independent Romanian consumer cooperatives, those branch cooperatives established in the Romanian villages which joined a central organization of the Hungarian cooperatives prospered and

rendered good service to the Romanian villages under the protection of
the head office. The people of Naszód were the ones to initiate the
movement at the turn of the century. Their representative, one
Daniello, got in touch with the managers of the Hangya in Budapest
and at Enyed/Nagyenyed [Aiud], as well as with the main cooperative
of the Saxons in Nagyszeben. At the main office of the Saxons he was
told that they would not accept Romanian members because the Saxon
cooperative central office could only serve the interests of the Saxon
nation. But the central office of the Hangya at Budapest and Enyed
were more than willing to accept the proposed Romanian cooperatives
as members, first of all because — according to the Romanian report —
this association was not strictly along nationality lines, and "those 900-
odd consumer cooperatives which had been established throughout the
country in the space of ten years were founded among the nationalities
without any national discrimination whatever."[51] Both Budapest and
Enyed accepted the Romanians on the basis of complete autonomy.
"Thus," the author of the report wrote, "we could prepare our ground
rules, organize, and manage our cooperative the way we liked. This
should have a reassuring effect on those who showed some hesitation,
whether because of our nationality or because they feared loss of
autonomy."[52] The Hangya main office was very helpful to the new
Romanian cooperative, and the help provided by it was always to the
advantage of the members whether at the moment of foundation, at the
time of shipments, or when representation was needed before the
authorities. The management of the cooperative resorted to the
following sensible argument to undo those Romanians who objected to
joining a "foreign" head office: The correspondent of the newspaper
stated:

> We must accept help from wherever it comes. Let us not
> reject it merely on the grounds of national sentiment, merely
> because this help happens to come from a foreign association....
> We must keep turning in the direction from which we may
> expect help to improve our own and our nation's material
> situation because, as you well know, nowadays it is economics
> that plays the most important role in the life of nations.[53]

Several Romanian villages did indeed understand the rationality of the
argument and joined up with the Hangya center in Budapest. In
addition to Naszód, the Romanian communities of Solymos [Şoimuş],
Kisrebra [Rebrişoara] and Szálva [Salva] also founded consumer and
profit cooperatives on the Hangya basis. Eventually 25 more Romanian

villages established similar organizations. Oltszakadát, a village in the county of Szeben, where Judge Prie was able to obtain significant state support, thanks to the Hangya organization, had such a cooperative.

Where there were no autonomous Hangya branches, great poverty often prevailed. This was the situation in villages built near large estates. The Romanians of such villages lived under deplorable conditions particularly in the central counties of Transylvania and the northeastern areas. The Romanian researcher we have quoted several times ascribed the great poverty to the considerable power of the Hungarian landowners, but he added that "to a certain extent, it can also be attributed to the lack of concern, understanding and scruples on the part of the intelligentsia, many of whom exploit the peasants just as much as the foreigners."[54]

Of course, it would be unfair to generalize regarding the poverty of the villages, or regarding the attitude of the great landowners. According to the publication of the Iuliu Enescu brothers, almost every community had its own property. The wealthiest communities were the Saxon settlements in the counties of Brassó, Nagy-Küküllő, Szeben, Beszterce-Naszód, Temes, Torontál, Krassó-Szörény, Bihar, and Arad. Of course, the excellent soil in the latter counties contributed to the prosperity of the villagers. The poorest villages were to be found in the counties of Szolnok-Doboka, Alsó-Fehér, Máramaros, and Torda-Aranyos.[55]

On the other hand, we know of individual Hungarian landowners who did help the population of the villages in the vicinity of their estates with charitable deeds; this was the case with Károly Torma, the governor of Zaránd [Zarand] county, landowner Károly Huszár of Honoros [Honoriei] and Lugoskisfalu [Satu Mic], as well as Count Domokos Zichy, landowner at Major [Maieru] and several others. The good deeds of Huszár impressed even one of the representatives of the normally anti-Hungarian Romanian press. As soon as he settled in a Romanian village of Krassó-Szörény he immediately gave away 48 *holds* of land to the village. Then he sold them 156 *holds* of pastures at half price, and the villagers also received wood from a forest area covering 334 *holds*. Later Huszár sold them 453 *holds* of land on installment at a very modest price. He had a house built for a poor widow and her five children, saving them from utter ruin. He also contributed considerable financial aid for the construction of the denominational Romanian school and of the new church.[56]

There were Hungarian landowners like Huszár in other regions as well who were also liked by the Romanian peasantry for their good deeds. Particularly good relations evolved between the Hungarian landowners and the Romanian peasants in Máramaros county. These good relations were expressed in one way or another more than once, to the great astonishment of the Romanian press. In early 1909 the newspaper of Brassó noted with dismay that "the Romanian gentleman, the Romanian who wears trousers has a bad reputation" among the Romanian people of Máramaros. "There is no better lord than the Hungarian," they often claimed.[57] This loss of prestige and the new sympathies signal the beginning of the end, noted the correspondent of the Brassó paper. The Romanian newspaper of Beszterce reprinted portions of the article because, as it stated, "it is a great pity, but in our region we have also heard some peasants declare that our lords are worse than the foreigners." Therefore, the Romanian paper called upon the intelligentsia to be more attentive to the people, "because the people are troubled by the attitude of the intelligentsia."[58]

The Causes of Poverty Among the Romanians.

The lesson from the data above indicates that large masses of the Romanian peasantry were relatively well off, from the Compromise of 1867 to 1890, and from 1900 to the outbreak of World War I. In certain counties, however, there were very poor Romanian villages surviving under miserable conditions. As we have seen, the contemporary Romanian leaders attributed this poverty in part to exploitation by the Hungarian large landowners, and in part to alcoholism. The most commonly-voiced explanation held the Hungarian state and Hungarian rule responsible for everything negative. According to another opinion, the true cause of Romanian misery lay in alcoholism. "The number one cause of our poverty is the uncontrolled use of alcoholic beverages," observed a Romanian weekly which launched a campaign against social diseases immediately after its first issue.[59] The author of the article found the second most important cause of impoverishment in the tendency to luxury in many parts of the country — a tendency manifesting itself particularly in the mode of dress. Dr. Denes Loginu, a Romanian attorney, traced the wave of emigration to America to the same causes, in addition to others.

> The nonchalance of the peasant, his abhorrence of books and learning, the lack of practical education and role models, the people's sinful distrust of the intelligentsia, the abuses committed by the intelligentsia against the people and their indifference to the people's woes, the boundless trust in foreigners, the refusal to listen to advice, alcoholism, laziness, rancor and quarrels,

the peasants from Moldavia. Upon hearing the news from Moldavia, the residents of the highlands did not use the pronoun "they," but rather "us." As he explained in one of his articles, Iorga was amazed "to see the manifestations of such feeling of national solidarity." But soon he grew terrified, as he realized "that this solidarity was not 'national', but pertained to a social class." The peasants from the highlands felt solidarity with the peasants from Moldavia, "not because they were Romanian, but because they were all peasants."[71]

The second fact was even more important than the first. The excitement that accompanied the *Jacquerie* soon drew the attention of the readers in Romania and Hungary to the difference between the situation of the peasantry of Romania, and the Romanian peasantry of Hungary. Given their favorable living conditions, the Romanian peasantry of Hungary felt no urge to rise up. In most places its economic situation was satisfactory, or even decidedly good. On the other hand, in free Romania the peasantry felt compelled to rise up because of its misery. Iorga felt compelled to note that the circumstances

> ...under which this uprising took place prove better than anything that we were facing a phenomenon of elemental power. This phenomenon was elicited by economic causes which alone are capable of stirring up the masses, for it is only hunger that places arms into the hands of the poor against the rich.[72]

Even Romanian leaders living under Hungarian rule were compelled to admit this fact. The constantly-voiced accusations regarding oppression by the Hungarians and regarding the difficult fate of the Romanian people of Hungary, were now emptied of all content at the sight of the episodes of the peasant war taking place in the free Romanian kingdom. Their enthusiasm for Romania and for conditions in Romania began to wane. They no longer regarded the Kingdom of Romania as that "wonderful country of dreams," in the capital city of which, in Bucharest, "the sun rises for every Romanian."[73] They viewed their own situation with all the greater self-confidence and feeling of superiority. Their attitudes and their statements regarding Romania revealed that they had been disappointed in their expectations, inasmuch as it seemed that "there was nothing to expect from that side." This was what prompted Iorga's criticism. He blamed them for looking down on Romania, for not caring about Romania, for relying excessively on their own powers.

Slavici, who lived in Romania at that time, addressed an open letter
to Iorga, pointing out the reasons why the Romanian leaders in
Hungary behaved this way. He referred to his own experiences since he
had moved to Romania. At one time he had been the editor-in-chief of
the *Tribuna* of Nagyszeben. He knew the conditions of the Romanians
of Hungary well, but he was also familiar with conditions in Romania.
He could not reconcile himself to these. He too felt that "our brothers
who remained in Hungary had nothing to expect from the Romania they
love so much." They had been saddened by the Bucharest exhibition of
1906, "whereas the events of this spring (referring to the *Jacquerie* of
1907) alienated them from Romania." In many ways the Romanians
living within the Habsburg Empire were ahead of their brothers in
Romania.

> The great masses of Romanians in Romania have degenerat-
> ed on account of the misery to which they have been subjected
> whereas, as you well know, this is not the case in Transylvania,
> or in Hungary, or in the Bánát, or in Bukovina — except perhaps
> in certain provinces which have been overrun by the Jews. In
> Romania the peasants work in vain, the boyars live as leeches
> not only on the land, but on those who cultivate it. The Roman-
> ians who live on the other side of the border have nothing to
> learn from their brothers over here. God protect them from
> getting into the situation in which these are now.

One must fight against the bad attitudes prevailing in Romania.
"Those among our brothers [in Transylvania] who are convinced that
they can expect nothing from Romania are merely showing good
judgement."

In his reply Iorga did concede that Slavici's letter contained no
assertion, however painful, to which he himself could not subscribe.[74]
But the Romanians of Transylvania must understand that they cannot
segregate themselves from the Romanians in Romania. Their future
will become identical, for the basis of this future is the creation of
national solidarity, which depends on Romania, for this is where the
bulk of the army is. This last observation by Iorga was a veiled hint at
the fact that, in the long run, it was the Romanian army that would
decide the fate of the Romanians living under foreign rule.

For the time being the attention of the Romanians of Hungary did
indeed focus inwards, towards further improvement of their own
economic, cultural, and political lot. Instead of the social problems of
Romania they were preoccupied with further purchases of land, the

organization of mass demonstrations against the electoral law draft, with school problems. The newspapers of Romania, on the other hand, continued to focus on the situation of the Romanians of Hungary which they now began to describe as exemplary in several ways. These almost-flattering statements regarding the Romanians of Hungary, about the economic achievements of the peasantry and of other social classes, voiced in a tone of sincere admiration, were becoming increasingly frequent. The assessment of these achievements become even more widespread after 1910. In 1911 a Bucharest daily reported on the conversation of one of its correspondents with the head of the Romanian Orthodox parish of Nagyszeben. The church leader opened his statement by insisting that the Romanian peasantry of Hungary was much better off than that of Romania. The church leader declared:

> The material conditions of the Romanian peasant of Hungary, are incomparably above that of the peasant in Romania. The state of our culture, which cannot even be compared with that of the peasant in Romania, contributes a great deal to this distinction. Almost every peasant among us is able to read and write, and lives under relatively hygienic conditions.[75]

The convictions of the historian Iorga were similar to that of the church leader from Nagyszeben. He expressed his feeling on this subject at the beginning of the following year in a well known essay:

> We must note one thing, and that is that the Romanians of Hungary live under far better economic circumstances than we do, the Romanians of the Kingdom.... Our peasantry is far poorer, far more burdened and far less educated than the Romanian peasantry of Hungary.[76]

At the end of the same year another Bucharest newspaper went even further; comparing the circumstances of the Romanians from Romania, from Bessarabia, and from Hungary, the latter were judged to be best off. In Austria and Hungary the Romanians were continually developing, economically and culturally:

> National consciousness and pride have found roots even among the peasantry, while the Romanians of the Kingdom of Romania are very far from it. The social and economic life of the Romanian peasantry living in Austria-Hungary is incomparably superior to that of the peasantry of Romania.[77]

As these observations show, the statements regarding better
economic conditions for Romanians in Hungary applied mainly to the
peasantry. For one thing, it was indeed the peasantry that had the
greatest social significance as a class, for they constituted 85% of all
Romanians. If the material conditions of this class were favorable this
meant that the normal development of a clear majority of Romanians
living under Hungarian rule was assured. The question remains, what
were the material conditions of the approximately 15% of the population
constituting the middle class in the period of the Dual Monarchy?

We may count among the Romanian middle class the artisans,
merchants, and intelligentsia, including civil servants and employees of
the churches as well as those who made a living partly as landowners
and partly as professionals. These were able to take advantage of the
economic opportunities in the Dual Monarchy period just as much as the
peasantry. The evolution of these strata and their economic growth
proceeded as freely and unhampered as did the well-to-do Romanian
peasantry. They were not hampered in their evolution, in the discharg-
ing of their work, or in their attainment of material well-being by any
generally-applied controls. All these strata began to thrive in the period
of autocratic Austrian rule, but it was only in the period following the
Compromise that they were able to fully develop and prosper.

The Romanian Artisans.

In general, the stratum of the Romanian artisans evolved under
Hungarian and Saxon influences. The Romanian population of the
towns, very sparse at the beginning, needed first of all artisans and
craftsmen. But Romanian youths, seldom opted for a career in the
crafts. Therefore Romanian community leaders began making collective
efforts to render these occupations more popular. In a general directive,
Romanian cardinal Andrei Şaguna instructed his priests and deacons to
encourage Romanian youths to take up artisanship or crafts.[78] The
artisan associations, eventually organized in every town, had the same
objective. The most distinguished members of the Romanian community
volunteered to lead these associations. In Brassó and Kolozsvár [Cluj]
it was the local deacons who became the organizers and first leaders of
these associations. The first leader of the association of Kolozsvár, in
1873, was a professor of the Romanian language at the University,
Gregoriu Silaşi. The importance of this new Romanian stratum was
understood not only by the Romanians of Hungary, but by those across
the border as well. Therefore, in addition to the moral and material
support provided by Astra, which the Romanian association had been

generously giving to the artisans from the beginning, the organizations of Romania also provided all kinds of encouragement to the slowly-multiplying young artisans. The Bucharest Association for Assistance to the Romanian University Students in Hungary, sent a yearly subsidy of 400 forints for the keep of Romanian apprentices in Transylvania. In 1883 the 52 members of the trade association of Kolozsvár took care of the keep of 30 to 32 apprentices.[79] Romanian trade associations were eventually formed at Balázsfalva, Arad, Beszterce, Fogaras, Hátszeg [Haţeg], Lugos [Lugoj], Nagyszeben, Szászsebes, Szelistye, Poján [Poiana], Szerdahely [Miercurea], and Varadia [Vărădia]. There were such associations in practically every town of any size, particularly near the Romanian borders. In 1907 a Romanian artisan association was formed in Budapest. As evidence of the freedom of assembly, we may note that the artisans of Budapest, began to meet immediately, after they submitted the statutes of the association to the authorities, without even waiting for the approval of the statutes, and "functioned in honest Romanian style," as we may read in the Romanian calendar for that year.[80]

It is very difficult to follow the numerical growth of Romanian artisans, for no compilations of data pertaining to them have been published. According to the data that are available, the stratum of Romanian artisans grew most rapidly in Brassó and Szeben. According to a Saxon compilation, between 1870 and 1895 the number of Romanian artisans increased from 96 to 168 in Brassó, and from 15 to 75 in Szeben.[81] In the years preceding World War I their numbers increased proportionately in many other places. In 1910 the total number of Romanian artisans already reached 26,376.[82] The Romanian intelligentsia, also increasing in numbers, employed primarily Romanian artisans as a matter of national solidarity; thus the livelihood of this stratum was ensured. The state or local authorities did not harass them on account of their nationality. We find no reference in the columns of the weeklies or dailies to any excessive taxing of Romanian artisans, or to the withdrawal of licenses issued to them. Nor was there any linguistic restriction imposed upon them which might have prevented them from using exclusively their Romanian mother tongue in the practice of their trade or in their dealings with the Romanian artisans' associations.

There were hardly any sizable Romanian industrial plants in Hungary. A few entrepreneurs lived in Brassó or Nagybánya [Baia Mare]. Some smaller Romanian enterprises could be found in the area of the Érchegység. Later, a few large Romanian enterprises were launched in Budapest and Szeben, as well as in Vienna. Large enterprises in the hands of the Romanians, however, remained relatively few and of modest proportions to the end, but not because their development was hampered by the state; nobody insisted on Hungarianizing them. Towards the end of World War I there were altogether 1,780 industrial enterprises in the areas to be attached to Romania later on; 26% to 29% of these were under Romanian ethnic control.[83]

Romanian Trade.

In contrast to small and large manufacturing, the impact, role, and opportunities of the Romanian trade sector were relatively far greater. This situation was mainly the consequence of an earlier favorable development. A number of families of Macedonian-Romanian and Greek origins had moved from the Balkans to settle on Hungarian territory in the 18th century, and some members of these families soon established flourishing trade companies in several cities. Romanian and Greek merchants found unexpected prosperity in Brassó, Szeben, Budapest, Miskolc, Nagyvárad [Oradea], Arad, Temesvár [Timişoara], and Vienna. The Greeks had become Romanized and in this way had strengthened this stratum of the Romanian population. Romanian researchers are in agreement that these well-to-do merchants had a "determining" influence on the general cultural development of the Romanians of Romania.[84] Their political impact was also decisive. Their sons found careers as priests, doctors, lawyers, and members of other professions. Since they were financially independent to start with, they soon attained a leading political status in Romanian public life. Şaguna the famous Romanian cardinal, Manuil Gojdu [Manó Gozsolu] the great Romanian legal mind who established a foundation named after him, the Mocsonyi family which played an influential political role, the great merchant Manole Diamandy of Brassó, one of the founders of the *Tribuna*, were all of Macedonian-Romanian descent. With the exception of Şaguna, they all owed their influence in Romanian public life to their wealth.

Brassó was the foremost center of Romanian commerce from the beginning. Here the Romanians gave the Saxons considerable competition. They soon managed to gain practically a monopoly over exports to Romania on account of their nationality, and creamed off the most profit from the commercial process. There was a time when 90% of the exports to Romania were handled by the Romanian merchants of Brassó. After the Compromise, in the 1880's and 1890's, the Brassó Chamber of Commerce was dominated by Romanian merchants. Even

the president of the Chamber was a Romanian: the well-known Manole
Diamandy, the greatest economic power among the Romanians of
Hungary, according to Slavici.[85] But there were a good many other
Romanian merchants in Brassó whose prestige almost equalled that of
Manole. The first owner of an automobile, towards the end of the last
century, was a Romanian merchant named A. Petru Popovici. The
Brassó center of Romanian commerce gave considerable support to the
Memorandum movement, which turned the issue of the Romanians of
Hungary into a European issue.[86]

In addition to the general economic conditions, the growth of modern
commerce is a function of constitutionality, freedom of commercial
competition, and the availability of capital. All these factors favored
Romanian commerce in Hungary. Constitutionality and free enterprise
were guaranteed by the laws and executive agencies of the state for
everyone, without regard to nationality or religion. Riots, vandalism,
and racial or anti-Semitic excesses were very rare and when they did
occur — for instance, during elections — they were engineered mainly
by Romanians against Jewish chandlers and innkeepers. Complaints or
any data indicating demonstrations or vandalism perpetrated against
Romanian stores or Romanian merchants are few and far between.

The fiscal policy of the state likewise did not discriminate against
commerce controlled by ethnic groups other than Hungarian. There
would be no point in looking for racial or ethnic considerations in
Hungarian fiscal measures. The notion that some merchants should pay
higher taxes because they were Romanian or Jewish, or because they
did not conduct their bookkeeping in the official language of the state,
never occurred to the Hungarian authorities. No law of any kind
compelled the Romanian merchants to put signboards in Hungarian or
to conduct their bookkeeping in that language. Nowhere have we found
information or complaints to that effect. It was entirely up to the
Romanian merchants whether they wished to advertise their wares
exclusively in their language, or in both Romanian and Hungarian. In
most cases they preferred to place their names only in Romanian in the
advertisements or on signboards, without including a single word or
letter in Hungarian; nor did it occur to anyone to prevent them from
resorting to Romanian national slogans for the sake of promoting their
business. For months, even years, one could read on the page of
classified ads of the Romanian weekly of Szászváros: "Come, let us join
hands, those of us in whom a Romanian heart beats, and let us buy only
from Romanian merchants."[87] The Hungarian state, or its institutions, did not hamper in the least the economic freedom of the Romanian merchants, or their potential to develop materially along ethnic

lines. This was one reason for the flourishing Romanian commerce, a clear testimony to the excellent financial situation of this stratum of Romanians, particularly in the decades preceding the outbreak of World War I. According to data compiled in 1918, even numerically the Romanian merchants controlled a considerable portion of the commerce of these areas. Of all the commercial ventures and companies the following percentages were in Romanian ethnic hands:

County	Percentage of Romanian Merchants
Brassó	14.56
Arad	44.27
Bihar	6.13
Fogaras	85.10
Krassó-Szörény	58.33
Beszterce-Naszód	49.09
Hunyad	46.66
Szeben	40.84
Szilágy	40.73

Of all commercial employees 17.29% were Romanian, that is 3,803 out of a total of 21,990.[88]

Undoubtedly, in many places the Romanian merchants did not attain a fair share corresponding to their percentage of the total population. Nevertheless, they did achieve tremendous progress, considering that it was only after 1867 that they began to appear at all in most towns. According to a Saxon compilation there were 110 Romanian merchants in Brassó in 1870, and by 1895 there were 200. The number of Romanian merchants in Szeben increased 500% in the same period.[89]

Romanian Financial Institutions.

The Romanian banks undoubtedly played an important role in the development of Romanian commerce in Hungary. They were the ones to provide the funds, the loans to the Romanian merchants; they were the ones who made it possible for the Romanian intelligentsia and peasants to buy up the Hungarian holdings offered for sale.

As we have already seen, the first such bank was founded in Nagyszeben by Roman Visarion in 1872. It was named Albina — the bee. In its first year of operations it had barely a few thousand forints of deposits, but eventually this amount increased at a rapid pace. By 1874 deposits totalled 121,856 forints; in 1882 they reached 762,549 forints; and in 1892 they attained 1,473,799 forints. The base capital increased correspondingly. At its foundation the institution had a base capital of 90,492 forints, and within a few decades this capital amounted to millions. In 1909 the base capital and the reserves totalled 4,803,093 crowns, and in 1912 around six million crowns. The following year it reached the seven million mark.[90]

Soon every sizable township had a Romanian bank on the model of the Albina:

	Number of banks
1892	28
1895	52
1899	73
1906	149
1914	221

By the end of that year they circulated almost 300 million in various financial transactions.

How do we explain the development of the Romanian banks of Hungary? These financial institutions were concerned basically with the transfer of money. They used the funds deposited with them for interest to disburse loans at a higher rate of interest. But no bank can rely exclusively on deposits. Its solvency, the amount of loans it can disburse, and the cost of sums loaned all depend on how much rediscounted credit it receives from a central bank or from other large banks. The central or money-issuing bank of the Dual Monarchy was the Austro-Hungarian Bank; the Romanian financial institutions received rediscounted credit from this bank and from certain big Budapest banking houses. It was clear, therefore, that if the Austro-Hungarian Bank or the large Budapest banking houses were to withdraw from satisfying the rediscount requests of Albina and similar institutions, as a matter of national prejudice or of deliberate anti-Romanian policy, then the evolution of Romanian banking would come to a standstill. The evidence, however, indicates that neither the Austro-Hungarian Bank nor the Hungarian banks of Budapest resorted to such a policy.

Indeed, if we page through the official periodical of the Romanian banking association there can be no hesitation regarding these facts. The data from the years preceding World War I are especially instructive in this regard. At the end of the fiscal year 1909-10 the Banca Poporală of Dés [Dej], according to its published accounts, received

307,785 crowns in rediscounts on a base and reserve capital of 100,000 crowns. Similarly:

Bank	Base or Reserve Capital (in crowns)	Rediscount
Drăganul of Belényes [Beiuş]	205,700	437,439
Orientul of Dobra	54,685	432,947
Progresul of Marosillye [Ilia]	130,379	255,381
Sebeşana of Szászsebes	235,003	478,216
Albina	4,803,093	14,009,394[91]

We found amounts comparable to that of Albina in the accounts of Victoria, the Romanian Bank of Arad, which received 3,305,379 crowns, on a base of 2,200,000 crowns, also in 1909. The ratio between the base capital and the rediscount credit remained comparable in later years as well. At the end of 1912 Albina received 7,178,840.83 crowns on a base of 422,291, the Drăgonul received 712,247 crowns on a base of 422,291, the Victoria of Arad 6,265,816.84 on a base of 3,500,000 crowns. In 1913 the credit dropped somewhat, whereas in 1914 it was generally on a level with the base capital. As the above data reveals, the Romanian banks often received twice as much rediscount credit as their base capital and reserve combined.

All these loans were easily granted to the Romanian banks not only by the Austro-Hungarian Bank but by some large Budapest banking houses as well. The largest credits were granted to Albina, and Albina in turn rediscounted the drafts of the smaller Romanian banks. A Romanian specialist on the subject wrote:

> The Hungarian banks, appreciating the solid foundation of our own banks, easily granted them rediscount credits.... After all, in 1914, the rediscount was equal to the amount of the base and reserve capitals. The high rate of rediscount was justified by the fact that Romanian economic life in Transylvania, in full process of development, required more capital than what the deposits could provide.[92]

Enescu also noted that, in addition to the Austro-Hungarian Bank which provided 60% of the rediscount credit, the Credit Bank of Budapest, the Hungarian Commercial Bank of Budapest, the First

the union as "the hanging of the Romanian nation." A few years later his colleague, representative Sigmund Borlea, used even stronger language in his attacks against the Hungarian government and its agencies. Since the Minister of Finance had handed down a decision against the request to nullify the fees pertaining to the transfer and entry into the land register of the estate donated for the welfare of the Romanian secondary school at Brád, Borlea came out strongly against the decision and against the government. The speech he delivered, reprinted in the newspaper, included the following tenets: "This [the demand for a fee] is the shame of the century and the debasement of humanity; the height of crudity and savagery, shame, and dishonor on such a government. Let this be the last offense thrown into the face of the Romanian people." At the same time he appealed to the Romanians to donate for the benefit of the secondary school at Brád, since "the tyrants of the world are persecuting and battering" the Romanian nation.[116]

The anti-government and anti-Hungarian pronouncements of Romanian representatives and county officials did not result in reprisals against those who uttered them. They may have elicited occasional distrust, but no one gave serious consideration to limiting the autonomy of counties or municipalities. Prime Minister Andrássy, and the Hungarian, Saxon and Székely representatives from Transylvania were well aware of the feelings of the Romanians and their irredentist endeavors, even when the latter were expressed only in somewhat veiled forms. But in 1877-78, at the time of the Russo-Turkish war and thereafter, as a result of the role Romania played in the war, the irredentism of the Romanian intelligentsia of Transylvania did surface in several places. The more sanguine Romanian youths, especially in the counties of southern Transylvania, expected the Romanian army to move right in for the occupation of Transylvania, once Plevna was taken.[117]

This no longer timid attitude of a good part of the Romanian intelligentsia rendered the government distrustful of any purely Romanian leadership at the county level. Therefore, from the eighties on, the government introduced the practice of placing higher posts in Hungarian or Saxon hands. Saxon or Hungarian governors were appointed to head counties with overwhelming Romanian majorities; yet the Romanian deputy governor and the largely Romanian civil service remained at their posts. Thus, for instance, the Saxon Guido Bousznera became governor of Fogaras county in 1892; next to him and subordinated to him we find the following officials: deputy governor Daniel Gremoiu, chief notary Ion Turcu, deputy notaries Aron Popa-Radu and

Nicolae Csato, prosecutors Mór Kapocsányi and Andrei Miku, president of the orphan's court Alexandru Nagy, chief clerks Ion Florea and Artúr Benedek, public guardian Lajos Bőhm, county physician Dr. Ştefan Pop, cashier Gregoriu Negrea, controller Ion Ganea, and census-taker Adolf Klósz. The sheriff of the district of Törcsvár, Jacob Popaneciu, was also Romanian as were the sheriff Ştefan Hocsa and the physician Dr. Nicolae Cîntea. In the district of Árpás [Arnaşu] the sheriff Aldulea Metian and his deputy Carol Rusz were also Romanian.[118]

The situation was about the same in other counties with a Romanian population. Romanian sheriffs, deputy sheriffs, and other leading county and municipal officials were still able to function undisturbed in the year of the Memorandum, 24 years after Transylvania was reunited with Hungary.

The Romanians in leading positions in the counties and municipalities were always able to intervene in defense of autonomy without hesitation or fear of reprisals, whenever they felt Romanian interests were at stake. At the end of 1884 the permanent commission of Fogaras recommended that the pay of the notaries of the villages and of district doctors in the employ of the community be disbursed from the sums deposited into the municipal treasury because the individuals concerned could retrieve their salary from there more regularly. This proposal, however, was rejected by the administrative committee, which was dominated by Romanians; they felt the approval of such a proposal would convert the Romanian notaries into instruments of the central government, or the government might be able to replace them by Hungarian notaries, inasmuch as "our notaries," observed the Romanian source, "are not familiar with the official state language."[119] Romanian national sentiment was even more marked in Naszód. When the news of the Romanian victories of 1878 arrived, the Romanian officials, the professors, students, and firemen's band paraded in closed ranks, praising the heroes of the Romanian battles. "The official circles [i.e. the Hungarians]" observed the chronicler of the demonstration, "knew nothing about these events which took place among us [i.e. at Naszód]."[120] There was only one way, this could have happened: Naszód's leaders were all Romanians. The same factor explains the participation of the Hungarians in the demonstration at Balázsfalva. There, upon receipt of the news of the fall of Plevna, Romanian as well as Hungarian residents lit up their houses to celebrate — so complete was the Romanian leadership there.[121]

In addition to the positions at the county or town level, a good number of Romanian intelligentsia occupied the post of notary in the villages. If we go by the 1884/85 yearbook of the notary publics, in most counties with a Romanian population the majority of notaries had Romanian surnames. Lacking a census of nationalities (the editors of the yearbook were not interested in the nationality of the notaries), we must go by these surnames: In this 17th year of the union, there were 41 Romanian notaries in Arad county, 22 in Beszterce-Naszód, 35 in Hunyad, 53 in Krassó-Szörény, and 29 in Szeben.[122] Actually, the total was probably far larger since many places, including Szolnok-Doboka and Torda-Aranyos counties, had failed to send in data to the editors of the yearbook. Moreover, even surnames that did not have a Romanian sound frequently belong to Romanians as well. If we reflect upon the significance of these data — Romanian notaries, Romanian sheriffs, Romanian deputy governors, county offices dominated by Romanians — we may conclude that in the period of the Memorandum, and of the sharpest press attacks against the Hungarians, certain Romanian counties in Hungary actually enjoyed Romanian administrative autonomy.

The Irredentism of Romanian County Officials.

In a report written after World War I, a Romanian member of the intelligentsia provides interesting proof that Romanian national autonomy did exist; he writes regarding the causes on behalf of which Romanians took advantage of this autonomy. In 1887 the report's author was vacationing at the Mehádia spa where he got acquainted with Simon Popescu, a professor of religion from the Sf. Sava secondary school in Bucharest. During the conversation Popescu inquired about everything: where was he from, who was the notary in his small village, who was the postmaster, who the sheriff, and what was the relationship among them. Once he had obtained all this information from his new acquaintance, and found out that all the individuals mentioned were Romanian, he handed over 100 forints and asked for a favor. His request was as follows: a package would soon be delivered in his village, addressed to a certain Béla Fegyverneky; he was to send an envelope from that package to six addresses provided to him (of which five belonged to lawyers). If there were any problems he should refuse the package and await the arrival of the addressee, Béla Fegyverneky. The new acquaintance of the professor of religion from Bucharest accepted the mission and, on his return to the village, awaited further developments. A few months later he received a letter from Bucharest advising him that the package was on its way. Not long there-after the Romanian postmaster received an order from the sheriff to the effect that a package addressed to Béla Fegyverneky should not be delivered to anyone until he, the sheriff, was notified of its arrival. The notary of the village was named János Topan. He had been reassigned there from Arad county because of his ardent Daco-Roman sentiments. The sheriff of the district was likewise a Romanian, Petru Viua. He had been transferred from Oravica [Oraviţa] because back there he would "turn even the stones into Romanians." As soon as the aforementioned package arrived and the sheriff was notified, the notary and the sheriff went to the post office. The Romanians, all three officials of the Hungarian state, wrote up a memorandum about the fact that a package had arrived for an unknown, non-existent recipient. Therefore they opened the package and noted that it contained old newspapers. These old newspapers were actually copies of the notorious irredentist proclamation issued in Bucharest in 1885. The sheriff took ten copies, the notary five. The remainder was taken over by the member of the Romanian intelligentsia who had been entrusted with the mission in Mehádia, and he duly sent them to the given addresses. This was how the irredentist proclamation was distributed among Romanians of the Bánság.[123] The contents of the proclamation are well known: the authors call upon the Romanians living on Hungarian territory to take up arms against the Hungarian "oppressors" and kill them.

The above Romanian account sheds light on Hungarian policy vis-à-vis ardently-nationalist Romanian officials of the Hungarian state. If someone such as Petru Vuia, former sheriff of Oravica should, in the words of the Romanian chronicler, "turn even stones into Romanians," he exposed himself, at the most, to the danger of a transfer. His job was not in jeopardy for having translated his Romanian nationalist feelings into acts. As we can see, even if transferred, it would be to another Romanian region, rather than to some distant province of the country among a different ethnic group. Petru Vuia was still posted to Krassó-Szörény in 1892, the district where he had participated in the dissemination of copies of the Romanian irredentist proclamation. We can imagine the possibilities for disseminating this proclamation in those counties where the majority of the notaries and of the sheriffs were Romanian. But since the Hungarian political police were not totally incompetent either, the Hungarian authorities were aware, or at least suspected (after all, the Romanian newspapers wrote about the matter rather openly) the role played by officials of Romanian nationality in the spreading of anti-Hungarian irredentist movements. Nevertheless, it did not occur to them to dismiss the Romanian officials and substitute Hungarians for them. If someone was caught performing a forbidden act, that person was sentenced, but other Romanian officials went unharmed. Until World War I, even until 1918, in most places we find officials of Romanian nationality who remained Romanian, even while working for the Hungarian state.

At first sight, on the basis of this evidence it remains a mystery why the Romanian press kept sounding accusations, complaints, or protests against the Hungarian state. Yet there was scarcely a Romanian newspaper which did not accuse it of oppression, of forceful Hungarianization, or of relegating the Romanians into the background and preventing their progress. Occasionally the Hungarian press responded to these charges. It pointed to the employment of Romanian civil servants, the enrichment of Romanian peasants, the development of general culture among the Romanians, the invalidity of the generally-voiced Romanian discontent. All this had no effect. "We are unhappy," wrote the *Tribuna* of Nagyszeben in reply, "and it does not matter whether the Hungarians recognize or not the validity of our discontent. But we are unhappy, and this is the only relevant fact the throne [i.e. the government in Vienna] and the Hungarians must bear in mind."[124] Later, in the years immediately preceding the outbreak of World War I, when even the Romanian press had to recognize the favorable material position attained by the Romanians living under Hungarian rule, it was more difficult to provide grounds for the anti-Hungarian charges of the Romanians. As we have seen, after the Romanian *Jacquerie* of 1907 a number of Romanian newspapers described how much better off were the Romanian peasants of Hungary than their brothers living in Romania. In the spring of 1913 the leaders of the Romanian Economic Association also made observations to this effect. They studied the economic conditions in Hungary and declared, on the basis of their observations, that the Romanian peasants of Hungary lived under favorable conditions, and that the rumors regarding the oppression of the Romanians did not conform to reality. A Romanian newspaper of Arad deemed the declaration an "unforgivable political blunder" and accused the Association of ignorance, stubbornly insisting on the fact of Hungarian oppression.[125]

If indeed the Romanian peasants of Hungary did not have serious reasons for dissatisfaction, we find genuine grounds for the complaints of the Romanian intelligentsia. They were often unfairly overlooked when it came to appointments to government positions. More than once a Hungarian official was appointed to an important post instead of a Romanian, merely as a result of political influence. In 1910 there were 181,788 civil servants in Hungary and only 6.35% of them were of Romanian nationality.[126] That percentage corresponds to barely one-third of the Romanians living in the country. If we take the size of

the ethnic group into consideration, their proportional representation
should have reached 20%; on the other hand, in that case, Romanian
irredentism would have assumed frightening proportions, endangering
the Compromise and Hungarian rule. The Hungarian governments
were not about to take such a chance, all the less so since the bankrupt
Hungarian lesser nobility were looking for positions which they
deserved because they had participated in the war of liberation with
heart and soul. They regarded the Romanians seeking government
positions as dangerous competition, not only from a nationalist point of
view, but also from an economic one. They counted on the sympathy of
the government against the Romanians, and seldom in vain. Hence
Romanian members of the intelligentsia were often unable to find civil
service jobs, even though many of them had completed university
studies, at home or abroad. They experienced discrimination on the
basis of nationality. It was mostly they who set the tone for the anti-
Hungarian Romanian press. Since they could find employment
commensurate with their education only with difficultly or not at all,
many of them moved to Romania, where they became the principal
proponents of the anti-Hungarian mood.

The Hungarian governments considered these Romanian complaints
unjustified. They felt that there were enough officials of Romanian
nationality in office. Indeed, it was possible to find Romanians
everywhere within the administration — in the judicial system and the
ministries, even at the highest levels. They did not have to conceal
their ethnic background. The aforementioned author writes that "most
of them achieved their rank because they were top caliber, because of
their undeniable professional qualifications." Their competence was
recognized and their nationality was no obstacle to their career. The
Hungarian governments felt this was enough, in and of itself, to
demonstrate their understanding and generous policy with regard to the
Romanians. They were aware that the German and Russian governments dealt differently with the nationalities under their rule. When
a German administration was set up in Alsace-Lorraine, all the leading
civil service posts were given to Prussian officials.[127] Nor did tsarist
Russia spoil the Romanian population of Bessarabia by giving them
Romanian officials. All this, however, was no comfort to the Romanians
who had applied for those positions. True enough, they did not lack a
means of livelihood because the Romanians of Hungary benefitted from
the favorable economic predicament. Those who were unable to enter
the civil service had no difficulty finding a place in the professions: in
industry, in banking, in commerce, in the editorial offices of newspapers.
Nevertheless, the bitter aftertaste of having been overlooked and kept

down, did not go away easily; after all, wherever they looked, they could find other Romanians doing quite well in relatively high administrative posts.

Romanian Officials and the Professional Intelligentsia in 1914.

If we examine the state civil service and the autonomous administrations on the basis of the census of 1914, we get the following picture of the Romanian presence: in Budapest, among the judges sitting on the Hungarian Royal Supreme Court and the Court of Appeals we find Dr. Alexandru Onaciu, Dr. George Plopu, Dr. Kosmutza, and Dr. Silvius Rosa. Judge Iosif Pop of the Supreme Court died in 1910. The Romanian calendar of the following year commemorated him in the following terms: "He was an honest soul, an ardent nationalist who, even in those high circles which he had attained thanks to his competence, always supported the just demands of the Romanian action with force and courage."[128] We find Romanians in the ministries as well:

In the Ministry of the Interior there was section chief Vasile Dumbrava, chief accountant Todor Labențiu, and interpreters Nicolae Diamandi and Dr. Leontin Pallade. In the Statistical Office there were under secretary Dr. Ion Bud and clerk Ion Lucaciu. In the Ministry of Finance we find under secretary Dr. Titus Dragonescu, chief accountant Ion Nicara, the secretary of the Direction of Finances of the county of Pest Iuliu Moldovanu, and reporters Dr. George Medici and Dr. Felix Dumitreanu. In the Ministry of Religious Affairs and Education we find section chief Dr. Petru Ionescu, reporter Victor Papp-Szilágyi, councillor George Cioara, auditors Nicolae Chizan and Ion Roșca, controller George Tartis, and clerks Romul Cristea and Nicolae Tifan. In the Ministry of Justice there was the clerk Dimitrie Lazarel. In the Ministry of Defense, the chief of Section I, Colonel of the General Staff Alexandru Aldea, the intendant Alexandru Abraham in Section VI, the intendant Otto Damianu in the Budget office, assistant secretary Dr. Vasile Nicoara in section 20/e, apprentice reporter Iuliu Pușcariu in section 23, clerk Traian Bogyi, and Second Lieutenant Aurel Căpitan. In the Ministry of Agriculture there were ministerial councillor Ion Șerban as chief superintendent, chief engineer Livius Martian, and veterinarians Tiberiu Cristea and Ilarius Noaghea. There were high ranking Romanian officials at institutions other than the ministries. For instance, in the Committee on the State Administration there was Judge Alexandru Brabat and Dr. Eugen Barbul at the University Library. There were seven Romanian officials in the Central Direction of the Railroads. There were Romanians even at the royal palace, two crown guards and two royal guards.

In the joint army the president of the military tribunal, Jenő Pap, was also Romanian.[129] The joint army provided good opportunities for Romanian youth even after the compromise. Those who understood German, or were willing to learn, were well received in the officer schools. The Romanian newspapers regularly published announcements and articles regarding the requirements of a military career, admission to officer school, and the favorable conditions prevailing there. More than once they explicitly appealed to young Romanians to apply in as large numbers as possible for admission to officer school. Interested young Romanians could gain much information regarding the lifestyles of Romanians serving in the joint army, regarding respect for the soldier's national sentiments, regarding their chances for promotion, etc. On the occasion of the hundredth anniversary of the foundation of the 62nd Infantry Regiment, stationed at Marosvásárhely, a Romanian group dressed in Romanian national costume and decorated with the Romanian national colors put on a show of folk dances. Just before that, Captain Nestor Onciu addressed the Romanian troops in Romanian, with great enthusiasm. Half the regiment was Romanian. In addition to the Captain, four or five Romanian officers served with the regiment named after the Bavarian Prince Ludwig. The dances were organized and led by First Lieutenant Alexandru Baies. The Prince and his retinue, took part in the ceremony as did the municipal and county officials; they watched the Romanian folk dances with pleasure.[130]

Officers of Romanian nationality were not by-passed in promotions. In the joint army they could attain the highest ranks faster than the Hungarians. Occasionally, Romanian newspapers recorded the activities of the Romanian staff officers with pride. In 1882 Leonida Pop, a Romanian officer from Naszód, was promoted to general, and the following year was appointed to head the Emperor's Military Cabinet. In 1903 there were two Romanian generals on active duty: one in Galicia, the other in Transylvania, at Gyulafehérvár [Alba Iulia] the capital of a county with a Romanian majority.[131] It should come as no surprise, then, that the military bands of the regiments stationed on Transylvanian territory occasionally played the Romanian anthem of Transylvania, "Romanian Awake from Your Slumber."

As the above examples indicate, Romanians living under Hungarian rule did not experience any handicap in the joint army on account of their origins. It seems that the highest Austrian circles trusted their loyalty to the state and their devotion to the monarchy. The leaders of the joint Ministry of Foreign Affairs also trusted Romanians. In 1894, the joint Minister of Foreign Affairs, Gusztáv Kálnoky, appointed Constantin Teodor Dumba, a Romanian, as the Monarchy's chargé d'affaires in Bucharest. Later Dumba was appointed to Washington and to Stockholm as the Ambassador of the Austro-Hungarian Monarchy. A Romanian newspaper of Transylvania devoted space to a discussion of his Romanian background and of his estates in Romania.[132]

Thus, in the offices of the joint ministries of the Monarchy, there was no mistrust of any sort towards employees of Romanian nationality. As mentioned, a diplomat of Romanian background was appointed to head the mission in Bucharest, the capital of the country which was lending support to anti-Hungarian irredentism; and this was in 1894, at the time of the Memorandum trials which stirred up so many passions. This appointment was the handiwork, it so happens, of the Minister of Foreign Affairs Kálnoky, the scion of an ancient Székely family of Transylvania. It is plain from all this that the Hungarian Kálnoky had the same trust in Dumba as his Austrian successors, notwithstanding the fact that the legation in Bucharest was indeed an important and sensitive post from the point of view of Hungarian interests, one where the personal attitudes and convictions of the ambassador played an enormous role. Yet all this presented no obstacle to Dumba's appointment nor to his eventual assignment to the United States and to Stockholm.

There was likewise no manifestation of distrust on the part of the Hungarian prime-ministry when the Romanian desk in the translation bureau was filled by a native Romanian. It was up to him to decide what kind of information was to reach members of the Hungarian government about materials published in the Romanian press of Romania and of Hungary. He was the one to evaluate and select the material which the ministers and heads of departments who knew no Romanian had to read in Hungarian translation. And he decided, in late 1893, that the materials on the debates which lasted for days in the Senate and House of Representatives in Bucharest need not be communicated to official circles in Hungary. The subject of the debates was Transylvania, the relationship between Romania and the Monarchy, the demands of the Romanians of Transylvania, and the objectives and methods of the irredentists — all matters of prime interest to the Hungarian government. Since the Romanian translator did not translate the pertinent materials, the members of the government gained no knowledge of the parliamentary speeches delivered in the Romanian capital, and of the vitally important revelations regarding the irredentism of Romanians living in the Hungarian state — precisely at the time of the Memorandum trials.

The Romanian experts were well-acquainted with the chauvinist, racist methods employed in Romania to fill any state position, in contrast to Austro-Hungarian practice. There the deciding factor was whether or not the candidate was a pure, native Romanian (*romăn din nașcere*). If he was not, he could not expect an appointment. Even recipients of academic awards had to be of Romanian ethnic background. The case of Dr. Loebell, Professor of Medicine, provides clear evidence on this point.

Loebell had been the most outstanding student of the Romanian scientist Victor Babeș, who transferred from the University of Budapest to Bucharest. Loebell decided to follow him, and became Professor Babeș' First Assistant; later he moved to the University of Iași, where he lectured in pharmacology. He was a respected lecturer, regarded as a pride of the university. His appointment to tenure, however, was vetoed by the Romanian government because his background was not Romanian but Jewish. The professors at the University of Iași gave him their unanimous backing and protested against the government measure. In vain! The government did not heed the protest. In fact, the government went a step further: it ordered Dr. Loebell to resign from his post because the government intended to fill it with a native Romanian.[133]

The racist chauvinism applied in the case of Jews and other nationalities of Romania found support in the columns of the Romanian newspapers of Hungary. The representatives of this press noted with disdain the Hungarian measures which did not discriminate among candidates for vacant posts on racial or ethnic grounds. The style in which one of the Romanian weeklies of Transylvania described the role of Hungarian civil servants of Romanian ethnic background — when it came to anti-state agitation — is quite illustrative.

A gendarme of Romanian background filed a denunciation against eight peasants from Debra for singing anti-Hungarian songs.

The sheriff from Marosillye, also of Romanian background, forwarded the denunciation to the office of the royal prosecutor. The Romanian prosecutor at Déva [Deva] placed charges against those denounced. The council, presided over by a Romanian judge and with the participation of another Romanian voting judge, decided to accept the charges. The royal treasurer and his son, also Romanians, appealed the decision. It was up to the whole bench of judges, complemented by a Jewish judge to boot, to save the principle of an unrecognized Hungarian state.[134]

This sarcastic, arrogant description reveals not only the ethnic chauvinism of the writer, but also sheds light on the lack of chauvinism among the Hungarian authorities when it came to filling state positions. Gendarme, prosecutor, head of jury, voting judge, lawyer for the defense — each of them was a Romanian employed in one of the most important institutions of the Hungarian state. This was practically beyond the comprehension of the author of the article; after all, he was well aware of conditions in Romania and of the sentiments of Romanians who served the Hungarian state.

In addition to judgeships, a number of important positions in other areas were filled by Romanians as well. There were a number of Romanians on hospital staffs. At Lugos the commander of the gendarmes was a Romanian (Ion Rusz). In addition to state civil servants there were a number of officials at the county and municipal levels who were elected and confirmed, as well as notaries and district physicians in the villages. In 1914, the 47th year of Hungarian rule, there was no lack of Romanian officials in any important field. The registry reveals the following financial officers: the financial councillor at Brassó, Ion Hobian; the internal revenue controller at Brassó, Jacob Paptea; the financial deputy secretary at Lugos, Valeriu Tabacaria; the chief accountant at Lugos, V. Petrovics; the treasurer of the internal revenue office at Oravica, Mihai Opra; the councillor at the direction of finances at Marosvásárhely, Ion Mirulescu; the tax collectors at Gyulafehérvár, Ignea and Victor Velicen; Valeriu Mureşan, the deputy secretary of the direction of finances at Nagyvárad; Ion Cipu, the deputy financial director at Sepsiszentgyörgy [Sfîntu Gheorghe]; and the secretaries of the direction of finances at Temesvár, Zamfred Roşescu and Dr. George Pintea. In addition to these there were a number of Romanian officials at lower level posts with various tax agencies.

With regard to the employment of Romanian judges the Hungarian state was acting in accordance with Act 1868: XLIV, the so-called Nationalities Law. As regards the jurisdiction of the judges the general prescriptions of the Nationalities Law were complemented, in specific terms, by Act 1869: IV. Paragraph 4 of this Act contained the following regulation:

Special attention should be paid, in filling judgeships, to appointments to district courts and to specific benches within those courts; in addition to the background specified in para-

graphs 6 and 7, due regard should be paid to the nationalities
residing in the judicial district, in accordance with paragraph 27
of the law of 1868: XLIV.

Accordingly there was always a fair number of Romanian nationals
on the courts and in administration. According to the census of 1914
the judges included the following Romanians: county judges Dr.
Honor Curucin at Felsővisó [Vişeul de Sus] and Inreu Pascu at Szatmárnémeti
[Satmar], notary of the council and judge in service Dr. Emil Haţiegan
in Kolozsvár, count judge district judge Alexandru Ancean at Szamosújvár [Gherla], judge on court of appeals Mózes Szava at Déva,
district judge Dr. Nicolae Pap at Algyógy, district judge Victor Javian
and register of lands Sebo Negru at Hátszeg, district judge Victor
Ancean at Körösbánya [Baia de Criş] district judge Nicolae Onucsan at
Puj [Puiu], notary of the district court Nicolae Mognean at Vajdahunyad
[Hunedoara], judge of the court of appeals Romulus Presia at Gyulafehérvár, notary of the court Sempronius Muntean and judge of the court of
appeals Romulus Papp in Kolozsvár, district judge Dr. Alexandru
Bohoczel at Bánffyhunyad [Huedin], judge of the court of appeals Iuliu
Muntean at Nagyszeben, judge of the court of appeals Pompeius Miksa,
district judge Alexandru Broban, and deputy district judge Elemér
Hosszú at Szászsebes; district judges Iuliu Moldovan and George Repede
at Dicsőszentmárton [Diciosănmartin], judge of the court of appeals
Petru Ungur at Kézdivársárhely [Tîrgu Secuiesc], deputy judge of the
court of appeals Victor Constantinescu at Székelyudvarhely, judge of the
court of appeals Dr. George Popa at Arad, assistant judge of the district
Dr. Sever Barbura at Borosjenő, district judge of the council at the
circuit court of Temesvár and chief royal prosecutor Dr. Alecu Gojdu at
Temesvár, district judge Emil Popotiu at Detta [Deta], district judge
Alexandru Tripan at Karánsebes, judge of the court of appeals Nicolae
Comsia at Lugos, judge of the court of appeals Aurel Radu at Temesvár,
and district judge Ion Candrea at Lippa [Lipova].
    There were probably further Romanians in addition to these,
inasmuch as the registries provide no indication of ethnic background.
In fact, many names with a Hungarian sound (e.g. Pap) or even with a
Slavic sound (e.g. many of those ending in "vics") may have belonged to
persons with a Romanian background; on the other hand, certain names
with a Romanian sound may well have belonged to individuals with
Hungarian sentiments.   According to the registries the following
Romanian officials were employed by the autonomous governments in
1914:   at Tövis [Teiuş], sheriff Dr. Aurel Szava; at Arad, public
prosecutor Dr. Ilieş Prokupás and Titus Vakuleszku, sheriff of Ternova

[Kökényes], in Arad county; at Beszterce, prosecutor Dr. George Linul and sheriff Ladislau Gheţie; at Óradna [Rodna], George Hojda; at Brassó, public prosecutor Dr. Eugen Metianu and notary of the orphan's court Petru Muntean; at Fogaras, public prosecutor Dr. Andrei Micu; at Árpás, in the county of Brassó, sheriff Emil Botta; at Déva, clerk of the orphan's court Valeriu Candrea; in the county of Hunyad, the sheriffs Amosz Gligor, Dr. Iván Bágya, Victor Rimbás, and Vasile Jasza; at Lugos, chief county notary Pavel Şerbul; at Bozovics [Bozovici], clerk of the orphan court Dr. Nicolae Prostean and sheriff Samuil Argelas; at Resica [Reşiţa], sheriff Ion Csimponeriu; in the county of Máramaros, Lord-Lieutnant Vasile Negrea; at Mármarossziget [Sighetul Marmaţei], county public prosecutor Dr. Ion Mihalyi and deputy prosecutor Dr. George Mihalka; at Szeben, chief county notary Ştefan Stroia and deputy notary Oprea Steflea; at Nagydisznód [Cisnădie], sheriff Dr. Ion Miclea; at Szelistye, sheriff Petru Dragita; at Szerdahely, sheriff Dr. Robert Baku; in Zilah [Zalău], chief county notary Dr. Octavian Felekan; at Temesvár, president of the orphan's court Dr. Ilieş Bob; at Várszó [Varsea], sheriff Coriolan Pincu. Leading officials at the municipal level were: at Szászváros, chief municipal notary Dr. Constantin Sotiv; at Szászsebes, clerk of the orphan's court and in charge of the register, Vasil Aldea and controller George Cretariu; at Temesvár, municipal engineer Stan Vidrighin and councillor Nicolae Dreia, municipal judge at Abrudbánya [Abrud]; at Brassó, municipal notary Dr. George Baku. Romanian municipal leaders were in a majority at Karánsebes and Lugos. At Lugos we find the mayor Dome Fiorescu, the chief notary and deputy mayor Dr. Ion Baltescu, chief of the internal revenue office Izso Kirtza, chief clerk Antal Rubian, controller Nicolae Petrovits, auditor Coriolan Brediceanu, tax officer Traian Lupu, public guardian Petru Calesian, recorder Remus Milkovits, executors of estates Adrian Damea and Szilard Cserogar, director of municipal parks Ion Csingitze, and controller of weights and measures Alexandru Damaszkin. At Karánsebes we find the mayor Octavian Bordan who was also the president of the orphan's court, councillor Aurelian Dobosan, chief notary Teodor Dragomir, treasurer Petru Punkov, auditor Iosif Andrei, tax recorder Petru Florian, archivist Ion Duru, and director of parks, George Jumanea.[135]

It is interesting to note the ethnic composition of the body of functionaries in towns with a mixed Saxon-Romanian population. Only on the rarest occasion did the Saxons allow Romanians to participate in municipal agencies. At Beszterce, Medgyes [Mediaş], or Segesvár [Sighişoara] the municipal leaders were exclusively Saxon, even though the number of Romanians in these cities grew by leaps and bounds in the period of the Dual Monarchy.[136]

In some towns and counties with a mixed population the leaders of the various nationalities managed to reach some agreement regarding representation. Such agreements were reached inászváros in the county of Szeben, and some smaller localities. In Szászváros an agreement came about in 1899 involving the Saxons, Hungarians, and Romanians. According to this agreement the Saxons received 26 posts on the municipal council, the Hungarians 23, and the Romanians 19. The Saxons being the majority, the office of mayor was reserved for them; one senatorial position was reserved for a Hungarian, the other for a Romanian. The nominations were effected by the municipal club or council of the particular nationality. Each ethnic group accepted the obligation not to nominate candidates for any position reserved for another nationality. Peace prevailed between the nationalities for a long time as a result of the agreement. After 1907, however, the Saxons gradually departed from the spirit of the pact. In 1909 the second senator of the city died. According to the pact the position belonged to a Romanian, since it had always been a Romanian who occupied it. This time, however, the Saxons nominated a Saxon candidate, whereas the Hungarians presented a Romanian candidate, but one who was not popular with the Romanian club. The Saxons were worried about the growing number of Romanians in the city. The Romanians became extremely upset. "The Hungarians," observed the Romanian paper,

did not present a strictly Hungarian candidate, and thus have lived up to the agreement in form if not in spirit. This is not the case with our Saxon compatriots. Because of them even the post of chief notary was taken away from our man; they have now presented a Saxon candidate without any ado and are taking over a Romanian position by force.

Since the Romanians boycotted the elections, the Saxons won, hence the position reserved for a Romanian was filled by a Saxon official. "But their victory," writes the Romanian chronicler, "was a shameless robbery of a position reserved for Romanians by contractual agreement drafted and signed by both parties." Repelled by such "animal greed", on the following day the Romanians solemnly rejected the pact, inasmuch as the signers, particularly the Saxons, had already set it aside.

Because of them we have lost everything that is valuable to us in this town; let us therefore return the favor in kind: We don't care, from now on, whether the Saxons or the Hungarians are in charge. Since, however, of the two evils the Hungarians were not as greedy in regard to us, let us return the favor by leaving them the opportunity to obtain any position they desire. Therefore, in the future, they may count on Romanian support. The Saxons will be able to obtain the position of mayor only if the Hungarians do not want it. The Romanians will no longer lay claim to any position in the municipality — let the Saxons and the Hungarians fight it out. The Romanians will support the Hungarians because, whatever they say, as partners they did not trample over the agreement as rudely as the Saxons did.[137]

The following year, much as in the case of Szászváros, the Saxons of Szeben likewise turned against the Romanians; disregarding an earlier agreement, they elected only one Romanian magistrate to the county assembly of Szeben instead of three. In following years the tension between Saxons and Romanians of Szeben became even more acute.[138]

Romanian professionals were not excluded from the post of district physician in the counties. We have seen that until 1898 they could practice medicine in the country even with diplomas acquired abroad (Bucharest, Paris). The situation did not deteriorate even after the equivalency examination was introduced, since this examination was not designed to make candidates fail. The Hungarian universities did not introduce anything like a *numerus clausus* in the admissions examinations. We know of no law, no directive, no practice, the purpose of which would have been to deter Romanian candidates or to ban them from learning, i.e. from obtaining diplomas. We find no complaint to this effect among the offenses listed by the Romanians. According to the medical yearbook of 1914 we find the following Romanian district or regional doctors among the district or hospital doctors in state service: at Balázsfalva, Alexandru Bordia; at Tövis, Aurel Ijac; at Fletót [Tauţ], Demitru Popa; at Máriaradna [Radna], district physician Athanaz Bredean; at Ószentanna [Comlăus], Vasile Cucu; at Borgóprund [Prundul Bîrgaului], Nicolae Hanganutz; at Nagyilva, Tivadar Miron; at Nagyasz [Osoi], Szilard Titieni; at Naszód, Teofil Tance; at Belényes, hospital physician Coriolan Nyes; at Geszt, deputy circuit physician Alexandru Roscu; at Gyergyótölgyes [Tulgheş], Emil Ternovean; at Fogaras, George Moldovan and physician in charge of the hospital Dr.

Titus Tertin; at Törcsvár, Valeriu Negrila; at Boica [Băiţa], Coriolan
Moldovan; at Brád, Tiberius Tisu; at Déva, head physician at the
hospital Nicolae Motin; at Hátszeg, career physician Leo Pareca; at
Hátszeg, Eugen Selariu; at Körösbánya, Nicolae Robu; at Puszta-Kalán
[Călan], staff physician (retired) Ion Popa; at Szászváros, county
physician Victor Markovinovich; at Vajdahunyad, district physician
Ágoston Dragits; in Kolozsvár, physician of the regiment Ilieş Kimpian;
at Boksángbánya [Bocşa], district physician Petru Barlovan; at
Karánsebes, chief physician in the reserves Virgil Budintian; at
Mehádia, Virgil Nămoian; at Nadrág [Nădrag], Ilieş Petrasko; at
Grevicsbánya, district physician Ion Mangoica; at Teregova, district
physician Valeriu Olariu; at Déda [Deda], Petru Neagos; at Avasfelső-
falu [Negreşti-Oaş], Coriolan Circa; at Nagytalmács [Tălmaciu], Ion
Petrascu; at Szászsebes, Athanaz Oana-Moga; at Újegyház [Nocrich],
Hilar Russan; at Vármező [Buciumi] in Szilágy county, Valeriu Ostatea;
at Bethlen, Iuliu Chitul; at Dés, Leonidas Domide; at Kápolnokmonostor
[Copalni Mănăştur], district physician George Iuliu Anca and circuit
physician Agoston Cârlig; at Magyarlápos [Tîrgu Lăpuş], Valeriu
Mustea; at Buziásfürdő [Buziaş], circuit physician and work insurance
controller physician Nicolae Dian and district physician Romulus
Peretiu.[139]

In addition to the Romanian physicians in the employ of the county,
or the state, there were others, of course, who had a private practice
among the Romanian population. These could continue their practice
without interference: they were not discriminated against in tax
assessments or in any other way on account of their nationality. While
the Saxons of Szeben refused to accept any Romanian in the hospitals
of Szeben in spite of a large number of applications, there were some
Romanian doctors in state hospitals. In 1912 the Romanian newspapers
published several articles discussing this grievance, but to no avail.

In spite of the anti-state and anti-Hungarian attitude of many
Romanian villagers in the years preceding World War I, the Hungarian
authorities did not prevent the Romanian communities from selecting
Romanian notaries. Thus the career of notary was also open to
members of the Romanian intelligentsia. Occasionally the magistrate
forced his own candidate onto the village, but this was not a general
phenomenon. In many places, however, notaries of Romanian nationality were not selected because the applicants lacked the qualifications
required by law. When, however, some Romanian — often a native of
the very village — did acquire the required qualifications, the village
selected him for notary with great pleasure. This was the case, for
instance, in the Magura community, county of Naszód, in 1908. The

community had a notary public post serving several villages. Since 1873 they had elected ten notaries. "The voters of the district," we may read in the Romanian report, "always voted up to expectations; within the realm of possibilities and of the law, theirs was always the vote of conscience dictated by their soul." Yet, in spite of this, only one notary out of ten was a native of the community during the 35 years. "The reason for this," writes the Romanian paper, "is that we did not have people with the background required by law, and thus we always had to choose from among strangers." Finally, when a vacancy occurred in 1908, one of the candidates was not only a native of the community, but had the prescribed qualifications as well. The Romanian priests of the community prepared everything. They visited George Hojda, the chief magistrate (likewise a Romanian), who may have had many reasons for resentment. They asked for his support. The judge was willing to give it and, indeed, "it was largely owing to him that the voting had such a fortunate outcome." From among some Jewish (according to the Romanian paper) and Romanian candidates of pro-Hungarian sentiments, the local Romanian candidate got elected.[140] Very simply, the Romanian notary was elected by public proclamation, as was the sub-notary in Szohodol [Sohodol] community, next to Abrudbánya, where the elections also took place amidst the goodwill of the magistrate and the great enthusiasm of the populace.[141] The election of a notary in the district of Burjánfalva [Păuliş], Hunyad county, took place under similar circumstances. The magistrate of Déva "behaved honorably, in a liberal manner. They elected the Romanian Petru Popa as notary of the community of Kavecs."[142]

On the eve of World War I the Hungarian state and its authorities did not attempt to curtail the numbers of Romanian notaries, to transfer or dismiss them. No such procedure was resorted to even in the counties neighboring Romania. As late as 1914, in Fogaras county which had an almost purely Romanian population and was adjacent to Romania, we find that the Romanian ethnic group lived its own life under an almost exclusively Romanian county administration and with very many notaries of Romanian nationality. In 1908 the Romanian newspaper of Szászváros noted with pleasure that at the county assembly of Fogaras "the Romanians enjoy almost the same power as they had at one time at the assembly of Zaránd county."[143] The ratio of Romanian notaries of the county could not have been unfavorable from a Romanian point of view, since in 1914 the leadership of the association of notaries was as follows: president, Ion Marinescu; vice-president, George Ursu; chief notary, Ion Tulbura; assistant notaries, Daniel Şerban and Ion Voda; treasurer, Matei Felea.[144]

In the county of Brassó-Szörény the situation was similar. Elsewhere the ratio of Romanians was somewhat less, but there was a good
number of Romanian notaries everywhere; a list of their names would
cover many long pages.

The significant presence of Romanian notaries gave rise to interesting situations in hundreds of communities. Most Romanian villages
lived completely under the domination of the Romanian intelligentsia.
There was not a single Hungarian in these villages who could have
monitored the administration or social life of the village. The Romanian village was usually dominated by the well-know trio of priest, judge,
and notary. The most ardent and anti-Hungarian Romanian daily, the
Tribuna, decorated all editions of its calendar with group pictures of this
village triumvirate dressed in their national costume. In the group
picture the priest is seated, the judge and notary on each side, and the
caption supplied by the editors of the calendar reads: "Picture taken
from life" [O icoană raptă din viața noastra].[145] Indeed, the calendar
was expressing a fact: in the period of the Dual Monarchy hundreds
and thousands of Romanian villages lived under the domination of the
Romanian intelligentsia. Depending on the district, there may have
been one or more Hungarian gendarme squads, one or more Hungarian
school teachers, here and there. But in most cases, especially prior to
1900, it was not possible to find members of the Hungarian intelligentsia in Romanian villages; sometimes not even after 1900. Unfortunately, we do not have complete registers from all counties, like the one
we can compile regarding Torda-Aranyos county, bearing on this
particular issue. Here, according to the calendar from 1914, and judging
by the surnames, 71 villages were led by a purely Romanian intelligentsia; not a single member of the Hungarian intelligentsia lived there.
For instance, in Mezőszentmargita [Sînmărghita] Ion Vlasza Jr. was the
notary, Avram Pop was the judge, and Gregoriu Nikola the Uniate
priest.[146] It is quite likely that the situation was similar in the 71
communities of the county that had a mixed population, even as late as
1914. In Fogaras, Beszterce-Naszód, Hunyad, Krassó-Szörény, Arad,
Bihar, Máramaros, and other counties we would find the same situation
in hundreds of villages. In fact, the situation amounted to Romanian
administrative self-government.

The Romanianization of Villages with a Mixed Population.

The facts above explain what has seemed unexplainable and
unbelievable to many until now: how several hundred Hungarian
communities became Romanianized in the second half of the 19th

century. According to the uncontestable computations of a great
Hungarian scholar, the Romanization process of 309 villages was carried
out from 1850 to 1900, in the Hungary that was denounced before the
world as the "oppressor."[147]

The process got underway during the period of Austrian autocratic
rule. Many members of the Hungarian lower nobility became impoverished after the emancipation of the serfs in the counties with a mixed
Romanian-Hungarian population. The homes and belongings of the
lower nobility and of Hungarian peasants got destroyed as a consequence of the events of the freedom fight of 1848-49. The fight failed
and the impoverished and defeated Hungarians were further weakened
by the continued oppression of the victorious Austrians. In many
villages with a mixed population, even the church estates of the
dispersed Hungarians were handed over to the Romanians. Romanians
dominated the village, the district, the county. In many places this
continued to be the case even after 1867 because, as we have seen, the
Hungarian government did not harm or replace the officials of Romanian national background. Among these there were quite a few like
Petru Vuia who, according to the Romanian assertion quoted above, was
able to turn even stones into Romanians. What can we expect regarding
the situation of the Hungarian peasant living in a village with a mixed
Romanian-Hungarian population, especially in areas where the
Romanians constituted the majority? The notary public was Romanian,
as was the judge, the magistrate of the district, and the officials of the
county; the Romanians kept together and supported one another on an
ethnic basis. On the other hand, the Hungarian state paid no attention
to him; in areas with a Romanian majority even solidarity was lacking
among the Hungarians. Neither the state nor other institutions granted
him assistance just because he was a Hungarian. if he needed money
or a loan, the only bank nearby was Romanian. If he turned to this
bank as a Romanian he was immediately granted the loan and was able
to purchase land or home; the notary, the magistrate, the county
officials suddenly became his well-wishing supporters. Between the
Hungarian left to his own devices and the Romanian peasantry which
enjoyed economic, social, and numerical superiority, it was the latter
that had the potential to assimilate others. Indeed, the Romanians took
advantage of the situation. Most villages with a mixed Romanian-
Hungarian population became Romanianized in the period of the Dual
Monarchy; after all, the primary condition of assimilation, a superior
economic and social situation, was in favor of the Romanians. These
villages were mostly those of the counties of Hunyad, Szolnok-Doboka,
and Szilágy, but a similar evolution could be observed almost every-

where. The journalist of the *Tribuna* was hinting at such instances
when he stated with arrogant self-confidence that "there are villages,
and entire regions, which were not Romanian before, yet have a purely
Romanian population today."[148]   Thus the Romanians were well
aware of their advantageous economic and social situation, and in spite
of the dissatisfaction constantly harped upon for the benefit of the
outside world, they knew a process of Romanianization was taking
place. When they wished to impress, as in the preceding instance, or at
the time of the Romanian exhibition in Bucharest, they even bragged
about the matter.

In view of this process we cannot help but wonder: How come the
Hungarian state did nothing to counter this process? After all, it must
have been aware of it. The newspapers and certain specialists often
revealed details or the more noteworthy episodes, and even suggested
ways of remedying the situation, occasionally referring to measures
adopted by other states or nations. The Hungarian leadership had two
options. One would have been the solution adopted by the Saxons
within the country, and by the Russian and German governments
abroad, for the benefit of their own people. The Saxons, as well as the
Russian and German leaders strove to promote the material and ethnic
interests of their own people by resorting to a variety of administrative
measures and aggressive methods. They did everything to achieve their
objective, from prohibiting settlement and making the purchase of land
difficult, to state purchases of land and mass resettlement programs.
Their measures were essentially in contradiction with the spirit of
liberalism prevailing in the second half of the 19th century. The other
option was to grant complete economic freedom, the principle of "laissez
faire, laissez passer," in accordance with the tenets of classical liberalism.

Within Hungary the Saxons of Transylvania were subjected to a
population pressure similar to the one the Hungarian population
experienced. As a Romanian specialist observed, from the end of the
19th century on, as a "result of the higher birthrate and of increasingly
improving economic conditions, the Romanians slowly began to weigh
down on Saxon villages and estates."[149]   The Saxons did not take
the matter lightly. They resorted to every possible means to prevent
purchases of land by Romanians or their settlement in Saxon areas. In
the community of Szépnyír [Sigmir] they would not allow the Romanians to construct homes. Mihaiu Olinea had to appeal to the Minister
in order to obtain a permit to build. In the community of Besenyő
[Viişoara] only those Romanians who converted to the national religion
of the Saxons, to Lutheranism, were allowed to build homes. In

communities with a mixed Romanian-Saxon population, the Saxons refused to hand over even one penny to the Romanians from the proceeds of the timber sold from community woods. In Szászlekence [Lechinţa] they likewise excluded the Romanians from all community rights. The Romanians once again went to the Minister with their complaints. The Minister did order that the rights of the Romanians be respected, but the local Saxon authorities refused to comply.[150] In other places there were even stranger goings-on. For instance, the Romanian inhabitants of the community of Repesz managed, over the years, by means of quiet perseverance, to purchase more than a hundred *holds* of land from the border areas of the neighboring Saxon community. They fenced in the lands they purchased, built homes and outbuildings on them, and planted orchards. The Saxons tried everything to halt the spread of the Romanian peasantry. They saddled the new Romanian settlers, under various pretexts, with one fine after another; yet they did not succeed in scaring the Romanian peasants away from their newly acquired holdings. Then the Saxons resorted to more aggressive devices. On November 21, 1908, seventy Saxon farmers armed with guns, pitchforks, and axes stormed the Romanian properties. They destroyed all the gardens, tore down the barns and other economic structures, and chopped down the trees. "Only at the time of the Mongols and of the barbarian hordes did such things happen," wrote the irate Romanian weekly.[151]

The Saxons of Transylvania were not the only ones to resort to aggression against the economic interests of other ethnic groups. The Romanian peasant who read newspapers could often read about the measures the German government in Berlin had adopted to thwart land purchases by Polish peasants living under German rule. The holdings up for sale were purchased by the German state which then settled Germans on the property. Moreover, the state earmarked large sums to assist Germans in purchasing Polish holdings.[152] The Romanian newspaper of Szászváros described this measure as a "most accursed system of regulations." Later the Prussian Minister of Agriculture sponsored a law regarding the expropriation of Polish holdings. In vain did the most famous intellectuals around the world protest against this measure, in response to an appeal by the Polish writer Henryk Sienkiewicz; the law was applied in several instances by the Prussian government, and the lands appropriated from the Poles were resettled by Germans.

Hungarian Economic Policies.

The leaders of the Hungarian state opted for the most liberal economic policies. They placed no restraints on the freedom of sales of estates, even with regard to foreigners. While non-citizens could not purchase land in Russia or Romania, anyone could do so in Hungary. The data regarding land purchase by Romanians, for instance, reveal the name of one Arthaxerces Tzaran, a resident of Romania, who bought more than 6,000 *holds* of forests in the vicinity of the community of Magyarbodza [Buzăul-Ardelan], in Háromszék county.[153] The leaders of the Romanians and Russians protected the land of the nation, and reserved them primarily for their own nationals. But the Hungarian governments of the Dual Monarchy acted differently. Their attitude deserves nothing but praise from the Romanians, certainly not accusations. Accusations would rather have to come from the Hungarian side. After all, in the period of the Dual Monarchy, the Hungarian nation lived under conditions more miserable than the Romanian. Emigration to America involved a much larger proportion of Hungarians than Romanians. For instance, among the immigrants to reach New York towards the end of February 1906 — were 779 Hungarians as opposed to 127 Romanians.[154] Thus Hungarians emigrated out of proportion to their numbers in the old country, while the number of Romanian immigrants was well below average. The discrepancy was so obvious that even the nationalist Romanian press had to deal with the issue: "The greater portion of those emigrating to America are of Hungarian nationality, because they will not put up with misery and are not as accustomed to suffering as we are," wrote the Romanian weekly of Szászváros, rather misinterpreting the causes of the phenomenon. As we have seen, the real reason for emigration was the greater misery of the Hungarian peasantry; and we find conclusive evidence of this misery both in the ratio of day laborers of Hungarian extraction, and in data from pawnshops.

Purchases of land by Romanians, loss of ground by the Hungarian peasants, and the ever-increasing rate of emigration finally induced the Hungarian government to undertake some resettlement. Between 1881 and the First World War, 21 settlements altogether were founded on estates belonging to the state or on lands bought with funds from the Settlement Foundation created by legislative act. Thus, in a period of 20 years, some 2,000 individuals were granted land in newly-created settlements. This meager result pales in significance when contrasted to British, French, Danish, or German efforts at resettlement, or with the complete Romanianization of 309 mixed Hungarian-Romanian villages. At the time of World War I the Hungarian Settlement Foundation had reserves of about 700,000 crowns, and seven million in debts, whereas the Germans had 900 million, the British 2,400 million, the French 100 million, and even small Denmark 57 million earmarked for resettlement programs.[155] It is obvious that the Hungarian government regarded the resettlement of landless Hungarian peasants, inclined to emigrate, as a minor issue.

When the mass emigration of the Székelys at the turn of the century aroused Hungarian public opinion, there were demands from all sides for effective state intervention. Effective remedy would have required land reform, but that was something all Hungarian governments shunned with horror because of their composition and their class interests. Instead of this, and under the influence of the Székely conference at Tusnád [Tuşnad] and similar activities, the Ministry of Agriculture set up the so-called sub-office of the Székely land. Its objective was to mitigate the misery of the Székely population by introducing new strains of cereals and animals to their land and by establishing farming associations. This sub-agency caused no harm whatever to the Romanians who lived in the area; in fact, it may have helped them, since its work was of general interest. The agency functioned for only a few years, because World War I put an end to its operations. Even so, its short lived operations elicited envious and resentful comments on the part of one of the Romanian newspapers. Although the misery and impoverishment of the Székely population was common knowledge among the journalists of the time, the Romanian daily of Brassó damned the government for giving "the superfluous funds of the state to the pampered, lazy, and haughty Székelys."[156]

In the third year of World War I some of those who acquired wealth by war profiteering embarked on large-scale buying of estates. They bought the lands of individuals who had become impoverished as a result of the war. Then the government finally intervened and, in November 1917, limited the sale of estates; in other words, state permits were required prior to further purchases of holdings. That this measure was not directed only against Romanians can be ascertained from an interesting episode. The chairman of the committee which controlled the sale of estates in Transylvania was the same Count István Bethlen who had written a thorough study on the purchase of estates by Romanians; nevertheless, he authorized some purchases which resulted in the acquisition of holdings by Romanians even in those final years of the war.

Thus the Romanians of the Hungarian state were able to increase their holdings throughout the period of the Dual Monarchy until the collapse of 1918.

If we follow the development of the economic conditions of the various strata of Hungary's Romanian population from 1867 to 1918, all data point to an important fact: the Romanian masses, as well as a considerable segment of the Romanian middle-class and the intelligentsia, lived under definitely favorable economic conditions. In fact, these conditions improved from decade to decade. The Hungarian state did nothing to hurt the livelihood or thwart the economic progress of Romanians. To the contrary. It unquestionably promoted the enrichment of the Romanians and the growth of their economic power in many instances: in the case of the holdings of the 150,000 peasants of the Romanian border guard communities, in the case of the Romanians of the Királyföld, in the development of Romanian agriculture, in the discount loans granted to Romanian banks, etc. The Romanian peasantry living in Hungary was socially and economically better off than the Romanian peasants living in Romania or in Bessarabia under tsarist rule. The Hungarian state did not discriminate between the Romanian and the Hungarian peasantry, to the point where the latter lived under comparatively unfavorable conditions. The Romanians, with the help of financial institutions operating on an ethnic basis and of other economic organizations — associations, casinos, etc. — provided material support and chances of development for other Romanians in every area of economic life. Moreover, they demanded, and received, from the Hungarian state all the material advantages due to the Romanian nationality on grounds of equal rights and of liberalism. The Hungarian peasantry, on the other hand, had no financial institutions or economic organizations operating on the basis of nationality or of race. The Hungarian peasant received no support from any quarter merely on account of being a Hungarian — neither from the state nor from private organizations. While Romanian organizations kept tabs on the economic situation of their own nation and did not abandon their fellow nationals in areas with a mixed population, the Hungarians did not have such organizations at their disposal, with the exception of the EMKE, established in 1885. In areas of mixed settlement the Hungarian peasants, the intelligentsia, the landowners, and the Székelys could not count on any kind of support on account of being Hungarian. As regards economics, state and society operated on the basis of total liberalism and did not indulge in economic chauvinism. On the other hand, the Romanians and the Saxons were both operating on the basis of economic chauvinism; the former promoted Romanian objectives with the support of economic organizations, and promoted them effectively, thanks to the benevolent consent of the Hungarian state and society.

Endnotes

1. A. Bărbat, *politica economică ungurească și dezvoltarea burgheziei române în Ardeal* (Cluj, 1936). Extras din revista "Observatorul Social-Economic", Cluj, Nos. 3-4, 1936.

2. Petre Suciu, *Probleme ardelene* (Cluj, 1924), p. 37.

3. Ion Slavici, *Românii din Ardeal* (Bucharest, 1910), p. 32.

4. Dénes Sebess, *Adotok a magyar agrárpolitikához a jobbágyság felszabadítása után* [Contribution to The Study of Hungarian Land Policies since the Emancipation of the Serfs] (Budapest, 1908), p. 23.

5. Ion Slavici, *Lumea prin care am trecut* (Bucharest, 1930), p. 65.

6. Ion Slavici, *Politica națională română* (Bucharest, 1915), p. 27.

7. "Din istoria fondurilor năsăudene," *Revista Bistriței*, 1903 Oct. 31, 1903.

8. *Magyar Törvénytár* [Hungarian Book of Statutes], 1898, articles XVII, XVIII, and XIX.

9. The justification for the proposed law on ownership of forests, in Sebess, *op. cit.*, pp. 56-62.

10. *Revista Bistriței*, 1909, No. 31.

11. *Ibid.*

12. *Revista Economică*, 1901, p. 371.

13. "Comunitatea de avere dela Caransebeș în primejdie," *Libertatea* 1910, No. 371.

14. "Statut über den Organismus und Wirkungskreis der Vermögen Gemeinde in ehemaliger Rosener Banater Grenz. Regiments-Bezirke Caransebeș, 1892" in Sebess. *Op. cit.*, p. 63.

15. Ion Enescu and Iuliu Enescu, *Ardealul, Banatul, Crișana și Maramureșul din punct de vedere agricol, cultural și economic* (Bucharest, 1920), p. 32.

16. Ioan Cavaler de Pușcariu, *Notițe despre întâmplările contemporane* (Sibiu, 1913), pp. 130-31.

17. *Tribuna*, July 19, 1884, No. 68.

18. *Ibid.*, January 30, 1885, No. 14.

19. Silvestru Moldovan, *Țara noastră* (Sibiu, 1894), pp. 129-30.

20. *Ibid.*, p. 223.

21. *Ibid.*, p. 241.

22. *Ibid.*, p. 260.

23. Silvestru Moldovan, *Zărandul și Munții Apuseni ai Transilvaniei* (Sibiu, 1898), p. 46.

24. Slavici, *Românii din Ardeal*, p. 32.

25. Suciu, *op. cit.*, p. 37.

26. *Tribuna* February 25, 1890, No. 34.

27. *Cărțile săteanului român.* Păcatele noastre de Petre Suciu. (Cluj-Gherla, 1903), pp. 15-16.

28. *Ibid.*, p. 5.

29. *Ibid.*, p. 28.

30. Suciu, *op. cit.*, p. 5.

31. László Tokaji, *Eladó ország* [Country for Sale] (Kolozsvár, 1913), II. GXLIII.

32. József Papp, "Epizódok a románság történetéből a magyar uralom alatt" [Episodes from the History of the Romanians under Hungarian Rule] *Magyar Kisebbség* [Hungarian Minority], Vol. 1 (1931), p. 152.

33. István Bethlen, *Az oláhok birtokvásárlásai Magyarországon az utolsó öt év folyamán* [Purchases of Estates by Romanians in Hungary in the Last Five Years], (Budapest, 1912).

34. "Sună dobele, sună," *Libertatea*, 1903, No. 12.

35. "Luptă pentru pământ," *Tribuna*, November 19, 1912, No. 40.

36. *Gazeta Transilvaniei*, October 31, 1912.

37. "Un salut," *revista Bistriţei*, 1906, No. 46.

38. "Prelegeri economice," *Ibid.*, 1909, No. 7.

39. *Ibid.*

40. *Ibid.*, February 5, 1910, No. 49.

41. "Economia," *Gazeta Transilvaniei*, October 13, 1912.

42. *Libertatea*, 1904, No. 20.

43. *Revista Bistriţei*, 1908, No. 32.

44. *Ibid.*, 1909, No. 3.

45. Ion and Iuliu Enescu, *op. cit.*, pp. 70-74.

46. "Un primar distins," *Gazeta Transilvaniei*, January 22, 1911.

47. Papp, *op. cit.*, pp. 126-27 on the basis of the September 10, 1910 issue of *Voinţa Naţională*, published in Bucharest.

48. Gheorghe Dragoş, *Cooperaţia în Ardeal* (Bucharest, 1934), p. 24.

49. *Ibid.*, p. 47.

50. Ibid., p.60.

51. "Despre insoţirile de consum," *Revista Bistriţei*, 1909, No. 8.

52. *Ibid.*

53. *Ibid.*, 1909, No. 10.

54. Gheorghe Dragoş, *op. cit.*, p. 70.

55. Ion and Iuliu Enescu, *op. cit.*, pp. 121-23.

56. Elemér Jakabffy, *Adatok a románság történetéhez a magyor uralom alatt* [Data to the History of the Romanians under Hungarian Rule] (Lugos, 1931), p. 260 on the basis of the April 13, 1913 issue of *Foaia Poporului Român*.

57. This proverb is quoted in a Romanian newspaper.

58. "În atenţiunea cărturarilor noştri," *Revista Bistriţei*, 1909, No. 9.

59. *Revista Bistriţei*, January 31, 1903, No. 3.

60. "Questiones perpetuae," *Revista Bistriţei*, March 14, 1903.

61. *Ibid.*, No. 1.

62. "Cum ne judică strănii?" *Ibid.*, March 6, 1909.

63. Suciu, *Probleme ardelene*, p. 10.

64. Pál Balogh, *A népfajok Magyarországon* [Ethnic Groups in Hungary] (Budapest, 1902), p. 1036.

65. "Unde au fost buni Români," *Libertatea*, 1911, No. 36.

66. "Un prefect model," *Tribuna*, March 21, 1907.

67. *Ibid.*, March 24, 1907.

68. "Cuvântul profesorului universitar dela Iaşi C. Stere în chestia ţărănească." *Tribuna*, March 24, 1907.

69. "Revoluţia din România," *Libertatea*, 1907, No. 14.

70. *Călindarul poporului Român pe 1908*. Budapest, pp. 120, 141.

71. Slavici's article in the *Tribuna* on April 3, 1907.

72. Speech by Iorga. *Monitorul Oficial*, June 29, 1907, p. 21.

73. The well-known slogan of Romanian nationalists in Hungary, formulated by Slavici for the first time in an 1884 issue of the *Tribuna*.

74. Slavici published the letter referring to the July 15, 1907 issue of *Neamul Românesc* and Iorga's reply in *Închisorile mele* (Bucharest, 1921), pp. 303-4.

75. The August 22, 1911, issue of *Universul*, reprinted in Jakabffy, *op. cit.*, p. 5.

76. January 30, 1912, of *Neamul Românesc*, reprinted Jakabffy, *op. cit.* p. 8.

77. In the December 10, 1918, issue of *Avedărul*, reprinted in Jakabffy, *op. cit.*, pp. 10-11.

78. Ion Lupaş, *Istoria bisericească a românilor ardeleni* (Sibiu, 1918), pp 224-226.

79. *Observatorul Social-Economic (Revista lunara)*. Cluj, 1931, p. 322 ff.

80. *Călindarul poporului Român pe 1908*, Budapest, pp. 152-154.

81. *Gazeta Transilvaniei*, January 16, 1897, No. 3.

82. Petre Suciu, *Clasele noastre sociale în Ardeal* (Turda [Torda], 1930), p. 18.

83. "Comerţul în Transilvania," *Patria*, December 3, 1920.

84. Slavici, *Românii din Ardeal*, p. 37.

85. Slavici, *Lumea prin care am trecut*, pp. 85-87.

86. I. Colan, *Casina română din Braşov, 1835-1935* (Braşov, 1935), p. 106. There are details regarding the flourishing Romanian business activities in Braşov on pages 149-162.

87. *Libertatea*, 1908, No. 14, and throughout the year, without anyone raising eyebrows over the issue.

88. "Comerţul în Transilvania, *Patria*, December 3, 1928.

89. *Gazeta Transilvaniei*, January 16, 1896, No. 3.

90. Information regarding Albina can be found in P. Petrescu, *Monografia institutului de credit şi de economii 'Albina'* [n.p., n.d.], and the accounts under the column "Revista Economică" in the official paper of the union of banks (by volume).

91. *Revista Economică*, 1918, pp. 36-37, 73, 110, 148, and 203.

92. Petre H. Nicolae, *Băncile româneşti din Ardeal şi Banat* (Sibiu, 1936), p. 68.

93. Enescu, *op. cit.*, pp. 214-215.

94. "Economia," *Tribuna*, January 16, 1912.

95. "Szegény Erdélyország" [Poor Transylvania], *Pesti Hírlap* January 21, 1912.

96. *Călindarul poporului pe 1900*, Sibiu, p. 95.

97. "Sine Astra con itur ad astra," *Revista Bistriţei*, August 15, 1908, No. 31.

98. "O credinţă falsă, care trebue stirpită din popor," *Libertatea*, 1902, No. 50.

99. For instance in Vaida's speech of 1923 at Buzău or in Slavici's work, *Închisorile mele*.

100. Tokaji, *op. cit.*, p. 17.

101. P. Suciu, *Clasele noastre sociale in Ardeal*, p. 11.

102. "O grea problemă," *Gazeta Transilvaniei*, May 14, 1912, No. 95.

103. Slavici, *Lumea prin care am trecut*, p. 33.

104. "Cronica externă," *Gazeta Transilaniei*, 1869, No. 23.

105. Puşcariu, *op. cit.*, p. 116.

106. "Falnicul Zărand," *Libertatea*, 1904, No. 34.

107. *Gazeta Transilvaniei*, 1897, No. 48.

108. "Urmările încrederei românilor," *Ibid.*, 1869, No. 79.

109. A *magyar királyi belügyminisztérium tiszti névtára* [The Roster of Officials of the Royal Hungarian Ministry of the Interior] (Buda, 1873), pp. 110-111.

110. *Ibid.*, pp. 113-114.

111. Puşcariu, *op. cit.*, p. 156.

112. *Ibid.*, p. 136.

113. *Ibid.*, p. 156.

114. *Ibid.*, p. 43.

115. "Discursul d-lui Dr. Iosif Hodoşiu," *Gazeta Transilvaniei*, 1869, No. 22.

116. The summons "26 August baia de crisiu," *Ibid.*, September 7, 1872.

117. Sextil Puşcariu, *Răsunetul războiului pentru independenţa în Ardeal* (Bucharest, 1927), p. 12.

118. *Az Athenaeum nagy képes naptára* [The Great Illustrated Calendar of the Athenaeum] (Budapest, 1892).

119. *Tribuna*, December 16, 1884, No. 195.

120. Puşcariu, *op. cit.*, p. 26.

121. *Ibid.*, p. 27.

122. A *magyarországi községi és körjegyzők évkönyve az 1884-85 évekre* [Yearbook of the Community and District Notaries of Hungary for the Years 1884-85], ed. Ferenc Vágó, (Nagyvárad, 1885).

123. "De După culise," *Biruinţa*, July 28, 1929.

124. *Tribuna*, November 4, 1884, No. 154.

125. In the May 10, 1913 issue of *Românul*, reprinted in Jakabffy, *op. cit.*, p. 206, under the title "Tudatlanság vagy misztifikáció" [Ignorance or Mystification].

126. P. Suciu, "Problema oraşelor ardelene," *Societatea de Mâine*, Vol. I (1924), p. 42.

127. "L'Alsace, Lorraine et l'Empire Germanique," *Revue des deux mondes*, Vol. XXXVIII (1888), pp. 721-757 and XL, pp. 241-291.

128. "Morţii noştri," *Călindarul poporului Român, 1912*, p. 181.

129. "Conspectul românilor din Budapesta după profesiune," *Călindarul poporului Român, 1914*, pp. 102-105.

130. "Unsere braven 'ficieri'," *Telegraful Român*, 1898, No. 80.

131. *Libertatea*, 1903, No. 16.

132. "Un român — ministru plenipotenţiar al Austriei," *Gazeta Transilvaniei*, 1913, No. 45, p. 3.

133. Endre Barna, *România nemzetiségi politikája és az oláh ajkú magyar polgárok* [Romania's Nationalities Policies and Hungarian Citizens of Romanian Background] (Kolozsvár, 1908), p. 33.

134. *Libertatea*, 1903, No. 16.

135. *Közigazgatási nemzeti kalendárium. Hivatali és irodai használatra az 1914. évre* [National Administrative Calendar for Official Use, for the Year 1914] (Budapest, n.d.), pp. 164-165.

136. *Ibid.*

137. "Dragii noştri Saşi!," *Libertatea*, 1909, No. 38.

138. "Dreptate săsească," *Libertatea*, 1913, No. 52.

139. Alfréd Pesti, *Magyarország orvosainak évkönyve és címtára* [Yearbook and Register of Physicians in Hungary] (Budapest, 1914).

140. "De pe apa Ilvei," *Revista Bistriţei*, 1908, No. 9.

141. "Alegerea de notar," *Libertatea*, 1907, No. 6.

142. "Alegerea de notar," *Libertatea*, 1909, No. 1.

143. "Din Ţara Oaşului," *Ibid.*, 1908, No. 1.

144. *Községi és közjegyzők zsebnaptára* [Pocket Diary for Community and District Notaries], ed. Mihály Posch, (Budapest, 1912-14), pp. 197-199.

145. For instance, on the cover of the *Călindarul poporului pe 1914*.

146. *Erdélyi Kalendárium az 1914-ik rendes évre* [Transylvanian Calendar for the Year 1914] (Torda, 1914).

147. Pál Balogh, *op. cit.*, p. 1037.

148. "Chestiunea naţionalităţilor," *Tribuna*, 1885, No. 240.

149. Dragoş, *Progres*, p. 127.

150. "Rele peste rele," *Libertatea*, 1906, No. 2.

151. "Vandalisa," *Revista Bistriţei*, 1908, No. 46.

152. "Din pildele altora," *Libertatea*, 1905, No. 51.

153. Tokaji, *op. cit.*, p. xxi, p. 1.

154. "Bietul pribegici," *Libertatea*, 1908, No. 8.

155. Béla Kenéz, *Nép és föld* [The People and the Land] (Budapest, 1917), pp. 122-123.

156. "Trecut şi viitor," *Gazeta Transilvaniei*, 1913, No. 1 (January 1, 1914).

Chapter II

The Right to Use the Romanian Language on Hungarian Territory

Apart from mere survival, the most important issue for any ethnic group living under the rule of a different nation is whether it is free to use its own language wherever its most important transactions take place. All nationalities yearn for the unlimited right to their own language, spoken or written, in all areas of public and private life. In addition to allowing unhampered economic progress, a nationalities policy may be said to be liberal insofar as it allows minority groups on its territory the freedom to use their own language.

The Nature and Provisions of the Law on Nationalities.

During the period of the Compromise, the Hungarian statesmen intended to live in peace not only with Austria, but with the nationalities as well. Consequently, on the proposal of Ferenc Deák, the Hungarian parliament voted in favor of the well-known Act 1868: XLIV dealing with "the equal rights of nations." The law received royal sanction on December 6, 1868, was proclaimed in both legislative houses on December 7, and was published two days later in the Record of Laws. This was the law that regulated the official use of various national languages in Hungary beginning in 1868.

The Act on nationalities addressed the use of minority languages in 29 Articles. Having designated Hungarian as the official language of the state, it prescribed the publication of authenticated translations of all laws into the languages of the nationalities (Article 1). In Articles 2 through 5 it regulated the spoken and written use of the languages of the nationalities by the authorities. In Article 6 it stated that "in their official contacts with the communities, assemblies, associations, institutions, and private individuals, representatives of the authorities are to use the language of these entities, as far as possible." Further on, the law guaranteed the nationalities the free usage of their language, spoken or written, in the various courts of law (Article 7 through 16), defined the use of language in schools, communities, and

81

local assemblies. In Article 20 it declared that the local assemblies
were free to choose their language of record and of transactions.
According to Article 21 "the officials of the communities were required
to use the language of the residents in their contacts with them."
Further provisions (Articles 22 through 25) prescribed the use of the
mother tongue for individuals and communities in their petitions and
applications addressed to various authorities; moreover, the law granted
the right to establish schools with a national character, and their equal
status with state institutions at the same level. Finally, under Article
27, the law defined a principle of decisive importance for the observation
of the above prescriptions:

> The most decisive consideration in appointments to offices
> will continue to be individual competence and ability; national
> background cannot be an obstacle to assuming any office or title
> in the country. On the contrary, the central government will, as
> far as possible, strive to employ in its courts of law and adminis-
> trative posts, representatives of the various nationalities who are
> perfectly familiar with the required languages and who are
> otherwise qualified for the post.

If we examine this Act in the light of the treatment of minorities
prevailing throughout Europe at the time, its democratic and profoundly
liberal spirit becomes immediately apparent. French, German, and
English authors alike praised it. According to the Frenchman Louis
Eisenmann, the provisions of the law gave evidence of a "spirit of
generosity and a sincere desire for justice," hence the law was "très
libérale."[1]

The Frenchmen Vincenty and Ruyasen, the Germans Harold
Steinacker and Isbert, and the Scotsman Carlile Aylmer Macartney also
commented positively on the liberal nature of the law. Yet foreign
scholars were equally unanimous in contrasting the spirit of the law
with its neglect after 1868, largely on the basis of statements by
members of the nationalities in Hungary.[2] During the Dual Monarchy
and with astounding unanimity after 1918, the nationalities in the
country insisted that the Hungarians had never observed the provisions
of the Act.[3]

Indeed, the lawmakers failed to provide for certain key eventualities.
First of all, they neglected to specify penalties for disobeying the law.
They also failed to formulate certain portions of it clearly and without
ambiguity. The first issue — not specifying penalties — can be
accounted for by the liberal spirit of the times. As we know, the

advocates of liberalism attributed a decisive role to reason in the observation of the laws. They were convinced that reasonable individuals would observe reasonable laws even without punitive sanctions, and such sanctions were likewise omitted from other laws of the period. The second mistake was the use of the phrase "as far as possible," where categorical imperatives would have served better. The lawmakers prescribed that the civil servants should speak the language of their constituents "as far as possible," and the government was also required, "as far as possible," to appoint representatives of the nationalities to various leading positions.

Hence the application of the law depended on the respect for the law on the part of Hungarian authorities and civil servants, or, rather, their goodwill towards specific ethnic groups. Whether such goodwill existed or not, was to a large extent a function of the attitude assumed by the nationality in question. In other words, the application of the law on nationalities, its partial or total neglect, also depended on the attitude of a given nationality towards the Hungarians. Thus, to look at the issue objectively, it is obvious that the nationalities had to bear the responsibility, along with the Hungarian state and its agencies, for the disregard of certain provisions of the law, or the failure to apply them.

Eisenmann hit the nail on the head when he referred to the "generous spirit" of the lawmakers; because, indeed, their contribution demonstrated precisely that quality. Let us take another look at the circumstances. In 1848-49 the Hungarians had lost the War of Independence against the Habsburgs basically because a large fraction of the nationalities, especially the Romanians of Transylvania, sided with the Austrian imperial family which had earned the contempt of all liberals in Europe and was rightly regarded as reactionary. As a consequence of their stand, tens of thousands of Hungarians lost their lives. Nagyenyed and other towns in Transylvania were wiped out because the nationalities in certain areas — the Serbians in the southern districts and the Romanians in Transylvania — massacred the Hungarians. Twenty years of autocratic rule by Austro-Germans and Czechs followed. Again it was the Hungarians who suffered most, whereas the nationalities, primarily the Romanians, grew stronger at the expense of the Hungarians. Then came a turn favorable to the Hungarians, resulting from the rapid deterioration of Austria's international position and the consequent need to conciliate the Hungarians. When preparations for this peace were undertaken, the Emperor revealed to the Romanian bishop Şaguna the seriousness of the undertaking and the events likely to take place. The Emperor advised him to adjust to the new situation: The Romanians should enter into peace negotiations with the Hungarians leaders.[4] If he, the Emperor of Austria, was forced to take such steps, then the Romanians should not feel bad about doing the same. The Romanians, however, were reluctant to take the initiative: They insisted on the autonomy of Transylvania and on Romanian leadership, on the grounds of their numerical superiority. Consequently, instead of conducting negotiations with the Hungarians, mainly with Ferenc Deák and Gyula Andrássy, they attempted to prevent an Austro-Hungarian Compromise. In 1867, when this compromise came about not withstanding, the representatives of the Romanians finally called upon Deák, a few days before the coronation, and asked for his support in protecting the special interests of the Romanians of Transylvania.

Deák received them kindly and carefully read to them the proposals regarding the future of Transylvania. He added that the Romanians were somewhat late with their requests; had they come up with them a year earlier, their requests could have been met. Since the Romanians referred to the example of Croatia, Deák pointed out the difference. In Croatia there was but one nationality, whereas in Transylvania there were three. One must take into consideration not only the wishes of the Romanians, but of other nations as well.[5] Then came the coronation, and discussion of the proposed legislation so decisive for the future of the Romanians got underway in 1868. Even then the Romanians exhibited an attitude which could only have increased the distrust the Hungarians had felt and reawakened their sad memories of 1848-49. On May 15, 1868, they issued a proclamation at Balázsfalva in which they rejected the basic law sanctioned by the ruler and demanded its repeal and the restoration of the conditions which prevailed before 1865. Thus they set an example for the other nationalities, who reacted similarly. Soon they went even further. They joined hands with the Pan-Slav representatives and, according to Romanian sources, discussed the possibility of overthrowing the Dual Monarchy and dividing Hungary up into cantons on the Swiss model, by nationality. When it came to the proposed law on nationalities, they presented counter-proposals which would have placed the Hungarians under the nationalities — under the Romanians in the case of Transylvania — except for the Hungarians in the region between the Danube and the Tisza. According to Puşcariu:

> This seemed unrealistic, given the stage the Hungarians had reached thanks to their successes. Therefore, neither the Saxons of Transylvania, nor the Germans of Hungary, nor even the Slovaks joined the resolution. The Romanians of Transylvania

should have insisted on the language laws of Szeben rather than
join the counter proposal of the nationalities which was inappropriate for them.[6]

Hence the attitude of the Romanians, whether before the nationalities' law or during the debates, was not likely to inspire confidence
among Hungarians. In spite of this, the nationalities' law defined
significant rights regarding the use of the languages of the nationalities,
including Romanian. Deák, Eötvös, and the Deák-party hoped that the
law, which was indeed generous, would contribute to reconciliation
between Hungarians and the nationalities. Unfortunately, this did not
happen. The adamant attitude of the Romanians merely elicited further
distrust among the Hungarians. At the beginning of 1869, after the
Romanians withdrew from the discussion of the proposed law on
nationalities; they declared political passivity at their meeting held at
Szerdahely, along with the Serbians and the Ruthenians. Thus they
openly indicated that they did not recognize the new constitutional
setup and had no intention of fitting into it. "We Romanians," the
official paper of the Romanian bishopric of Nagyszeben was to state,
"lacked sufficient political maturity to unanimously accept the legal
basis for our development and thus to draw the attention of the leaders
of the state to our power."[7]

The Use of Romanian in the Early Seventies.

Even though, as we have seen, the attitude of the Romanians
towards the Hungarians and the Hungarian state could not be described
as conciliatory in any sense of the term, nevertheless, the language
provisions of the law were observed in every respect for many years.
The *Tribuna* of Nagyszeben in 1885 wrote:

In the first years of the Dual Monarchy, Romanians enjoyed
well-defined conditions more or less suitable to our national
development within the lands of the Hungarian crown, because
of the practice that had evolved during the provisional regime
and on the basis of the laws brought about by the constitutional
parliament in Hungary.
Our school system — protected by the shield of the church,
was safe from government intervention.
In our villages, the Romanian language became the official
language without ado. The taxpayers' right to vote seemed a

sufficient guarantee that eventually we will attain self-rule, at
least at the community level.

Everywhere in the courts the Romanian inhabitants could
find people who understood their language, knew their needs and
customs, and were favorably disposed towards them. They
accepted all petitions in Romanian, and issued their decisions in
the same language.

In the provinces with a Romanian population, there was a
host of Romanian officials to whom we could turn in complete
confidence; and nobody questioned our right to use our own
language in public affairs.

Even at the highest court (the Royal Curia) and in the
departments of the ministries we had representatives who could
provide accurate information about our problems and could
intervene with complete goodwill on our behalf.[8]

The former editor of the *Tribuna*, Slavici repeated the above
statements almost word for word in his autobiography written after
World War I.

As a consequence of practices introduced at the time of the
provisional regime, and on the basis of the law on nationalities,
Romanians had the right to use their language in administration
and before the courts of law. In 1872, this right was respected,
and the suits brought by Romanian parties could be pursued in
Romanian to the highest levels where the decisions or sentences
also were handed down in Romanian. The rights of the
Romanians were recognized even better in administration.[9]

The data provided by the contemporary Romanian press confirm the
facts in these two statements. In those years, wherever Romanian
leaders so proposed, Romanian was declared the official language of
record and of conducting business. Such was the case in the counties of
Zaránd, Belső-Szolnok, Hunyad, Arad, and elsewhere. In Belső-Szolnok
there were Hungarians among the county leaders; even the governor,
Károly Torma, was a Hungarian. But since the Romanians were in the
majority, Gabriel Manu proposed the complete application of the law on
nationalities at the meeting of September 13-14, 1869. In his proposal,
he demanded that all correspondence of the county with the central
government take place in Romanian. Civil servants and judges should
communicate with the people in Romanian. The administrator was in
favor of the motion, which was adopted at the county assembly even

though the Hungarians, in a minority, objected.[10] Similar measures were adopted in the counties of Zaránd, Fogaras, and Naszód.

Thus it is clear that the language provisions of the law were carried out in this early period, ensuring the official use of Romanian in the prescribed manner. The Romanians spoke Romanian in the villages and at the county assemblies. The Romanian counties communicated with the central government in Romanian, the courts issued their decisions to Romanian parties in Romanian, and the civil servants transacted business with the people in Romanian.

Of course, the application of the law did not always go smoothly. Where the Romanian ethnic group had a decisive majority — as in Fogaras, Hunyad, and Szolnok-Doboka — the use of Romanian derived naturally from the letter and spirit of the law. In the counties with a mixed population, however, the difficulties and obstacles soon became manifest. There were some, among both Hungarians and Saxons, who objected to the liberal provisions of the law and attempted to sabotage it. Such attempts took place in 1872 at some Hungarian and Saxon institutions. Certain Saxon courts settled all cases in German, and the Royal Court at Gyulafehérvár decided that it would only accept an oral defense in Hungarian in civil and criminal cases brought through an attorney.[11]

Upon hearing this, the president of the Royal Tribunal of Marosvásárhely, Baron Károly Apor, went on a fact-finding tour to the lower-level courts of Királyföld and other areas with a Romanian population. He intended to observe personally how the law was being carried out. Everywhere during his visit he explained the principles of the official interpretation of the law. He emphasized that:

> parties may use their own language before the new courts, may present written petitions, and are entitled to have the record of their interrogation kept in their mother tongue. The decisions of the judges are likewise to be handed down in the language of the parties concerned. The compulsory use of Hungarian is limited to official correspondence, and the keeping of records and registries.[12]

Not everyone was pleased with Baron Apor's interpretation of the law, and the matter led to further debates. The Minister of Justice ended the controversy in an instruction handed down to the president of a court, in the Királyföld. First of all, he pointed out the objective of the law. The official state language being exclusively Hungarian, in accordance with the unity of the state, the objective of the law on nationalities was:

> to prevent difficulties that may arise out of the use of the official language, and to meet the just and warranted demands of the various nationalities.... Consequently, the provisions of the law according to which the parties may use their own language before the courts must be applied in practice as well: the discussions must be conducted in the language of the parties concerned. The courts will send their appeals to the higher courts in Hungarian. The required registries, inventories, and records should be in Hungarian, but the interrogation of the parties, of witnesses or of experts, and the record of the interrogations will be conducted in the language of the parties concerned, as provided by Article 8 of the law.

The courts were obliged to carry out the instructions of the Minister without further argument. This was the case with the Tribunal of Brassó, and the district courts as well. The contemporary Romanian account notes that, as a consequence, "Romanian presentations are accepted even from lawyers, the record is conducted in Romanian, and decisions are handed down in Romanian. At the main hearing the prosecuting attorney presents his charges in Romanian if the accused is Romanian."[13]

The year 1872 brought favorable results in other aspects of the use of the Romanian language. A good example of this was the happy outcome of the struggle of the Uniate priest of Kőhalom [Rupea] in defense of the Romanian language. Kőhalom, originally founded by Saxons, became a large community with a mixed Hungarian-Saxon-Romanian population at the time of the Compromise. The authorities in the community asked the Romanian priest to provide data on Romanian youth liable for military service. A printed form was enclosed, requesting the priest in charge of the registry to fill out the appropriate items. The language of the form, however, was German and Hungarian. The priest rejected the request because the questionnaire was not in Romanian. Then the chairperson of the community sent a message to the priest: Let him bring the questionnaire to the office so that the data may be entered there. Once again the priest sent a negative reply, because the oral invitation was not issued in the official, proper form. He proposed that the chairperson come to the parish where the registry would be made available to him, in the presence of the priest. Nor was this the first time that the priest had confronted the

authorities: in the church he had threatened with excommunication
those Romanians who participated in the election of representatives in
spite of the proclamation of passive resistance. In fact, he had been
denounced to the authorities at the time. Now, once again, the matter
was reported to the same Minister. In his reply, the Minister ordered
the authorities "to take the trouble and translate the questionnaire into
Romanian and hand it over to the priest, thus putting an end to all
further correspondence in the matter." Thus the Minister took the side
of the priest who was defending the rights of the Romanian language.
As the journalist reporting the incident observed with satisfaction:
"those who had hoped for more, perhaps even the jailing of the priest,
had to be satisfied with this much."

The Romanian weekly of Brassó added a rather interesting comment
which serves to illustrate well the struggle around the use of that
language.

> Let all priests follow this example. The priest from Rupea
> was probably not the only one among the many thousands who
> received questionnaires in German and Hungarian. Why was he
> the only one to take up the cudgels? Let us hope it is not
> because they are weak and give in to every justice of the peace
> who acts illegally, because of indifference, or fear of the regime.

Are they afraid of those in the church hierarchy who should be the
very ones to protect them against abuses? "If some do nothing for lack
of competence, then it is the deacon in charge who ought to take a stand
in the name of all of us and reject all writs that are not in Romanian."
Our language and our nation must be defended in a different way:

> let us stay away from the authorities, and they will stay away
> from us. Rights can be secured only by taking a stand and
> defending that stand courageously. *Audaces fortuna juvat,
> timidesque repellit.* [Fortune favors the brave and shuns the
> timid]. As can be seen, determination elicited respect for the just
> demands of the priest, and the case obtained victory.

From now on this is the way to demand "respect for completely equal
rights, until such time as we obtain political rights as well."[14]

In the same year the equal status of the Romanian language was
accepted without a struggle at the provincial assembly of Kolozs county.
Ladislau Voida moved that henceforth the invitations to the assembly
be issued to the Romanian members in Romanian. His motion passed,

particularly since Romanian was already a language of record, along
with Hungarian.   From then on the Romanian members of the
provincial assembly received their invitation in Romanian.[15]

In 1873, a district court in the county of Arad rejected Slavici's
Romanian-language application, on the ground that the judge was
unfamiliar with the language. Slavici, who was only an aspiring lawyer
at the time, did not leave the matter at that. The higher level courts
declared themselves incompetent to decide the issue. Then Minister of
Justice Teodor Pauler was challenged in parliament. In his reply the
Minister expressed regrets for not being able to find enough judges who
spoke Romanian. Subsequently, Romanian-language petitions came to
be rejected in other places as well.[16]

The application of the law on nationalities had as its first, almost
physical prerequisite, that qualified Romanian or Romanian-speaking
persons be appointed to administrative posts and the courts of the
counties with a Romanian population. Since, according to our sources,
there were many Romanians in the courts at this time, the rejection of
petitions in Romanian occurred presumably because they came before
new appointees unfamiliar with the language. In all probability, the
Hungarian judge mentioned above who spoke no Romanian replaced
some recently-deceased Romanian judge. In this case we are indeed
dealing with the fading of spirit of the law on nationalities, even if it
was not a case of ill-will or deliberate "Hungarianizing."

Inasmuch as, from the end of the 1870's and especially after the mid-
eighties, Romanian writers and newspapers kept complaining that the
nationalities law was not being observed and, hence, the use of
Romanian was no longer possible, let us examine language usage at
various levels and places.

The Use of the Language in the Villages.

The use of ethnic languages at the village level was covered by
Articles 20 through 24 of the law. According to these, civil servants
were "obligated" to resort to the language of the residents. The local
assemblies were empowered to determine what language should be used
in the conduct of business and in the minutes of the assembly meetings.
Petitions from the villages or by private individuals could be in the
mother tongue or in the official language of the state.

As a consequence of the democratic principle of self-government at
the community and county levels, the officials of both communities and
counties were elected by the local population. Consequently, where
there were enough Romanians with the right qualifications and where

the residents of the community were aware of their rights and made use of these, there was no impediment to the use of their language. Where the community assembly declared Romanian the official language of the community, this settled the issue most of the time. Where the ignorance of the members of the assembly, their negligence, or the ill-will of the leaders (where these were not Romanian), or again in villages with a mixed population where some of the residents objected, the written use of the mother tongue often encountered difficulties in the long run. One thing is certain, however: under the Dual Monarchy the officials of the Romanian communities continued to communicate with the residents in their mother tongue to the end, and the Romanian residents could use their language freely at the townhall. Whether the village was led by a Romanian notary or otherwise, the use of the language was not curtailed in official oral communications. No such complaints can be found in most Romanian newspapers.

By this time, however, the use of the ethnic languages in the administration of communities, the minutes of assembly meetings, and in petitions and correspondence ran into difficulties in many places. In counties with a mixed population, the elected deputy county high sheriff often spoke no Romanian. Sometimes he learned the language, sometimes not. In the latter case he expected to receive documents in Hungarian, even from those communities where the language was Romanian. Thus the struggle over application of the law got underway.

We find a pertinent example in Slavici's memoirs. In the mid-seventies, in Arad county, a lawyer by the name of Tabajdi was elected deputy county high sheriff. Speaking no Romanian, he expected the civil servants to submit all documents in Hungarian. He became unpleasant towards those who did not satisfy this demand, and praised those who did. The notary of Ópálos (Păuliş), a Romanian citizen prior to 1867, shifted allegiance after the Compromise and strove to please the deputy county high sheriff. Thereupon the residents of the community filed a complaint against him to the county authorities. Tabajdi went out to inspect the village personally. There the residents awaited him with Slavici, their legal counselor. The community was well-off: the deputy county high sheriff did not impress them. Confident in the justice of their cause, they were not even afraid of him. When the county leader entered the townhall without removing his hat, one of the village leaders also donned his and bid others to do likewise. The notary scolded them, but the villagers refused to remove their hats. This was the atmosphere in which they proceeded to record the complaints against the notary. The deputy county high sheriff found the complaints unwarranted. Slavici then explained that the complaints were justified, since the law had not changed and the Romanians had the right to demand documents in their own language. "I insist," shouted one of the peasants, "that the document I sign should not be in a language I don't understand." The debate became heated, the deputy county high sheriff joined in, and in the end the peasants assaulted him. He had to jump out of the window along with his retinue, for fear of his life. He ran home and immediately dispatched soldiery into the village to quell the "rebellion." But the soldiers found peace and quiet when they arrived. A thorough investigation was conducted and Slavici was cited for agitation, but the examining judge exonerated him. "Tabajdi's efforts were in vain," the hero of the story notes, "since even Hungarian circles disapproved of the measures he took regarding the use of Romanian."[17]

Thus the Hungarian judiciary and society hardly approved the rolling back of the Romanian language in administration. On the contrary, they found the stand adopted by the Romanian villagers understandable. "Even the most fanatical Hungarian nationalists," continued Slavici, "were forced to recognize that the deputy county high sheriff was wrong; civil servants are required to use the Romanian language."[18] Accordingly Tabajdi was "almost forced to declare that he would be satisfied if his subordinates were to translate the most important documents into Hungarian, so that he might check them." For a while the leaders of the village composed their documents in Romanian and Hungarian, because they intended to be on peaceful terms with the deputy county high sheriff. Eventually, however, they grew tired of doing double work, and gradually, on the suggestion of the notary and the judge, the assemblies of the community council resolved, here and there, that Hungarian was the language of record. Slavici wrote:

> Thus the Romanian language was gradually removed from administration. One could say that it was not the Hungarian government itself that ordered the use of Hungarian, but the Romanians who voluntarily surrendered their rights to their own language.[19]

In counties with a mixed Romanian-Hungarian population similar cases began to occur more frequently towards the end of the seventies, especially if there were compact masses of Hungarian residents. In many villages of the counties of Arad, Bihar, Szatmár, Szilágy, and Kolozs the practice of using Hungarian along with Romanian, and eventually of Hungarian alone evolved. The law was not flagrantly disregarded, since most of the time the civil servants managed to persuade the villagers to use Hungarian as the language of record. There is no doubt, however, that we are witnessing the fading of the spirit of the law, and eventually its complete disregard.

The question remains: Why was the law gradually disregarded, and why weren't punitive measures adopted? In other words, why was this subtle transgression of the law not prevented? Obviously, there always have been and always will be individuals who do not respect the law; but if the affected party takes prompt action for redress and the society and regime in question ensure that those who disobey the law are punished, then the laws would remain effective everywhere and at all times.

In view of the Romanian-Hungarian relationship, it is not difficult to find an answer to the question above from the materials provided by the Romanian press. The leaders of the Romanian ethnic group marched out of parliament during the debate on the nationalities law. On several occasions, they declared and demonstrated clearly by their attitude that they would not recognize the Hungarian constitution of 1867, the Dual Monarchy. As the protests against the constitution brought no results, they embarked upon passive resistance in 1869. In other words, they stayed away from elections, sent no representatives to parliament, and delivered sharp attacks against the Hungarian state publicly and in the press.

In spite of this, as we have seen, for a good many years, the Hungarian state and its agencies honestly carried out the provisions of the nationalities law as regards to the use of the language. For four or five years after 1868, or until the mid-seventies, the Romanians enjoyed limited self-determination in many respects in administration and justice, and complete self-determination in church and school matters, according to the *Tribuna*'s own admission. Obviously, the Hungarians had embarked upon this generous nationalities policy with certain expectations in mind, certain ulterior motives. As Dezső Szilágyi, later Minister of Justice, noted:

When we gave our compatriots speaking a different language, everything we recognize as their right; we did it on the assumption that they would also give the Hungarian state what every citizen owes to it. It is painful to note that we have been disappointed. Our nationalities did not appreciate the generosity of the Hungarian nation, and did not meet our expectations. Thereby they absolved us from the obligation of carrying out the commitments we had assumed conditionally. Should they give up their antagonistic behavior, their separatist strivings, and loyally adjust to the Hungarian state, thereby reassuring us that the weapons we place in their hands will not be used against us, then we will know our responsibility even today.

But no such change occurred in Romanian attitudes either in the early years of the Dual Monarchy or later. Bishop Şaguna died in 1872. Upon his death there was no one who would lead the Romanians from the barren soil of passivity onto the path of cooperation. On the contrary, the policy of passive resistance was bolstered that very year. The Romanian congress of Gyulafehérvár once again proclaimed its faith in passive resistance, demanding autonomy for Transylvania.

A few years later a decisive turn occurred in Hungarian domestic politics. Upon the death of Eötvös, the government party lost strength. It united with the center-left led by Kálmán Tisza in order to undertake a successful struggle against the growing strength of the independence movement. Thus Tisza and the newly-formed Liberal Party assumed the leadership and brought about significant change on the Romanian issue, especially the issue of language.

There were several advocates of centralized power in the Tisza cabinet — an issue which had already played a part in 1848 — the most prominent among them being Minister of Religious Affairs and Education, Ágoston Trefort (1872-1888). They considered the extensive self-government at the county level to be most detrimental to the progress of the country. They had no confidence in the conciliatory intentions of the Romanians, and regarded the law on nationalities as legislation that merely gave the nationalities opportunities for exploitation and misuse. Hence they did not intervene seriously in cases where certain Hungarian officials or individuals circumvented the law. What is more, in some cases the government itself clashed with the letter and spirit of the law, since it was not on friendly terms with the Romanians advocating passive resistance. The Romanian lawyer Nicolae Strǎvoiu correctly summed up the disadvantages of passivity at the meeting of the representatives of Romanian voters held at Szeben in 1876. He explained, among other things, that passivity forces the government to take action against the Romanian population. "Political abstention denies the right of existence of any government. No one can expect advantages from an adversary, only blows. Action elicits reaction, a punch elicits a counterpunch."[20]

During the Russo-Turko-Romanian War of 1877-78, the pro-Romanian demonstrations in the country merely reinforced the distrust already present among some members of the government. Even before

1867, and more than once in the seventies, the Romanian newspapers expressed unequivocally their wishes regarding the union of Transylvania with Romania. The Romanian weekly *Albina*, published over a period of eleven years in the Hungarian capital, wrote in its last issue of January 12, 1877:

> It is not possible that everything our readers found in the columns of this newspaper did not have extended roots in the bosoms of Romanians, pointing the way from Babylonian captivity to the Promised Land, towards the rule of Romania and the race of Trajan.[21]

The Hungarian government must have taken note of this and of the pro-Romanian demonstrations of 1877-78 through its Press Office. We have seen in the preceding chapter that the demonstrations attained greater proportions where the leadership of the communities — as in Naszód and Balázsfalva — was entirely Romanian and could act pretty much as it pleased, thanks to its autonomy. As Puşcariu wrote, the officials may not have known about the nationalist demonstrations in Naszód, but surely they received news about the events in Szeben or Brassó, since these took place in full view of the local Saxons and Hungarians. The photographs of the Romanian ruler Carol I, of his spouse, and of Ion C. Brătianu were pasted on the walls of every Romanian house. Romanian women wore caps similar to the one worn by a unit of the Romanian army. The university students at Budapest sent a message of greetings to the Romanian prime minister Brătianu. Two teachers of the high school at Naszód wrote a book about the Eastern campaign in which they described the pro-Turkish feelings of the Hungarians in the following terms:

> The Hungarians promote and teach the most explicit feelings of brotherhood towards the Turks, to whom they are related on account of their Asian origins, their barbarism, and their practice of oppressing conquered nations.[22]

These facts gave unequivocal indications of the feelings and yearnings of the Romanians. Hungarian society, the local authorities, and the government itself took cognizance of this with growing irritation. After such precedents, the process of limiting the use of nationalities' languages in the villages got underway in some countries with a mixed population. This also explains the Article of the Act of 1879, XIII, regarding the compulsory teaching of the Hungarian language as a subject at non-Hungarian teachers' colleges and in the primary schools.

The situation did not change, however, in the villages of the Romanian or predominantly Romanian counties. The inhabitants of the Romanian villages of Fogaras, Beszterce-Naszód, Hunyad, Szolnok-Doboka, Brassó, and Szeben used their own language in the offices of the community and at the local assemblies, as prescribed by the nationalities law. Where Romanian was the language of community affairs all announcements, summonses, receipts, notifications, registries, and documents of all sorts that were issued by the town halls of the villages and towns were exclusively in Romanian. We have seen that most notaries in the counties were Romanian, as were the justices of the peace and leaders in general. The use of the mother tongue could suffer no curtailment under the protection of such a self-government. We have seen that in Fogaras, the administrative committee of the county voted down a proposal regarding notaries' salaries, because the Romanian notaries knew hardly a word of Hungarian and the committee would not allow them to fall under the sway of the government because of this.[23] And if the Romanian notaries spoke no Hungarian, it is clear that the language of administration at the community level was Romanian. The conditions were similar in other counties with a majority of Romanian-speakers.

If the notary heading the community was not of Romanian background, he nevertheless had to be familiar with the language of the community, in accordance with the regulations regarding examinations administered to notaries. The candidates had to take the examination in front of the county examination committee. The governor, the prosecuting attorney, the president of the orphans administration, the inspector of taxes, and the superintendent of schools were all members of this committee. We have already seen that these officials were often Romanian. The examination was both written and oral. The oral examination was open to the public. We read in the regulations:

> In addition to the official language of the state, this examination must extend to the candidate's familiarity with the language prevailing in the district and indicated in his application.... The certificate of capacitation... must specify in which communities of what notarial language he may be employed, given his linguistic background.[24]

Therefore, as we have seen from the examples presented in the preceding chapter, if in some village the notary was not Romanian this merely signified that no Romanian candidate with the required preparation could be found. But every notary spoke the language of the people, and it would have been most difficult to change the notarial language already determined in the community.

The free usage of Romanian in the communities prevailed throughout the period of the Dual Monarchy. Nevertheless, Hungarian was introduced as the notarial language here and there, in the nineties. But there was no more basic change or departure from tradition, as the data below clearly indicate.

At the turn of the century, some Romanian leaders launched an aggressive movement to politicize the Romanian population of Transylvania. First, the newspaper *Tribuna Popurului* of Arad, founded in 1896, then from 1902 on, the weekly *Libertatea* of Szászváros undertook to persuade the masses. The Romanian intellectuals backing these periodicals realized the negative consequences of passive resistance. They rejected it primarily because it penetrated into areas where it entailed considerable sacrifice of rights: e.g. in the counties and the communities. Abstention from parliamentary elections gradually began to have repercussions in the counties and villages as well. Romanian intellectuals no longer attended the assemblies at the county level and neglected the affairs of the community, giving up a chance to arouse consciousness of the value of citizens' rights among the inhabitants of the village. "The most fatal consequence of our withdrawal," observed the newspaper from Szászváros, "is that we deprived ourselves of the most appropriate means to provide a political education for our people and to mold them into citizens conscious of their rights as individuals within the nation."[25]

The editors of this weekly immediately launched a program for ensuring the use of their national language. In a series of articles, they informed their readers about the rights the law provided to Romanian villages. They pointed out that another language might displace Romanian as the notarial language only where Romanians were ignorant or indifferent, where they brought restrictions on the use of their language themselves. The periodical doggedly continued its work scolding, yet, encouraging the Romanians to insist on their rights. Even after a policy of political activism was adopted in 1905, it continued to scold with ever-greater impetus the indifference of the Romanians towards the use of their own language. "This was the way we Romanians behaved," it wrote in 1907, "and we have voluntarily surrendered almost all those partial rights which the law on nationalities granted to our language at the community and county levels."[26] The line adopted by the Romanian weekly was not without results. In many places, the leadership of the Romanian communities brought about new resolutions proclaiming Romanian as the language of notaries and of administration. This was the case, for instance, in the community of Sikló [Şiclău] in Arad county. Here nine-tenths of the residents were Romanian, the remainder Hungarian. Formerly, Hungarian had been introduced as the notarial language by a tricky notary. In 1910, however, the representatives of the community, who were almost exclusively Romanian, declared that Romanian would be the official language of the community in every respect. The weekly of Szászváros took this opportunity to once again scold those Romanian communities where such measures had not been adopted — for instance, some ten communities in the county of Hunyad where Hungarian remained the official language of administration. According to one author difficulties arise only where people are weak. "Where they are strong, they can force the community leaders to issue summonses, receipts, and minutes of meetings exclusively in Romanian."[27] In 1912, it repeated almost verbatim the admonition enunciated many years earlier: "It is because of our indifference that we lost most of those rights the law guarantees even today in public life, especially in the communities and the counties."[28]

Thanks to this affectionate, scolding, chiding, and encouraging tone of the Romanian weekly of Szászváros, we obtain a generally accurate picture of the use of the Romanian language in Transylvania. Scanning the scattered data and short articles we also obtain a picture of the use of Romanian at the village level in the years preceding World War I. This Romanian source, which certainly did not display great love towards the Hungarians, indicates that in the Romanian villages of the county of Szeben, some parts of Brassó, in Beszterce-Naszód, Hunyad, and Fogaras the language of registry and of official business was Romanian. In other words, the villages received every document, summons, bulletin, receipt, etc., in their Romanian mother tongue. The minutes of community meetings were kept exclusively in Romanian. In 1912, the periodical stated this in such a way as to imply that *only* in these counties were these rights still enjoyed, "since we lost many of our rights due to neglect and to the misguided policy [passive resistance] of our predecessors." It went on to state:

> The nationalities law passed in 1868 provided us, after all, with rather nice rights at the community and county levels. But instead of accepting these as a foundation or a beginning on which we could stand solidly to widen our base and wring out further concessions so that by now we would have twice as many

rights as the law had given us, we allowed even those rights
provided by the law to become dormant in our hands."[29]

According to the linguistic map compiled by the *Libertatea*,
Romanian was the official language in the villages of the above five
counties around 1912. According to Hungarian officials and contemporary sources Romanian was the official language in the villages of some
other counties as well, for instance in Kolozs, Szolnok-Doboka, Temes-
Torontál, Arad, Krassó-Szörény, and Máramaros. Undoubtedly the law
was disregarded in many places, and a significant fraction of the
Romanian villages was unable to take advantage of the law either
because of its leaders' indifference or as a result of pressure from above.
On the other hand, equally reliable Romanian sources indicate that in
the Romanian villages of five large counties Romanian remained the
only official language to the end, throughout the Dual Monarchy. It is
most likely that villages in other counties also enjoyed the official use
of Romanian, as we may surmise from the presence of civil servants,
judges, and doctors of Romanian background.

*Language in the Counties and in Communications
with Higher Authorities.*

As we have seen, in most communities of the counties with a
Romanian majority, the right to submit applications in Romanian
remained uncontested. Where Romanian was not the official language,
but the notary was familiar with it, petitions and other transactions in
Romanian had to be accepted by the notary in accordance with the law.
   According to contemporary data, the right to submit petitions in
Romanian was actually observed in Hunyad, Szeben, Brassó, Fogaras,
Beszterce-Naszód, Krassó-Szörény, and even Arad county. We have seen
that in 1914, and even during World War I, there were officials, even
justices of the peace, of Romanian background among the civil servants
of the Romanian counties. Where the Hungarian officials could not
speak Romanian, the petitions were handed over to officials familiar
with the language. In fact, in 1906, the deputy county high sheriff of
the county of Temes inaugurated a course in Romanian for the benefit
of county officials. The course lasted five months, and 40 officials
signed up to learn Romanian, in order to understand the people. It was
taught by Alexandru Mihuţa, a professor with the Hungarian State
Teachers' College in Temesvár.[30]
   In the counties enumerated above, documents submitted by the
denominational schools in Romanian were also accepted, as were

applications emanating from private individuals. In 1910, the administration of Hunyad county requested the superintendents of the individual dioceses to furnish data regarding the salaries of teachers at their schools. The weekly from Szászváros published guidelines on how to respond to this request. "The county leaders wrote in that letter that if the school committee should provide documentation in some language other than Hungarian, a translation must be included." Some priests, misinterpreting the instructions, sent in all the documents in Hungarian. The paper (whose editor, Deacon Ion Moṭa, was a member of the county assembly) explained that the county officials had requested Hungarian translations because the documents were intended for the pension fund in Budapest, where they had to be understood.

When, however, I, as president [i.e. of the parish] reply to the county at its request, and I write in order to meet the request of the county, then I will write *only in Romanian*[31] because the county will accept the Romanian language[32] and has no right to demand that I write in Hungarian.

There should have been officials who spoke Romanian in every ministry in Budapest as well. Yet, because of what the paper referred to as intolerable politics, this was not the case at that time.

Still, the committees in the parishes should refrain from writing in any language but Romanian in their communications with the county and the school superintendents, as otherwise they are running roughshod over their church's right to use Romanian as its official language.

The paper advised that where the superintendent of schools will not accept documents in Romanian, they should be sent directly to the joint ministry.[33]

The same year the Romanian weekly analyzed another interesting issue: the language of the census questionnaire sent out by the justices of the peace. One justice of the peace requested a report on the state of the libraries at denominational schools. A Romanian priest responded in the official language of the church, i.e. in Romanian, and placed his response in an envelope, addressed it in both Romanian and Hungarian, and mailed it. Since other Romanian priests sent in their responses mostly in Hungarian, the justice of the peace scolded the priest who wrote in Romanian, and even commented on the fact that the Hungarian address on the envelope was written in smaller characters. The

Libertatea self-righteously condemned this attitude on the part of the justice of the peace. "Thus one may see to what extremities the unbearable hatred of the Hungarians towards the Romanian language has gone," the newspaper argued.

The Hungarian version on the envelope was included not as the actual address, but merely as a translation for the benefit of those postal workers who could not understand Romanian. There was no mistake made in using small characters, or setting it between parentheses. It is a manifestation of ignorance and repulsive chauvinism on the part of the official to bring this matter to the attention of the priest.

The paper published this article under the heading: "The audacity of a justice of the peace who attacks our right to our Romanian language."[34]

Until the turn of the century, it was even possible to send applications to the ministries in Budapest, in Romanian. In 1885, the direction of the Romanian commercial high school of Brassó, submitted the written questions proposed for the final examination for the high school diploma to the Ministry of Education only in Romanian. The document went through official channels by way of the consistory of the Romanian archdiocese of Szeben.   Although the consistory forwarded the Romanian questions as asked, it sent instructions to the director of the school requesting a Hungarian translation thereof. It probably feared that the Ministry would reject an examination in Romanian. This was not what happened, however. While the consistory and the school in Brassó were exchanging communications, the Ministry of Religion and Education returned the exclusively Romanian text with its seal of approval. "Which means," added the Romanian paper, chiding the archdiocese on account of the incident, "that it was not the government that insisted on the use of Hungarian, but the consistory that went overboard in its excess of zeal."[35]

Another incident is mentioned in a newspaper of Szászváros. In 1895, Ion Moța, a collaborator of the *Foaia Poporului*, appealed a decision he felt was illegal; the appeal to the Hungarian Ministry of Interior was in Romanian, without a Hungarian translation. The Ministry had the Romanian appeal translated into Hungarian, and handed down a favorable decision.[36]

If we consider that this event took place in the midst of the tension provoked by the "memorandum affair," we must regard the measure taken by the Hungarian Minister of the Interior as noteworthy.

Regarding the issue of the language of communication with the authorities, the decision taken by the Hungarian Minister of Education, Albert Apponyi, was also interesting. The board of directors of the Romanian secondary school for girls of Nagyszeben, which was supported by the Greater Romanian foundation Astra, corresponded with the Superintendent of Schools in Romanian. The Superintendent objected, upon which Astra turned to the Minister of Education. The Minister authorized the school to correspond with the Superintendent and other authorities in Romanian and Hungarian, in a parallel manner.[37] It was still possible to submit applications in Romanian and obtain a favorable response in 1914, after all, as we have seen from the data provided in the Romanian calendars, there were ethnic Romanian officials in every Hungarian ministry.[38]

The Use of the Language in County Assemblies
and Municipal Offices.

The use of Romanian in county assemblies and municipal offices evolved even more interestingly. We have seen above that in the decades following the Compromise, the use of the mother tongue continued undisturbed, guaranteed by the Law on Nationalities. The leaders of the Romanians of Transylvania, however, extended the principle of passive resistance to the county assemblies at times. Consequently, they were often conspicuous by their absence, and people gradually became accustomed to this absence and to the fact that the issues were discussed only in Hungarian and German. When Romanians nevertheless made an appearance at the assemblies and attempted to use their mother tongue, they were often interrupted. Where the Romanians stalwartly defended their rights, they succeeded in having those rights respected most of the time. Many examples of this are mentioned in the newspapers.

An interesting scene took place at Lugos in the spring of 1884, at the meeting of county officials, where Hungarian members were in a majority. The filling of two vacant posts was on the agenda. When the matter of commissioning an appointment committee came up, the Romanians, in a minority, demanded that their candidate, C. Brediceanu, be included on the committee. The Hungarian majority objected. Then the Romanians made deafening noises. The county high sheriff, who was chairing the meeting, shouted, rang the bell, lost his temper, but was unable to restore order. Someone loudly scolded in Hungarian, the Romanian members who were shouting at the top of their lungs. In response, Popovici, a Romanian member of the assembly, said to the county high sheriff in Romanian: "Speak in Romanian, for we don't understand Hungarian." The county high sheriff answered that it was not he, but notary Schönfeld, who had scolded the Romanians. Popovici then said, "to our knowledge, you are the county high sheriff and the chair of the assembly as well. Since Romanian is the language of registry, speak Romanian." The county high sheriff remained silent. Popovici continued: "Speak Romanian! If you can't, you are not qualified to fill a position which includes presiding at this assembly, the language of the assembly being Romanian as well." In the course of the heated discussion one of the Romanian members declared in Hungarian that the Romanians will never give in. The Romanian article which reported the incident observed with considerable satisfaction that as a result of "the determined and manly statements, as well as because of the obstreperous shouting" the county high sheriff had to give in and accept Brediceanu as a member of the selection committee.[39]

According to the contemporary Romanian account, the Romanian members of the county assembly at Lugos not only spoke in their mother tongue, but adopted an aggressive tone vis-à-vis the county high sheriff, referring to the law. No one prevented them from using their mother tongue at the meeting. The situation was the same at the county assembly of Torda in 1890. Here contributions to the EMKE society was on the agenda of the meeting. Prior to the meeting the Romanian members had agreed on the principles of their intervention. Thus, at the meeting of January 28, Ioan Raţiu, in the name of the Romanians, protested against the discussion of contributions to the association in "our melodious Romanian language," to quote the words of the newspaper.[40] The protest bore fruit, the item was taken off the agenda. A similar Romanian stand prevailed on this issue at several county assemblies.

According to Romanian sources, at the turn of the century, the situation was as follows, county by county:

"In the county of Beszterce-Naszód," wrote Dr. Valeriu Moldovan "it is taken for granted that everyone should speak their mother tongue at the county assembly."[41] The same conditions prevailed in those counties where three nationalities lived side by side, i.e. in Brassó, Nagy-Küküllő, and Szeben. All members used their mother tongue at meetings of the assembly. A second group was made up of those counties where the Hungarian majority faced a strong minority: in Hunyad, Krassó-Szörény, Arad, Alsó-Fehér (to avoid confusion, not the majority of the general population, but a majority among members of the administration is meant). In these counties the Romanians "have already partly secured" the use of their language.

There was a third group of counties where the Romanians formed but a small minority. Here the right to use the language was an issue of secondary importance; the main objective was control over the administration and exposing official abuses.

The situation as regards the use of Romanian at the county level is clearly revealed by this overview. After the turn of the century the Romanian members of the administrative machinery spoke Romanian in Brassó, Beszterce-Naszód, Nagy-Küküllő, Arad, Krassó-Szörény, and Hunyad, in accordance with the provisions of the Law on Nationalities. There were struggles, moreover, in Alsó-Fehér and Szolnok-Doboka. Whenever the usage of spoken Romanian was granted, it also became a language of the minutes: that is, the minutes were kept in Romanian in addition to Hungarian and German.

At the administrative centers of Déva and Dés, the county seats of Hunyad and Szolnok-Doboka, the law on nationalities was applied as follows: After the Compromise the Romanian members continued to speak in Romanian for many years; later, as a result of the policy of passive resistance, there was no one left to make use of this right, since the Romanian members stayed away from the meetings. Thus the right to intervene in the mother tongue fell in to disuse.

Around the turn of the century, militants and activists wanted to avail themselves of the right to intervene in the mother tongue at the county assemblies. From 1901, they intervened more and more frequently in their mother tongue. Déva and Dés soon became the scene of interesting debates. Some of the Hungarian members at the assemblies objected to the use of another language in a place where, for a long time, only Hungarian had been spoken. But because of the praiseworthy perseverance of the Romanians and of respect for the law, the county leadership soon allowed the provisions of the Act to prevail. Within three years, the use of Romanian was once again taken for granted at Déva.

It was mainly Dr. Aurel Vlad, one of the principal representatives of the activist tendency, who spoke in Romanian at the meeting of the Hunyad county assembly in 1901. On one such occasion a couple of delegates shouted "in Hungarian!" But the county high sheriff who was chairing the meeting "intervened on behalf of Dr. Vlad and requested the Hungarians to allow him to speak in Romanian, because he had the right to do so."[42] The speaker was able to continue his speech in Romanian without further interruptions. The following year, in 1902, many Romanians spoke in their language at the county assembly at

there were Romanians even in the Budapest ministries, not to mention the Romanian ethnic officials at the county, municipal, and other levels.

The Use of Romanian in the Courts.

The measures of the law on nationalities regarding the use of language in the courts were applied in rather the same manner as at the community level. That is, there were courts where all the prescriptions were honored to the very end, and there were others where the laws were observed only partly or not at all. Unfortunately, details regarding this issue cannot be found in either Romanian or Hungarian sources. The Romanian papers reflect the following situation:

Until the mid-seventies the laws were observed generally and everywhere, as high up as the Royal Tribunal — as we may note from the *Tribuna*, other newspapers, and from Slavici's autobiography. In other words, Romanian clients could resort to their mother tongue everywhere, orally or in writing. The language of the documents submitted was Romanian, as were the sentences handed down by the courts.

It would appear from the complaints that towards the end of the seventies the sentences were couched exclusively in Hungarian in some courts of law. From then on the practice of the judges tended more and more in that direction. But since — as we have seen from the census of 1914 — there remained Romanian judges throughout, it is most likely that at some of the lower courts the judges of the Romanian background issued their sentences in the mother tongue of the clients as late as the years immediately preceding World War I. According to elderly, retired Hungarian judges, such was the case in more than just one instance. In theory, legally, and in practice, sentences could be handed down in Romanian as the law prescribed wherever there were Romanian judges.

Regarding the language of the dockets, we have somewhat more data at our disposal. According to Slavici, in the mid-seventies, one of the district courts in the county of Arad rejected dockets submitted in Romanian on the ground that the judge was not familiar with the language. It seems that this was a rather isolated case. In other places, the courts accepted dockets in Romanian well into the eighties, both at the district and at higher levels.[53] In 1902, Ioan Manteanu, the editor-in-chief of the weekly *Libertatea*, submitted an application in Romanian to the tribunal at Déva which had jurisdiction over press matters, requesting that all charges against him be dropped. The application was accepted. Similar incidents could be gleaned from other Romanian papers. We may conclude that some courts accepted documents in Romanian during the entire period. Of course, the opposite also happened between 1875 and 1914: The relevant prescriptions of the law on nationalities were often disregarded.[54]

On the other hand, the right to resort to spoken Romanian remained. Accounts of suits involving the press as well as other suits provide ample evidence of this. Most of the time Romanian defendants made use of their mother tongue proudly and demonstratively.

Between July 4 and 9, 1889, the Court of Szatmár heard a press suit brought by Vasile Lucaciu, a Romanian priest. According to the account of the Romanian newspaper of Brassó, Lucaciu spoke Romanian in front of the tribunal. The official witnesses followed his example, and "all, with united force, made certain that Romanian speech echoed in front of the tribunal." Romanians, fuelled by a sacred enthusiasm, took no heed of the threats uttered by the president of the tribunal, but "with a pride worthy of the name Romanian, resorted exclusively to their mother tongue." The accusations and intrigues were brought to light, the court absolved Lucaciu, "and the Romanian language carried the day."[55]

Thus a defense exclusively in Romanian did not hurt the chances of the Romanian defendant; in spite of his demonstrative attitude the court acquitted him. When it came to passing sentence, the decisive factor was not the nationality of the defendant or his language, but the justice of his cause. If justice was not on his side, the sentence would be adverse. This was the case with the defendant in the famous suit of the "Memorandum" in 1894: Much like Lucaciu, he spoke exclusively in Romanian throughout the trial, in the presence of several hundred foreign observers.

In 1902, George Novacovici, a Romanian university student, also presented his defense in Romanian. The charge was that he had attacked the Royal Hungarian prosecutor who had offended the memory of Avram Iancu, the leader of the Romanian rebels in 1848, in a sharply worded article. Novacovici's hearing took place on April 8, 1902. Although he knew Hungarian well, he nevertheless spoke exclusively in Romanian during the entire hearing. His justification was "that I want to avail myself of the right granted to me by law to speak only in my mother tongue, Romanian." His stalwart demeanor did not hurt his cause. The tribunal of Kolozsvár acquitted him of the charge.[56]

Dr. Valeriu Braniște, professor and newspaper editor, and the delegate Dr. Nicolae Șerban likewise used their mother tongue before the tribunal. The latter stood as a defendant in front of the Royal Tribunal of Brassó in 1911. He began his lengthy pleading with the following words:

I am a lawyer, but as a defendant I have the right to speak in Romanian. This language is dear to me, and I insist on making use of my rights, to such a degree that I would not give up the right, fully aware that this boldness will only render my situation even more serious.[57]

The specific examples above illustrate that during the Dual Monarchy, the use of Romanian in front of Hungarian courts was not restricted. Romanians could rely on their language freely in Kolozsvár, Szatmár, or Brassó, if they wished, and its exclusive use entailed no disadvantage for them.

The Use of Romanian in the Churches and the Schools.

In the period of the Dual Monarchy, the Hungarian residents of Romanian background, belonged to either the Uniate (united with Rome) or the Eastern Orthodox Church. The Romanian national character of these two churches was officially recognized by Hungarian legislation in the period following the Compromise. Consequently, Romanian was officially recognized as the language of the two churches.... Uniate and Orthodox priests spoke Romanian within and outside the church, communicated in Romanian with the authorities and the congregations, published and distributed ecclesiastic and religious publications in Romanian, and placed Romanian inscriptions on the walls of churches and other religious buildings, as well as on tombstones.

Instruction was also in Romanian at the primary schools, secondary schools, and at the higher institutions maintained by the churches. For a decade following the Compromise, the language of the state did not even have to be taught as a subject. The situation was modified in the second decade. The Hungarian National Assembly passed a law in 1879, which required that Hungarian be taught as a subject in the denominational primary schools. Act XXX of 1883, extended this requirement to the secondary schools. But in the higher theological seminaries of the Romanians, Hungarian never became a required subject during the entire period, even though these institutions received considerable state subsidies. On the other hand, Romanian language and literature were among the required subjects.

Between 1867 and 1918, the majority of the schools in the country were denominational; in the schools sponsored by the Romanian churches teaching in Romanian was preserved to the end. Although the

so-called "Apponyi Laws," adopted in 1907-08, increased the number of
hours devoted to the teaching of Hungarian, they did not interfere with
the use of Romanian as the language of instruction. The registries, the
minutes of faculty meetings, and all documents pertaining to the
internal affairs of the schools were exclusively in Romanian. It did not
even occur to the Hungarian authorities to require the parallel use of
Hungarian in order to facilitate state supervision.

According to Article 15 of the nationalities law, the language of
instruction at the state schools would have to be determined by the
Minister of Education at all times. But the same Article made it
mandatory for the Minister to strive to provide as far as possible,
instruction in their mother tongue, "the citizens from ethnic groups
living together in significant numbers" in schools sponsored by the
state. This prescription pertained to the schooling provided for the
nationalities, obligating the state to set up primary and secondary
schools in native languages of residents.

Nowhere were these provisions of the law actually carried out during
the Dual Monarchy. Hungarian leaders left instruction in mother
tongues in the hands of the churches. The state schools, which formed
25% to 30% of all schools, taught all subjects in Hungarian. The
language of instruction in some of the community schools was
Romanian in the first years of the Dual Monarchy; but later in many
communities, the leaders handed the schools over to the state, and the
language of instruction became Hungarian. The Romanian pupils no
longer studied in their mother tongue in these schools.

According to the law, the state was supposed to set up Romanian-
language primary and secondary schools in areas with a Romanian
majority; to bypass the Romanian language and introduce Hungarian
as the language of instruction in these schools was one of the biggest
mistakes of Hungarian educational policy in this period. One reason
why the law was disregarded, no doubt, was the nationalist illusion
which expected to win over the indifferent or anti-Hungarian nationalities through education. Many Hungarians were aware of the antagonistic attitude of the Romanians, including the Romanian plans for the
partition of the country. Several Hungarian dailies and weeklies
regularly published articles regarding the Romanians, and these often
mentioned Romanian irredentism. When, at the time of the 1872
elections, some candidates of the Independence Party made promises to
support the "just demands" of the Romanians, in order to win their
votes, lead articles in the Deák-party newspaper of Kolozsvár warned
them about the possible consequences. The candidates should not forget,
the newspaper wrote, that the demands the Romanians called "just"

included "Daco-Romania all the way to the Tisza River." Whoever supported these demands was playing with fire, "setting fire to his own house."[58]

Like other papers, this newspaper also revealed the Romanian connections of the irredentist movement. It revealed in one of its articles, that the Romanian nationalists of Transylvania identified themselves with these strivings in Romania, the ultimate objective of which was the "partition of the Hungarian homeland."[59]

Dezső Szilágyi and others believed that actually granting all the rights guaranteed under the law of nationalities would become yet another weapon the Romanians could use against the Hungarian state. This was essentially the reason why the aforementioned prescriptions of the law on nationalities were not observed.

The Use of Romanian Place Names and Family Names.

Generally speaking, the names of towns and villages evolved among nations as a result of a long linguistic and historical development. The same goes for family names. For these reasons place names and family names become an organic part of the vocabulary of individual nations. Their unrestricted usage in private and public life is part and parcel of the freedom to use one's language. Their restriction, or any attempt to modify them, would constitute outright duress against a given nation or ethnic group. Such measures usually elicit strong emotional reactions.

As a general rule of linguistics, individual names come about in accordance with the special nature of a given language. Whether it is a matter of original designations, or of borrowing from a foreign language, the peculiarities of the language come through. In rare cases it may happen that a foreign place's name is adopted into another language without change. Paris, the capital of France, has the same name in German, English, and Romanian, but its pronunciation varies according to the peculiarities of the language. In the case of other capitals the modification may go beyond the pronunciation and extend to spelling: for instance, the capital of England, London, is Londres in French, Londre in Romanian. The Swiss city near the French and German borders is Bâle in French, Basel in German. Venice is called Venedig in German, Venise in French, and Venetis in Romanian, although it is Venezia in Italian. All nations would consider it a barbarism if they were forced to change the age-old name of their city for a foreign name.

If family names that evolved over the course of centuries are arbitrarily changed when copied into another language, it is likewise a matter of aggression. The international consensus is to write foreign names according to their original spelling, without modification. Georges B. Clemenceau, Winston Churchill, and Otto von Bismarck have identical names in all languages; they are written in their original form the world over.

In areas where several nations or ethnic groups live side by side, the towns they inhabit jointly are called by different names. Thus a town or village may have as many names as there are ethnic groups. The names usually originate with the first settlers. Residents who arrive later, accept the name given to it by the earlier settlers, or adopt it according to the spirit of their own language and pronounce it differently.

Such was the situation in Hungary. In areas inhabited by different ethnic groups, the place names had several variants. In Transylvania and the neighboring counties where Hungarians, Germans, and Romanians live side by side, most localities had Hungarian, German, and Romanian names. The seat of the county of Kolozs was called Kolozsvár by the Hungarians, Klausenburg [Kolozsvár] by the Germans, and Cluj [Kolozsvár] by the Romanians. Of course, three different names evolved only where three ethnic groups lived together in close proximity. Consequently, groups that arrived later adopted the names used by the indigenous population. This fact becomes clear from etymological analysis and toponymy.[60]

Let us provide some specific examples of the aforementioned facts.

1. The following names were taken over by the Romanians from the Hungarians without change: Déva, Apahida, and Arad.
2. Hungarian names modified by the Romanians in their spelling were: Kisfalud = Chişfalud or Chişfalău, Nagylak = Nădlac, Újlak = Úileac or Uilac, Széplak = Seplac, Középlak = Cazărlac, Szatmár = Satmar, Dicsőszentmárton = Diciosânmartin, Szentandrás = Sentandras, Szentkirály = Sâncraiu/Sîncrai, Szentimre = Sântimreu, etc.
3. Hungarian names transformed in accordance with the nature of the Romanian language were: Bükkös = Bichiş, Gambuc = Gambuţ, Hari = Hariş, Herepe = Herepeia, Csesztve = Cisteiu, Mindszent = Mesentea, Igen = Ighiu,

under foreign rule. The true implications of this situation become clear if we compare the use of Romanian in Hungary to its use in other countries.

The Use of Romanian in Other Countries

While the Romanians of Hungary could make free use of their language in public and private life, in most neighboring countries the nationalities could not do this at all, or only with considerable restrictions. As a memorandum published in Bucharest makes clear,[67] the close to one million Romanians living in Serbia were not allowed to speak Romanian in public places. Young Romanians were compelled to attend evening courses organized by the Serbian authorities to learn to speak and sing in Serbian. The authorities resorted to every possible means to wipe out the use of Romanian. The churches could hold services only in Serbian. Romanian family and Christian names were Serbianized, as prescribed by an episcopal circular to Serbian priests. Romanian family names were altered in Serbian schools and offices: Sandul became Sandulović, Iancu — Iaincović, Iorga — Iorgović, etc.

The one million Romanians in Bessarabia suffered a similarly miserable fate. Services could not be held in Romanian; only at funerals was it permissible to recite a few words in Romanian, for the benefit of the deceased.[68] The newspaper of Brassó noted:

> The entire Romanian nation gazes beyond the Prut River in mourning, because brothers waste their lives in a small land taken away from us by force and guile.... Bessarabia, a piece of the holy land we call fatherland, is groaning under the arbitrary rule of a tyrannical tsar, and we do not have the power to change the sigh of pain frozen on the cold lips of the Bessarabian peasant into a revolutionary song.[69]

The readers of Romanian papers in Hungary read not only about the sad fate of the Romanians in the Balkans and in Bessarabia; occasionally the Romanian press carried news about the French or the Poles living with in the German Empire. While in many hundreds of Romanian villages in the Transylvanian counties public affairs were conducted in Romanian and the language could be freely used in county and popular assemblies, or in the municipal offices; the following lines appeared in the Romanian weekly of Szászváros regarding the use of language by Frenchmen living under German rule: "In Alsace-Lorraine the Prussian government decreed that when there are at least two individuals on the communal committee able to speak German reasonably well, the official language becomes German, and all documents are to be issued in German."[70] A few months later, the same paper reported about another Prussian law which ordered that in areas of Poland belonging to the German Reich, speakers at popular assemblies might speak only German.[71]

The nationalities policy of the independent kingdom of Romania deserves special attention, if only because the Romanian press and the leaders of the government which gained its independence under the rule of Carol I often condemned the Hungarian policies on nationality in harsh words. They almost constantly accused the Hungarian governments of oppressing Romanian language and culture. Let us, therefore, take a closer look at the opportunities this Romanian regime, which demanded complete national freedom for the Romanians of Hungary, offered to its own minorities.

The scholar dealing with the issue meets his first surprise when he picks up the official report of the census of 1900. This census contains no data regarding nationalities.[72] According to the Director of the Statistical Office, pertinent data were not included; because nothing was to be gained from examining the use of languages spoken within the country. Therefore, there was no minority issue in Romania. The population, numbering 5,956,690, was classified into two groups: Romanians and stateless. The first group, Romanian citizens with full rights, numbered 5,489,296. The second group, the stateless who did not enjoy full rights and were not granted citizenship, numbered 278,560, of whom 256,488 were Jews.

If we compare these statistics to data obtained from other sources, it becomes immediately evident that they do not hold water scientifically, that they are deliberately biased. This is clear even from the census itself. Regarding the population of Dobrudja, annexed by Romania in 1878, we read that it "consists of foreign settlers," who became Romanian as a result of the annexation. We also find out how the population was misrepresented; they were Turkish in the majority, but there were a goodly number of Bulgarians, Russians, and Greeks among them. Without any doubt the 129,217 inhabitants of Dobrudja belonged to non-Romanian ethnic groups at the turn of the century.

In addition to the nationalities in the Dobrudja, there were more than 50,000 Csángók living in Romania. A nationalist Romanian writer discovered their presence with astonishment in 1906. "It was my misfortune to find in the villages of Moldavia, Romanians who could speak no Romanian," he wrote among other things:

In fact, I found entire villages where there was only this kind of Romanians. In this part of Romania you might believe you are in a Hungarian village: the language is Hungarian, the customs are Hungarian.... Our beloved Moldavia is an anthill of foreigners where the lard of the Hungarians and the garlic of the Jews play their part.[73]

According to these data Romania did have a minorities problem although official circles refused to recognize it. The state was declared a "nation state," and the foreign nationalities, constituting about 16% of the population, were to be Romanianized by every possible means.[74] The chauvinist measures adopted with regard to the Hungarian Csángók were particularly obvious.

As we have seen, Romanians under Hungarian rule could use their language freely in the churches, in the schools, and in public life; the Romanian government, however, forbade the Csángók from using their mother tongue in every area of public life. Religious services were held entirely in Romanian; the priests delivered their sermons and recited all prayers in Romanian. Most did not even know Hungarian. There were one or two who understood the mother tongue of the congregation, but the Romanian bishop of Iaşi would not allow them to use the language in their sermons. Thus the priests who understood Hungarian could not even use that language to communicate with the faithful. Eventually, the bishop relented and the priests were allowed to take confession from the dying in their mother tongue. Hungarian was banned from the schools as well: the children could study only in Romanian. At the seminaries the language was also Romanian.

The Csángók were not allowed prayer books in Hungarian. When a Roman Catholic priest obtained Hungarian prayer books, they were confiscated by the authorities. The Csángók were not even allowed to use their mother tongue on tombstones: all inscriptions had to be in Romanian.

The same procedure applied regarding place and family names. Instead of the place names used by the Hungarian people, names with a Romanian sound were mandated officially. The village of Báródbeznye became Bezneaca, Dormánfalva became Dormăneşti, Barátos [Brateş] became Brăteşti. If anyone added the local name in parenthesis after the official name, the item was not delivered by the Romanian postal services.

The Romanian authorities meant to eradicate all traces of Hungarian descent by writing Hungarian family names with a Romanian spelling in official documents. Thus the internationally known family

name Bartók became Bartoc, Kádár became Cadar, Baka became Boaca,
Bode became Bodea, Barkóczi became Barcacian.[75] Names with a
Hungarian sound disappeared and the Romanian authorities could then
consider their bearer even more Romanian.

Romanian chauvinism did not stop at forbidding the use of the
native language to nationalities living of Romanian soil; at times it
even intervened against foreign visitors using a foreign language. In
1906, an ethnographic fair of all Romanians was organized Bucharest,
and the Saxon chorus "Transylvania" was invited to participate. At the
ceremonial concert the chorus sang in German. After its performance
the Romanian historian and university professor Nicolae Iorga, first
secretary of the famous Romanian Cultural League, stood up in his box
and shouted to the members of the Saxon chorus "It was beautiful! Why
don't you sing in Turkish next time!" Upon this the Romanian audience
whistled and booed, shouting "Down with them [i.e. with the German-
speaking performers]!" Dozens of university students ran to Iorga's box
and, lifting him onto their shoulders, carried him triumphantly around
the arena serving as stage. Iorga, who had provoked the demonstration,
shouted to the cheering masses from the shoulders of the youths: "I
objected to those who pretended to be French, but now we must not
allow the German language to become the new fashion."[76]

The infamous chauvinistic policies of Romania — the complete ban
on the use of the mother tongue by Csángók, Turks, and other nationalities — met with the approval of the Romanian press of Hungary. What
is more, this press occasionally demanded even harsher policies against
the Jews and other nationalities. While it constantly attacked the
Hungarian authorities, resorting to the extremist slogan "all or
nothing!", in Romania itself it favored complete Romaniani-zation. This
fundamental inconsistency did not go unnoticed in either country. In
1911, the author of an article in a Romanian periodical expressed his
astonishment. "It seems," wrote Radu Ciomag in a Bucharest periodical, "that our brothers [the Romanians of Transylvania] have double
standards. One for the world at large, and another for their own use.
They condemn chauvinism in their country, but they accept it in
Romania." It is understandable that the Romanian paper *Românul*,
published at Arad, rejected the argument of the Bucharest essayist, even
though right on target, with the fury of someone caught in the act.[77]

To summarize the use of the language by Romanians living under
Hungarian rule we may note that, at the time of the Compromise, the
leaders of the Hungarian state adopted a nationalities law that was
more liberal and democratic than any known in Europe at the time. In
the years following the Compromise, with the exception of a few of its

articles, this law was observed and carried out with respect to the Romanian population. But a few years later, by way of reaction to the anti-constitutional and anti-Hungarian attitude of the Romanians, a process got under way which led to the exploitation of the law and a mockery of its spirit in many locations. Some of the measures, including Article 17 regarding the establishment of state schools in the languages of the minorities, and Article 27 regarding the appointment of administrators from the ranks of the minorities, were never applied at all. Yet, as regards the Romanians, over three-quarters of the provisions of the law were observed in practice throughout, from 1867 to 1918. Where the law was circumvented, the passive resistance mounted by Romanians was at least as much to blame as the impatience and distrust of Hungarians, in the opinion of the Romanians themselves. As regards the use of the mother tongue, the Romanians of Hungary enjoyed far more extensive rights than the Csángók of Romania, Romanians living in third countries, or the French and Poles living under German rule. According to Romanian sources, the Hungarian state adopted policies that were more understanding and more democratic than the ones adopted by the Serbian, Romanian, Russian, or German governments vis-à-vis their own nationalities.

Endnotes

1. Louis Eisenmann, *Le compromis austro-hongrois de 1867* (Paris, 1904), p. 551.
2. Imre Mikó, *Nemzetiségi jog és nemzetiségi politika* [The Rights of Nationalities and Nationalities Policies] (Kolozsvár, 1944), pp. 342-344.
3. In several works by Iorga and Lupaş, as well as in high school textbooks *Şcoala românească din Transilvania şi Ungaria*. Onisifor Ghibu, the Romanian university professor well-known for his anti-Hungarian feelings, wrote in 1915: "From the moment the law on nationalities went into effect until now the law has never been observed." *Extras din Revista Generală a Învăţământului* (Bucharest, 1915), p. 20.
4. Puşcariu, *op. cit.*, p. 85.
5. *Ibid.*, pp. 112-113.
6. *Ibid.*, p. 125.
7. La începutul anului," *Telegraful Român*, 1899, No. 1.
8. *Tribuna*, October 17-29, 1885, No. 237.
9. Slavici, *Lumea prin care am trecut*, pp. 64-65.
10. "Din comitatul Solnocului interior in Oct," *Gazeta Transilvaniei*, 1869, No. 78.
11. "Tribunale care interpretează legile," *Gazeta Transilvaniei*, 1872, No. 56.
12. "Limba română în statut," *ibid.*, 1872, No. 632.
13. *Ibid.*

124   Sándor Bíró

14. "Asia ce face toti practii — și Rupea," *ibid.*, 1872, Nos. 78, 81.

15. "Esperturi despre luptele și gravaminele românilor," *ibid.*, 1872, No. 101.

16. Slavici, *Lumea prin care am trecut*, pp. 69-70.

17. *Ibid.*, pp. 66-69.

18. *Ibid.*, p. 70.

19. *Ibid.*, p. 72.

20. Teodor V. Păcățian, *Cartea de aur sau luptele politice-naționale ale românilor de sub coroana ungară.* (Sibiu, 1902-1915), Vol. VI, pp. 655-656.

21. Ion Lupaș, *Contribuțiuni la istoria ziaristicei românești ardelene* (Sibiu, 1926), p. 21.

22. Pușcariu, *op. cit.*, 9, pp. 24-25.

23. *Tribuna*, December 14, 1884, No. 195.

24. Vágó, ed., *op. cit.*, pp. 207-208.

25. "Curentul neu," *Libertatea*, 1902, No. 22.

26. "Visul nostru," *ibid.*, 1907, No. 36.

27. "Notărirea dela Șiclău," *ibid.*, 1910, No. 8.

28. *Ibid.*, 1912, No. 28, p. 5.

29. "Drepturi pentru limba noastră," *ibid.*, 1912, p. 53.

30. "Pilda vrednică," *ibid.*, 1906, No. 5.

31. Italics in the original.

32. Italics by the author.

33. "Cum să scriem la comitat în treburile scolilor?" *Libertatea*, 1910, No. 49.

34. "Cutezanta unui solgabirau în a ataca dreptul limbii române," *Libertatea*, 1910, No. 33.

35. *Tribuna*, Oct. 29, 1885, No. 237.

36. "Monumentul lui Avram Iancu," *Revista Orăștiei*, September 5, 1885, No. 39.

37. József Papp, in *Magyar Kisebbség*, 1931, No. 10, p. 879.

38. "Conspectul românilor din Budapesta după profesiune", *Călindarul poporului pe 1914*, p. 102-105.

39. *Tribuna*, May 9, 1884, No. 21.

40. *Gazeta Transilvaniei*, 1890, No. 18.

41. Valeriu Moldovan, "Lupta în comitate," *Libertatea*, January 25, 1902.

42. *Libertatea*, 1902, No. 2.

43. "Șovinismul brutal," *ibid.*, June 7, 1902, No. 24.

44. "Dela congregația," *ibid.*, 1903, No. 41.

45. "Noutăți, *ibid.*, 1904, No. 1.

46. "Lupta românilor la Dej," *ibid.*, 1904, No. 2.

47. "Drept are," *ibid.*, 1904, No. 3.

48. "Dela Dej," *Libertatea*, 1904, No. 4. At the funeral of Ion Brătianu in 1927, the same Alexanderu Vaida-Voevod was to declare that, thanks to the intervention of the great statesman, the Romanian parties of the Regat were able to reach an agreement regarding the Transylvanian issue: "From then on, in obedience to instruction received from Brătianu, the leaders of the Romanian parties of Transylvania guided the struggles of the Romanians according to instructions from the party in power in Romania." Thus the leaders of the Romanians of Transylvania were in constant contact with the governments of

Romania (*Viitorul*, November 30, 1927). Mihali, who was likewise active in Dés, wrote in 1929 that the Romanian Party of Hungary carried on its struggle in accordance with instructions received from Bucharest, and liaison with Bucharest was an organic part of the politics and tactics of the Romanian National Party.

49. "Dela congregaţie," *Libertatea*, 1910, No. 11.

50. "Lupta românească la Arad," *ibid.*, 1913, No. 46.

51. *Ibid.*, 1903, No. 49.

52. "Dela oraş," *ibid.*, 1902, No. 43.

53. "Şovinismul deschide căreri noi," *ibid.*, 1912, No. 37.

54. "Mai nou," *ibid.*, 1902, No. 54.

55. "Amintiri din anul, 1889," *Gazeta Transilvaniei*, 1890, No. 1.

56. "Procesul Novacovici," *Libertatea*, 1902, No. 17.

57. *Românul*, November 23, 1911. See Jakabffy, *op. cit.*, pp. 80-81.

58. *Kelet*, 1872, No. 145, published in Belső-Szolnok county (the paper for the Ferenc Deák Party in Kolozsvár).

59. *Ibid.*, 1872, No. 205.

60. István Kniezsa, "Keletmagyarország helynevei" [Place Names in Eastern Hungary] in *Magyarok és románok* [Hungarians and Romanians], Vol. I, eds. József Deér and László Gáldi (Budapest, 1943), pp. 158-159. This was the yearbook of the Hungarian Historical Institute for 1943. Kniezsa shows that 58% of the 3,836 Romanian names listed in the work of S. Moldovan and N. Togan, *Dicţionarul numirilor de localităţi cu poporaţiune română di Ungaria* (Sibiu, 1909), were derived from the Hungarian. 21.3% of all names have a purely Romanian origin, 12% Slav, 4.2% German, while the derivation of 304 names remains unknown. Of the 511 place names mentioned in contemporary sources to the end of the 13th century, there were only three of Romanian origin, whereas 423 were Hungarian. Of the Romanian place names mentioned before 1400 A.D. 1,355 were of Hungarian and 76 of Romanian derivation. These data demonstrate that the overwhelming majority of place names were taken over by the Romanians from the Hungarian language.

61. *Revista Bistriţei*, 1908, No. 32.

62. "O horărîre dreaptă," *Libertatea*, 1909, No. 7

63. "Numirile comunelor," *Unirea*, February 10, 1912.

64. "Ştie româneşte," *Revista Orăştiei*, October 26 - November 7, 1896, No. 44.

65. "Coresondenţa," *Libertatea*, 1903, No. 43.

66. "Praznicul cultural dela Arad," *ibid.*, 1911, No. 18.

67. *Universul*, January 11, 1913, in Jakabffy, *op. cit.*, pp. 181-182.

68. "Starea socială a românilor besarabeni," *ibid.*, October 17, 1912.

69. "Trecut şi viitor," *Gazeta Transilvaniei*, 1913, No. 1.

70. "Pilda rea a apăsării," *Libertatea*, 1908, No. 38.

71. "Adunări mute," *ibid.*, 1908, No. 51.

72. L. Colescu, *Rescensământul general al populaţiunei României* (Bucharest, 1905), analyzed in detail by Endre Barna, *România nemzetiséqi politikája és az oláh ajkú magyar polgárok* [Romania's Nationalities Policies and Hungarian Citizens of Romanian background] (Kolozsvár, 1908).

73. *Sezătared Săteanului*, (Bucharest), 1906, No. 9-10, pp. 286-290.

74. On the basis of his analysis of the regions inhabited by minorities Endre Barna estimated the total number of non-Romanians at almost one million. *Op. cit.*, p. 22 ff.

75. *Ibid.*, pp. 71-72.

76. On the basis of the August 29, 1906, issue of *Dimineaţa* and other Romanian newspapers. In Barna, *op. cit.*, p. 161.

77. *Românul*, October 25, 1911, No. 234, states that Ciomag's essay appeared in the periodical *Noua Revistă Română*, published in Bucharest. The comments by *Românul* are deplorably lacking in purity of principles.

Chapter III

Romanian Churches in the Hungarian State

The history of ethnic groups demonstrates that, in addition to material factors, it is religion that determines the evolution of a given ethnic group. Many a nationality owes its survival as a nation and even its progress, to its religion and its clergy. Thus it is hardly possible to arrive at an accurate picture of the evolution of any ethnic group without taking a close look at its religious life.

Romanian Churches Before the Austro-Hungarian Compromise

The so-called Romanian churches played a decisive role in the national development of the indigenous Romanians. The term "Romanian church" refers to the Orthodox Christian Church and to the Uniate Church which broke away from it in 1699. Even before the Compromise of 1867 these churches had entirely blended with the national, cultural, and political aspirations of the Romanians. The priests, teachers, and theologians of the Uniate and Orthodox Churches were responsible for awakening the national consciousness of the Romanian bourgeoisie. The movements of 1848 were directed mainly by the leaders of these two churches, who were likewise responsible for setting the foundations of Romanian public education in the period 1849 to 1867. The Hungarian statesmen of the Compromise period were perfectly aware of these contributions of the Romanian churches. When Hungarians finally took political control over their own affairs, it was up to the Hungarian statesmen whether to allow further development of the mostly anti-Hungarian Romanian churches, or to paralyze the Romanian nationalist work of the churches by imposing various restrictions. The following details illustrate this dilemma.

Besides freedom of religion, churches are able to carry out their particular tasks well only if they have an adequate organization and the necessary financial strength, as well as freedom of organization and movement. Hence the objective of the state's religious and ecclesiastic policies, if well-intentioned, is to ensure the above conditions at all

127

times, while a state with a negative attitude would constantly strive to deprive the targeted churches of the conditions favoring their operation.

Hungary's Romanians were granted religious freedom by the end of the 18th century. The Hungarian laws of 1848 not only confirmed this freedom, but also granted their churches equal treatment and equal financial support. During the autocratic Austrian rule the two Romanian churches were markedly better off than the Hungarian churches, because the regime was ill-disposed towards the latter. The Orthodox Church was in an especially favorable situation as a consequence of the trust Emperor Francis Joseph manifested towards Andrei Șaguna, the Romanian Orthodox bishop and later archbishop. The bishop obtained this trust primarily because of the role he had played in 1848 when, during the Hungarian War of Independence, he lined up the Romanians against the Hungarians and, late in 1848, requested the intervention of the Russian troops stationed in the Romanian principalities to suppress the Hungarian fight for freedom.

In August 1865 when, because of Austria's deteriorating international position, the Austro-Hungarian Compromise became inevitable, Francis Joseph summoned Archbishop Șaguna and, in the course of a lengthy audience, informed him of the coming Compromise. The Emperor's counsel was that the Romanians adjust to the new situation — that is, to try to make peace with the Hungarians. After the audience the Archbishop declared to the Romanian official Popp, who came to inquire about the results: "We were thrown as prey to the Hungarians."[1]

Thus Hungarian statesmen received considerable leeway from the Emperor as regards policies towards the Romanians in Hungary. In other words, the continued development of the Romanian churches now depended to a large extent on the goodwill and generosity of the Hungarian statesmen. The evolution of the two Romanian churches was first of all a function of organization, and secondly a matter of finances. Both churches were Romanian, even officially speaking, and they wished to preserve this character by means of a separate administration and a solid financial base. Were these aims to encounter obstacles erected by the Hungarian state, such obstacles would certainly have been taken as a manifestation of a negative attitude.

The events indicate that the Hungarian state not only manifested goodwill, but gave decisive assistance and continued support to the progress of the two Romanian churches, their national character not withstanding.

Setting Up an Independent Archdiocese of the Uniate Church

The national character and progress of the two Romanian churches depended primarily on whether it was possible to keep the Romanian Uniate Church separate from the Hungarian Roman Catholic one, and the Romanian Orthodox Church separate from the Serbian Orthodox Church. The interests of the leaders of the Romanian churches and of their Romanian character demanded that they be preserved from the influence of non-Romanian co-religionists. Therefore Romanians always insisted on the complete separation of the Uniate Church from the Romanian Catholic Church in Hungary, and of the Romanian Orthodox Church from the Serbian. If these demands were met, the Romanians would no longer have to fear the absorption of their churches by Hungarian Catholics or Serbian Orthodox.

At the time of the Compromise this issue first came up in connection with the Romanian Orthodox Church, since the Romanian Uniate Church was already separated from the Hungarian Catholic Church in 1853. Indeed, on November 26 of that year Pope Pius IX recognized the Romanian archdiocese of the Uniate Church in Gyulafehérvár in his encyclical *Ecclesiam Christi*. The diocese of the old Uniate Church of Nagyvárad, as well as two new dioceses formed at Lugos and at Szamosújvár were placed under it. The Archbishop of Esztergom, the head of the church in Hungary, issued a statement relinquishing jurisdiction over the Romanian dioceses, thereby recognizing the independence of the Romanian archdiocese.

Thus by the time of the Compromise the Romanian Uniate Church was independent of the Primate of Esztergom, and embodied purely Romanian interests. Since the establishment of the archdiocese of Gyulafehérvár and of the two new dioceses took place under Austria's autocratic rule, it was up to the new Hungarian government to recognize their existence. The Hungarian government formed in 1867 took cognizance of this independence and gave legal recognition to the archdiocese and the two new dioceses by Act XXXIX of 1868. What's more, the Minister of Religious Affairs and Education, Baron József Eötvös, issued liberal instructions guaranteeing the election of the Romanian archbishop of Balázsfalva at all times by the Romanian priesthood, free from any outside interference. Thereby he preserved the Romanian Uniate priesthood's right to elect its leader in democratic fashion. Ion Vancea was elected archbishop in 1868, and Dr. Viktor Mihályi in 1893. The details of the electoral procedures were specified in directive number 2288/1892 by Minister of Religious Affairs and Education, Albin Csáky, in the spirit of Eötvös. In accordance with

these instructions, three candidates would be selected at the electoral
synod; and the King would appoint the Archbishop from among these
three. In practice, the King always appointed the candidate who
obtained the plurality of the votes.

Thus the Hungarian government ensured the election of the
Archbishop in a liberal and completely democratic fashion. All
possibility of government interference was excluded. The Romanian
priests enjoyed rights in the selection of their leader, a practice
Hungarian priests could not boast of, since the Hungarian Catholic
bishops obtained their sees by appointment, without having to ask the
clergy.

The Romanian Orthodox Archbishopric

The evolution of the Romanian Orthodox Church is even more
interesting. This church was promoted to an Archbishopric by the ruler
Francis Joseph in 1864. This recognition was tantamount to granting
independence, that is, to separation from the Serbian Orthodox Church;
but since the ruler had taken this step during Austrian rule, once again
the constitutional regime which came about as a result of the Compromise had to legislate anew. Thus Act IX of 1868 was adopted, by which
the Hungarian parliament recognized the separate nature and self-rule
of the Romanian Orthodox Church. What's more, at the motion of the
Romanian member of parliament and ministerial councillor, Ion
Puşcariu, parliament adopted Article 6 of the law, designating the
Orthodox Church as a Romanian "national" church. There were
objections to this proposal, but the majority voted in favor at the end,
since it was backed by Eötvös. During the debates the "parliament of
Hungary," wrote Puşcariu, "manifested a very favorable disposition
towards the Romanian church under the leadership of the free-thinking
Minister Baron Eötvös."[2] The law was adopted thanks to the sympathy of the Hungarian parliament, and the independence and self-rule of
the Romanian Orthodox Church was legally sanctioned. A legislative
congress of the Romanian Orthodox Church was convened on the basis
of this law. After lengthy debates this congress approved the famous
Organizational Rules — a constitution which regulated the government
of the church in detail. The draft of the aforementioned constitution
had been worked out by well-known Romanian politicians such as
Vincenţin Rabeş, Cosma Partenie, Alexandru Mocioni [Mocsonyi], and
others. By integrating certain Protestant principles and certain ulterior
political motives, the laity was given a chance to control the government of the church. According to the constitution adopted by the

congress, the congregation would have a determining role in managing ecclesiastic affairs. The lay delegates were to form two-thirds of all ecclesiastic bodies, including the synods of deacons, of bishops, of the archbishop, and even of the national synod. All vacant posts in the church would be filled through elections. As a subsequent appraisal of this constitution notes:

> within the framework of the Organizational Rules, the congrega-
> tion, like sovereign people, decide freely the external affairs of
> the church. It freely controls and oversees ecclesiastic and
> educational matters, as well as its foundations. It elects all
> officials, from the bell-ringer to the highest dignitary, the
> Metropolitan.[3]

The application of the principles enunciated in the Organizational Rules provided the people, or rather the intelligentsia, with almost unlimited powers within the Romanian Orthodox Church. In the name of the people, and often in opposition to the clergy, they became the deciding factor at elections, and in all internal and external affairs of the church.

Lay control was not in accord with the wishes of Şaguna. His own proposal was based on principles of church tradition and in the spirit of church canons. Two among these were especially important. One related to elections in the church, the other to the composition of the supreme body. Şaguna was an advocate of indirect elections, because he wanted to avoid demagoguery. In his opinion direct voting entailed abuses, as manifested in political life: clashes result from slanders and vested interests, and these unavoidably degenerate into demagoguery. He wanted to make the Synod of Bishops the supreme body of the church, in accordance with the spirit of church canons. But the lay majority at the congress summoned in 1868 radically altered the original plan of Şaguna. There were meaningful modifications. As one leading member of the congress was to observe later, the so-called Organizational Rules "was the work of the congress of 1868, rather than that of Şaguna, both in form, and in its most essential parts. Thanks to its higher educational level the lay element succeeded in introducing a secular mentality even into the church."[4]

Şaguna and his immediate collaborators knew right well that the great masses of the Romanian people were not mature enough to make a correct application of the liberal constitution advocated by the majority at the congress. They foresaw that the constitution of the church "placed excessive powers into the hands of the people before they had a chance to obtain the education needed for the correct use of these powers."[5] The majority at the congress, however, was not in the least affected by this consideration. They well knew that it is not really the people who would take decisions within the church, but the intelligentsia, and those who controlled the press and the banks.

These factors explain why Şaguna and other representatives of the Orthodox Church felt that the Organizational Rules of 1868 were not orthodox or canonical. They were familiar with the situation of Orthodox Churches in other countries where the faithful were not granted significant rights in face of the bishops or of the secular ruler. This derived naturally from the Ceasaro-Papist nature and spirit of the Orthodox Church. Thus the Orthodox Romanians of Hungary, led by political and ethnic considerations, turned away from some Orthodox traditions and elaborated their church constitution on the basis of democratic self-government in the Protestant spirit.

The big question remained: would the Hungarian government consent to this strongly political regulation favoring the self-government of the Romanian Orthodox Church, in the spirit of Protestantism? The Romanian sources describe the details of the approval of the Organizational Rules as follows:

"Minister Eötvös appointed a board to evaluate this proposed rule. It was composed of two undersecretaries, Gedeon Tanárky and George Ivanovics [a Romanian]. This board, under the personal direction of the Minister, read out and discussed the entire Organizational Rules article by article. Once they had discussed the whole document and noting the essentially liberal concepts it embodied the Minister declared: "I will let His Majesty sanction this law so that they may one day say that it happened under a liberal Hungarian minister who did not want to appear less liberal than your congress."[6]

Indeed, so it happened. On May 28, 1869, the Hungarian King sanctioned the Organizational Rules, with minor modifications, at Schönbrunn. Puşcariu, who provided the above description of the role of Eötvös, also gave an account of the modifications. According to him, he and Ivanovics felt they should immediately agree to the modifications, since these did not interfere with the rights of the church, and mostly because they were afraid that if sent back to the Romanian congress the whole Organizational Rules might be jeopardized. Eötvös worked on his own, and he rarely accepted advice from his younger ministerial colleagues. He carried out what in his opinion was positive from an idealistic, liberal point of view — with touchingly pure motivations by today's standards. After his death the more important ecclesiastic affairs were presented to the ministerial council by Andrássy who, being a pragmatic politician, was more inclined to resist. When he found out that the bishops of the Romanian Orthodox Church were elected by the diocese synods in accordance with the Organizational Rules submitted by Eötvös and sanctioned by His Majesty, he would not believe it at first. When section chief Mandics placed the actual text in front of him, he exclaimed: "Poor Eötvös, he was always dreaming of American institutions, but even in America this is not the way things are."[7]

We may imagine the happiness of the Romanian church leaders when they received the news of the approval of the Organizational Rules. They knew better than Eötvös what this sanction meant from the Romanian point of view. A Romanian church historian wrote:

> The Orthodox Romanians were convinced, that through this most favorable basic law of their autonomous archdiocese, they have secured power; and a safe preserve for their nationalist aspirations, at least as far as church life was concerned; and this independence gave them the opportunity to extend it to educational, cultural and economic areas too, within limits.

Indeed, the pride and awareness of independence of the Romanian Orthodox was enhanced by the approval of the law. The following year, in 1870, the official paper of the church, the *Telegraful Român*, could write: "The Orthodox are subject only to God and to their autonomous archdiocese."[8] Such expressions of complete freedom did correspond to the situation in which the Orthodox Church found itself on Hungarian territory as a consequence of the Organizational Rules. It functioned in a straightforward manner, meeting no obvious obstacles during the entire period of the Dual Monarchy. Understandably when, decades later, the leaders of the church surveyed the fortunate outcome of their progress, they felt unbounded gratitude towards the first Hungarian government for its approval of the broad self-rule. Partenie Cosma, the executive director of Albina, described the policies of the government at that time as follows:

> We mention with sincere recognition those statesmen who brought about the first constitutional government, especially Count Gyula Andrássy, the former Prime Minister, and Baron József Eötvös, the former Minister of Religion and Education. They not only included the autonomy of our church among the laws of the state and secured the approval of our Organizational Rules, but always exhibited goodwill and a sense of fairness

towards our church in all matters. They treated our church on
a footing of equality with other churches in our country. That
government even created a special section in the Ministry of
Religion and Education to deal with Romanian Orthodox
Christian matters, along the lines of the one dealing with Roman
Catholic issues, where our ecclesiastic and school problems could
find expert solutions, in an objective and patriotic spirit. We had
an under-secretary in that Ministry, Georghe Ivanovici, a
ministerial councillor, Ioan Puşcariu, Esquire, and a section chief
named Roşiescu.[9]

As the years passed it became obvious to the initiated that the
self-government worked out in the Rules was threatened not by the
state but by the Romanians within the church. Indeed, the Hungarian
state did not intervene in the affairs of the church. The leaders of the
Orthodox Church tackled all key issues of their ecclesiastic life as they
saw fit: the election of the dignitaries, the training of priests, the
organization of the dioceses, church discipline, the administration,
upkeep, and direction of all church institutions. The fears of Şaguna
and his immediate collaborators became verified. After Şaguna's death,
most believers were unable to take advantage of the rights granted
them under the Organizational Rules. Intense party strife arose already
over the selection of his successor. The consensus candidate of the
church was Nicolae Popea, Şaguna's most faithful and talented disciple,
but the secular intelligentsia, with Babeş in the lead, prevented his
election. They resorted to slanders, underhanded tactics and distortions
published in the press, leading to the triumph of demagoguery within
the church.

After Roman Miron was elected archbishop in 1874, there were no
more elections to that office for over a quarter of a century. Electoral
fraud in filling vacant sees and in the election of priests became
rampant. The election of the bishop of Arad in 1875 was a particularly
notorious case. As we may read in a study of the Orthodox Church, in
this election:

all institutions and practices of the church were trampled
underfoot. More particularly, no regard was paid to the canonical preparation of the candidates, their qualifications, their style
of living, or to clerical seniority. No notice was taken of
canonical requirements and of personal qualities, even though
prescribed by the church and required by the spirit of an
enlightened age....[10] The new bishop of Arad, for the sake of

whose election these abuses had been committed, was Ioan
Meţianu, the eventual successor to Archbishop Roman Miron.
He was of a secular turn of mind, aggressive and fond of
intrigue, as became evident during his over 25 years of tenure as
bishop. He governed the see as a tyrant and filled the vacant
posts with his own people at discretion. The abuses during the
elections at Arad occurred in other episcopal elections as well.
The culprits were usually lay persons who committed themselves
to one candidate or other, slandering their opponents with false
political and social accusations.[11]

Most often these lay persons resorted to political slanders as a
welltried weapon against candidates not to their liking. Since the
antiHungarian campaign of the Romanian press was well under way
from the beginning of the seventies, all that was needed in order to
slander anyone was to claim that the person in question was subservient
to the Hungarian government or some Hungarian authority. It was but
one more step to the even more serious charge: the individual was in
the government's pay. These rumors were spread often by the very
persons who themselves may have been suspected of such behavior.
Archbishop Roman Miron had his fair share of such accusations during
his entire period in office. Although elected by a large majority, the
first slander was soon uttered by his competitors: he owed his election
to the government. One of those who refuted this charge had been a
delegate to the congress. He published the following statement in the
official paper of the church upon the death of the archbishop: "As a
former delegate to the congress I deny with all my might that the
government exerted any kind of influence on the delegates on behalf of
the victorious candidate."[12] The government had no opportunity to
intervene even if it wanted to. Besides, Roman Miron had outstanding
qualifications, recognized among others by the historian Iorga.
    The campaign of slander directed against Roman Miron had
religious and political roots, for the archbishop was dissatisfied with the
behavior of the laymen in the church and in politics. On more than one
occasion he spoke disapprovingly of the "unlimited freedom" which the
Organizational Rules accorded them. He saw lucidly that most laymen
did not make good use of the rights granted them. Ten years after the
introduction of the Organizational Rules, the Orthodox archbishop still
felt this factor was the principal reason for the difficulties of the church.
In addition to the financial woes, it was these uninformed members who
constituted the main obstacle to the progress of the church. "Our
people," stated the Archbishop at the opening of the Synod in 1879,

"especially the peasants, but occasionally even those from the professional classes, cannot use well and correctly rights guaranteed to them in church life through the new organic institutions." Nothing can be accomplished until the faithful learn how to use these rights well. If the financial problems pass, and the faithful learn how to use their rights:

> then we may become justly proud of the constitution of our church, for it may provide the most favorable results in every area of church life. Then by uniting us into a national church and fulfilling our beautiful liberal institutions, unlike anything to be found in any other church, our wishes will become completely realized.[13]

This observation of the Archbishop of the Orthodox Romanians of Hungary regarding the unparalleled liberality of the church institutions was so conformed to the true state of affairs that it was constantly and proudly repeated by the clerical and secular press of the Romanians of Hungary. Thus, when the seminaries for Orthodox priests were placed under the supervision of the main body of the Ministry of Public Education in Bucharest, the best-known periodical of the Orthodox Romanians in Hungary expressed amazement and disapproval.

> The state may not regulate theological instruction, only the Synod is entitled to supervise theological instruction. The directives issued by the main council of public education in Bucharest regarding theological education constitute an attack against the church. We, Romanians of Austria-Hungary, who do not have the good fortune to live under the Romanian and Orthodox government — what would we do if our government allowed itself to interfere in church matters?[14]

Indeed, the Hungarian state never interfered with theological instructions. Consequently, the instructors at all higher educational institutions of the Romanian church taught what and how they pleased. The Hungarian state did not even require that Hungarian language be part of the curriculum. During the entire Hungarian administration, the Hungarian language was not a compulsory subject at Romanian seminaries, while the Romanian language and literature were.[15]

The Political Role of the "Nation-Church" Congress

The Hungarian state did not interfere in the internal affairs of the self-governing bodies of the Orthodox Church even though some of these bodies had assumed a political character from the start. The Nation-Church Congress set up in accordance with Chapter V of the Organizational Rules was particularly political. This body met once every three years. One of its functions, according to Article 154, was:

> to take care that freedom of worship and self-government of the Romanian Orthodox Church are preserved; moreover, to regulate all ecclesiastic, school and foundation affairs, as well as the election of the archbishop and of the officials of the archdiocese.

In accordance with this regulation, approved by the Hungarian state, a body of Orthodox Romanians, consisting of about one hundred members — only one third of them clergymen — met in the fall of every third year. These representatives elected by the people met and functioned in the period of the Dual Monarchy as a political assembly, as the very choice of terms used by the Romanian newspapers indicate. The reports on the meetings of this Congress always assumed a political tone. The members of the assembly were referred to as "representatives," their contribution was called "intervention," and these interventions began with the parliamentary formula: "are you aware that...." The matters discussed at the Congress resembled the speeches delivered by Romanian representatives in the Hungarian parliament, the only difference being that they spoke out even more freely at the Nation-Church Congress, since not a single representative of the Hungarian authorities was present. On the other hand, since they did not have much to say about freedom of worship, or about church autonomy, for these were never seriously infringed; they focussed on educational and national issues. They besieged the speaker of the Congress with interventions along these lines, as they did the presidents of the episcopal consistories too, which met more often. In 1883, the sixteenth year of Hungarian rule, Dr. Nicolae Pop intervened at the Episcopal consistory because, he claimed, from July of that year the authorities had been sending out forms to Romanian schools, for statistical purposes, printed only in Hungarian. In a sharp tone Pop demanded: was the president aware of this? The procedure was in open disregard of Act XLIV of 1868 and, moreover, it made it impossible for Romanian schools to assume responsibility for the accuracy of their replies. At the same meeting "representative" Candrea "intervened" to ask whether the bishop was aware that, in certain communities the Romanian language was not being taught in the community and state schools? And, if he was aware, what action had he taken? Thus challenged, there was not much the president could do: he promised to provide an answer to the query at the next meeting, "if he receives the necessary information."[16] In the case of the forms printed in Hungarian, the following year, in 1884, the forms received by the Romanian schools were once again printed in three languages, as had been done in the past. Even so, there was cause for grievance: the Romanian daily *Tribuna*, well-known already at that time, was upset about the style of the Romanian version of the forms. The Hungarian nation cannot consider itself cultured it tolerates such "barbarisms," observed the paper.[17] Thus the Romanians took advantage of every opportunity for criticizing and attacking the Hungarian authorities at the meetings of church bodies, as well as in the press. In final analysis, the autonomy of the Orthodox Church served political rather than ecclesiastic ends during the entire period of the Dual Monarchy. The meetings were dominated by the lay majority who more than once outvoted the church leaders, forcing their will on the church itself. Their will was usually the Romanian national interest, and only on the rarest occasions were matters of purely ecclesiastic nature on the agenda. Spiritual issues, always central to the church, could never sufficiently tie down the attention of the church delegates, and these were usually relegated behind national and political issues. The *Tribuna* of Nagyszeben admitted it:

National feeling takes precedence over religious feeling within us Romanians, and we would find ourselves alienated from a church that did not form a defensive shield for our national development. Our priests should be, above all, disseminators of Romanian culture and peaceful advocates of the national spirit, for otherwise we are not interested in them.[18]

Archbishop Miron and some others disapproved of this interpretation; they realized that passionate involvement in politics relegated the true spirit of the church into the background, subordinating it more and more to political considerations. They were particularly dissatisfied with the Nation-Church Congress, for this body hardly produced anything beyond protests against the laws of 1879 and 1883. It worked out a few hurried regulations, but was incapable of any lasting contribution in the areas of religion or culture.

The Political Concepts of Archbishop Miron

The Archbishop of the Orthodox Romanians objected not only to the emphasis on politicking within the church; at the beginning of the eighties he even objected to that Romanian nationalist tendency which aroused distrust between Hungarians and Romanians by demanding autonomy for Transylvania and by struggling against the Dual Monarchy. Like Şaguna, he believed in active participation; that is, he disapproved of the policy of passive resistance declared in 1869, and of the boycott of parliamentary elections. He was in agreement with the Romanian lawyer Nicolae Strǎvoiu, according to whom passive resistance denied the right of existence to the Hungarian government and rejected the constitution and the whole system of the Dual Monarchy. He believed Romanians should struggle for their rights by standing on a constitutional platform. When, in 1881, those attending the Nagyszeben congress of electors, reasserted the policy of passive resistance and the demand for the autonomy of Transylvania, the Archbishop issued a circular to his disciples. He explained that he disagreed with the decision reached at Nagyszeben because passive resistance and the demand for Transylvanian autonomy implied the denial of the constitutionality of the state. Romanian political activity could not be directed against the constitution, for many Romanians, including the officials of the church, had taken an oath of allegiance to it.

Some members of the Romanian intelligentsia and part of those directing the political movement, namely the Babeş and Mocioni groups, joined Archbishop Miron, while others remained adamant. A sharp struggle developed between the partisans of conflicting tendencies for the sake of winning over public opinion. Archbishop Miron and his followers, a group of about fifty, held a conference in Budapest on March 14, 1884, and announced the foundation of a "Moderate Romanian Party." The new party recognized the Dual regime and Transylvania's union with Hungary without reservations, but accepted all other items of the program of Nagyszeben. Its weekly, the *Viitorul*, busied in favor of peaceful Romanian-Hungarian coexistence. The mottos of the paper, activism and respect for the law, fraternity and equality, expressed the essence of their program. The paper claimed that passive resistance and exaggerated anti-constitutional demands were a mistake, for the latter endangered the interests of the homeland. Being a good Romanian had to be reconciled with being a good patriot. The common ground was acceptance of the Constitution. One must fight against all abuses and unlawful acts standing on this secure foundation. Hatred, over

sensitivity, and chauvinism must be avoided in the course of the
struggle. The actions of certain individuals must never be ascribed to
the entire nation; one must not blame the whole Hungarian nation for
the actions of a few.[19]

Had the archbishop and his group been able to rally the majority of
Romanians, a meaningful Romanian-Hungarian rapprochement might
indeed have taken place. But, in spite of its auspicious beginnings, the
attempts in this direction failed, mainly because *Tribuna*, the daily of
Szeben with its hate-mongering and ruthless tactics directed from the
Kingdom of Romania and subventioned by the Liberal Party in
Romania, took only two years to discredit the prestige of the Moderate
Party and of Archbishop Miron.[20] The influence of *Viitorul*, appealing to reason and moderation, remained far behind that of the *Tribuna*,
with its ability to arouse the passions of the masses; indeed, so often
reason remains ineffective against passion. The *Tribuna* attacked the
Viitorul in a series of articles and drowned the members of the
Moderate Party in a flood of suspicions and slanders. The main target
of the attacks was Archbishop Miron himself. The paper criticized his
political concepts, and his methods of running the church. It organized
an opposition within the church. Later, it openly egged on the clergy
against him. A contributor to the paper asked the academic question,
"what should Romanians do if their church leaders use their power and
influence to support the Moderate Party?" His answer was: "We must
listen with childlike obedience to the advice of our church leaders, but
we must always do the opposite of what they say.... This behavior is
particularly recommended to the priests who are obliged to obey their
superiors."[21] Not only priests, but all good Romanians must turn
against the leaders and followers of the Moderate Party. They are so
dishonorable that they have no honor even towards one another. Those
who say evil about them deserve the respect of all Romanians, whereas
those who do not accept the program proclaimed at Szeben are confronting the true leaders of the nation, and therefore must be castigated. By
rejecting certain points of the Szeben program, they have sided with the
Hungarians, and this is the cardinal sin, for it amounts to betrayal of
the people. Hatred towards them is justified. "We have the right to
hate them," continued the paper:

> and we have the right to despise and systematically persecute all
> those among us who have closed ranks with the Hungarians
> either openly or in secret. This hatred, contempt and systematic
> persecution are as certain as the light at the break of dawn.[22]

The effects of the systematic attack by the *Tribuna* were not long in being felt. Archbishop Miron and his followers were becoming manifestly isolated. The weekly of the Moderate Party, the *Viitorul*, ceased publication in 1885. "It perished of the disease of moderation," wrote the victorious *Tribuna*, which became by far the most widely read paper of the Romanians of Hungary. Other Romanian serials were unable to compete with it. Although the Archbishop did everything to counteract its influence, it even had an effect on the internal life of the church. The Archbishop prohibited the Orthodox clergy from subscribing to it, and solemnly warned the members of the Nation-Church Congress about the dangers of the line represented by the paper:

> Do not lose sight of this fateful tendency promoted with great passion of late and continuing today, designed to destroy the prestige of the hierarchy, and weaken discipline and spiritual relations within the church; yet those are the factors to which we owe the fact that our Orthodox Church, the only refuge of our nationality, has survived even under circumstances far more detrimental than the ones prevailing today.[23]

Of course, the official paper of the Orthodox Church, the *Telegraful Român*, and certain circles of the clergy supported the Archbishop against the campaign of slander. Many experienced the terror unleashed by the *Tribuna* on their own skin. Others disapproved of the sharply anti-Hungarian articles, or of the project of the anti-Hungarian memorandum to be handed over to the Emperor. Archbishop Miron himself did not support the Memorandum movement. Like other Romanians filling jobs in the Hungarian administration and like the members of the Babeş-Mocioni group, he felt the memorandum, intended for Vienna while by-passing the Hungarian government, would be harmful, and the whole movement was a mistake. Still, when those who signed the memorandum were condemned by a tribunal in 1894 he, along with the Uniate bishop of Szamosújvár, Ioan Szabó, presented a petition for pardon to the ruler. Indeed, the King pardoned the condemned in 1895. The signers of the memorandum paid by spending a year and half in jail for denying the constitution of the country and turning directly to the ruler with their complaints, on the grounds that they rejected the Dual Monarchy.

Thus the Memorandum movement was a fiasco. On the basis of the Constitution the ruler could not and did not receive the Romanian delegation which presented its appeal to him not as the constitutional monarch of Hungary but rather as the Emperor of unitary Austria.

This attitude of the ruler justified Archbishop Miron and his followers who had felt from the beginning that the project was misguided, because they had always felt that demands for the autonomy of Transylvania were an error in tactics. According to the official paper of the archdiocese, the point of the Romanian program regarding Transylvanian autonomy and Dualism "were Platonic wishes, sweet but unrealizable dreams which everyone with a healthy judgement must realize cannot be fulfilled under normal circumstances." As a matter of political wisdom, the paper stressed, these items should be suspended for the sake of the achievement of other demands, and later revived at a more appropriate time. All the more so, since the Romanians cannot guarantee autonomy. That issue can only be resolved by the force of circumstances. "We don't know," continued the author of the article with weighty foreboding, "when the conjuncture with such potential may come about. But when it does come, the Romanians will not be satisfied with the autonomy of Transylvania, but will come up with other demands."[24]

As the article makes clear, the official church paper under the direction of Archbishop Miron objected only to sounding the demand for autonomy at a given time. It approved of the notion of autonomy and felt that under given circumstances even further demands could be realized. These further, unspecified demands were clearly a reference to the final objective of Romanian irredentism: the division of Hungary and the union of all Romanians.

An editorial expressing such controversial and radical ideas, published without a signature — that is, as an editorial opinion — could not have appeared without the knowledge and consent of the Archbishop. Hence Archbishop Miron must have agreed with the arguments contained in the editorial. Consequently, he too sympathized with the extremist Romanian demands presented at Szeben and with the concealed irredentist wishes, objecting merely to the tactics and bad timing of the struggle. The *Tribuna* and the extremist tendency of Romanian public opinion were wrong in labeling the Archbishop a traitor.

The Archbishop expressed his political concepts even more clearly in the so-called "Millennium Circular" published in 1896 in the official paper of the church.[25] The Hungarian government organized great festivities and a national exhibition at Budapest on the thousandth anniversary of the Hungarian conquest of the land. The churches of the nationalities were invited to participate. The Committee of Nationalities, which was under Romanian leadership, protested against the millennium celebration in a manifesto. In his circular Archbishop

Miron did not openly protest, but he unquestionably made significant concessions to anti-Hungarian Romanian public opinion. The contents of his circular also demonstrated that he identified with the arguments published in the official paper of the church regarding the autonomy of Transylvania.

In this circular the Archbishop first of all contrasts "the always martial and heroic Hungarian race" which immigrated from certain parts of Asia, with those "tame and peace loving" nations from whom they conquered the land. The celebration of the conquest which took place a thousand years ago amounts to the glorification of the Hungarian race, which in turn has been identified with the Hungarian political nation. Not only do the state authorities invite the leaders and faithful of the Orthodox Church to participate in the celebration, but "in a sense they even force us to participate." Yet it is impossible for the faithful of the church, especially its more "educated elements," to participate with heartfelt warmth in this celebration "which almost totally overlooks the interests of our being and of our progress in former times and at present."[26]

If the Hungarian race has the right to celebrate, the other nations of the country also have the right to "meditate over the millennial celebration and show even greater concern about fate." Not a single non-Hungarian nation wants to "blend into the ruling Hungarian race, nor even to vanish behind the general cover of the united political nation." On the contrary, each nation wants to preserve "its language, its religion, its customs as manifestations of its own character." Only on these conditions can the citizen remain a faithful son of the fatherland, a faithful citizen of the Hungarian state.

No matter how difficult the situation of the Romanians, "precautions, political maturity, and even good manners" demand that the acrimony in social and public life be suspended for the duration of the celebrations. The people should not harken to those who have usurped the role of leaders of the nation and whose every ambition is directed at "keeping this nation, more solid in its common sense than sharp-witted, in a constant state of excitement by planting hatred, distrust, and hypocrisy in their hearts." For the sake of a united stand the Archbishop orders that the priests organize "their own celebration" at each service. Let them give thanks to God in this celebration, for "in spite of all the sufferings of the past thousand years God has found us worthy of preserving our most valuable treasurers: our church and our nationality." Let us request that God grant us this power in the future as well. Let the clergy pray for the ruler, the army, for the cessation of the quarrels between nations and churches. Our own celebration will be observed on April 28 and May 10, before the regular church service, beginning at 9 in the morning, in ceremonial attire. We may rightfully refer to this celebration, in a historical and ecclesiastic sense, "as a millenary liturgy" — noted the Archbishop. Then he prescribed the details of the service, at the conclusion of which the people's hymn composed for the ruler [probably the *Gott erhalte*] must be sung. The circular should be read out by the priests a week before the celebration in the church, and the significance of the holiday explained to the faithful.

In the circular the Archbishop also stressed that more cannot be expected from the proud population or from the church under the present circumstances. If some want to participate in the millennial celebrations elsewhere, on their own account, they may do so as private individuals, without any constraints on their freedom as citizens, but not as representatives of the church. If the state authorities should insist that some organization of the Orthodox Church participate at a given political event as the representative of the church, in ceremonial attire, the church authorities may comply only on a basis of a prior request and special authorization, to which they are then obliged to adjust.

The reading and analysis of the circular make it obvious that Archbishop Miron accepted the state invitation to participate in the celebration only in appearance. Instead, he organized his own interpretation of a millennial holiday of historical-ecclesiastic import, in which the faithful would pray for the survival of the Romanian Orthodox Church and the Romanian nationality. The diplomatic language, at times deliberately vague and ambiguous, enabled him to list the main Romanian complaints, from the occupation of the ancestral home of the Romanians to the process of Hungarianization, the use of "force" and the obstacles to Romanian vital interests and progress, without mentioning, albeit hinting, that the Hungarians were responsible for all this. The circular rejected official participation on the part of the Orthodox Church in the celebration of the millennium, by tying participation to conditions which could not be met, if only because of lack of time. Hungarians and Romanians alike interpreted the circular in this sense. Several Hungarian papers attacked Miron, pointing to the thinly veiled anti-state contents of the circular. The *Tribuna* also criticized those sections of the circular which referred to the self-appointed leaders who teach the people to hate. Believing the charge was levelled at itself, the *Tribuna* accused the Archbishop of having assumed the leadership of the church with the assistance of the Hungarian government, caring little about the fate of the church and the schools. Iorga and other Romanian nationalists looked at the issue in more nuanced terms. According to Iorga, Archbishop Miron "could represent a nation vis-à-vis its natural adversaries in a dignified manner."

After the death of Archbishop Miron the leaders of the Orthodox Church did not alter their political perceptions. They continued to support the political demands of the Romanians in their long-range objectives as well as their day-to-day political struggles. Nor was there an absence of open or veiled attacks against the Hungarian regime, even though the system of state supplemental pay for priests of both Romanian churches was instituted in the first decade of the 20th century. The material conditions of the Romanian clergy improved nationwide, but all this did not decrease the anti-state and anti-Hungarian mood of the church leadership, since the main demand, autonomy for Transylvania, continued to be rejected by the Hungarians. In 1898, the year the state began to supplement the income of the clergy, and article in the official paper of the church contained the following precept: "those in power now mock us, beat us, and physically destroy us, what is more, they bury us politically as a nation because it is forbidden to us, at the risk of our lives, to appear as a nation to the outside world."[27]

Occasionally one of the Romanian churches took some conciliatory steps towards Hungarian public opinion. This was the case of the Orthodox Romanian bishop of Arad, Ioan Pap, who participated at the unveiling of the statue of Lajos Kossuth at Arad. The Romanian press attacked him for this and qualified him a traitor. A national boycott was declared against him. Aurel Vlad and one other Romanian deputy declined an invitation of the Orthodox Archbishop because they did not want to sit at one table with the Orthodox bishop. In 1909 the Nation-Church Congress held in Nagyszeben took up the issue of the bishop of Arad's participation at the Kossuth ceremony. The adopted resolution reads:

> The representatives of Congress, condemn the bishop of Arad for taking part in the unveiling of the statue of Kossuth and appeal to him to abstain in the future from all activity which might bring him into conflict with public feeling regarding the interests of the Romanian race and of the church.[28]

If a bishop of the church was subjected to such querying for having participated in an unveiling ceremony, one can imagine the terror to which mere priests were subjected to when it came to everyday political issues. In agreement with the nationalist press the laymen dominating the Orthodox Church recognized only one correct attitude: to support and serve Romanian political goals with every available means. In 1905, the candidates running on the platform of the activist line demanded unconditional backing from every Romanian priest. In many places in 1905 the priests made their congregation swear in church that they will vote only for the Romanian national party. The venue for a voters' meeting in Szászváros was the Orthodox Church. The Romanian priest of the village of Penes, campaigning on behalf of the Romanian candidate Vaida-Voevod, told his congregation that whoever did not vote for Vaida-Voevod deserved fire and the bullet.[29]

Of course, there were priests who defied the threats and voted for a pro-government Romanian candidate. In 1909 the government designated the Romanian teacher Iosif Siegescu as candidate in Oravica. Some Romanian priests promised their support. The Romanian press, however, unleashed a veritable campaign of hatred against them. The Romanian paper of Szászváros wrote:

> Such priests, could not commit a bigger sin vis-à-vis God than the sin they commit against their own people when they bend before the Satans and anti-Christs of Budapest. We will blacklist by name all priests who dare to vote in the elections for the sinful and divisive Siegescu. We will print his name within a black frame, as one who is dead to our people.[30]

The editors of the paper kept their word, and for years they published the names of those who voted for other than the candidate of the Romanian National Party under the column "Blacklisted."

Poring through the religious press and the political dailies edited by the clergy[31] the question is bound to arise: Was there any clerical activity at all that can be described as Christian, that was exempt from hatred? Undoubtedly there was, only it was hardly mentioned. Hundreds of churches were built or renovated thanks to the willingness of the faithful to sacrifice or from the contributions of the communities, testifying to good pastoral work. Occasionally these achievements were also given space in the columns of the religious press: for instance, the church-building perseverance of the Orthodox priest of Rákosd [Răcăştie], as a result of which the new church was consecrated on October 25, 1898, in the presence of twelve clergymen. The priest had collected the funds over a period of years. He was apparently on friendly terms with the Hungarian residents belonging to the Reformed Church, for the Reformed Minister Kállai represented them at the consecration ceremony. Members of other religions also contributed to the decoration of the church. Among the latter we find the Hungarians, Mrs. István Nagy and her brother Domokos Cserni, who donated gifts for the consecration.[32]   Over a period of twenty years, 104 new churches were constructed and 205 were renovated in the area of the Orthodox bishopric of Arad. The treasury of the church also grew considerably. In 1875 the bishopric had a capital of 580,786 forints, increasing to two million by 1895.[33] In addition to subsidies from the communities and the state it was most likely the congregation, persuaded by pastoral work, that contributed to the construction of these new churches.

Decline in Religious and Moral Life.

The several hundred churches Romanian Orthodox members built during the Dual Monarchy and the steady growth of their financial resources are undeniable proofs of outward progress; but religion and morality were unable to keep up with this material progress. In fact, the trend was rather the reverse, and not by accident. If a supposedly Christian church spreads not love and understanding but hatred, if its leaders and administrators reinforce the influence of the secular press which proclaims a policy of hatred, the consequence can only be the atrophy of religious and moral feeling. Such was the case of the Romanian Orthodox Church of Hungary. The unlimited leeway in administration granted to laymen, and the all-pervasive nationalism and chauvinism necessarily bore fruit. Interest in religion declined not only among the faithful, but among the clergy as well. They performed their religious duties nonchalantly, less and less concerned with the spiritual welfare of their flock. They devoted all their energies to the awakening and fostering of nationalism, and since this activity was condoned by the top officials of the church no remedy could come from above. Occasionally Archbishop Miron addressed warning words to the clergy, but without significant results. Nor did his bishops help him much in this endeavor. The bishop of Arad, Mețianu, refused to take serious measures to uplift religious and moral life; the Episcopal Consistory committed innumerable abuses under his administration, and the bad example spread to the clergy of the dioceses.

The Romanian Orthodox Christians who felt responsible for upholding the true calling of the church attempted to intervene on several occasions. The periodical of Arad already quoted, *Biserica și Şcoala*, was deeply involved along these lines throughout the period. The editors of the periodical soon identified the source of the troubles.

Already in the late 1870's they noted with anxiety that the behavior of the Orthodox clergy was seriously remiss. "We confess with deep irritation that the priests — and the exception proves the rule — had allowed themselves a great deal of liberty since the introduction of the constitutional regime." In fact, they took more and more advantage of their liberty. The diocese is constantly rocked by conversion movements, or by quarrels between clergy and their congregation. They have neglected church discipline. In seven years the synods have not adopted a single rule as regards discipline.[34] The churches are empty. The choruses are disbanding. Priests do not deliver sermons regarding the liturgy.[35] Similar observations can be found in the issues of the following year. The author of one study pointed out that the sermon should be the most important part of the service; "but, to our misfortune, the sermon is not taken seriously, or is neglected altogether in our Romanian Orthodox Church." In other churches the pulpits resound from the sermons delivered by the preachers, from the proclamation of the evangel. In contrast, Romanian pulpits are deeply silent. The art of preaching is in decline among Romanians. Where sermons are still being delivered they cause more harm than good; but there are places where the sermon is bypassed completely.[36]

An even more depressing article appeared about conditions in 1883. In this article the author drew a parallel between the external and internal conditions of the church. Materially the Orthodox archdiocese grew stronger after the passage of the Act 1868: IX, which ensured its autonomy. "The liberal constitution of the church had been drafted on the basis of that law — a constitution so liberal that even Protestant denominations are envious of it." The constitution encourages meetings, discussions for the advancement of religious and general education. This autonomy of the church must be defended. Yet the religious objective of the archdiocese is different: to spread the verb, religion, and morality. But what are the priests doing? Very little indeed; they deliver no sermons in church. The recipients of scholarships to seminaries learn everything except what the church really needs, the art of preaching. Many priests are outright enemies of the religion and of church rituals. Immorality has begun to take hold of many priests. "And have the synods done anything to improve morals?"[37] Indeed, priests spent little time on religion or morals, because they were too busy with politics. There were more than fifty priests among the 156 delegates to the Nagyszeben Congress of the representatives of Romanian voter in 1884.[38]

Though the Romanian clergy did not lead in strictly religious work, in preaching or teaching morals, it played an important role in the

Instead of refuting the charges raised by Maneguţiu, the church officials immediately deprived him of his job, bypassing the prescribed due process altogether.[45] Yet the manifestations of corruption did not cease. In 1903 even the *Budapesti Hírlap* reported on the event, and its observations were repeated by the Romanian paper *Drapelul* without comment or refutation. The Romanian paper of Szászváros did add some comments, however: "For those of us who are privy to some of the secrets of the church, who hear everyday deeply concerned priests mention the desecration of our own system of justice, we declare ourselves in solidarity with the meaningful silence of *Drapelul.*"[46]

Indeed, the system of justice of the church was replete with scandals. Maneguţiu was immediately deprived of his job and means of livelihood, whereas the Orthodox deacon of Fogaras, Dan, however, was allowed to remain at his post for a long time, even though he had embezzled funds innumerable times and committed other crimes to the consternation of the faithful. Complaints lodged against him with the church authorities fell on dead ears, no disciplinary action being taken for a long time. He was finally forced to retire when, on July 30, 1905, the state tribunal at Brassó sentenced him to five years in jail for 54 instances of embezzlement and forged checks.[47]

The faithful who were dissatisfied with the administration of Meţianu lodged complaints against the archbishop and the consistory of the archdiocese on several occasions. As noted, even the newspapers voiced their critical opinions every once in a while. They refrained from attacking him openly because they were happy with his stand on the main issue, serving the objectives of nationalism. Nevertheless, Meţianu was irritated by the charges placed against him, and the dissatisfaction of the clergy. He wanted to put an end to all "opposition." He had fresh disciplinary measures adopted, most of which were aimed at smothering internal criticisms. The most serious sin, in this new set of disciplinary rules, approved on October 29, 1906, to be severely punished, was "disloyalty towards the church." Among other sins we find "whispering campaigns and slanders against the leaders of the church, ecclesiastic bodies, institutions, and circles" [point 3], as well as "conspiracy and collaboration against the integrity and constitution of the church." Those guilty of such sins were to be punished more severely than those who neglected their official duties or did not meet their responsibilities. Thus the Archbishop could feel more secure, confident that the Hungarian state would not interfere with the autonomy of the church.

All these developments were the logical consequence of serving Romanian national interests above all else. Religion and morals continued to deteriorate, because leaders of the archdiocese were completely preoccupied with political struggles, protests against the Apponyi Laws, and the proposed revision of the electoral process. They had no time to study cases such as the behavior of Mănase, the Romanian Orthodox priest of Piski [Simeria Veche], during his frequent visits to Szászváros. The daily *Libertatea* of Szászváros finally wrote up the case which so scandalized the local Romanians, hoping that the machinery of church discipline might thereby be set in motion. The aforementioned priest, cap in hand, yelled in a drunken fashion and danced a wild jig in front of many spectators while the local military band was playing. The public roared with laughter, but the Romanians were embarrassed. The perpetrator of the scandal was finally removed by the police. The scandalized faithful denounced the priest at the see in Szeben where the complaint was merely acknowledged at that time.[48] Such cases vividly illustrate that the Orthodox Church did not use the amazing autonomy granted to it by the Hungarian state to foster a truly Christian way of life, but rather to benefit Romanian nationalism. The Romanian author who, in his French-language work published in 1916 wrote that as a consequence of Şaguna's Organizational Rules the Romanian church in Hungary "formed a true state within a state," was quite correct.[49]

A few years later the Romanian newspaper of Szászváros reported another instance of abuse. The priest of the community of Balomir in the vicinity of Szászváros, one Nicolae Suciu, having reached old age, announced a competition for the position of assistant priest. He meant to have his grandson "elected," even though the latter lacked the required qualifications. Since the community was rather well off, there were quite a few young men with the required theological preparation who expressed an interest; however, "as a consequence of the intervention of some church organizations, they withdrew their applications and did not compete." Merely a "moralist," who had attended secondary school for only a few years, the grandson could only have obtained a position with the smallest congregation, according to the Organizational Rules. This case was yet another indication that the people did not understand or make good use of the Organizational Rules. But it would be the task of the church hierarchy to make sure that the Rules, "that wise law, be carried out in an ideal way.... The responsibility for this failure must be divided three ways," wrote the correspondent of the paper of Szászváros: "the consistory of Szeben, which ran roughshod over the precepts contained in the Organizational Rules and allowed the moralist to apply in a parish barred by those Rules," the priest Suciu, and the people of Balomir [Balomirul de Cîmp].[50]

Of course, the people did not and could not make use of the rights granted them. In any case, they were beginning to get fed up with the one-sided and not particularly Christian behavior of the nationalist priests. It was at this time that the first Baptist churches were set up in Romanian areas. The Romanian peasants, disillusioned with their own church, turned eagerly to the Baptist preachers. The consequence was the spread of Baptist teachings and the conversion of large numbers of Orthodox Romanians. This frightened the Orthodox clergy, all the more so since the more intelligent believers occasionally pointed a finger straight at the priests, by means of letters to editors. In 1912 an Orthodox correspondent from the town of Brád made the following pointed observations: "For some time now the Baptists, the sect of the 'converted' whose members have abandoned their ancestral faith, are becoming increasingly numerous among us...." Romanian priests, on the other hand, did not preach on this issue. Of the six Romanian priests in Brád "none took it upon himself to preach some Sunday about the correctness of our faith and the errors of the 'converted.'" It is fortunate, at that, that there is a decent church chorus; when it sings, the pews are filled. "How happy would we be if our priests were to preach to us as well, in a manner uplifting our soul and strengthening our ancestral faith; then the church would always be full."[51]

This description by the correspondent from Brád of the troubles affecting the Romanian Orthodox church was fitting. The main problem was the neglect of the evangel and, consequently, the apostasy of large numbers of faithful. All this derived naturally from the fact that the Romanian Orthodox church used its autonomy for national and political goals, from 1868 all the way to the end of World War I.

Though Hungarian leaders were aware of these activities of the Romanian Orthodox Church, they respected its autonomy granted by the law to the end. It was the will of the laymen that prevailed during elections for head of the church, in the internal organization of the church, in the operation of its diverse bodies, in the seminaries, in the absolute freedom enjoyed by the religious press, etc. The Orthodox leaders publicly acknowledged the positive attitude of the Hungarian state. What's more, when parts of Hungary became attached to Romania after 1918, and the Romanian government crudely interfered even in the elections of the Orthodox synod in 1924, the frightened and indignant Romanians of Transylvania recalled the respect for the law exhibited by the former Hungarian regime. In that year the government attempted to appoint the members of the Orthodox diocese of Arad. The Bucharest regime did what the "oppressive" Hungarian authorities never even thought of doing. The newspaper *Románia* wrote:

> The political administration, particularly that of the county of Arad, from the prefect on down to the village notaries, interfered openly in the elections with the help of elements of the state police, and infringed on the moral and constitutional rights of the voters in an unheard-of aggressive manner.

Finally, they even closed the synod down. When the minutes of the synod were published in the official periodical of the diocese, the prefect of Arad censored the publication, obliterating entire pages from the *Biserice şi Şcoala*. The indignation of the leaders of the Romanian Orthodox church knew no bounds. An eyewitness observer wrote:

> Let anyone try to find a similar case, in the 48 annual volumes of our official publication, beginning with the introduction of Şaguna's Rules: When did anyone dare censor the minutes of the synod of the diocese! The Hungarians refrained from doing it even during the World War. Now the Liberals [members of the political party of Romania then in power] are doing it, in the sixth year of peace and national independence. How base and lacking in self-respect!

A week later the paper differentiated between the Hungarian and Romanian procedures even more clearly. Bucharest's methods were used during the elections to the synod.

> They forged the results of the election, destroyed the records of the voting district, and threatened the voters; the delegates to the synod of Arad, both ecclesiastic and secular, resigned their mandate in protest against the infamous procedures, unprecedented in the history of the church on the other side of the Carpathians.... The officials of Prime Minister István Tisza never dared lay a finger on a church publication in order to censor it, much less censor the minutes of the synod, even in the period of the most severe siege during the Great War.[52]

It is clear, therefore, that the Hungarian state respected the autonomy and freedom of the Romanian Orthodox Church to the very end, and exercised control or set limitations only in certain specific cases, as in the case of the control of Romanian synods after 1916 and the appointment of government commissioners. The First World War reached Transylvania when it was invaded by the Romanian army. The Romanian clergy in Hungary openly sided with the invading Romanian troops, in spite of the oath they had taken, to such an extent that the military authorities demanded closer supervision of the Romanian churches. Consequently, the commissioner would appear at authorized meetings, deliver a short speech, and depart. Many of them did not even know Romanian. Furthermore, church autonomy was subjected to limitations in the area of education. Other than these, the Orthodox Church had no grounds for complaint regarding autonomy.

The Romanian Uniate Church

Similarly, for a long time the Romanian Uniate Church had no cause for complaints. The head of the Hungarian Roman Catholic Church had no jurisdiction over the Uniate Church. The two churches were identical or similar only in their structure and teachings, otherwise they were entirely distinct. The Romanian Uniate Church was definitely Romanian, whereas the Roman Catholic Church was Hungarian as regards the majority of its congregations; but there were, among the followers of both churches, members of other nationalities as well. This caused no serious difficulty within the Roman Catholic Church, since it never functioned as an exclusively Hungarian national church. Slovaks, Germans, and others all prayed in their mother tongue at Mass, which everywhere was said in Latin. Not so in the Romanian Uniate Church. Since that church was Romanian even officially, the members of Hungarian nationality and language were subjected to constant Romanianization, for everywhere the Uniate clergy held Mass in Romanian; when they occasionally departed from this rule for the benefit of the faithful speaking a different language, the priests involved became the targets of violent attacks, especially in Transylvania.[53] This attitude of the church resulted from the fact that the clergy intended to Romanianize those with a Hungarian background, whereas they wanted to retain as Romanians those with a Romanian background who spoke only Hungarian as a result of residing in predominantly Hungarian areas. From the turn of the century, Hungarian public opinion demanded ever more insistently that a separate Hungarian Uniate bishopric be set up for the benefit of the Hungarian members of the creed. Naturally, the Romanian priests and the official bodies of the archbishopric did everything in their power to prevent the establishment of a Hungarian-language diocese. They feared that such a bishopric would attract all the Hungarian members

of the church, and thus not only would the numbers of their congrega-
tion decrease, but the process of Romanianization would suffer as well.
The Hungarian Uniates persisted, collecting signatures among the
Hungarian-speaking members of the church and organizing a pilgrimage
to Rome. The Hungarian Uniates of 67 communities in the region of
Nagyvárad joined the movement and requested the establishment of a
Hungarian bishopric from Rome. The Romanian press, government
agencies, and the irredentist organizations of the Romanians of
Bucharest also went into action. Everywhere they advertised that the
projected bishopric was yet another device for Hungarianization
advocated by the Hungarian government, since the number of Hungarian Uniates was negligible. The Romanian historian Nicolae Iorga even
wrote two pamphlets in French on the issue, and the world press echoed
the Romanian complaints for months. In response the Hungarians
pointed out that a Hungarian bishopric was intended precisely to
prevent the further Romanianization of the Hungarian members of the
church. After all, the Romanian bishopric of Nagyvárad included many
Romanianized Hungarians. The oldest roster of the bishopric indicated
that of 264 priests and seminarians, 148 were of Hungarian mother
tongue. In 1912, after almost two decades of struggle, Rome finally
agreed to set up a Hungarian bishopric. Now the Romanians readily
admitted that there were many Hungarians in the Romanian Uniate
Church. Their continued protests were aimed merely at limiting the
number of communities assigned to the new diocese. The semi-official
paper of the Romanian diocese wrote:

> We recognize that there are many among us who have lost
> their Romanian background altogether, either because they
> never used the Romanian language, or because our pastors, not
> unlike some landlords, did not guard their flock.... Therefore, for
> those who so fervently requested the diocese, let it come into
> being, but only for them; no Romanian communities should be
> attached to the new diocese.[54]

Along with the Hungarian government, the Holy See gave considera-
tion to this legitimate Romanian request. Though at the time of the
1910 census some 304,318 Uniates had declared themselves to be
Hungarian, only 217,540 of them were assigned to the Hungarian
Uniate diocese set up by the encyclical *Christi fideles Graeci*. The new
diocese received the name Hajdúdorog and, in addition to the Hungarian
Uniates of the region of Nagyvárad, it included the faithful from the
Székely region. There were still a few complaints regarding the

The Uniate Church fostered Romanian nationalism as much as the Orthodox Church did. Much like the Orthodox clergy its priests took part in Romanian political movements, conferences, and protests. Representatives of both churches may be found among the signers of the *Memorandum*. They were in complete agreement regarding the ultimate aim of Romanian nationalism. Their common theoretical ground, anti-Hungarian irredentism, even erased the doctrinal differences between the two churches, as clearly demonstrated by the agreed-upon practice according to which, if both churches were represented in a given village, the Orthodox and Uniate priests acted as alternates in their clerical functions.[59]

Nevertheless, the leadership of the Uniate Church was more flexible and less aggressive than the Orthodox. Though their nationalist aims were identical, their devices and attitudes often differentiated them. There was no corruption mentioned in the Uniate Church. But the distinction obvious to all was their financial situation.

The Financial Situation of the Romanian Churches.

Apart from effective organization, the evolution of the Romanian churches was also a function of their financial means. Their financial situation was not equal, whether in the period preceding the Compromise or thereafter. Its history explains why the Uniate Church was always the wealthier of the two. During the Dual Monarchy, however, both churches increased their holdings steadily. They acquired landed estates, managed foundations, applied for and received subventions from the state. It can be easily ascertained that both the Orthodox and the Uniate Churches were far more prosperous by the end of the Hungarian rule, in 1918, than they had been in 1867, at the time of the Compromise. Thus this period of Hungarian rule was not economically detrimental to the Romanian churches in any way.

Most of the wealth of the two churches came from their estates. Their holdings kept increasing. Let us compare the statistics from the turn of the century with those from the First World War. The Romanian Uniate Church of Hungary owned 143,408 cadastral *holds* of central estates in 1900 — including episcopal, archiepiscopal, and clerical lands. Of these 138,964 were in Bihar county, 2,150 in Alsó-Fehér, 661 in Kis-küküllő, and 245 in Szolnok-Doboka. There were also 1,388 cadestral *holds* of estates in Transylvania. The church and pastoral holdings in the entire archdiocese — not counting the estates of the church schools — amounted to 65,388 cadastral *holds*. Thus the amount of land held by the Uniate Church exceeded 200,000 cadastral *holds*, more exactly 208,746.[60]

The Romanian Orthodox Church owned far less. The estates owned by the administrative centers and by the monasteries barely exceeded 10,000 cadastral *holds* in all, whereas church and pastoral lands of the dioceses amounted to about 50,000 *holds*. The Romanian Orthodox Church, therefore was much poorer than Uniate Church.[61]

A decade and a half later, towards the end of the First World War, both Romanian churches could boast of considerable increases in their holdings. That year the Uniate Church held 226,582 cadastral *holds*, whereas the Orthodox Church held 89,838.[62] The Uniate Church acquired almost 20,000, whereas the Orthodox Church acquired over 25,000 additional cadastral *holds* in the intervening period. These estates produced a sizable revenue. The estate of the Uniate diocese of Nagyvárad, for instance, brought in a yearly income in excess of 400,000 crowns.[63]

The income of the larger church estates served primarily to cover the expenses incurred by the central administration. Often there were not enough funds to cover the needs of the poorer parishes or to support the more deserving priests. Similarly, administration, construction and equipment of new buildings, repair of old churches, construction of new ones and their expenses in new districts, such as the Uniate bishoprics of Szamosújvár and of Lugos, were often left uncovered. Tidy sums had to be collected or secured by means of donations. Wealthy Romanians from either Hungary or Romania occasionally donated enormous sums for Romanian cultural or religious purposes in Transylvania, to enable the Romanian churches to build new churches and schools. There were no legal impediments to accepting such donations. Permission had to be obtained only for more extensive collection campaigns. Among the Romanian complaints we have found none regarding any refusal to grant such a permission.

Yet the church estates, collections, and donations still did not suffice to cover the expenses of the Romanian churches. After 1867 the Hungarian state had to provide subsidies to the Romanian churches. The Hungarian Minister of Religious Affairs and Education earmarked regular assistance for Romanian religious purposes from the purely Roman Catholic Religious Foundation and from the state treasury. These sums enabled the Romanian churches to grow, their central administration to function, and the seminaries to remain open; it also allowed them to construct and repair churches, and covered the emergency expenditures of church dignitaries and active priests as well.

Since the Religious Foundation had a Roman Catholic source, the minister used this fund mainly for the support of the Uniate Church, whereas the state treasury provided for the Orthodox church. The extent of Hungarian state subventions can be determined with a fair degree of accuracy from the official publications of the two churches, from the budgets of the Uniate dioceses, and from the minutes of the synods and congresses of the Orthodox Church. In addition to these sources, the secondary works, as well as letters of thanks from Romanians in the archives of the Hungarian Ministry of Religious Affairs and Education testify to the extent of state assistance.

It can be determined from the budget of the Uniate Church at the time of the Compromise that the Religious Foundation provided the primary financial base of the Uniate diocese of Szamosújvár. In response to the application of Bishop Ion Vencea, the Hungarian Ministry of Religious Affairs and Education met the expenses incurred by the seminary of Szamosújvár with a yearly contribution of 14,800 forints. There was also a 10,000 forint annual subvention to the parishes. Also, 17,224 forints were awarded for the construction of the Uniate Church of Szilágysomló. The bishopric of Szamosújvár continued to enjoy support not only from the Foundation but from the state treasury as well. For instance, the Hungarian Minister of Religious Affairs and Education purchased the site of the episcopal palace.[64] Years later, in 1911, when Dr. Vasile Hossu was appointed bishop, the Hungarian government once again made a sizable contribution; this time the sum donated for the construction of institutions in the diocese amounted to 600,000 crowns.[65]

The Romanian Uniate diocese of Lugos received even more extensive assistance from the Foundation, and later from the state treasury. Neither the bishop nor the see had offices when the diocese was set up. Bishop Ioan Olteanu obtained 35,000 forints from the Foundation for the episcopal residence. This contribution enabled the church to purchase a large house with a garden, and an estate of 9 *holds* on the outskirts of the town, constituting the principal estate of the diocese. The house was converted into an episcopal residence. It was once again the Foundation that provided 10,000 forints to meet the cost of the repairs and conversion. It was also the Foundation that made it possible to find a place for the see. In 1879, at the request of the Bishop Dr. Victor Mihalyi, the Foundation disbursed 8,000 forints for this purpose. This contribution was used to purchase the two treasury-owned houses adjoining the episcopal residence, and these were to constitute the see. A few decades later, when these buildings were deteriorating, Dr. Dimitru Radu obtained a fresh contribution of 41,451 crowns and 70 fillers from the Foundation, to renovate the houses and place them under a common roof with the episcopal residence.[66] The special state assistance remained the most important basis for the development of the dioceses even under the successor to Dr. Radu. The new bishop, Dr. Vasile Hossu, requested and received an assistance of 200,000 crowns for various church and school purposes. Thus the financial situation of the dioceses continued to improve. Thirty-nine new schools were built under his long tenure of office, during the very era of Apponyi.[67]

In addition to the Religious Foundation, the Uniate Church received tidy sums from the state treasury. The bishops of Lugos and Szamosújvár regularly received 20,000 crowns annually, and pay for the canons of the church also came from the state treasury. Before the First World War the bishopric of Gyulafehérvár received a yearly 38,000 crowns, the bishopric of Nagyvárad 30,000, the bishopric of Lugos 37,000, and the bishopric of Szamosújvár 38,970 for the pay of the canons. In addition to these regular sums the dioceses also received extraordinary contributions. In 1917 Bishop Hossu was granted 20,000 crowns in addition to the 21,000 crowns he received regularly for expenses. During the war the bishops of Lugos and Szamosújvár received 133,000 crowns assistance each.[68]

The Romanian Orthodox Church also received considerable sums from the state treasury. In addition to extraordinary grants for special purposes, the bishops and archbishops, the offices of the Orthodox administration, the sees, and the seminaries survived mainly thanks to state support. These were disbursed annually and regularly as part of their budget. In the years preceding the First World War the main archdiocese of Szeben received 68,400 crowns, the Arad diocese 40,000, the Nagyvárad diocese 37,000 and the Karánsebes diocese 34,000 crowns of yearly state assistance. Thus the Hungarian state contributed 179,400 crowns annually to ensure the viability of the central institutions of the Orthodox Church.[69] Moreover, the Orthodox Church received additional sums earmarked for church and educational institutions, amounting to roughly 150,000 crowns a year. Of this sum 100,000 crowns were earmarked for the archdiocese at Nagyszeben, 29,300 for the diocese at Arad, 19,800 for the diocese at Karánsebes, and 900 crowns for the pastors of the latter two dioceses. Such assistance, in addition to the regular supplemental pay the clergymen received from the state, was not unusual.

In the years immediately preceding the First World War and during the war itself, the Hungarian state increased the subsidies considerably. In 1912 the subsidy for the Romanian Orthodox see of Nagyvárad was

increased from 12,000 to 29,000 crowns. This extra help enabled the see
to fill two positions of "section chief" and raise the salaries of the staff
in general.[70] The following year the same see received 37,000 crowns
of extraordinary subsidy from the state to cover urgent needs. In 1917
the subsidy for the Romanian Orthodox see of Nagyszeben increased
along with the rest. In 1918, the last year of the war, the see of
Nagyszeben received 91,700 crowns, that of Arad 70,000, that of
Nagyvárad 50,000, and that of Karánsebes 70,000. These sums were
disbursed at a time when the Romanian delegates had already declared
their intention to break away from the Hungarian state; in fact, Dr.
Frenţiu, the Orthodox bishop, received his disbursement on January 13,
1919, that is fully six weeks after the secession meeting held at
Gyulafehérvár.[71]

It was likewise state support and the Religious Foundation that
provided for the maintenance of the offices of the see, as well as for
personnel and supplies. The largest sums under these categories went
to the Uniate sees of Lugos and Szamosújvár.

While financial support for church dignitaries and for the central
administration got off to an early start and afforded a decent standard
of living, help for the parish priests left a lot to be desired for a long
time. The lower clergy, the priests in charge of smaller or larger
parishes, survived under most deprived conditions. This was particularly true of the Orthodox priests, since their church was not as well off as
the Uniate Church. Where the priests had to rely exclusively on the
"stola" or their plot of land, they must have made a very meager living
indeed. The faithful in the Uniate diocese of Lugos give their priests
stolas worth only ten to twelve forints at the time of the Compromise.
In other dioceses the situation may have been better, or worse in the
case of Orthodox dioceses. There was an unquestionable need for
Hungarian state subsidies; without it the condition of Romanian priests
in the first twenty years of the Dual Monarchy, when the general
population was living under more modest circumstances, would have
been unbearable.

Very soon, therefore, the Romanian church leaders turned to the
state for salaries to the clergy and to the staff of the central offices. The
first steps in this direction were taken during the Austrian autocratic
regime. In 1850, Şaguna requested state pay for all employees of the
church. Since during the 1848-49 revolution the Romanian Orthodox
clergy, led by Şaguna, lined up the Romanians on the side of the House
of Habsburg and against the Hungarians, he drafted a special memorandum to explain how the Romanian Orthodox Church was entitled to
such support, inasmuch as the Romanians, beginning with their clergy,

had performed a great service for the Habsburgs. Still, it took the Viennese central government eleven years to award 25,000 forints. Of this sum 24,000 were earmarked for the clergy, and one thousand was awarded to the seminary.[72] In 1864, for the first time, 25,000 forints were awarded to cover the expenses of the central diocese.

When the Austrian autocracy was replaced by the Hungarian regime in 1867, Dr. József Eötvös, the Hungarian Minister of Religious Affairs and Education, accepted the continuing disbursement of this sum, at Şaguna's request. Neither Eötvös nor any other member of the Hungarian government thought of taking revenge for the anti-Hungarian role of the Romanian clergy in 1848-49 by withholding the subsidies awarded by the Austrian government. In addition to assistance for the clergy, the parliament, already in the early 1870's, granted an additional 100,000 forints to the Romanian Orthodox Church. The Orthodox bishop of Karánsebes, Ion Popasu, wrote a special letter (number 163), dated March 1, 1871, to thank the state for its support, which he acknowledged "with unrestrained happiness and infinite satisfaction."[73]

The bishops, however, managed to withhold illegally various amounts from the sum meant for the clergy. They were able to do this because each year, until 1884, the sum intended for the clergy was disbursed to the central authorities of the church, who in turn were accountable to the state for the distribution of the sum.[74] In 1884 the government deprived the archbishoprics of the right to distribute the sum because of the abuses. The Orthodox Romanian deacon, Nicolae Maneguţiu, related the antecedents of this government decision in a book published in 1902. According to Maneguţiu it was the unprecedented abuses of the central office of the Romanian Orthodox Church that compelled the Hungarian government to resort to this measure. The Romanian clergy only knew what their church leaders were willing to reveal to them about the matter. They were told that "the Hungarians have denied and withdrawn the subvention for the Romanian Orthodox clergy in an arbitrary manner." "They told this lie to the clergy," continued Maneguţiu, "because the officials of the consistory had to find a cover for their criminal activities."[75]

The truth was that during the distribution of the state subvention each official of the consistory retained 1,200 forints. Moreover, since they were trained priests, their names also appeared on the rolls as clergymen, hence they received an additional 200 to 400 forints. Each deacon received 200 forints, and priests 50 to 70 forints. According to the guidelines issued by the Hungarian government, priests with more years of schooling, with families, and with children attending school, should have been on top of the list. But the deacons decided otherwise. They included on the list priests who were illiterate, who knew nothing of the subvention, and who were willing to sign [sic] anything placed in front of them because they were only too happy to be tolerated. These illiterate priests were on the lists, but once they signed a receipt written in the Cyrillic alphabet, which they could not understand, the deacons collected the sums in their stead. The better-educated priests filed hundreds of denunciations requesting that the government put an end to such abuses. Finally the government sent an inspector to the consistories. After a three-week examination tour "the inspector reached an absolutely just verdict: subsidies to the clergy should continue, but the distribution should be carried out by the government rather than the consistories which had committed the abuses." The church leaders failed to inform the clergy of this verdict; rather, they misled the clergy, pretending that the government had withdrawn the subsidies arbitrarily and without cause. They went further: the leaders proposed that the synod reject the subsidies provided by the government if the latter insisted that the distribution not be entrusted to the consistories. The misguided synod accepted this proposal.[76]

This measure of the consistory of Nagyszeben resulted in some confusion in the disbursement of the state subsidies to the lower clergy. The government refused to hand over to the consistory the sums earmarked for the clergy, but this did not prevent it from disbursing the allotted amounts directly to the clergy, nor did the government stop disbursing the usual sums to the bishops and to the consistory. Until the voting of the Congrua Law, many letters of thanks testify to the support given to the bishops of Arad, and to Nicholas Popea, the bishop of Karánsebes, among others. The priests of the Orthodox Church received regular annual compensation, on the basis of Act XIV of 1898 regarding subvention to the clergy.

The Congrua Law divided the clergy into two groups, according to their level of education. The state complemented the incomes of the priests in the first group, those who had gone through all eight forms of the secondary school before attending the seminary, with an annual 1,600 crowns. Priests who attended the seminary without completing their secondary education fell under the second category and were awarded a state subvention of 800 crowns. By approving the Congrua Law the Hungarian state meant to make up for the loss in income resulting from the nationalization of the registry process. Before 1895 the registries had been kept by the clergy. Clergymen were the ones to record births, marriages, and deaths — a service for which they received remuneration. In 1895 the so-called ecclesiastic policy laws regarding civil marriage and the keeping of the registries by civil servants were approved; henceforth the clergy was deprived of these remunerations. The Hungarian state awarded the annual subvention, called the *congrua*, to the priests of various churches as a sort of compensation.[77]

The Orthodox Romanian clergy, instigated against the Hungarian state by the consistory of Nagyszeben, received the *congrua* with mixed feelings. During the "memorandum trials" this clergy, with but few exceptions, had conducted a mass campaign of agitation against the Hungarian state and the Hungarian courts. It was well aware that these activities could not be hidden from the Hungarian authorities. Hence it expected no financial support from the state; on the contrary, it feared reprisals. Instead, the state adopted the Congrua Law. Thus it is not surprising that a substantial portion of the clergy greeted the law with suspicion, suspecting some kind of a trap. Maneguţiu wrote:

> This was an unexpected boon to the lower clergy, the state overwhelmed the clergy with its munificence. According to the clergyman author of an article in the official paper of the church, the clergy had not even dreamt of such subvention and was wondering how it had deserved it.[78]

At the same time the Romanian clergy regarded the *congrua* as a kind of balm, and soon began to urge its disbursement. Indeed, this did not take long: On May 28, 1899, with a vote of 40 to 28, the main body of the Orthodox Church, the Nation-Church Congress, declared that it would ask for the *congrua*, but with one condition: it should be picked up by the consistory. The Hungarian state had no objection. The Romanian archbishop, Ioan Meţianu reached an agreement with Dr. Gyula Wlassics, the Hungarian Minister of Religious Affairs and Education, regarding the method of determining the state support to be awarded to the Romanian Orthodox parishes. Accordingly the secretary of the main see of Nagyszeben, Dr. Cristea Illes Miron, the future Patriarch of Greater Romania, was sent to Budapest. Cristea spent over seven months with the Second Section of the Ministry of Religious Affairs and Education; he did most effective work in his thorough examination of the Ministerial instructions pertaining to the application of the Congrua Law, and how it applied to other religious groups. As a result, the Romanian Orthodox clergy obtained everything it deserved according to the provisions of the law; in fact, significant subvention for some of the new parishes was also facilitated. The Hungarian Ministry of Religious Affairs and Education awarded the subvention even where

there were hardly any Orthodox Romanians. Thus the clergy of the
newly-formed parishes in Balázsfalva, Naszód, Beszterce, and Marosúj-
vár [Ocna Mureş] also received the subvention. Without it, acknowledged the decision number 179/1901 of the see of Nagyszeben, the
parishes established in those cultural centers "would have remained
without a priest."[79]

The yearly subvention soon completely altered the financial and
social situation of the Orthodox Romanian clergy. "Our church," wrote
Maneguţiu, "received a considerable sum under the title subvention,
and the thirst of the priests for this unexpected manna was like the
thirst of the earth for drops of rain after an extended drought."[80]
Within a few years the financial situation of the hitherto-impoverished
Orthodox clergy improved substantially. Therefore, in his report 123
dated January 26, 1904, Archbishop Meţianu requested the Ministry of
Religious Affairs and Education "that the available funds be turned
over for the construction of churches and other buildings in the poor
parishes." The decision of the Minister favored the interests of the
priest, but support for the parishes also got underway.

The amount of the *congrua* increased several times by the end of
World War I. For instance, in 1907, according to the official accounts
of the dioceses, the priests received 674,177 crowns and eight fillers in
the main see of Nagyszeben, 292,492 crowns in the diocese of Arad,
121,800 crowns and 62 fillers in that of Karánsebes. In 1907, during
the regime of the Minister of Religious Affairs and Education, Count
Apponyi, the Orthodox priests received altogether 1,088,469 crowns and
70 fillers under the title congrua. Seven years later the amount of the
congrua more than doubled, to reach three million crowns.[81] The
increase took place on the basis of Act XXXVIII of 1913. This law
provided compensation for seniority, in five year increments; priests
with the required educational background received a pay of 3,000
crowns after 25 years of service. In 1917, in accordance with regulation
1870, they also received a 500 crown clothing allowance. In the same
year, they received an allowance for every child on the basis of Act IX.
In 1918 these sums were raised to 1,000 and 600 crowns respectively.

Since the Uniate Church was considerably better off, its priests were
awarded the *congrua* only later. In this church for a long time, the
financial burdens of the priests were borne almost entirely by the
Religious Foundation. The Uniate priests of the diocese of Lugos
received a subsidy amounting to five times their local income in 1867.
The Foundation also took care of the moving expenses of the priests
[*oeconomicalis* assistance], it often paid the tax on clerical lands, medical
expenses incurred by the clergy, assistants appointed to help elderly

priests, the keep of mounts needed to visit distant parishioners, etc.
Such were the subsidies given to the poorer priests of the archdiocese of
Gyulafehérvár, and to those of the dioceses of Lugos and Szamosújvár.
In 1872 the average amount of the subsidies was 50 forints per
individual, equivalent to the price of a cow.

The state subsidy was handed over to the Uniate bishop in a lump
sum from 1900 on.[82] The final determination of the amount of
congrua to be awarded to Uniate parishes took place in 1908, along with
the parishes of the Roman Catholic Church but, as we have seen, Uniate
priests received the sums corresponding to the *congrua* even earlier.

Five years later, after the approval of the five year increments, the
financial situation of the clergy had improved to such an extent that the
official paper of the archbishopric called upon them to work overtime.

> Our clergymen will even receive five year increments from
> now on; although the government's proposed law to this effect
> has not yet gone through the legal formalities, the moneys have
> already arrived, and this is the main thing. Today our priests
> receive a yearly salary of 3,000 crowns, which is infinite progress
> compared to the past when, only fifteen years ago, they received
> next to nothing. In those times the priest had to mind his parcel
> of land carefully to support himself and his family. The *congrua*
> and the related five-year increments have improved his condition
> immeasurably.
>
> Yet the question remains, now that they no longer have to
> worry about making ends meet, what will our priests do for the
> sake of the people and the church? In our region the churches
> stay closed all week long, except on Sunday, and our clergy pays
> not the slightest heed to the spiritual welfare of the people
> during the week. Now that they are able to live more at ease
> will they even bother to continue preaching and practicing the
> rituals?
>
> These questions must be answered by acts, because a heavy
> responsibility would weigh upon our church dignitaries if our
> priests, in exchange for a salary of 3,000 crowns a year, were
> expected to do no more than fifteen years ago, when they earned
> almost no cash whatever.[83]

The question now arises: Could the increment provided by the state
be viewed as preventing the Romanian priesthood from continuing to
act on behalf of Romanian nationalism and be involved in politics? Was
it not the objective of the *congrua* to hang as a sword of Damocles over

the head of the Romanian clergy, which was running the risk of losing its freshly-tasted ease if it did not refrain from political involvement?

The law specified the circumstances under which the increment could be withheld. According to paragraph 7 of the Act of 1898: XIV a priest deprived of his parish by due process, or condemned for moral turpitude or anti-state activities, was not entitled to the *congrua*. The *congrua* could be withdrawn for a maximum period of three years during the loss of the parish. It could be permanently withdrawn only from someone who had been repeatedly sentenced for moral turpitude or anti-state activities. In every case, the accused priest had to be tried in his own ecclesiastic court. The Minister could withdraw the congrua only after the ecclesiastic trial had been concluded. According to Article 9, if the ecclesiastic authorities took no action within three months, upon the Minister's request, the latter had the right to decide regarding the withdrawal of the congrua on the basis of the data available to him. He had the right to do the same if the ecclesiastic court dismissed the charges despite valid grounds. But in such a case the church authorities still had the right to appeal the Minister's decision in the local courts. The concept of anti-state activity was defined in Article 13 of the Act of 1893: XXVI, describing the goal of the objectionable acts in precise terms. Activities directed against the constitution, the national character, the unity, the independence, the territorial integrity, and furthermore the misuse of the official language of the state were defined as anti-state activities.

The above prescriptions seem extremely harsh at first reading. Indeed, part of the Romanian clergy refused to accept them. At the general meeting of the main body of the Romanian Orthodox Church held on May 28, 1899, to deal with this specific issue there were 26 votes for the motion to reject the *congrua*. No doubt one of them was the vote of the Romanian chronicler who, in the 1900 edition of the *Tribuna's* popular calendar, described the *congrua* as persecution of the church.[84] Other Romanians were less pessimistic regarding the *congrua*. They saw favorable signs in the attitude of the Hungarian government up to that time. The church leaders in Szeben knew right well that in 1895 the Hungarian government had not withheld subsidies from those officials of their Orthodox see and those professors of theology who had been sentenced in connection with the Memorandum trial.[85] Even earlier, the government had continued to support Romanian priests who had been sentenced by the courts, because it did not consider a leading role in some political movement as grounds for withholding assistance. We know how important was the 1881 meeting of Romanian voters in Nagyszeben for the development of the move-

ment against the constitution of Hungary. This was where the program
of the Romanian National party was elaborated, as was the demand for
the autonomy of Transylvania and other demands. Nicolae Popea, the
Romanian deputy bishop, presided over this meeting. Yet the government raised no objections when, shortly thereafter, Popea was elected
bishop at Karánsebes; in fact, the government forwarded his name for
confirmation.[86] These and similar facts convinced the majority of
Romanian leaders at Szeben that the *congrua* constituted no threat to
the political and ethnic independence of the Romanian clergy. Indeed,
the events gradually proved them right. The *congrua* was disbursed
year after year without serious confusion or negative consequences. The
law of 1898, in the thirtieth year of Hungarian rule, did not even
prescribe a knowledge of the Hungarian language for the priests
benefitting from the *congrua*. That requirement was stipulated later,
by Act 1909: XIII, but even then it allowed a five-year grace period for
those priests who were otherwise qualified and who strove to meet the
linguistic requirement.

When the Romanian leaders mounted mass demonstrations against
the laws promoted by Apponyi, the Minister of Religious Affairs and
Education, some Romanian priests did not participate. Most likely they
feared eventual reprisals, the loss of their *congrua*. A lawyer (probably
Victor Onişor) published a series of articles about the situation of the
clergy in a Romanian weekly from Beszterce dealing mainly with social
and financial issues. "Dependence deriving from state supplement pay
is not so dangerous," he wrote in his introductory article, "because the
fears relating to the loss of the *congrua* are baseless and derive from
lack of knowledge of the legal situation."[87] The *congrua* does not
subordinate the priest to the state.

> The law prescribes this income not for certain political
> services or for certain opportunism, but in exchange for priestly
> functions.... The increment can be obtained only on the basis of
> the law and if the required conditions are present. No minister
> or other entity has the power to grant this increment on grounds
> different from the circumstances as defined, and once the pay is
> granted it can be lost, once again, only as a result of specific
> occurrences defined by the law. The knowledge and understand-
> ing of these facts must awaken in the clergy an awareness of the
> significance of their vocation and of their independence vis-à-vis
> the state. The state requires no service from the clergy, because
> they are not employees of the public administration, are not in
> a relationship of dependence from the state or the police. They

are merely required to perform their pastoral duties, not as a demand of the state, but as a requirement of their vocation. In spite of any pay increment granted by the law the legal situation of the priests has not changed in any way; they remain subordinate to the same higher institutions of the church as before.[88]

The events of subsequent years proved these arguments correct. In 1910 and 1911, the Romanian clergy once again participated in Romanian political movements in even greater numbers than earlier. One of the vice-presidents at the voters' conference in Nagyszeben, in 1910, Nicolae Ivan, also happened to be the top official of the see of the archdiocese of Nagyszeben (hence his pay came from the Hungarian state). At the plenary session of this conference the Hungarian state was under intense attack. In the series of mass rallies held in Romanian areas in 1911 the tone of the attacks was even more radical. The Romanian clergy who benefitted from help or incremental pay provided by the Hungarian state participated in masse, at the rallies held in larger towns and villages. Roman Ciorogariu, the director of the seminary, six deacons, a professor of theology, fourteen parish priests, and others attended the February 16 meeting at Arad. They denounced the government in sharp tones in a resolution adopted by the popular assembly, and expressed their adherence to the program of the Romanian National Party (one of whose points aimed at changing the country's constitution). The Romanian priests of Brassó (Dr. Softu, Vasile Ştefan, Ioan Priscu, etc.) and twenty priests from nearby villages were present, yet not a single one had his *congrua* withdrawn by the state for having participated in the assembly.

These facts lead us to believe that the risk of the *congrua* being withheld was indeed slight, and the Hungarian state did not resort to it as a political weapon. Our opinion of the contributions and financial solidity of the Romanian priests may be identical or similar to that of the Romanian historian Nicolae Iorga, as expressed in 1926:

In Transylvania, under Hungarian rule, the priestly vocation was one of the most sought-after. With the granting of the *congrua* the income of village priests improved sensibly, and their financial situation became satisfactory. Financial independence contributed greatly to their moral standing before both the people and the authorities. Moreover, a career as priest served the ends of national independence as well. The important role played by the clergy in our political struggles is well known.[89]

The satisfactory situation of the clergy was the result of the Hungarian state's contribution to the livelihood of over 3,500 individuals — priests and their families. In the first year of World War I there were 1,943 priests in the Orthodox Church. More than 1,500 priests were functioning in 1,475 parishes and 1,600 affiliate parishes of the Uniate Church.[90]   The Hungarian state ensured the financial independence of the Romanian clergy even though it was aware of its anti-state and anti-Hungarian attitudes. Very seldom did the state declare the *congrua* forfeited, though it may have had good reason to do so more often, for the Romanian archdiocese committed serious abuses in issuing the certificates needed to apply for the *congrua*. The archbishop issued certificates even to some who were not entitled to them. Had the attitude of the government been negative it could have resorted to serious reprisals.   Instead, it was satisfied with the archbishop's declaration to the effect that he had signed the objectionable false documents without reading them.[91]

The sources describing the financial situation of the clergy also mention state help to Romanian seminaries and theological faculties. The seminaries of the Uniate Church were subventioned from the Religious Foundation, the Orthodox ones from the state treasury. The Foundation took care of the board, clothing, and even medical expenses of the theologians. Sometimes it even covered the traveling expenses of Romanian theologians studying abroad. The novices from dioceses without a seminary were kept by the Foundation at the Roman Catholic seminary of Nagyvárad or Szatmár, or at the Uniate seminary at Ungvár [Uzhgorod]. The seminary of Szamosújvár was subsidized by both the Foundation and the state treasury. The latter also covered the expenses of the renovation of the seminary at Balázsfalva in 1916-17.[92] The salaries of the Romanian professors of Orthodox theology were paid out of the state treasury. Part of the sum earmarked for this purpose was disbursed to the consistories, and part of it directly to the individuals through the internal revenue bureaus.[93] Moreover, the state granted certain sums for the university studies of Romanian Orthodox theologians on an annual basis, and these sums enabled four theologians to study at Hungarian or foreign universities, year after year. Dr. Onisifor Ghibu, Nicolae Regman, George Tulbure, Lazăr Triteanu, Iosif Enescu, Cristea E. Miron, Iosif Blaga, and others benefitted from scholarships awarded by the state.

In addition to state subsidies for the clergy and for the training of priests, the Religious Foundation and the treasury often took care of the expenses of the parishes. Every time a parish wanted to build a new church, or repair the old one, the foundation or the treasury was the most important source of funds, besides the collections taken. Many parishes of the Uniate Church were kept afloat by the Hungarian authorities or the Foundation. For instance, the Foundation was in charge of 77 parishes and over 20 Uniate institutions in the diocese of Nagyvárad and of 45 parishes in the diocese of Lugos, while 30 more parishes were supported by the Hungarian Ministry of Finance or the Ministry of Agriculture. In other words, the churches and other religious buildings in these parishes were built by organizations subventioned by the state. The Foundation covered the expenses incurred in connection with the construction of a particularly large number of churches in the Uniate diocese of Lugos. The program started under Ioan Olteanu, when new churches were built at Izgár [Izgar], Petrománу [Petroman], Rakovica [Racoviţa], and Vermes [Vermiş], all from the funds of the Foundation. When Olteanu undertook to visit this region and requested a travel voucher from the Minister of Religious Affairs, he wrote in his application:

> I find the present moment most appropriate for the suggested tour of inspection, because I can show the faithful facts regarding the completion of churches recently consecrated thanks to the Hungarian government, regarding the extent to which our government is taking care of us, and with what favors we are being overwhelmed.[94]

Later, under bishop Dr. Mihályi, thirty new churches were constructed, 24 repaired, and 33 school buildings added in the same diocese. The greater part of the expenses were borne by the Religious Foundation. Moreover, the Minister also awarded grants from the treasury to those underprivileged Uniate parishes which were not supported by the Foundation. Thus there were several hundred parishes in Transylvania where new churches were constructed and old ones repaired with the assistance of the Foundation or of the treasury.

In addition to helping the Uniate parishes, the government did not reject requests for assistance from the Orthodox parishes. According to the records of the Ministry of Religious Affairs, the government contributed to the construction of churches in the following Romanian Orthodox parishes in the decade preceding World War I: András, Bernád [Bernadea], Borsómezõ [Inuri], Burjánfalva, Béganyiresd [Breazova], Birda [Birola], Csarnóháza [Bulz], Dés, Erzsébetváros, Felsõcsertés [Certege], Felsõpoumbák [Porumbacul de sus], Gerend-keresztúr [Grindeni], Halumány, Istvánlak, Kisbecskerek [Becicherecu Mic], Köröstarján [Tărian], Kislaka [Chişlaca], Les, Lüki [Iteu],

Mártonhegy [Şomărtin], Maroskeresztúr [Cristeşti], Mezőbergenye
[Berghia], Marosaszaó [Ususău], Nagydisznód, Nagydevecser [Diviciorii
Mari], Oláhtyukos [Ticuşu Nou], Pakles, Pokola, Pürkerec [Purcăreni],
Szakadát [Săcădat], Szirbó [Sîrbova], Sellemberk [Şelimbăr], Szarakszó
[Sărăcsău], Tîrgovesti, Terebes, Torontáloroszi, Unip [Temesújnép],
Vámosláz [Chişlaz], Vársonkolyos [Şuncuiuş], Valkány [Vălcani] and
Zöldes [Zeldis] as well as the convent of Csiklovabánya [Ciclova
Montană] and the cloister of Marionforrás.

The following churches were repaired thanks to financial assistance
from the Hungarian state: Alcina [Alţina], Alsógezés [Ghijasa de jos],
Alparét [Bobîlna], Arany [Uroiu], Budafalva [Ungureni], Bendorf
[Beneşti], Boholc [Boholţ], Brulya [Bruiu], Buziásfürdő, Berekszó
[Bîrsău], Csicsóújfalu [Ciceu-Corabia], Csíkardál, Csulpesz [Ciulnăz],
Erdőhát [Găunoasa], Gajnár [Poeniţa], Jakabfalva [Iacobeni], Kőhalom,
Kupsafalva [Cunşeni], Kosztafalva [Costeni], Kisdebrecen [Dumbrava],
Köved [Cuiad], Kálbor [Calbor], Kutin [Cutin], Kossó, Mogos [Mogoş],
Magyaró [Aluniş], Mezőtelegd [Tileagd], Milova [Milova], Nyárádszentbe-
nedek [Murgeşti], Nyárfás [Plopiş], Oláhszentandrásfalva [Săcel], Obád
[Obad], Omlód, Prázsmár [Prejmer], Ruszka [Rusca], Szelecske [Sălişca],
Sepsiszentgyörgy, Sövénység [Fişer], Szászahuz [Săsăuşi], Tiszavina,
Temesújnép [Unip], Telekirécse [Recea Nouă], Újváros [Noiştat], and
Zsombor [Jimbor]. The same applied to the lodging of the priests at Aga
[Brestovăt], Felsőkápolna [Căpîlna], Hortobágyfalva [Cornăţel], Jánosda
[Ianoşda], Kóródszentmárton [Coroisînmărtin], Marosorbó [Oarba de
Mureş], Magyarcséke [Ceica], Ördögkút [Treznea], Rákos, Sövényfalu
[Corneşti], and Temesvukovár [Vucova]. It was also thanks to the
financial support of the Hungarian state that the Romanian Orthodox
churches of Alsódoboly [Dobolii de Jos], Budapest, Dés, Falkusa
[Fălcuşa], Felsőorbó [Gîrbova de Sus], Felsőkastély [Coşteiu de Sus],
Hegyeslak [Hăzeşti], Kisbecskerek, Marosilye, Székelyandrásfalva, and
Székelyföldvár [Războeni-Cetate] were equipped or furnished. In
addition to the above, Hungarian state support made it possible to
repair the steeples of the Romanian Orthodox churches at Márpod
[Mariapod], Offenbánya [Baia de Arieş], and Szászkézd [Saschiz]; it also
enabled the Orthodox churches of Dés, Skoré [Scoreiu], and Újegyház to
purchase bells. In some Orthodox parishes such as Rogoz [Rogojel] and
Illenbák [Ilimbav] state assistance was requested and obtained for
fencing the churchyard.

The construction and maintenance work of the Romanian parishes
was carried out, apart from state assistance, with contributions obtained
at the community or municipal level. In most Romanian communities
the process encountered no difficulties whatever. Since the notary, the

judge, and the community council were in the hands of Romanians, they easily approved the contributions requested by the dioceses. Nor did these requests encounter difficulties in towns with a mixed population. In Szászváros the council approved the wood for a new cross,[95] in other areas they approved the cash. If this did not suffice, the religious leaders turned to the authorities for permission to solicit funds. We have found no indication among all the Romanian complaints that any such application was denied. The Hungarian authorities approved such applications courteously. The collection for the construction of the Orthodox cathedral at Nagyszeben was an interesting case in point: It has taken over a period of almost half a century, from 1857 to 1906. The collection had been launched by Şaguna, who retained part of the contribution the Austrian government issued to the clergy. The fund for the cathedral amounted to 22,400 forints by 1868. From that year the Hungarian government undertook to contribute the same amount, even though it knew that the Austrians had been forwarding the money as a reward for the participation of the Romanian clergy in the anti-Kossuth fight in 1848-49. On December 31, 1900, the fund had swollen to 507,837 crowns and six fillers, of which almost half had come from the Hungarian state. At the time of construction the state added yet another 15,000 crowns. Thus the famous Romanian Orthodox cathedral of Nagyszeben is a 50% product of Hungarian state help.[96]

Hungarian society also contributed to the success of fund-raising for Romanian church construction. Occasionally even Hungarian landlords had Romanian churches built at their expense. In 1872 Count Domokos Zichy, the Hungarian landowner of Major in Beszterce-Naszód county, while visiting the community of Kisilva, summoned the Romanian teacher, Gabriel Nechiti, who was also curator of the church, and asked him: "Do you all want to build a church?" "Of course we want to," the man answered, "but we are too poor." "I will have the church built, you only need to bring the materials," said the Count, and kept his promise. He took care of all expenses, and the beautiful church was erected.[97] Károly Huszár, the Hungarian landowner of Lugoskisfalu, acted in a similar manner. According to Hungarian sources several members of the Wesselényi family had churches built in many a Romanian community. The governors of certain counties with a Romanian population also went out of their way to support the Romanian churches and meet their financial needs. On the occasion of the consecration of the Romanian Uniate Church of Dés, the Uniate bishop of Szamosújvár delivered a special speech of thanks to Dr. Zoltán Dézsi, the governor of the County of Szolnok-Doboka, for all the assistance he had provided to Romanian religious causes.[98]

In smaller communities, the Romanian dioceses met almost all of their more-significant expenses from benefit performances. There is scarcely a daily or weekly which does not mention the success of some such performance. These reports indicate that in villages with a mixed population, Hungarians always participated in goodly numbers in soirées organized for the benefit of Romanian religious purposes, and supported these with sizable donations. In 1897, for instance, the Uniate priest of Körösbánya publicly expressed his gratitude to associate judge, János Nagy, the notary, Mészöly, the notary public, Károly Pap, and the Minister of the Reformed Church, Szegedy, who had all donated for the benefit of the diocese at the ball organized by its leading clerics.[99] A few years later the committee of the Romanian diocese of Retteg [Reteag] organized a benefit for the Uniate Church. Fifteen of the guests paid in excess of the face value of the ticket, and nine of the fifteen were Hungarians. "We express our special thanks to the professionals from other ethnic groups who honored us by their presence," wrote the author of the report.[100] In 1912 the Hungarians of Abrudbánya showed up in considerable numbers at the local Romanian ball.[101] And the columns of the Romanian papers mention hundreds of similar occurrences throughout the period of Hungarian rule, demonstrating that in most places Hungarian society did not isolate itself from the Romanian.

Having achieved a satisfactory, and even steadily-improving financial situation, the Romanian churches could carry on with their work in peace. This work, as we have seen, was more ethnic and national than Christian, and the Hungarian authorities were well aware of this. They also knew how pervasive abuse and corruption were within the Romanian churches, particularly the Orthodox one. The leaders of this church disregarded the Organizational Rules whenever their interests so dictated. Bishop Mețianu ruled the church in an arbitrary and tyrannical manner. He modified the decisions of the consistory at the time of their execution. When this high-handed application of the rules was criticized at the episcopal synod he stood up and declared: "I am the law and rules of our church."[102] In spite of all this the Hungarian authorities continued to respect the autonomy of the Romanian Orthodox Church, the freedom of movement of church officials, their right to assemble or tend to their flock, and the observance of the holidays of their church throughout the period, as stipulated by the law. Romanian church autonomy and freedom of worship were not empty slogans, but reality, and this is confirmed by the Romanian press and the minutes of religious assemblies which make no mention of any infringement of these rights. Nowhere have I run across complaints to the effect that individuals who belonged to the Romanian Uniate or Orthodox Churches were forced or intimidated into conversion to another faith, forced to share in the financial burdens of other religions or to construct churches that did not belong to them. Nor is there evidence that the authorities interfered with the holidays of the Orthodox Church, which came later than the holidays of the Western Christian churches. The Orthodox Christmas, Easter, and Ascension Sunday did not normally coincide with the same holidays of the Gregorian calendar, rather, these Orthodox holidays were celebrated later, and sometime this led to chaos. Occasionally Roman Catholics and Protestants leaving their church on a holiday met Romanians working in the village or on their plots. This had a disturbing effect on Hungarian Christians, as it did on the Orthodox when, coming out of their church on an important holiday they found offices and stores open. Occasionally even a megalomaniac policeman might prevent the Orthodox Romanians from working on their plots on a Western holiday. This was the case with a Hungarian policeman at Zernyest [Zărneşti] who forbade Romanians from working on the Christmas Day of the Gregorian calendar. His supervisors, however, had him transferred by way of punishment.[103]   At Déva, Hungarian and Romanian merchants concluded an agreement to observe each other's holidays; the Romanian merchants kept their shops shut on the Christmas Day of the Western Christians, and the Hungarians did the same on the Christmas Day of the Orthodox, which, according to the Julian calendar, fell 13 days after the Christmas of December 25 in the Gregorian calendar. The agreement implied mutual tolerance, and nipped in the bud any possibility of either party spoiling the holiday.[104]

The authorities were generally considerate of the religious sensitivities of the population. On St. John's Day the military partici-pated in the Orthodox religious ceremony in the larger towns such as Brassó or Szeben, with a parade or a gun salute; after the ceremony they returned to their barracks while the military band played Romanian tunes.[105]

Dignitaries of the Romanian church were accorded receptions fitting to higher church and public office by the authorities. More than once, if some high ranking Hungarian official arrived at the episcopal see, he paid his respects to the Romanian bishop. In 1913 the Hungarian Minister of Religious Affairs and Education Béla Jankovich paid a personal visit to the Romanian archbishop. After words of greeting from the Archbishop, the Councillor Ion Micu Moldovanu stood up and delivered a speech in Romanian "so that the Minister too may have an opportunity to enjoy the sweet sounds of our Romanian language."[106]

The situation of the Romanian churches on Hungarian territory can be understood from the data above. But the circumstances of the Romanian churches under Hungarian rule become even clearer if we compare them to the predicament of the Romanian churches in neighboring countries.

The Religious Situation of the Romanians in Neighboring Countries.

Let us take a glance first of all at the religious situation in the independent Kingdom of Romania, where 91% of the Romanians belonged to the Orthodox Church. This fact was recognized by the constitution of the country, since the Orthodox religion was declared the dominant religion, and the church a state church. The state guaranteed freedom of worship to other religions on condition that their "practice not conflict with public order and good morals." Even the Uniate Church was not recognized as official; those members of this church who moved from Hungary to Romania were listed as Orthodox. The official religion enjoyed certain privileges; only the Orthodox Church and its clergy could benefit from state subventions. The secular state authorities decided on important organizational, financial, and disciplinary issues of the church. Its bishops and its Metropolitan were elected by the so-called Great Electoral College [*marele colegiu electoralu*] according to the law the Romanian Orthodox Church adopted in 1872. This College consisted of the Holy Synod and members of the Romanian senate and house of representatives. The state and politics exerted unlimited influence over the church, which played an entirely subordinate role. The meetings of the Holy Synod were summoned by royal decree. The agenda of the meetings had to be drawn up with the approval of the Minister of Religious Affairs and Education. Royal decrees took care of church discipline and launched the periodical of the church; this publication was regulated by state legislation, as applied by the Minister.[107]

While the Romanian Orthodox Church of Hungary was independent of the state, dealt with issues on the basis of autonomy, and waged intensive theoretical and practical struggle against the state, the Orthodox faithful and clergy living under Romanian rule could not even dream of such rights. The Holy Synod had no autonomy whatever, vis-à-vis the various regimes. These regimes decided as they pleased on most issues confronting the church. They elected metropolitans and deprived bishops of their sees. In the case of the Metropolitan Serafim, the Holy Synod was, in the words of the historian Iorga, "subject to jealousies among the principal popes allied with the government, and even cowed in a servile manner before all governments."[108] These conditions were typical not only of the Romanian Orthodox, but of the relationship between the Serbian and Russian Orthodox churches and their respective states, since they were a logical consequence of the ceasaro-papist organization of the official church. Clear evidence of this was the measure adopted by the Serbian government towards the Metropolitan Mihal, the head of the Serbian Orthodox Church. The Metropolitan, along with some bishops, raised his voice against a new stamp act proclaimed by the government. On the request of the cabinet, the ruler removed the Metropolitan from his position by decree, without due process, and had him interned in a monastery. His position was filled by someone else. The Serbian clergy unanimously backed the deposed Metropolitan. The citizens of Belgrade sent a delegation to the ruler, and even the tsar intervened on behalf of the popular Metropolitan, all to no avail! He had the audacity to object to a law, and had to disappear into a monastery.[109]

The moral scandal that broke out in 1911 sheds a sharp light on the relationship between the Romanian state and the Orthodox Church. Bishop Gherasim accused the Metropolitan of Romania of immorality, plagiarism, and heresy. The government removed both from their positions, although everyone recognized that the bishop who raised the charges was correct and above reproach. According to one Romanian paper, the Metropolitan represented all those who "either compromised with the dirty regime in the bosom of the church, or simply fled by leaving the church." They had difficulty finding a qualified person to fill the vacant position of Metropolitan, because it turned out that the majority of the bishops had been bribed by the government to ensure their vote during the decisive meeting of the Holy Synod. Rumor had it that a Romanian bishop from Transylvania would be approached to fill the see of the Metropolitan. One newspaper in Bucharest described this as unrealistic, since the Romanian bishops of Transylvania "are sovereign rulers within their church who can be removed from their see only by death." They would surely not accept the high office, because they realized how offensive this would be to Romania. The Romanian nation and the Romanian Orthodox Church indeed had the right to feel offended, since inviting a bishop from Transylvania was tantamount to admitting that "there was not a single person worthy of filling the office of Metropolitan in the entire Orthodox Church of Romania."[110]

A comparison of the situation of the Orthodox churches in Hungary and Romania leads to interesting conclusions. The 6.7 million Orthodox members of Romania had two archbishops and six bishops. The three

million Romanians in Hungary had two archbishops and five bishops in
the Uniate and Orthodox Churches combined; in other words, the
Romanians of Hungary, whose numbers were only about half of the
Romanians of Romania, had almost the same number of church leaders
as their brothers in the Kingdom of Romania. The comparison of the
number of parishes leads us to similar conclusions: In Romania there
were 6,636, in Hungary 6,136. On the other hand, the number of priests
differed considerably; they were far more numerous in Romania than in
Hungary, where they could choose between many parishes. Thus a
career as priest was more attractive and enjoyed greater prestige in
Hungary.[111]

The churches in Hungary and in Romania agreed in one respect:
support for Romanian nationalism and fostering it by whatever means.
In Hungary this meant a common fight by the two Romanian churches
against the state, and the Romanianization of Hungarians living among
the Romanian population for the sake of enhancing Romanian power.
As the newspaper of Brassó was to write:

> The people of Romania recognize but one church: The
> Romanian Church.   In spite of all the differences that have
> evolved between our religions, we represent one and the same
> church, the calling of which is to defend and cultivate our
> national unity. Thus a common fight is our obligation.[112]

The Orthodox Church also felt it to be its national mission to
Romanianize the non-Romanians living in Romania. The periodical of
the church wrote:

> The Holy Synod must strive to integrate into the Romanian
> nation, the foreign ethnic elements assembled in our country, so
> that they may become true sons of the Romanian nation. This
> can be achieved only if the foreigners who are already Romanian
> citizens become Romanian Christians through the church as
> well.[113]

Such was the chauvinist final objective of the Romanian state.
The Romanian subjects who did not belong to the Orthodox Church,
especially the Hungarian Csángók, who were Roman Catholic, and the
Jews, soon felt the impact of the chauvinist policies of the Romanian
state in all areas. Although the constitution guaranteed freedom of
worship, the practice was different. Jewish school children had to spend
half a day in school even on Saturday, hence could not observe their

religious holiday. Romanian chauvinism was particularly obnoxious with regard to the Csángók who were forced to observe the holidays of the Orthodox Church. Their language was banned from church. The bishop of Iaşi authorized the printing of the catechism only in Romanian for the benefit of Hungarian children, in accordance with the Law on Education of 1893.

The Romanian government endeavored to Romanianize the Hungarian-speaking Csángók by every means at its disposal. It instructed the Romanian bishop appointed by the state to send into the Csángó villages only priests who could not understand Hungarian. The priests who were already stationed there received different instructions: "It is forbidden to pray, sing, or deliver sermons in Hungarian in the churches." According to the ban issued by the bishop they were not even allowed to speak Hungarian in their private communications with the faithful. The Hungarian press did raise the issue on several occasions. Endre Barabás, familiar with Romanian conditions, dealt with the sad predicament of the Csángók in a monograph and a series of articles. He pointed to the flourishing condition of the Romanian national churches in Hungary and to the differences between the religious policies of the Hungarian and Romanian states. Yet the Romanian press in Hungary felt, without exception, that the religious policies of the Romanian government of Bucharest vis-à-vis the Csángók, were entirely justified. The *Libertatea* of Szászváros, edited by the Orthodox deacon Moţa — that is, by a church official — responded to one of Barabás's articles by stating that the Csángók could no longer speak Hungarian, hence it was necessary to resort to Romanian at church. But even if they were Hungarian and could speak the language, we must still not forget that "Romania is a nation-state, not a multilingual state like Hungary. The sixteen communities declared to be Hungarian (although in fact Romanian-speaking) would not have the gall to request that Romania change its educational laws."[114] Thus the author of the article was of the opinion that since the Csángók spoke only Romanian they had to be "truly Romanian," but when it came to the Romanians of Székely-land who spoke only Hungarian, the same paper took the stand that the language spoken by the people is not a criterion of nationality. And not only this newspaper, but the entire Romanian press adopted the same stand when the issue of the Hungarian Uniate bishop came up in 1902, even though, as we have seen, the Hungarians intended this institution only for a defensive role.

The situation of the Orthodox Romanians living in the Orthodox countries of the Balkans or in Russia was the saddest of all. Everywhere a ceasaro-papist regime prevailed; the Orthodox Church and the

Serbian, Bulgarian, Greek, and Russian Tsarist state were as one. As
far as Romanian minorities were concerned, this meant the total
annihilation of Romanian national feeling by the Orthodox Church-
state. None of the states allowed the Orthodox Romanians to organize
on an ethnic basis. The nearly 500,000 Romanian Orthodox living on
Serbian and Bulgarian territory did not have a Romanian church or
clergy, either in the second half of the 19th or in the first decades of the
20th centuries. They had to attend mass said in Serbian or Bulgarian.
Serbian priests Serbianized even Romanian family names.[115] In
1913 the situation of the Romanians of Serbia was described to the
Romanian parliament in a memorandum, with a wealth of details. "The
Romanian churches have disappeared, and the Romanian priests have
gradually been replaced by Serbians, as a consequence of which
Romanians have to attend service in the churches of Serbia exclusively
in Slavic language." By circular number 765, dated August 18, 1899,
the Bishop of Timocul instructed priests to give "purely Serbian
national names to Romanian children, and he compiled a list of such
names for this purpose."[116]

The fate of Romanians living on Greek territory, and of Macedo-
Romanians living on Turkish territory in areas with a Greek majority
was even worse. The Greek government and state church tried
everything to turn the Romanians into Greeks. It persecuted
Romanians living on its own territory, while exerting constant pressure
on neighboring Macedo-Romanians as well. According to Romanian
sources the Greeks hired gangs of criminals to perpetrate tortures and
slaughter in areas inhabited by Romanians. According to the newspaper published in Brassó:

> For a period of fifty years the Romanians of the Ottoman
> Empire were subjected to constant pressures and harassment, as
> manifested in the refusal to provide religious services, in
> excommunications from the church, in libelous denunciations to
> the Ottoman authorities, or in far more terrifying slaughter and
> other atrocities. No crusade has ever been directed with greater
> determination and deliberateness than the one against the
> Romanian churches and their followers in the Ottoman Em-
> pire.[117]

But the situation of the Romanians in Bessarabia, in Tsarist Russia,
was no rosier, as Romanians in Hungary were well aware. The Russian
state and Orthodox Church would not allow church organization on an
ethnic basis. It was forbidden to speak or pray in Romanian in the

churches. In 1908 the rumor spread that the Tsar would authorize
Masses in Romanian, and a Romanian priest in the province of Izmail
gave a sermon in Romanian without awaiting official confirmation of
the news. The next day he disappeared from the bosom of his family,
and was never heard from again.[118]

Surveying the ecclesiastic life and the evolution of the churches of
the Romanians in Hungary, we must conclude that throughout the Dual
Monarchy, Romanian churches evolved without encountering obstacles
from outside. The majority of Romanian priests had intervened on the
side of the Habsburgs in the Hungarian freedom fight of 1848/49,
against the Hungarians. The Austrian autocratic regime initiated
regular state subsidies for the Romanian Uniate and Orthodox churches
from the revenues of Hungarian lands, by way of reward. It also
agreed, in theory and in practice, to the organizational separation of
Orthodox Romanians from Serbians, and of the Romanian Uniates from
Hungarian Catholics, by setting up the Romanian Orthodox archbishopric and by recognizing the archbishopric of Gyulafehérvár of the Uniate
Church. This separation placed the two Romanian churches on an
ethnic foundation. All this took place as a reward for the anti-Hungarian stance of the Romanians in 1848-49, and to set up Romanians as a
bastion against any possible anti-Habsburg action on the part of
Hungarians. In 1867, because of international considerations, the
House of Habsburg achieved a peaceful coexistence with Hungarians,
and also gave them a free hand with regard to Romanians. The
Hungarian statesmen could have placed obstacles to the development of
Romanian Churches to lessen their national character. Instead, at the
time of the Ministry of Baron József Eötvös, the Hungarian government
consolidated the national basis on which the two Romanian churches
were organized. By approving the Organizational Rules providing
autonomy for the Orthodox church, the Hungarian state erected a
powerful fortification protecting the Romanian Orthodox and enabling
them to settle matters of church and nation in peace during the whole
period of Hungarian rule. The Hungarian authorities respected this
autonomy to the end, even though the Romanian church had become a
state within a state as a result of it.

The Hungarian government not only agreed to continue to pay the
subvention initiated by the Austrians, but also subsidized the churches
increasingly year after year. The government alleviated the financial
burdens of the Romanian churches at first with special contributions,
and later with the *congrua*. Bishoprics, central religious institutions,
priests, and parishes benefitted from the assistance provided by the
Religious Foundation and the state treasury. Many bodies, buildings,

Sándor Bíró

and churches of the Uniate and of the Orthodox were set up or built
entirely out of Hungarian government contributions. The government's
help to Romanians was not aimed at curtailing the political role of the
Romanian clergy, nor did it have such an effect.
By recognizing organization on an ethnic basis, by increasing
government allowances, by the unlimited freedom of operations granted
to ecclesiastic bodies, by unfettered freedom of religion and conscience,
the Hungarian state adopted a well-meaning and liberal religious policy
which was in sharp contrast to the religious policies of Serbia, Romania,
Russia, or Bulgaria.

Endnotes

1. Puşcariu, *op. cit.*, p. 86.
2. *Ibid.*, p. 121.
3. *Telegraful Român*, January 27, 1898, No. 6.
4. Eusebiu Roşca, *Monografia mitropoliei ortodoxe române a Ardealului* (Sibiu, 1937), pp. 161-163.
5. "Sinodele parochiale," *Telegraful român*, 1899. No. 4.
6. Puşcariu, *op. cit.*, p. 135.
7. *Ibid.*, p. 136.
8. Lupaş, *op. cit.*, pp. 194-197.
9. "Sfinţirea catedralei ortodoxe române din Sibiu," *Deşteptarea*, May 24, 1906.
10. Roşca, *op. cit.*, p. 29.
11. *Ibid.*, p. 163.
12. "La biografia răposatului metropolit Miron," *Telegraful Român*, 1898, No. 118.
13. "Foaie bisericească, scolastica etc.," *Biserica şi Şcoala*, 1879, p. 122.
14. *Biserica şi Şcoala*, 1877, pp. 341-342.
15. Onisifor Ghibu, *Şcoala românească din Transilvania şi Ungaria* (Bucharest, 1915), p. 84.
16. *Tribuna*, April 21, 1884, No. 6.
17. *Ibid.*, October 18, 1885, No. 228.
18. *Ibid.*, October 29, 1885, No. 237.
19. "Către oun cetifori," *Viitoriul*, 1884, No. 1.
20. This role of the *Tribuna* is described in detail by Sándor Bíró in his work *A Tribuna és a magyarországi román közvélemény* [the *Tribuna* and Romanian Public Opinion in Hungary] (Kolozsvár, 1942).
21. "Presiuni electorale," *Tribuna*, May 21, 1884, No. 20.
22. *Tribuna*, December 31, 1884, No. 199.
23. Roşca, *op. cit.*, p. 24.
24. "Autonomia Transilvaniei," *Telegraful Român*, 1896, No. 21.
25. *Telegraful Român*, 1896, No. 42. "Cerculariu către clerul şi poporul orthodox român din archidiecesa Transilvaniei," Sibiu.

26. *Ibid.*
27. *Telegraful Român*, 1898, No. 37.
28. Papp, *op. cit.*, pp. 94-95.
29. *Libertatea*, 1905, Nos. 2 and 10.
30. "Închinătorii," *Ibid.*, 1909, No. 8.
31. The adamantly nationalistic weekly *Libertatea* was edited by the Orthodox deacon Moţa.
32. "Sfinţirea bisericei din Răcăştie," *Telegraful Român*, 1898, No. 130.
33. *Ibid.*, 1899, No. 22.
34. "Purtarea preoţilor în societate şi cu poporul," *Biserica şi Şcoala*, 1877, pp. 74-75.
35. *Ibid.*, 1877, p. 138.
36. *Ibid.*, 1878, p. 25.
37. *Ibid.*, 1883, pp. 285-286, and 296.
38. *Tribuna*, June 8, 1884, No. 35.
39. Roşca, *op. cit.*, p. 24.
40. *Tribuna Poporului*, October 22, 1898, No. 212. Roşca, *op. cit.*, p. 161.
41. *Telegraful Român*, 1896, No. 12.
42. *Tribuna Poporului*, February 28, 1899, No. 32. Roşca, *op. cit.*, pp. 28, 340.
43. Roşca, *op. cit.*, p. 32.
44. Nicolae Maneguţiu, *Alamanachul Sfîntului Nicolae* (Sibiu, 1902), p. 198.
45. Roşca, *op. cit.*, p. 30.
46. "Săracii de noi," *Libertatea*, 1903, No. 48.
47. "Protopopul Dan condemnat şi pensionat," *Libertatea*, 1905 No. 28.
48. "Din public," *Libertatea*, 1911, No. 21 and 25.
49. Mircea Şirianu, *La question de Transylvanie et l'unité politique roumaine* (Paris, 1916), pp. 273-274.
50. "Din Balomir," *Libertatea*, 1909, No. 51.
51. "Scrisoare din Brad," *Ibid.*, 1912, No. 24.
52. "Scandalul liberal dela Arad," *Romania*, May 16, 1924.
53. According to the Romanian deacon Nistar from Marosvásárhely. "Întâmpinare," *Românul*, April 26, 1912.
54. *Unirea*, September 7, 1912.
55. *Deşteptarea*, July 18, 1912.
56. *Unirea*, October 1, 1912.
57. Jenő Szabó, *A görög-katolikus magyarság utolsó kálvária útja* [The Last Calvary of the Uniate Hungarians] (n.p., n.d.).
58. *Libertatea*, 1913, No. 25.
59. Roman R. Ciorogariu, *Zile trăite* (Oradea, 1926), p. 50.
60. *A magyar korona országainak mezőgazdasági statisztikája* [Agricultural Statistics Pertaining to the Lands of the Hungarian Crown], Vol. *Végeredmények* [Final results], (Budapest, 1900), tables on pp. 23-33.
61. *Ibid.*, pp. 34-41.
62. *K. Statisztikai Közlöny* [Royal Bulletin of Statistics]. New series Vol. XXVII, pp. 25-33, and pp. 35-41, new series 39, p. 163. József Vencel, *Az erdélyi román földbirtokreform* [The Romanian Land Reform in Transylvania](Kolozsvár, 1942), p. 43.

63. *Tribuna,* February 23, 1912.

64. *Şematismul,* No. 46.

65. *Unirea,* December 28, 1911.

66. *Şematismul,* compiled from the annual reports of the Romanian Uniate church.

67. *Unirea,* April 20, 1912.

68. On the basis of documents in the archives of the Ministry of Religious Affairs and Education.

69. Onisifor Ghibu, *Viaţa şi organizaţia bisericească şi şcolară in Transilvania şi Ungaria* (Bucharest, 1915), pp. 26-28.

70. "Ajutor de stat pestru consistoriul gr. ort. român din Oradea-Mare," *Telegraful Român,* 1912, No. 23.

71. Archives of the Ministry of Religious Affairs and Education, 233.970/1918.

72. Roşca, *op. cit.,* p. 268.

73. Archives of the Ministry of Religious Affairs and Education, 4893/1870.

74. Roşca, *op. cit.,* p. 268.

75. Maneguţiu, *op. cit.,* p. 78.

76. *Ibid.,* pp. 78-80.

77. Roşca, *op. cit.,* p. 269.

78. Maneguţiu, *op. cit.,* p. 163.

79. The autobiography of Dr. Cristea Illes Miron, quoted in Jakabffy, *op. cit.,* p. 148.

80. Maneguţiu, *op. cit.,* p. 164.

81. Ghibu, *op. cit.,* pp. 37-40.

82. *Călindarul poporului pe 1902,* p. 115.

83. *Unirea,* February 25, 1913, quoted in Jakabffy, *op. cit.,* p. 190.

84. "Prigonirea şcoalelor şi bisericilor" *Călindarul poporului,* 1904 (Sibiu), Vol. XV, p. 104.

85. Archives of the Hungarian Ministry of Religious Affairs and Education, document 72.664-1895.

86. Roşca, *op. cit.,* p. 22.

87. "Situaţia preoţilor şi învăţătorilor," *Revista Bistriţei,* 1908, No. 47.

88. *Ibid.,* No. 49.

89. "Criza da preoţi în Ardeal," *Neamul Românesc,* March 24, 1926.

90. Ghibu, *op. cit.,* pp. 36-37, and 70.

91. Roşca, *op. cit.,* pp. 272-274.

92. Archives of the Ministry of Religious Affairs and Education, 173.677/1916 and 180.486/1917 documents.

93. Ghibu, *op. cit.,* pp. 26-28.

94. Report by Olteanu, in the Archives of the Ministry of Religious Affairs and Education 12.982/1873.

95. "Dela Oraş," *Libertatea,* 1902, No. 46.

96. Roşca, *op. cit.,* pp. 184-188.

97. "Un învăţătar veteran," *Revista Bistriţei,* May 9, 1908, No. 17.

98. *Revista Bistriţei,* 1903, No. 27.

99. "Dare de seamă şi mulţumite publică," *Gazeta Transilvaniei,* 1897, No. 45.

100. *Revista Bistriţei,* 1903, No. 9.

101. "Din Munții Apuseni," *Gazeta Transilvaniei*, March 16, 1912.
102. Roșca, *op. cit.*, pp. 29-30.
103. *Călindarul Poporului pe 1902*, p. 104.
104. "Un pact frumos," *Libertatea*, 1903, No. 1.
105. *Gazeta Transilvaniei*, 1897, No. 5 and 8.
106. *Libertatea*, 1913, No. 47.
107. Much pertinent data may be found in Vol. I of *Biserica Ortodoxă Română*, a religious periodical. This periodical was launched in 1874, when the daily *Telegraful Român* of the Romanians of Hungary had already reached twenty volumes.
108. Nicolae Iorga, *Istoria românilor. Integitorii* (Bucharest, 1939), p. 314.
109. *Biserica Ortodoxă Română*, Vol. V, pp. 835-838.
110. In *Scara* (a semi-official paper of the government) of October 1, 1911, quoted in Elemér Jakabffy, *A románok hazánkban és a román királyságban* [The Romanians in Our Country and in the Kingdom of Romania] (Budapest, 1918), p. 7.
111. Jakabffy, *op. cit.*, p. 14 and Iorga's already quoted remark.
112. "Solidaritatea națională biserclicor românești," *Gazeta Transilvaniei*, 1913, No. 25.
113. "Raportul comisiumei Sfîntului Sinod," *Biserica Ortodoxă Română*, V, p. 685.
114. "Unele altela," *Libertatea*, 1910, No. 31.
115. "Un mou regat albano-român," *Românul*, 1912, November 3, (No. 233).
116. *Universul*, January 11, 1913, quoted in Jakabffy, *Adatok*, pp. 181-182.
117. "Macedonia Macedonenilor," *Gazeta Transilvaniei*, 1913, Nos. 12 and 14.
118. "Starea socială a românilor besarabeni," *Românul*, October 30, 1912.

Chapter IV

Education and Cultural Development among the Romanians of Hungary

The character of a nation finds expression above all in its language and culture. All nations cling to their cultural heritage, at first instinctively, then consciously, as they realize that their identity as a nation is intimately connected with it. A nation becoming conscious of its national identity, its culture, language, traditions, history, customs, etc., strives not only to retain these but is eager to see them flourish. In fact, one of its major preoccupations is to pass on its national culture to posterity. This preoccupation is tantamount to national self-preservation, since a nation passes on its culture to its youth in order to preserve its national character for the future. It is for this reason that schools play a decisive cultural role in the life of nations.

However, the transmission of culture takes place not only in a school setting; cultural organizations, associations, the press, and the theater also assume an important role in defining and spreading popular culture. The cultural development of the people is the result of the combined work of all these entities. Hence the cultural situation of Hungary's Romanian population was determined by its schools, its associations, its press, and theater. We need to survey their work to gain an understanding of this situation.

Primary Schools

The Nature and Number of Schools

As in most other countries, education in Hungary, during the Middle Ages and well into modern times, was in the hands of the churches. Before 1867 there was not a single state elementary school, since all schools were run by the churches. Apart from the need for religious instruction, establishing schools hinged on financial considerations; churches which were financially better-off developed a network of schools sooner. The Uniate and Orthodox churches were rather late in organizing their educational system, as compared to the Roman

189

Catholic and Protestant churches. Since it was in a relatively better financial situation the Uniate Church established schools in the middle of the 18th century, before the Orthodox Church. From the middle of the 19th century the number of Uniate schools began to grow rapidly, and an increasing number of Romanian children received a regular primary education. At the time of absolutist Austrian rule, under the wise leadership of Archbishop Şaguna, the education provided by the Orthodox Church, which had been lagging somewhat, attained a level comparable to that of the Uniate Church. Even then not every village had a school, but where there was one, it now functioned more regularly. The Hungarian element took over political control in Hungary as a result of the Austro-Hungarian Compromise. The Hungarian leaders established the foundations of primary education in the country as early as 1868, when parliament approved the public education system proposed by Baron József Eötvös, the Minister of Religious Affairs and Education. This proposal led to Act XXXVIII of 1868 regarding education in public (including religious) schools, which anticipated similar basic measures in the United Kingdom, France, and Italy.

As a Romanian author notes, this Act was based on two principles: compulsory schooling for all, and freedom of choice of instruction.[1] Parents who disregarded the principle of compulsory schooling were penalized according to Article 4 of the law and fined by the Treasury. Freedom of choice of instruction was guaranteed under Article 6. It stated that "parents and guardians are free to have their children educated in the home, or at a private or public institution sponsored by any church, wherever that educational institution may be located."

Article 10, pertaining to support for the schools, stated that "institutions of public education in our country may be established and financed in a manner determined by law, by religious groups, various associations, individuals, communities, and the state." According to Article 11, the religious groups could establish schools, appoint their own teachers, and determine their own textbooks and curriculum in every community where they had followers. The curriculum had to, however, include subjects required by the state, and they had to receive equal time.[2] The church sponsoring the school was free to determine its language of instruction. In addition to this law, Article 26 of Act XLIV of 1868 granted churches the right to establish and finance schools, and emphasized that public schools established by religious denominations enjoyed equal status with similar-level state schools.

As can be seen from this text, the Act attempted to provide public education primarily through denominational schools. The denominations were mentioned first in the list of those financing schools. The right to set up schools in the community was granted first of all to the denominations. The list then went on to mention associations, communities, and, in last place, the state. According to Article 23, the communities had a duty to establish a school wherever the denominations did not maintain a public school in accordance with the prescriptions of the law. Wherever state schools came into being they were usually converted Hungarian religious schools.

According to this master plan, the establishment of state schools was a last resort. According to Article 80, the Minister could call for the construction of "educational establishments required by local conditions purely with state funds" if and when it deemed these necessary. The small number of state schools demonstrates that in most places they were not deemed necessary. Forty years after the adoption of the Act, state schools still continued to be no more than 14.1% of all primary schools.[3] In 1918, in formerly Hungarian areas then inhabited by Romanians, only 28% of all schools were state schools, while the others were denominational.[4]

Through the above Act the Hungarian government broadly guaranteed the establishment of Romanian denominational schools. If a community school was organized in a locality that already had a denominational school, those residents who contributed to the maintenance of such a school by paying over 5% of their income tax for the purpose were, according to the provisions of the Act, exempted from the burden of having to support the community school. Thanks to this exemption, Act XXXVIII of 1868, the residents of Romanian communities could not be made to bear the burden of providing for the maintenance of two schools at once. On the contrary, the Act allowed real estate taxes in the community earmarked for education to be turned over to the denominational school if there was no community school.

The Romanians raised no objections to this Act, either then or later. In 1877 the periodical *Biserica şi şcoala*, in a survey of the more important basic laws, criticized only those parts of the Education Act that related to state supervision, since the Romanian attitude at the time was not to recognize the government's right to any kind of supervision. Even so, the periodical stressed that it did not intend to attack the Act on public education which "provides many attractive rights to the denominations." Unfortunately, "our denomination," it added, "does not have the means to take advantage of these rights, and therefore our schools can develop to the extent advocated by the country's law only by making supreme efforts."[5]

If applied to the Romanian Orthodox Church, this statement was entirely warranted. At that time, in the seventies, this church had but meager resources. According to the census taken at the turn of the century the Orthodox parishes owned teachers' or school plots amounting to a total of 6,736 *holds*, an average of no more than 3.5 *holds* per parish.[6] It was difficult to finance a school and pay a teacher in accordance with the prescriptions of the law, which required a well-lit room, limited the number of pupils per classroom, and prescribed the preparation of the teachers. It is clear that if the Hungarian state had been antagonistic to Romanian denominational instruction, it could have found pretexts enough for putting a stop to all instruction in the Romanian language at the primary level. But Eötvös sincerely wished to see Romanian denominational instruction thrive, and therefore he manifested infinite patience towards those schools which did not meet the requirements set by the law. For decades his successors exhibited the same kind of patience with regard to the deficiencies of Romanian schools. It was thanks to this attitude that the schools sponsored by the Romanian churches managed to take hold and do a creditable job instructing Romanian children in their mother tongue.

After the adoption of Act XXXVIII of 1868, the Romanian parishes organized denominational schools wherever they could. According to Romanian church laws, every parish with over 30 children between the ages of 6 and 12 was obliged to set up a primary school.[7] Within a few years the two churches established more than 2,000 primary schools where instruction took place solely in Romanian. In a few hundred villages, Romanian language community schools were set up instead of denominational schools. No prior authorization of any kind was required for setting up a school. The church administration simply reported the existence of the new school to the Ministry, which took cognizance of its existence, and thus the school became official.

On the basis of the annual reports of the Hungarian Ministry of Education, and the evidence provided by Romanian ecclesiastic organizations, the number of schools with Romanian as the language of instruction was as follows during the Compromise period:[8]

1869	1872	1877	1880	1884	1890	1906	1911	1914
2569	2878	2773	2756	2843	2582	2985	2813	2901

Thus, the number of schools with Romanian as the language of instruction did not vary considerably in the period from 1868 to 1914. Two to three hundred schools may have become defunct, but within five or ten years an equal number of new ones were founded. From 1869 to 1872 the original figure, 2,569, increased by 309. By 1890 the figure had decreased by 292. Before the Apponyi Laws there were almost three thousand; when these laws were introduced the figure once again dropped by several hundred, but by the first year of World War I there were 348 more schools than in 1869. Romanian Orthodox Church schools increased from 1552 to 1640, especially after the Apponyi Laws, between 1911 and 1914.[9]

By making full use of the provisions of Act XXXVIII of 1868, and thanks to the benevolence and understanding of Hungarian governments, the churches were able to maintain an impressive number of primary schools with Romanian as the language of instruction. The schools established at the beginning usually had but one teacher and a tiny classroom. The room was often no more than an ordinary hut built of adobe. Moreover, the children attended schools only in the winter months. Instruction took place without textbooks or any other kind of instructional material. Fines collected by the authorities were used to cover the cost of whatever equipment and instructional material was available. Fines were assessed because of deficiencies and, according to Article 4 of the Act on Public Education, such moneys were reserved for the school fund. Apart from fines, the cost of maintaining the schools was borne by the community itself, though there were additional contributions in the form of profits on school land (wherever there were such lands), private donations, and state subvention.

The Uniate schools functioned without serious difficulties, because the church was considerably better off and received assistance from the Catholic Religious Foundation, which enjoyed as official status in the Hungarian state. But the majority of the Orthodox schools could exist only because of the leniency and understanding of the authorities. Ten years after the adoption of the Eötvös Act on Public Education, in 1878, the periodical of the Orthodox theological institute of Arad, described these schools as follows:

Our schools are most primitive; they do not meet the requirements set by law; nor do they satisfy the demand for educational services — they fail altogether to fulfill their lofty mission. In fact, in some places they are outright scandalous — repulsive, tiny, dark, filthy; except for one of two toilets these schools have absolutely nothing. They do not have the necessary materials, textbooks, or anything at all that is required for effective learning. The school is often too far from where the children live. Neither the townspeople, nor the parents are truly con-

cerned; in fact they are tired of the school. The people think of
it as a serious burden and a nuisance; instead of expressing
interest, feeling enthusiastic, or making sacrifices, the people
eagerly await an opportunity to rid of it.[10]

A few decades later, by 1902, the situation had improved somewhat.
In a conference held on May 1, 1902, Demeter Comsa, president of the
Association of Orthodox Teachers, stated that only about half of the
schools were clean, and that their yards and equipment generally met
the standards required by law. The rest were unclean. At many schools
the floors and windows were not washed or swept for months at a time.
The podiums, blackboards, and benches were seldom cleaned. Few
schools had a furnace. The courtyards were choked with weeds, rags,
and filth. No one wanted to take the responsibility for these shortcomings: the priest blamed the teacher, the teacher blamed the judge, the
judge blamed the notary; but it was the teacher who received most of
the blame. Few deacons took the trouble to supervise the priests with
sufficient enthusiasm and perseverance to encourage, in turn, the
priests to mind the schools. Many large and prosperous Romanian
communities did not maintain their school building. In Felkenyér
[Vinerea], for instance, the school was the most beautiful structure in
the village, yet it was sadly neglected because the parish did not
maintain it. "This is a sin that reflects on all of us," concluded the
president of the Association of Romanian Teachers.[11]

In the years preceding World War I the situation of the Romanian
schools had improved a great deal as compared to the seventies. But
even then, about 30% of the schools fell far short of the standards set by
the law, and 700 to 800 schools could have been closed down for non-
compliance. In many places the buildings were entirely inadequate, or
even outright hazardous. In one village, instruction took place in rented
rooms, since the school did not have its own building.[12] In many
instances the two Romanian churches could only muster a common
school, which was then dominated by the larger of the congregations.[13] In the eighties the bishops of Nagyszeben and Balázsfalva
had reached an agreement regarding schools to be built and maintained
jointly. They stipulated that in those Romanian communities where one
of the denominations could not build a school on its own because of the
small size of its congregation, the two churches would pool their
resources and bear the expenses jointly. The costs would be divided
proportionately. Following the agreement in principle between the
highest church officials, many communities reached an agreement at the
local level regarding a combined school. For instance, in the community

of Tordas [Turdaş] near Szászváros, the priests of the Orthodox and Uniate churches reached an agreement in 1897. They agreed, in Szászváros, in the presence of their deacons and other church officials, that the Uniate school in Tordaş would close down, but members of the Uniate Church would contribute proportionally to the extension of the building of the Orthodox school, and the new, enlarged school would then serve the educational needs of Uniate children as well. Consequently, a nice new school building was built, and it was dedicated on October 25, 1898. The Romanian notary, Ioan Roşu, contributed considerably to the construction and opening of this new combined school.[14]

The Hungarian Ministry of Religious Affairs and Education did not forbid such agreements. What mattered was that the school building satisfy the standards set by law. Although the Act of 1868 did not provide for such combined schools, the Ministry allowed them to function because it stood for the principle of unlimited freedom of instruction, and denominational schools had the right to accept anyone as students. Not a single school was closed down on this account. Repeated postponements were granted where there was any possibility that the standards set by the law would eventually be met. As regards the Romanian schools, the Apponyi Laws were carried out only three or four years after their adoption. Since in many places Romanians refused to accept the curriculum prescribed by the state — which was a prerequisite of state support ensuring the normal pay of teachers — about 300 Romanian schools were closed down as a result of these laws. By then Romanians were in a much better economic situation than they had been at the end of the 19th century, hence they were able to satisfy the requirements of the law in most places. Elsewhere denominational schools were transformed into Romanian-language community schools. When six Romanian schools of the Székely-land were closed down as a result of these laws, the Romanian weekly of Szászváros commented sadly "that these schools were lost through our own fault rather than because of the regime. In one place the priest failed to inform the people in time as to what must be done, while elsewhere the people refused to undertake sacrifices."[15]

Cases of neglect were rather frequent in the Dual Monarchy; but ingenuous Romanian school officials soon found the remedy. They sought patrons in the Romanian kingdom who were prepared to make sacrifices and were willing to provide financial support to the schools. This support was at times given in secret, but at other times was even mentioned in the press. In 1898 readers of the official paper of the Orthodox Church could read the good news that lady Elena Turnescu,

a resident of Romania, had donated 1,000 lei for the construction of the
Romanian school in the community of Markos [Márkoş][16]   Even
greater publicity was given to Constantin Mille, the editor of *Adevărul*,
a Romanian daily, who launched a collection for the Romanian schools
of Hungary by means of an appeal published in his paper; the campaign
continued for a while until a few thousand lei had been collected. The
sum was then transferred to the Romanian schools of Hungary, which
were not prevented by anyone from accepting donations from abroad.
As the Romanian daily of Transylvania was to write, "Indeed, no one
can be prevented from accepting a gift from whoever they wish."[17]
The sponsors of the Romanian school of the community of Kaca [Caţa],
near Kőhalom, acted in a similar manner in 1914. Their school, the
most beautiful in Transylvania, was constructed entirely from funds
collected in Romania. Dr. Ioan Ursu, a Romanian professor at Iaşi
University, and the Mircea brothers from Bucharest contributed all the
funds needed for the construction of the building in Romanian national
style. A ceremony, including a dramatic performance, was organized at
the school on January 7, 1914, in their honor, and it was attended by
one of the brothers. He enjoyed himself until the wee hours of the
morning and provided yet another contribution for a piano. In the
morning the youths, carrying Romanian national banners and singing
national songs, accompanied him to the station whence the generous
donor travelled straight back to Bucharest.[18]

Financial support from Romania, was, of course, a cumbersome and
slow solution. Church officials who knew the people well and had
organizational talent also knew that a faster and more secure way of
obtaining support for the schools was awakening the Romanian
peasantry's willingness to sacrifice — all the more, as economic
conditions of this segment of society had been steadily improving.
When the Hungarian Minister of Religious Affairs and Education
decided to raise the salary of teachers and obliged the sponsors of the
Romanian schools to follow suit, Cristea Miron, the Bishop of Karánsebes, appealed to the people to take up the cause of the schools. Not
hundreds of thousands but millions were donated, and schools were built
or restored in over sixty communities, while the salaries of 272 teachers
were adjusted to meet the norms of the state.[19]

A multitude of data proves that the Hungarian government did not
use the dilapidated state of the Romanian schools, their deficient
equipment, the non-compliance with the requirements of the law, or
assistance obtained from Romania and confessed in the press, as
weapons against the schools. Otherwise it could have found a thousand-
and-one reasons for closing them down. It resorted to this measure only

when there was no hope that the given school could ever be legally viable. The good intentions of the government are shown by the fact that it is continued to allow access to the Romanian schools; indeed, the Romanians raised no complaints on this account. In accordance with Eötvös's Laws on public instruction, no ministerial authorization was required for setting up a new primary school. The organization or construction of a school was merely reported to the Ministry by the church authorities. Schools thus registered were considerate the equivalent of schools, their public nature was taken for granted, and there was no need to make a special request to legalize their status.

The Students

According to Article 6 of the Eötvös Act anyone could register in a Romanian primary school. Freedom of choice of instruction was unlimited during the entire period: in other words, parents could send their children to whichever school they wished. The school administration could take in any pupil it wished without regard to religion or nationality. Thus, there were no legal impediments to accepting pupils of Hungarian ethnic background or of another religion, for that matter. In many communities with a mixed population there was but one denominational school, with Romanian as the language of instruction, catering to the children of Hungarian parents as well. Where the number of Hungarian residents did not exceed one hundred, or was under one hundred and fifty, there was usually no state school with Hungarian as the language of instruction, hence Hungarian children in that village had no choice but to attend a school where the language of instruction was Romanian. In villages with a mixed population Hungarian children who were in a minority attended stale-supported Romanian schools. These children did not study in their mother tongue — they could read and write only in Romanian. The process often resulted in the Romanianization of the children. The Apponyi Act XXVII of 1907 was designed to remedy this situation by stipulating that if there were twenty or more children of Hungarian background attending a Romanian school they had to be instructed in Hungarian.
Comparing the number of Romanian schools with the number of Romanian inhabitants or the number of Romanians of school age, we may ask: A public elementary school with autonomous jurisdiction and with Romanian as its language of instruction catered on the average to how many Romanian residents or Romanian children? In the years preceding World War I, one school catered on average to 90 - 110 children. There was one Romanian denominational school for every

1,100 inhabitants of Romanian extraction. The ratio was less favorable
for the members of the Orthodox Church: according to the official
church census, in 1914 there were 1,640 Romanian language public
schools for 1,885,173 inhabitants. In 1913-14, in the 47th year of
Hungarian rule, there was one Orthodox school with Romanian as the
language of instruction for every 1,149 Orthodox residents[20]   In
Romania in the same period there were 4,913 schools for 7,771,914
inhabitants, that is one public elementary school for every 1,582
inhabitants![21] Thus the Romanian students could attend the primary
school sponsored by their own church and receive instruction in
Romanian, since in the years preceding World War I, 75% of the purely
Romanian communities had a denominational public school where
instruction took place in that language. In 1914, of the 1,867 parishes
of the Orthodox Church 1,395, or almost 75%, had their own school.

In general 75% was the ratio for the population as well:[22] on the
average 75% of children of school-age living under Hungarian rule could
attend public denominational schools where the language of instruction
was Romanian.   What percentage of school-age children actually
attended is a different matter. In 1913/14, according to the already
quoted official publication of the Romanian Orthodox Church, 128,959
of the 280,786 children of school age who belonged to the church
(between the ages of 6 and 15) attended denominational schools where
the language was Romanian, whereas 59,935 attended other schools.
About 90,000, that is more than 30% of all Romanian school-age
children, attended no school at all,[23] which meant that when World
War I broke out not quite one-fourth of the children of school age
belonging to the Orthodox religion attended school in other that their
mother tongue, whereas the others attended their own schools or did not
attend at all.

Some Romanian children attended state schools where the language
of instruction was Hungarian, and sometimes denominational schools
where the language of instruction was German. They were sent there
because their parents felt it necessary to learn these languages. They
could not expect to accomplish this in a Romanian-language school
because, as one of the Romanian papers of the Bánát noted: "our
schools leave a lot to be desired in comparison with foreign schools when
it comes to direction and supervision."[24] Of course, from the start the
Romanian press prodded all Romanians to support only their denominational schools. Indeed, this propaganda had its effect. Yet there were
areas where the parents actually believed the state had more to offer,
hence neglected the Romanian denominational school.[25]

The Eötvös Act XXXVIII of 1868 which ensured freedom of choice of instruction, that is the right of the parents to select the school of their choice, remained in effect throughout the Hungarian regime. Registration at state schools, as we shall see below, was never compulsory, and parents continued to send their children where they wished. Anyone could be registered in any school without special permission.

Hundreds and thousands of children of Hungarian background were registered in schools where instruction took place in Romanian. The recently acquired Romanian national feeling continued to be reinforced even under Hungarian rule among the children of Romanianized Hungarian families. It occurred to no one to restrict the parents' right to chose schools on account of ethnic or religious differences, or even to favor state schools. We find no complaints in the official publication of the Orthodox Church, even after the introduction of the Apponyi Laws, albeit this publication never failed to report grievances.[26]

The Situation of the Romanian Teachers

In the first years of the Compromise the Romanian denominational schools were directed by the churches without any state interference. They trained and certified their own teachers without state supervision or control. Their teachers' colleges followed a curriculum of their own. Until 1879, that is in the first twelve years of Hungarian rule, the government issued no directives, not even regarding the teaching of the official language. It was the Romanian church authorities that placed teachers once the latter had completed their preparation at Romanian teachers' colleges.   No state authorization was necessary, either beforehand or afterwards, to enable a teacher to occupy a post or to gain tenure.[27]

Thus the Hungarian government granted broad rights to the Romanian churches regarding the schools for the training of teachers, their selection, and the granting of tenure. The Romanian churches took full advantage of these rights. Where trained teachers were not available they employed individuals who had completed a few years of elementary school. In 1877, ten years after the beginning of Hungarian rule, only 32 out of 216 teachers were certified in the schools under the jurisdiction of the Orthodox consistories of Arad and Nagyvárad. Altogether 184 teachers, of whom 97 had never attended a teachers' college, taught without certification. Thirty-three posts could not be filled even with untrained teachers.[28]

From 1879 the government began to supervise the work of Romanian teachers' colleges and the situation of the teachers more systematically. The aim of this supervision was, on the one hand, to ensure familiarization with the official language, resulting in the effective teaching of the language at the primary level and, on the other hand, standardizing teachers' salaries.

Hungarian educational policy sought to attain the first objective by adopting Act XVIII of 1879, *Regarding the Teaching of Hungarian at Institutions of Public Learning*. This Act prescribed the education of teachers capable of teaching the official language. It also made the teaching of Hungarian compulsory in the primary schools to the extent the teachers were able to master and teach it. According to Article 1 of the law, Hungarian had to be taught in sufficient number of periods in teachers' colleges where Hungarian was not the language of instruction, so that every candidate would be able to master it sufficiently in speaking and writing during the course. Young teachers who completed their studies after the above date could only obtain an appointment if they could master Hungarian sufficiently to be able to teach it as a subject in a primary school. The Hungarian superintendent of schools had to sign a certificate to that effect. If this was not the case, he did not sign the certificate, which remained invalid without his signature.

The teachers who graduated after 1872 were allowed a longer period in which to acquire the official language: four years from the date the law entered into effect. Teachers certified before 1872 who were older than 25 at the time the law was adopted were not required to learn the official language. They could continue to function to the end of their lives and Hungarian was not taught in their schools. But from 1883 on they could teach only in villages with a exclusively Romanian population. According to the law the villages with a mixed population of Hungarians and Romanians could employ only teachers who were able to teach Hungarian as a subject.

According to Act XVIII of 1879, after 1883, villages with a mixed population could employ only those Romanian teachers who, could teach Hungarian effectively even if they were less than 25 years old. The officials of the two Romanian churches objected to the law, because they claimed, the overwhelming majority of Romanian teachers could speak no Hungarian at all.[29] They were afraid that these teachers would find themselves in dire straits.

As we have seen, only those who completed their studies after 1872 were obliged to acquire the official language in four years. Older teachers, and even those over 25, were not compelled to learn the language. They could continue to function in peace in exclusively Romanian villages. Those teachers over 25 who did not know Hungarian well were scheduled to take proficiency examination in 1883.

The law concealed no serious danger to the nationalities. It contained no sanctions against those who did not familiarize themselves with the official language within the period allowed. They could continue to teach even if unsuccessful on the proficiency examination; at most, they were required to sign up for another course in the subject.

Indeed, the application of the law indicates that it was not designed as a measure against the Romanian schools. The government did not merely prescribe the need to learn the official language, but took care to provide the means as well. It organized courses at government expense for the benefit of Romanian teachers. The teachers received a per diem allowance for the duration of the course. The first such courses were offered at Arad, Kolozsvár, and other cities of Transylvania in 1879. The per diem, including a free sojourn in larger towns with opportunities for entertainment, proved so attractive that many signed up for the courses. But, as we may read in the Romanian school periodical, only teachers with a smattering of Hungarian were admitted, whereas the remainder were rejected.[30] The latter were not pleased, for they would have preferred greater compulsion to take the course.

The question is, what fraction of the Romanian teachers did not know Hungarian in this period? According to the Romanian bishops, the overwhelming majority had some knowledge of the language. Comparing this assertion with the data contained in the reports presented by the Minister of Religious Affairs and Education to parliament every year, we may conclude that in the 13th year of the Hungarian regime there were about 1,500 Romanian teachers on the territory of the Hungarian state who spoke not a word of the language, whereas about 600 had a smattering of it. Only a few hundred Romanian teachers knew enough to teach it as a subject. The frequently-organized courses, as well as the new crop of teachers graduating from college, gradually increased the percentage of those who knew Hungarian. But the slow and ponderous application of the law was also demonstrated by the statistics; in 1884 there were 450 who knew no Hungarian at all; in 1889 the number dropped to 221, and at the turn of the century there were still over 100 Romanian teachers with no knowledge of Hungarian. Yet they could retain their post in spite of their ignorance of the official language, and no serious measures were taken to introduce Hungarian in their schools.

Of course, this could only happen thanks to the large measure of understanding and indulgence on the part of the Hungarian authorities. The results of Hungarian language examinations confirms this assumption. We are acquainted with the process at one of these examinations from a debate which took place before Romanian public opinion. The examination in question was administered in 1883 at the seat of Hunyad county, in Déva. Of the hundred Romanian teachers who took the exam, 49 passed and 51 failed. The president of the examination committee was László Réthy, the Hungarian superintendent of schools. After the publication of the final results, the Romanian weekly *Gazeta Transilvaniei* of Brassó attacked superintendent Réthy "for the excessive severity he manifested at the examination." It presented the issue as if Réthy had deliberately failed the Romanian teachers on specific instructions from the government. Then a Romanian teacher took the side of Réthy in the Orthodox periodical of Arad, refuting the attack in the Brassó paper.

> Superintendent Réthy greeted us with the deference and good will one can expect of top officials; in fact, he was even considerate of our weaknesses to some extent. And this is not merely my personal opinion, but also that of several colleagues who were present at the examination.

It is true that many teachers failed, but this was not entirely due to the strictness of the Hungarian superintendent. "Without meaning to insult in the interest of objectivity my colleagues, or to downplay their merits as Romanian teachers, it must be admitted that among those who passed there were some who could speak not a word of Hungarian."[31]

Most proficiency examinations in Hungarian took place under similar circumstances, but without serious protest. Witness the fact that in the minutes of the meetings of Romanian church organizations, no grievances were recorded in connection with this issue.

In addition to intervening in the above matter, the Hungarian Ministry of Religious Affairs and Education also tried to intervene in the matter of teachers salaries at denominational schools, whether Romanian or of some other nationality. The consideration that prompted the Ministry and the government in this endeavor was the attempt to determine a minimum salary for teachers; higher pay would oblige the administration of schools to take advantage of state subvention and at the same time grant the state greater control over schools for the nationalities. The Hungarian government tried to attain this objective with Act XXVI of 1893, which prescribed minimum salaries churches were to grant their teachers. If the school-sponsoring church could not pay the required salary, it received state subvention. In return the law stipulated that the teachers had to adjust to the provisions of Act XVIII of 1879 regarding the teaching of Hungarian.

The law of 1893, however, did not make the teachers beholders to the state, since they continued to be employed by the school-sponsoring church to the end of their careers. Thus, someone who could not teach Hungarian effectively lost the government subvention but retained the post, since the school was not closed down. Unsatisfactory teaching of the Hungarian language did not entail the closing down of the school, since the state did not require those who knew no Hungarian to teach the official language.

This liberal measure is noteworthy, all the more so since at the same time the government of Romania penalized with the greatest severity those Greek schools where it felt Romanian was not being taught adequately. In 1905 the government closed down the private Greek schools of Tulcea and Constança, because some pupils at these schools knew very little Romanian. In the eyes of the Romanian state this was sufficient proof that no care was taken to teach Romanian in those schools. Among the justifications adduced for closing down schools, the teaching of geographical and historical principles also played a part. It was alleged that these subjects were taught "in disregard of historical truth, against the interests of our people." The Greek school at Sulina was closed down roughly on the same grounds. Thus Romania was far removed from the spirit of liberalism and patience which the Hungarian government manifested towards the Romanian schools.[32]

The Apponyi Laws

A change came about in the situation of the teachers as a result of the famous Apponyi Laws, particularly Act XXVII of 1907 which dealt with the "Legal Status of Non-state Public Schools and the Salaries to be Paid to Community and Denominational Public School Teachers." The goal of this law, according to the preamble provided by the Ministry, was to ensure a decent livelihood for public school teachers, as well as to safeguard state and national interests. The first sixteen paragraphs of the law contained significant new measures affecting the material and legal status of teachers.

In the first years of this century the financial condition of the teachers was far less secure than that of other professionals. Hungarian and non-Hungarian denominational teachers had to struggle to survive. At the meetings of Romanian teachers' associations the teachers demanded pay raises ever more insistently; they also demanded assurances of being paid on time. Their demands became known to Hungarian authorities from reports in the press and those submitted by school superintendents. Such demands were voiced, for instance, at the

Uniate Teachers' Association (named Mariana), which met at Besztterce
on October 22, 1906. On this occasion a teacher named Bogdan voiced
the general demands of the Romanian teachers. He pointed out that the
pay of a teacher at a Romanian denominational school was below that
of a bank-teller. In behalf of the teachers he demanded that the pay of
Romanian teachers at denominational schools be raised to the level of
state teachers salaries.[33] The complaints concerned not merely the
negligible amount the Romanian teachers were paid, but also the fact
that this pay was not disbursed. In many villages the teachers received
only part of their pay, and they had to fight to obtain even that. In the
community of Földra [Feldru], for instance, the teachers at the
Romanian denominational school received their pay only once every four
or five months, and even then it was only partial pay.[34] Hundreds of
similar cases can be cited from the period.

Such were the conditions that led to the famous Apponyi Law XXVII
of 1907. Article 1 of this law defines the teachers at the community and
denominational primary schools as civil servants, and that their pay is
determined and supported by the public administration. In the
following articles it defined in detail the amount of their salary, its
nature and breakdown, the manner of paying and the sum to be
received as state subvention. Even more important than the amount of
salary defined by the state was its collection, as well as the possibility
of obtaining state subvention. The application of these two principles
soon improved the financial lot of the Romanian teachers.

Since taking advantage of state subvention entailed, according to the
terms of the law, increased supervision by the state over the effectiveness of the teaching of the official language, as well as over the
employment of teachers, Romanian society received the Law of Apponyi
with a great deal of resentment and bitterness. The teachers themselves, however, were happy about the legal measures regarding their
pay, and neither they nor the authorities of the church protested against
these provisions. Indeed, the latter could not protest, because they were
well aware of the difficult financial situation of the teachers, their
associations had been trying to improve for so long. The church
authorities could do but one thing, something they might have thought
of sooner: They called upon the parishes to raise the pay of the teachers
to the level prescribed by the Apponyi Law.

The entire Romanian press went on a campaign to this effect, citing
those parishes which had already satisfied the requirements of the law
as examples. Of course, by so doing they implicitly recognized the
validity of the above prescription of the law, about which the teachers,
who were most directly concerned, also had no doubts. "The pay raise

for teachers is required not only by the law," stated the Romanian weekly from Beszterce, "but by our age as well; after the pay of all civil servants, including the janitors, had been normalized, it was finally the turn of the educators of our people, those who carry the torch of enlightenment."[35] The press, the church officials, the autonomous Romanian communities all competed with one another in promoting the cause of the Romanian teachers by demanding that their pay be normalized by the church authorities themselves, without having to rely on state subvention. Indeed, they soon achieved significant results. In a good many communities the salaries could be easily raised since, as we have seen, large masses of Romanians had attained financial security by then. Romanian banks and associations, growing in numbers in endowment, as well as the Romanian politicians in charge made sure that denominational teachers got paid wherever they intervened. Unfortunately, they did not think of it often enough; the altruistic feelings, so widespread at the beginning, had been increasingly displaced in the years preceding World War I, by concern for profit-making and the accumulation of capital. As the *Tribuna* freely noted, the resources of the Romanians of Hungary "had increased to such an extent during the previous six decades, that they should suffice to meet the general educational needs of the Romanians." But the Romanian committee had not dealt with the matter in time, and the banks provided little financial support. "Our Romanian financial institutions," continued the same periodical, "would do better to provide help for our schools rather than increase their endowment year after year from their net profits."[36]

The banks rarely took this advice. The help they offered usually took the form of a one-time donation of a substantial lump sum on special occasions rather than regular contributions to help meet the expenses of the schools. Instead, the pay raise of the teachers at Romanian denominational schools was promoted by the Romanian Raffeisen associations.

The Apponyi Law was carried out three years after its adoption. Those in charge of the schools had three years, from 1907 to 1910, to normalize the pay of their teachers by providing the salary required by the law. Where the communities did not normalize the salaries after this period and did not apply for state subvention, the school-sponsoring church lost its rights of sponsorship.

During these three years the impact of the Apponyi Law on the financial situation of the teachers resulted in obvious improvement. In many places the parishes raised the teachers' salaries, while elsewhere they applied for and received state subvention. In the academic year

1911/12, according to the official statistics of the Romanian Orthodox
Church, only 33 out of 418 in the diocese of Arad, 76 out of 242 in the
diocese of Nagyvárad, and 41 out of 266 teachers in the diocese of
Karánsebes were not receiving salaries prescribed by law. In other
words, in the first year of the application of the Apponyi Law, in 776
out of 926 Orthodox Romanian schools the salaries of the teachers had
been raised, whereas the prescribed salary could not be granted in only
150.[37] Unfortunately, the data from the main see of Nagyszeben are
not included in the official report of the church, hence we cannot gain
an accurate picture of the situation throughout the church. The
estimates are that in 1910/11 at least 50% of the Romanian schools were
able to provide for the salary raise out of the resources of the school-
sponsoring church. The Romanian population had sufficient financial
clout to raise teachers' salaries everywhere, yet this endeavor fell short,
partly for lack of organization, partly because of greed. Therefore the
dioceses gradually turned to state subvention. They did not do so
eagerly, but were compelled by the situation and by the law to accept
the curriculum determined by the Ministry in order to become entitled
to state subvention. In the beginning they feared that state subvention
would lead to excessive interference in the affairs of the schools. But,
as we shall see below, this worry dissipated in a few years, and soon not
only the poorer parishes, but even the more prosperous ones applied for
partial or complete state subvention. From then on the main source of
complaint was rather that the state subvention applied for was not
always granted. Nevertheless, according to the official reports of the
Romanian churches, Hungarian state subvention to Romanian schools
increased each year after 1910. Subvention to primary schools
sponsored by the Romanian Orthodox Church amounted to 390,679.52
crowns in 1911/12, 517,720.60 crowns in 1912/13, while in 1913/14 it
reached 778,990 crowns. In other words, it increased by 99.4% in three
years. The rise in teachers salaries in certain dioceses was even more
marked: the state subvention to teachers in the diocese of Arad grew
by 129%, and by 228% in the diocese of Karánsebes.[38] The subvention to teachers in the schools sponsored by the Romanian Uniate
Church was even greater; according to Ghibu the total amount of
Hungarian state subvention to all Romanian primary schools amounted
to about two million crowns in 1915.[39]

Thus the teachers at Romanian denominational schools had attained
a comfortable standard of living in the years preceding the World War.
Act XVI of 1913, which placed teachers in different pay categories, and
defined the base pay, fringe benefits, and child allowances, went into
effect on January 1, 1913. On the basis of this so-called János Zichy

Law the Romanian teachers, like their Hungarian counterparts, received 3,200 crowns annually, a turn ensuring one a decent standard of living at the time. In addition to the salary, the Romanian teachers enjoyed all the benefits granted to Hungarian public and denominational school teachers by the state: they received a pass entitling them to half-fare on the railroads, they became pensioners and, after one year of military service performed in a volunteer capacity, i.e. as officer candidates, like the Hungarians, were promoted to officer if they passed the examination. Among the many complaints there were none about discrimination in the administration of officer examinations to members of ethnic groups[40]

Their favorable financial situation, however, did not prevent the teachers, for the most part, from maintaining the nationalist atmosphere prevailing in the Romanian schools.

The Atmosphere of the Romanian Schools

The atmosphere of the Romanian primary schools in the first decades after the Compromise was characterized by undisturbed manifestations of the Romanian national spirit. From 1867 to 1880, for twelve years, Hungarian was not even taught as a subject in the Romanian denominational schools, and the Hungarian government did not interfere in matters of instruction.[41] There was no systematic primary schooling in today's sense of the word. As we have seen, the schools were lacking in appropriate space, in textbooks and other teaching materials, and most of the teachers lacked adequate preparation. In 1874, 184 of the 214 teachers in the areas of the Orthodox consistories of Arad and Nagyvárad lacked certification, and 97 of them had never attended a teachers' college.[42] Assuming that the situation was similar in other Romanian dioceses, as is likely, at least 75% of the teachers at Romanian denominational schools taught without regular training. They were able to teach only the most basic skills: the "three r's" and singing. Their pedagogic competence and didactic skills were far behind what teaching at a higher level would have warranted. The Romanian church and education officials were well aware of this. The official paper of the Orthodox archdiocese continually encouraged the teachers to read and study the educational review. Unfortunately, the constant propaganda had little effect. *Foaia Pedagogică*, the only such review, tried in vain to awaken the teachers' interest in pedagogical matters. Very few of the almost 2,000 Orthodox parishes subscribed, while the teachers themselves were not ready to use money out of their own pockets. The Uniate teachers had no educational review at all.

This need not have deterred them from reading the only Romanian educational review, but it seems the teachers were generally uninterested in methodological issues. This is confirmed by the periodical of the Orthodox Romanian church which "deplored the lack of interest in the only educational review."[43]

Under these circumstances the Romanian schools meant little in terms of a learning experience, but all the more from the point of view of fostering nationalist feeling. There were hardly any textbooks. Later the schools began to use textbooks published in Romania, since the textbooks at denominational institutions were selected by the school-sponsoring church, and no government authorization was required. But in most places instruction continued to take place without books, the amateur teachers trying to teach the children to read and write under primitive circumstances. The teaching of the Romanian language, religion, and singing had the greatest impact in the schools. Religion was taught by the priest, while singing did not require any particular skill, especially since church and national hymns were widely known. The best known Romanian song, taught in all the schools, was the anti-Hungarian Romanian anthem "Awake, Romanian, from your slumber."

The priests and teachers with certification, represented a pronounced irredentist sentiment. This becomes clear from contemporary press reports, especially in the church periodical edited by professors of the theological institute of Arad which trained priests and teachers. The ideas of the collaborators of this periodical were marked by a complete identification with Romania, openly advocating irredentism and making a conscious effort to isolate the Romanians from Hungarian public life. The readers of the periodical — priests, professors and teachers — could sense from most of the articles published that everything that happened in Romania was relevant to the Romanians, whereas what took place in Hungary was at best, of marginal importance. In vain do we look in this periodical for reports on Hungarian literary, educational or even religious movements. On the other hand, the readers constantly received detailed information on internal and cultural affairs in Romania, and even on the contents of speeches delivered in the Romanian parliament. It is obvious that the editors and contributors of the periodical, and even its readers, were completely attuned to what was happening in Romania, where they felt truly at home, whose affairs preoccupied them. They were not concerned with Hungarian problems, and did not even try to find out about them; after all, they hardly had the means to do so, since they spoke no Hungarian and the official language of the state was not taught in the primary schools or at the seminaries. The intensity of their irredentism was of course enhanced by being sealed from Hungarian affairs. This became particularly obvious on the occasion of the Russo-Turkish war of 1878, when the Romanians of Hungary expressed their glee at the Romanian victories in nation-wide irredentist demonstrations. The periodical which, according to its title, dealt with ecclesiastic and educational issues, published a short poem on this occasion, in which it referred to Romania as the queen of queens and demanded that Romania secure the territories which had belonged to it at one time.[44]

The Introduction of Hungarian as a Subject in the Schools

At this time the Hungarian government felt the time had come to introduce Hungarian as a subject in Romanian denominational schools. Apart from other reasons, the pertinent Article of Act XVIII of 1879 was deemed necessary in order to end the isolation of the Romanians from Hungarian society. One of the requisites was indeed acquaintance with the Hungarian language, with the help of which the Romanian masses might be able to escape from the charmed circle of Romanian politics and of the press reflecting the Romanian mind. The preamble to the law points towards this veiled objective in stating: "It being necessary that all citizens be given the opportunity to become familiar with Hungarian, as the official language..." etc. In accordance with this law, students at Romanian teachers' colleges were to be taught Hungarian. Hungarian language was to be introduced in all the schools to the extent there was a generation of teachers capable of teaching it.

The Romanian delegates and the school-sponsoring churches launched a major struggle against the law. They insisted unanimously that it was not possible to teach a language other than the mother tongue in the public schools. It could not be done in the Romanian schools, if only because so many of the teachers knew no Hungarian, and therefore could not possibly teach it. According to the Romanian delegate Nicolae Strǎvoiu, teaching Hungarian in Romanian schools would be a luxury because the Romanians had not attained the necessary level even in their own language. In view of the situation of the Romanian schools at this period, the statement of Strǎvoiu did indeed conform to reality.

On the basis of the knowledge available to us today we may contend that at the time the law was proposed, debated, and adopted neither Hungarians nor Romanians were candid about their motives. The Hungarians did not reveal the results they expected from the application of the law: to draw the Romanian ethnic group closer to the Hungarian way of life and away from the charmed circle of Romania.

There were even Hungarians who naively expected that knowing Hungarian would lead to feeling Hungarian. Thus the Romanian delegates could charge that "the objective of the law is the Hungarianization of other nationalities" (Alexander Roman) or that "the law was a crime against the nationalities" (George Popu).

The Romanians likewise kept quiet about the underlying motive of their struggle against the law, namely that they did not even want to have Hungarian taught in the Romanian schools. As we have seen, the Romanian leaders tried systematically to isolate the Romanian masses from Hungarian ways and keep them exclusively under the influence of Romania. Apart from the atmosphere of the schools this is also indicated by the fact that they objected to having the official language taught in the primary schools, claiming that the right place for teaching languages was in the secondary schools; yet, in 1883, when it was the turn of the secondary schools to undertake the teaching of Hungarian, Romanians fought against this new law with the same vigor they showed in opposing Act XVII of 1879.

It is interesting to note that while the Romanian press unanimously supported the protests of the Romanians of Hungary against the laws of 1879 and 1883, the government used all available means to introduce the official language into the schools of the Kingdom of Romania. A few years after the introduction of Hungarian as a subject in the Romanian primary schools of Hungary, the Romanian parliament adopted the law about the organization of public education: in its preamble, the basic principles governing the relationship between schools and the state were spelled out. State and school are intimately related. The supervisory role of the state is not limited to policing the institution, but extends to maintaining the nation's traditions. If the state did nothing to "defend" the Romanian language this would amount to an abuse of the principle of freedom of instruction. The sorry fact, that in sizable portions of the country the residents "still do not know the language of their country, hence are unable to communicate with other citizens of the nation, can no longer be tolerated. All citizens must become acquainted with the common language, because without it they cannot know their rights and duties as citizens, and are therefore exposed to tyranny. Without a knowledge of the official language the individual "cannot be a free, independent citizen."[45]

Indeed, school affairs in Romania were regulated according to this principle. Romania tolerated no language other than Romanian in its public schools. The children of citizens of other than Romanian background could study only in schools where Romanian was the language of instruction. The children of parents who were not yet

Romanian citizens (Greeks, Germans, etc.) could attend private schools, but even there they had to study Romanian, as well as geography and history taught in Romanian by native-born Romanian teachers, in accordance with the curriculum prescribed by the state.

Hungarian public education followed different principles. As we have seen, the government was extremely patient and lenient towards those of its citizens who spoke a different language. This explains why Act XVIII of 1879, intended to introduce them to the Hungarian language, was put into practice only decades later. It was carried out completely only after the adoption of the Apponyi Laws, around 1910. Even at the turn of the century, that is a full twenty years after the law was passed and thirty years after the beginning of Hungarian rule, there were several hundred Romanian primary schools where Hungarian could not be taught because the teacher was not familiar with the language.[46] Even where Hungarian was taught, instruction took place in Romanian because Hungarian was just another subject like geography, composition, etc.[47] Thus the compulsory teaching of Hungarian as a subject did not meet the expectations at all, partly because it took a long time to put the law into practice and few Romanian children ever learnt the language. In the 1907/08 academic year, almost 40 years after the law passed, only 38.11% of the graduates of primary schools where Romanian was the language of instruction could speak Hungarian.[48] Even most of these had probably learnt the language in the home rather than in school.

The Irredentism of Romanian Teachers

The atmosphere in the Romanian denominational elementary schools changed not a wit after the introduction of Hungarian as a required subject. The teaching of national songs had already deeply marked the children in a Romanian nationalist sense. This influence only increased after the Act of 1879. The songs, taught earlier without any manual, were published in book form in 1881, and they became one of the most popular readings of the Romanians of Transylvania for decades to come. Even the title of the individual songs in this collection "published for the benefit of both sexes"[49] promised a lot. In three thousand or so Romanian primary schools operating freely on Hungarian territory the Romanian children sang songs with titles like "Awake, Romanian, from your Slumber," "The March of Unification," "The March of Iancu," "To the Romanian Army," "Long Live Romania," "To Free Romania," "The Romanian Fatherland," etc. The text of these songs carved the basic principles of Romanian national consciousness deeply into the souls of the children. The pupils at Romanian primary schools learnt and sang for decades about the "barbarian tyrants" (i.e. the Hungarians), the anthem of the Romanians rising against the "cruel enemy" of the Romanian people; singing the march of Iancu they marched along with him in imagination, in order to chase away the barbarians (i.e. the Hungarians) with "cleansed weapons." Every day thousands upon thousands of "Romanian children hailed the Romanian army with lyrics of the song "The Free Romanian" or "the Romanian Homeland" which extends wherever the sweet sounds of the ancestral language can be heard, in the country which is called "great" (Greater Romania). For years and decades they hailed "the sweet Romanian language so dear, more harmonious than any language in the world." The Hungarian state did not close down a single school on account of these songs, not even on account of those whose title and lyrics required "hailing" everything that was Romanian — the Romanian nation, the Romanians of Moldavia and Wallachia, the beloved Romanian language, or "Romanian unification, which we all desire." No Hungarian official sought to ban this collection of songs which appeared in several editions and circulated in many thousands of copies all over the country. The Romanian teachers, beginning with the author of the anthology himself, were well aware of this freedom, and took full advantage of it. The 1900 edition was still printed explicitly for "the youths of the schools," — an indication of the leeway for a Romanian national education in the denominational schools of Hungary.[50] Finally one of the Hungarian ministers of Religious Affairs and Education had enough of the school use of this collection, and banned the book from the school premises. Yet it could go on being used outside of the schools and the songs became more popular than ever in the years preceding the war.[51]

Of course, this national spirit of the Romanian primary schools thrived thanks to the teachers and other representatives of Romanian cultural life. Nor did the Romanians make any secret of the extent to which they adopted the cultural life of Romania itself. As the *Tribuna* of Nagyszeben explained in 1885 "the cultural cornerstone of the Romanians of Transylvania is the Romanian state,"[52] and everyone took this for granted. The teachers were completely captivated by this line of thought, not only outside the schools but within the school premises as well. Their concepts manifested themselves in the political arenas as well, as certain evidence indicates. When the authors who had besmirched the Hungarian state were sentenced by a Hungarian court in the famous "replica trial," the teachers of the Romanian primary school at Borgóprund cabled a message of support to the condemned. Hence the Minister suspended them from their post.[53]

The political attitude and irredentist mentality of the Romanian teachers were so well known that unless these manifested themselves blatantly the authorities looked the other way and did not resort to any punitive measure. Hence the atmosphere of the Romanian schools reflected the ideals of Romania much as before. The children learnt to read, write and compose in Hungarian for two or three periods a week. In most Romanian primary schools nothing more was expected. In fact, as we have seen, in very many Romanian schools where the teacher did not know Hungarian even this much could not happen.

After the nineties the irredentism and anti-Hungarianism of the Romanian primary schools became even more pronounced; from year to year the teachers became more involved in Romanian social and political movements. They led the choruses and bands of the villages, organized the cultural events, mustered people for political gatherings. The conventions of the teachers' associations were excellent occasions for manifesting the Greater Romania yearnings of the teaching corps. For instance, the Romanian denominational teachers of the Orthodox diocese of Arad assembled at Nagyhalmágy [Hălmagiu] on July 18 and 19, 1902; after the meeting the 130 or so teachers boarded a train for a pilgrimage to the tomb of Avram Iancu. Here they kissed the cross on Iancu's grave, and the oak of Horia. "After all this," wrote one of the Romanian newspapers, "they all returned to Brád singing the sounds of our national anthem."[54] There is no record whatever to the effect that this mass demonstration of the teachers had elicited any kind of intervention on the part of the Hungarian Ministry of Religious Affairs and Education, even though the superintendent of schools had, on several occasions, reported such manifestations. In the course of teaching Romanian language, Romanian history, and Romanian geography — not to mention the teaching of national songs — the teachers injected into the minds of the children respect for Iancu and Horia, "the brave leaders of the noble Romanian nation in its struggle against the barbarian Hungarians."

The 1906 Bucharest Fair

In 1906 the stratum of the middle class composed of the clergy and teachers among the Romanians of Hungary, and the educated Romanians in general expressed their irredentist feelings in an unusually strong and far-reaching manner; and since this demonstration led to the proposal of the famous school law of Apponyi, it warrants a more detailed discussion. That year, on the occasion of the fortieth anniversary of the rule of King Charles, Romania hosted a great fair in

Bucharest. The neighboring countries were invited to the fair, in order
to enable the Romanians of the Balkans, of Bessarabia, of Bukovina,
and of Hungary to participate. The Romanian middle-class of Hungary
took part in the fair in large numbers.[55] A sizeable fraction of the
participants consisted of priests and teachers, that is of Hungarian
citizens serving under the supervision of the Hungarian Ministry of
Religious Affairs and Education. The first group, organized by the
teachers' association of the four dioceses of the Bánát, took the trip from
the Bánát under the leadership of Dr. Putici, the deacon of Temesvár.
They were joined by members of the teachers' associations of Maros and
of Karánsebes, 600 teachers from the areas of Máramaros and Szatmár,
and over one thousand from the core of Transylvania. On the afternoon
of August 27, twenty-five choruses took part in the Romanian choral
completion organized in the Arenele Române of Bucharest. Sixteen of
these came from Hungary, whereas Romania itself mustered only seven.
With few exceptions, the leaders of the Romanian choruses from
Hungary were teachers from denominational schools. Priests and
teachers spoke without inhibitions about unification with Romania at
the ceremonies held in their honor. The Hungarian government as well
as public opinion in Hungary received detailed accounts of the behavior
of the Romanians from Hungary in Bucharest based on the extensive
reports published in the papers of Romania, the descriptions of the fair
provided by Hungarian visitors, the reports which appeared in the
Hungarian press, and the dispatches of the Austro-Hungarian legation
in Bucharest. The attitude of the Romanians of Hungary towards the
Hungarian state created a deep and painful impression in Hungarian
official circles. Romanians from various countries organized special
exhibits within the framework of the general fair. The Romanians of
Serbia, Bessarabia, Austria, and Turkey exhibited objects of strictly
ethnological significance in the room or hall reserved for them, in such
a manner as not to offend or provoke the countries whence they came.
They exhibited folk costumes and household or religious objects. Above
the place of exhibit they wrote the name of their country — Serbia,
Austria — or the name of their province — Bessarabia, Macedonia. The
Serbian flag was displayed in the exhibit hall of the Romanians from
Serbia. The wardrobe in the hall was decorated with the Serbian colors,
captions were exclusively in Serbo-Croatian, and under the captions the
Serbian crowned seal was splendidly displayed above the portraits of
Serbian King Peter. Not a single ribbon bearing the Romanian colors
was to be seen anywhere at the Serbian exhibit. Similar restraint
marked the halls where the Romanians of Bessarabia, Bukovina, and
Turkey held their exhibits. In each place the Romanians displayed

their exhibits with the colors of the country whence they came. At the fair of the Romanians from Bessarabia the captions were strictly in Russian; Romanian language or Romanian colors were nowhere to be seen. The Romanians of Bukovina, under Austrian jurisdiction, likewise refrained from using Romanian colors in their exhibit hall: on the contrary, they displayed the Austrian flag, the description of the exhibits was in Romanian and German, and the placenames were also given in their official German version. Thus the Romanians of all these areas went out of their way not to offend their country or province — Serbia, Austria, Russia — by displaying the Romanian national colors. The cautious, almost timid behavior of the Romanians from these countries indicated to what extent they feared sever reprisals, which they already knew from personal experience.

The Romanians of Hungary felt otherwise. They arranged their exhibit hall in such a manner that visitors could not possibly determine the country of which they were citizens. Unlike other groups of Romanians the inscription at the entrance simply read "Romanians from the other side of the border." Every exhibit was practically wrapped in Romanian colors. Neither the inscription above the entrance nor the list of exhibits nor the national seal or flag indicated that the Romanians exhibiting in the hall lived in Hungarian territory. Both the outside appearance of the hall and its interior showed only that the Romanians of Hungary did not belong to the Hungarian state, that they took its seal, its colors, its constitution, its official language for nought, that they were not afraid of official reprisals, that they considered the areas of Hungary they inhabited as separate Romanian states. The Hungarian authorities and public opinion found this attitude not only offensive, but downright provocative, since the Romanians of all other countries were loyal to their respective governments. They respected the name of their state, its colors and official language.

The Hungarian authorities found this attitude all the more provocative since they had raised no obstacle of any kind to the travel of large numbers of Romanians to Romania, while the Russian state had forbidden its subjects from participating in the fair. The provocative behavior was further enhanced by the irredentist speeches with which the Romanian authorities and organizers greeted the groups from Hungary. Most of the praise and exhortation were reserved for the teachers from Hungary. Speakers from the Romanian side described the teachers as "the heroes of the cause of the whole Romanian race" (Alex D. Florescu) who fight for a "united Romanian national culture." The

teachers could rest assured, they were told, of complete support of the
part of the Romanian brothers. In their reply the Romanian teachers
from Hungary expressed "deep-felt emotions" which they dedicated to
the "flowering of the Romanian race" (Dr. Putici). They expressed
heartfelt gratitude for the beautiful Romanian national flag presented
to them, and proudly insisted that the borders no longer meant
anything, that the Romanians of Hungary shared a common heart with
the brothers from Romania, "which beats for one another, for the same
idea, without fear" (Voina, the Deacon of Brassó). Romanian priests
leading the groups of teachers assured those "from the mother country"
that they were "raising sons dedicated to the national idea" (Greceanu),
and once they returned to their homes (i.e. in Hungary) "they will fight
ten times as hard for the interests of the race" (Amzea). They felt
moved by the encouragement that there was no way of preventing "the
unification of hearts and souls that were already in harmony" (i.e. those
of the Romanians), because it was a matter of "historical and social
necessity" (Dr. Stica), that the "Carpathians did not separate, but rather
unite" (Barbu Delavrancea), that the Transylvanians were "returning
home to Romania" (Florescu), that the Romanians had organized the fair
to knock down "the international boundaries that separated the
Romanians" (I. Brătescu). The Romanian papers of Hungary wrote
about the fair in a similar vein. "The Romanian choruses," wrote the
weekly from Szászváros, "proclaim in their songs that 'unification is
written on our banners' and proudly profess that they know but one
tricolor flag in the world, their own."[56]

All these professions of faith aroused the ire of Hungarian public
opinion, and astounded Hungarian officials as well. They felt there had
to be a response, for these declarations unequivocally threatened the
territorial integrity and the borders of the country. Moreover, these
manifestations played into the hands of extremist Hungarian nationalists who had always deplored the liberalism of the Hungarian policy
with regard to the nationalities and the autonomy granted to the
churches and schools of the nationalities, particularly the Romanians.
They pointed out that the Romanians living in other lands —
Bessarabia, the Balkans — did not enjoy half as many rights, yet
behaved in a loyal manner. What would the Serbian, German, or even
the French state do if its own citizens were to show such contempt for
their country's flag, its seal, or its official language when abroad?

Such were the immediate antecedents of the drafting of the Apponyi
School Laws. During his entire political career Count Albert Apponyi
had fought for a stronger assertion of the Hungarian national character,
for a clearer national expression with the Hungarian state as well as in

the joint army. One point of his program as Minister of Religious Affairs and Education was to increase control over the non-Hungarian schools, and transform their spirit for the benefit of the Hungarian state. He did not intend to close these schools down, but merely to alter the anti-Hungarian spirit which prevailed in them. This was the basis objective of his directives and laws.

His first measure affecting the Romanians, and which created a major stir, was issued in the Fall of 1906. In a circular the minister ordered a four-day pay cut for all those Romanian teachers who had postponed the opening of the academic year by four days on account of their extended sojourn at the Bucharest fair. The semi-official paper of the Bucharest government reported on the punishment in an article title "Rabid Hungarians." In the deduction of the amount corresponding to four days' pay the author of this ominous article saw evidence that "the work of mad Hungarianization was nearing completion by repressing self-consciousness, by brutally throttling racial and national feelings as well as the language."[57]

Apponyi Against the Irredentism of Romanian Schools

With his circular Apponyi seemed to express his disapproval of the behavior of the Romanian schoolteachers from Hungary during their visit to Romania, penalizing them with a four day pay-cut. Not long afterwards he embarked on the final elaboration of his famous law proposal. In this proposal he was guided by the idea of preventing future manifestations of the irredentist spirit within the schools of the nationalities that were contrary to the interests of the Hungarian state. In his justification of the proposal he explained that the state recognized the right of the churches to sponsor schools and even helped them financially to exercise this right; but there is one condition to this aid and to the recognition of the churches' mission: Every school should provide faultless education in patriotic citizenship."[58]

After several modifications, and considerable struggle inside and outside parliament, the proposal was adopted in 1907. This became the Act XVIII of 1907 mentioned already several times. All nationalities, but especially the Romanians, protested against this Act in a series of mass rallies, and heatedly denounced some of its measures in the House of Representatives. The rally at Szászváros, for instance, was held in front of the church, and the pupils of the Romanian primary school were brought out. But neither the series of rallies nor the interventions in parliament prevented the proposal from being adopted. What is more, the consensus in the House of Representatives was that the original text of the proposal was rather mild in places. Thus several representatives proposed even stronger compulsory measures.[59] Apponyi, however, rejected the extremist proposals, seeking a balance between the motions raised and preserving the rights of the nationalities along with the defense of Hungarian interests.

The most heatedly debated parts of the law were Articles 15 through 21. In fact, these were basically the measures for which the law was written in the first place. All these measures were aimed at realizing the new concepts enunciated in Article 17:

> Every school and every teacher, regardless of the type of school he is attached to and whether or not that school receives state subvention, is required to express and reinforce in the souls of the children attachment to the Hungarian fatherland and consciousness of belonging to the Hungarian nation, as well as morality and religion.

As outward expression of this spirit, the seal of Hungary is to be placed above the main entrance to the school and in the classrooms. Illustrations from Hungarian history are to be pasted on the walls of the classrooms, and on national holidays the flag bearing the national seal must be flown from the building. In addition to these symbols, only the seals of the district and of the community, or religious symbols may be displayed. The government will provide Hungarian flags, seals, and illustrations for the denominational schools of the nationalities at its own expense. The deliberate failure to carry out these measures is a misdemeanor, punishable by a fine of 500 crowns.

These measures were aimed at changing the anti-Hungarian atmosphere of the schools of the nationalities. We have noted the system of irredentist ideas permeating the national songs taught in the Romanian schools of Hungary; we have noted the feelings expressed at the Bucharest fair, indicating that the Romanians regarded Romania as their "fatherland," their "true country" and their "home" — and most Hungarian members of parliament had not forgotten the news about this Bucharest fair. Hence they voted unanimously in favor of the measure which prescribed that every teacher should "express and reinforce in the souls of the children the idea of attachment to the Hungarian homeland and of the consciousness of belonging to the Hungarian nation." The Romanians knew they had exceeded the measure in Bucharest. In protesting against the Act they selected their arguments far more carefully than during previous protests. In their parliamentary speeches as well as in their written petitions they stressed that these measures were "completely superfluous," and "generate a general lack of trust and feelings of animosity without good reason." After all, they had never questioned the "self-evident" task of the schools which "consists in reinforcing loyal attachment to the Hungarian homeland." Therefore, it was unnecessary to require this by legislation. They objected to the prescription regarding the compulsory use of the Hungarian flag and seal because, as they indicated in their petition of 1915, "the success of the operation of the school does not depend on decorating the school building with external symbols.[60]

Other measures of the law which were found highly objectionable related to the language of instruction, the number of periods devoted to the teaching of Hungarian, the approval of the curricula and textbooks, and the employment of teachers at schools receiving state subvention. According to Article 18 the language of instruction at the schools of the nationalities would continue to be determined by the organization sponsoring the school, but where there was no school with Hungarian as the language of instruction, yet at least 20 students spoke Hungarian as their mother tongue, they must be taught in Hungarian even in the denominational school. If 50% of the registered students spoke Hungarian as their mother tongue then the language of instruction at the school must be Hungarian, although the students who spoke no Hungarian could continue to receive instruction in their mother tongue. The Romanian members of parliament protested most vigorously against having to teach Hungarian children in Hungarian at the denominational schools, because they felt this measure jeopardized the autonomy of the church and the unity of the schools. "It is impossible to carry out, in practice, a system of public schools with two languages of instruction," wrote the Romanian Orthodox archbishop in his petition of 1915. Indeed, the Hungarian government did not insist that this measure be carried out, hence as the report of the archbishop had predicted, it was not applied to the territory of the archdiocese. This was also, the fate by and large, of the measure which prescribed Hungarian as the language of instruction of remedial courses.[61] As regards the extent to which Hungarian was to be taught, Article 19 of the Law stipulated:

> In primary schools where the language of instruction is not Hungarian, whether they receive state subvention or not, Hungarian is to be taught as a subject in every class according to the curriculum determined by the Minister of Religious Affairs and Education, in consultation with the denomination sponsoring the school, to such an extent that the child whose mother tongue

is not Hungarian should be able to express his or her thoughts orally and in writing, in Hungarian, in an understandable fashion, upon completion of the fourth year.

Therefore the Ministry prescribed a curriculum according to which Hungarian had to be taught as a subject between 13 to 39 periods a week in schools where Hungarian was not the language of instruction, depending on the number of teachers. This meant a weekly 13 periods in schools with a single teacher, 21 1/2 periods in schools with two teachers, 26 1/2 periods in schools with three teachers, 32 periods in schools with four or five teachers, and 39 periods in schools with six teachers, or an average of two hours and ten minutes a week per form. The instruction of the official language, which did not exceed three forty minute periods a week at most, was regarded by the Romanians as a "pedagogic impossibility" and they protested against it assiduously.

The Law also introduced new measures affecting the curriculum of schools receiving state subvention, the authorization of textbooks, and the employment of teachers at those schools. According to Article 20, in community schools where the language of instruction was not Hungarian the teachers could receive state subvention only if the Hungarian language, arithmetic, Hungarian geography, history and government were taught in accordance with the curriculum prescribed by the Minister, for the prescribed number of periods, with the help of textbooks approved by the Minister as well. Only readers and teaching materials with a patriotic content, approved by the Minister, could be used in these schools. Complementing the above prescription, Article 21 of the law stipulated that if the state contributed over 200 crowns to the pay of a teacher at a community or denominational school, then the consent of the Minister of Religious Affairs and Education was required for his or her appointment. The Minister could withhold his approval for state reasons.

Further provisions of the Act dealt with disciplinary measures against denominational school teachers, and with forms issued by the school administrations. These measures provided for separate state disciplinary procedures in addition to the procedures applied by the ecclesiastic courts. Moreover, they prescribed the mandatory use of school forms in Hungarian schools and bilingual forms in the languages of the nationalities.

The Apponyi Laws constitute a serious attempt on the part of the government to harmonize the schools where the language of instruction was other than Hungarian with the interests of the Hungarian state. Among all the nationalities, the Romanians fought against it most insistently, because they were most intent on preserving the irredentist, anti-Hungarian spirit of the schools. They placed the greatest obstacles in front of the Law, postponing its application, and not applying certain measures of the Act at all. As became obvious during the war the Law did not even come close to achieving the results some Hungarians had hoped it would.

The provisions regarding the salary of teachers and the situation of the schools were not carried out until after 1910. At the request of the Hungarian Minister of Religious Affairs and Education the Romanian archbishop of Nagyszeben instructed the schools under his jurisdiction to carry out the provisions of the Law with his directive 11.410 of September 30, 1910. Some of these provisions were realized under interesting and rather typical circumstances.

Until 1907, before the Apponyi Laws, the teachers at Romanian denominational schools were not expected to swear allegiance to the Hungarian constitution, nor were they committed to the observance of Hungarian laws. Once Act XXVII of 1907 declared that the teachers at denominational schools were civil servants, the official oath affecting civil service status applied to them as well. Consequently, in each county, the Romanian denominational teachers had to appear at the county seat to take the oath. Contemporary observers tell us of the conflicting feelings the Romanian teachers exhibited in the process. In Hunyad county some teachers on their way to Déva, the county seat, stopped at Cebe [Cebea] to place a wreath decorated with the Romanian national colors on the tomb of Auram Iancu. The ribbon tying the wreath bore the following inscription: "The ideas of your soul will remain in our souls forever. The Romanian teachers."[62] In other words, the Romanian teachers vowed that even after taking the required oath they will continue to teach according to the principles advocated by Iancu. No doubt these same teachers were among those who, the following day, took part in a luncheon, having ceremonially taken the oath on the Constitution in front of the county high sheriff and the superintendent of schools. At the luncheon they caused a scandal. While the orchestra played the Hungarian anthem some teachers remained seated to show their contempt.[63] We have found no data indicating whether the said teachers were or were not reprimanded for their disrespectful attitude.

The teachers could demonstrate with impunity against the anthem because in Hungary there were no legal prescriptions regarding respect due to the national anthem as there were in Romania. The Minister of Education of Romania issued special directives in 1902 and 1903 regarding the proper gestures towards the national flag and the national

anthem. Directive 11.270 of September 27, 1902, required teachers at
all Romanian schools to stand up and remove their hat upon hearing
the national anthem, wherever they may be at the time. As for the
national flag, they were to salute it wherever it was displayed, whether
in company or alone. Directive 7104 of August 8, 1903, stipulated
respect for the national anthem as a manifestation of national education
in the schools. It also prescribed that the portraits of the king and
queen be displayed in every classroom. The national anthem must be
played to open every school ceremony. The principals of schools where
they neglected to play the national anthem would suffer the "most
serious" consequences.[64]

Even the Apponyi Laws had not forced such measures on the
teachers at the romanian schools of Hungary. As we have seen, the
purpose of the Law was defense against Romanian irredentism. It took
a long time to apply its provisions, and they were carried out in the
community schools earlier than in the denominational schools. One
superintendent or another may have exceeded his authority in applying
the law, and attempted to introduce Hungarian as the language of
instruction in the community school. This was the case of the superintendent in Fogaras who ordered that teaching should take place in
Hungarian in the community schools under his jurisdiction. The
Romanians appealed the directive of the superintendent, but the county
committee rejected their appeal. Then the Romanian leaders of the
communities carried their appeal even higher, directly to Minister
Apponyi; "and the Minister," we read in the report, "recognized the
rights of the Romanian language in those schools, and annulled the
decision of the county, declaring that it was based on a mistaken
interpretation of the law... thus the Romanian language will be
preserved in those communities."[65]

Not everywhere did the officials of the community defend the former
language of instruction of their schools so proudly. In many places they
were negligent. In the community of Parád (Spini) near Szászváros the
school board, composed exclusively of Romanians, with the priest in the
lead, took no action when the successor of the retired teacher Chirca, in
1907, suddenly decided to teach in Hungarian. "Whose fault is it? Of
the Hungarians?" asked the author of an unsigned article in the
Romanian weekly.

> No. The Hungarians are not at fault here. They are a brave
> people who know how to work and reap for their nation every-
> thing they can, wherever they can! This is all very fine on their
> part, for their own sake! We are contemptible ones who give

them what they have not even asked for! There have been attempts to Hungarianize the community schools in Fogaras county also, but the Romanians stood up and declared: 'Hold it! We are not giving up our rights!' And the Minister came and said 'You are right, your mother tongue dominates in those schools, and it will continue to dominate.' Indeed, those schools have been saved.... We are always accusing the Hungarian governments of mutilating our rights wherever they can, but in all honesty we must admit that we have lost far more, here and there, on account of our own weakness.[66]

Such were the conditions, as confirmed by the members of the school board in the community of Novákfalva (Glimboca). This board refused to acknowledge the appointment of a new female teacher because she knew no Romanian. The Romanian priest, Iuliu Musta, declared that not even the Minister had the right to send into the community a schoolteacher who was not wanted, because the Minister would trespass on the autonomy of the community thereby. A concerned Romanian teacher denounced the priest for this statement, on the grounds of incitation. The district court of Karánsebes, the court in the first instance, sentenced the priest to three days in state custody, but the case was appealed, and when it ultimately went before the Royal Hungarian Court at Temesvár, Musta was absolved, and the sentence thrown out.[67]

The same spirit prevailed when the Act was applied to the Romanian denominational schools. We have seen that the Romanian archbishop of Nagyszeben issued his directive regarding the execution of the Law in the Fall of 1910. In a two-year period most schools had adjusted to most instructions contained in the Law. Here too it happened that some superintendent or other exceeded the requirements of the Law. For instance, superintendent Elemér Szabó tried to persuade the teachers at the Romanian schools of the Olt region that they had to celebrate March 15 in their schools, even though the Law prescribed no such thing; but the superintendent was denounced in the columns of the *Tribuna*, and he was soon transferred.[68]

It happened sometime that, at the request of the Romanian Orthodox archdiocese, the Minster desisted from applying the Law. This was the case with regard to a provision of Act XLVI of 1908, which provided that the Minister would receive the statements in the report cards and register forms of the primary schools in Hungarian; hence the Minister had only authorized the Hungarian version of the forms. The archdiocese of Nagyszeben then requested the Minister to modify his decision and to recognize the validity of the Romanian version as well. A favorable response was finally obtained inasmuch as the Minister changed the forms which until then had been exclusively in Hungarian and accepted the proposal of the holy see.[69]

How did the Romanian primary education fare after the Apponyi Laws were applied? The Romanian sources provide the following interesting picture.

Romanian Primary Education After the Application of the Apponyi Law

The situation of the Romanian primary schools did not change up until 1918, i.e. after the introduction of the Apponyi Laws, which were attacked for many reasons, some of them just others not.

All subjects except Hungarian were taught in Romanian in all Romanian denominational schools, whether they received state subvention or not. Hungarian language as a subject was taught by the so-called "active" method, using only Hungarian, and certain materials from arithmetic, history, geography, and government were included in the context of this subject. Arithmetic, history, government, and geography, however, were taught solely in Romanian. The Romanian church authorities only authorized textbooks in Romanian for the teaching of these subjects.[70]

From 1910/11 Hungarian language, arithmetic, history, government, and geography had to be taught according to the syllabus issued by the Minister in the schools subsidized by the state. In other words, the number of periods devoted to each subject and the topics to be discussed were defined by the Minister.

The instructions regarding the schedule, specified that once the students learned these subjects in their mother tongue, they also had to learn brief summaries in Hungarian during the Hungarian language period.[71] But these subjects were taught solely in Romanian, i.e. the Romanian schools were not bilingual in this respect.[72] The register and the report cards, however, had to be provided in both Hungarian and Romanian.

Except for Hungarian language, all subjects were taught according to the curriculum of the school-sponsoring organization in the schools that did not receive state subsidies. The subjects in the official curriculum, however, had to be given equal coverage in the church curriculum. The total number of periods of instruction was somewhat greater in the state primary schools than in the denominational schools.

The situation regarding textbooks was best described in directive 11.4210, dated September 30, 1910, issued by the archdiocese of Nagyszeben. According to this directive:

> Act XXVII of 1907 does not require that all the textbooks used in our schools be approved by the ministry, but prescribes merely that the manuals for teaching arithmetic, history, government, and geography used in state-subsidized schools be provided with the ministerial seal of approval; as for the schools that were not subsidized by the state, only the manuals of Hungarian language need bear the ministerial seal of approval. As regards the manuals for religion, Romanian language, and natural science, these need not be subjected to approval by any organization save the church; schools not subsidized by the state may use any manual (except for Hungarian-language ones) reviewed and approved by the episcopal synod or consistory. Only books expressly banned by the Minister may not be used in any school[73]

The official paper of the church stressed the same principles. "Any textbook approved by the holy see or the episcopal synod may be introduced into schools that are not subsidized by the state. The textbooks intended for these schools need not be approved by the Minister."[74]

Thanks to state subsidy and the support of the authorities schools experienced fewer financial problems than before the Apponyi Laws. No special effort was required to obtain state subvention once the conditions prescribed in the law had been met. Ghibu notes that "the state aids the denominational schools too, but in that case the syllabus for five subjects (Hungarian language, history, geography, government, and arithmetic) is determined by the state."[75] The government did not adhere firmly to the other conditions required for winning support, and many Romanian schools received the subsidy even though their classrooms were not up to par. In 1913/14 there were still 191 classrooms on the territory of the Orthodox archdiocese that were inadequate.[76] The number of schools receiving state subsidies increased year after year. The parishes which could not provide salaries for teachers as stipulated in the Apponyi Law often preferred to give up their schools rather than accept the conditions for state subsidies. Thus a few hundred schools were closed down and replaced partly by community, partly by state schools. The teachers left unemployed as a result of the closures were rehired either by the community or by the state. From the time of the first application of the Act to the beginning of World War I, 35 teaching positions were eliminated in the area of the Orthodox archdiocese, but 39 new ones were established.[77] Most often the teacher at the one-teacher school was rehired at a school with several teachers.

In places where the Romanian parish did not apply for state subvention but raised the teacher's salary on its own, the Apponyi Law ensured the collection of the school tax from the residents. Everyone had to pay a surtax of 5% for the upkeep of the school. This 5% was paid to the state only if there was no denominational school in the parish. "Where the school tithe cannot be collected by the church organizations," wrote Ghibu, "the office of the parish transfers the tax-roll to the administration, namely the sheriff's office, which then collects the tax by executive order."[78]

Romanian church and school authorities sometimes abused the right to apply the law, as far as taxes were concerned. In some communities their officials collected the school surtax even from individuals who were exempt. For instance, every Uniate parishioner was forced to pay a 15% tax in 1906 and a 30% surtax in 1907, earmarked for the Romanian Uniate school of Óradna. Although this special tax had been rejected by the community assembly, the officials collected it by executive order, and confiscated various objects from those who refused. Twenty-four Romanian parents lodged a complaint against the officials to the county high sheriff, requesting that the confiscated objects be returned to them.[79] There is plenty of evidence that this was not an isolated incident.

The Romanian schools did not undergo considerable change as regards financial support or the language of instruction. The greatest changes introduced by the law were with regard to the teaching of Hungarian, as well as increased state control over Romanian teachers. In fact, the law of 1879 regarding the teaching of Hungarian was only now put into effect completely. There was no longer any school in which Hungarian was not taught. Yet the pupils in the first grade at Romanian denominational schools were taught to read and write only in Romanian since, according to the ministerial curriculum, Hungarian did not have to be introduced at this level. Hungarian was introduced in the second year, with the method of "active" teaching. Of course, the results depended mainly on the competence and good intentions of the teachers, when work was to be overseen by the superintendents.

This control focussed first of all on the teaching of Hungarian or, better said, on assessing the results obtained in teaching the language. It seems the control was rather strict at the beginning. But the

Hungarian superintendents, as Ghibu noted, had no "direct authority" over Romanian schools. Their observations were relayed to the Minister who communicated these to the consistory. The consistory then adopted measures to put a halt to practices criticized by the superintendents through its own ecclesiastic and school administration.[80]

The question remains: did the Apponyi Law achieve its true objective, i.e. to change the atmosphere of the Romanian schools? Did it succeed in replacing the sympathy for the notion of a greater Romania, by the patriotic spirit "of belonging to the Hungarian homeland" in the souls of Romanian children or at least managed to weaken irredentist sentiments? On the basis of plentiful evidence available to us the answer can only be in the negative.

The deep-rooted Romanian national sentiment of the teachers changed not a bit; after all, neither these sentiments nor their outward manifestations were forbidden by the Law. Thus the teachers could continue to represent Romanian nationalism freely, and even to raise their pupils in this sense. At the folk festival organized on February 12, 1909, the teacher at the Romanian school of Mirkvásár [Mercheaşa] had girls dressed in Romanian colors dance Romanian national dances on the stage of the school.[81] This activity could not be faulted by the state, since there was no law barring ribbons with the Romanian national colors. The activities of the Romanian teachers at Kaca might have been judged far more severely. In this community the Romanian school had been built from donations by the Mircea brothers of Bucharest, as the Romanian press related on several occasions. The intellectual influence of the donors naturally had its impact on the activities of the teachers. This was noted by the professors from Romania who passed through the area in the spring of 1912, on a visit to Hungary. The professors were enchanted by the activities they witnessed at the Romanian school and their impact on the village. The residents of the Romanian village were deeply imbued by Romanian culture. "The portrait of our king [Romania's] may be found in every home," wrote the participant who gave an account of the visit," and there are Romanian books everywhere, as in a small library."[82] In this case the Greater Romania mentality was not limited to the school: The portrait of the foreign ruler became a household item in the homes of Romanians living in the Hungarian state.

From 1913 on the Greater Romania mentality of the schools began to thrive again, in spite of the strict measures of the Apponyi Law, and became stronger than ever before. From 1907 to 1913 the Romanian teachers felt hesitant, timid, and depressed. As Nicolae Sulica, a controller of the holy see of the Orthodox Church, noted towards the end of 1912, the superintendent pushed the image of the respectable Romanian deacon into the background of the perception of the teachers, while the name of the Minister of Religious Affairs and Education often overshadowed that of the chief dignitary of the church.[83]   Many teachers believed that the Law had to be taken seriously, and tried to comply with the stipulations regarding the teaching of Hungarian. Apart from this, some teachers sincerely wanted their pupils to learn Hungarian in school, if only for the sake of retaining state subsidies. There were even some who began to teach Hungarian in the first grade for the sake of better results, although the curriculum imposed by the Minister mandated Hungarian only in the second grade.[84]   Many teachers in the counties of Szatmár and Beszterce-Naszód acted this way; for instance, Iuliu Danciu, teacher at Kackó [Cîtcǎu], requested that the periods devoted to Hungarian be increased from 13 to 26, to enable him to teach the language better. Similar manifestations and strivings revealed the vulnerability of teaching primary school exclusively in Romanian, as a result of the introduction of the Apponyi Laws.

It soon turned out, however, that the measures of the Law regarding the teaching of Hungarian need not be taken literally. The first modification in this request was offered by the Hungarian Minister of Religious Affairs and Education himself in his instructions attached to the curriculum.   According to these instructions the curriculum determined only the general subjects, whereas the time devoted to specific topics "must follow from the nature of things." In judging the effectiveness of teaching, the superintendents were instructed to "bear in mind the environment of the school which at times may affect the results adversely, even when the teachers are self-sacrificing and enthusiastic."   According to this basic principle the teachers were instructed, in turn, to bear in mind "the living conditions of the child, to adjust to the natural, social, and economic environment, and pay particular attention to the spiritual development and the sphere of knowledge of the pupil."[85]

Thanks to this concession the Romanian teacher soon felt the way open to liberation from fear of the law. "We must not feel demoralized, there is no need to observe the law literally," they kept insisting more and more frequently. According to the instructions regarding the curriculum, it was possible to refer to the environment, to the spiritual needs and the sphere of knowledge of the students. Indeed, a child living in a purely Romanian environment was not in a favorable position to learn Hungarian: his sphere of knowledge extended only to his mother tongue. Therefore even the superintendents, in compliance with the ministerial instructions, had to admit that the poor results or complete lack of results obtained in teaching Hungarian was not necessarily the teacher's fault, but merely a consequence of the unfavorable environment. Thus there was the possibility of substantially easing the measures regarding the teaching of Hungarian, and the predicament of the teachers improved as a result. They could explain the meager results, yet safeguard their financial interests (that is, the continued disbursement of state subsidies), while still performing their duties as teachers according to their Romanian conscience. When Hossu, the Uniate bishop of Szamosújvár, made an appearance at the general assembly of the Uniate teachers at Nagyiklód [Iclod] on October 20, 1912, he offered words of encouragement, referring to the above possibilities in veiled terms: "It is true, the laws of the land demand that Hungarian be taught in incomparably larger measure than heretofore, but this is not unfortunate; I am convinced that even so we may achieve satisfactory results."[86]

By 1913 the majority of the Romanian teaching corps had reached a consensus regarding the tenacious nibbling away at the most important components of the Apponyi Law, leading to effective sabotage in many places. More and more argued that it was not possible to realize the objective enunciated in Article 19 of Act XXVII of 1907: children could not learn enough Hungarian within four years to express their thoughts in words and in writing in an understandable manner. This consensus was phrased as a resolution by the Orthodox teachers meeting in 1913, and their resolution was soon adopted by the Uniate teachers as well. In this resolution the teachers unanimously declared:

The objective stipulated in Article 19 of Act XXVII of 1907 cannot be achieved, even at the cost of affecting the health of the teachers," and given the environment of the Romanian schools "all their efforts devoted to the teaching of Hungarian had not once resulted in attaining the degree of proficiency required by Article 19 of Act XXVII of 1907.[87]

By the resolution the Romanian teachers unanimously adopted the stand of *non possumus*. Hence the objective of the Law was definitely not achieved, because the only logical response would have been to deprive all Romanian teachers of state subsidies. This was not the objective of the Hungarian government, however, and it did not even think of resorting to such a measure. Thus everything remained as before. The teachers taught the children parts of the prescribed syllabus in Hungarian mechanically, while the remainder was not even attempted, since it had been declared impossible. Those teachers who at the beginning had been hesitant, timid, or perhaps excessively enthusiastic and eager to instruct their pupils in Hungarian gradually rallied to the majority view. In connection with the teachers' conference of 1913 Ghibu noted with satisfaction: "Today our teachers no longer fall so easily into error as they had during the first years of the entry in vigor of the Apponyi Law; in fact, they recognize their own errors and seek to eliminate these completely."[88]

They found the way of eliminating the errors completely by consistently neglecting the teaching of Hungarian, using the environment as an excuse, and by an increased emphasis on the Romanian way. The latter was openly expressed at the Romanian teachers' convention held in Kolozsvár in 1913. One speaker among several clearly pointed out that as far as the Romanian teachers were concerned there is nothing but the Romanian nation, the Romanian language, and Romanian history. He declared:

> For us teachers, we have nothing but the Romanian nation, which includes all members of our race wherever they may live, whose aspirations are the same everywhere.... The Romanian language and literature are the common treasure of this nation.... Let us bow our heads in front of that glorious past which we have learnt to know from the holy book of the history of our race, and let us have faith in a bright future. Our calling and our work are not restricted to the four walls of the school, but compel us to defend ourselves against every alien influence aimed at our race and schools, whether it appear under the form of bilingualism or under any other form.[89]

According to this analysis, after a few years of hesitation and depression the teachers turned back once again on to the road of yearning for national unity with the Romanians of Romania. They continued to live and teach according to the principles, spirit, and aspirations of the slogan "one nation, one race, one culture," within the schools as well as outside of them. In face of this mentality a partial, or even complete application of the Apponyi Laws (although they were never completely applied) could not have elicited any real change. On the contrary; the evidence is overwhelming that the provisions regarding increased teaching of the Hungarian language as well as those pertaining to the display of the national flag and seal on school buildings only enhanced the anti-Hungarian irredentism of the Romanians. One sign of this anti-state and anti-Hungarian irredentist sentiment was the frequent removal of the Hungarian seal displayed on school-buildings, at night by unknown culprits. The seal would be found broken in some stream or at the garbage dump. Such vandalism could be carried out without serious repercussions, since the authorities of the "oppressive" Hungarian state usually limited themselves to launching an investigation, and the investigation would normally not lead to any results, whereupon the pertinent report would be filed away and a new seal displayed, at state expense, in place of the broken one.[90]

Romanian antagonism manifested itself not only against the Hungarian seal, but against the Hungarian language and Hungarian ideas as well. A Romanian journalist from Hungary, Maior, recalled his interview with the famous Romanian playwright Ion Luca Caragiale, in 1912, under the title "Remembering." Caragiale expressed regret at having forgotten the Hungarian language which he had understood fairly well at one time. Maior strongly objected to these regrets. He declared that he himself considered it a sin to learn Hungarian. "I tried hard to convince him that Hungarian was without any esthetic merit, that it wasn't even a civilized language, merely an Asiatic one" which caused downright pain with its ear-damaging sounds. Upon which Caragiale commented: "You are just as chauvinistic as they are."[91]

It is obvious that a Romanian who did not recognize the Dual Constitution of 1867 of the Hungarian state would resent as unbearable oppression everything that was justified and constitutional in the eyes of the Hungarian government. According to Hungarian concepts, as formulated by Ferenc Deák, all residents of Hungary combined to form the Hungarian political nation, of which every Hungarian citizen was politically a member (as far as citizenship, rights, obligations were concerned), regardless of his or her mother tongue. Moreover, this concept recognized the separate nationality of the citizens whose language was not Hungarian. The textbooks of history, geography, Hungarian language, and Romanian language designed for use in the Romanian primary schools naturally embodied this concept, reflecting a basic concern with the preservation of the state. But the Romanians, rather than recognize the Compromise of 1867 and the Dual Constitution, chose to regard it as illegal and considered the inclusion of these concepts in the textbooks at Romanian schools as most offensive and as an unbearable manifestation of Hungarian chauvinism. Thus Ghibu, the former superintendent of schools of the Romanian Orthodox archdiocese of Transylvania, quoted in one of his works certain excerpts from these textbooks "upon reading which the chest of the Romanian feels tightened." Expressions such as: our country is called Hungary; Hungary is our homeland; the nations of our country combine to form

the indivisible Hungarian political nation; the residents of the country
are differentiated by their nationality and their religion; in our
homeland different languages are spoken of which the most significant
is Hungarian because it is the official language and the language of
general communication; etc. — "all point to the process of Hungarianization." Ghibu regarded such expressions as frightening examples of
aggressive Hungarianization and of an excessively patriotic education.
He even criticized readings written for the purpose of practicing the
language, one of which could be summarized as "Romanians are also
sons of our dear homeland, Hungary" or the notion that "the Hungarian
is a good person" — something that was unacceptable to Romanians.[92]

To representatives of this line of thought the measures introduced
by the Apponyi Laws could only appear as the most intolerable
aggression, and it became a matter of conscience for every self-respecting Romanian to circumvent them and to protest against them within
the country and abroad. The charges and attributes heaped upon
Apponyi indicate the depth of this hatred: "the vampire of the schools,"
and "the hangman of the freedom of education and religion,"[93] were
among the mildest. Apponyi's conference in Vienna was drowned out
by persistent shouts and whistling on the part of Romanian university
students there, and spread a hateful reputation of him abroad. In the
final analysis the Apponyi Law proved completely inadequate to
restrain the anti-Hungarian irredentist spirit. Even if it had been
carried out successfully for an extended period of time with all factors
in its favor, it would still not have achieved the desired results because
of the international predicament.

Thus, from 1913 on, the Romanian irredentist spirit once again
dominated the Romanian primary schools. Undoubtedly Romania's role
in the Balkan War of 1913 contributed to this; the great success which
Romania reaped at the peace of Bucharest filled the Romanians of
Hungary with enormous satisfaction and expectations. From then on
the teacher-conductors of the village choruses sang the well-known work
of the composer Ciprian Porumbescu on every ceremonial occasion a
beautiful melody which emphasized with growing conviction the
expected unification with Romania — "Unity is inscribed on our
banners."[94]

Romanian Primary Schools During World War I

The situation of the Romanian schools was considerably eased during
the first years of the war. Already in late 1914 the Hungarian Prime
Minister, István Tisza, wrote a letter to Meţianu, the Romanian

archbishop of Nagyszeben, promising to modify the Apponyi Law. At the same time the superintendents of schools were instructed to be particularly considerate of the environment. Encouraged by the letter from Tisza the Romanian Orthodox Church, through its office of education, elaborated a proposal for modifying the law and Meţianu forwarded it to the Prime Minister at the beginning of 1915. In this historically most interesting proposal the leaders of the Romanian Orthodox Church pointed out the measures they found objectionable and unrealistic and which were not put into practice due to circumstances — for instance, Articles 18, 19, and 21 — and described in detail the Romanian position on these issues.[95] The proposal was studied by the Ministry of Religious Affairs and Education. Tisza honestly wanted to see the Law modified, partly because he himself felt that many of its measures were unfortunate, and also because he hoped to propitiate the Romanians by concessions. This hope, however, diminished as the war progressed. The army commands and law and order agencies reported that many Romanian teachers had escaped to Romania and enlisted in the Romanian army. This fact, as well as Romanian entry into the war in 1916, prevented the modification of the Apponyi Laws.

On August 27, 1916, Romania declared war on the Central Powers, and that same day Romanian troops crossed the Transylvanian border. There was no sizable Hungarian force stationed in Transylvania, hence the Romanian troops were able to advance rather rapidly. The majority of the Uniate and Orthodox teachers, up to 80% in some areas, rallied to the advancing forces — i.e. the enemy troops from the point of view of the state. The Romanian teachers, always imbued with the spirit of irredentism, saw in the advance of the long awaited Romanian troops the final realization of the concept of a Greater Romania, and eagerly awaited the opportunity to carry out the assignments given them by the Romanian military commands. These assignments and orders were of a military nature, and in most cases had to do with the control, spying upon, and denunciation of the Hungarian population remaining in the area. But the Romanian forces were only able to occupy, for a short while, the counties adjacent to the Romanian border, and a few months later had to retreat even from these border areas. The Romanian denomination teachers who had collaborated with the Romanian army and carried out their military orders dared not remain at their post. They knew they would have to account for their acts in front of the Hungarian authorities. After all, not only were they subjects of the Hungarian state, but civil servants living on state subvention. Thus several hundred Uniate, Orthodox and other Romanian teachers left with the retreating troops for Romania, and their schools remained without a staff. Serious and incriminating charges were lodged against them once the Hungarian authorities returned, even regarding the attitude of some Romanian teachers who had remained at their post.

At this time army headquarters sent a memorandum to Apponyi, the Minister of Religious Affairs and Education, requesting him to make sure that only completely loyal teachers be allowed to remain in the areas along the borders, for military and security reasons. Accordingly, Apponyi contemplated nationalizing the Romanian schools along the border. He informed the Romanian archbishopric of Nagyszeben about this plan on August 2, 1917, since the nationalization would affect mostly the Orthodox schools under its jurisdiction. In his directive Apponyi referred, first to the "painful events connected with the invasion of the Romanian army," then continued:

> The attitude exhibited by the great majority of the teachers at denominational schools during the invasion convinced me that patriotic intentions had not prevailed in the schools of the aforementioned areas.... This consideration prompts me to nationalize the schools, which I undertake in order to build a strong cultural boundary line for the homeland; in order to bring this about, the communities most indicated are the ones whence the denominational school teachers had departed voluntarily with the enemy, or whose denominational and community school teachers are under disciplinary investigation. I will make sure that the teachers posted in the state schools thus created are familiar with the mother tongue of the people.[96]

The consistory of the archdiocese of Nagyszeben repeatedly tried to persuade the Minister to alter his decision, but in vain. To solve the school issue along the borders, the Minister dispatched a commissioner who attended the meeting of the Romanian consistory on November 17, 1917. Here the latter pointed out the reason, personally and *viva voce*, why the government insisted on the nationalization of the schools concerned: it had been requested by the army corps high command, which urged the establishment of a "cultural zone."

The final episodes of the war prevented further action. The cultural zone project of the Hungarian government, elaborated at the most critical moment of the war, remained dead letter; it could not be carried out after the collapse of 1918.

Elaborated under war conditions and for military considerations the project has been presented later, in the histories of Romanian educational institutions, as if it had been definitely carried out. It has been described as the culmination of the Apponyi Laws, as a deliberate measure of forceful Hungarianization, the brainchild of Hungarian chauvinism aimed at Romanian denominational schools. This was the way the topic was introduced even to the League of Nations in the mid-twenties, when the representatives of the Hungarian minority in Romania complained about a Romanian cultural zone in the land of the Székelys. Of course, they failed to mention that the chauvinist idea of an actual cultural zone was first realized in the Old Kingdom of Romania towards the end of the 19th century, with a view to Romanianize the Bulgarians of Dobrudja and the Hungarian Csangók of Moldavia. That project had been worked out and carried out according to the concepts of Spiru C. Haret, the Romanian Minister of Education.

The Minister completely reorganized education in the Kingdom of Romania at the end of the 19th century. The principal objective of the reorganization was the complete Romanianization of all foreign ethnic groups in the country. He intended to attain this objective with the help of kindergarten, primary, and secondary schools. The basic tasks had to be solved at the kindergarten level. Aware that the majority of the inhabitants of the Dobrudja, attached to Romania in 1878, were not of Romanian background, and likewise aware of the existence of the Hungarian Csangók in Moldavia, he focussed the efforts of the Romanian kindergarten and primary schools on these two areas. Thus he established the first kindergartens in Dobrudja and in the villages inhabited by the Csangók, and devoted special attention to the primary schools in these areas as well. These regions were considered a "cultural zone," where the principal tasks of the kindergartens, primary schools, and secondary schools was to Romanianize the non-Romanian nationalities. Haret started from the assumption that the Bulgarians of Dobrudja were already Romanians as a consequence of the "reattachment" to Romania but unfortunately they were not familiar with the language because of their foreign background. Hence, the most immediate task of the kindergartens was "to familiarize the children with our language, as their age permits." Thanks to these kindergartens "the education of the children in the villages with alien residents becomes uniform sooner. The primary schools would then have an easier task; otherwise they would have to face enormous obstacles — the ignorance of our language." Yet the primary schools, imbued with the national spirit, would be able to overcome this obstacle. The primary schools have to be national, or nothing.

Consequently, the Romanian government established altogether 168 kindergartens in the period 1897 to 1910. About one hundred of these were set up in the non-Romanian villages of the provinces of Constanţa

and Tulcea in Dobrudja, while twenty more were set up in the Hungarian villages of Moldavia. The Law of December 11, 1909, made
attendance at these kindergartens mandatory, thereby ensuring that the
Bulgarian and Hungarian children would learn Romanian fast. In the
greater part of the country, the purely Romanian counties, the government set up only 48 kindergartens, whereas it set up 120 small
"cultural zone" inhabited by three nationalities.[97]

A Kindergarten Act was also adopted in Hungary in 1891, stipulating that minding the non-Hungarian children be combined with their
introduction to the official language of the country. But the law did not
apply to those parents who were able to care for their children in their
homes, nor did it specify any punitive sanctions against delinquent
kindergarten teachers. Its main objective was probably to make it
easier for the state schools, where instruction was to take place in
Hungarian.

*The Relationship Between Romanian Denominational Schools and
Hungarian State Schools*

According to the concepts of Eötvös a primary education was mainly
the responsibility of the denominational and community schools. He did
not even strive to establish state schools. Until the end of the century
his successors likewise seldom manifested any enthusiasm for setting up
state schools. But since in some places the denominations — especially
the purely Hungarian Reformed Church and the Unitarian Church —
could not or did not want to accept the sacrifices entailed by sponsoring
schools, the state assumed responsibility for the personnel expenses
involved and, renting the existing school space of the denominational
schools, organized state schools. Entirely new state schools were set up
beginning in the eighties, especially in communities where there were
no schools at all. In 1869 there was not a single state school, whereas
in 1880 1.6% of all schools belonged to the state. In 1900 the state
schools still did not exceed 10%. It is obvious that financial considerations prevented the state from increasing the number of state schools.

Since the first state schools in Transylvania and east of the Tisza
River were usually set up where the Hungarian Reformed and Unitarian dioceses had given up their schools and leased the premises to the
state, they catered to a purely Hungarian population and naturally the
language of instruction was Hungarian. These dioceses had usually
signed contracts with the state, retaining the right of ownership to the
school buildings. At the same time, however, fearing a return of
Austrian autocratic rule, in which case the Austrians might decide to

introduce German as the language of instruction, they prescribed that the school institute Hungarian as the language of instruction, whereas the teacher to be appointed should be of the same religion as the members of the diocese and be able to fill the post of cantor as well if necessary. During the entire period of the Compromise, 170 Reformed and 38 Unitarian denominational schools were thus ceded to the Hungarian state.[98]

Hence the state schools replaced denominational schools of the Reformed and Unitarian churches, at least at the beginning. From the eighties on, however, the government began to set up state schools in communities where none of the denominations had schools. As soon as they set up schools in areas inhabited by Romanians the question of the language of instruction arose: should it be Romanian or Hungarian? In accordance with the letter and spirit of the nationalities law (Article 17) the state was obliged "to the extent possible" to make sure that the ethnic groups living in larger concentrations are able to obtain an education in their mother tongue. There is some evidence that until the eighties the teachers at all community schools established in Romanian villages resorted to Romanian as the language of instruction. It seems that after 1883 Hungarian became the language of instruction at community schools in many a village. This prompted the Romanian Orthodox representative Candrea to intervene at the April 1884 meeting of the Romanian Episcopal synod of Nagyszeben.[99] Candrea asked the members of the synod whether they were aware that Romanian was not being taught in the state and community schools of Romanian communities? Yet other data, however, suggest that in many villages the teachers at the community schools still taught in Romanian, even after the introduction of the Apponyi Laws. In the newly-established state schools the language of instruction was Hungarian.

By setting up state primary schools with Hungarian as the language of instruction in villages with a Romanian population, Hungarian educational policy unquestionably overlooked Article 17 of the law on nationalities, according to which Romanian children had to be taught in Romanian even in the state schools. With its system of primary schools with Hungarian as the language of instruction even in areas inhabited by the nationalities Hungarian educational policy committed a serious mistake, with unfortunate consequences. This mistake is mitigated by the fact that the state did not force anyone to transfer from denominational to state schools. Nevertheless in the final analysis primary schools in ethnic areas, with Hungarian as the language of instruction even if few in number, were equally useless from the Romanian and the Hungarian point of view. Children living in a purely

Romanian environment seldom learned Hungarian, while the policy elicited a lot of ill-feeling. The assumption was easily made: by mandating Hungarian as the language of instruction the state wanted to Hungarianize the Romanians. So it appeared, indeed, although, with hindsight, one may say that anyone expecting Hungarianization of the Romanians to result from a few hundred state schools was incredibly naive; after all, there were nearly 3,000 purely Romanian schools in the country. Indeed, the illusion of Hungarianizing through schools was entertained by some Hungarians, as we may note from speeches and declarations here and there. The nationalities, primarily the Romanians, were prompt to make use of these declarations abroad, accusing the Hungarians of constant aggressive and crude attempts at Hungarianizing and of cruel oppression of the nationalities. At the same time, however, they dispelled the worries and anxieties of those who actually believed the complaints aired abroad, by describing the actual situation in a calming way: "We have admitted several times that we do not feel ourselves threatened in our existence by the Hungarians," confessed an important anti-Hungarian Romanian weekly.[100] Basically the Romanians did not truly believe they were being Hungarianized, yet took advantage of the relevant declarations by some Hungarians; and one of the most frequently used issues was precisely the issue of state schools with Hungarian as the language of instruction.

Towards the end of the century, the establishment of the kindergartens had become an issue used against Hungarian educational policies, as well as state schools with Hungarian as the language of instruction. Yet the drafting of the Kindergarten by Act XV of 1891 was not expressly intended as Hungarianization. Only those children in the age group three to six who could not be minded properly in the home were compelled to attend kindergarten.[101] There the children were taught to pray, sing, and play various games. According to the oft-criticized Article 8 of the Kindergarten Act "in the kindergartens and homes for children, the occupation of those whose mother tongue is not Hungarian will be combined with the introduction of Hungarian as the official language." The proposed Act spelled out, in its preamble:

that knowing how easily small children acquire other languages in the course of play, it seemed appropriate to stipulate that those children whose mother tongue was not Hungarian be introduced to it, as the official language of the state, thereby facilitating the task of the primary schools in carrying out Act XVIII of 1879.[102]

This specific measure of the Act on kindergartens concealed no real danger regarding the nationality of Romanian children, for the law included no sanctions against those kindergarten teachers who might decide to disregard the provisions of the law. On the other hand, it proved once again a most useful weapon against the Hungarian state in the hands of the Romanians. Most likely it was the lack of success in carrying out the provisions of Act XVIII of 1879, as well as the lack of achievements in state primary schools with Hungarian as the language of instruction in villages inhabited by the nationalities that prompted the government to propose this law. In this respect the Kindergarten Act was indeed a consequence of Act XVIII of 1879. It goes without saying, however, that instruction exclusively in Hungarian in state primary schools, as well as the above provision of the law on kindergartens, hurt the Hungarian state far more than they helped.

After the turn of the century, state schools and Romanian denomination schools worked side by side more often. Naturally, at the beginning this situation existed only in the larger communities with a mixed population. For a long time the two kinds of schools lived side by side in peace, the Hungarian children attending the Hungarian state school, the Romanian children attending the denominational school. This process was not rigid, however, since it often happened that Romanian parents would send their children to a Hungarian state school, whereas Hungarians parents would send theirs to the Romanian denominational school for the sake of learning the language. Romanian newspapers frequently attacked those parents who sent their children to Hungarian state schools. This issue did not cause particular tension between state and denominational schools, however, until the Apponyi Laws.

The situation changed after the adoption of Act XVIII of 1907, by which time there was a state school with Hungarian as the language of instruction alongside the Romanian denominational school in many a small village with a Hungarian and Romanian population. Since the Romanian parishes often could not pay the higher salaries prescribed by the Apponyi Law, they had but two alternatives: either they requested state subvention, or they applied for the establishment of a state school in lieu of the denominational school. Thus the struggle between state and denominational school got under way.

The evidence concerning this competition between Hungarian state schools and Romanian denominational schools is noteworthy. In several hundred relatively prosperous Romanian parishes the teachers' salary was raised, hence the survival of the Romanian denomination school was ensured. The state seldom set up a school in such places. Where, as a consequence of the excessive zeal of some school superintendent, a

Hungarian state or community school was nevertheless set up, it
usually remained empty. Such was the case in the community of
Szentandrás in Hunyad county, where Romanians residents had built
a beautiful new school, dedicated in the fall of 1911, after the Apponyi
Law. The community also had a state school with Hungarian as the
language of instruction, but the Romanians, taking advantage of the
principle of freedom of instruction, did not send their children to the
state school, and the latter remained empty. One night unknown
parties shattered its windows and doors because, as we can read in the
report, "some over-emotional people felt irritated by the fact that the
state teacher remained in the village, took walks, and received his pay
for doing nothing, as if to provoke the Romanians."[103] The two
schools in Palos [Paloş] competed in a similarly violent manner. Here
the Hungarian leadership organized a community school with Hungarian as the language of instruction, in addition to the somewhat weak
Orthodox school which had two teachers. After a struggle which lasted
ten months the Hungarian school was closed down, "since the brave
Romanians refused to send their children there."[104]

Judging by the evidence of many similar occurrences the Hungarian
state did not intervene at all in the local competition between the
Romanian denominational and the Hungarian state school. Rather than
limit freedom of instruction by forcing children to attend a Hungarian
school it preferred to allow the state or community school with
Hungarian as the language of instruction to wither away or close down.
It may have happened, in isolated cases, that some megalomaniac
village teacher tried to lure away the pupils of the Romanian denominational school to the Hungarian school with one device or another, but
such measures were inevitably followed by countermeasures. All the
more so, as the Romanian press and the church and school authorities
could fight unhampered for the Romanian denominational school and
against the Hungarian state school. The Romanian press could
announce, without the least fear of incurring official sanctions or
consequences, "a complete national boycott, the refusal of all assistance
or service" to those who requested a state school in lieu of the denominational one.[105] The boycott was observed strictly. "We must never
forget the sin of the wicked ones," explained the *Libertatea*. "You must
be adamant, merciless, vindictive and aggressive all your life and not
let your anger against the wicked ones [i.e. those who requested a state
school dissipate]." Where such measures are taken, the evil ones either
move away or break down.[106]

This response was prompted by the steps taken in many a Romanian
community to set up a state school. Indeed, in many places the village

elders had requested a state school instead of the denominational school. For instance, in 1908, the Romanian community of Karács [Carciu], in Hunyad county, led by the priest Indrei, decided to join the state school of Körösbánya. Until that time it had maintained a denominational school in conjunction with the village of Cebe, but now it decided to sever this old relationship and sent a delegation to the sheriff in order to request approval of its new resolution.[107] A similar occurrence took place in the village of Sibisán [Sibişani] near Alvinc [Vinţu de Jos]. Here the salary of the teacher of the Romanian Orthodox school was raised in 1908 by the community as well as the consistory, but in the summer of the following year the people had second thoughts about the teacher, rebelled against the denominational school, and requested a state school instead. The deacon, however, refused to record their resolution to this effect. When the Romanian residents found out, they sent a delegation to the superintendent at Enyed and, informing him of the stand taken by the deacon, insisted that a state school be set up in the village.[108] The Romanian residents of Lónapoklostelke [Paglesia or Pîglişa or Pâglişa] in Szolnok-Doboka county acted in a similar manner; many among them protested against the new Romanian school, and asked that a state school be set up in the village.[109]

From these and other incidents not mentioned here it becomes clear that the national consciousness of the Romanian villagers did not always regard the setting up of state schools with Hungarian as the language of instruction as a threat. On the other hand, it is obvious that the state refrained from intervening against the freedom of instruction of the Romanian population. In the history of the competition between Hungarian state and Romanian denominational schools, there is no example of the state closing down the Romanian schools in order to force its own state school onto the residents of the community. The evidence indicates that the state school was always requested by the Romanians themselves, partly because it was set up entirely at state expense, without burdening the local residents. Where the population gave up the denominational school, apart from its weaker national consciousness the reason was its reluctance to undertake financial sacrifices. There is no instance in the Hungarian school system where the residents of some community had to bear a double tax burden, i.e. to contribute to the support of a state school in addition to supporting their own denominational school.

Once the Apponyi Law was applied, competition between state and denominational schools became a permanent feature in many places. Each had its advantages and disadvantages. Until 1914 the language of instruction in the state schools was in Hungarian only. On August

13 of that year, in his directive 114.000, the Minister of Religious Affairs and Education ordered that the mother tongue of children of non-Hungarian parents must be taught as an auxiliary language and as a subject.[110] From then on the rights of the mother tongue prevailed to some extent even in the state schools. Earlier, there was no such guarantee, while the children were required to learn the official language reasonably well. The denominational schools provided an education entirely in Romanian, whereas Hungarian was not taught well. The parents could freely assess the advantages of each system, and decide as they saw fit. The description provided in one Romanian newspaper in 1912 is rather typical of the issue: "The Romanians do not support the Romanian school even where there is one, preferring to send their children to foreign schools. At Lugos only 40% to 50% of the children of school-age attend the Romanian denominational school." One reason for this phenomenon, according to the paper, was that the Romanian schools fell behind the foreign (Hungarian and German) schools as regards direction, supervision, and control. But the real reason was that, according to the growing conviction of some social strata among the Romanian population, "under the present circumstances familiarity with Hungarian is absolutely essential, and since this can only be obtained at Hungarian schools, they send their children there."[111]

According to these statements the parents took advantage of the freedom of instruction to the very end. Never during the whole period of Hungarian rule was there any law or directive forcing parents who declared themselves to be Romanian to send their children into schools with Hungarian as the language of instruction. In the competition between schools true freedom of instruction prevailed in the primary as well as the secondary schools.

Secondary Schools

While the task of the Romanian mass education was largely met by almost 3,000 primary schools with Romanian as the language of instruction, the objectives of Romanian secondary education were served by far fewer institutions. The following Romanian secondary institutions functioned on Hungarian territory in the years preceding the world war: six men's and two women's teachers' colleges, three vocational schools, four girls' high schools, one commercial school, two midwife training schools (there were in fact state institutions, but the material presented to the Romanian students was in Romanian), moreover one junior high and four senior high schools. These Romanian secondary schools could be categorized in terms of their sponsors as community schools, association schools, foundation schools, Royal Catholic schools, and denominational schools. The Romanian character of these schools was provided, in addition to the nationality of those sponsoring them, by the nationality of the teachers and the language of instruction. With one or two exceptions, all the secondary schools mentioned had Romanian as their language of instruction, and, but for Hungarian language and literature, all subjects were taught in Romanian. Given the peculiarities of Romanian society and the significance of the schools, we must differentiate between specialized schools and general high schools. The impact of the former was limited to strata with a certain occupation, whereas the latter had an impact on Romanian society in general as a result of the wide-ranging activities and influence of the Romanian intelligentsia that graduated from them.

The Teachers' Colleges

The Romanian churches sponsored six men's and two women's teachers' colleges. The colleges of Nagyszeben, Arad, and Karánsebes catered to Orthodox students, whereas the ones of Balázsfalva, Nagyvárad, and Lugos catered to Uniate candidates. The institutions at Szamosújvár and Nagyvárad were not only exclusively Romanian Uniate but were Royal and Catholic as well, hence the Ministers of Religious Affairs and Education actually intervened in the administration of the two schools as a consequence of the close relationship between the state and the Roman Catholic Church. In addition to the aforementioned schools, Romanian Uniate colleges were established in 1914 at Lugos, and in 1915 at Szamosújvár.[112]

The Romanian Uniate teachers' colleges had more rights than their Orthodox counterparts. In some of the latter, including the Royal Catholic colleges of Szamosújvár and Nagyvárad, certain subjects were taught in Hungarian, and the certifying examination was conducted by a representative of the government. The teachers were priests with the required competence. The Royal Catholic colleges were made possible by contributions from the Religious Foundation. Hungarian had to be taught in accordance with Act XVIII of 1879, in other words, to such an extent that the candidates should be able to teach it once they graduate. Hungarian language was taught at a rate of four periods a week each year.

In the Romanian Orthodox colleges the candidates had to pass the certifying examination in front of a board appointed by the consistory.

The representative of the church consistory was also the president of the committee and of the board of examiners.

The college bearing the name of Andrei Şaguna was considered the most prestigious Romanian teachers' college. Even from a financial aspect its teachers stood above their colleagues at other Romanian colleges. According to Ghibu, the Minister had offered to adjust the pay of the other teachers to a level commensurate with that of state professors, but only on condition that four subjects be taught in Hungarian at the Romanian colleges. The church authorities rejected this proposal, and Romanian continued to be the language of instruction at the teachers colleges.

Vocational Schools

According to Act XVII of 1884, the community was to set up a vocational school if there were over fifty apprentices in a given locality, provided the church had not already done so. The community school thus created was maintained by a surtax of 2%. These were four-year schools, the first being a preparatory year. Although, according to the law, the language of instruction at these schools could only be Hungarian, in reality other languages were used. Thus three Romanian vocational schools were functioning on Hungarian territory, of which two were community supported and one denominational.[113]

The Romanian Commercial High School and Junior High School at Brassó

In 1869 the Orthodox St. Nicolae parish of Brassó established both the Romanian commercial high school and the junior high school. The foundation of these two schools was made possible by a resolution of the Romanian parliament on June 6, 1868, according to which the government of Romania was to increase aid to the Romanian parish of Brassó as its residents had requested; the additional sum enabled the parish to open the two schools. In 1874, once the commercial high school was in full operation, the Hungarian government granted it public status and authorized it to administer the matriculation exam. The school was maintained thanks to assistance from Romania to the end, as was the junior high school. All subjects were taught in Romanian.

Girls' High Schools

There were four girls' high schools with Romanian as the language of instruction of Hungarian territory: at Balázsfalva (Uniate), Belényes (Uniate), Arad (Orthodox), and Nagyszeben, the latter supported by the Romanian cultural association Astra. Hungarian was taught at these schools, but all other subjects were taught in Romanian. The institution maintained by Astra at Nagyszeben was the most significant among these. From 1894-95 this school offered extension courses for those students who had already completed high school, and Romanian language and literature were required at these courses while the official language was only an elective. Moreover, Hungarian was not even an elective in the home economics course designed by Astra in 1907 (which included a chef's course), according to the announcements in the Romanian papers. The Romanian girls at this school were required to wear Romanian national costumes at all times.[114]

Midwifery Schools

Midwifery schools on Hungarian territory were run by the state. In spite of this, the subject was presented in Romanian to Romanian ethnic students at Nagyszeben and Kolozsvár.[115] The Romanian students numbered 107. In addition, to these, midwifery courses were occasionally offered at other locations. In 1903, the state hospital at Déva offered a two-months winter course, primarily in Romanian. The announcement in the Romanian weekly of Hunyad county read: "the language of instruction at the school is Romanian, and only if necessary would it become Hungarian or German. Let all villages where there are no trained midwives send one to study here, because they would be doing a good thing."[116]

The Management of the Romanian Secondary Schools in Transylvania

There were five Romanian secondary schools on Hungarian territory at the time of the Compromise. Four of these had all forms, from first through eighth, while one offered only the first four forms. The four major ones, in the order of their foundation, were: 1) the Romanian Uniate secondary school of Balázsfalva; 2) the Uniate secondary school of Belényes; 3) the Andrei Şaguna Orthodox secondary of Brassó; and 4) the Foundation secondary school of Naszód. The Orthodox junior secondary school of Brád opened last.

All of these schools, with the exception of the one at Naszód, were established by the churches. The oldest and most significant was the secondary school of Balázsfalva, since it had an impact not only on the Romanians of Hungary, but on those of Moldavia and Wallachia as well. Launched in 1754, it became a true center of Romanian cultural life within half a century.

Chronologically, it was followed by the Uniate School of Belényes, founded by the Romanian Uniate Bishop of Nagyvárad, Samuel Vulcan, in 1828. Ten years later it was in full operation. The Romanian secondary school of Brassó was initiated by the Orthodox Bishop Andrei Şaguna in 1851; it became a full-fledged high school by 1865. The first class of the secondary school of Naszód opened in 1863, and that of the junior secondary of Brád in 1869. Thus, when the Hungarian government took control over the country in 1867, three Romanian secondary schools were fully operational, while the ones at Naszód and Brád were in process of formation. The formation of the latter two was not hindered by the change in sovereignty: the secondary school at Naszód was fully operational by 1870, while the junior secondary at Brád had opened a year earlier.

These secondary schools proved to be a great financial burden for their sponsors even though each of them, with the exception of the one at Brassó, owned several thousand *holds** of land. The school at Balázsfalva had the most solid financial foundation, based as it was upon the combined revenues from the nearly 10,000 *holds* of estates of the Balázsfalva Uniate archdiocese and on the Alexandru Sterca-Şuluţiu Foundation. The Uniate school of Belényes could rely on the revenues from the more than 100,000 *holds* of estates owned by the Uniate bishop of Nagyvárad. Although the diocese had other priorities, it took the school under its wings from the eighties on. The upkeep of the Foundation high school at Naszód was covered by estates totalling 12,254 *holds* owned by the borderland Cultural Foundation. The junior secondary school at Brád likewise had an estate of 2,416 *holds* which covered, albeit modestly, the greater part of its expenses.[117]

The Andrei Şaguna School had no solid financial foundation. Its expenses were borne by members of the Romanian parish of Brassó, who paid a regular contribution yearly. Nevertheless, these contributions came in rather irregularly, and sometimes not at all. Therefore the Romanian Orthodox parish of St. Nicolae turned to the Romanian government for support. At one time the parish had received estates

---
* One *hold* equals 1.23 acres.

from the Voivods of Moldavia and Wallachia. Now they requested regular financial contributions from the legal heirs of these Voivods, i.e. the Romanian government. From 1861 on the Romanian government regularly disbursed a certain sum to cover the expenses of the school each year. In 1875 Minister of Religious Affairs and Education, Ágoston Trefort, prohibited by his directive 559/1875 the continued acceptance of the annual assistance provided by the Romanian government. Still, the assistance continued to come in, although in secret; but in 1898 this secret was disclosed and the Hungarian government launched an investigation. The investigation confirmed the fact and revealed the details of the Romanian transaction. Then the Hungarian government reached an agreement with the Romanian government regarding further assistance for the schools of Brassó. The Romanian government was to deposit almost one million crowns in the Hungarian Central Bank of Budapest, in the account of the church of St. Nicolae of Brassó. From 1900 the schools received an annual stipend of 38,000 lei from this account, forwarded by the Hungarian treasury.[118]

The Romanian secondary schools were also helped by the numerous scholarships awarded to their students. The yearly contributions of Romanian associations, banks and foundations, as well as the regular salary adjustment disbursed by the Hungarian treasury after 1906, also increased the endowments. Foundations serving the cultural objectives of Greater Romania, such as the Godu Foundation, the Commonwealth of Karánsebes, as well as smaller funds earmarked for scholarships covered the expenses of many hundreds of needy Romanian students each year. In the academic year 1906/07, for instance, almost half of the students of the Romanian boarding school of Belényes had all or 50% of their expenses paid. In Brassó 35 of the 45 students making use of the mensa had their fare covered by contributions from the foundations. Greater or lesser sums were received by a number of students at other institutions as well.

The Status of the Romanian Faculties

The true worth of any educational institution is determined primarily by the competence and preparation of its faculty. The value of their work derives, on the other hand, from the freedom granted them in instruction. The evolution of the status of the Romanian high school teachers in Hungary was a function of Hungarian educational policies and of the Romanian communities in charge of the schools.

Until 1883 the training of high school teachers was entirely in the hands of those sponsoring the schools. The Uniate teachers were certified by a particular committee of the archdiocese of Balázsfalva set up for this purpose, whereas the Orthodox instructors were certified by the pertinent committee of the Orthodox archdiocese of Nagyszeben. The individuals were then hired by the appropriate sections of the school-sponsoring institutions — the wards representing the schools in the case of Brassó and Brád, and the consistories in the case of the Uniate schools.[119] No ministerial authorization of any kind was required for the selection, hiring, and granting of tenure. The Foundation school of Naszód, where the instructors were appointed by the Hungarian Minister of Religious Affairs and Education, on the recommendation of the Borderland Foundation, constituted an exception in this respect.

The situation of the instructors was modified by Act XXX of 1883. This Act prescribed that all instructors at secondary schools were to pass an examination by the state examining board once they completed their university studies. In other words, while until then the preparation of the teachers took place outside the universities, the new law specified that it could be obtained only through the universities. From 1883 Romanian teacher candidates had to obtain their diplomas from Hungarian universities. The Romanian churches, the Orthodox Church first of all, protested against this provision of the Act, by way of Archbishop Roman Miron, because "it takes the preparation of the teachers out of the hands of the churches."[120] But Article 70 of the Act enabled the candidates to pass their examination in their mother tongue for a while. The Minister of Religious Affairs and Education was authorized by this paragraph of the law to allow the examination boards, for a period of ten years after the law goes into effect and at the recommendation of the leadership of the denomination concerned, to offer the examination in some subjects entirely or partly in a language other than Hungarian. All candidates, however, had to pass an examination in Hungarian language and literature, as prescribed by law in the sixteenth year of Hungarian rule.

The Act concerning the secondary schools also provided state support for teachers and schools on certain conditions. These conditions entailed increased state control and direction in proportion with the amount of state support. Since the Romanian secondary schools, on the one hand, did not necessarily have to rely on state subsidy and, on the other hand, did not want to give the state an opportunity to intervene to any considerable extent in their administration, they did not take advantage of the offer of state subsidy until 1906. At that time every Romanian secondary school was granted salary adjustments for its faculty, by the state, under interesting circumstances. Regarding the details of the state subsidy the bulletin of the Andrei Şaguna high school in Brassó reads as follows:

Romanian teachers were not happy to see their Hungarian colleagues teaching in state schools with the same educational background, and at the same level, better paid, even though their teaching load was less. As a result the Romanian teacher was obviously in a position of inferiority vis-à-vis his Hungarian colleague. But Minister of Religious Affairs and Education Count Apponyi partly rectified the situation in 1906 by eradicating the causes for resentment. In a ministerial directive he declared that all church authorities sponsoring secondary schools may apply for subsidy for their teachers without any condition and without jeopardizing the autonomy of the schools thereby. Then the teachers would be paid like the teachers at state schools at the same level; divided into pay categories and steps.

When the matter came under study the school committees and boards, as well as the consistory of the archdiocese decided, under directive 10.431 of October 30, 1906, to accept the subvention provided it could be surrendered at any time; hence the teachers at the schools at Brassó and Brád began to receive their pay supplement as of July 1, 1906. The matter, however, was not settled that easily with the administration of the school at Brassó. Here there was great opposition on the part of some who feared that the government would exert a negative influence on the schools once the agreement was concluded.

From the text of the directive of the Minster of Education it could not be concluded that he intended to curtail the autonomy of the schools, or to interfere in school matters. It is true, however, that the subsidy hung over the professors like the sword of Damocles, and they had to be aware that the sword could be used against them as well, that they would at least have to be more circumspect in the future. But the spirit and atmosphere of our schools, or the political tendency of the teachers did not alter in the least as a consequence of the implementation of the rules pertaining to state subsidy and this constitutes powerful evidence of the purity of feelings and sense of honor of the teachers concerned.[121]

The teachers at other Romanian secondary schools received their subsidy under similar circumstances; for instance, the committee at the high school of Brád decided regarding state subsidy in a similar manner. Their report reads:

> The school board, consisting of the prominent residents of Zaránd, suggested to the officials of the secondary school that they accept the pay supplement, since the directive of the Minister is in harmony with the laws already on the books, and does not curtail church autonomy any further. The consistory of the archdiocese opted for acceptance on October 30, but reserved the right to give it up immediately, should the autonomy of instruction be affected in any way.[122]

The teachers at other Romanian secondary schools received their pay supplement in a similar manner, and this supplement was disbursed by the state regularly until 1918. The faculty at the five Romanian secondary schools received a total of 426,860 crowns of pay supplement, and all this, as we have seen, without affecting their autonomy in any way.[123]

Count Albert Apponyi, Minister of Religious Affairs and Education, brought about a positive and comforting change in the financial situation of the faculty of Romanian secondary schools in Hungary. Once his directives were implemented, the Romanian teachers were on a par with their Hungarian colleagues as far as pay was concerned. In other respects too they enjoyed equal status. The Romanian teachers were accepted as members of the pension fund; consequently, after thirty years of service, they received a pension from the Hungarian treasury which afforded them a decent living. For instance, the president of Astra, Andrei Bârseanu, a former teacher at the secondary school of Brassó, received a pension from the Hungarian state. Along with their Hungarian colleagues the Romanian teachers were issued an identification card which enabled them to purchase tickets on state railroads at half fare. The correspondence and publications of Romanian secondary schools were exempted from tax, stamp, or franking expenses, much as those of the Hungarian denomination schools. Romanian teachers were not discriminated against when it came to promotions in the army, particularly appointment to officer rank, on account of their nationality; we have found no complaints to this effect in the contemporary press.

On the basis of the evidence presented above we may conclude that Hungarian educational policy was fair and humane towards Romanian teachers in Hungary. The government provided them with a decent livelihood and pension, and did not discriminate between Hungarian and Romanian instructors. The teachers at Romanian secondary schools owed their improved situation precisely to Apponyi, the very person denounced in the Romanian press of Hungary as well as of Romania as the executioner of the Romanian school system. Their consolidated financial situation allowed the Romanian teachers to continue to indulge in school activities promoting the idea of a Greater Romania freely throughout the period of Hungarian rule.

The Spirit of the Romanian Secondary Schools

The Romanian secondary schools served the cause of nationalism from the very start of the Romanian national idea, and their history is practically identical with the history of Romanian national aspirations. The teachers at the Romanian Uniate secondary school of Balázsfalva — especially Simion Bărnuțiu and George Barițiu — exerted a decisive influence through their literary, journalistic, and political activities, in the strictest sense of the term, on the national and political evolution of the Romanians of Hungary. It is no exaggeration to say that the history of the Romanian secondary schools is equivalent to the history of Romanian nationalism.

Naturally, the secondary school at Balázsfalva, which was the oldest and boasted of the most distinguished faculty, was the only one to embody Romanian national and cultural movements at the beginning. It had a decisive influence, especially in the period 1834 to 1850, when it developed the traditions which were eventually adopted and faithfully copied by other Romanian secondary schools.

What did these traditions peculiar to Balázsfalva consist of? According to the Romanian author Slavici the focus at the school had always been on demonstrating the Romanians' right to Transylvania, and to prepare intellectually for the exercise of this right.[124] By stressing the Latin origins of the Romanian people and the notion of historical continuity, according to which Romanians, as the descendants of the Dacians and of the Romans, inhabited Transylvania, without interruption, they set out to demonstrate that only the Romanians were entitled to rule over the area. This was the reason why Bărnuțiu insisted on natural rights in his lectures at Balázsfalva, and his colleague Timotei Cipariu tried to excise from the Romanian language all words which did not have a strictly Latin etymology. They meant to present the past and the future of this concept appropriately to their students and, through the press, to Romanian readers in general.

Next to this concept of the teachers at Balázsfalva we find another concept deriving naturally enough, at least in part, from the former; this

notion, which arose in the 1830s, was unification with the Romanians
on the other side of the Carpathians. The Romanian instructors at
Balázsfalva were in close contact with the leaders of Romanian
nationalist movements in Bucharest from the beginning. Barițiu and
Cipariu, two young teachers from Balázsfalva, travelled to Bucharest in
1836. As one of their future colleagues was to write later, they went
there "because they were both enthusiastic young instructors at the
time and they wanted to experience Romania as persons deeply involved
in the increasingly powerful manifestations of Romanian nationalism."[125]   This trip was decisive from the point of view of the
evolution of the Romanian school at Balázsfalva and, in the long run,
of the evolution of Romanian nationalism in Hungary. The two young
teachers made the acquaintance of Romanian nationalist leaders in
Bucharest who already harbored the notion of a Romania uniting all
Romanians under one rule. As soon as this notion became a concrete
political project sponsored by the Romanian aristocrat Ion Câmpineanu
in 1838, the political irredentism of detaching Transylvania from
Hungary was hatched.[126]

By then Barițiu was at Brassó as teacher and editor of the first
Romanian political weekly. He remained in close touch with Balázsfalva and his former colleagues, as well as with Romanian politicians
in Bucharest and Moldavia. Undoubtedly he was the one to communicate, in 1838, the concept of a Greater Romania to the faculty of the
school at Balázsfalva. Thus, in the 1840's the national spirit and
tradition of the Romanian secondary school at Balázsfalva consisted of
the notion of the national unity of all Romanians in addition to the idea
of the Latin origins of the Romanian people and their right to Transylvania. From then on, Romanian literature, history, geography, and all
subjects in any way related to the objectives of Romanian nationalism
were taught at the secondary school of Balázsfalva.

The role played by Balázsfalva, the students at the school, and
Bărnuțiu, one of its former instructors, in the events of 1848-49, is well
known. It was Bărnuțiu and his disciples who turned the Romanians
of Transylvania against the Hungarians. They were the ones to line up
the Romanians on the side of the Habsburgs and against Kossuth, and
it was under their influence that part of the Romanian intelligentsia of
Transylvania became anti-Hungarian. Bărnuțiu and his disciples acted
logically in turning against the Hungarians, since the latter constituted
the main obstacle to the unification of Transylvania with the two
Romanian principalities. Therefore they protested against the reattachment of Transylvania to Hungary, because this union made the
realization of the unification plan more problematic, to say the least.

The Romanian national idea at the secondary school at Balázsfalva had manifested itself by 1848 in the notions that the Romanians are the descendants of the Romans, that they inhabited Transylvania before the arrival of the Hungarians, that they had a better right to Transylvania than the Hungarians, that in order to unite Transylvania with the Romanian principalities it would be necessary to fight against the Hungarians who were intent on preventing this unification — all these notions derived logically from the preceding one.

When the secondary schools at Brassó, Naszód, and later at Brád, opened their gates, during the last years of Austrian autocratic rule, they took over the traditions of Balázsfalva ready-made, and elaborated on them in their own manner. At the time of the Compromise every Romanian secondary school embodied the concept of a united Romania. The majority of the faculty felt they belonged to Romania, considered the reattachment of Transylvania to Hungary illegal, and regarded the Hungarians as their natural enemies.

The greatest Romanian poet, Mihai Eminescu, who studied briefly at Balázsfalva and Belényes,[127] encountered these ideas already there. It was under the impact of these Romanian ideas from Transylvania that he changed his name from Eminovici to Eminescu. From the writings of Slavici we know how passionate was the sentiment of nationalism he harbored.

The passionate Romanian national ideas which dominated the Romanian secondary schools did not alter, of course, when Hungarian rule was introduced. Judging from the annual reports of the secondary school at Balázsfalva, the Hungarian government did not interfere in the educational process taking place at the school for ten years, until 1876.[128] In the period from 1867 to 1876 teaching continued within the framework elaborated before the reattachment. The students learnt the subjects that were most important from the point of view of the Romanian national idea, such as history and geography, from the "lecture notes of the teachers." In accordance with the principle of autonomy of the secondary schools the syllabus for the courses was drafted by the administration of the school. While in the Hungarian schools geography and history meant the geography and history of Hungary, the professors at the Romanian secondary school of Balázsfalva taught mainly the geography and history of Transylvania and of the Romanian principalities i.e. of Romania, once the two principalities were united. From 1867 to 1876 the syllabus for geography was *Transylvania and the neighboring lands*, and history likewise was *The History of Transylvania and of the Neighboring lands.*[129] These subjects were taught in the second, third, and eighth years.

Judging from the annual reports from the secondary school at
Balázsfalva it is clear, that for almost ten years after the beginning of
Hungarian rule the syllabi of history and geography courses covered
mainly Transylvania and, among the neighboring countries, mainly
Romania. That is, Romania was the ideal for both instructors and
students; the Romanian people were regarded as one nation, some
members of which lived on this side of the Carpathians in Transylvania,
and some on the other side, in Romania. Hungary was mentioned in
the syllabi of the history and geography courses only as a "neighboring
land" — even though the Romanians were its citizens from 1867 on. In
other words, the Transylvanian autonomy demanded in the political
arena was applied de facto by the instructors in the curriculum,
inasmuch as Transylvania was studied as a separate country and
Hungary was considered a neighboring land.

For almost ten years, the Hungarian state and its educational policy
did not intervene in any way in the affairs of the Romanian secondary
schools, with the exception of the one at Belényes. Consequently the
activities of Romanian teachers were anti-Hungarian and favored a
Greater Romania. The students raised in this spirit expressed their true
feelings on several occasions. On May 15 ceremonies and anti-Hungarian demonstrations were held at the site of the former Romanian
People's Assembly. At the May Day festivities in 1868 a student in the
senior year at the secondary school of Belényes tore up the Hungarian
flag. At the same time the Romanian students at Brassó deployed
under the Romanian flag for the May Day parade. Besides these acts
of lesser significance the irredentist and anti-Hungarian character of the
Romanian secondary schools was revealed in its true colors by the
demonstrations of 1878. That year the Romanian army captured the
fort of Plevna from the Turks, and following the Congress of Berlin,
Romania became a completely independent state.

The satisfaction of the Romanians was extreme. The teenagers
particularly in the counties of southern Transylvania such as Brassó,
Szeben, and Balázsfalva, actually expected the Romanian army to march
into Transylvania at any moment. They believed that after the capture
of Plevna the Romanian troops would turn about and capture Transylvania as well. All of Balázsfalva became a single army of demonstra-
tors, with students and teachers in the lead. At Naszód the faculty of
the Romanian secondary school organized even more impressive
demonstrations. The faculty and students, along with the municipal
employees, all of whom were Romanian, marched up and down the
streets singing Romanian national songs. Then the teachers addressed
speeches exhorting the Romanian masses. Two of the teachers from

Naszód, Dr. P. A. Alessi and Massimu Popu, even wrote a book about the Russo-Turco-Romanian war. The book was published in Graz, Austria, as a matter of precaution, undoubtedly because it contained very sharp attacks against the Hungarians. Indeed, Hungarian public opinion was pro-Turkish. "The Hungarians exhibit unconcealed feelings of sympathy towards the Turks, to whom they are related by their Asian origins, their barbarism, and the tyranny they manifest towards the subjugated nations," wrote the two Romanian intellectuals living on Hungarian territory.[130]

Thus the idea of a Greater Romania dominated the atmosphere of the Romanian secondary schools. Since at that time the Hungarian government did not even require the teaching of Hungarian as a second language (this would take place only in 1883, in the 16th year of Hungarian rule), it was not taken seriously in any of the Romanian secondary schools. It was taught, but mostly for the sake of appearances, if not in outright mockery. "Hungarian represented no danger to us, since we never really studied it," wrote Gheorghe Bogdan-Duica, professor at the University of Kolozsvár, after World War I. "For weeks on end we tortured the item entitled 'The Poor Miserable Hare' as the author of the book and our swarthy Professor Feneşanu knew well; although his face was black, he was a good man."[131] Thus the Hungarian language caused no serious worry to the faculty or students of the Romanian secondary school at Brassó. At Balázsfalva the situation was pretty much the same. At Belényes the superintendent of the school district of Nagyvárad noted this neglect of the Hungarian language during his visit in the academic year 1874/75. Since the Uniate bishop of Nagyvárad, the patron of the institution, as well as the school itself received assistance from the educational fund, the superintendent recommended to the ministry that, for the sake of teaching Hungarian effectively, he should decree that some subjects be taught in Hungarian. The Minister of Religious Affairs and Education communicated the opinion of the superintendent to the Bishop who, in his circular 1.277 of November 14, 1875, took steps regarding the teaching of history and geography in Hungarian, retaining free use of the Romanian language. Thus, even before the Secondary School Act of 1883 stronger state control prevailed and more room was made for the teaching of Hungarian at the school of Belényes than in the other Romanian secondary schools.

The Secondary School Act of 1883

Under the impact of the provisions of Act XXX of 1883 the Romanian secondary schools of Hungary began to function more uniformly. This Act, dealing with "the secondary schools and the preparation of their faculty" regulated in detail, the operation of secondary schools where the language of instruction was not Hungarian. Articles 7 and 8 of the Act were the most relevant. According to Article 7:

> The denominations have the right to decide the language of instruction in the secondary schools they sponsor. If this language is not Hungarian, they are required, in addition to teaching the language of instruction and its literature, to provide for the teaching of Hungarian language and literature as well in sufficient contact hours to enable the students to master these subjects. They will submit to the Minister of Religious Affairs and Education the syllabus and schedules pertaining to the teaching of the Hungarian language and literary history, in order to facilitate control. In secondary schools where Hungarian is not the language of instruction, Hungarian language and literary history will be taught in Hungarian in the junior and senior years, and the graduation examination in these subjects will also be administered in Hungarian. As regards this final examination, the provision of the law will enter into effect with the examinations of 1885.

The provisions of Article 8 regulated the extent to which the schools retained autonomy:

> At the educational institutions sponsored by the churches the final objective in each course and the extent of knowledge to be imparted, as well as the methods of instruction, the curriculum, and the textbooks will be determined by the authorities of the denomination who, in each case, will submit these to the Minister of Religious Affairs and Education. The number of contact hours they determine, however, may be no less than the number applied at the institutions directly under the jurisdiction and direction of the Minister of Religious Affairs and Education; this constitutes merely a minimum standard for the denominational schools.

Other provisions of the Act dealt with disciplinary matters applying to students and teachers, the conditions for obtaining state subsidies, as well as the modalities of state supervision. In the denominational schools the disciplinary measures regarding students and teachers, as well as the procedures and regulations, were to be determined by the church officials. They were required, however, to submit these and any modifications thereto to the Minister of Religious Affairs and Education for acknowledgement. Supervision was carried out throughout the school districts by the superintendents or by special commissioners sent out from the Ministry. The Minister would examine the textbooks selected and, could confiscate them if warranted. He would ensure that the school funds are appropriately spent. Article 72 of the Act prohibited the secondary schools from accepting donations from foreign states, their rulers or governments.

Of course, the officials of the Romanian churches in Hungary, the Romanian press, and other Romanian entities protested vigorously against the Act. They protested even before the Act was passed. "Is Herod enraged once again? Does he demand Ion's head?" the great Romanian church and school periodical quoted Chrysostom as masthead to the article denouncing the new law. Presumably Herod was the Hungarian state which strove to integrate by this Act the Romanian secondary schools, the head of Romanian nationalism, i.e. the head of John the Baptist, into the educational system of the country. Roman Miron, the Orthodox archbishop of Nagyszeben, protested against the law in the name of the church because, as he said, "the church has always been the defender and shield of Romanian language and nationality." He objected to taking the preparation of the faculty out of the hands of the church, moreover to the right now granted to the state to intervene in the denominational secondary schools.[132]

Protests against the Act appeared not only in the press, but at mass rallies as well. Members of the Romanian intelligentsia organized protest rallies at Arad, Balázsfalva, and Brassó, making sharp sallies against this more recent measure of "Hungarianization." Five Romanian members of parliament, however, sent an open letter to the Romanian voters to reassure them and appeal to them not to hold meetings of protest against the law, because there was no cause for alarm. The desires of the nationalities are taken into consideration in the house of parliament, "and as for our nationality, this law represents no danger to it," they asserted.[133]

The implementation of the law bore out these statements of the Romanian members of parliament. The Romanian protests had been directed not so much against the teaching of Hungarian language and

literature, but rather against state control and against the preparation
of the faculty at Hungarian universities. As we have seen, Hungarian
language was already part of the curriculum, even if not taken in
earnest. The new thing about the law, that Hungarian language and
literature were to be taught in Hungarian in the junior and senior years
of high school, and that the final examination would be administered in
Hungarian as well, amounted to no extraordinary burden, particularly
if the results were assessed fairly. The Romanians knew from experience that everything depended on the supervision. They could not know
aforehand whether this supervision would be stricter than in the past.
Their conscience bothered them some because they knew right well that
a thorough, strict, or perhaps antagonistic state control would quickly
ruin the Romanian secondary schools; a thorough investigation would
have easily revealed the assistance the schools were receiving from
Romania, the secret irredentist contacts, as well as the anti-Hungarian
ideas entertained by Romanian students and faculties. It was understandable, therefore, that the section of the Act regarding state
supervision made them feel nervous.

As soon as the first set of examinations administered by state
entities was over the spirits were gradually calmed. The visits by
officials had an unexpectedly positive impact. This impact was
particularly apparent in the evolution of the secondary school at Brád,
which was surviving under impoverished circumstances. The intervention of Hungarian controllers resulted in improvements. "Visits were
carried out with good will and conscientiously," we may read in this
regard, and they "exerted a beneficial influence on the development of
the secondary school at Brád." According to the report by the delegate
from the Hungarian ministry, superintendent Veres from Nagyszeben
who visited the school for the first time in the academic year 1886/87:

> neither the number, nor the preparation of the faculty, nor their
> salary, met the stipulations of the law. The next inspector
> succeeded, thanks to his well intentioned advice and his personal
> intervention, in achieving that the board of the secondary school
> carry out the improvements required by the spirit of the
> times.[134]

Of course, where the inspection revealed anti-state activities there
were consequences, as in the case of the Uniate secondary school of
Belényes. On June 1 and 2, 1888, Lőrinc Schlauch, the Roman Catholic
bishop of Nagyvárad, visited Belényes to administer the sacrament of
confirmation. All public buildings, including the Uniate Romanian

The center of the cultural life of all people (i.e. the Romanians) is naturally to be found in Romania. The same paper a few month later noted:

> We have never made a secret of our love for our brothers across the Carpathians, nor the satisfaction with which we noted the growing power of the Romanian state, the state which, in final analysis, constitutes the cultural center of attraction for the entire Romanian nation.[145]

This being the situation, the faculties of Romanian high schools in Hungary naturally did everything in their power to disseminate Romanian culture among their students, and this Romanian culture, as we have seen, was basically irredentist, hence anti-Hungarian. According to the Romanian perspective the Romanians, as representatives of the proud Latin race, stood far above the Hungarians. One of the great merits of the Romanian nation was its fight against the barbarians, the Hungarians among them. The most glorious period of Romanian history was the reign of Voivod Mihai Viteazul when he conquered Transylvania and united all three principalities under his rule. The Romanians of Hungary adopted this perception of Romanian history. For years the Romanian press advertised a painting depicting Voivod Mihai's triumphal march into Gyulafehérvár in 1599, with the following caption: "There is no day more glorious in the whole history of the Romanian nation than the day when Mihai Viteazul, having taken Transylvania, marched into Alba Iulia as conqueror and lord of the land."[146]

Romanians assessed the history of the nations of Transylvania strictly from a Romanian nationalist point of view. According to this perspective the Romanian nation of Transylvania was represented as one which, in spite of its noble origins, was groaning under the yoke of the barbarian Hungarians, against whose tyranny it was constantly protesting by means of national uprisings. The completely false view according to which all major Hungarian leaders from King Matthias to Ferenc Deák, along with György Dózsa and Gábor Bethlen were of Romanian descent, was just the logical consequence of this perspective of history, which was considered objective history, and it was taught to the Romanian students even in courses on world or Hungarian history. Of course, this distorted perception did not prevail in Hungarian secondary schools, hence the Romanian press constantly accused the Hungarians of falsifying history. They consistently encouraged Romanian parents to send their children to school at Naszód, Balázsfalva, and Brassó. If not all eight forms, at least children were told to attend the last two forms in some Romanian secondary school where they would "get to know and love Romanian literature, as well as the true history of their own nation."[147]

Indeed, the Romanian secondary schools provided an education in the spirit of a Greater Romania, since their students learnt "the true history of our nation" which, as we have seen, was irredentist and anti-Hungarian. There were ample opportunities within the autonomy granted Romanian schools for this peculiar Greater Romanian "education of the nation" to manifest itself. The right to decide the curriculum was one of these autonomous rights. The school-sponsoring Romanian churches put the curriculum together in such a manner that the number of periods devoted to the various subjects suited the needs of schools with Romanian as the language of instruction. The teachers at these schools taught most subjects in either greater or lesser number of periods than their counterparts in the Hungarian schools. According to the table of comparison provided by Ghibu, only religion, physics, and handwriting were taught in the same number of periods in the Romanian and Hungarian schools at Balázsfalva. In the state school Hungarian language was taught in 30 periods, Latin in 49, Greek in 19, Geography in 10, Natural Science in 8, whereas in the Romanian school only 27 were devoted to Hungarian, 40 to Latin, 13 to Greek, 6 to Geography, and 11 to the Natural Sciences.[148] It is characteristic of the freedom of choice in the Romanian schools that the faculty even had the right to increase the number of periods according to local requirements. For instance, in 1908, the teacher of Greek at the Naszód Romanian secondary school raised the number of periods devoted to Greek in one of the forms from 2 to 4; however, the Romanian students objected, and went on strike for two days to mark their disagreement.[149]

The Hungarian state subsidies accepted in 1906 did not alter the mood of the Romanian secondary schools one iota. "The spirit and atmosphere of our schools, the tendencies of our faculties did not change a bit as a result of the restrictions deriving from the subsidy," noted the editor of the school yearbook at Brassó.[150]

In the years preceding the World War this mood once again found expression, as it had in the past, in the case of the principal Oniţiu. A boyscout troop was formed by some students at the Romanian schools of Brassó in 1912/13. The scout leaders immediately sought contact with the scouts of Romania. They procured the bulletins and publications of the command of the Great Legion of Romanian Boyscouts, because they wanted to organize on the same model. They almost literally followed the basic principle announced in the *Tribuna* thirty years earlier, according to which the Romanians must strive first and foremost not to separate themselves from their brothers in Romania. The scouts from Brassó succeeded in establishing contact with the scouts from Romania in the second year of World War I when the attitude of Romania had become ambiguous and when "the central powers looked upon Romania's neutrality with distrust anyway," wrote Romanian chronicler.[151]

The contacts with Romania established by the Romanian students of Brassó bore fruit in 1916. Romania entered the war and rapidly occupied the counties of Transylvania along the border. Romanian troops entered Brassó. The scouts from the secondary school immediately reported to the commander of the Romanian forces and offered their services. From then on, during the entire period of Romanian occupation, they were most active in maintaining law and order in Brassó. We read in the bulletin that:

> the police kept a close watch on the movements of the foreign population [Hungarian and German] antagonistic to the Romanian army, apprehended the whispering conspirators no matter how circumspect they may have been, and denounced them to those in charge of the supervision of public order.

They carried out the directives issued by city hall and supported their faculties especially, M. Bogdan, Dr. Stinghe Stere, and Papus, who were the first to take an oath of allegiance to Ferdinand I King of Romania.[152]

The Romanian forces were able to hold on to Brassó for only a few months and then had to withdraw from Transylvania. The faculty of the Romanian secondary schools of Brassó was in a serious predicament. During the Romanian occupation the faculty, along with many students, had severely compromised themselves vis-à-vis the returning Hungarian authorities. What would the "barbarian" Hungarians do to them, what would Apponyi do to the schools and their teachers who had carried out the orders issued by the Romanian headquarters so openly and enthusiastically? Tortured by this dilemma and worried about the possible consequences, the principal of the secondary school, Dr. Iosif Blaga, joined the departing Romanian forces and left Hungary along with ten of his colleagues. Of the seventeen professors at the two secondary schools only three, those who felt themselves less compromised, remained at their post. They too probably waited with anxiety: what reprisals would be taken against the schools which, from the

Hungarian point of view, had been hotbeds of treason? Would Apponyi close them down? A few months later the Romanian professors could breathe easier, for Apponyi did not close down the schools; in fact, he helped the new professors, chosen to replace those who had departed for Romania, to receive the state subsidies, which they were able to retain until the collapse of 1918.[153] The schools could continue to operate undisturbed under the aegis of the Hungarian authorities; twenty Romanian students, in the academic year 1916-17 and 28 in 1917-18 received their high school diploma.[154] Judging from these facts, the Hungarian government did not take revenge for the attitude of the professors at the Romanian secondary school of Brassó.

The Students at the Romanian Secondary Schools

No restrictions were imposed on the influence of the Greater Romanian idea prevailing in the Romanian secondary schools of Hungary since, in accordance with the principle of freedom of instruction, anyone could register at these schools. Anyone of any creed, any ethnic group, whether Hungarian, Romanian, German, or Jew, could be admitted to a Romanian secondary school. Consequently one may find students of different religions, nationalities and even from different countries among the student body of the Romanian secondary schools throughout the period of Hungarian rule. What more, certain schools, such as the ones at Brassó and Balázsfalva, became veritable gathering points for Romanian students from different countries. The yearbook of the secondary school at Brassó states:

> Our Romanian cultural institution has acquired a special
> character distinguishing it from other secondary schools because
> of its very geographical location along the old borders and close
> to the nucleus of our race, so that our sons from every area
> inhabited by Romanians may converge to their alma mater... to
> enjoy greater freedom in the compilation of the curriculum and
> the distribution of the subjects. Students from all the Romanian
> provinces come to Brassó where they are not forced to study
> subjects for which they feel no need, such as Hungarian language
> for youths coming from Romania.[155]

These lines were written by Ion Clinciu, a graduate of the Brassó secondary school, who presents his personal experiences regarding the freedom of instruction prevailing in the schools and safeguarded by the laws of Hungary. The yearbooks of the Romanian secondary schools provide ample evidence to indicate that this freedom of instruction prevailed at all schools, without restrictions. According to the yearbook of the secondary school of Brassó, in the academic year 1895/96, the student body included Christian Kertsch from Ploeşti, Adolf Kraushaar from Bucharest, and George Feneki from Breţcu. Among the student body at the Uniate secondary school of Balázsfalva we find Aurel Deac from Poiana Arieş [Aranyospoján], Joan Astalus from Cergăul Mic [Kiscserged], Joan Vasas Cherestes from Santiona, Alexandru Ciachi from Ostrovul Mare [Nagyosztró], Joan Feher from Seplac [Széplak], George Chelemen from Turdaşul Român [Oláhtordos], Alex Csergedi from Blaj [Balázsfalva], Emil Jozon from the same place, Alex Mesaros from Turda, Emil Pataky from Stoiana [Esztény], Ştefan Banfi from Somostelnic [Szamostelke], Ştefan Halmagyi from Comana Inferioara [Alsókomán]. The purely Hungarian sound of the surnames indicates that these students were of Hungarian background, albeit Romanianized. The strictly Romanian transcription of the placenames shows that the administration of the Romanian secondary school enjoyed unlimited editorial freedom. German and Jewish students could attend the Uniate kindergarten of Balázsfalva freely: among them we find Wlwarth, Lőzinger, Szinberg, Trencsiner, Heisikovits, Schmidt, Benedek, Harghes, Hajek, Schramm, Ambrus, and Bartha. Among the student body of the girls' high school we find Amalia Mezei, Ottilia Rics, Emilia Birtolon, Gizella Bretter, Elena Halasz, Ida Simon, Emma Stromayer — all students from other than Romanian background. Indeed, this was the case everywhere. According to the yearbook from 1906-07 there were 61 Orthodox, two "Helvetians," two Jewish and 7 Hungarians in addition to 440 students of the Uniate creed at the secondary school of Balázsfalva. Four of the Romanian students came directly from Romania. In the same year, the 405 students registered at the secondary school of Belényes were divided as follows: 203 Uniate, 143 Orthodox, 16 Roman Catholic, 1 Jewish, 9 from Romania, 1 from Russia, and 1 from Greece. The 88 students at the junior high school included 16 from Romania, but there were also some Hungarians and Jews. Among the 95 students at the Romanian commercial school of Brassó we also find Romanian citizens, altogether 12, and 5 Jews. In that academic year only the Romanian school at Brád had no students from Romania; two students from Romania are mentioned in the yearbook at the Naszód secondary school along with 12 Hungarians, 6 Germans, and 7 Jews among a student body of 276.

The above data provide clear evidence that students of all ethnic backgrounds, languages, and creeds could attend the Romanian secondary schools of Hungary, since the freedom of instruction guaranteed in the Hungarian laws on education was a living reality. Similarly, the freedom to register any student studying at home was a reality. According to the Romanian yearbooks mentioned above there were sixteen such students at Balázsfalva, 9 at Belényes, 6 at the high school in Brassó, 2 at the junior high school, 2 at the commercial school, 7 at Brád, 10 at Naszód. They were examined in the autonomous Romanian secondary schools and provided with state approved certificates much as in the state secondary schools with Hungarian as the language of instruction. The criteria for admittance were defined by the school-sponsoring organization and everybody was admitted who did not create a disturbance for Romanian interests. The state did not intervene in this area at all.

The Romanianization of Hungarian Students

It was generally accepted that Romanian parents who had almost assimilated under the influence of the great masses of Hungarians in areas with a Hungarian majority decided to send their children to Romanian secondary schools. In these schools children not only regained their Romanian identity but were converted into young people with ardent Greater Romanian ideas and embraced anti-Hungarian sentiments. In addition to saving those members of their ethnic group who were in danger of being Hungarianized, they promoted the process of Romanianization of those Hungarians who, after 1850, during the period of Austrian domination, lived in areas with a mixed population. According to the 1906 exhibit of the Romanians from Hungary at the Bucharest fair altogether 309 Hungarian villages had been Romanianized in the counties of Szolnok-Doboka, Torda-Aranyos, Hunyad, Beszterce-Naszód, Arad, Szilágy, and other counties, during the second half of the 19th century.[156] Thus this Romanianization took place mainly under Hungarian rule, altering the ethnic complexion of entire regions. We have seen that as early as 1885 the *Tribuna* gave an account of this process of Romanianization of the Hungarians, noting with satisfaction that "there are villages, and even entire regions, which were not Romanian before, whereas now they are inhabited by purely Romanian people."[157] Among these were the seven Romanian villages of the county of Hunyad which had been Romanianized since the 18th century.[158] Hungarian public opinion and the government were well aware of this. In spite of this neither the Minister of Religious Affairs and Education nor the government as a whole thought of barring the children of such parents from the Romanian secondary schools and forcing them to attend schools with Hungarian as the

language of instruction. The Romanian secondary schools achieved
success in other ways as well. As we have seen, Aurel Deac, Alex
Csergedi, Alexandru Ciachi (Sándor Csáki), Ioan Astalus, and their
companions who, in spite of their Uniate religion, were all of Hungarian
background, could enroll at the Romanian secondary school of Balázsfalva. Their Romanian feelings were reinforced on Hungarian territory
in a secondary school where Romanian was the language of instruction,
under the tutorship of teachers with irredentist feelings who were
receiving a complementary salary from the Hungarian state.

The students at Romanian secondary schools absorbed irredentist
anti-Hungarian ideas not merely from the lectures of their teachers;
their Romanian ethnic consciousness was enhanced in self-improving
circles, thanks to the books available in youth libraries, but mostly
thanks to the Romanian press. According to the 1906-07 yearbook of
the Romanian secondary school of Balázsfalva, "in addition to the
regular meetings, the members of the self-improvement circle read
together, every week for two hours the newspapers and periodicals to
which the circle subscribed." What were these publications like? The
youth library received 14 strictly Romanian political dailies and
periodicals, ten of which came from the Kingdom of Romania. Among
these they had access to Iorga's famous irredentist serial, the *Neamul
Românesc*. In addition to the press products from Romania the library
received, free of charge, the 22 volumes of publications of the Romanian
Academy. Where the youth library did not receive these papers the
students had access to them through the faculty library. It is easy
enough to imagine the impact of these papers, given the tone of extreme
hatred most Romanian journalists evinced towards Hungarians and the
Hungarian state.

The school officials of the Hungarian government did not interfere
with the inner life of the students at Romanian secondary schools.
What newspapers the students read, what gown or cap they wore, etc.
was left entirely up to them. At times the dormitories of the secondary
schools resounded from anti-Hungarian songs. These incidents were
seldom reported to the Minister. But when someone contributed to the
students' boarding expenses, it was brought to the Minister's attention.
According to an item in one Romanian weekly, in 1908 Minister of
Religious Affairs and Education, Count Apponyi sent a letter of
appreciation to Simion Catarig, a Romanian peasant from Naszód, and
to his wife, thanking them for donating 1,000 crowns towards the
boarding of students at Naszód.[159]

The number of Romanian secondary school students did not fluctuate
significantly during the period of Hungarian rule. The student body

came, in general, from the same social strata. The largest number of students, on a steady rise during the last decade and a half of Hungarian rule, attended the high school of Balázsfalva: there were 440 students in the academic year 1906-07, and 559 in 1913-14. In the latter year altogether 149 students took the high school graduation examination in their mother tongue at Brassó, Naszód, and Balázsfalva. The last mentioned alone awarded 64 diplomas. When the enrollment was excessively large, the Romanian secondary schools set up parallel classes for which no prior or *post facto* ministerial authorization was necessary. Judging from the numbers, the Romanian secondary schools were not overcrowded, although the five schools were too few for a total population of almost three million Romanians. Romanian parents often preferred to send their children to Hungarian schools because they felt that the children would surely learn the Hungarian state language there. The best known leaders of Greater Romania after 1918 — Iuliu Maniu, Alexandru Vaida-Voevod, Octavian Goga, Roman Ciorogariu, Miron Cristea — had all completed their secondary studies at Hungarian state or denominational schools. All these facts refute the well-known thesis of Romanian authors regarding forced Hungarianization, i.e. the repression of Romanian feelings among Romanian children. Surely these schools could not have been so aggressive in their Hungarianization if the Romanian students graduating from them included political celebrities so active in Romanian public life.

It is undeniable, however, that the Hungarian government did not encourage the establishment of Romanian secondary schools. After the Compromise, the Romanians attempted to set up a secondary school at Nagysomkút [Şomcuta Mare], and later at Karánsebes, with Romanian as the language of instruction. The government did not oblige and, what was a more serious mistake, it did not set up secondary schools with Romanian as the language of instruction on its own, even though it should have according to the stipulations of Article 17 of the Law on Nationalities. It is obvious that this mistaken educational policy caused the Hungarians more harm than good. Even from a Hungarian point of view it would have been advantageous to set up state secondary schools with Romanian as the language of instruction in which the curriculum, the textbooks, and the faculty would have been selected by the state itself. The Hungarian government hindered the establishment of new schools because it considered the irredentism of the Romanian intelligentsia enough of a threat to the Hungarian state as it was. Moreover, neither the admission of students nor the setting up of parallel classes met with obstacles in the Romanian schools already in existence. Consequently the Romanians could make good use of the institutions that did exist and which granted diplomas, recognized by the state, to quite a few. Nor were there any obstacles to admitting them to secondary schools with Hungarian as the language of instruction. The Romanian teenagers could acquire the knowledge, that is the diploma which certified the acquisition of this knowledge, necessary to enter an institution of higher learning, whether in their mother tongue or in the language of the state. Naturally, the ratio of the Romanian students attending schools with Romanian to those attending schools with Hungarian as the language of instruction varied as time went on. For instance, in the academic year 1911-12, 45% of the 4,256 Romanian secondary school students attended schools with Romanian as the language of instruction as opposed to 55% who attended Hungarian schools.[160] Thus the reproduction of the Romanian intelligentsia was ensured. The members of this intelligentsia prepared for careers in the church at universities with Romanian as the language of instruction, while they attended German or Hungarian universities to prepare for other careers.

Institutions of Higher Learning

From 1867 to 1918 a total of six Romanian theological institutes functioned on Hungarian soil, three were Orthodox and three Uniate. The three Orthodox seminaries were at Szeben, Arad, and Karánsebes. The Uniate institutes at Balázsfalva and Nagyvárad taught in Romanian; the Uniate institute at Szamosújvár taught the seminarians in Latin. The Hungarian state, as we have seen in our chapter on the churches, did not interfere at all with the internal life of the Romanian seminaries, hence Romanian churches enjoyed the greatest autonomy in this area as well. Whether the seminarians needed to study the official language was left entirely up to the church authorities. Indeed, since Romanian church authorities felt no need to have the official language taught, it was not taught at these seminaries during the entire period of Hungarian rule[161]. On the other hand, Romanian language and literature were required subjects.

The Hungarian state contributed financially towards the upkeep of the seminaries. The Orthodox seminaries received financial help from the treasury, whereas the Uniate seminaries received it from the Religious Foundation. In the case of the Uniates the assistance often consisted of scholarships for the students of theology. For instance, each year the Religious Foundation covered completely the tuition of 32 Romanian Uniate seminarians belonging to the diocese of Nagyvárad.[162] Since the diocese of Nagyvárad was able to set up a seminary institute only in the years immediately preceding World War I, the candidates who received scholarships from the Foundation attended Hungarian Catholic seminaries. They were at the center of a great scandal at the Catholic institutions of Nagyvárad and Ungvár in 1912. They refused to sing along or behave in a respectful manner when the country's anthem was sung on the occasion of the national holiday. Since their attitude provoked increasing tension at these institutions the administration expelled them. For weeks and months on end the Romanian press editorialized about the matter, passing over in silence one of the most important factors, namely that these seminarians were studying at state expense as guests at institutions with a Hungarian and Catholic character, where they should have adapted to the traditions of the host institution, if only as a matter of courtesy.

Generally speaking, the Romanian theological institutes were focal points for Romanian ideas. The most important role among them was played by the Orthodox theological institute of Nagyszeben and the Uniate seminary of Balázsfalva. Both promoted the most ardent Greater Romanian ideas. Since the Hungarian government did not apply any kind of pressure on these institutions, there was every opportunity for training the seminarians in an irredentist sense. True to their tradition, the Uniate theologians of Balázsfalva expressed their Greater Romanian feelings at occasional literary soirées. Of course, one item on the program for such a soirée, in early 1902, was the anti-Hungarian march "Awake Romanian from your Slumber" which, as we may read in the Romanian paper, "echoes the feelings not only of the Romanians of Transylvania, but of all oppressed and victimized Romanians."[163] The Orthodox theologians did not lag behind their Uniate counterparts. Similar declarations were occasionally made at the seminaries of Nagyszeben, Karánsebes, and Arad as well. At the end of 1911, for example, the seminarian Stefan Meteş delivered a two-hour lecture at the Orthodox seminary regarding the work of the Romanian historian Nicolae Iorga. Iorga was the best known spokesman of anti-Hungarian Romanian irredentism whose periodical, the *Neamul Românesc*, even the Hungarian government was forced to ban from the country. Of course, Meteş spoke of Iorga with much enthusiasm, pointing out his contributions to the cause of all Romanians, on account of which the Romanians of Hungary should show him particular affection.

There were no Romanian institutions of higher learning on Hungarian territory apart from the seminaries. The Romanians launched a movement for the establishment of a Romanian state university as early as 1848. In 1849, the Austrians had promised to establish such a university at Balázsfalva, but did not keep their promise. Since in 1850 rumor had it that the Austrian government, instead of the Romanian university it had promised, planned to establish a German university at Nagyszeben, the Romanians protested. They declared that the establishment of a German university would constitute a dangerous experiment jeopardizing the development of Romanian national culture and leading to the deculturation of the Romanians.[164] The German university was not set up, but the Austrian government continued to desist from setting up a Romanian one.

After the Compromise, Article 19 of the Law on the Nationalities provided for setting up chairs for teaching the languages spoken in the country and the pertinent literatures. From 1862/63 there was a chair of Romanian language and literature at the University of Budapest, and a similar chair was established at the University of Kolozsvár in 1872, in accordance with the prescriptions of the Law on the Nationalities. The first professor to occupy the chair at Kolozsvár was Gergely Szilasi [Grigoriu Şilaşi] who, in spite of his Hungarian name, was one of the most ardent Romanian nationalists. His counterpart at Budapest and the occupant of the chair until the end of the century was the parliamentary deputy Alexander Roman, a member of the Romanian Academy of Bucharest.

Thus the Romanians of Hungary had no separate university with Romanian as the language of instruction. Romanian students registered either at the Hungarian universities in Kolozsvár and Budapest, or at German-language universities in Vienna or elsewhere. The Romanian students had ample opportunities for cultivating their national sentiments at these institutions.

The situation of the Romanian students at Hungarian universities was marked by a complete lack of restrictions on enrollment, opportunities for free tuition and other expenses, and the freedom to express their national consciousness. Thanks to these three factors the university students of Romanian background flourished at Hungarian and German universities.

Admission to the Hungarian universities of Budapest and Kolozsvár was not restricted. Among the Romanian complaints we find none regarding obstacles to admission, or some kind of a "numerus clausus" applying to the nationalities. One could register without hindrance for courses in the faculty of medicine, of law, or any other faculty. We have seen that in order to qualify as law professor the Romanian candidate had to be certified by a committee created for this specific purpose by the higher church authorities. The Romanian professorial candidates did not have to attend a Hungarian university until 1885, and even then, for a decade after the law entered into effect, they could continue to take their final examination in their mother tongue with the permission of the Minister.[165] In other words, Romanian students preparing to become professors had to take an examination in what was for them a foreign language only from 1893 on, 25 years after the start of Hungarian rule; from then on they were examined on their knowledge of Hungarian as well. Even then, however, the Romanians were able to avoid this easily at the beginning. Most Romanian medical students completed their studies at Vienna, Paris, or even Bucharest, yet could practice medicine freely in Hungary on the basis of their foreign diploma. There was no official impediment to this until 1898, inasmuch as the validity of the diploma obtained abroad was recognized without ado. In 1898 Minister of the Interior, Dezső Perczel, issued a directive requiring the validation of foreign diplomas through an examination administered in Hungarian.[166]

Romanian students seldom complained about bias on the part of the professors at Hungarian universities, nor did they have a reason for so doing. They experienced no problems either at Budapest or at Kolozsvár if they studied; there was no discrimination on account of ethnic background.

Another interesting issue was the financial resources available to Romanian students; were they not hampered in their studies by lack of funds, given the oft-mentioned destitution of the Romanians?

Scholarships for Romanian Students

Financially speaking, the Romanian students had many opportunities available to them. Apart from the slow but steady material improvement of Romanian social strata, the Romanian students coming from a poor home had various scholarships at their disposal. Those of Orthodox faith could rely, first of all, on the enormous financial resources of the Goidu Foundation, whereas the dependents of the Border Guards could rely on the income of the foundation of the border regions of Naszód and Karánsebes, on the banks, the Astra, the churches, the Romanian associations, and sometimes even on state support. Manuil Gojdu was a Romanian attorney born in Nagyvárad who became the governor of the county of Krassó-Szörény in 1861, and judge of the Hungarian Royal Court in 1869. On November 4, 1869, he established a foundation bearing his name and based on his considerable properties, for the benefit of Romanian students of the Orthodox

faith. The real estate property consisted of a building in Budapest on
Király Street, a villa in Rákos, acreage, and valuable stocks. The base
capital of the foundation grew from day to day. On the one hand, the
stocks rose in value, on the other hand the villa at Rákos and the
surrounding garden, required by the state railroads, was appropriated
for 125,000 forints instead of its appraised value of 54,174 forints.[167]
As a result of its rapid rise in value the principal of the foundation
amounted to two million forints by the turn of the century. On January
1, 1907, it was 7.340,317 crowns and 73 fillers, invested in three
buildings in Budapest, one at Nagyvárad, and in valuable stocks.

One third of the income (i.e. interest) from the fund was distributed
in accordance with the will of Gojdu as scholarships to Romanian
students of Orthodox faith. The foundation was administered by
dignitaries of the Romanian Orthodox Church and distinguished secular
personalities. From October 18, 1882, the funds were handled at the see
of Nagyszeben, which became the treasury of the foundation, although
its offices were set up in Budapest. The latter was also the address
where the students had to apply for their scholarship every year by
August 5. Any Romanian student of the Orthodox faith at a primary
of secondary school, but particularly at an institution of higher learning,
who could prove hardship, became eligible to apply. The scholarship
could consist of anywhere between 60 and 500 forints, depending on
which school the student had selected. The scholarships were disbursed
in four installments each year by the bursar at the Budapest office. Not
overmuch was expected from the applicant. The main requirements
were to complete his studies, remain faithful to the Orthodox Church,
and to take courses in Romanian language and literature if these were
offered. Even in case of failure the scholarship was merely suspended.
If the candidate passed the makeup examination he retained his
scholarship. It was withdrawn only if he failed a second time.

Actually, most scholarships went to students attending institutions
of higher learning. Altogether about 3,000 Romanian students received
Gojdu scholarships from the time the Foundation was established to
World War I; and most of the recipients attended a university. In the
academic year 1906-07 the recipients included 30 doctoral students, 58
law students, 20 medical students, 14 in the humanities, 14 technicians,
4 students in forestry, 2 veterinarian students, 12 cadets, 2 studying to
become notaries, 1 student at a general commercial academy, 1 at the
commercial academy in Croatia and, finally, 17 secondary school
students. Hence in the academic year 1906-07 there were 161 university students and 17 high school students receiving scholarships amounting to a total of 71, 786 crowns and 5 fillers.[168]

In addition to the Gojdu Foundation, in the decade and a half preceding World War I, the Central Scholarship Fund of the Naszód border region granted a yearly average of 20 to 22 scholarships to university students, while the Commonwealth of Karánsebes granted scholarships to the same number of students in forestry and other fields. From 1908 the Romanian cultural association Astra provided free room and board to 16 Romanian university students at Kolozsvár, in addition to other scholarships. The sizable sums donated each year by the Romanian banks for so-called cultural purposes added to these opportunities. In 1911, 4.75% of the net profits of the banks, that is 190,504 crowns, were earmarked for cultural purposes,[169] and assistance to university students was one of these purposes. Assistance to university students also came from Romania; some of this was announced openly and disbursed by Romanian organizations, while other help was provided in secret, in a manner and quantities still unknown. For a long time the scholarships offered from Bucharest to Romanian students at Hungarian universities could be announced in the newspapers without any jeopardy. A special association was formed in Bucharest to assist students from Hungary, the very name of which indicated its function: "The Transylvania Company to Help Romanian University Students from Across the Carpathians."[170] This association covered the expenses of many students, in exchange for which the students were told which university to attend. The scholarships and the conditions for applying were announced in Romanian newspapers in Hungary. For instance when a scholarship for a medical student became vacant in June 1885 the association placed an advertisement in the largest Romanian paper in Hungary and called upon students to apply for it. The application had to be sent to Bucharest. Only Romanian students from Hungary were eligible. The successful candidates received a yearly 1,600 lei, and they had to pursue their medical studies at the University of Vienna.[171]

We know from Slavici's autobiography that, in addition to the above association, the Junimea of Romania also gave assistance to Romanian university students from Hungary. Slavici was able to support himself thanks to the stipend provided by Junimea, a monthly 12 pieces of gold, forwarded at first by Eminescu, and later through the intermediary of Jacob Negruzzi. This stipend enabled Slavici to cover the expenses of his studies at the University of Vienna.[172]

To summarize, 200 to 250 Romanian university students received scholarships sufficient to cover their studies (tuition, room, and board) in the years preceding World War I. About the same number may have received greater or lesser stipends from the Romanian associations in

Bucharest, or from the Romanian government itself. For the time being this can only be surmised, on the basis of circumstantial evidence, since specific data is not available given the nature of the subject.

The Hungarian state provided annual scholarships to Romanian seminarians; the Roman Catholic Religious Foundation covered the expenses of 32 seminarians of the Uniate diocese of Nagyvárad and of 15 more from the diocese of Lugos.[173] Each year, upon graduation from an Orthodox theological institute, four theologians could attend a university in the country or abroad, thanks to Hungarian state scholarships.[174]

Thus the needy Romanian university students in Hungary could avail themselves of various kinds of financial opportunities to cover their studies expenses. Their best opportunity came from Romanian society in general, which was becoming more prosperous year after year. The students could overcome their financial difficulties with relative ease and concentrate on completing their studies.

What were the national sentiments of the Romanian students studying at Hungarian universities? To what extent did the Hungarian university have a negative impact on the evolution of their Romanian sentiments? Since most Romanian students pursued their studies at Kolozsvár or Budapest, we will focus on the conditions at these two universities. The University of Vienna lying outside Hungarian jurisdiction, the possibilities open to Romanian students there do not fall within the scope of our investigations.

*The Predicament of Romanian Students at
the University of Kolozsvár*

The predicament of the Romanian students at the Hungarian University of Kolozsvár was naturally more precarious than at Budapest. Kolozs was a largely Romanian county, but the city of Kolozsvár itself was 90% to 95% Hungarian, all the more so since the best known cultural and other institutions of the Hungarians of Transylvania had been located there for centuries. Kolozsvár was viewed as the capital city of the Hungarians of Transylvania because of this as well as on account of its geographical position. Its Hungarian character was underscored by the university established there in 1872. Being the hub of a region that was mainly Romanian, its situation reflected that of Transylvania as a whole. The Hungarian population of Kolozsvár, in the midst of a mainly Romanian county, must have felt as did Hungarians of Transylvania in general, surrounded as they were by a Romanian majority. Therefore the Hungarians of Kolozsvár were quick to react to any manifestation of Romanian nationalism, especially since they were aware of the plans to detach Transylvania to form a Greater Romania.

Under such conditions the predicament of the professor of Romanian language and literature of the University of Kolozsvár was as delicate as that of the Romanian students. This chair was occupied by Gergely Szilasi [Silaşi], who took part in every Romanian movement. In 1873, not long after the opening of the university, he became president of the association protecting the interests of the Romanian apprentices of Kolozsvár.[175] Soon he was able to rally the Romanian students at the university as well: they organized the Julia Literary Society under his guidance and leadership, on a Romanian national basis. Occasionally the society received kudos from the Romanian press, which rendered it suspect to the Hungarian public. Since the mentor and leader of the association was Professor Szilasi [Silaşi] himself, the suspicions aroused by the society reflected on him. For instance, the fact that he delivered a speech in 1876, at the opening session of the Julia, replete with strong Romanian sentiments, was held against him. Moreover, he was criticized for his lectures in Romanian as well, although this was a natural thing. After a warning from the Minister of Religious Affairs and Education, and the Rector of the University, Szilasi realized that the suspicions surrounding his activities derived from his involvement with the Julia Society, hence he resigned from it. But his official resignation did not signify that he was no longer interested in the student organization, and he continued to guide it from behind the scenes. Of course, this could not be kept secret, and only increased the distrust of the Hungarian public towards him. Since both the Julia Society and Szilasi were more circumspect from then on, the excitement gradually abated and, until 1884, Romanian students could cultivate their national sentiments in peace.

The year 1884 brought a most significant turn in Romanian public opinion in Hungary. The Romanian daily *Tribuna* was launched that year with the objective of silencing those Romanians who were inclined to appease the Hungarians and, moreover, of preparing ideologically for the union of the Romanians of Hungary with those of Romania. The irredentist leaders of young Romanians had decided to launch the paper in theory already in 1871 at their mass gathering in Putna [Pûtna]. It was shortly before the Putna gathering that the unification of the Italians and of the Germans had taken place. One of the Romanian organizers, Slavici, noted in connection with the meeting that "the idea that sooner or later all Romanians would unite in a single state was not far-fetched. We were of the opinion that this unification would take place in the natural course of events.... But the main thing was to be prepared for it, as the Italians and the Germans were prepared." The objectives of this preparation were served by the daily *Tribuna* whose aim was to establish the cultural unity of Romanians as a necessary prerequisite for a political union.[176]

The *Tribuna* was one outcome of the struggles at Putna; it was launched on April 26, 1884, at Nagyszeben. From the very first it struck such an aggressively anti-Hungarian tone that both Hungarian and Romanian readers had to harken. In Kolozsvár, so important to the evolution of Hungarian opinion in Transylvania, the Hungarian university students naturally rattled by the tone and demands of the newspaper. The paper demanded autonomy for Transylvania, cursed the Hungarians for having "turned back into barbarism" one part of the country (Transylvania) since 1867,[177] and boldly agreed with the Saxon observation according to which young Romanians were "brought up with an anti-state mentality".[178] It strove to enhance the anti-Hungarian feelings of the Romanians with every stroke of the pen. Nor was this difficult to accomplish: Romanians read the news published in the *Tribuna* with growing interest, and soon one Romanian from Kolozsvár began to correspond about local matters in the daily from Nagyszeben. At the same time, among the books advertised by *Tribuna* was one by Szilasi [Silaşi], in which the Romanian professor of the Hungarian University of Kolozsvár attempted to refute the arguments of Hungarian scholars.[179] All this drew the attention of the Hungarian students to the activities of Szilasi and of the Julia Society once again. It took but one spark to set the place on fire, and this spark was provided by the preparations of the Romanians of Kolozsvár for the celebration of May 14.

In the evening of May 14, 1884, university students and leaders of the local intelligentsia gathered at the Hotel Biasini to commemorate the events of May 15, 1848, the day Romanians met in Balázsfalva to declare the autonomy of Transylvania. As a consequence of this declaration the Romanians seized arms against the Hungarian regime of the time, on the side of the Habsburgs. Now, on the eve of May 15, 1884, the students planned to commemorate the day of the mass rally at Balázsfalva. They had commemorated this day on previous occasions, without the Hungarians becoming particularly aroused; but at the beginning of 1884 the *Tribuna* with its provocatively anti-Hungarian tone constituted a fresh sensation. When correspondents from Kolozsvár began to publish in the paper as well, the Hungarian university students, regarding this as a provocation, began to demonstrate. In the evening of May 14, a sizable crowd of Hungarian students marched to the apartment of Professor Szilasi [Silaşi], the former leader of the Young Romanians, and protested noisily. They protested against the Julia Society, then against the Romanians celebrating at the Hotel Biasini, then once again they wanted to return to Szilasi's apartment, but were prevented from doing so by the police. These demonstrations lasted for days and, on one occasion, the Hungarian students ceremonially set an issue of the *Tribuna* on fire, in the middle of the marketplace. Finally, both the police and the council of the University took measures against the organizers of the protest, and order was restored.[180]

As a consequence of the demonstrations, however, the Julia Society and Professor Szilasi, became even more objects of suspicion. This led to the dissolution of the society in 1884, whereas Professor Szilasi, who had taught for 14 years, was sent into retirement. Thus the Hungarian youth of Kolozsvár and the Hungarian public in general regarded the Julia Society as anti-Hungarian, demanding its dissolution. This demand is best explained by the anti-Hungarian behavior of the Romanian students which, to put it mildly, was inconsiderate. The Hungarian public accused the Romanian students of anti-Hungarian and anti-state activities, and the validity of these charges was confirmed, among other things, by the attitude of the Romanian students at the time of the Memorandum trial.

In 1894 the Hungarian state attorney's office sued those Romanian leaders who, while Hungarian citizens, had rejected the constitution two years earlier by sending their writ of accusation against the Hungarians to the Emperor of Austria; this memorandum was also eventually published in the press. The Romanian students at the University of Kolozsvár embarked upon political action of considerable significance. Although the ground rules of the university, barred students from engaging in political struggles they issued a proclamation, appealing to the people to express solidarity with those accused at the trial, whose cause was their own cause. The authors of the proclamation also instructed the people of the neighboring Romanian villages to come to Kolozsvár on the day of the court proceedings *en masse* and show their solidarity towards the accused. Furthermore, they instructed the people of more distant communities to send delegations at the expense of the community. Moreover, every Romanian village was to draft a statement of unity and encouragement and send it to the accused, copies of which were to reach the editorial offices of the *Tribuna*. The clergy of the two Romanian churches were asked to explain the meaning of the Memorandum trial to the Romanian people on the Sunday of St. Thomas during mass, beseeching God to promote the cause of justice.

Armed with the above proclamation the 42 Romanian students of the University of Kolozsvár set out to agitate among the people of the Romanian villages in the vicinity of the city. The Romanian press published enthusiastic communiqués about the success of their enterprise, forcing the administration of the University to take disciplinary action; the council of the university barred the Romanian students from taking the examinations, on the basis of Articles 80 through 94 of the ground rules. Then the students affected appealed to the Hungarian Minister of Religious Affairs and Education. On the intervention of Prime Minister Dezső Bánffy, their appeal was allowed, the rights of the University students restored, and the disciplinary action halted.[181]

The dissolution of the Julia Society did not put a stop to the self-improvement of the Romanian students in a nationalist direction. Nor was this the main purpose of the order to dissolve, but rather to put a stop to the anti-state and anti-Hungarian agitation. Soon, however, a new formation replaced the dissolved organization: as one of the Romanian deputy ministers recalled after the war, the Romanian students at Kolozsvár found the means "to set up their organization once again in secret, in the guise of the 'Romanian Casino' of Kolozsvár."[182] The new association was of course more dangerous from a Hungarian point of view, because it operated secretly and could not be monitored.

In the decades preceding World War I, the Romanian students at the University of Kolozsvár lived their Romanian national life without serious conflict. They met regularly at the Romanian Casino to discuss their national affairs and reinforce their national consciousness. They spoke Romanian amongst themselves on the street, at social gatherings, and within the university. Occasionally some Hungarian student objected to the use of Romanian, especially if it was spoken loudly and demonstratively, and this may have resulted in greater or lesser confrontations. For instance, in 1911, some Romanian students were speaking their language and reading a Romanian newspaper in one of the classrooms. In line with the tone of the Romanian press at the time, they used strong epithets to characterize the Hungarian state. One of the students, a "Jewish-Hungarian" according to our Romanian source, objected to the loud Romanian speech and the reading of the Romanian newspaper. Words were exchanged, leading to an argument and to a general fight. The Romanian students were beaten, and the Hungarian students demanded that the university administration forbid the use of Romanian on the campus. The administration did not comply with the request of the Hungarian students. The provost summoned the

Hungarian students who had participated in the fight, scolded them severely, and praised the Romanians, saying: "You have shown that you are aware of your rights; and you cannot be faulted for defending them; I will not allow any attack upon those rights."[183]

The Romanian Students at the University of Budapest

While at the University of Kolozsvár the relationship between Romanian and Hungarian students became tense on account of the general situation in Transylvania, the atmosphere at the University of Budapest was calmer. Since Budapest was cosmopolitan, the national movements of the Romanian youths aroused but mild interest. Moreover, the Romanian students behaved less demonstratively in the capital city of Hungary. The first professor of Romanian language and literature at the University was the member of parliament and editor Alexandru Roman who led an active struggle against the Hungarians and on behalf of the Romanians both in the press and in the House of Parliament. He demanded autonomy for Transylvania on several occasions and, in the years following the Compromise, fought passionately for the federalization of the Monarchy, intent on changing the constitution. He was sentenced to one year in jail in 1870 for agitation against the constitution. He sat out his sentence at the prison in Vác, where he fell ill. The Hungarian Minister of Justice, Boldizsár Horváth, granted him a furlough of six weeks from the prison to enable him to restore his health.[184] After his release he continued to function as a professor at the university. His sentence and prison term were not held against him either by the administration of the university or by the Minister of Religious Affairs and Education as incompatible with his professorship. In fact, he was granted tenure in 1872. From then on he carried out his functions as the professor of Romanian language and literature undisturbed until the end of his life.[185]

The Romanian students at the University of Budapest expressed their national sentiments in their reading club, the Petru Maior. The club was founded during the Austrian autocratic regime, before the Compromise of 1867. Its ground rules, however, were not ratified by the Board of the University. After the Compromise the students submitted their request for approval to the Minister of Religious Affairs and Education. Their first application was denied because Article 5 of their ground rules stated that non-university students could be admitted as regular members of the club. The Hungarian ministry stipulated that this article be deleted. The leaders of the club eventually complied, and the modified ground rules were ratified by the Minister on January 29,

1873. From then until the Memorandum trial the club functioned in peace. The members published a paper, held reading sessions, and discussed all the implications of the Romanian question at their meetings. In the academic year 1891-92 the club published Ghiță Pop's work, *Horia*, in which the author praised the hero of the peasant rebellion on 1784. Gradually the Romanian students drifted into Romanian political movements. They held readings and debates with political contents not only in the club room, but even in the private rooms of some restaurants. In the tense situation which prevailed after the Memorandum trial, this activity of the club did create some stir. Hence the Hungarian Minister of the Interior suspended the activities of the club by his directive 17-24 of December 29, 1895, and ordered an investigation to determine to what extent the club had overstepped the objectives and boundaries defined in its ground rules.

The investigation revealed the facts mentioned above, and for a while the Ministry of the Interior hesitated about whether to authorize the club to resume its activities. Finally, in view of the mood of conciliation which prevailed at the time in Hungarian domestic affairs, he withdrew his suspension on July 9, 1896, and the club could begin to function under new rules.[186]

The club was typical of Romanian national movements before 1918. Closed to Hungarians, its irredentism was often in the open, manifesting itself in disguised animosity towards the Hungarian state, as on the occasion of its fiftieth anniversary, celebrated in April 1912: the activities of the club were praised in exalted language in the presence of Romanians from Vienna, Czernowitz [Cernăuți], and other cities. Its true objectives were expressed openly by one of its members at the Second Congress of Romanian Students held in Craiova in September 1912. Delegates sent by Romanian students in the neighboring lands participated at the congress. The university students in Hungary were represented by Vasile Stoica from the University of Budapest. According to the press Stoica delivered a long speech praising the work of the Romanian university students of Hungary and comparing the Petru Maior to the Romanian student association of Vienna, the România Jună. In his conclusion he expressed the expectation that "our dream, the union of all Romanians, will become reality much sooner than we think."[187] At that time Vasile Stoica was the president of the Petru Maior.[188] The club had a three-room library and 146 members, a majority of whom (77) were medical students. According to the semester report of the club, its objective was "to keep alive love for the nation and, in this connection, to bring about the union of souls of all Romanians."[189]

Thus the Petru Maior faithfully embodied the Romanian irredentist spirit of the students at the University of Budapest to the end. Other Romanian residents of Budapest helped in this endeavor. While Romanian public opinion regarded Professor Siegescu, who occupied the chair of Romanian language and literature, as a renegade, the assistant professor at the University, Dr. Iosif Popovici, enjoyed the complete trust of the students. He was one of the spiritual mentors of the club.

Before the millenary celebration there was yet another Romanian professor at the University of Budapest. This was the distinguished professor Victor Babeş, the well-known Romanian bacteriologist, who had a chair and a laboratory. In 1887 he was invited to teach at the University of Bucharest. His departure was deplored in some Romanian circles, but others felt it was absolutely necessary. Slavici, the editor-in-chief of the *Tribuna*, declared that as far as he was concerned, this was a matter of principle: Babeş could not remain at Budapest, he had to move to Romania, otherwise he could no longer be regarded as a Romanian. "Although he has a chair and a laboratory at Budapest, the hub of Romanian life is in Bucharest, hence he has no choice."[190] Naturally, as long as he stayed at the University of Budapest, Babeş had been a role model for the Romanian students there.

During the whole period, the students of Romanian ethnic background at the University of Budapest were able to edify each other within a club formed on an ethnic basis and prepare themselves for whatever calling they expected to fill in Romanian society. The Hungarian university authorities did not interfere with the operation of the club which, except for a brief interruption in 1896, remained open up until the collapse in 1918.

Summary

Surveying the broad evolution of Romanian schools in Hungary the reader can form an interesting picture. As we have seen, the Romanian students of Hungary could acquire Romanian culture at all levels in their own primary and at a few secondary schools, as well as the completely independent theological seminaries; whereas students at Hungarian universities could acquire it in their own national clubs, taking over and building upon the culture of the preceding generation. Since freedom of instruction was never impinged upon, students could register wherever they wished and study in their mother tongue without hindrance. The new Romanians (i.e. originally Hungarians) also had the right to retain their freshly acquired national identity for their children; that is, the right to Romanianize or assimilate was not denied on the territory of the Hungarian state. In villages with a mixed population the Hungarian minority continued to merge into Romanian society. Although Article 18 of the Apponyi Act XXVII of 1907 did provide for instruction in Hungarian to Hungarian children, this provision, as we noted, was not carried out.

The Romanian schools were supported partly from the financial resources of Romanian social classes, partly by open or secret donations from Romania, or by assistance from the Hungarian state. In exchange for state support the primary schools were obliged to offer five subjects in accordance with the syllabus provided by the Ministry of Religious Affairs and Education, albeit in the mother tongue of the students, whereas state support for the secondary schools did not entail any similar obligation.

For a long time the teachers and professors could continue to function without interference by Hungarian officials. In spite of their irredentist and anti-Hungarian attitude the educators received state subsidies and enjoyed rights equal to those of their Hungarian colleagues.

By the Acts of 1879, 1883, and 1907 the Hungarians state provided for teaching of Hungarian as a subject in the primary and secondary schools. The first Act was fully implemented only after 1907, and even then its provisions were applied strictly only until 1913. Thereafter Hungarian was taught less and less in the Romanian schools.

Primary, secondary, and higher Romanian institutions spread irredentist and anti-Hungarian ideas to all strata of Romanian society throughout the period of Hungarian rule. The Hungarian state prescribed the teaching of Hungarian in order to curtail and prevent the spread of these ideas, and this led the state to commit mistakes. The most obvious of these were: Hungarian as the only language of instruction at state primary schools and vocational schools; the prevention of the establishment of further Romanian secondary schools; instruction at state secondary schools exclusively in Hungarian. Apponyi's Act was meant to weaken anti-Hungarian irredentist ideas, while providing for patriotic education at Romanian schools. This was also the objective of the measure adopted after the Bucharest fair of 1906, according to which the emblem and flag of Hungary were to be displayed at Romanian schools on holidays. Apponyi also fomented the establishment of new state schools without, however, intervening aggressively in the competition between Romanian denominational and Hungarian state schools.

The measures adopted did not achieve the goal on maintaining the Hungarian state or defending its concept. Because of the clever propaganda mounted by the Romanian media the measures taken by Apponyi appeared, abroad, as if they had been adopted for the sake of crude and aggressive Hungarianization. While the Romanians carried on such a clever struggle against Apponyi's measures, they knew right well that the Romanians were culturally far worse off in all the neighboring countries. There was not a single school with Romanian as the language of instruction in Serbia, Bulgaria, or Russia. Moreover, the Romanian press did report on the measures adopted by Germany to force Poles and Frenchmen to study only in German.[191] German school officials insisted that even religious instruction must be given in German in the Polish schools, while Romania itself resorted to similar methods. Cultural policies in Romania made no allowance for the rights of nationalities who constituted about one sixth of the population of the country, and tried to Romanianize them by instructing them only in Romanian.

While the official language was the language of instruction in almost every country, there were Romanian schools in Bukovina under the Austrian regime. In theory the Austrians granted certain rights to these Romanian schools but, as we may read in the situation report provided by one of the Romanian newspapers, Austrian officials went out of their way to repress the Romanian language and to encourage German. Since they operated covertly, with more refined methods, they caused less of a stir than the policies attributed to Apponyi; hence, in the opinion of the author of an article, it was even more dangerous from the Romanian point of view.[192]

Comparing Hungarian educational policies and the Romanian schools of Hungary with the policies of neighboring states and the Romanian school situation there, we are bound to conclude: Hungarian educational policy provided immeasurably greater opportunities for the instruction of Romanians in their mother tongue than the governments of neighboring countries. Because of the irredentist ideas entertained in the Romanian schools, Hungarian officials had to resort to measures which, in the long run, did not achieve their goal, and caused the Hungarians more harm than good.

Romanian Cultural Organizations

In addition to the schools, the cultural needs of Romanian society in Hungary were met by Romanian associations, theatrical performances, and the Romanian press. These three types of institutions preserved, strengthened, and developed Romanian national consciousness among the adult members of Romanian society. The best known associations were Astra, the Romanian National Cultural Association of Arad, the Romanian People's Educational Association of Máramaros, the Progresul Association of Fogaras, and the Romanian Theater Foundation Society. Furthermore, there were about 25 women's associations, 113 choral and music groups, and 33 reading societies (casinos) by 1907. The Romanian press consisted at that time of 49 papers of which 20 were political, 4 social, 6 ecclesiastic and educational, 4 literary, 8 economic, 4 humoristic, and 3 technical. The cause of the theater in Romanian language was served by cultural associations in Hungary and by companies from Romania.

Astra

Astra was the most significant social group of the Romanians of Hungary. Its name was an abbreviation of "Asociaţiunea Transilvană" — the first syllables of the two words. It was founded in 1861, under the Austrian autocratic regime. Ioan Puşcariu, who was to become a judge in the Hungarian Royal Court, took the initiative to set up the association along with the leaders of the two Romanian churches, Andrei Şaguna and Alexandru Sterca-Şuluţiu. Their first application for authorization was rejected by Frederick Lichtenstein, the governor of Transylvania because, as he stated in his response, he could not authorize the creation of a national association since the "projected association... would serve exclusively nationalist purposes by which the Romanians would quite openly segregate themselves from the other nationalities living alongside them." On the governor's instructions the Romanian organizers of the association modified the ground rules: according to Article 4, persons of any creed or nation could now join. The ground rules were finally approved. According to Article 2, the objectives of the association were "the promotion of the culture of the Romanian people in every field, by the elaboration and publication of studies, awards in various scholarly and artistic disciplines, scholarships, and similar means." Already at the time of formation the general assembly of the association elected, as its first honorary members, distinguished personalities from Moldavia, Wallachia, and Bucharest. Among them we find Simion Bărnutiu, a professor from Iaşi, Prince Bibescu Brâncovan, Dr. Petru Câmpean, a resident of Berlin, A. Tr. Lăureanu, a university professor from Bucharest, Ioan Maiorescu, also a professor from Bucharest, Dr. Ilarion Papiu, secretary of state from Moldavia, a few Hungarians and, in general, all those credited with some special contribution to Romanian culture. Maiorescu, Lăureanu, and Papiu were all aware of the plans which cropped up since 1848, even officially at times regarding the unification of Transylvania with the two Romanian principalities.

The work of the association consolidated during the first years of the Hungarian regime, and expanded freely; its impact was soon felt by all Romanians of Hungary. At the beginning it had but three sections, and these sections had some difficulty getting off the ground. The jurisdiction of these sections was decided at the general meeting at Balázsfalva in 1877, but it was not until after 1895 that they began to function effectively. Later, particularly after the turn of the century, Astra had five sections, namely 1) literary, 2) historical, 3) scientific, 4) educational, and 5) economic, each of which had a specific task. The literary section set up public libraries and printed popular editions. It also concerned itself with Romanian orthography and made proposals to the Romanian academy regarding standardizing the spelling of Romanian words. On the basis of this proposal the Romanian Academy did, indeed, pronounce on the rules of Romanian orthography applicable to all Romanians. The historical section also studied the placenames in the Romanian regions of Hungary and, in 1903, announced a competition for a dictionary of geography and toponymy as pertaining to the Romanian counties of Hungary. In 1906 it entrusted Silvestru Moldavan and Nicolae Togan with the compilation of the dictionary, and their collaborative work appeared in 1909.[193] The scientific section organized, from 1903, popular readings with the help of audio-visual aids. The speakers hired projected pictures pertaining to Romanian history and folk culture to Romanian audiences in the towns and villages. For instance, in 1906 Moṭa, the Orthodox deacon of Szászváros, held lectures at the churches of Romanian villages in the vicinity, in the course of which he projected on canvas the portraits of the King and Queen of Romania.[194] The economic section compiled data pertaining to the life style of Romanian peasants in Hungary, and studied the issue of continuing education for peasants. It also dealt with the issues of emigration and socialism and, later, employed a lecturer in economics to discuss development in the villages.

In addition to the operation of these sections, Astra was able to achieve other results as well. It established a secondary school for girls at Nagyszeben. Between 1895 and 1904 it compiled the first encyclopedia in the Romanian language, published in three thick volumes. The project employed 172 paid contributors, 90 of whom were from Romania. By commissioning this encyclopedia, Astra demonstrated that it had greater powers of initiative and more cultural potential than any cultural association in Romania with the exception of the Romanian Academy.

The Romanian National House in Nagyszeben was another achievement of Astra. The construction of the National House had been resolved in 1897. The expenses of its construction were covered by special collections. It was inaugurated on August 19, 1905, at the time of the plenary meeting of the association. On this occasion Astra organized a grand ethnographic, historical, and cultural exhibition on the newly opened premises. It was the artifacts and date from this exhibition that were loaned for the Bucharest fair of 1906 discussed previously.

Astra became increasingly active; after 1907 and its financial footing expanded as well, to over half a million crowns, a sum increased by further donations and funds. The data presented at the plenary meeting held in 1912, just before World War I, revealed an increased appreciation of the work of the association. In 1912 it had 13,022 members, including regular, honorary, founding, contributing, and other kinds. It is typical that most of the contributing members, 115 out of 144, were from Romania. According to the annual report of the select committee there were 67 branches in 1911 which organized altogether 714 popular events attended by 150,000 persons: 218 cultural, social, moral, and religious events, 86 financial, 15 linguistic or literary, 26 industrial or commercial, 29 events dealing with health, and 42 with legal matters. Most speakers were clergymen, teachers, or lawyers. The economic experts of the association delivered 87 popular lectures in 45 communities. Moreover, Astra created two Raffeisen cooperatives, a course in viticulture at Alsópián, and a course in orchardry for clergymen. It organized 18 literacy courses at various branches of the associations attended by 430 illiterate Romanians. Certain branches organized exhibitions. Others distributed several thousand pamphlets among the peasants at the district assemblies of the organization. By the end of 1911 the association could boast of 442 puplic libraries, holding a total of 26,335 volumes. They published popular works for the public libraries, in altogether 15,000 copies in the year 1911. For instance, the publications intended for the youth libraries were printed in 11,961 copies. The library of the association was organized according to the system of the library of the Romanian Academy in Bucharest. By the end of 1911 Astra had 958,587 crowns and 31 fillers in its treasury, including several large contributions donated that year. One significant sum was the 10,000 crowns donated by Vasile Stroescu to establish a library for the benefit of the Romanian students at the University of Kolozsvár.[195]

As the data indicates, the Astra of Hungary provided impressive services on behalf of the cause of Romanian culture in Hungary.

Obviously, such activity and progress could not have taken place under anything but the most propitious circumstances. We cannot help but notice the wonderful opportunities the association enjoyed throughout Hungarian rule. From the time of the Compromise the Hungarian state not only allowed it to organize, but actively supported it. It contributed 400 forints annually and, until 1899, the association accepted this contribution with thanks. That year, at the plenary meeting in Déva, the leaders of the association declared that they will no longer request this assistance, because the state had undoubtedly made this contribution with the ulterior motive of "intervening in our cultural affairs as well."[196]   Nevertheless, immediately before the World War, the economic lecturer of the association accepted financial support from the Minister of Agriculture who assumed the expenses of the course in viticulture at Alsópián.[197]

Thus, in general the Hungarian authorities good naturedly supported the operations and progress of the associations. The ground rules elaborated during the anti-Hungarian Austrian autocratic regime remained in effect unchanged until 1895; the Minister of the Interior did not even inquire about them. In 1895 the ground rules were submitted to the Minister of Religious Affairs and Education in connection with a trial; the Minister, in consultation with the Prime Minister, called upon the central committee of the association to change the name of the association and certain expressions in the ground rules to meet the new requirements of public law. Early in March 1897, at its extraordinary plenary meeting held at Nagyszeben, the association deleted the term "of Transylvania" from its title and, expanding and modifying the ground rules, resubmitted these for approval. The new ground rules were approved as early as August 13, of that year. Consequently Astra could now expand its activities to cover all areas of Hungary inhabited by Romanians. According to Article 2 of the ground rules the objectives of the association became far broader:

...The promotion of education for the Romanian people, especially the initiation of studies and research; the publication of literary, scientific, and artistic works; the establishment of public libraries, museums, and special collections; donations of various scientific, artistic, and industrial awards; grants of scholarships; the organization of exhibitions, public lectures, and readings; the establishment of boarding and other schools, or assistance to those already in existence by organizing departments in various disciplines and providing specialized instructors; moreover, diverse legal ventures to promote the literature and ideas of the Romanians of Hungary, as well as their training in sound economic management.

As we may note from this most extensive set of objectives, the association actually assumed and carried out tasks befitting a scientific and popular Romanian national academy. The impact of its enormous accomplishments on the Romanian population became particularly apparent at the plenary meetings it organized occasionally in one Hungarian town or other. The most memorable of these were the meetings at Nagyszeben in 1905, at Dés in 1910, and at Balázsfalva in 1911. The National House was consecrated at Nagyszeben in 1905. A meeting of great significance from the point of view of the national consciousness of the Romanians of Szolnok-Doboka county was held at Dés in 1910. On this occasion the Hungarians at Dés were most courteous towards Astra, making the auditorium of the county hall available to it. The Hungarians also put up the guests who arrived for the meeting.[198] The Romanian processions at the general meeting of Balázsfalva in 1911 amounted to demonstrations. This was the fiftieth anniversary of the foundation of Astra, and preparations for the meeting had been going on for a whole year. About 6,000 guests took part, including archbishops and leading political figures from Romania, with Nicholae Iorga, the best-known spokesman of anti-Hungarian irredentism in the lead. During the celebration, which lasted three days, "there was no sign of life other than Romanian," according to the offical report. The Hungarian government gracefully contributed to the celebration by ensuring a strictly Romanian framework for it: not a single gendarme was in sight, since the organizers had set up their own police apparatus for the occasion. Even the author of the official publication thanked the government for it, in the name of the organizers, because "during the celebration it was hardly possible to see a gendarme on the streets of Balázsfalva." The celebration did turn out to be a perfectly Romanian national moment.[199]

Occasionally, some local authority refused to grant permission for setting up a branch of the association. On such occasions, however, the Ministry invervened and allowed the appeal, contributing to the implementation of the right to organize, as guaranteed by law. This was the case when Astra set up a branch at Gyergyóbékás [Bicazu Ardelean]. The sheriff rejected the ground rules presented by the branch, and this rejection was upheld by the governor. When the First Secretary of Astra appealed the ban to the Minister, the latter decided in favor of Astra, and the branch did come into being in 1912, on the edge of the land of the Székelys, along the Romanian border.[200]

Apart from these minor incidents the authorities did not hinder the activities of Astra anywhere during the Hungarian period.

The activities of Astra did contribute, in the long run, to the retention of large numbers of Romanians within the fold of national consciousness. According to the revelations published after World War I, its whole work had an irredentist impact on the Romanians of Transylvania. Carol II, King of Romania, remarked during a visit to Blaj [Balázsfalva] in 1936 that "Even fifty years ago this cultural association had erased all boundaries keeping Romanians apart.... Yesterday Astra had prepared the unification."[201]

Other Associations

There were other associations serving Romanian national intersts. Both the Arad association and that of Máramaros were active on behalf of the culture of the Romanian people and for the support of certain strata of Romanian society. We have found no evidence of any Hungarian government measures hampering their activity. Their ground rules were approved by the authorities without undue delay. Even when there was some objection, approval never took longer than one year or two, including the required modifications. The casinos and women's associations also operated on behalf of the above national goals. The inside information about these organizations can come only from Romanian works published after 1920. If the casinos were anything like that of Brassó, then it is clear that extremist irredentist sentiments were given vent even in these cultural institutions. According to the evidence in the general work on the casino at Brassó, the portraits on the walls of the casino as well as the activities of its members testify to the closest collaboration with Romania. It was not the portrait of the ruler of Hungary that was hung on the walls, but that of Carol, the ruler of Romania, with the caption: "The Lord of all Romanians (Domn al românilor)." In addition to the portrait of Carol, the walls of the casino were also adorned with the portaits of Emperor Trajan, Decebal, and particularly that of Voivod Mihai Viteazul, the latter being, as the chronicler says, "the symbol of the unity of the nation." In order to mislead the authorities, the casino officials always emphasized that they were not interested in politics. Yet they constantly dealt in politics, and not only the politics of Hungary but those of Romania too. In 1880, when the attempt to asassinate the Romanian Prime Minister, Ion C. Brătianu, ended in failure, the members of the casino sent him a decorated album to celebrate his escape. In 1894, on the eve of the Memorandum trial, a confidential

nent Romanian theater, yet never pressed hard for its construction, probably because the cause of the Romanian theater was better served by the amateurs or the actors from Bucharest.

The Romanian Press

From the point of view of the national interests of the Romanians of Hungary and their cultural values the Romanian press, without a doubt, played a decisive role. After all, the Romanian press was the real power which controlled and harmonized the Romanians of Hungary, mustering them on behalf of particular Romanian interests. Hence the significance of this press was enormous. The first political weekly was founded in 1838 by a professor from Balázsfalva, Gheorghe Barițiu, in Brassó: this was the famous *Gazeta Transilvaniei.* During the events of 1848, further Romanian weeklies were established, although many of these were but short-lived. The famous organ of the Romanian Orthodox Church, the *Telegraful Român,* came into existence at the beginning of the autocratic regime, whereas further political weeklies were founded towards the end of that period, but not for long. The first Romanian political daily, the *Tribuna,* of Nagyszeben, was launched in 1884.[210] At the same time the *Gazeta Transilvaniei* of Brassó was converted into a daily as well. Thereafter Romanian weeklies and dailies of various types were founded in rapid succession.

All these serial publications gave vent to anti-Hungarian Romanian irredentist ideas more or less in unison. As Iuliu Maniu noted in 1923, "it is mostly to the Romanian press that we owe preservation of our national and political traditions, of our language and culture, and that the spirit of the people could dedicate itself to national demands in the former occupied areas.[211] Of course, all this could not have happened without freedom of the press and the lack of censorship that prevailed in Hungary, as we shall see in the next chapter.

The issue of the financing of the Romanian press in not entirely clear to this day. We know for certain that the expenses of some periodicals were covered by moneys received from Romania. In the case of others we can only suspect this but have no hard evidence. In any case, the history of the Romanian press is in its very infancy. It is certain, however, that many Romanian serials could not have survived merely from subscriptions, hence they had to rely on assistance from the outside. The deficits of the famous *Tribuna* of Nagyszeben were covered by contributions from the Romanian Liberal Party at first, and by the Romanian Conservative Party later.[212] The fines imposed on Romanian journalists as a result of sentences in press trials were also paid thanks to contributions from Romania. Everyone knew that the expenses of the official publications of the Romanian National Party were covered from sums made available by the Romanian government. Romanian financial support could often be determined from the very contents of a paper. For instance, the Bucharest branch of the Romanian Cultural League ordered the popular *Poporul Român* for the Romanians of the counties of Bihar, Szatmár, and Máramaros in 70 copies.[213] Other papers were supported by the Romanian banks, or occasionally a well-to-do Romanian patron. Very few Romanian papers were able to survive from subscriptions. The oft-quoted *Libertatea* of Szászváros may be among the latter; it circulated in over ten thousand copies after ten years of publication, and the popular illustrated magazines, such as the *Foia Interesanta*, were sold in even greater numbers.[214]

These Romanian papers may have been political, cultural, social or economic; as regards the state and the Hungarians, however, they exhibited a rather uniform attitude, determined by Romanian irredentism. Hence they were invariably anti-Hungarian. Although everyone was aware of this, the Hungarian state, as we shall see, guaranteed freedom of the press to all citizens, Romanians included.

The Cultural Policies of the Neighboring States

While the Romanians in Hungary could boast of almost 3,000 Romanian primary schools, half a dozen Romanian secondary schools, a highly developed Romanian nationalist press, and flourishing Romanian associations, the ruling establishment in the neighboring states mercilessly repressed the culture of their minorities. The minorities living in Romania, tsarist Russia, and the Balkan states had practically no opportunity to develop.

Let us first look at the cultural situation of the minorities in the Kingdom of Romania. The Romanian government set up a school system quite different from the system of denominational schools in Hungary. Only instruction in Romanian was available to children of Romanian citizens. The overwhelming majority of schools were uniform public schools with Romanian as the language of instruction. Moreover, the Romanian government contributed to the establishment of certain private schools, of which there were two kinds. The first kind consisted of schools where all instruction was in Romanian. The children of Romanian subjects could also be admitted to these schools which were obliged to go by the curriculum prescribed by the state. The teachers had to have the same preparation as those teaching in state schools.

The other kind of private school was not allowed to enroll children of Romanian subjects. The language of instruction could be other than Romanian, but in addition to Romanian language, geography, and history had to be taught in Romanian and according to the official syllabus. Only native Romanian teachers trained by the state and bearing a license issued by the Romanian Minister of Public Education were authorized to teach these subjects. In these private schools the principal had to demonstrate his preparation and his knowledge of Romanian orally and in writing before assuming his post; he was personally responsible to the authorities for everything that happened in the school.

It is typical of the chauvinism which characterized the cultural policies of the Romanian state that even such highly restricted private schools were not authorized for the benefit of the Hungarian Csángók or the Bulgarians. The children of the Csángók who spoke Hungarian, as well as the children of the Bulgarians of the Dobrudja had to attend primary schools where only Romanian was taught and where Romanian-ization was the primary goal. In 1905 the same consideration prompted the Romanian government to close down the Greek private schools, which had been authorized for the benefit of children of Greek background in the Dogrudja, under false pretenses.

The Romanian government manifested a similar chauvinism when it came to newspapers published in languages other than Romanian. Among the few such newspapers there was one weekly in Hungarian and one in Greek. The Hungarian weekly, published in Bucharest, was Roman Catholic, since the majority of Roman Catholics in Romania came from among the Csángók. The Romanian author Bogdan Petriceicu Hașdeu accused this weekly, in one of his articles, of nationalist bias and of spreading Hungarian nationalist propaganda. After that the Romanian postal services refused to deliver the paper to the subscribers in the Hungarian areas of Moldavia, depriving the Csángók of the opportunity of reading the only paper that appeared in their mother tongue. The weekly published in Greek suffered an even worse fate. The Romanian government closed it down in 1906, without explanation, after which the *Iris* ciould never again be published on Romanian territory. It then moved to Hungary, where its publication encountered no difficulty whatever.[215]

Apart from Hungary and Romania itself, the largest number of Romanians, almost one million, lived in tsarist Russia. Their national culture, however, was subjected to complete Russification. The tsarist regime tolerated no Romanian school or newspaper of any kind in Bessarabia, which had been absorbed into the Russian Empire. "In the whole of contemporary Bessarabia there is not a single Romanian school," wrote the Romanian paper of Hungary in 1912.

> They have no school secular or denominational, state or private whether in the villages or in the towns.... The Russian state does not allow courses in Romanian even at the lowest level in the primary of secondary schools.... They tolerate nothing that might lead to some kind of Moldavian national culture. There is not a single true Romanian daily which might foment Romanian culture or might defend the cause of our brothers.[216]

A few weeks later a daily in Bucharest compared the situation of the Romanians of Hungary with those of Bessarabia. It described the fate of the latter in the darkest colors. It pointed out that there was no common denominator in the situation of the Romanians under Hungarian rule and those under Russian rule. While the struggles of the Romanians in the Austro-Hungarian Monarchy indicate that "they live as a nation," the "silence of the tomb" among the Romanians of tsarist Russia demonstrates their "national apathy."

> It seems a funeral eye-patch covers the Romanian nation in Bessarabia. We do not know their exact numbers. Their complaints do not reach the Romanian press. Their fate cannot be compared with that of the Romanians living in Austria-Hungary. The latter form a large mass that continually develops, economically and culturally. Their national consciousness is as a higher level than that of the Romanians living in free Romania.[217]

Of course, some Romanian experts, university professors or scholars, were aware of the conditions in Bessarabia. The most distinguished among them was Constantin Stere, a Romanian professor from Iaşi born in Bessarabia. In Romanian public opinion he represented those who felt that Russian expansionism was a greater danger than the Hungarian "oppression" which threatened the Romanians living in the Monarchy. From time to time Stere brought the attention of the public to the fate of the Romanians of Russia. As one who had experienced the tsarist regime personally, he had a clear idea of the essence and methods of the Russian nationalities policies. He wrote an interesting article on this subject in January 1913, dealing with the consequences of a possible war involving Russia and Austria-Hungary. The world press, hence the Romanian public, felt the system of alliances would soon clash. Occasionally the Russian press wrote favorably about the national demands for the dissolution of the Monarchy, including the attachment of the Romanians under Hungarian rule to Romania. Stere sharply confronted these Romanian "national prophets" encouraged by the Russian press. "The Romanians of Transylvania," he wrote, "were able to retain their national identity even after a thousand years of Hungarian rule, and can keep struggling with every hope of obtaining victory." But what would be the situation should the Russians win? "The fate of our nation in face of the victorious wave of Pan-Slavism would never be in doubt. Russian language would be introduced in education, administration, and the courts." Forty-five thousand members of the Romanian intelligentsia would be deported to Asia. A deadly silence would prevail all over the country.[218]

The cultural situation of the Romanians in the Balkan states was hardly better than the situation of those in Bessarabia. Close to half a million Romanians lived in Bulgaria and Serbia, 300,000 in Serbia alone. "They do not have a single Romanian school or assembly, wrote the newspaper *Românul* in 1912.[219] The Serbian government will not let them travel to Romania to find work, because they may return harboring Romanian feelings. Romanian feelings and Romanian culture are forbidden to them. "They would be fortunate to live under a regime like the one in Transylvania." The Romanian peasants had often tried to set up Romanian schools, but the Serbian government had always prevented them. In 1896 Covecievici, a Serbian prefect, had launched a witch-hunt against books in Romanian. Whoever was found with a Romanian book in his or her possession was in trouble. These measures were taken to ensure the continued domination of Serbian culture. The Romanian language was described as a gypsy language, and the government intended to eradicate it everywhere. School, church, and administration were turning the Romanians into Serbians. This plan might have succeeded for lack of Romanian cultural tools.[220] All manifestations of Romanian feeling were cruelly repressed. The police of Negotin punished all manifestations of Romanian nationalism by administering beatings. In the village of Isacova "the police maimed a Romanian peasant because they discovered the portraits of King Carol and the Queen in his home."[221] Romanians under Hungarian rule knew well that no harm would befall anyone who hung the portraits of the Romanian ruling couple in their homes.

Summary

The enormous difference separating the national culture of the Romanians of Hungary from the cultural situation of their brothers under Russian, Serbian, or Bulgarian rule is clear from the evidence above. While the Romanians of Russia and of the Balkans could not maintain a single Romanian school, nor publish a single Romanian newspaper, those of Hungary had almost 3,000 primary schools with Romanian as the language of instruction, a flourishing system of secondary schools, and theological seminaries independent of the state. Theoretically, the primary and secondary schools with Romanian as the language of instruction were maintained by the churches. In reality the Romanian banks and social institutions, as well as the Romanian state and well-to-do private citizens made significant sacrifices to assist them. Although Hungarian laws prohibited financial support from abroad, this was often condoned and, in some cases, as in that of the Romanian schools of Brassó, the regular disbursement of such support was promoted by an international agreement.

The Romanians in Hungary needed more Romanian secondary schools and even a university, in proportion to their numbers. The Hungarian state did not help to establish these, because the Romanian primary, secondary, and higher institutions already in existence operated to the end with intensely anti-state and anti-Hungarian ideas. Romanian teachers and professors taught their students to hate the Hungarian state and people, and to feel as if they belonged to Romania. Although the Hungarian government was aware of this, it did not resort to aggressive moves against the Romanian schools. The government introduced the teaching of Hungarian as a requirement only twelve years after the Compromise in the primary schools, and sixteen years after the Compromise in the secondary schools. Hungarian was not taught at all at the Romanian seminaries during the entire period of the Dual Monarchy, even though the Hungarian state made significant contributions towards their upkeep. The faculties of primary and secondary schools did not take the teaching of Hungarian seriously. The Act of 1879 was implemented only under the impact of the Apponyi Laws much later. The stricter prescriptions of these laws, adopted in response to the irredentist demonstration held in Bucharest in 1906, remained dead letters, as did the so-called cultural zone adopted because of the Romanian attack of 1916. These defensive measures aimed at neutralizing aggressive Romanian irredentism proved ineffective and hurt the Hungarian state considerably abroad.

Hungarian education officials allowed hundreds of Romanian teachers completely unfamiliar with the language to pretend to teach it for decades. As late as the decade immediately preceding the World War there were over one hundred teachers who knew not a word of Hungarian. In spite of this they benefitted from the rights granted to public school teachers along with their colleagues: they received complementary pay from the state upon request, an identification card entitling them to half-fare on the railroads, and state pensions. Occasionally they were mildly scolded for their Romanian nationalist sentiments, their irredentist or anti-Hungarian behavior, their participation in political movements, but most of them suffered no serious ill consequences.   Even their participation in irredentist manifestations in Bucharest, in 1906, did not elicit severe reprisals. The behavior of the teachers who remained seated during the playing of the national anthem after they had taken the official oath in 1907 likewise remained unpunished. These facts indicate that the adminis-tration was understanding and humane towards Romanian teachers and professors to the end.

The education of students in a Romanian nationalist sense at seminaries and universities was ensured by professors of theology or by Romanian students' associations that were not controlled by the state. The expenses of the students were covered by the Gojdu Foundation with a capital of millions, by scholarships offered by the church or by associations, as well as by aid coming from the Kingdom of Romania. The Romanian seminaries received considerable state support. In spite of this the professors of theology remained just as irredentist in mentality as the teachers at the high schools who also received state subsidies.   The admission of Romanian university students was not restricted by any entrance examination. Their anti-Hungarian attitude was well known.

Romanian adult education was directed by various Romanian associations. The Romanian press was not subjected to censorship. The Astra society, which could carry out its irredentist activities without hindrance in any part of the country inhabited by Romanians, had the greatest impact.

The number of Romanian illiterates in Hungary, a country accused of the oppression of Romanian schools and of Romanian culture in general, was relatively less than in the "free" kingdom of Romania. The first Romanian encyclopedia was published by Romanians of Hungary in Nagyszeben. The Romanians of Hungary appeared at the Bucharest fair of 1906 with twice as many choral groups as the Kingdom of Romania was able to muster.   Hence the Romanians of

302   Sándor Bíró

Hungary were, in many respects, culturally better off than their
counterparts in Romania itself.

Endnotes

1. Ghibu, *Viaţa şi organizaţia*, p. 106.
2. *Ibid.*
3. *Magyar Statisztikai Közlemények* [Hungarian Statistical Bulletin], Vol. 31, p. 30.
4. *Dezbatările Senatului*, Mo. 85/1925, p. 1911.
5. *Biserica şi Şcoala*, 1877, No. 2, p. 10.
6. *A magyar korona országainak mezőgazdasági statisztikája* [Agricultural Statistics of the Kingdom of Hungary] (Budapest, 1897-1900), Vol. IV, 34-41. According to Ghibu there were 1867 Romanian Orthodox registry districts). *Viaţa şi organizaţia*, p. 28.
7. Ghibu, *op. cit.*, p. 108.
8. The printed annual reports of the Hungarian Ministry of Religious Affairs and Education, compared with Ghibu, *op. cit.*, and the same author's *Anuarul pedagogic*, 1913, as well as with the data in *Protocolul Congresului Naţional Bisericesc din Sibiu*, 1916.
9. *Protocolul Congresului Naţional Bisericesc din Sibiu*, 1917, p. 163.
10. *Biserica şi Scoala*, 1878, p. 406.
11. *Libertatea*, 1902, No. 19 and 26.
12. "Şcoala din Feldru" *Revista Bistriţei*, 1908 No. 7.
13. Ghibu, *Viaţa şi organizaţia*, p. 108.
14. "O frumoasă armonie," *Telegraful Român*, 1898, No. 129.
15. "Glas de durere din Secuime," *Libertatea*, 1913, No. 15.
16. "Un dar şcolar," *Telegraful Român*, 1898, No. 109.
17. *Tribuna*, February 10, 1912.
18. "Din Cata," *Libertatea*, 1914, No. 15.
19. *Memoriei prea fericitului Patriarh Miron* (Caransebeş, 1939), p. 16.
20. *Protoculul Congr. Naţ. Bis. Ord. Intrunit din Sibiu, LA 17/30 Julie 1916* (Sibiu: 1917). *Date statistice anuare*, pp. 133 and 163.
21. *Anuarul Statistic al Romániei*, 1924, pp. 11 and 234.
22. *Protocolui*, 1916, pp. 139 and 152.
23. *Protocolui*, 1916, pp. 156-57.
24. *Drapelul*, September 7, 1912.
25. *Ibid.*
26. *Protocolui*, 1916, pp. 142-151. *Raportul general al consist. mistrop. ca senat scolar.*
27. Ghibu, *Viaţa şi organizaţia*, p. 114 ff.
28. *Biserica şi Şcoala*, 1877, p. 98.
29. *Biserica şi Şcoala*, 1879, pp. 50-51.
30. *Ibid.*, 1879, pp. 217-18.
31. "Examinare din limba maghiară," *ibid.*, 1883, No. 39.

32. Barna, *România nemzetiségi politikája*, pp. 62-64.

33. *Revista Bistriței*, October 27, 1906, No. 41.

34. "Școala din Feldru," *Revista Bistriței*, 1908, No. 70.

35. *Revista Bistriței*, March 28, 1908.

36. *Tribuna*, February 10, 1912. See also Jakabffy, *op. cit.*, pp. 96-97.

37. Data in *Protocolul*, 1916, pp. 152-53 (paragraphs 3 and 5).

38. "Suma ajutoarelor la salar," 1916, *ibid.*, p. 153, point 6.

39. Ghibu, *Viața și organizația*, pp. 118-20.

40. *Ibid.*, pp. 120-23.

41. *Tribuna*, October 29, 1885, No. 237.

42. *Biserica și Școala*, 1877, p. 98.

43. "Foaia pedagogică," *Telegraful Român*, 1898, No. 72.

44. "Către țara românească," *Biserica și Școala*, 1878, pp. 406-07.

45. Barna, *op. cit.*, pp. 43-47, based on "Raport asupra proiectului de organizațiune generală a învățământului public."

46. *Képviselőházi Iromànyok* [Parliamentary Documents], 1906-11, No. 442, p. 326.

47. "Unele-altele" in *Libertatea*, 1902, No. 35; and "Ucazul lui Wlassica," in *Libertatea*, 1902, No. 27.

48. *Magyar Statisztikai Közlemények*, Vol. 31, 330.

49. Ion Dariu, *Arion, sau culegere de cânturi naționale spre întrebuințarea tinerimei de ambe sexe* (Brașov, 1881).

50. Ion Dariu, *Carte de cântece pentru tinerimea școlară*, (Brașov, 1900), 168 VIII. The author outlines the method in the preface to the 1881 edition. He recommends that the teacher explain the text to the children before teaching them the melody. The text of the songs quoted may be found under items 1, 11, 21, 32, and 57. Number 21 is "Vivat Romania," no. 28 "La armata română," no. 29 "La România liberă," whereas no 57. is "Să trăiască."

51. Ion Băilă, Trecutul Ardealului," *Adevărul*, March 16, 1929.

52. *Tribuna*, 1885, no. 241.

53. *Biserica și Școala*, 1893, p. 403.

54. "Din viața reuniunilor îvățătorești," *Libertatea*, 1902, No. 31.

55. Both Hungarian and Romanian newspapers of August and September 1906 provide detailed reports on the exhibition. Endre (Barabás) Barna, in his book *Magyar tanulságok a bukaresti kiállításról* [Lessons for Hungary from the Bucharest Fair] (Kolozsvár, 1906), deals with the issue on the basis of the reports in these newpapers, as he does in his other work titled *România nemzetiségi politikája* [The nationalities policy of Romania] (Kolozsvár, 1908). Our data, comes from the survey of the Romanian press in the latter work.

56. "Un vis," *Libertatea*, 1906, No. 44.

57. *Țara*, September 23, 1906, quoted in Barabás, *op. cit.*, p. 168.

58. *Miniszteri indokolás*. *Képviselőházi Iromànyok* [Ministerial Justification. Parliamentary Documents], 1906-11, No. 421, p. 75.

59. *Képviselőházi Napló* [Parlimentary Journal], Vol. VIII, 364-417.

60. *Protocolul*, 1916, pp. 101-103.

61. *Ibid.*, pp. 105-107.

62. "Mormântul lui Iancu incununat," *Libertatea*, 1907, No. 37.

63. "Jurământul învăţătorilor noştri," *ibid*. The author of the article (without a doubt one of the teachers who took the oath) refers to the playing of the anthem as "total impertinence."

64. Barna, *op. cit.*, pp. 68-69.

65. "Dreptul limbii române," *Liberatea*, 1908, No. 12.

66. "Aşa ne bate Dumnezeu," *ibid.*, No. 14.

67. "Osînda nimicită," *Liberatea*, 1910, No. 40.

68. Ghibu, *Şcoala românească*, p. 43.

69. *Protocolul*, pp. 145-46.

70. Ghibu, *Anuarul Pedagogic* (Sibiu: 1913), p. 166.

71. *Ibid.*, p. 169.

72. "Circulară," *Telegraful Român*, August 23-September 10, 1912. In the above circular the holy see placed several issues on the agenda of the convention of the Romanian Orthodox teachers for that year. It included the following instructions for discussing the issue of "The relationship of Romanian to Hungarian in our schools." The former is a language of instruction and a subject, whereas the latter is only a subject. Our schools are not bilingual. The topics pertaining to the Romanian language are not discussed in Hungarian as well. The syllabus of other subjects is to be discussed first in Romanian and in Hungarian only thereafter, during the Hungarian period, in brief abstracts.

73. A Hungarian translation is published in Endre Barabás, *Az erdélyi és magyarországi román egyházak és iskolák élete és szervezete a világháború előtt* [The Life and Organization of Romanian Churches and Schools in Transylvania and Hungary before the World War] (Lugos, n.d.), p. 51.

74. "În atenţiunea învăţătorilor noştri," *Telegraful Român*, September 4/17, 1912.

75. Ghibu, *Viaţa şi organizaţia*, p. 107.

76. *Protocolul*, 1916, p. 154.

77. *Ibid.*, p. 162.

78. Ghibu, *Viaţa şi organizaţia*, pp. 119-120.

79. "Duşmanii şcoalii confesionale din Rodna Veche," *Revista Bistriţei*.

80. Ghibu, *Viaţa şi organizaţia*, pp. 116-17.

81. "Corespondenţa," *Libertatea*, 1909, No. 14.

82. "Lauda comunei româneşti Cata," *Românul*, May 5-April 22, 1912.

83. *Gazeta Transilvaniei*, 1912, No. 150.

84. Ghibu, *Anuarul Pedagogic*, 1913, p. 166, ff.

85. Directive 11.433 of the consistory of the Romanian Orthodox archdiocese of Nagyszeben, dated October 28, 1910. The Hungarian text can be found in Barabás, *op. cit.*, pp. 52-53.

86. "Adunarea generală învăţătorilor din jurul Gherlei," *Românul, 1902, No. 229*.

87. Ghibu, *Şcoala românească*, p. 67.

88. *Ibid.*

89. *Românul*, August 24, 1913. The Hungarian translation can be found in József Pap, *Epizódok a románság politikai életéből* [Episodes from the political life of the Romanians] (Lugoi, 1932), p. 174.

90. "Pajura ungurească zvîrlită în pârâu," *Libertatea*, 1910, No. 8.

91. "Amintiri," *Românul*, June 30, 1912.
92. Ghibu, *Şcoala românească*, pp. 54-67.
93. "Apponyi grăeşte," *Libertatea*, 1907, No. 41.
94. According to M. Gr. Posluşnicu in his *Istoria muzicii la români* (Bucharest: 1900), this composition of Porumbescu was called "the anthem of unification." pp. 455-477.
95. "Raprezentaţiunea în afacerea cu revizuirea art. de lege XXVII din 1907," *Protocolul*, 1916, pp. 95-119. It is published with parallel texts in Romanian and Hungarian as proposed in 1915. The Hungarian text is quoted verbatim in Piroska Magyari, *A magyarországi románok iskolaügye* [The School Issue of the Romanians of Hungary] (Szeged, 1936), pp. 65-74.
96. Lazăr Triteanu, *Şcoala noastră 1850-1916. Zona culturală* (Sibiu, 1919). Extensive excerpts are published in Barabás, *op. cit.*, pp. 55-57. All our data regarding the cultural zone are from this work.
97. Lui Spiru C. Haret, *"Ale tale dintru ale tale."* La împlinirea celor ani (Bucharest, 1911), pp. 96, 100, 103.
98. *Tribuna*, 1884, No. 6.
99. *Ibid.*
100. *Ibid.*, September 29/October 11, 1885, No. 222.
101. *Biserica şi Şcoala*, 1891, p. 317.
102. *Képviselőházi Iromànyok*, 1887-92. Vol. XXII, document 765, p. 59.
103. "Spargerea şcolii de stat din Santindreş," *Libertatea*, 1911, No. 48.
104. "Din Paloş," *Libertatea*, 1913, No. 41.
105. "Din Sîngeorzul roman," *Libertatea*, 1907, No. 50.
106. *Ibid.*
107. "Trădătorii se arată," *Libertatea*, 1908, No. 37.
108. "Oameni rătăciţi," *Libertatea*, 1909, No. 35.
109. "Lucruri slabe," *Libertatea*, 1911, No. 20.
110. Ghibu, *Viaţa şi organizaţia*, pp. 123-24.
111. *Drapelul*, September 7, 1912. In Jakabffy, *op. cit.*, pp. 131-32.
112. Ghibu, *op. cit.*, pp. 111-114; 132-33.
113. *Ibid.*, p. 167.
114. *Dimineaţa*, July 23, 1906. Quoted in Barna, *România nemzetiségi politikája*, p. 127.
115. Ghibu, *Şcoala românească*, p. 83.
116. "Şcoala de moşit în Deva," *Libertatea*, 1903, No. 30.
117. The data are taken from the reports of various schools in different academic years and from the catalogs listing publications in Hungary.
118. Andrei Bârseanu, *Istoria şcoalelor centrale române gr.-or. din Braşov*, 1902, and *Anuarul Liceului Ort. Roman "Andsei Saguna" din Braşov*, 1925.
119. Ghibu, *Şcoalo românească*, pp. 136-48.
120. *Biserica şi Şcoala*, 1883, pp. 65-66.
121. *Anuarul* quoted in Barabás, *Az erdélyi és magyarországi roman egyházak és iskolák*, pp. 32-38.
122. "O întîmpinare," *Libertatea*, 1906, No. 51.
123. Ghibu, *op. cit.*, p. 80.
124. Slavici, *Românii din Ardeal*, p. 80.

125. Lupeanu's report on the trip to Bucharest by Bariţiu and Cipariu in *Cultura Creştină Revista Lunara*, January 1925.

126. P. P. Panaitescu, "Planurile lui Ioan Câmpineanu pentru unitatea naţională românilor," *Anuarul Institutului de Istorie Naţională* (Cluj, 1924-25) Vol. III, 63-106.

127. Ion Slavici, *Amintiri* (Bucharest, 1924), p. 47.

128. *Program'a gimnasiului Sup. Gr. Cat. din Blasiu pe a. şcol. 1868-69* (Blasiu, 1869). Under the same title in subsequent years.

129. *Ibid.* In every academic year, including 1875, the title for the two courses was "Geografia Transilvaniei şi a ţărilor învecinate" and "Istoria Transilvaniei şi a ţărilor învecinate." "Geography of Hungary" is first mentioned in the academic year 1875/76, but history was taught from handouts even in that year.

130. Puşcariu, *Răsunetul războiului*, pp. 25-28.

131. "Cronica literară," *Libertatea*, 1903, No. 5.

132. *Biserica şi Şcoala*, 1883, pp. 65-66.

133. "O epistolă," *ibid.*, p. 116.

134. "Gimnaziul român gr.-ort. din. Brad," *Libertatea*, April 12, 1902.

135. *Transilvania, Banatul, Crişana şi Maramureşul, 1918-1928*, Vol. II, 990.

136. Ghibu, *Viaţa şi organizaţia*, p. 136.

137. *Anuarul Liceniui Ortodox Român. "Andrei Şaguna" din Braşov*, 1925, p. XVII.

138. *Ibid.*, p. XVIII.

139. Ghibu, *Viaţa şi organizaţia*, pp. 116-117.

140. *Anuarul*, p. XVII.

141. *Ibid.*, p. XVIII.

142. *Gazeta Transilvaniei*, February 5, 1897, No. 18.

143. I. Colan, *Casina română din Braşov, 1835-1935* (Braşov, 1935), p. 106.

144. *Tribuna*, June 10, 1885, No. 120.

145. *Ibid.*, September 5, 1885, No. 192.

146. "Un frumos tablou," *Unirea*, October 12, 1912.

147. *Libertatea*, August 2, 1902, No. 32.

148. Ghibu, *Viaţa şi organizaţia*, p. 136; Barabás, *op. cit.*, p. 32.

149. *Revista Bistriţei*, 1908, No. 12.

150. *Anuarul*, 1925, XCIV.

151. *Ibid.*, pp. XXIV, XXIX, LXIX.

152. *Ibid.*, p. XCCCI.

153. *Ibid.*, pp. XXIV, XXIX, LXIX.

154. *Ibid.*, p. XCCCI.

155. *Ibid.*, p. 43.

156. This description of the exhibition was published in Barabás, *România nemzetiségi politikája*, pp. 136-137.

157. "Chestiune naţionalităţilor," 1885, No. 240.

158. Puşcariu, *Notiţe*, p. 37.

159. *Revista Bistriţei*, 1908, No. 42.

160. Ghibu, *Şcoala Românească*, pp. 78-79.

161. *Ibid.*, p. 84.

162. *Tribuna*, February 23, 1912.

163. *Tribuna*, December 28, 1911. Quoted in Jakabffy, *op. cit.*, pp. 158-159.

164. Dimitrie Gustie and Emanoil Bucuţă, eds., *Transilvania, Banatul, Crişana şi Maramureşul 1918-1929* (Bucharest, 1929), Vol. II, p. 851.

165. Article 70 of Act XXX, 1883.

166. *Călindarul poporului Român pe 1900* (Sibiu), Vol. XV, p. 95.

167. Puşcariu, *Notiţe*, p. 167.

168. *Analele fundaţiunii Gozsdu*; see also "Ce e românesc în Budapest," *Călindarul Poporului Român pe 1908*, pp. 150-52.

169. *Revista Economică*, April 12, 1913. Jakabffy, *op. cit.*, pp. 199-200.

170. Societatea Transilvania pentru ajutorul studenţilor români din tările de peste Carpaţi.

171. *Tribuna*, June 1/July 1, 1885, No. 138.

172. Slavici, *Lumea prin care am trecut*, p. 75.

173. *Tribuna*, February 23, 1912, and the church summaries of the Uniate Church.

174. Eusebiu Roşca, *Monografia Institutului seminarial teologic-pedagogic. "Andreian,"* (Sibiu, 1911), pp. 249-51.

175. *Observatorul Social-Economic* (1931), p. 322.

176. Slavici, *Admintiri*, p. 115.

177. *Tribuna*, 1884, No. 15.

178. *Ibid.*, No. 13.

179. "Apologie," *Tribuna*, 1884, No. 15-17.

180. These protest demonstrations were reported in No. 17-20 of the *Tribuna*, 1884.

181. Dr. Aurel Maniu, "Memorandiştii," *Cuvântul*, May 16, 1929.

182. Article by under-secretary Ghiţă Pop in *Adevărul*, March 15, 1932.

183. "Au românii drept să vorbească româneşte la universitatea din Cluj?" *Libertatea*, 1911, No. 16.

184. Ion Lupaş, *Contribuţiuni la istoria ziaristicei româneşti ardelene* (Sibiu, 1926), p. 20.

185. Ghibu, *Şcoala românească*, p. 89.

186. Dezső Albrecht, "A román diákmozgalmak története" [The History of Romanian Student Movements], *Magyar Kisebbség*, No. 8, January 16, 1929.

187. Jakabffy, *Adatok*, pp. 132-34.

188. *Românul*, April 12, 1913. Quoted in Jakabffy, *Adatok*, pp. 198-99.

189. *Ibid.*

190. "O chestiune de principiu" in the Foita column of the *Tribuna* 1887, No. 65.

191. "Românii din Basarabia," *Tribuna*, February 29, 1912; *Românul*, 1912, No. 233; "Pilda Polonilor," *Libertatea*, 1906, No. 47.

192. "Germanizarea şcolilor primare din Bucovina," *Românul*, October 18, 1912.

193. Silvestru Moldovan and N. Togan, *Dicţionarul numirilor de localităţi cu propraţiune română din Ungaria* (Sibiu, 1909).

194. "Prelegerile economice," *Libertatea*, 1906, No. 21.

195. Jakabffy, *op. cit.*, pp. 163-73.

308 Sándor Bíró

196. *Călindarul poporului pe 1900*, p. 106.
197. "Economie," *Gazeta Transilvaniei*, October 18, 1912.
198. "Singurul adevăr," *Libertatea*, 1910, No. 39.
199. *Serbările dela Blaj 1911* (Blaj), p. 422.
200. "Scrisoare din Bicaz," *Românul*, March 16, 1912, No. 51.
201. *Foaia Noastră*, September 27, 1936, quoted in Zoltán Tóth, *Az 'Astra' románosító tevékenysége a Székelyföldön* [The Romanianizing Activities of Astra in the Land of the Székelys] (Kolozsvár, 1942), p. 9.
202. Ion Colan, *Casina română din Braşov 1835-1935* (Braşov, 1935), pp. 106-09, 162.
203. Ion Breazu, *Matei Millo în Transilvania şi Bánát 1870*, in, *Fraţilor Alexandru* and Ion I. Lăpedatu, *La împlinirea vârstei de 60. ani* (Bucharest, 1936), p. 202.
204. Slavici, *Românii din Ardeal*, p. 63.
205. "Bârsan oprit şi iarăşi îngăduit," *Libertatea*, 1908, No. 8.
206. "Teatrul Românesc al fruntaşilor artişti din Bucureşti pe la noi," *Libertatea*, 1913, No. 46; and the *Călindarul poporului pe 1914*, p. 88
207. Breazu, *op. cit.*, p. 199.
208. *Călindarul poporului pe 1914*, p. 122.
209. *Ibid.*, 1907, p. 113.
210. This evolution of the Romanian press has been summarized in Sándor Bíró, *A Tribuna és a Magyarországi román közvélemény*.
211. *Aurora*, March 2, 1923.
212. Ion Breazu, "Literatura Tribunei," in, *Dacoromania* VIII, 1934/35, p. 31.
213. *Românul*, February 18, 1912.
214. "Zece ani," *Libertatea*, 1912, No. 1.
215. Barna, *op. cit.*, pp. 17-18. Data regarding the schools are to be found on pages 47-50.
216. "Starea socială a românilor basarabeni," *Românul*, October 30, 1912.
217. *Adevărul*, December 10, 1912. Quoted in Jakabffy, *A románok hazánkban és a román királyságban*, pp. 10-11.
218. "Perspectivele războiului Austro-Rus şi România," *Gazeta Transilvaniei*, 1913, No. 9 and 10.
219. *Românul*, November 3, 1912, No. 233.
220. *Universul*, January 11, 1913. Jakabffy, *Adatok*, pp. 181-82.
221. Românii din Serbia," *Gazeta Transilvaniei*, January 16, 1913.

Chapter V

The Civil Rights of the Romanians of Hungary

Since continuous evolution and change are characteristics of all organic forms, individuals and national communities are also subject to continuous change. The circumstances of the Romanians of Hungary changed from year to year, from decade to decade. Continuous development may be noted in their financial situation, their culture, their relations to the state. In countries dominated by a single nation such changes are often to the detriment of other nations. The nation in control of the state is always inclined to regard its own interests as paramount and to disregard the interests of others. Naturally, the nation that feels oppressed will defend itself against its second-class status and against futher deterioration of its situation. Since the leadership of the state is not in its hands, it cannot defend itself by armed might. Self-defense may be carried out through the individual and civil rights of the citizens. Civilized and truly liberal states have always granted their citizens the right to legal defense against oppression threatening them. Since the French Revolution, these rights are usually referred to as civil or human rights.

Romanians living under Hungarian rule also felt the need to resort continually to defense. According to their perception, the measures adopted by individuals or authorities were directed specifically against them. At such times they resorted to any means available to effect the withdrawal of the harmful measures or obtain compensation for the harm suffered.

What rights did the Romanians of Hungary enjoy? The answer is not to be found in the statute books or the ordinances in print, but rather in what actually took place in practice. It often happens that the practical application of the rights guaranteed by law encounters difficulties when resorted to by a given ethnic group. Therefore, as regards to the rights of the Romanians; the evidence presented in Romanian sources, press reports, and secondary works is most important, for these are the materials from which we may determine the degree to which these rights could be applied. Judging from this material, the Romanians of Hungary actually enjoyed individual

freedom, freedom of the press, freedom of assemble, and freedom of
worship throughout the period of the Dual Monarchy. In addition to the
above rights enjoyed by all citizens of Hungary, the Romanians, as a
separate nationality, enjoyed rights peculiar to their nation. These
rights concerned the use of Romanian national symbols and contact
with Romanians on the other side of the border. In addition, the
Romanians also enjoyed political rights, the right of local autonomy; and
when these rights were curtailed in any way they resorted to the
Hungarian system of justice to defend themselves. The evidence in the
Romanian press indicates that the principle of equal rights applied to
the Romanians as well.

Individual Freedom

This basic freedom was enjoyed by the Romanians of Hungary until
the very end. They had the right to take decisions, to move about freely
on the territory of the state, to reside where they pleased. During the
era of the Dual Monarchy there were no measures, whether it be states
of siege, martial law, forced labor, or quartering of troops in private
homes, limiting the freedom of the individual. Consequently, the
Romanians of Hungary lived in complete freedom as individuals, doing
what they pleased within their homes; they were not troubled by a
police state or other monstrosities threatening individual freedom. We
have found no complaints along these lines in the Romanian press or in
historical works about the Romanians of Hungary.

The Right to Property

The right to private property was completely respected throughout
the period by the Hungarian state. Everyone was free to do as he or she
pleased with his or her property or wealth, within the limits of the law.
These rights were enjoyed not only by individuals but by legal persons
as well. Expropriation was very seldom resorted to, and only when it
was definitely in the public interest. Buildings or estates in private
hands were never expropriated under the guise of any national or state
reason. As regards the Romanians, we know of but one case of
expropriation: the estate of the Gojdu foundation at Rákos. The
foundation owned a villa and adjoining fields, which were expropriated
for the purposes of the Hungarian state railways. Expropriation meant
that the railways purchased the villa and the fields at a price three
times their appraised value. The holdings of the Gojdu foundation
increased considerably as a consequence of this expropriation.[1]

Freedom of the Press

Freedom of the press was the most important and significant of the rights of the Romanians of Hungary. The application of this right was determined primarily by the fact that in the period of the Dual Monarchy, from 1867 to 1918, the institution of prior censorship of the press was unknown in Hungary. This kind of preventive censorship had been practiced by the Austrian authorities with regards to the Hungarians as well as the Romanians before the Compromise of 1867, but after the Compromise the Hungarian state put an end to it. Journalists were held responsible for contravening laws only after their articles were printed. Sentences in press matters were passed by juries. It is possible to determine the exact measure of freedom of the press enjoyed by Romanians from the operations of the Romanian press and from the proceedings against the authors of articles appearing in various Romanian papers.

What were the measures that restricted freedom of the press? In other words, what was the nature of the articles for which the authors were held accountable? What could be published in the Romanian papers appearing on Hungarian territory without entailing prosecution? Furthermore, what sentences were handed down, and to what extent did the execution of these sentences inhibit or frighten the representatives of the Romanian press?

We get a very interesting picture from the answers to these questions. Most of the time Romanian newspapermen got into trouble for the reasons described in paragraph 172 of the BTK (Criminal Law Code). This paragraph referred to agitation against an ethnic group:

> Whoever addresses or disseminates a direct appeal against a law, or against ordinances and decisions issued by authorities acting within their legal competence, in a manner determined in paragraph 171 (at some assembly, publicly, verbally, or by the distribution or exhibition of printed materials, documents or illustrations) is punishable by incarceration up to two years and by a maximum fine of 1,000 forints. The same punishment may be meted out to someone who, in the manner defined under paragraph 171, stirs up any social class, nationality, or religious denomination against another, as well as the one who agitates against the institution of private property and marriage.

The concept of nationality mentioned in the text was defined, in principle, by the Supreme Court, in the following terms: "by separate nationality is meant those ethnic groups that are identifiable by their language and their historical past, and who insist on retaining their mother tongue."

On the basis of the quoted measures, if some Romanian newspaper published an article agitating against the Hungarians, or against the constitution of the Hungarian state (the Compromise of 1867 and the Dual Monarchy — that is against the leading role of the Hungarians within Hungary), the state prosecutor might initiate a press trial. The first press trial against the *Tribuna*, initiated in 1884, was caused by an article published in its November 30, 1884, issue. The article was by the Romanian writer, Ion Slavici, who had returned to Nagyszeben from Romania in the wake of the resolutions adopted by Putna. He debated the issue of the official language of the state in connection with the sentence passed over two Saxon armed robbers. Among other things, he wrote: "They force us inevitably into blind animosity towards the Hungarian state; and we must seek opportunities to shake it to its foundations by any means necessary, to rally and unite with all its enemies everywhere, and to turn people against the Hungarian state wherever we go." The prosecutor placed charges against Slavici. The trial came before the jury at Nagyszeben, and the members of the jury were of Saxon nationality. They found the charges unwarranted, and Slavici was exonerated. In the first year of its publication not a single author of any article in the *Tribuna* was found guilty. The prosecutor did not even place charges when the *Tribuna* published the following words in the fall of 1884:

> If it is not possible to strengthen the Romanian race within the Hungarian state then the only alternative that remains to us is the annihilation of said Hungarian state; the struggle for this annihilation, alliance with the enemies of the Hungarian race, appear to us as organic necessities.[2]

After 1885, in view of the attitude adopted by juries composed of Saxons, the Hungarian government referred press trials to the Hungarian court at Kolozsvár. This was where most press trials launched against certain Romanian journalists for agitation against the Hungarians or against the Hungarian state came up for adjudication. The reasons given by the prosecution for initiating these trials are illustrative. For instance, another press trial was launched against the *Tribuna* in 1885, on account of an editorial which appeared in its November 28 issue. The author of the editorial explained the objectives of the Romanians of Hungary in polemics with the *Kolozsvári Közlöny*.

The *Kolozsvári Közlöny* claimed that if the Romanian demands were met, this would be tantamount to the realization of union with neighboring Romania. First the Romanians would request autonomy for Transylvania. Then they would demand the recognition of the special rights of the Romanians within the autonomous state. After this demand was met, they would join, at the first opportunities, with the related and neighboring state if there were such a thing, and if not, they would achieve complete independence and secession. The *Tribuna* noted that the semi-official paper of the Kolozsvár was mostly correct in writing that "whatever concession granted us Romanians, we would use to prepare union with our brothers on the other side of the Carpathians and for the establishment of the Greater Romanian state extending between the Danube, and Dniester [Nistru] and the Tisza." Our answer is: "the semi-official paper of *Kolozsvár* is right in assuming that the Romanians are imbued with the desire of national unification. This desire is most natural, and it has penetrated the large masses of Romanians far more deeply than the Hungarians realize." According to the *Tribuna* the only way to fight against this desire would be for the Hungarians to grant all the rights the Romanians demanded. In vain did the Hungarian newspaper point out that the autonomy granted to the Croatians did not make them content; and, therefore, the state and its leaders must retain their Hungarian character. The Romanians would never reconcile themselves to such a solution. It would lead straight to civil war.

> This land is not the home of the Hungarians, nor of the Romanians, but the home of us all. The Hungarians should not keep coming with the claim that it is Hungarian and nothing but Hungarian, because by so doing they force the Romanians to demonstrate stubbornly that it is either Romanian or a waste-land.[3]

As we have seen, there were serious grounds for the press trial. The state had to defend itself against such tones which, resorting to emphatic words and grandiloquent style, spread daily among the avid Romanian masses. The need for self-defense also forced the Hungarian prosecutor's office to initiate yet another press trial at the end of the same year, with similar arguments. The cause for legal action was the following sentence:

> If the Hungarians could, in spite of the Pragmatic Sanction and against our will, unite Transylvania with Hungary; it is

difficult to convince the Romanians that they may not, likewise
in spite of the Pragmatic Sanction and the will of the Hungarians, strive towards the unification of Transylvania with some
other state.[4]

Indeed, the Hungarian state initiated the above actions as a matter
of self-defense. The freedom of the press which prevailed in Hungary
made it possible for the Romanians to express their yearnings and
complaints in extreme form, although they were occasionally held
accountable for it. Contrasting the mildness of the sentences imposed
with the impact of the agitation on the minds of the people, it becomes
obvious that the sentences were not excessive, nor did they have an
inhibiting effect. In cases of press offenses, prison terms or fines were
handed down. But the state prison, particularly the one at Vác, was not
in the least a deterrent in that period. We know this from the book
titled *My Prisons* by Slavici, the editor-in-chief of *Tribuna*, published
after World War I.[5] The book reveals the situation of the journalist
sentenced to a jail term. Slavici was not arrested after sentence was
passed; the court allowed him time to travel to Bucharest and settle his
pending affairs. He was allowed to specify the date when he intended
to report at Vác. Slavici actually reported on the day he had specified.
This was not the prison at Vác, but a separate building which the
Hungarian state had rented specially for those sentenced in press trials,
political trials, or for duelling.

Slavici was assigned to a private room, the only window of which
opened onto a clean courtyard. The furniture consisted of a bed, two
chairs, a small table, and a wardrobe. The bed was equipped with a
horsehair mattress, a feather pillow, and an eiderdown. An employee
of the prison cleaned the room for the fee determined in the regulations.
Slavici was allowed to order his meals from the outside, so his wife
moved to Vác with their two-year old son, and stayed in a furnished
room not far from the prison. She cooked and kept her husband
company in the daytime as he was allowed to spend the entire day in
his room in the company of his family. Other inmates had the same
situation. Their afternoons were usually spent in the garden behind the
house. Here they could entertain each other or receive visitors. If the
weather was pleasant and they felt like having an excursion, they went
to the island of Szentendre across from Vác. The boat and oarsmen of
the prison were made available for the purpose. Slavici frequently
availed himself of the privilege. On such occasions he would walk,
accompanied by a guard, to the banks of the Danube where his wife and
child awaited him. Here they embarked in the boat and the oarsmen

sped to the island where the family stayed together in "complete freedom" to enjoy the pleasant weather and picturesque surroundings. Slavici wrote:

> This was not some kind of privilege granted me alone but an indulgence to which all those sentenced for longer terms were entitled, because the purpose of the punishment was not the destruction of body and soul, and certainly not to make the prisoner immoral and an even greater threat to society.[6]

During the prison term Slavici's wife was nearing her time for giving birth to another child. Slavici, the great enemy of the state, was seized with considerable anxiety. He would have liked to remain by the side of his wife in her hours of need. The prison warden advised him to turn to the Minister of Justice and request leave for that period. Slavici turned in the request which was immediately granted. The Minister instructed the prison warden, by cable, to have the prison doctor examine Mrs. Slavici, and assign a permanent doctor to her; Slavici was granted leave for the period of the delivery. Thus Slavici spent two weeks by the side of his wife and could go anywhere he pleased in the town without being subjected to guard or police supervision or surveillance. The delivery took place without complications under the supervision of the prison doctor. Two weeks later the newborn was baptized in the presence of twenty Romanian university students from Budapest who had travelled to Vác to honor the editor-in-chief of the *Tribuna*. Once the anxiety surrounding the arrival of the baby had dissipated, after his furlough of two weeks, Slavici returned to the small house which symbolized detention.

During his entire term of imprisonment Slavici busied himself as he pleased. He was entitled to read any book or periodical. The director of the prison loaned him books from his own library gladly; but even at this time Slavici preferred to deal with the affairs of the *Tribuna*, and edited the text of the Eudoxiu Hurmuzaki archives to be published in Bucharest. The printers in Bucharest sent the galleys straight to Vác where Slavici performed the proofreading, often with the help of the prison warden. Sometimes, instead of proofreading, he wrote articles which he sent off immediately to the *Tribuna*, criticizing in strong words the "anti-Romanian nationalities policies of the Hungarian government."[7]

Slavici's recollections of his experiences at Vác constitute an accurate description of the predicament of Romanian journalists sentenced to jail terms. Had the objective of the Hungarian press policy been to repress freedom of thought by instilling fear, the incarcerated journalists would surely have been treated differently. As Slavici noted, the punishment was not aimed at the "destruction of body and soul," hence the condemned were treated with kid gloves. The treatment in the state prison at Szeged was somewhat less lenient, yet the human dignity of the inmates was respected. Lucaciu, the most radical representative of Romanian irredentism, could continue to write his sociological treatise during his entire period of incarceration there. "While his fellow-prisoners read or entertained each other," writes the author of the monograph on Lucaciu, "he wrote at his simple table, absorbed in his subject, and the writing filled up the pages line by line."

The journalists knew well that prison was not a terrifying experience, hence they were not afraid of the sentences meted out and, once released, they continued their agitation. They made full use of the freedom of the press. Though the biographer of Lucaciu refers to this as merely "the beginning of freedom of the press," he immediately adds that "the Romanian leaders used this freedom to speak to the masses. It hardly mattered that they may be sent to jail as a result of their articles censored after publication; the main thing was the impact of the articles."[8]

The other manner of punishment was fines. This was not a deterrent either, considering the financial situation of the various strata of Romanian society, improving year after year, and the generous financial support granted by the Romanian government. Thus, fines did little to restrain the authors of articles in Romanian newspapers from sharp attacks against Hungarians and the Hungarian state. Agitation committed verbally also entailed but mild punishment. A few examples will shed light on the procedures of the Hungarian judicial system.

In 1896, in the community of Kürtös [Curtici], county of Arad, there was a torchlight parade on the occasion of the millenial celebrations. Palcu Dumitru, a resident of Kürtös watching the parade, shouted to the marchers; "Down with the Hungarians!" When questioned about his outcry, he gave the following explanation: "I have the right to speak this way, because this land is not Hungarian, but Romanian." The tribunal in the first instance absolved him for lack of proof, but the prosecutor appealed the decision. The Supreme Court sentenced him to three months in jail and a fine of 50 forints.[9]

On May 16, 1902, after the laying of laurels at the foot of the statue of Andrei Mureşanu in Brassó, the Romanian printer Drăghici shouted: "Long live the Romanians, let the Hungarians croak!" He was sentenced to one month in state prison and fined 100 crowns.[10]

Florea Berdean, a Romanian landowner from Újszentanna [Sîntana], requested a ticket in Romanian at the local railroad station in 1909. He was refused, because the cashier could not understand Romanian. Then, within earshot of several witnesses, the Romanian landowner shouted: "This government keeps the Romanian people in jail and is a true curse on the country. The whole country has to be partitioned, as was done with Poland!" He was sentenced to 15 days in jail for these weighty statements.[11]

We could cite similar incidents over many pages. But the ones already mentioned should suffice to show that agitation in words was penalized less heavily than inciting articles published in the press. The courts were probably more concerned about the impact of the agitation; articles in the press could be read by large numbers who, in turn, created public opinion, whereas the impact of oral statements remained isolated.

Of course, whether the sentences were mild or severe often depended on the tensions of the moment in the relations between Hungarians and Romanians. Trials regarding agitation were by jury. The members of these juries were usually persons who read newspapers and were not always immune to the influence of the views published there. Hungarians who understood Romanian sometimes read the original article, others obtaining information from reports in the Hungarian press. The anti-Hungarian tone of the Romanian press, pandering to feelings of hatred, appeared even meaner when reinterpreted in the Hungarian press. This appearance was occasionally reflected in the decisions handed down by the juries. It also happened, however, that the Hungarian press deemed the sentence for agitation too harsh. This was the case when, in 1905, a court in Kolozsvár condemned the author of a Romanian poem to one year in jail; the Hungarian daily *Kolozsvári Napló* objected to the sentence. The Romanian paper of Szászváros quoted the reaction of its Hungarian counterpart with some satisfaction. "The excessively harsh sentence has elicited great astonishment everywhere," and added, "after this anyone would understand and sympathize with the rebellious bitterness of the nationalities."[12]

A year in prison was indeed an unusual sentence for agitation. Only during the "Memorandum trial" were longer sentences passed over a Romanian accused. Vasile Lucaciu was sentenced to five years and several of his companions to two years each. As we know, the condemned did not have to sit out their sentences, since they were to benefit from an amnesty after a year and a half.

Most press trials were initiated for arousing hatred against the Hungarians. The justification of the prosecution for the press trial against the author of the article "Romania for Us" published in the *Foia Poporului* of July 23, 1893, may be considered typical. According to this justification, excerpts from the article present "Hungarian rule," the "Hungarian nation," and the "Hungarians" as the most adamant enemies and destroyers of the Romanians, administering them blow upon blow and torturing them with illegal and unjust oppression, persecution, and political terror. Since these endeavors attributed to the Hungarians were appropriate to incite those Romanians who are more easily misled to hate the Hungarians, they bear all the traits of the crime "agitation against a nationality." On the basis of paragraph 172, the prosecutor initiated a press trial against the author of the above article and the editor-in-chief of the periodical.[13] The usual punishment for such articles was incarceration in a state prison for a few months, half a year at most. Sentences were also handed down by the courts because of anti-Semitic agitation. The Romanian poet Goga sat in the prison of Szeged for such an article. In cases of agitation against the constitution or the integrity of the state, the sentences were more severe.

In spite of the press trials, freedom of the press offered the Romanian ethnic group broad rights and opportunities. The Romanian journalists regularly enjoyed the rights and opportunities below without the risk of a trial:

a) The proclamation of racial boycott by Romanian society.
b) Harsh criticism of the Hungarian state, the Hungarian authorities and institutions, as well as of the Hungarian character and culture, to the point of ridicule.
c) Unlimited praise and glorification of Romanian ethnic traits.
d) The distortion and vilification of Hungarian history.
e) Various ways of expressing allegiance to Romania.

a) *Proclamation of Racial Boycott*

Romanian racial boycott was proclaimed soon after the Compromise. The authorities had no mind to intervene. The boycott was directed primarily against those who befriended Hungarians or spoke Hungarian, or gave some evidence of understanding towards the Hungarians and their aspirations. Widespread racial boycott got underway especially after the launching of the *Tribuna*. "We have the right to hate, show contempt towards and systematically persecute all those who collaborate with the Hungarians whether openly or secretly," wrote the *Tribuna*. "This hatred, contempt, and systematic persecution is as certain as light at daybreak."[14]

It naturally followed from this basic principle that the Romanian press attacked every Romanian who frequented Hungarian establishments. They resorted to all kinds of slander, falsehood, and acts of terror towards such persons. "We give him no bread when he is hungry, nor water when he is thirsty, and lock our doors when he asks for lodging" — that is, every Romanian who befriends Hungarians and frequents Hungarian society. Soon statements appeared in the Romanian press by individual Romanians protesting against the accusation of having committed treason by contacts with the Hungarians. Judging from items in the Romanian press, membership in a Hungarian casino, the organization of a ball with Hungarian participation, contributing to collections for the Hungarian Red Cross, dancing the *csárdás*, etc., constituted such *crimen laesae nationis*. These acts, not serious in themselves, entailed serious consequences. One point of the program of the weekly *Libertatea*, launched in Szászváros in 1902, was to educate the Romanian people to terrorize. In the first issue of the paper we read that the "*Libertatea* considers as one of its most important missions to teach our people the art of terrorism. Whereas terrorism in the hands of the authorities is a sinful weapon, terrorism in the hands of the people is the shield of the common good."[15] During its long life the paper did, indeed, carry out this task without once incurring a press trial. There was complete freedom to announce boycott and terror, and the state prosecutor did not intervene against anyone for so doing, although even the editors of the *Libertatea* were astounded by some of the consequences of this persistent education for aggression. The incited masses did not always resort to aggression when the editors of the Romanian paper deemed it appropriate, as in the case of the inhabitants of two Romanian communities in Hunyad county.

The Romanians of the community of Pánk [Panc], along the Dobra River, quarrelled with the likewise Romanian inhabitants of Roskány [Roşani]. The latter turned to the courts, because they laid claim to some parts of the forest and meadows used by the inhabitants of Pánk. Their rightful claim was recognized by every court; hence the residents of Roskány won the suit and awaited the execution of the verdict. But when the judge arrived to mark division, the Romanian peasants of Pánk chased him away by force. On the request of the inhabitants of Roskány he returned to the contested area, this time accompanied by 14 gendarmes. Those of Pánk set up barricades along the way and greeted

the approaching gendarmes with shots and a shower of stones. Those
who had no gun were armed with scythes and pitchforks. The gendarmes returned the fire, but seeing the determination of the crowd,
they soon retreated, making way for a military unit which finally
succeeded in pacifying the rebels. The editors of the Romanian paper
bent on preaching aggression did not approve. "This is a most painful
event," they concluded; "all the more painful, as the verdict of the judge
did not result in any injustice, for all three courts had decided in favor
of those of Roskány."[16]

Of course, when the people resorted to aggression for a Romanian
national or political objective, approval was not long in coming. When
the Romanians decided to become politically active, and some of their
candidates launched their electroral compaign, it was accompanied by
tremendous intimidation. The intimidation was directed against those
about whom it was known or suspected that they would vote for the
opponent, though the opponent was Romanian as well, but one who
based his campaign on the program of the government party. Woe to
the one who voted for him. His home was set afire at night by
"unknown culprits," his animals were driven away, or he himself beaten
half to death. After one such election campaign, the paper advocating
agression noted with satisfaction that success at the polls was due to the
terroristic intervention of the Romanian voters. "The people of the
electoral district deserve every praise," insisted the paper from
Szászváros. At other times it merely noted the fact of aggression,
without resorting to praise: "they beat a few judges from the village
who did not speak out for the village masses but sided with the lords,"
it wrote curtly.[17]

In the long run this terrorism became a powerful weapon in the
hands of Romanian national leaders. It was resorted to in a similar way
before and after almost every election. The weeks preceding the voting
witnessed true revolts in many places. The politicians tried to persuade
those suspected of not favoring the Romanian candidate to change their
intentions, but means of all kinds of threats. Romanian priests,
notaries, teachers, and various campaign managers all indulged in such
psychological terror. They threatened the voters thus identified with
death, with arson, with the theft of their property, etc. For weeks on
end, the papers published articles about the villages in which some
noteworthy incident took place. After an unsuccessful campaign certain
Romanian papers would list the name of every Romanian priest and
teacher whose attitude had not been sufficiently adamant in their
obituary section.[18] It happened that under the impact of such
articles, the priest would make the Romanians swear in church to vote

for the Romanian candidate. When the peace negotiations between Vasile Mangra and István Tisza became known, and the majority of the Romanian priests and deacons of the county of Bihar came out in support of Mangra (who had launched a movement in favor of coexistence with the Hungarians), the newspaper from Szászváros described them as enemies of the people "prepared to smear the clean name of the people" and "serve Mammon rather than God."

> The actions of the priests and deacons of the poor people in the vicinity of Nagyvárad must receive their just reward, much as the Romanians of Valea Iepii had done to the Marian priest; for all those who wrote in favor of the madman Mangra are so many Marian priests dangerous to our very lives.[19]

The case of this priest was well know: during one of the election campaigns he busied himself in favor of the government candidate. Under the influence of the Romanian newspapers his parishioners locked him out of his church, and refused to allow him to hold service. Everyone avoided him as if he were suffering from the plague. His servants left him and his neighbors denied him all help. This situation lasted for half a year, when the priest finally decided to move away from the village. The *Libertatea* was running no risk when calling upon its readers to perform similar acts boldly.[20]

b) *Criticism of the Hungarian State and the Hungarians.*

Along with the exercise of the previous right, the Romanian papers consistently directed harsh criticism at the Hungarian state and its agencies. Such criticism seldom resulted in prosecution. The following assertions, for instance, could be made scot-free: The Hungarian state embodies an unjust political system; Hungarians are not fit to lead the state; the administration up to this point has really barbarianized certain regions of the country; — Hungarians are midgets compared to other nations, a mongrel, savage race from Asia who are naturally unable to absorb European culture; the civil servants are petty, corrupt and abuse their power; the Hungarian language hurts the eardrums and is uncultured — it sounds like the braying of a donkey. According to a popular Romanian anecdote, few people who spoke Hungarian would ever make it to heaven. The Hungarian peasant of the anecdote is lazy and dirty. The calendars published by various newspapers were filled with descriptions of Hungarians as repulsive. Such materials appeared especially frequently in the calendar of the *Tribuna*, which was widely disseminated in rural areas, for decades. The combined objective of the articles, anecdotes and photographs which appeared in these calendars was to provide a debasing view of the Hungarians. Whenever Hungarians or Székelys were mentioned in the anecdotes, they were described as stupid, foolish, and ridiculous: An acquaintance from the city could locate the house of farmer János by the fact that his yard was filled mostly with dirt, rather than by the number.[21]

In another calendar, satyrical drawings of Hungarian patriotic demonstrations pretending to be "actual photos" represented men with frightfully hooked noses and criminal features, or women looking like furies, all designed to make the Hungarian patriotic holidays seem ridiculous.[22] Neither the editors of the papers, nor the authors of the articles, nor the publishers were penalized for all these assertions and distortions. Nor did the Romanian delegate Alexandru Vaida-Voevod come to harm in 1908 for reading out, in the Hungarian house of parliament, the following poem:

> Everything is in vain, in vain... you will perish/ scum from Asia that tramples on all rights.... /For ten cursed centuries you lived like parasites/bloodthirsty bedbugs feeding on this country./ And it has put up with a lot, but forgotten nothing/because the Romanian is *cine mintye*.[23]

There were times when even the Hungarian prosecutor's office felt prompted to raise official charges for slanders against the Hungarian nation. For instance, charges were prompted by an article about the Hungarians publishing in the paper *Românul*. Among other things, the author noted that:

> as a result of their Asian origins the state concocted by the Hungarians on the Hungarian steppe has remained Asian in all its customs: attempts at regicide, continuous rebellions, incessant aggression against individuals and their property. In other words, the history of Hungary continues to show that both Hungarians and the Hungarian state have preserved, in their savage spirit, their Asian origins. The Hungarian way of thinking has preserved two essentially Asian traits: animal servility towards those above, and cruel tyranny to those below.[24]

Most states would have punished the author of such an article with a sentence longer than just half a year in state prison. The authors of such articles were charged by the Hungarian courts because they attempted to depict not just a few Hungarians who abused their powers, but all Hungarians, the entire Hungarian nation, in baleful colors. The injustice of such allusions was admitted on one occasion by the *Tribuna* itself. When in 1911 some Romanian leaders undertook preparatory talks with the Hungarian Prime Minister Károly Khuen-Héderv[á]ry in view of a Romanian-Hungarian reconciliation, the Romanian paper pointed out the greatest obstacle to

...brotherly collaboration with the Hungarians. During our centuries-long struggles we were conscious of the fact that the Hungarians are our relentless enemies. Indeed, it would be rather difficult for us now to accept the notion that we have been fighting not against the Hungarian nation, that it was not the nation that was our real enemy, but only a certain social class, the members of which, clothed in Hungarian national garb, exploited not only us, but the Hungarians as well....

Only the press could prepare the agreement. Hungarian and Romanian journalists must mutually approach each other. Let us get acquainted, and let them promote the struggle against these obstacles in their papers. Only this way could they stop "the spread of those lies which they used to disseminate formerly, with a specific objective."[25]

As is well known, Romanian-Hungarian reconciliation got scuttled because of the influence of politicians from Romania. Hatred continued to spread. Iorga praised the process in the Romanian parliament: "The Romanians did not make peace with the Hungarians, which is only as expected. This was dictated by their past, and will become their future."[26]

c) *Glorification of the Romanian Race*

While the Romanian press depicted the Hungarians in the most repulsive light and with the coarsest attributes, it constantly published odes to the virtues of the Romanian race. "You must be proud to be born Romanian" the Romanian papers repeated with increasing frequency. The Romanian nation was described as the only Latin race in Eastern Europe, hence the only worthy representative of Western Civilization. According to an assertion oft-repeated in the Romanian press, the Romanian people were the most homogeneous of Eastern Europe and called upon to perform the most important role. Their duty was to spread Western civilization towards Russia and the Balkans.

There was no language sweeter or more harmonious in the world. The Romanian race was far superior to the neighboring races, particularly the Hungarians. In face of the attempts at Hungarianization it posited the "pride of the Romanian race of a higher order," looking down from above at the lower order of Hungarians.[27]   The Romanian nation represented true culture and true order in contrast to Hungarian barbarism. While the Hungarians harrassed the Romanians with laws such as the Apponyi Law, Romania would not grant its Jews citizenship and excluded them from the body of the nation "in a most humane manner."[28] Hence the Romanians were the representatives of true civilization and humanism. The Romanian nation was pure, law-abiding, hospitable, patient, and endowed with the most outstanding qualities, after all it "descends from a majestic tribe."[29] It deserved to be addressed as "His Majesty the Romanian People."[30]

The glorification of the Romanian race served two purposes. One was to reinforce national pride to such an extent that it would become immune to any kind of Hungarian influence, including Hungarianization. An Easter article in one of the Romanian papers was typical of this endeavor. According to the author of the article, while celebrating the resurrection, the Romanians should implore God

> ...to spread national pride in their soul and to avoid aliens who ended up on Romanian soil, and to look down upon them since they stem from a lower order of nations than the Romanian; whereas those among us who agree to serve the alien, let us bear them with the most profound contempt.[31]

The other objective was to justify the Romanians' right to rule over Transylvania, by stressing their outstanding qualifications. The *Gazeta* of Brassó stated outright that the "poor and unfortunate" Romanian nation was called upon "to rule over these areas" because of its excellent qualities and the sharpness of its intellect.[32] Of course, the term "nation" was meant symbolically, because what the intelligentsia and the landowning class in charge of the Romanian press had in mind was its own role as leaders and rulers of the people. Under the term "nation" they referred to their interests and ambitions; by praising the excellent qualities of the Romanian people they were merely voicing their own image of themselves. They knew right well that the masses had no notion of the mission and strivings of the Romanian National Party.[33]

d) *Demeaning Hungarian History*

The Romanian press and publishers enjoyed the highest degree of freedom to distort Hungarian history and present it in a loathsome light. Hungarian history was nothing but the history of the continuous exploitation of the Romanian people and of barbarous tyranny, as far as the Romanian dailies and other publications were concerned. Hungarian historians were dismissed as simply "falsifiers of history". According to the Romanian weekly from Szászváros, "it is common knowledge that Hungarian scholars are greater falsifiers of historical evidence than the scholars of any other nation;"[34] therefore, Romanian historians should not even engage in conversation with them. True historical science was represented by Romanian scholars, and this was the history the Romanians must cultivate and learn. This history reflected historical facts faithfully. The Romanian nation has occupied the land of the heroic Dacians for two thousand years, and all the savage nations of the world had to cross this land to steal away their fruits. One of these nations were the Huns, "an incredibly savage nation related to the Hungarians."[35]

Moreover, the way the Hungarian chieftain Árpád was presented in history was a "lie." The Hungarian occupation of the land was "highway robbery," "a millenial theft and a cursed phenomenon."[36] András II was a mean ruler because he gave the Saxons the right to exploit the forests at the expense of the Romanians. Lajos Kossuth, the leader of the struggle for independence in 1848, was the executioner of the Romanians whereas the rulers of Transylvania were their oppressors. The best known and greatest Hungarian historical figures, those whose accomplishments could not be belittled, were almost all Romanian descent, according to the Romanian interpretation: King Matthias, György Dózsa, Gábor Bethlen, and even Ferenc Deák. In 1848 the Hungarians were bent on causing chaos and anarchy, whereas the Romanians' tribunes came to the rescue of the threatened imperial throne, fighting for order and civilization.[37]

In March 1848, when the Hungarians launched the revolution and seceded from Austria; they had a grand army, strong forts, and a well stocked treasury; whereas the Romanians had nothing but heroic determination, loyalty towards the Habsburg dynasty, and could offer but their naked arms.[38] Even such an outstanding figure as the Romanian poet George Coşbuc wrote in this vein about the Hungarian fight for independence in 1848/49, presenting the facts in a completely distorted light. Yet everyone with some knowledge of history was aware that in the first half of 1848 the Hungarians had neither a separate army, nor a treasury, nor even strong forts, for these were in the hands of the Austrian forces. They declared their independence from Austria not in 1848 but in 1849. The Romanian press, however, persisted in presenting Hungarian history in a negative light, as yet another device to foment the hatred felt by the Romanian people towards the Hungarians. Still, not a single Romanian jounalist or publisher was penalized during the entire period of Hungarian rule on account of having thus distorted Hungarian history or depicted it in negative terms. Naturally, because of the reckless distortions and belittling, even the purest figures of Hungarian history now appeared hateful to the Romanians. It is not surprising, therefore, that the Romanians felt glory was involved in the act of some who, on October 6, 1903, the Hungarian day of mourning for the martyrs of Arad, spat on the portraits of Lajos Kossuth and of the executed generals in the Faller restaurant at Máriaradna. The only penalty was their exclusion from the Hungarian casino.[39]

Expression of Belonging to Romania

Freedom of the press in Hungary even provided the opportunity to express belonging to Romania in various forms. No press trial was directed against journalists or publishers in the Dual Monarchy for availing themselves of this opportunity.

The notion of belonging to Romania was first popularized in its cultural aspects. The initiative was taken by the *Tribuna*. This paper succeeded, by dint of persistence, to spread the notion that "for the Romanians the sun rises in Bucharest," in just a matter of years. This was tantamount to accepting the cultural leadership of Romania. "Today our gaze is constantly directed towards Bucharest," wrote the paper,

and our most important endeavor is to make sure that, as regards to our general culture, we do not turn away from our more cultured brethren whose spiritual accomplishments we want to spread here /in Hungary/.[40] In another issue the *Tribuna* stated: We have never made a secret of our love for our brethren on the other side of the Carpathians, nor of the satisfaction with which we view the steady progress of the Romanian state, which constitutes the center of attraction of the entire Romania nation.[41]

All Romanian, papers and publishers followed the example set by the *Tribuna*. It became standard practice from then on to praise Romania and express love towards the Romanian state in every way in the press, and sometimes even in books. The papers published regular columns devoted to Romania and events taking place there. This column usually bore the title "Din țară" /from the country/, implying that "the country" could only be Romania. On the other hand, when referring to Budapest, it usually specified "the capital city of Hungary."

We have seen that the songbook prepared for Romanian children and published on Hungarian territory could announce without any ill consequence "Vivat! Vivat! Vivat Romania!" It could say long life, or up with the Romania army, after all there was no preventive censorship, and the prosecutor's office could find no grounds for proceedings in such language, nor even in that other song which extended the borders of Romania, in its text, to wherever the "ancient and sweet" Romanian language was spoken.

Nor is it surprising that the most militant Romanian Uniate priest, Vasile Lucaciu, when appointed to head the parish of Lácfalu [Sisești], immediately launched a nationwide collection for funds to build a church which he intended to name the Church of the Union of All Romanians. No one interfered with the collection carried out by mail and through the press, nor even with the fact that the priest wrote an account of the two-year long collection campaign, of the construction of the church, and its significance, in a separate monograph. Thanks to the freedom of the press and of opinion, this little booklet, *The Church of the Union of All Romanians*, could be published in Hungary without consequences; the author was not reprimanded by the state even though, according to his pamphlet, he sought to express symbolically, through the construction of the church, "that which the poets had sung, that which every Romanian soul yearns for — the majestic, sacred, and blissful union of all Romanians." In his consecration sermon in front of the assembled Romanians who listened to his words with astonishment, he provided an even more outspoken explanation:

I consecrate this church to the sacred union of all Romanians. With its construction begins the struggle of the Romanians of Hungary for their liberation and for union with the mother country. As God has helped us to erect this proud and imposing church, so let Him help us build up the soul of the Romanians, to make them fit for their liberation and for the brotherly handshake with Romanians wherever they may live.

The state attorney did not initiate proceedings against him, either for his consecration speech or for the publication of the booklet, even though the Hungarians of Nagybánya brought to the attention of the Prime Minister the irredentist behavior of the militant priest in a special petition.[42]

The prevailing freedom of the press and of expressing opinions explains how it was possible to openly identify with Romania — the common attitude of all Romanians of Hungary. As mentioned, the attorney's office did not launch proceedings for articles advocating ethnic union or unification. The Romanian weekly of Szászváros could report without running risks regarding the banquet held after the consecration of the Orthodox church at Petrozsény, where the main theme of the toasts was the "racial ties that bind us to the brothers across the Carpathians. ...We have but one religion, we speak the same language, and the same great ideal guides all Romanians," stated the report. Nor was anyone surprised that guests from Romania who had only to step over the nearby border attended the consecration: Colonel Gheorghe Lambru, the commander of the regiment of Gorj, and his deputy, moreover the principal of the Romania secondary school at Tîrgu Jiu along with many of the professors. By their very presence, the guests from Romania made profession of faith to unification.[43]

The Romanian press of Hungary could disseminate without suffering penalties the anthem of the union with Romania which began with the words "Union is inscribed on our banners." This same song was sung at the Bucharest fair of 1906 by the choral groups from Hungary, accompanied by storms of applause on the part of the Romanian audience.[44] This song was what fired up the Romanians during a soirée organized in one of the Romanian inhabited villages of Transylvania where the theme of unification "inspired the souls of those present with the spirit of national unification."[45] In 1913 the Romanian orchestra conductor, Ionel Rădulescu started his concert performance at Szászváros with this anthem; and when he was recalled to Romania by telegram, the people came to bid him farewell at the railroad station singing the same anthem. Along with the review of the concert, the newspaper published an improvised poem according to which "from the four corners of the Romanian world we hear the selfsame echo: 'Long live Romania!' "[46]

Of course, the best opportunity for an unhampered expression of the feeling of belonging to Romania came during visits to Romania. It is typical of the freedom of the press which prevailed in Hungary that the Romanian newspapers there could give reports of these experiences. Indeed, they could do this freely; because they were not threatened by any kind of reprisal on the part of the Hungarian state for their contacts with Romania or for reporting the feelings expressed while over there. In 1906 Voina, the deacon of Brassó, told a large audience in Bucharest, according to the report in the press: "We have but a single soul which throbs for one another, for the same idea. Therefore, we shout without fear, from the bottom of our heart: 'Long live Romania!' " Of course, the Romanians of Hungary took advantage of their visits to Romania to pay their respects to the leaders of the kingdom in person. The Romanian paper, *Tribuna*, published in Arad, could tell its readers about such a visit by Dr. Teodor Mihali without worrying that the Hungarian authorities would consider this an offense against the state. The subscribers to the paper and other interested Romanians would indulge in guesses as to just what transpired between the leader of the Romanian National Party in Hungary and the King of Romania. The carefully worded communiqué in the *Tribuna* merely served to arouse the curiosity of the readers: "Dr. Mihali, on a visit to his relatives in Bucharest, stopped over in Sinaia to pay homage to His Majesty the King and the Queen."[47] Paying homage to the king who stood at the helm of the Romanian state was nothing new as far as the Romanian leaders in Hungary were concerned. After all, as we have seen, the portraits of the King and Queen adorned many homes in Transylvania, and without any penalty at that, because the Hungarian authorities did not forbid this manifestation of homage to a foreign head of state even if they were aware of the irredentist significance of such a demonstration. In Romania anti-Hungarian irredentism was out in the open and widespread. Therefore, anyone who travelled there from Hungary for a shorter or longer period was exposed to even more marked irredentist feelings. Travelling to Romania was an everyday occurrence not restricted by the Hungarian authorities at that time.

The evolution of the feeling of belonging to Romania culminated in unhindered contacts of the Romanians of Hungary with the Romanians of Romania. During the entire period of the Dual Monarchy no limits were set on personal contacts between citizens of the two countries or on travel in or out of the country. Often the Romanians who lived along the border would just cross some mountain-pass and visit the Romanian regions near Hungary without a passport. This was even facilitated by the demographic factors because, the population was Romanian everywhere along the Hungarian-Romanian border except for the land of the Székelys. The Romanian shepherd knew every path over the mountains, as had their ancestors in the 18th century when they immigrated in such large numbers from the Romanian principalities into Transylvania, to the point where they soon outnumbered the

Hungarians and the Saxons in the province. Even a passport was not always a requirement for such travel because anyone could obtain an identification card allowing him or her to cross the border. The issuance of this identification, like that of the passport, fell within the jurisdiction of the county. As we have seen, there were a good many Romanians among the county leaders who naturally would not reject applications for such identification. In fact, even if the issuance of passports encountered difficulties in some of the counties, the Romanian applicant could simply come to some county along the border, especially to Szeben or Fogaras, where he could easily obtain the identification allowing him to cross. Consequently, numerous Romanians visited Romania each year, and experienced no trouble crossing the border. The limits set on travel across the border after World War I were completely unknown at that time. We seldom encounter complaints in the more prestigious Romanian serials about refusal to issue a passport or hampering travel to Romania. Thousands of Romanians travelled from Hungary to the great fair in Bucharest in 1906, and only once were passports refused to one of these groups, a group from Szászváros. "This is repulsive, latter-day barbarism against freedom of culture," commented the Romanian weekly from Szászváros. Nevertheless, the group was able to leave without a passport; they dispatched one member to Nagyszeben with a physical description of each member of the group, and there the competent authorities of the county issued the identification allowing them to cross the border without further ado.[48] Thus even this complaint was finally remedied. Therefore, the Romanians of Hungary could be said to have had the right to travel to Romania with relative ease, whether with passport or with an identification card.

Travel in the other direction was equally smooth. It was possible to visit Hungary from Romania either with a passport or with a simple identification allowing the bearer to cross the border. Romanian visitors literally flooded Hungary at all times. Journalists, scholars, politicians, army officers, and even various members of the royal family could cross the border with equal ease in order to visit their ethnic brothers in Hungary.

The Romanian historian Nicolae Iorga, one of the main organizers of the Bucharest fair of 1906, the greatest enemy of the Hungarian state and the First Secretary of the Cultural League of Romania, visited the regions of Hungary inhabited by Romanians many times. In 1906 he was accompanied on his trip to northern Transylvania by the Romanian lawyer, Victor Onișor. According to Iorga's account in the weekly of Beszterce, no one even questioned his presence. No Hungarian authority challenged him to identify himself. His only unpleasant experience was a result of his long beard, because of which Romanian women mistook him for a Jew and called him "dirty." Iorga was to describe the episodes of this journey in a lengthy volume. Before the publication of the book, he had already held several conferences in Bucharest about his experiences in Hungary. He noted during one of these conferences that the Romanians were a "cultured people" whereas the Székelys were "barbarians thrown among us by the circumstances." He concluded by the following appeal for unification: "We must awaken the soul and work for the fraternal unification of all the fragments that compose our nation." These observations of Iorga were reprinted in the Romanian papers of Hungary;[49] in fact, the entire text of the conference was published as a separate pamphlet in Naszód. Thus the Hungarian authorities undoubtedly found out; yet Iorga continued to visit Hungary in subsequent years without any impediment.

The above statement and many other acts of Iorga are indications of his animosity towards the Hungarians. The Hungarian authorities were well aware of the ideas of the professor from Bucharest and of their harmful effect on the Romanians of Hungary — harmful at least from the point of view of the state and of the Hungarians. Still, when the general assembly of Astra opened in Balázsfalva in 1911, Iorga was allowed to participate on the third day of the celebrations. He had just arrived on the express train from Bucharest. When he entered the hall, all Romanians stood at attention, as if they had been greeting the King himself. Iorga sat on a small chair behind the president's rostrum, and gazed with great love, if not a little satisfaction, at the Romanian faces beaming towards him.[50] As the First Secretary of the Cultural League, Iorga paid visits of a similar nature and with similar intent to the Romanians of Bukovina living under Austrian rule; but since he reported on his visits there in the same vein, the Austrian authorities expelled him from Bukovina forever.[51]

In addition to scholars, journalists, and officers, members of the Romanian royal family often visited the areas of Hungary inhabited by Romanians. From Sinaia, where they spent their summers, they occasionally came over to Brassó and the vicinity, and were always greeted with loud cheers by the Romanian population. Some Hungarian papers suspected a specific purpose behind these "high level" visits, and even surmised — as indeed it happened — that these royal visitors arrived on Hungarian territory occasionally in the company of high-ranking officers, and perhaps not always merely to admire the beauty of the scenery. The Romanian papers protested indignantly against the "base suspicions" of the Hungarians.[52] But they knew quite well, among each other, why Ion Brătianu, the Prime Minister of Romania, had paid a visit to Brassó in the company of Sazonov, the Russian Minister of Foreign Affairs, in the second half of June 1914. In fact, the news spread like wildfire among the Romanians of Hungary.

Contacts between the Romanians of Hungary and the Romanians of Romania, as we know, did not cease even during World War I.

Freedom of Assembly and Association

This freedom was one of the most important rights of the Romanians. In the chapter on culture we have discussed the mass rallies and gatherings held by the Romanians of the Hungarian state in order to protest various Hungarian laws on education. There being no state of emergency or preventive censorship during the entire period of Hungarian rule, only rarely did the authorities intervene to restrict the right of assembly. According to the prevailing regulations, if citizens intended to meet for whatever reason; they had to announce their intentions at least 24 hours in advance, either to the sheriff in the villages, or to superintendent of police in the towns. They would also communicate the venue and the program, requesting that the announcement be acknowledged. The pertinent authority had to respond to this announcement within the shortest possible delay. An acknowledgement in writing was tantamount to authorization; but if the acknowledgement was not forthcoming, permission was denied. Denial of authorization could be appealed all the way up to the Minister.[53] As regards the right of assembly, Romanians were content to demand that it be regulated in a uniform way so that they would not be exposed to the fickleness of the local authorities. They presented the issue as if the exercise of this right encountered the greatest difficulties. On the contrary, however, items in the Romanian press indicate that the freedom of assembly was almost invariably respected throughout the period: very seldom was authorization denied. Before the well-known ordinance of Minister of the Interior Károly Hieronymi (with which he dissolved the Romanian National Party in 1894), even Romanian political gatherings could take place wherever and in whatever form the organizers desired. "Until Hieronymi came with his draconian regulations, it wasn't so difficult for us," noted the lawyer, Dr. Aurel Vlad.

Before those regulations we could witness effective manifestations of the will of our nation. From the sixties to the years of the Memorandum, the Romanians availed themselves fully of the right to assemble. Then, in the suddenly tense atmosphere, some

local authorities were less forthcoming in the matter of authorizing political meetings, in a few instances.[54]

Indeed, before the Memorandum the Romanians availed themselves
fully of the right to assemble, and within a few years the situation
returned to normal. After 1905, when the Romanian National Party
gained a new lease on life and modified its anti-state program, once
again mass rallies of Romanians were organized. Hundreds of rallies
were held in 1906, 1907, 1908, 1910, and 1911, to enable delegates to
the parliament to present their annual and other reports. There were
victory parades following the elections, protests against the Apponyi
Laws, and mass rallies in connection with the proposed law on electoral
rights, in rapid succession. The mode prevailing at these rallies was
virulently anti-Hungarian. After the elections in 1906, at Szászsebes,
the large majority of Romanian voters, their hats doffed, paraded down
the streets escorting the successful candidates, and lined up along the
market where they sang, "Awake, Romanian, from your slumber."
According to the report in the Romanian press:

> speaker after speaker spoke openly, breathing fire into the hearts
> of the people at the town market, then marched around the town
> singing, and then once again speeches, making noise to their
> heart's content; yet there was not a single gendarme of twisted
> mind to intervene or forbid such demonstrations, as long as they
> were otherwise peaceful.[55]

Similar observations may be read in another Romanian weekly
regarding the mass rallies at Románszentgyörgy and Bethlen where the
Romanian voters of the area were summoned to defend their right to
vote. At these mass rallies the Romanian speakers attacked the
government's proposed electoral law in rousing speeches; during the
speeches the sheriff was present, as was the entire body of civil servants
in Bethlen, yet "they did not interrupt the speakers with a single word
or gesture."[56] The Romanian delegates presented their reports to
their constituency in such a manner as to provide political schooling for
the masses. The *Libertatea* would have preferred to hold such meetings
once a month because, as it noted, then "these rallies would become
most effective cultural and political training, and provide a stimulus for
improving the Romanian people in every respect."[57] The most
outstanding in the series of mass rallies and general assemblies in the
coming years were the ones held at Szászváros in 1910, the anniversary

meeting of the Astra already discussed, and the protest meeting of 1912 at Gyulafehérvár.

A great Romanian rally was held at Szászváros in the spring of 1910. From 4,000 to 5,000 Romanians participated in the rally, along with representatives from the Hungarian municipal authorities. They listened to Goga's speech. It did not backfire against the illustrious poet, even though he stated, within earshot of his listeners:

> You know how Christ was beaten, spat upon, and crucified, only to ascend to heaven thereafter. But, brothers, the fate of our Romanian nation resembles that of our divine guide in many ways. Our own people have been tied down, beaten, spat upon, and crucified between two thieves, in the same way.[58]

Preparations for the mass rally of the Astra at Balázsfalva were rather interesting. The organizers of the rally had reached an understanding with the Hungarian authorities to the effect that the gendarmes dispatched to Balázsfalva would not be posted along the streets. Indeed, during the entire period of the meeting no gendarmes were seen on the streets; as if embarrassed, they modestly retired to a public school building so that the distinguished guests from Romania would not even notice them, as arranged beforehand by Iuliu Maniu directly with the Hungarian Prime Minister. The report on the celebrations states:

> In order to avoid any unpleasantness, and in order to avoid the hateful supervision of the state, the master of ceremonies, Dr. Maniu, personally called upon Prime Minister Khuen-Héderváry, in order to show him the program of the activities. The program was approved and Maniu was given assurances that the administration would cause no difficulty in the execution of details.[59]

Indeed, the celebration went on without interference.

At first the authorities would not allow the protest rally planned for Gyulafehérvár in 1912; but, upon instructions from the Hungarian Minister of the Interior, permission was finally granted. Some 20 to 30,000 people gathered; the popular paper of the Romanian peasantry noted:

> The Romanians were unable to find accomodations for the night on account of the large multitude and had to sleep under the

stars. This seldom happens in our own country where no sooner do 20 or 30 peasants assemble the local authorities immediately intervene to disperse them, chase them away, and stop them from voicing their opinions, from writing a memorandum, or from protesting in any way. In Hungary, in spite of all the intimidation by the gendarmes, Romanians gather by the tens of thousands to defend their rights effectively.[60]

After World War I, the statements of some Romanian politicians of Hungary confirmed that this right to assemble really existed. For instance, Alexandru Vaida-Voevod told the grand assembly of the National Peasant Party held at Temesvár in 1923 that at the time of Tisza, the Hungarian authorities "did not ban a single meeting of the Romanian National Party."[61] Vaida was telling the truth. We may complement his declaration with data concerning the antecedents of the mass rally at Gyulafehérvár on December 1, 1918. The Romanian army had not yet occupied Transylvania at that time and the transportation network was still in Hungarian hands. The Hungarians knew from the proclamation summoning the mass rally that the Romanians intended to declare their secession from Hungary. Nevertheless, as noted by the official paper of the Romanian National Party of Transylvania, the Hungarian authorities did not prevent the rally, but instead provided "special trains to enable all our delegates to reach Alba Iulia in time."[62]

This last mass rally ended the freedom of assembly enjoyed by the Romanians of Hungary. They declared the unification of the Romanians of Hungary with Romania and, a few months later, the Romanian army did indeed occupy most areas inhabited by Romanians in Eastern Hungary.

We have seen in the first chapter that, as regards the right to assemble, the Romanians of Hungary enjoyed real freedom in accordance with the prescriptions of the laws. The numerous associations formed by Romanians in Hungary and their unhindered and effective operation all indicate that this freedom existed not just in theory, but in practice.

The Freedom of Worship

We find no mention of any infraction of the freedom of worship in the Romanian press during the entire period of Hungarian rule. Although complaining about the infringement of autonomy of the church in connection with the introduction of the school laws, the minutes of church meetings likewise do not provide evidence of any infractions against the freedom of worship. Not a single Romanian was forced to convert to another religion or to attend service at a church alien to him. Nor did it occur to anyone to order Romanian children to attend a church of a different religion. Romanian ecclesiastic meetings were held to the end of the World War I free from interference. In 1917, towards the end of the war, after the Romanian army broke into Transylvania, the Orthodox synod summoned to discuss the nationalization of the Romanian Orthodox schools was dismissed by the Hungarian representative and barred from continuing its sessions. This, however, was not a religious issue, but one of national security.

In the chapter on the churches we have seen how the Romanians took advantage of their church autonomy. Most Romanian priests indulged in anti-state actvities. Sometimes the candidates of the Romanian National Party held their campaign speeches on church premises, and sometimes even motion pictures were projected there. The priests concerned suffered no harm as a consequence, because the authorities respected freedom of worship in spite of all abuses. It is evident, therefore, that freedom of worship remained a reality for the Romanians on Hungarian territory to the end.

In addition to the rights of citizens, the Romanians of Hungary enjoyed various national rights as members of a separate nationality. Most important and significant among these was the right to display Romanian national symbols.

The Display of Romanian National Symbols

Every nation has symbols expressing its special national character, symbols which are revered as such. These include the national flag, the national anthem, and national heroes whose feats are in harmony with the yearnings of the nation. Under alien rule the use of these national symbols is hampered in every way if the rulers harbor ill-feelings towards the minorities within the country, for the people manifest their right to a national existence and their national aspirations through these symbols, which have extraordinary potential for reinforcing a sense of identity. Hence, an important aspect of the nationalities policy of any state is its attitude towards these national symbols.

parliament declared the demise of the legitimate dynasty, the revolution was on its way, the civil war was under way with all its consequences.... Two months after the outbreak of the revolution, the prospect of the imperial forces defeating the rebels by themselves diminishing day by day, the Romanians gathered at Balázsfalva and declared their intention: that they were prepared to spill their blood and put their possessions on the line in order to end the revolution and restablish law and order on the basis of the Pragmatic Sanction.[77]

The Hungarian public and the authorities realized that the Romanians used these arguments to transform the events of 1848 to suit their purposes. After all, in the first half of May there was no such thing as a Hungarian army and, as everyone knew, the demise of the dynasty did not take place until the spring of 1849. Therefore, and because of its obviously anti-Hungarian character, the Hungarian Minister of the Interior banned the Romanian celebrations of May 15 at Balázsfalva in 1885, while the celebration was allowed to continue in other cities. In the calendar of the *Tribuna*, in the column titled "National Holidays," anyone could read for years the self-same text: "Although Hungarian rule punishes us severely and persecutes us for all kinds of national actions and will not allow us to hold meetings, even this year the majestic day of May 15 was celebrated in a dignified manner in many Romanian provinces, including Brassó, Szeben, Kolozsvár, and Nagyvárad." In Kolozsvár after a festive religious service, there was a soirée.[78] This could not have been held without the knowledge of the police, after all the program of the soirée was announced in the papers beforehand. It follows, therefore, that the Hungarian authorities, in spite of the interesting assertions quoted above, did allow the celebration of May 15, albeit not in the form of an anti-Hungarian demonstration.

In general, as regards the use of national symbols, we may state that, according to the evidence collected from the Romanian press, the Romanians of Hungary enjoyed extensive, opportunities to express their national yearnings.

The Political Rights of the Romanians

From the point of view of self-defense of ethnic groups living under alien rule, the measure and use of political rights is always critical. It is with regard to the curtailment of these rights that we find the largest number of justified complaints by Romanians in Hungary. Once the

Hungarian house of parliament had defeated their request for the autonomy of Transylvania after the Compromise, the majority of Romanians opted to give up the utilization of their political rights. In 1869, at a conference at Szerdahely, most Romanians from Transylvania declared political passivity with regard to elections at the national level. In other words, they decided what they would not field candidates for parliamentary elections nor represent themselves in parliament. They justified their decision on the ground of the existing election laws and of the aggressive government intervention at the polls. They declared they would not participate in the parliamentary elections, because the unjust provisions of the electoral laws and the abuses committed by government made it almost impossible for Romanian candidates to succeed. On the other hand, they intended to continue participation within the autonomous bodies of the communities and of the counties, and did in fact remain active at those levels.[79]

Against the arguments for passivity, the activists remained in a minority. Their leader was Andrei Şaguna, the famous Romanian Orthodox archbishop. Şaguna was consoled only by the fact that the Romanians in areas of Hungary outside of Transylvania remained politically active and sent delegates to the Hungarian parliament in Budapest regularly.

In reality, the decision in favor of passive resistance was reached not because of the actual injustices of the electoral system, or the aggressive government intervention at the polls. By passive resistance they strove to achieve Romanian self-government in Transylvania, much as the Hungarians had done during the period of the Austrian autocratic rule.

The years passed and it soon became obvious that passive resistance entailed negative consequences for the Romanian population. These consequences were summarized in a classic formulation by the *Libertatea* in 1902, the weekly of Szászváros published by that group of Romanians who advocated political participation. According to their formulation, the most deplorable consequence of passivity was that:

> we have deprived ourselves of the most effective tool for the political schooling of our people, a schooling which could have helped mold them into citizens aware of their national and individual rights.... Today the situation is that the over-whelming majority of the masses from which the National Party has to recruit its militants do not have the faintest idea of the mission and demands of the party.

As a consequence of passivity, the people never even found out what rights they had within the state, let alone how to use those rights. As a consequence of passivity the people forgot their leaders and at times became victims of all kinds of candidates who lost campaigns in some other electoral district. They no longer support the former leaders of the National Party and, what is even worse, "their hatred towards their oppressors, against whom they had had to fight so hard during the electroral campaigns at one time, has abated, and even died down almost completely." Indeed, this was the case: these arguments of the group from Szászváros were conforming to reality in almost every respect. In many places the people, rather than stay away from voting, had voted for non-Romanians; there was no one to whip up the passions of the crowd during the campaigns, hence the anti-Hungarian fervor had indeed decreased considerably.

Through the weekly the activists launched an aggressive movement in favor of participation. They pointed out that passive resistance the electroral laws, had also become a:

> ...most solemn declaration of national weakness and contempti-
> bility. Because assuming that our voters are aware of their
> rights and that they are men, if we have the absolute majority
> of voters in 30 or 40 electoral districts; there is no power in the
> world that could pervent the victory of the national candidate, in
> spite of the strange laws and artfully designed boundary lines of
> these districts, unless the voters are stopped by force.

The erstwhile defeats suffered by the National Party during elections for parliament can be attributed to a failure to exercise those rights in full. In most cases "it was due to our own weakness or, better said, to our political immaturity and lack of orientation." The Saxons are a shining example of this truth. Why can't the government manipulate elections in a Saxon district without the Saxon's consent? After all, they resort to the same measures towards the Saxons. "But the difference lies in the fact that the Saxon voters are disciplined and aware of their rights, so they cannot be enticed away from their own candidates, whether by pressures or bribery." If the Romanians gave up their passivity then the electoral campaigns would reinforce the national consciousness of the Romanians and make the masses aware of their political rights.

> Thus before long, as regards the use of the right to vote, we
> have complete control over our voters, and it become impossible

for our adversaries to keep us down. I am not underestimating
the terror and force that can be used by the executive power; but
we can confront their terrorism with a far more powerful
terrorism, that of the masses of the people which the nation,
fully aware of its power, may resort to.[80]

This campaign of the activists soon carried the day. The activists
among the former leaders of the Romanian National Party were able to
control an increasingly large constituency. Soon the Romanian National
Party helped the young leader of the activist group, the lawyer Dr.
Aurel Vlad, enter the elections as a candidate at Dobra, in 1903.

The polling was preceding by a great deal of excitement. The laws
on franchise in Hungary tied the right to vote to certain property
qualifications; in other words, not everyone had the franchise, only those
with sufficient income. The rosters of the voters were revised each year,
to add new names or delete the names of those who no longer qualified.
While the Romanians had remained passive, little care was taken to
determine whether the new voters were truly eligible or not. After the
turn of the century, however, they became interested in determining the
number of Romanian voters in every electoral district. The control of
these rosters was the task of local authorities, according to the principle
of autonomy. Upon the announcement of activism the Romanian
leaders intervened first in the district of Naszód to check the roster of
Romanian voters in that area. For instance, in the village of Magyarne-
megye [Nimigea de Jos] they determined that of the eighty persons
registered to vote, many were no longer entitled to the franchise; hence
only 17 names were admitted onto the new roster. At the meeting of
the central voters' committee the Hungarians requested that they be
reinstated. On the counter-motion of the Romanian doctor, Ciuta, their
request was denied. Then the Hungarians carried their complaint, to
the effect that the Romanians were persecuting them and depriving
them of their franchise, all the way to the Ministry of the Interior. The
Minister also denied their request. Before they could request their
reinstatement once again, the deadline for appeals had passed; and thus
the Hungarian voters in this village lost their franchise on the motion
of Dr. Ciuta, who was consciously representing Romanian interests;
according to the census mentioned in the law, they were not entitled to
vote that year anyway.[81]

The Romanians effected similar controls in the area of Szászváros.
In 1903, after almost one year of publication by *Libertatea*, Aurel Vlad
launched his campaign at Dobra. Thanks to the prodding of *Libertatea*,
all the Romanian priests and civil servants supported his campaign.

There were plenty of interesting scenes during the campaign. Enormous crowds assembled on election day. Anyone about whom it was suspected that he did not intend to vote for Vlad was loudly berated. Soldiers and gendarmes were summoned to maintain law and order. In order to encourage the Romanian voters, they played the *Deseapta* during the actual voting. The militants of the opposite party attacked the supporters of Vlad, including their leader, the deacon Morariu, as we may read from the report; but the gendarmes dispersed them right away. The president of the election committee "behaved honorably and in a perfectly correct way."[82]

Thus Vlad was elected at Dobra by a landslide, and this victory considerably strengthened the hand of those advocating activism. Now they set upon to prepare general Romanian activism everywhere. All the Romanians of Hungary became active during the campaign of 1905, and from then on made full use of their political rights everywhere.

This was when the Romanian National Party of Hungary reorganized once again. The party had been originally organized on the basis of a resolution adopted at the voters' conference of 1883 in Nagyszeben. Although passive in parliamentary elections, the party carried out impressive social and especially journalistic activities. Taking advantage of its contacts with the parties and newspapers of Bucharest, it organized an information service to broadcast information towards foreign countries regarding the situation of the Romanians of Hungary. The party soon succeeded in shaping opinion abroad regarding the situation of the Romanians of Hungary, which sharply condemned the Hungarian government's systematic "oppression of the nationalities." The *Tribuna*, bringing the Romanians of Hungary completely under the influence of Bucharest, endowed the party with a great deal of prestige. The Hungarian authorities took note of the anti-Hungarian and anti-state activities of the Romanian National Party with increasing concern when the mood abroad became even more unfavorable due to the Romanian Cultural League formed in Bucharest in 1891. In 1892 the Romanian leaders took a memorandum to Vienna with the intention of placing it into the hands of the ruler, Francis Joseph. Their dailies had been editorializing on the significance of this move for awhile. Briefly stated, it meant that the Romanians, by-passing the Hungarian government in Budapest — since they did not recognize the legitimacy of Hungarian leadership in the country — turned with their complaints directly to the rulers of the Monarchy, the Emperor of Austria. This move meant open rejection of the constitution of the Hungarian state and of the Dual system brought about in 1867. At the time the Hungarian authorities could only suspect what we now know for certain

from the recollections of those who prepared the memorandum, namely that the whole movement was initiated and orchestrated by political circles in Romania. The ruler, would not accept the memorandum on constitutional grounds. Then the Romanian National Party, bent on turning the issue of the Romanians of Hungary into a European issue at all cost, took a very significant step. It published the text of the memorandum in the official paper of the party, in order to compel the Hungarian government to become aware, officially, of the dissatisfaction of the Romanians, and perhaps to initiate proceedings against them. The Party succeeded, since the shortsighted Hungarian government did indeed render this service to the Romanians. The government brought the leaders of the Romanian National Party to court and sentenced them in 1894, while resolving to dissolve the party. After the dissolution the Romanians could claim everywhere that the reason for the dissolution was the national character of the Party, which the Hungarian government would not tolerate. But a few years later one of the most prestigious leaders of the Romanians, Ioan Mihu, admitted that the facts had been presented in a false light. The dissolution of the Romanian National Party by order of the Minister occurred not because of the national or Romanian nature of the Party, but because it had overstepped certain boundaries in its activities and its manifestations.[83] Indeed, this was the case. The members of the Party not only openly demanded a change in the constitution of the country, but openly admitted their political contacts with circles in Romania in the columns of their newspapers. So the government considered it could no longer overlook its operations, hence the order issued by Minister of the Interior, Hyeronimi, to dissolve it.

In order to become active once again, the Party had to place itself on a legal footing; it changed the political program of 1881, reconciling it with the constitution of the country. As one member of the activist group had noted already in 1903, the first point of the program of 1881 regarding the autonomy of Transylvania "was a matter of constitutional law aimed at changing and breaking up the political unity of the Hungarian nation."[84] Once this part of the program was modified, the Romanian National Party could operate legally once again; and it soon operated throughout the country. Everywhere the Romanian candidates undertook to check whether the rights of the Romanian voters were respected. Wherever they detected abuses, they immediately intervened and turned to the appropriate authorities for remedies, obtaining rewarding results. In 1904 they elected members of the county assembly at Dobra. During the polling Hits, a notary of Dobra, distributed slips of paper to the voters, promoting the victory of the

after the World War I: the Romanian leaders of Transylvania acted according to instructions received from entities in the Romainan Kingdom on every important issue. These contacts with Bucharest became an integral part of the political life of the Romanians of Hungary. From the time of the Memorandum all important political issues were decided according to instructions from Bucharest.[95]

The power of the political leaders of the Romanians of Hungary was considerably enhanced by other foreign contacts as well. These contacts resulted from the propaganda campaign the Romanian press of Hungary carried on abroad, beginning soon after the Compromise. The basic principle of this propaganda effort was identical with the struggle the *Tribuna* of Nagyszeben launched at the beginning of 1884 against the Hungarians and against Romanians intent on fraternizing with the Hungarians. This principle was summarized by the *Tribuna* as follows; "We must bring this regime into ill repute."[96] The term regime referred to the Dual Monarchy and the Hungarian government in general. Every Hungarian mistake or abuse of authority was publicized abroad in an exaggerated, distorted, misinterpreted form. The papers of Bucharest reprinted articles from the Romanian papers in Hungary, whence they reached the foreign press — French, Italian, German, English, etc. The Hungarian government could ill defend itself against this campaign. What's more, since it misjudged the problem for a long time, it even contributed to the Romanian propaganda by its ill-advised measures and its numerous mistakes. The opinions in foreign countries, particularly among the Western powers, turned increasingly against the Hungarian state and its policy on nationalities. This became particularly obvious as the time of the Memorandum trial and later, when the foreign contacts of the Romanians proved even more rewarding for the Romanian cause. Celebrities, including prestigious representatives of the literary and scientific worlds, took a stand on behalf of the Romanians of Hungary one after another. Their one-sided interpretations stemmed from the Romanian press. Thus, in 1908, Björnstjerne Björnson spoke out against the educational policies of Count Albert Apponyi, his data were provided by the correspondent of the *Tribuna* of Arad, who suffered no harm for doing that.[97] The Romanian informants, of course, failed to provide comparative date, and the diplomats representing the Hungarian state consisted for the most part of Austrians, or of indifferent individuals from among the gentry or magnate strata who were bored and unable to furnish factual information or serve Hungarian interests.

Occasionally, the Hungarian government and individual Hungarian statesmen tried to make peace with the Romanians, but these efforts proved futile. According to the Romanians, they were futile because the Hungarians were unwilling to meet the justified demands of the Romanians; but according to authentic Romanian statements from after World War I, there can be no doubt that these efforts failed because of the intervention of circles in Romania. When the conversations between István Tisza and Romanian politicians got under way in 1914, "the Romanian National Party immediately informed the Romanian government, and undertook the negotiations in agreement with the latter."[98] When the negotiations led to no results, the Romanian press hinted at the real reason for the fiasco. The outcome of the negotiations, according to an article in *Luceafărul*, could not have changed the situation in any case, since the future

> ...is not subject to agreements between political leaders, for it is determined by the iron rails of the course of historial events. The times are more powerful than any individual will, because the soul of our Romanian masses can no longer be tampered with. Only the national principle rules over them and... agreements, pacts, ceasefires of any kind mean nothing in the cauldron of great events which drive us ineluctably towards the goal which had guided us but faintly until now.

The *Libertatea*, reprinting this eloquent statement, added: "indeed, it is so."[99]

The political clout of the Romanians of Hungary derived in part from areas outside of Hungary, and not much could be done to counteract that. With the shortsightedness peculiar to him, Francis Ferdinand believed that contacts with Romanian leaders could serve to reconstitute a united Austria. As the events were to demonstrate, he was the victim of a serious error in judgment. The Romanians were interested only in realizing a single objective, the unification of Transylvania with Romania.

Equal Rights Before the Law

In substance it is possible to answer the much debated question, whether the nationalities, specifically the Romanians, enjoyed equal rights during the Dual Monarchy, on the basis of the particular cases already cited. The authors of Romanian publications intended for foreign countries generally denied that equal rights existed. Their claims misled more than one well-intentioned foreign researcher. Much as in the matter of whether the law on nationalities was observed or not, comments on the administration of justice in Hungary also became critical. According to these comments, Hungarian justice was always prejudiced when it came to the affairs of the nationalities; its decisions were imbued by national hatred; and equal rights remained an empty fiction for members of the ethnic groups.

The Romanian sources cited in the preceding chapters lead us to question the one-sided assertions above. The decisions regarding complaints against electoral abuses, the dismissal of cases for lack of evidence, the authorization issued by the courts to allow the singing of the anti-Hungarian Romanian anthem, and similar decisions indicate that equality before the law was a demonstrable reality. We have quoted the meaningful statement of the Romanian weekly from Szászváros, according to which "it is not the name or the nationality of the lawyer that counts in the courts, but the facts."

Most Romanian complaints and criticism from abroad aimed against the Hungarian system of justice, naturally centered on press trials of a political nature. The accusation that the Hungarian juries and courts see the Romanians as political adversaries, hence smite them with unjustly severe sentences, was almost universal. But an analysis of the better known trials involving agitation or some other political factor, does not support this contention. If we examine the events leading to judicial proceedings, the article or act that became the object of accusation; we find that in the overwhelming majority of cases the proceedings were justified. No state has ever remained indifferent towards those who engaged in acts denying its constitution or jeopardizing the internal and external security of the state.

The ideology of the judicial system is best revealed by the sentences passed by the highest judicial forum, the Supreme Court (Kuria), and their justification. Courts at the first and second levels often introduced subjective considerations; but the sentences handed down by the Supreme Court were formed on the basis of a consistent ideology, and they faithfully mirrored Hungarian juridical views regarding equality in front of the law.

A typical example was the sentence pronounced by the highest court in the case of the Romaina Uniate priest, Vasile Lucaciu of Lácfalu, in a trial pertaining to agitation. The circumstances were also noteworthy. As mentioned, Lucaciu was of the boldest advocates of Romanian irredentism in the late eighties. While he launched a nationwide collection for a church "dedicated to the unification of all Romanians," he also took an active part in Romanian political movements. He belonged to the sharply anti-Hungarian group around the *Tribuna* and, at the conference of Nagyszeben in 1887, he was one of the principal

advocates of the memorandum to be sent to the Emperor. Upon his
return from the conference, he delivered a speech to Romanian voters,
over two hours long, in the course of which he passionately incited the
audience against the Hungarians, according to the prosecution. In that
speech he made assertions such as:

> They turned us into beggars. We are oppressed. The
> ministers unleash whole armies of oppressors upon us. We are
> excluded from everything, and our language commands no
> respect. The rights of the Romanians are trampled upon all over
> the country. We live without rights or justice. Romanians are
> not appointed to state schools. Those who are appointed must
> renounce their nationality. We are outlaws all our lives, because
> we are excluded from everywhere and deprived of our rights.

Lucaciu admitted having used these expressions, but he denied
having made the assertions attributed to him by some Romanians who
denounced him after the speech. Throughout his trial at the court in
the first instance, he used his mother tongue. In his Romanian defense
he protested vigorously against using Hungarian, referring to the law
on nationalities which guarantees the right to use one's mother tongue
in court. Upon cross-examination of the witnesses, the Hungarian jury
acquitted him of the charge. The prosecutor, however, well aware of
local conditions and of Lucaciu's feelings, appealed the decision. The
court in the second instance confirmed the acquittal, even though
Lucaciu continued to persist in his irredentist activities. The prosecution once again appealed, and the case came in front of the Supreme
Court. This Court reconfirmed the decisions taken by the lower courts
and it offered a detailed explanation.

The Supreme Court claimed that the multitude of life experiences
and famous court cases predisposed the court to exercise the greatest
circumspection in such matters.

It questioned if members of an audience are able to faithfully
recollect the contents of a long speech, the expressions, examples, or
similes used by the speaker, upon hearing the speech but one time,
without mixing these recollections with their own subjective reactions.

The speech that was the subject of the accusation lasted over two
hours. It was delivered partly in the everyday language of the people,
partly in literary Romanian. The almost two hundred listeners who had
assembled in the courtyard of the village restaurant could not have
heard the arguments of the speaker without interference. The judges

surmised that this was the case of the individuals who, after the speech, repeated it in front of the Hungarian authorities in "surprising detail."

Among those who made the denunciation, there were farmers who could not read nor write. Undoubtedly, they could not have understood a significant portion of the speech, since it was delivered in Romanian literary style, a style completely unfamiliar to simple people. Moreover, the accusers retracted some of their statements during the trial. According to his own admission, the government official who attended the meeting did not understand Romanian, hence he could not ascertain precisely the contents of the speech in question.

"For all these reasons we must accept as just the statement of the court in the second instance, according to which what is contained in the denunciation and in the testimony of the witnesses cannot be considered as the actual content of the speech of the accused."

The Supreme Court also observed that the speech, or its essential parts, was noted by several persons, even if not verbatim or in short-hand. A memorandum had been prepared on the basis of these notes, and authenticated for the purpose of publication in the Romanian papers. The judges assumed that this memorandum, attached to the records of the trial, reflected faithfully the ideas of the speaker.

They claimed that according to this text, the speech without the least doubt, "contained crude and improper expressions regarding the government and the administration." Nor could it be doubted "that the speech contained untrue, distorted, or exaggerated statements regarding the prevailing political, administrative, or economic conditions." Moreover, it cannot be doubted that some of the administrative shortcomings "and the general confusion which may arise in administration were described by the speaker in a one-sided and disloyal manner, as if it were exclusively the Romanian population which was subjected to those "sufferings." Nor can it be doubted that the speaker used those arguments which were to conform to reality to derive surprising and inappropriate conclusions, for the sake of depicting all these facts as injustices committed against the Romanian population.

> *"Yet all these devices, which cannot be viewed with approval, do not exceed the boundaries of normal political discourse which may be directed against the authorities and institutions of the country or against specific government and administrative acts, in a constitutional country; these may not, however, be directed against the Hungarians, or against other nationalities of the country."* [Italics by the author]

Thus, the judges concluded that the criterion mentioned in paragraph two of Article 172 was moot. In other words, it was not a matter of inciting against a nationality.

This most interesting explanation by the Supreme Court was complemented by the following statement of ideology:

> Although the accused speaks the official language of the state well, he nevertheless resorted to Romanian at the main hearing, rejecting the right to answer questions in Hungarian — he thereby resorted to a right guaranteed by law. ...Hence this practice of his legal right cannot constitute the object of special mention among the justifications adduced by the courts.[100]

These facts, reported in the Romanian book compiled with the aim of glorifying and praising Lucaciu, eloquently deny the accusations of prejudice often raised against the Hungarian judical system. It becomes clear from an analysis of the sentence that the highest Hungarian court was impartial. Although Lucaciu was one of the most inveterate enemies of the Hungarian state; the Supreme Court recognized his right to pronounce harsh judgments against the state and its institutions, even though the facts on which these judgments were based were "untrue, unfair, or distorted." Such arguments were also used by Hungarian politicians of the opposition without incurring criminal charges. Therefore, the Court could not condemn an accused of Romanian background; because if it did, it would deprive the accused of a right which Hungarians could resort to freely. Thus, the Court applied equality before the law without bias in the case of Lucaciu.

The former leaders of the Romanians of Transylvania themselves publicly admitted, after the First World War, the objectivily of the Hungarian courts and the application of the principle of equal rights in the Hungarian state. Comparing these procedures to the crude character of the system of justice administered by the new Romanian state and to the sentences passed by Romanian judges who received their instructions from the state or who were intimidated, they recalled with sighs their experiences gained at the courts of the former Hungarian state. In 1918 the Romanians of Transylvania proclaimed union with Romania, at the famous meeting of Alba Iulia [Gyulafehérvár], on the basis of the motion of Alexandru Vaida-Voevod. Several times in 1923 and 1924, the same Vaida-Voevod publicly compared conditions in the former Hungarian state to those in the Greater Romania that came about in 1918. "We were not slaves in Hungary. We had the shield of the laws to protect ourselves, and these were laws even for the

Romanians. Today they treat us as some alien element outside of the law."[101] The following year the same person declared, in front of the Romanian peasants of the community of Cricău [Boroskrakkó] in the electoral district of Ighiu: "Is it not true, brothers, that it was better under the Hungarians?" Some peasants answered: "It may be so, Sir, but it is also possible that things will improve in Greater Romania from now on."[102]

These statements by Vaida-Voevod reflected a widely held opinion in the country. "We are used to legality," a Romanian from Transylvania told the journalist from the daily *Timpul*. "We lived that way under the Hungarians, and we won thanks to legality. We do not want to perish for lack of the most basic rights in our own country, which we had imagined quite differently. Grant us legality!"[103]

We may consider the above statements by politicians and peasants who cannot be accused of being pro-Hungarian as decisive in any evaluation of the Hungarian courts of the period of the Dual Monarchy.

Rule of Law and Civil Rights in Other States

While the Romanians of Hungary could make full use of the human and civic rights guaranteed in the constitution, the residents of neighboring or more distant lands enjoyed no such advantages. Romanians who lived outside Hungary occasionally thought of the rights and opportunities enjoyed by their brothers in Hungary with yearning mixed with envy. Unfortunately, the Romanians of Romania, those living under Russian and Austrian rule, as well as those in the Balkan states, all lacked many of the rights enjoyed and sometimes abused by the Romanians of Hungary. The same may be said about the minorities dominated by other nationalities in more distant countries.

a) Let us first take a glance at the legal conditions prevailing in Romania. Even before World War I, part of the Romanian press pointed out that the supposedly democratic relations in the country bore not the least resemblance to conditions in truly democratic states. These papers compared public life in Hungary with that of Romania almost always to the detriment of the latter. Aware of the rights and freedoms prevailing in Hungary, they did not find conditions in Romania the least bit rosy or attractive for the Romanians of Hungary. "As things are," we may read in a newspaper published in Bucharest, "the Romanians of Hungary are not inclined to exchange the odious Hungarian rule with our twice as odious rule over here, where the gendarme and lawlessness dominate the scene." The Romanian leaders of Hungary were aware of this. "The oligarchy of King Carol bears no comparison with Hungarian rule."[104] The Romanians of Hungary would not be able to stand the present Romanian administration for even six months.[105]

Although the Romanian leaders in Hungary were aware of all this, for reasons of politics and propaganda, they did not bring the issue out in public. Had they openly admitted that the Romanians of Hungary had greater democratic rights than those of Romania, the anti-Hungarian irredentist propaganda would lose all credibility. Therefore, they did not publicize comparisons between the two regimes. After 1918, however, when the lawlessness customary in the old kingdom of Romania was also introduced into the Romanian areas formerly under Hungarian rule, they did voice their opinions. The best known spokesman of these views was Alexandru Vaida-Voevod, a former representative of the Romanians of Hungary. According to him, "an oligarchy more cursed than the Hungarian" ruled in old Romania.[106] While the country appeared to have the constitution, the regime was tyrannical in practice. The Liberal Party had stolen the rights of the people. "No party could hold meetings in the country, because the gendarmes and secret agents would bust it. They are trying to introduce their system on our side as well, in order to terrorize us."[107]

As mentioned, in actuality there was no such thing in Romania as the right to assemble. While in Hungary thousands could participate in meetings protesting government policies, even twenty or thirty peasants would not be allowed to meet in Romania. These conditions hurt first of all those Romanians who were comparing the two countries.

Under the circumstances the non-Romanian residents of Romania — the Csángók, Bulgarians, Greeks, and Jews — had practically none of the rights enjoyed by the Romanians living under Hungarian rule; they were subjected to complete Romanianization. As regards the Csángók, they were not even allowed to travel to Hungary. They could travel no further than the Romanian border. On one occasion a resident of Săbăoani [Szabófalva], gathering his courage in both hands, overstepped the boundary and visited Hungary. Upon his return the county police and the Ministry summoned, interrogated and harrassed him in order to discourage others from following in his path. At the same time the Romanians of Hungary could freely meet with their brothers across the border during the whole period.[108]

b) The Romanians of Bessarabia, under Russian administration, would also have been elated to enjoy even one fourth of the rights enjoyed by the Romanians of Hungary. They could not even dream of

104. *Adevărul*, October 18, 1911, quoted in Jakabffy, *op. cit.*, p. 768.

105. *Ibid.*, December 10, 1912; Jakabffy, *op. cit.*, p. 11.

106. *Universul*, November 22, 1922.

107. *Adevărul*, November 22, 1922.

108. Lóránt Hegedűs, *A székelyek kivándorlása Romániába* [The emigration of the Székelys to Romania], pp. 39-40, quoted by Barna, *op. cit.*, pp. 153-154.

109. *Pagini despre Basarabia de astăzi de N. Iorga. (Văleni de Munte)*, 1909, 1912, p. 9.

110. *Ibid.*, p. 20.

111. *Ibid.*, pp. 46-47.

112. *Ibid.*, p. 25.

113. N. Iorga, *Les Hongrois et la nationalité roumaine en 1909* (Văleni de Munte, 1909), pp. 27-28.

114. *Ibid.*, p. 44. Iorga comments on the order of expulsion as follows: "Donc, il existe cette théorie de droit international a savoir qu'un état a le droit d'interdire l'accès de son territoire à quiconque s'est permis d'émettre des idées hostile à ses intérêts." *Ibid.*

115. N. Iorga, *Histoire des roumains de la péninsule des Balkans* (Bucharest, 1919), p. 57.

116. Sălbătăcie germană, *Românul*, September 15, 1912.

117. "Jandarmii," *Telegraful Român*, 1898, No. 90.

118. "Perzecutarea tricolorului," *Românul*, September 19, 1912.

Chapter VI

Conclusion

The multitude of discrete items presented as evidence in the last chapter lead us to but one conclusion: The rights and freedoms of the Romanians under Hungarian rule constituted an effective protection against abuses. Thanks to this protection, they were able to successfully fight against injustice, against administrative excesses and against abuses. Their human and civil rights, therefore, were not empty words; they were respected, rendering their lives more secure, more beautiful, and their future more promising.

a) The press, which were free from preventive censorship, presented opportunities which extended to exaggerated criticism of the Hungarian state and society, to the formation of a national community of Romanians, to the proclamation of ethnic union with Romanians on the other side of the border, to making fun of Hungarian culture, and to the profession of unification of all Romanians in culture, in sentiment, and in ideas. Press trials were initiated only in cases of agitation against the territorial integrity of the state or against the Hungarian nation itself. In spite of all the rumors to the contrary, the sentences handed down by the courts did not have a deterring effect: witness the case of Lucaciu. The prescriptions concerning the treatment of prisoners did not jeopardize their health, their lives, or their human dignity. During his incarceration at Vác, Clavici was treated as if on vacation and was allowed to continue his literary and scholarly work, as was the other great enemy of the Hungarian state, Lucaciu, imprisoned at Szeged. Having sat out their sentences they continued to engage in irredentist, anti-Hungarian activities much as before. They criticized and attacked all official measures they deemed abusive or unjust. They contributed to the realization of irredentist goals throughout their life.

b) The Romanian ruling stratum guided and strengthened the political education of the masses with the help of the right of assembly and of forming associations. Thousands of political and cultural meetings or rallies took place without impediment. Until 1894 the right

to assemble was not restricted at all, and the hundreds of protest
meetings held in later years demonstrate that the Hungarian authorities very seldom withheld permission. The Romanian speakers at
political meetings almost always resorted to anti-Hungarian and anti-
government slogans, whipping up the passions of the masses. In spite
of this a meeting already in progress would almost never be dissolved,
although this was a daily experience for the opposition parties in the
Kingdom of Romania. The peasantry, which constituted the majority
of the Romanians of Hungary, supported the Romanian National Party,
fighting for irredentist objectives, with its nationalist sentiments, even
though it could not understand the program of the Party. The yearnings of the program were "so high, so idealistic," noted a Romanian
weekly, "that the underprivileged cannot reach them even with a pole.
Whereas we consider the necessities of day to day existence, in
connection with one of the more compact points, a matter of course."[1]

c) Equality before the law and the impartiality of the Hungarian
system of justice were particularly evident in the sentences handed
down by the Supreme Court and their justification. The episodes of the
trial of Lucaciu, permission to sing the Romanian national anthem, the
condemnation of electoral abuses, decisions favoring the Romanian side
in cases of conflict between Romanian and Hungarian interests, all
provide evidence to support such a statement. Vaida-Voevod expressed
a historical truth when he declared in 1923: "In Hungary we held the
shield of the laws in our hands; the laws were laws also for us." He
thus admitted that equality in before the law was actually practiced
during the period of the Dual Monarchy.

Thanks to these rights the Romanians grew stronger economically,
culturally, and in their national consciousness during this period. Their
peasantry and middle class prospered. Their economic, cultural, and
social institutions flourished. Effective protection by the laws shielded
them from the measures the Hungarian state or the Saxons occasionally
undertook against Romanian interests. Thanks to their rights the
consciousness of the Romanians kept rising, their interventions became
more decisive, their tone often aggressive. This became particularly
obvious in the years preceding World War I when the Romanians of
Hungary spoke of their plans for Romanian national unification almost
completely in the open. This fact was clearly shown by the words of
deacon Voina of Brassó: "we shout without fear, long live Romania!"
he said in 1906, expressing thereby the basic factor characterizing the
situation of the Romanians of Hungary: awareness of life without fear.

The definite fiasco of the initiatives taken by Hungarian statesmen from 1910 on regarding Romanian-Hungarian peaceful coexistence also support this view. At first, Prime Minister Khuen-Héderváry and later István Tisza repeatedly discussed the conditions of such coexistence with the leaders of the Romanian National Party. The Hungarian leaders of Transylvania also manifested extraordinary deference towards the leading cultural organization of the Romanians, the Astra. Part of the Romanian press registered this tendency with pleasure.

Increasingly often we hear from the bosom of the Hungarian people voices that fight against chauvinism. In contrast to the chauvinism of the renegades and of the Jews these voices penetrate slowly but surely into the Hungarian masses, destroying the idols set up by political speculators and smoothing the path towards an honorable understanding between all nations of the country, wrote the collaborator of the oldest Romanian paper of Transylvania.[2]

Some of the Hungarian statesmen, and the sensible segments of Hungarian society thus fought against chauvinism and nationalist illusions. They were true advocates of a sincere Hungarian-Romanian rapprochement. István Tisza promised far-reaching concessions, including a revision of the Apponyi Laws. But the demands on the Romanian side were tantamount to the secession of the Eastern parts of the country. As Tisza suspected, and as every historian knows today, the extremist demands presented by the Romanians of Hungary were inspired by the Romanian government in Bucharest. Essentially it amounted to political independence, the gist of the Romanian conditions. "All or nothing," commented the *Gazeta Transilvaniei* with regard to the communiqué issued by the Romanian National Party. "We can save our lives only by controlling all the conditions on which our national existence depends."[3]

This last sentence makes it appear as if the Romanian nation were in mortal danger, and that the only way to escape complete destruction would be to recognize the Romanian nation. Several thousand data presented in the preceding chapters all indicate that this perception of mortal danger was without foundation. Dozens of quotations from Romanians, masses of statements from the moment the *Tribuna* was launched, all go to prove that the Romanians did not feel themselves threatened by the Hungarians. But these confessions were for internal consumption only. The tone from abroad was quite different: it was the tone of a nation extremely embittered by aggressive Hungarianization.

It becomes clear from the Romanian press that the Romanian leaders made ample use of naive or irresponsible Hungarian statements regarding Hungarianization for propaganda purposes. When such statements were not available they simply considered every measure taken by the state as an attempt at Hungarianization: the introduction of the official language, Hungarian, as a required subject in schools, the equivalency examinations, the voting of the *congrua* for the priests — all these measures were described as Hungarianization. They came up with such statements in order to win over public opinion in the West, although they often boasted, for internal consumption, of the fact that the Romanians under Hungarian rule grew stronger.

This growth in power and this economic, cultural, and social development were undeniable facts. They could not have come about without Hungarian liberalism, without the existence of basic rights. Comparison with the situation of Romanians in other countries serves as incontrovertible evidence of all this. Let us consider these facts, comparing Hungary in 1867-1914 to Romania in the same period:

a) The constant improvement in the financial situation of the peasantry which constituted a majority of the Romanian population — their purchases of land. On the other hand, in Romania the continuous decrease in the standard of living of the peasants: a peasant war and the slaughter of 11,000 Romanian peasants in 1907.

b) Unlimited or almost unlimited freedom to assemble. Hundreds of meetings of protest throughout the country against the government. In Romania, no opposition party allowed to hold meetings; those who tried were dispersed by the gendarmes or by secret agents.

c) Freedom of the press and no censorship: Romanian newspapers and publications — printed without impediment in Hungary. In Bukovina the Austrians resort to preventive censorship against the Romanian press.

d) Unhampered contacts between the Romanians of Hungary and those of the Kingdom of Romania. In Bessarabia the Russians isolated the Romanians completely from their ethnic brethren in Romania: "The borders of merciless steel separate two different worlds." (N. Iorga).

e) Free use of the Romanian language in the courts, at county assemblies, in the church, at school and in the villages, whether in public or in private life. In Bessarabia and the Balkans the Romanian language was excluded from the church, the schools, public life, the press and, in the Balkans, even from private life.

f) The laws were "laws even for the Romanians;" the Supreme Court defended Romanian interests vis-à-vis Hungarian parties on the basis of equality before the law. The Supreme Court authorized the use of the anti-Hungarian Romanian anthem (photographs of the Romanian king in Transylvania). In Bessarabia and in the Balkans dictatorship prevailed. The Russian government carried out a resettlement program while Greek gangs went unpunished, murdering those Romanians who wished to retain their nationality.

In the final analysis: The Romanians under Hungarian rule became more powerful financially, in their national consciousness, and in the decisive stands they took during the period 1867 to 1914. "We are close to victory" (Stere).

On the other hand, in Bessarabia and in the Balkans, Romanians lived in a constant state of fear, deprived of all rights. Their fate was insecure, without any prospects for improvement. They did not have a single political representative.

The above items of comparison, taken from Romanian sources, show clearly how little truth lay in the statement: The Romanians in Hungary can only save their lives if their demands for political independence are recognized by the Hungarian state! Without the slightest doubt, it was not a matter of some mortal danger threatening the Romanian population, but rather of demands for control over the Eastern portions of Hungary, overthrowing the territorial integrity of the Hungarian state. This fact must by now be clear to the reader, on the basis of the data contained in this work.

Endnotes

1."Unele — altele," *Libertatea,* 1907, No. 19.
2.*Gazeta Transilvaniei,* May 20, 1911.
3."Comunicatul comitetului naţional," *Gazeta Transilvaniei,* 1913, No. 38.

Part II

The Hungarian Minority Under Romanian Rule, 1918-1940

Chapter I

The Economic Situation and Livelihood of Hungarians in Greater Romania

The economic situation of the Hungarian and Romanian populations changed drastically in the formerly Hungarian areas that came under Romanian rule as a result of the occupation of 1919 and of the Peace Treaty of Trianon in 1920. As we have seen, after the Compromise of 1867, the standard of living and status of all strata of the Romanian population improved steadily under the Hungarian regime. This fortunate progress of the Romanian population derived primarily from the economic liberalism of the Hungarian regime. Those in charge of Hungarian economic policies did not intervene in economic activities, thus all enterprises could develop free of government restrictions. Although after 1910 economic liberalism was replaced by state intervention in some areas, apart from the years of the World War, Romanian economic life could develop in a spirit of free competition during the entire period.

In contrast, the economic life of the Hungarian population which came under Romanian rule, was determined from the start by the tendency of the Romanian government to intervene. Indeed, the economic policies of the Romanian state departed from the path of economic liberalism and the enterprises in the country were increasingly subjected to state intervention. The measures adopted b y the state soon cut through the principles of free competition, and economic life came under government direction.

The direction of Romania's economic life was in the hands of the National Liberal Party even before the formation of Greater Romania. This party had vested interests in maintaining its economic advantages. The Romanian National Bank, innumerable enterprises, and various industrial plants, all served the financial interests of the Party. Afte r the formation of Greater Romania it was this party that laid the

377

foundations of the state's economic policies, and its first term in office determined economic trends in Greater Romania.

The Liberal Party's most prestigious economic expert was the famous member of the Brătianu family, Vintilă Brătianu. He laid the foundations of Greater Romania's economic policies.[1] According to his closest collaborators, he was an advocate of state intervention from the very beginning. He "demanded" that the state control all enterprises, and that these conform to the general goals of the state. Vintilă Brătianu formulated the Liberal Party's famous economic slogan "Prin noi înşine" (On Our Own), which meant that Romanian economic policies were to be adapted to national principles. In his opinion, "to realize this program, Romanian work and initiative had to be extended to all her territories in every shape and form... and all economic opportunities had to be reserved for Romanians."[2] As the Finance Minister of Greater Romania, from 1922 to 1926, he implemented the above principles consciously and consistently. In his view the Romanian state was the expression of an "integral nationalism, the role of which was to defend and guide the economic, financial, cultural, and social activities of the Romanian people." Thus he strove, by his economic policies, to his people "thanks to certain advantages granted to the Romanian elements in the exploitation of the country's resources."[3]

Vintilă Brătianu's policies determined the economic opportunities of the Hungarian population that had passed under Romanian rule. Consequently, the first attempt at land reform, devised by the Governing Council of Transylvania, was not carried out, because those who guided economic policies from Bucharest did not find it sufficiently radical. The above outlined viewpoint determined the execution of the Romanian land reform, the measures to enable the Romanians to acquire land and turn the Hungarian population into paupers, the policies on credit, the system of taxation and forfeiture, and in general all those measures that led to the prosperity of the Romanians and the impoverishment of the Hungarians in former Hungarian areas.

The leaders of the Romanians of Transylvania objected from time to time against Brătianu's economic policies. Responding to one of these objections, Brătianu made prophetic statements: "We undertake a policy," he said among other things, "which you and all those who will come to lead the state after us will be compelled to continue, provided you have Romanian souls: the policy of placing economic and financial matters on a national footing."[4]

This declaration of Brătianu was in fact realized through the economic policies of subsequent regimes. As we shall see, each regime strove to render the Romanian element financially stronger at the expense of the non-Romanian populations.

Brătianu's economic ideas were carried out by measures in conformity with these principles. This explains why the economic life of certain regions and ethnic groups differed throughout the period of Greater Romania. In certain regions there was great misery at a given moment, whereas there were considerable opportunities at the same time in other regions. In the Székely and Hungarian regions the extent of taxation and the strictness with which the taxes were collected usually differed from what obtained in the Romanian regions at the same time. In the matter of the extraction of minerals, in credit policies, in measures complementing the land reform, and in various ecclesiastic and cultural matters Brătianu's concepts prevailed to the end. After his death, one of his admirers noted, true to fact, "that his concepts and his example, his teachings and his actions, constitute the firm foundations of the organization of the Romanian state and of the Romanian people, as long as Romania stands."[5]

The financial situation of the close to two million Hungarians who came under Romanian rule was altered first of all by the Romanian land reform. In the first part of my work I described the process which resulted in the economic prosperity and continuous financial strengthening of the Romanians under Hungarian rule. We have noted the opportunities available to the Romanians as a result of the liberal Hungarian economic policies. In a matter of a few decades, by dint of hard work, with the help of their nationally-based banks, and with the help of unlimited credits provided by the Austro-Hungarian Bank and the Hungarian banks of Budapest, the Romanians were able to purchase several hundred thousand cadastral *holds*. Thus, under Hungarian rule, power began to slip out of the hands of the Hungarian landowners as a result of free competition, even before the World War. This process led to the rise of a class of mid-size Romanian landowners, while the smallholders had almost unlimited opportunities to acquire land as well.

The transfer of Hungarian estates into Romanian hands began in the first months of Romanian rule. The basic principles of the land reform were formulated at the Romanian national assembly of Alba Iulia [Gyulafehérvár] in 1918. According to this assembly's resolution:

all estates, particularly the large ones, were to be listed in a census.... On the basis of this census... the peasant should be able to acquire an estate (meadows, fields, and forests) large enough for him to work along with members of his family. The guiding principle of this land reform was, on the one hand, the redistribution of wealth and, on the other hand, the enhancement of production.[6]

The resolutions of Alba Iulia, defined the objectives of the land reform as the formation of peasant holdings and social equality. In order to understand what follows we must look at the data pertaining to land distribution in Greater Romania.

In the Kingdom of Romania prior to 1918, before the land reform, the small estates comprised 46.7%, the mid-size estates 10.9%, and the large estates 42.5% of agricultural land. Thus the middle and large estates combined amounted to 53.3% of the lands.[7] According to 1905 data, 1953 large landowners owned 3,002,100 hectares of land, whereas 2,608 mid-size owners owned 786,000 hectares. In other words, the large and mid-size estates totalled 3,788,100 hectares, divided into 4,171 estates, whereas 1,015,302 smallholders owned altogether 3,320,000 hectares.[8] The area controlled by large and middle landowners greatly exceeded the area under the control of smallholders.

In contrast, in Transylvania under Hungarian rule, in 1910, the area of land controlled by small estates exceeded the area of the large and mid-size estates. According to the breakdown, the small and mini-holdings totalled 5,509,778 cadastral *holds*, whereas the large and mid-size estates amounted to 4,438,082 *holds*, corresponding to 44.6% of the total.[9] The Romanian expert Alexandru Nasta recorded the division of land in Transylvania as even more favorable to the smallholdings, since according to him the proportion of estates exceeding 100 hectares was 37% in Transylvania, as opposed to 47.7% in Romania. In other words, the ratio of mid-size and large estates to smallholdings was greater in Romania than in Transylvania.

Consequently, in the old Romanian kingdom misery and land hunger were far more widespread than in Transylvania under Hungarian rule. According to Constantin Garofild, former Minister of Agriculture, Romania had seven million agricultural proletarians,[10] whereas in Transylvania there were only 473,974 landless peasants.[11]

If we look at land ownership in Transylvania we get the following picture: in 1916 the area of the mini and smallholdings totalled 4,037,496 cadastral *holds*. 24.8% or 1,001,300 cadastral *holds* were in Hungarian hands, whereas 66.2% or 2,672,822 cadastral *holds* were owned by persons of Romanian background. Furthermore, 81.2% of the 578,469 cadastral *holds* of mid-size estates were Hungarian-owned, while 93.7% of the 884,764 cadastral *holds* of large estates were in Hungarian hands.[12] Thus mid-size and large estates were seldom in Romanian hands, while the Romanians were more favored as regards the ownership of the socially so important small estates. In 1910, in the Hungarian areas other than Transylvania that were later attached to Romania, 76.5% of the holdings under 5 *holds*, 73.9% of the holdings between 5 and 10 *holds*, 63% of the estates between 10 and 50 *holds*, and 44.1% of the estates between 50 and 100 *holds* were in Romanian hands. In the same categories the Hungarians were incomparably worse off — that is, relatively speaking, the Hungarian masses did not own as much land as the Romanian masses. In other words, the Hungarian population was relatively more at the mercy of the large estates than the Romanian was.

This becomes clear from a closer examination of the data. In the category of those with a precarious living the percentage of Hungarians far exceeded the percentage of Romanians. For every 100 Hungarians with decent income there were 11.3 individuals living under the poverty level, whereas there were only 5 such individuals among every 100 Romanians. Thus there were far fewer proletarians than average among the Romanians in Transylvania.[13] According to the 1910 census, 53.8% of household servants in Transylvania were of Hungarian background but only 40% were of Romanian background. This makes it obvious that economically and socially the Romanians were better off than the Hungarians. The significance of this factor becomes even more obvious if we look at the various categories of estates from the point of view of agriculturally productive land. Since the major portions of the middle size and large estates consisted of forests and other areas that were agriculturally not productive, whereas all the area of the smallholdings was productive, it is clear that economically speaking the Romanians who owned most of the smallholdings were better off than the Hungarians. From 56.3% to 57.7%, or about 2.7 million cadastral *holds* of the agriculturally productive land in Transylvania and of the pastures, were in Romanian hands, whereas the Hungarians owned only 34.1% to 35.9% of the productive lands. In other words, the Romanians had a 0.9 to 2.3% advantage in relation to the ratio of the ethnic groups, whereas the Hungarians were at a disadvantage by 0.5 to 2.3%.[14]

As we have seen in the first part of this work, this situation derived from the unhampered economic evolution of the Romanian population. Relying on the banks and cooperatives of the Romanians, as well as on help from the Austro-Hungarian Bank and other banks, this largest and most valuable stratum of Romanian society was able to acquire the land it yearned for, while Hungarian peasants had no institutions operating on an ethnic basis to assist them. Since the state did not intervene in economic matters, the Hungarian peasants became poorer and were forced to emigrate in larger numbers than the Romanians.

It is obvious from the above that a fair land reform, applied without discrimination, would have benefitted the Hungarian peasants in Transylvania. The number of Hungarian paupers was relatively larger than that of Romanians, because the Romanian population lived under much more fortunate circumstances during the period of Hungarian rule.

Yet the Romanian law regarding land included clearcut measures favoring the Romanians of Transylvania, to the economic disadvantage of the Hungarians. The true purpose of these measures is revealed by comparing the land reform law in Transylvania with the one carried out in the old Kingdom of Romania, as well as from the application of the law. In any case, this objective was formulated by some Romanians already during the senatorial debates of 1921. Senator Elena Hossu-Longhin asserted that "if we want these areas to acquire a truly Romanian character, if we want to convert them into thoroughly Romanian districts, then we must give the Romanians possession of the land." His fellow-senator, N. Bataria, added that "by the Transylvanian land reform not only are we rectifying a social injustice, but we are establishing the foundations for the rise of the oppressed Romanian element. The land reform in Transylvania has to be viewed primarily in its national context."[15]

The preparatory work for the land reform, its provisions and application did conform to these objectives. The various strata of the Hungarian population that came under Romanian rule suffered enormous financial losses as a consequence of them. Their great material losses and impoverishment were in contrast to the prosperity of the Romanian strata.

The Situation of the Hungarian Peasants

As we have seen, under Hungarian rule the Hungarian peasant lived under relatively less fortunate circumstances in areas with a mixed population. This becomes clear from the statistics compiled in 1910. According to these, 46.6% of the owners of plots of less than 5 *holds* were Romanian, 29.2% were Hungarian. In contrast, 70.8% of the Hungarians were landless peasants, but only 53.4% of the Romanians. There were almost three times as many landless peasants as smallholders among the Hungarians, while the Romanian landless stratum exceeded the smallholders only by a few percentage points. It is clear, therefore, that a far larger proportion of the Hungarians were impoverished than of the Romanians.[16]

The Romanian leaders were presented with an excellent opportunity to gain the support and loyalty of the landless Hungarians upon the introduction of Romanian rule. Had the Romanian government demonstrated its good intentions by giving the landless access to land, then it most assuredly could have secured the support of these masses and their loyalty to the Romanian state forever: However, the preparatory measures for the land reform, the forced rentals, and eventually the way the reform itself was carried out all indicated that the Romanian leaders were guided by the old adage: "whoever owns the land owns the country and has the power." Consequently, the land reform served only to strengthen the influence of the Romanians and to deprive the Hungarians of their land.

The land reform in Transylvania differed from the land reform carried out in the old Kingdom of Romania both in its basic principles and in its application. In the old kingdom the upper limit of the amount of land to be expropriated was set at 2 million hectares. In contrast, no limit was set upon expropriation in Transylvania. Here confiscations were carried out until the various strata of Hungarian society had been deprived of their lands to a sufficient degree, from the Romanian point of view. The one-sided data published after the reform is inadequate to determine the true intentions of the land reform. For a long time the Romanian authorities refrained from publishing certain data altogether. For instance, to this day they have not published data regarding the ethnic background of those who acquired land as a result of the expropriations. This silence was suspicious already then. As a contemporary Romanian newspaper noted:

> In Romania... they do not know what the results of the land reform really are. This is mainly the fault of the authorities, since they do not feel it is their obligation to inform the public in the country. Only with the greatest effort can we gain access to information regarding land reform in Romania.[17]

The *Enciclopedia României* published at great expense in 1938 contains certain data not found elsewhere; but the ethnic background of those given land is still not indicated. As regards the northern part of Transylvania, data were compiled by the Hungarian authorities after the Second Vienna Arbitration Treaty of 1940, on the basis of an official census enabling us to obtain a thorough survey of hitherto unknown aspects of the land reform in Transylvania. On the basis of these data we may state that the Romanian land reform was intended to validate Romanian national interests, while social considerations were given second or third priority at best.   Of the aforementioned landless Hungarian peasants only 46,069 were given land, according to the Romanian data, whereas 242,540 of the Romanian landless acquired land. 14.8% of those who gained land were Hungarians, 78.1% of them were Romanian.[18]

Thus the land hunger of the Hungarian peasantry was given only token satisfaction. It became clear from the details of the expropriation process that the Hungarian smallholders and masses who expected to benefit from the dissolution of Hungarian-held estates actually suffered serious material losses.

The law bankrupted first of all those Hungarian families who had been resettled on Hungarian state-owned estates after 1885. Even the small-holders among these settlers were expropriated; once the division had been completed their acreage, averaging 20 cadastral *holds*, was reduced to only 5 *holds*, here and there. The expropriated lands were then given to Romanian peasants brought in as settlers from other regions. As a consequence of this land policy 1,802 Hungarian peasants were forced to emigrate.   The Hungarian peasants were further weakened by measures expropriating the public domain of the Székely region and the estates of the Private Properties of Csík.

The Székely population, the largest group of Hungarians which came under Romanian rule, had always lived under precarious material conditions.   There were no large estates in the Székely areas.   The population acquired a certain income and livelihood from the so-called commons, consisting mainly of forests. These forests were exploited in common, and even the poorest strata received part of the income. Hence the Székely commons served social ends par excellence, and benefitted practically the whole Székely community.

Among the commons, the Private Properties of Ciuc [Csík] played a special role. The origins of these Private Properties were identical with those of the borderland communities of the Romanian border guards. The enormous common estates of the Romanians of Năsăud [Naszód] and Caransebeș [Karánsebes], as we have seen, had been left by the Hungarian governments of the times in Romanian possession. The estates forming these two commons serving Romanian interests amounted to over half a million cadastral *holds*. The regularization of the commons of the Székely descendants of the Csík border guard regiment took place at the same time.

Their common estates were confiscated by Emperor Francis-Joseph in 1851 to punish them for having sided with Lajos Kossuth. After the Austro-Hungarian Compromise, and at the suggestion of the Hungarian government, the ruler returned these commons, called the Csík

Properties, to the Székely nation for keeps, with restricted rights of ownership.

The Romanian law regarding estates expropriated even these properties serving the common good. According to the prescriptions of section 13 of the law the community properties were to be confiscated, and according to other measures contained in the law the Csík Properties could be confiscated as well.

These measures led to the expropriation of a large portion of the pastures and forests of the Székely communities without regard to need or size. Many communities where the residents owned less than a *hold* of private land now lost their possessions entirely. Such was the fate not only of the forests, but of community pastures as well. For instance, the community of Menăşag [Ménaság] with its 502 heads of families, would have been entitled to 5,020 *holds* of pastures according to the law, yet of its 161 *holds* of pastures it was allowed to retain only 35. The community of Bîrzava [Borzsova] would have been entitled to 2,020 *holds* for its 202 heads of families, but it was allowed to retain merely 83 of its 827 *holds* of pastures. Similarly in Topliţa-Ciuc [Tapolca], where, instead of 4,000 *holds* of community pastures for its 400 heads of families, the community was allowed to retain merely 492 *holds*. The 250 heads of families at Şumuleu [Várdotfalva] kept only 371 *holds*, the 1,820 heads of families at Cioboteni [Csobotfalva] retained 269 *holds*, and the 213 heads of families of Lutoasa [Csomortán] retained 598 *holds*.[19] If we add up the losses suffered by the residents of Székely villages we must conclude that, under the guise of Romanian land reform, over ten thousand Székely peasants were deprived of their already meager livelihood.

The affair of the Csík Properties constitutes the saddest chapter of the economic deprivation of the Hungarian peasantry under Romanian rule. As mentioned, this common estate came about at the same time as the Romanian commons of Năsăud and Caransebeş. Their fate was also identical, except that the Székely commons had been confiscated between 1851 and 1869. From that moment on the Hungarian administration dealt evenhandedly with the property rights of the descendants of the border guards at Csík, Naszód and Karánsebes.

The Hungarian peasantry expected a similarly evenhanded treatment from the Romanian regime. The Transylvanian land reform law, dated September 10, 1919, had indeed exempted the "estates of the commons of former border guards" from expropriation, regardless of nationality. But the new law, dated July 23, 1921, exempted only the commons of the Romanians of Năsăud, without mentioning other similar commons. According to Articles 24 and 32 of the law:

The pastures of the communities of the former second Romanian border guard regiment of Năsăud, regularized by Act 17 of 1890, will remain exempt from expropriation. These pastures are used by every resident of the former border guard communities, even by those who cannot trace their ancestry to a border guard family.... The forests of the former second Romanian border guard regiment of Năsăud, in accordance with Act 18 of 1890, will remain as community forests exempt from expropriation. Every farmer of the communities may make use of these forests, including those who cannot trace their ancestry to a border guard family.

Later on, at the time of its application, the exemption in the law was extended to the commonwealth of the Romanian border guard regiment at Caransebeş.

The consequence of the discrimination between the commons of Romanian and Hungarian border guard families would soon become apparent. The agrarian committees in the first and second instances expropriated 27,000 cadastral *holds* of pastures and forests from the Properties for the benefit of Romanian communities, various churches, and Romanian individuals in the county of Ciuc. The management of the Properties appealed the expropriation measure. Since the injustice was blatant, management expected a just solution as a result of its appeal. The February 26, 1923 decision of the agrarian committee came as a blast. Instead of redressing the injustice the agrarian committee declared all lands of the Properties Romanian state property. It justified its decision on the grounds that the Székelys had received the property only as usufruct, and that they had lost even this right on account of their role in the revolution of 1848 and their "disloyal rebellion." In the opinion of the agrarian committee it had only been a matter of usufruct even after 1869, whereas ownership remained vested in the state. Since the Romanian state was the rightful heir to the Hungarian state, it considers itself the rightful owner of the commons. In any case, it was argued, this property used to belong to the Romanian principality of Moldavia before the so-called border rectification under Joseph II.

The decision was soon followed by execution. In April, 1923 the Romanian government dissolved the management of the Properties and took over its holdings.

The leaders of the peasants of Ciuc did not submit to the confiscation of the great peasant commonwealth and the wrong done to them. The management sent queries to both houses of parliament and to the ministries. In the name of the Hungarian Association István Ugron led a delegation to call upon Minister of Agriculture Alexandru Constantinescu. Later József Sándor, a representative, requested the Minister to right the wrong, at the head of another delegation. The Minister promised immediate measures, but his promise remained unfulfilled, like the previous one. Since all interventions proved unsuccessful the management of the Properties decided to file a complaint with the League of Nations, as a last resort. The complaint was drafted and printed in 1923. Then, on instructions from the government, the police inspector of Miercurea Ciuc [Csíkszereda] confiscated the printed copies of the memorandum as well as the manuscript, thus preventing, for the time being, the forwarding of the complaint to the League of Nations.

Soon there was a parliamentary intervention in the issue, and Constantinescu had to address the issue in parliament, on December 7, 1923. He referred to the actual considerations behind the move:

> Having examined the appeals, I have reached the conclusion that in this case it is not a matter of expropriation, but rather that the state has to take everything back for its own purposes. The agrarian committee has performed a magnificently patriotic task, rectifying injustices and miseries suffered in the past.[20]

Then the managers of the Properties took further steps. One of these steps was to contact the opposition Romanian Peoples Party which in an agreement with the Hungarian Party vowed to resolve the issue of the Properties. Unfortunately, when the Romanian Peoples Party did come to power, it forgot about its promise. Another attempt was made in 1928. At that time the government was in the hands of the Romanian National Peasant Party, under the prime-ministership of Iuliu Maniu. Since this regime constantly harped on its good intentions towards the peasants, and supported the creation of a separate peasant party among the Hungarians, the Székely peasants of Ciuc and the managers of the Properties turned to Maniu for redress. While Maniu accepted the memorandum presented by the leader of the delegation, he made this meaningful statement: "I will examine your alleged rights." The promised examination never took place. Then the managers finally realized that they could not expect a favorable turn on the issue from within the country. Resorting to the only remaining alternative, on July 20, 1929, they transmitted their complaint, bearing the signatures of Arthúr Balogh, the Senator from Odorheiu [Udvarhely], and of Gábor Pál, the Senator from Ciuc, to the League of Nations. The complaint pointed out the irregularities and the unequal treatment, in the handling of the matter in disregard of the Treaty on Minorities. By law, the agrarian committee had jurisdiction only in matters of expropriation; yet the committee had intervened to resolve an issue of ownership that had not been challenged by anyone, and which belonged to the courts. By so doing the Romanian government had seriously contravened its commitment, under the Minorities Protection Treaty of December 19, 1919 in as much as it had dealt differently with the Romanian and with the Hungarian commons that had identical origins.[21]

The signers of the complaint submitted additional materials to complement their arguments repeatedly. In these documents they revealed the antecedents of the affair, and their observations regarding the stand taken by the Romanian government. The government emphasized primarily its rights as heir to the Properties which, it argued, had belonged to the Hungarian government. It alleged that in 1869, at the proposal of the Hungarian government, Francis Joseph returned only the usufruct of these properties to the Székelys of Ciuc. Therefore, the Romanian government committed no injustice with regard to the commonwealth of the Székelys and did not show discrimination in favor of the commons of Năsăud and Caransebeş, since the latter, in addition to making use of the estates, were also their owners. As regards the commonwealth of the Székelys, it was not a matter of confiscation, but expropriation in accordance with the provisions of the agrarian laws.

In contrast, the appellants proved the veracity of their complaints, by pointing out that the Romanian government continued to pay the agreed upon rent for the buildings that had been the property of the commons until 1923, much as the Hungarian government had done before 1918. Thereby the Romanian government had recognized the private character of the commons, as did the Romanian administration of the county of Ciuc. What's more, when the former employees of the commons requested their pensions from the Romanian government after 1923, their request was denied with the explanation that they were not entitled to pensions since the Properties were an agency of the state. Neither the Hungarian state, nor the county of Ciuc had ever considered the Properties as property of the state. It is hard to believe that the Hungarian government would have granted the Hungarians far less rights with regard to these properties of the descendants of the border guard regiments than to the descendants of the Romanian border guard regiments that fought against it.

The Romanian government embarked on various delaying tactics. First, it questioned the jurisdiction of the League of Nations. Then it requested an extension of the trial date because, it claimed, it intended to settle with the signers of the complaint, and appointed a committee of six members for the purpose. The Council of the League complied with the request, delaying the discussion of the affair until the following session.

The Ministry of Foreign Affairs in Bucharest did, indeed, call upon the signers of the complaint to negotiate on July 19, 1931. Except for two of the signers, these showed up. The Romanian committee opened the negotiations by declaring that the signers of the complaint were not entitled to represent the Properties of Ciuc because that commonwealth had never constituted the property of the Székelys of Ciuc. The signers of the complaint rejected this objection and declared that they would not agree to any solution which would deprive the Székelys of Ciuc of their Properties permanently. Since the Romanian committee was not empowered to make further proposals, the negotiations reached a deadlock. The signers of the complaint reported the unsuccessful attempt to the League of Nations. Eight weeks later, at the request of the League, the Ministry of Foreign Affairs once again called upon the signers to come and negotiate. The starting point for the proposal on this occasion was the same as on the previous occasion: all properties taken by the Romanian state belong to it by right of inheritance. The Romanian committee did hint at the prospect of certain concessions, should the complaint be withdrawn. They would return certain buildings, they would disburse assistance to the churches, and would recognize the right of the employees to a pension. The signers of the complaint did not accept these offers, hence the negotiations came to an end once again. When the promoters notified the League of Nations, the latter placed the affair of the Properties on its agenda for September 4, 1931. But the Romanian government requested a delay once again, for the sake of further negotiations.[22] These negotiations were held in Bucharest on October 10, 1931, but without any positive outcome, since the Romanian government refused to return any part of the commons. The last attempt at a compromise took place in Braşov [Brassó], on November 4. On this occasion the signers once again requested a just resolution of the dispute over the Properties. They requested the return of the buildings, the return of the revenue derived from the already distributed lands and pastures, due compensation for the areas that could not be returned, and the restitution of the lands and forests held by the state as reserves, or an appropriate compensation for them. The state committee rejected all these requests and refused to recognize any building, forest, or pasture as the property of the Székelys of Ciuc. The state indicated its exclusive right of ownership with regard to these, and repeated the promises it had already made should the complaints be withdrawn.

The sponsors of the grievance, seeing the repeated failure of the negotiations and attempts at compromise, and the dilatory tactics of the Romanian government, requested the League of Nations to place the issue on its agenda. Thus the dispute was once again on the agenda for 1932. Then the Romanian government made a final attempt: it questioned the right of the League to bring a decision in the matter, claiming the Romanian courts had jurisdiction, and that the promoters of the grievance had made no effort to have their grievance examined by the courts. The League of Nations, however, rejected this interpretation of the Romanian government and, on the basis of a decision reached by a special legal committee, determined that it did have the right to settle the dispute and the aggrieved party was not obliged to seek redress in front of the Romanian courts.

The League decided the dispute on September 27, 1932. Its decision was essentially practical, avoiding the issue of property rights. The League's decision, nevertheless, recognized the justice of the complaint and the injustice of the procedure of the Romanian government, by declaring that the managers of the Properties be reinstated, and the municipal real estate be returned and handed over to the reinstated management. The Romanian government would also have to restitute 6,704 hectares of the pastures and forests still in its possession. It would recognize the right of the former employees to a pension in accordance with the rules applying to all civil servants.

The justification of the League's decision emphasized that this solution would preserve the legitimate interests of the minority while taking into account the supreme interests of the Romanian state. Thus the League did not deal with the essence of the infringement of rights, and its decision was intended to reassure the Romanian government. Naturally, the solution was painful to the promoters of the grievance and to Hungarian public opinion; but the Romanian government was more or less satisfied with the decision, even though this decision indirectly recognized the validity of the grievance. This decision repeatedly referred to "return" and "restitution" whereas — as Arthúr Balogh, the foremost expert on the affair, noted — a property can be restituted only if it does not belong to the one making the restitution. Thus, the rights of the Székely peasants were theoretically conceded, but in practice they had to be satisfied with a decision aiming at the restitution of only parts of their confiscated property.

Further difficulties cropped up when it came to carrying out the verdict. The Romanian government delayed the execution for a year and a half. Then, in June 1934, it presented a law proposal regarding the verdict of the League of Nations, giving Romanian authorities the right to dispose of the portion to be restituted to the Properties. The proposal did not list the Properties under dispute; moreover, it agreed to order restitution to the organizations in charge only in exchange for a statement by which the Székelys would surrender all other property in dispute. In his intervention the Hungarian senator Elemér Gyárfás declared that the "condition would represent an inordinate constraint" and would be contrary to the letter and spirit of the decision of the League of Nations. Therefore, in the name of the Hungarian population, he protested most strongly against the law.[23]

His protest, however, was in vain, because the law was adopted as proposed. Then the managers of the Properties once again forwarded a grievance to the League on October 25, 1934. They pointed out in their petition that the law the government had proposed and passed in 1934 was in conflict with the verdict of the League. It provided the Romanian authorities with the right of intervention and control over goods that have been returned, moreover it did not comply with the provision of the verdict regarding pension for the former employees of the Properties since the pensions it offered constituted but half or one third of the pensions due. Moreover, only 75% of the pension was to be paid, retroactively.

The renewed complaints, however, led to no results. By that time the prestige of the League had been thoroughly shaken by international events, and it could not even offer the Székely peasants of Ciuc what it had offered them a few years earlier. The final episodes of the affair took place in 1936. Valeriu Oțetea, the Romanian prefect of the county of Ciuc, summoned the committee in charge of the Properties to a meeting on June 15, 1936, for the sake of handing over the real estate to the owners, as prescribed in the law: the expanded committee, under the chairmanship of the prefect, included the state councillor Avramescu, Petre Suciu, the director of forests, as well as members of the committee in charge of the Properties. By way of introduction Avramescu declared that the Properties would only be restituted if the owners agreed to a statement explaining that by accepting the almost 12,000 *holds* of estates and the buildings, all their claims will have been satisfied, and they will demand no further compensation from the Romanian government. The persons in charge of the Properties rejected this demand, declaring they were not entitled to make such a statement.

Because of this conflict of opinions, the Properties were not turned over, and the negotiations were adjourned until July 1.[24]

Since the Romanian government attached conditions to the restitution, the managers of the Properties stated their position in a memorandum. They insisted, among other things, that:

> the board of directors, in the name of the commons it represents, is not authorized to issue the declaration of surrender demanded in Article II of the above law. This surrender was also prohibited by Article IV of the by-laws. Moreover, the board wants to avail itself of those legal recourses which entities, citizens or institutions, are entitled to under the constitution and by the laws of the country.[25]

Thus the fate of the Properties did not alter after the attempt to carry out the verdict of the League of Nations; in final account, nothing was returned to the peasants of Ciuc. The true purpose of the measures adopted by the Romanian government was to remove the Székely commons from the hands of the Székely population and place it into Romanian hands. The government gave presents of increasing value to Romanians, individuals or institutions, out of the confiscated estates. Of the 54,515 cadastral *holds* of estates in the northern region of the county the government gave 27,744 *holds* to the Romanian residents of the communities of Bilbor [Bélbor], Corbu [Holló], Tulgheş [Tölgyes], and Bicazu Ardelean [Békás]. Later some Hungarian communities also received certain areas: the 3,106 Hungarian residents of Miercurea Ciuc received 30 *holds*, and the community of Seplac [Széplak] received one *hold*. In contrast, the 1,419 residents of Bilbor had received 8,530 *holds*, and the 1,015 Romanian residents of Corbu received 6,632 *holds*. The ratio of estates granted to institutions was similar. Altogether 1,500 *holds* were distributed to the churches, of which 1,200 *holds* went to the Romanian Orthodox and Uniate churches, and 300 to the Hungarian churches.[26] The residents of Romanian communities also received lots, in addition to the forests and pastures, for building homes. Although the Transylvanian land-reform law expressly forbade awarding lands to absentee landlords, the community of Voşlobeni [Vasláb], 100 kilometers from the estate, received a valuable piece of the forest. A number of Romanian communities in Transylvania as well as in the old Kingdom of Romania received a piece of the commonwealth of the Székely peasants. Moreover, thousands of private individuals received terrains, or free wood in Ciuc county, without any payment. Some astute entrepreneurs plundered the forests ruthlessly, as a while consequence of which the estates of the Properties suffered irreparable damage. Enormous forests were wiped out completely; in the place of the once so beautiful virgin forest there remained nothing but denuded, slippery terrain, and bare mountains. Thus the commonwealth of the Székely peasants of Ciuc was almost totally lost to the Székelys. The expert on the issue summarized the morale of the story in his French language monograph:

> While lands amounting to 518,105 *holds* (or 297,910 hectares), which the rulers and lawgivers of Hungary had handed over to the border guards at Năsăud and Caransebeş once upon a time from estates belonging to the Hungarian state was now completely at the disposal of the Romanian population, the Romanian government deprived the descendants of the Székely border guards of their 62,800 *holds* estate (36,110 hectares), on the pretext that this estate had at one time been state property — which was contrary to fact. Of this illegally withheld property the Council of the League of Nations granted the government 51,217 *holds* (29,477 hectares) for permanent retention, ordering only that 11,651 (6,704 hectares) be restituted, representing 18.5% of the area and 1.5% of the value of the confiscated estate. As regards the 81.5% confiscated from the Székelys, it was distributed mainly to the Romanian churches and communities, the government retaining the remainder. This Romanian property serves only national ends to this day. More recent Romanian laws prescribe that the use of certain property must remain the privilege of the descendants of the Romanian border guards. In contrast, only a minor portion of the estates of the Székely border guards of Ciuc was retained by their descendants, and there is no sort of guarantee to ensure that even this portion will be used for the benefit of the Székely minority. This is the fate of those properties which had been reserved, by the royal decision of February 16, 1869, to improve the lot of the Székely nation. In obvious disregard of the Minorities Protection Treaty, close to 100,000 Székelys were deprived of their property. If we consider merely the value of the lands, the losses amount to at least 99 million gold francs.[27]

By the time the fate of the Properties of Ciuc was finally settled the true objectives and results of the Romanian land reform program were obvious to everyone in Transylvania. Indeed, as we know from the data gathered in Northern Transylvania, in every respect the land reform was designed to promote the economic welfare of the Romanian element, and to effect a decrease of the holdings of the Hungarian population.[28]

The official Romanian statistics indicate clearly that 22.6% of all holdings confiscated was handed over to peasants entitled to land. Thus the primary goal of the land reform was not to ensure the complete satisfaction of the peasants in need of land. 56.7% of all the confiscated holdings was earmarked to create a new sort of commons of forest and pasture areas. According to data from Northern Transylvania, at most 33.2% of the confiscated holdings was earmarked for the Hungarian regions. As regards the entire area attached to Romania this ratio was obviously lower, and could not have exceeded 20.3%.

The Romanian land reform, promoted in the name of "social goals" resulted in 533,982 cadastral *holds* of completely unused land. As we have noted, only about 27% of the Hungarian peasants, that is those members of the Hungarian ethnic group who were entitled to land, actually received some. It is clear that the confiscated holdings would have been amply sufficient to cater to the needs of all Hungarians entitled to land. Of the 533,982 cadastral *holds* of unutilized area, 170,011 formed the so-called public reserve, out of which the Romanian government rewarded Romanian churches, schools, and other institutions. The remaining 363,972 cadastral *holds* were managed by the state — that is, were reserved for Romanian purposes as well.

To what extent did the confiscation affect the small estates? The data collected in Northern Transylvania provide an interesting analysis. In the areas awarded to Hungary in 1940 — where two-thirds of the Hungarian minority lived — only 3,358 landowners were subjected to expropriation. 57.2% of these landowners, or 1,923 persons, were small and dwarf holders owning less than 50 cadastral *holds*, whereas 6.3% were smallholders owning between 50 and 100 cadastral *holds*. Moreover, 51.4% of landowners with less than 50 cadastral *holds* and 53.3% of landowners with between 50 and 100 cadastral *holds* were expropriated. Thus over one half of the dwarf and smallholders, mostly peasants, had been subject to expropriation. The affected smallholders were mainly Hungarian: 74.7% of those in the 1 to 50 *hold* range were Hungarian, as were 68.1% of those in the 50 to 100 *hold* range.[29] All this, in spite of the fact that, as noted from the data presented by Suciu regarding the areas of Hungary turned over to Romania, the Hungarians owned only 24.8% of the 4,037,496 cadastral *holds* of small and drawf holdings, as opposed to 66.2% owned by Romanians. It is obvious, therefore, that the land reform had a much more negative impact on the smallholder peasants of Hungarian background than on the Romanian peasants, whereas among those who benefitted from the land reform the Romanians outnumbered the Hungarians by far. 78.1% of the Romanian population benefitted, as opposed to 14.8% of the Hungarians, whereas the proportions of the general population in these areas was 58.7% Romanian and 31.2% Hungarian. A just land reform would have meant true social levelling, awarding land to those entitled to it among both nationalities in a manner that would have taken the ethnic ratios into consideration, as regards confiscation as well as redistribution. Thus the Hungarian population should have received not 14.8% but 31.2%, and the Romanian population only 58.7% instead of 78.15%. Hence Hungarian peasants under Romanian rule were treated unfairly both in regards to confiscation and in regards to redistribution.

Unfortunately, since the Romanian authors and the specialists on official assignment have not published exact data regarding the ethnic background of those losing or receiving land until now, we have no way of determining exactly how many Hungarian peasants lost how much land as a consequence of the biased application of the reform laws. Considering merely the data already presented, the confiscation of the land of the settlers, the nearly 100,000 Székely peasants affected by the confiscation of the Properties of Ciuc, as well as the expropriation of smallholdings resulting from purchases facilitated by the Altruista Bank, we may estimate the number of Hungarian landless, draft holders, and smallholders who suffered serious material damage, or were by-passed by the land reform, at close to 150,000. In the case of purchases facilitated by the Altruista Bank, the land of Hungarian smallholders was taken away without any compensation. Thus, in the community of Jarma [Jármal] (in Mureş-Turda [Maros-Torda] county) 132 *holds* were lost by the Hungarian smallholders; altogether 1,850 *holds* were taken away from 350 smallholders at Pata [Kolospata], Gheorgheni [Györgyfalva], and Bocin [Bocs]. In Aiton [Ajton] (in Cluj [Kolozs] county) 390 *holds* were taken from 39 smallholders in Sigheu Silvaniei [Szilágysziget], Chieşd [Szilágykövesd], Samşud [Szilágysámson, and Mocirla [Szilágymocsolya] 736 *holds* were taken away in the community of Boiu [Bún], Tîrnava Mare [Nagy-Küküllő], and 85 *holds* from smallholders of Someşeni [Szamosfalva] in Dezmir [Desmér].[30] These confiscations affected many thousands of Hungarian smallholders.

The Hungarian peasantry did not profit from the land reform, but lost out. The acreage received by the 46,096 Hungarians mentioned in the Romanian statistics was far below the quantity of lands expropriated from Hungarian dwarf and smallholders, or from the community lands which had been so beneficial to the Hungarian masses up to that time. Thus the Hungarian peasants saw their fate deteriorate rather than improve as a result of the Romanian land reform. This is demonstrated clearly by the measures the Romanian lawgivers took in the period following the land reform, for the sake of increasing its impact and achieving the Romanian economic objectives.

The curtailment of the holdings of the Hungarian peasantry and smallholders did not end with the land reform. According to the law on mineral rights, mineral waters were listed among the minerals, while the Romanian constitution specified that mineral wealth was the property of the state. Hence the exploitation of mineral waters in the Székely region, almost exclusively in the hands of the minority group, was now reserved for the Romanian state.[31] The economic measure adopted a few years later prove that turning mineral wealth over to the state affected only the peasants of the minority group, for when it came to applying the constitution and the law on mineral rights to the Moc people, (Romanians living on the Wester slopes of the Carpathians) a decree issued in 1927 allowed them to retain their rights to the gold mines.[32]   Of course, there was no such decree to maintain the acidulous wells in Székely hands.

By 1937 and 1939 further measures were adopted to confiscate properties in Hungarian hands. Towards the end of 1938 a military border region was established. The pertinent legislation enabled the state to expropriate any real estate in this region for military purposes. The communities and institutions were required to hand over all real estate that could be used for military purposes to the Romanian War Ministry, without compensation. Any real estate in the border region could only be brought into circulation by granting the state preemptive rights. Since the execution of the law affected mostly those areas where the majority of the population was Hungarian, it was obviously designed to make the real estate in Hungarian hands available for confiscation for Romanian purposes.[33]

In 1939 a further law was passed regarding the preemptive rights of the state. According to this law the real estate purchased in border areas or in areas with a mixed population could only be used for settlement purposes and could only be sold to Romanians — i.e. those defined as racially Romanian in the constitution — in parcels of 5 to 10 hectares.[34]

In 1937 a law was passed regarding the dissolution of the Saxon University and of the Community of the Seven Judges. Until then the property of these institutions served the general cultural welfare of the entire population of the Saxon region. 47.3% of the income from the property of the Saxon University and 56.3% of the income from the property of the Seven Judges went to the Romanian population, whereas 18.5% and 10.1% respectively were earmarked for the Hungarian population. The law of 1939 stipulated that the income from both properties could be used only for the benefit of the Romanians and Saxons living in the area of Királyföld. Hence the Hungarian residents were deprived of their rights and of their part of the income, although the government could have opted to adopt the measures applied by the Hungarian government in 1879 when it declared the Romanian villages an integral part of the Királyföld and awarded a portion of the income of the Saxon University to the Romanians. The Romanian government disregarded the possibility of equal treatment or of renewing the measure previously adopted by the Hungarian government.[35]

The same policies prevailed in the provisions of the law adopted in 1934. This law was designed to alleviate, by a series of measures, the predicament of the taxpayers who got into a difficult situation as a consequence of the world economic crisis. For instance, it granted a long period of grace for the payment of the taxes. But once again a deplorable distinction was introduced regarding the ethnic background of those in debt. The law excluded legal persons and community property from among the beneficiaries, hence these entities had to pay their debts in full on schedule. Yet the Romanian community property that belonged to the former second border guard regiment of Năsăud and the 13th border guard regiment of Caransebeş were exempted from the law. Various measures of the law applied to ease the debts of these two legal persons, whereas the communities of Székely region in Hungarian hands had to pay all their debts in the usual manner. Thus the Romanian lawmakers eased the situation of the communities serving Romanian interests, but not that of the commonwealths serving Hungarians.[36]

In addition to the above, more than once the Romanian laws provided special treatment to the poor Romanian population of the Old Kingdom, Transylvania, and other provinces. For instance, they promoted the welfare of some Romanian residents by providing wood for heating and construction free of charge. In 1937 the Moc people of the Arănies [Aranyos] valley were helped by a 75% discount off the regular fare on railroads. The poor masses of Hungarian ethnic background — including those living in misery in some parts of the Székely region — were never granted similar privileges.[37]

Thus the Romanian land reform and the complementary legislation always considered the interests of individuals with a Romanian background but seldom had any regard for the masses of peasants of a different ethnic background. This was also substantiated when the reserve lands that remained in government custody as a result of the land reform were put to use, and by the measures adopted in cases of individual expropriation when the injustices committed against Hungarian landowners were supposed to be righted by the Romanian courts.

As mentioned above, after the expropriation an enormous mass of land remained in government custody. The largest such reserves were located in the counties of Bihor [Bihar], Ciuc, Trei Scaune [Háromszék], and Satu Mare [Szatmár], and to a lesser extent in Odorheiu and Salaj [Szilágy]; 21.9% of the expropriated land in Ciuc county, 21% in Trei Scaune, and 24% in Satu Mare remained at government disposal. With regard to part of this area Constantinescu, the Romanian Minister of Agriculture, declared in the Romanian Senate on November 10, 1923, that:

we must keep the confiscated areas in Transylvania, from the Timiş-Torontal through Arad, to Satu Mare, to enable us to resettle those Romanians who live abroad or on our Alps, because I feel that they alone, representing the cradle of Romanian nationalism, are entitled to this land.[38]

Later Romanian sources expressed themselves regarding this matter in a similar vein, or even more clearly. According to the hefty commemorative album issued by the Romanian Peasant Party in 1928:

Although little of the land expropriated in Transylvania was fit for agricultural purposes, nevertheless significant reserves remained after the requests for property had been satisfied. We decided to resettle farmers there from areas where there was not enough land available.[39]

Later a Romanian, Victor Jinga, one of the best-known experts on the question of Romanian settlements and a former deputy secretary, was most outspoken regarding this objective of the Romanian land policies. According to him, the objective of the land reform measures in borderland areas was to change the numerical ratio between majority and minority populations.

The aliens who came here or were brought here, whatever language they speak, in whatever manner they worship God, have to be made to understand that this land is reserved for the complete and permanent rule of the Romanian people under the sun; and therefore, as a matter of obligation, in the interest of national self-preservation, we embarked on a determined and sweeping undertaking, the first and foremost part of which was to clean the space of the Romanian nation from all alien elements.[40]

In order to achieve this goal, according to the data by Jinga, altogether 111 Romanian settlements were established along the borders defined at Trianon. In these settlements the Romanians received a total of 69,223 cadastral *holds* of acreage, with an average of 13.9 *holds* per parcel. The number of resettled families was 4,973. It goes without saying that, in order to achieve the goal indicated above, not a single individual of Hungarian background received land in these areas.

There were instances during the execution of the land reform, whenever the Romanian authorities recognized the injustices committed at the expense of the Hungarian peasantry. Yet when it came time to pay the compensation awarded by the courts, the Romanian authorities balked. The case of the Romanian residents of the community of Hărău [Háró] was especially infamous.

The pastures of the community, belonging to the Csángók of Deva [Déva] and amounting to some 126 cadastral *holds*, had been exempted from confiscation by the land reform committee of the district. The committee at the county level, however, decided in the opposite sense; confiscating the pastures, it divided them among the Romanians of Hărău, the Orthodox churches of Deva and Hărău, and other institutions. The Hungarian peasants appealed. On March 29, 1926, their appeal was sustained by the agrarian committee and the confiscation was annulled. Decree 3,754 of April 15, 1926, added that the present decision of the county agrarian committee "be carried out promptly and the execution reported." But the agrarian committee delayed execution for weeks, until, on May 4, it received orders by telegram to reinstate the Hungarian peasants on their property. The restitution was scheduled for the following day, but then came another telegram suspending the execution. After a few months of indecision the mayor of Deva, under Decree 3,555 of September 17, 1926, handed down a decision barring the Hungarian peasants from possession of the pasture as per central directive 21,262/1926. The residents of Hărău then turned to the Romanian court at Timişoara [Temesvár] on March 7, 1927, the court mandated the superintendent of agriculture of Hunedoara county to restitute the pastures to the Hungarians. On April 12, however, an armed band of Romanians of Hărău numbering 100 to 120 surrounded the seven unarmed Hungarian peasants of Deva engaged in surveying the land, and assaulted them. One of the victims,

Péter Molnár, was pushed into the stream in a wounded condition, where he drowned.

After these events, on April 20, 1927, the Romanian police prefect of Deva visited the judge of the Hungarian settlement accompanied by another officer, and nailed on his door Decree 14,801 issued by the Casa Centrală section of the Ministry of Agriculture in Bucharest, barring the Hungarian peasants of Deva from the disputed pasture awarded to them by the court, and retaining these exclusively for the benefit of the Romanians of Hărău. Thus, in this case, while the Romanian court recognized the rights of a group of Hungarian peasants, the judicial decision could not be enforced, and the Minister of Agriculture ended by sanctioning the aggressive intervention of the Romanians of Hărău. A similar incident took place in the case of Béla Simény, a landowner of Uroi. The agrarian committee had exempted part of his land from expropriation by a legally valid decision, but the Romanians of Simeria Vecheo [Pisk] and Uroi [Arany] "chased him with pitchforks from the furrows he had started digging." Simény turned to the Romanian police prefect of Hunadoara county for support, but the latter declared that the "Agrarian Committee had brought about a decision which could not be technically enforced."

Soon after the above case, reported in the Hungarian press as "the crime of Hărău," there was a similar incident with the pastures of the commonwealth of Sîncrai [Kalotaszentkirály] in Cluj [Kolozs] county. The Romanian community of Săcuien [Székelyjó] had its eyes set on the pasture and, its demand recognized by the local agrarian committee of the county, the pasture was duly expropriated. The Romanians of Săcuien carried out the decision and took possession of the pasture. The peasants of Sîncrai appealed. The Agrarian Committee allowed their appeal and brought about a fair decision, returning the disputed area to the Hungarian smallholders in 1929. But the Romanians of Săcuien prevented the execution of the decision by force. Then the residents of Sîncrai filed a suit for interference with property. The final decision in the suit was handed down by the highest Romanian court, the Court of Appeals which rejected the arguments presented by the Romanians of Săcuien, declaring the Hungarian peasants of Sîncrai the rightful owners of the property under dispute. When the decision was to be carried out; however, the Minister of Agriculture intervened in person to prevent the Hungarian peasants from taking possession of their lands. He threatened to send the peasants to Hungary, while instructing the inspector of the gendarmes to bar the peasants from returning to their pastures. After, this it was no longer possible to carry out the verdict of the highest Romanian court in the case, the

Hungarian peasants of Sîncrai filed a complaint with the League of Nations. Thereupon the Romanian government sponsored a law on April 7, 1936, buying up, with the help of expropriation bonds, the 136 cadastral *holds* of pastures and forests of the commons of Sîncrai and, for the sum of 1.1 million lei, handed these over to the Romanian community of Săcuien, to be paid in installments over a period of ten years, at 5% interest.[41] The same happened with some of the properties of the Székely communities of Cîrța [Karcfalva] and its vicinity, which the Romanian communities had taken over by force while the Romanian authorities stood by. Complaints to the League of Nations once again resulted in forced purchase. Not once was the Romanian government willing to return the land to the Hungarian owners, not even when the injustice had been redressed by judicial process.

In the Székely region it also happened that the estates of certain Székely communities were used for Romanian purposes, beyond the provisions of the land reform. For instance, the government took away by a subterfuge the income from the Székelyhavas, forming the commonwealth of 127 Székely communities and called the "Ancient Commons of Marosszék," amounting to about 15,000 *holds*, and awarded it to Romanians. The law recognized that the property belonged to the 127 Székely communities in common, but it placed the county council of Mureş in charge of the property. The council was composed of appointed rather than elected members, and the majority of the appointees were Romanian. Thereafter the Romanian council used the income from the commonwealth for Romanian purposes as they saw fit. Consequently, the Székely communities were not only barred from managing their property, but were barred from its fruits.[42]

After 1934 there was a movement to place the spas of the Székely region under Romanian control. The Romanian Minister of the Interior moved to deprive the Székelys of part of the holdings belonging to the bathhouses at Tuşnad [Tusnád]. In 1935 the Minister summoned the council of four Székely communities to surrender part of the area to the Romanian Tourist Office, without compensation. When the community councils refused to comply with the request after repeated demands, the Ministry dissolved them on the grounds "that they brought about decisions which overlooked measures adopted by the higher authorities, to the detriment of the administration of the communities, endangering the security of the state."[43] Thus the Minister of the Interior described the stand of the leaders of the Székely communities, intent only on defending the interests of the Székely peasants, as endangering the security of the Romanian state. The Minister appointed new councils, consisting of resettled Romanians for the most part, which were willing to carry out the order of the Minister. Thus the land of the commonwealth of Tuşnad became the property of the Romanian Tourist Office, at no cost.

Taxation in the Hungarian Regions

In addition to the confiscation of Hungarian properties, Romanian economic policies contributed to the impoverishment of the Székely region, and of Hungarian regions in general, by a special tax system. According to the official bulletin of the Romanian Ministry of Finance, from 1924 to 1926 the direct taxes paid in Transylvania exceeded those paid in Romania itself by 205 million. During those two years the direct taxes in the old Kingdom decreased by 45 million in comparison with the previous fiscal year. Yet in the same period the total amount of tax revenue increased by 31.3%. In the area of the old Kingdom the rise was 28.4%, but in Transylvania it was 72%. This rise was most conspicuous in the Székely counties: direct taxes rose in Ciuc county by 76%, in Odorheiu county by 86.5%, and in Trei Scaune county by 110%.[44] During the same two years direct taxes in the old Kingdom increased by 1.9%, whereas they increased by 22.2% in Transylvania. Similar divergencies may be noted in the case of other taxes.

The distinctions between the Romanian and non-Romanian population was apparent not only in the assessment of taxes, but extended to their collection as well. According to the data in the official bulletin from 1934 to 1936, the collection of taxes was far more efficient in the Székely counties than in areas inhabited by Romanians. In the year 1934/35 the nation-wide average was 72.9% of the tax assessed. In certain purely Romanian counties of the Kingdom of Romania collection remained far below the national average. In the county of Buzău only 25.5% of the assessed tax was collected, in Dorohoi 51.8%, in Teleorman 59.4%. In the Székely region, however, which even according to Romanian authors, was one of the poorest in the country; the result of the tax collection was far above what obtained in Romanian counties. In the county of Trei Scaune 61.4% of the taxes assessed were actually collected, in Odorheiu 74%, in Mureş-Turda 103.8%, whereas in the poorest county, Ciuc 121.6% of the assessed taxes were collected. In the Romanian counties of Transylvania, as in the old Kingdom, lesser percentages were collected. In Alba [Alsó-Fehér] the ratio was 69.5%, whereas in Năsăud county, where the Romanian border guards had been able to retain their commonwealth of a quarter-million cadastral *holds*, merely 39% of the taxes assessed were collected. In contrast, in the county of Cernăuți, which had a predominantly Ukrainian population, tax collection must have been stricter, because according to the Romanian tables, 95.5% of the assessed taxes were collected.

The trend continued the following year. 75.5% of the assessed taxes were collected, but once again the rate depended on the ethnic background of the inhabitants of the county. In the Romanian counties 38.2% of the assessed taxes were collected; 55.4% in Teleorman, 57.2% in Dorohoi. In the Székely and Hungarian counties: 85.2% in Odorheiu, 96.8% in Ciuc, 99.98% in Mureș-Turda, 100.2% in Trei Scaune. In the Romanian counties of Transylvania the collection relented: 64.5% in Năsăud, 66.7% in Alba. In the county of Cernăuti, with a Ukrainian majority, the ratio approximated that of the Hungarian counties: 96.5%.[45]

One might assume that this difference in the rates of tax collection was a result of a favorable economic turn in the Székely and Hungarian areas. The official Romanian statistics indicate the opposite. In a period of ten years, from 1925 to 1935, the Székely counties lost a large fraction of their heads of cattle. The county of Odorheiu had 55,907 head of cattle in 1925, but the figure was down to 40,470 by 1935 — a loss of 23%. In the county of Trei-Scaune the decrease was from 54,638 to 38,074 — a loss of 30%. The number of milking cows decreased in the same period from 22,959 to 17,470. Among the Székely counties only Ciuc had sufficient cattle, but the number of pigs was far below the demand. From the point of view of meat and protein the population of Ciuc would have needed 45,000 pigs, whereas it owned a mere 14,569.[46]

It is obvious, therefore, that Romanian economic policies along the principles advocated by Vintilă Brătianu achieved the impoverishment of the regions with a Hungarian population. These policies aimed at accelerating the emigration of the Székely towards the old Kingdom of Romania by depleting their resources. Indeed, the Székely population, because of its needy financial condition already under Hungarian rule, emigrated in large numbers towards the areas of the Kingdom of Romania at that time. Towards the end of the twenties Romanian authors realized the advantages the enhancement of Székely emigration might offer for the Romanians and, after 1934, the Romanian authorities did their best to make the life of the peasantry in the Székely areas truly unbearable. In some places the Romanian civil servants stationed in the Székely areas exerted unbearable pressure on the population of the villages. They forced the Székely peasants to build churches for the benefit of a few dozen Romanian civil servants and a few other Romanians who had been settled there by the government and who belonged to the so-called Romanian National Church.

As we may read in the official calendar of the Romanian Uniate Church of Blaj [Balázsfalva] in 1938, churches had been constructed in Guşteriţal [Szenterzsébet], Aldea [Abásfalva], Dragu [Szentmárton], and Crăciuneşti [Karácsonyfalva] in the county of Odorheiu. The Ministry of Religious Affairs provided an assistance of 1,125,000 lei for the construction of churches, but these "had to be built for the most part from local contributions."[47] Yet the local residents were Hungarian; according to the calendar, there were altogether 66 members of the Uniate Church in Aldea [Abásfalva], 117 in Mărtiniş [Homoródszentmárton], 120 in Crăciuneşti [Karácsonyfalva]; these could not have built the churches out of their own resources. Paging through the registers of the governing councils of the Unitarians residing in this area we run across the following bitter observation: "the Romanian bourgeois class goes far beyond the requirement of love for one's neighbor in not merely requesting but demanding that the Unitarian Székely farmer carry the foundation stone of the Orthodox Church to be built in his village."[48] Of course, it was not just the Unitarians; Reformed and Roman Catholic peasants were likewise forced to participate in the construction effort. The political community was often ordered to take care of the construction and maintenance of the Romanian National Church building. More than once, within the same Székely village, a separate parish would be set up for the benefit of 15 to 20 Romanian parishioners — mostly teachers and other civil servants assigned there — in addition to the already established Romanian parish which likewise had but few parishioners.

The Romanian weekly published in Miercurea Ciuc, the *Gazeta Ciucului*, noted with irritation in 1937, under the headline "Mistakes in the Policy of Romanianization" that the Romanian Orthodox bishopric of Sibiu [Szeben] was establishing a parish for 15 Orthodox churchgoers at Ditrău [Ditró]. The paper explained that this was superfluous zeal, because the Romanian Uniate Church was already established at Ditrău, moreover, it was harmful, because now "the community had to provide financially for both churches."

By this time the majority of the Székely communities were led by Romanian teachers and notaries resettled in their midst. It was primarily these Romanians, not natives of the village, who were appointed to the community council. The councils were constituted in such a way that the Hungarian peasantry was hardly represented. Such a council would naturally be most generous in awarding the revenues and taxes of the community for Romanian national purposes.

In the official Romanian bulletin of January 23, 1940 (No. 19), we may read a directive authorizing the managers of the community of Sîndominic [Csíkszentdomokos], in the county of Ciuc, to provide a lot as a present for the site of a Romanian Orthodox Church. The justification for the request states unequivocally:

> that the construction of an Orthodox Church in the community of Sîndominic is not only for the beautification of the community, but is necessary from the national point of view as well, since it is the task of the church to bring the residents back to the ancestral faith.[49]

In such cases the residents of Székely villages constructed, at their own expense, Romanian churches called upon to Romanianize them.

The Székelys were forced to construct state schools with the same objective in mind. As we shall see in our chapter on school issues, the Székelys and Hungarians had to build, in addition to their own denominational schools, the Romanian public schools as well. This double school funding burden was considered quite natural by the person introducing the law of 1924 on public education because, as he explained:

> If a community has a minority school supported by the minority, but the community decides to establish a public school as well, the citizens of the minority group may not withhold their contribution on the grounds that they are already burdened by having to support their own school.[50]

In addition to the larger taxes assessed and the far stricter collection of these, in addition to supporting their own church and school, they had to build and maintain the National Churches and public schools established in order to Romanianize them. This terrible financial burden eventually became quite unbearable. All the more so, as the Romanian state employees transferred to the Székely region seized every opportunity to persecute the Székelys. By 1936 this activity of the Romanian civil servants had assumed such proportions that well-intentioned Romanians writing in the weekly of Ciuc admitted it was too much. One of them tried to express clearly the more impartial Romanian point of view:

> The Székely peasants are regarded as a chauvinistic minority group. All their ideas and moves are followed with suspicion. We do not realize at all that the unbridled nationalism with

which so many of us are persecuting the Székely peasant from
morning till night alienates him from us and forces him into an
antagonistic stance.... This is a profound error! Whoever
possesses the criteria for understanding the Székely peasant
knows that he expects sympathy and peace, not a policy of
irritations. Let us deal with him humanely, otherwise we turn
him into an enemy in our own home.... This is what those of us
Romanians who would die unless they swallowed one Székely a
day must understand.[51]

As a consequence of the economic policies of the Romanian
government in the Székely areas, the number of male and female
emigrants depleted the population increasingly year after year. Some
regions of the old Kingdom soon filled up with men and women
migrating from the Székely areas. According to certain computations
almost 50,000 Székelys found room in Bucharest, since living there was
much easier. They did not have to pay higher taxes there, nor were
they expected to maintain two kinds of churches and schools; in fact,
they paid lower taxes than in Transylvania. Moreover, Bucharest, as
the capital of Greater Romania, had embarked on the path of large scale
development, and the various works undertaken offered intelligent
Székelys good financial opportunities. At the same time migration in
the opposite direction got under way from the areas of the old Romanian
Kingdom: civil servants, teachers, notaries, and other Romanian state
employees flocked to the Székely villages and towns.[52] It was for
their sake that the Székelys had to build those Romanian churches. But
Székely emigration was directed not only towards the old Romanian
Kingdom. Many who had the possibility left for America. In 1936, for
instance, 110 Hungarians emigrated from the county of Trei Scaune, all
but one of whom went to America. In the absence of statistics during
the 22 years of Romanian rule, a precise picture of emigration cannot
be gained, but one could assume a massive Hungarian exodus.

Apart from emigration, the population of the Székely region and
other Hungarian areas was depleted by the low birthrate. The average
population increase in the county of Odorheiu in 1930 was 8.1 per
thousand, well below the 11.7 nation-wide average. By 1938 this rate
had decreased to 6.9. The rate was even lower in the county of Trei
Scaune; in some places it did not even reach 3.8 per thousand. The
population also decreased in the county of Ciuc. Indeed, most of the
migrants to Bucharest and other parts of old Romania came from this
area. A bus would depart from Ciuc-Caşin [Csík-Kászon] twice a week
carrying emigrants to Bucharest. In some communities the houses were

closed down, the doors and windows boarded up, because a third of the population had left for Bucharest and other parts of old Romania. Some left their families behind for a few years, and the head of family remained tied to Bucharest by income and interest. These two-homed beings replied to a pastor inquiring about their spiritual welfare: "Why should we build a cultural center here, when we have one in Bucharest?"[53]

While the population of Hungarian background fell into dire straits in the Székely region, in some areas of Transylvania with a mixed population the financial opportunities were more favorable.   In particular, where the Hungarians lived interspersed with Saxons, they were able to penetrate into the Saxon areas and set footing financially. At Mediaş [Medgyes], Braşov [Brassó], and other Saxon centers such as Sighişoara [Segesvár] the number of Hungarian residents increased during the Romanian rule, and their financial situation improved. There were even some areas in the Székely region where some fortunate cooperative venture led to financial betterment. In the county of Mureş two significant Hungarian institutions came about: the Agricultural Association of Mureş county, and the Transylvania Dairy Settlement. These two institutions earned immeasurable merits in the protection of the economic interests of the Hungarian peasantry.   After 1930 the Association engaged in large-scale agricultural extension work, organized exhibitions, formed smallholder's societies, acquired sowing machines and breeding animals, etc. In this work it relied on assistance from the Transylvanian Farming Union, which supported it financially and with its prestige.

The dairy settlement "Transylvania" was founded by the Association of Agricultural Cooperatives and Credit Unions in 1936.   The Association transformed the existing milk stores into cooperatives and organized the collection of dairy products from the villages. The dairies worked on the Danish model.   At the beginning 17 communities supplied the milk.   Later, 72 communities participated in the transportation of milk, as a consequence of which excellent butter could be manufactured at Tîrgu Mureş [Marosvásárhely].   Thanks to the efforts of the Association the price of milk rose, the income of the smallholders increased, and the quantities shipped in 1936 increased in value by 2.065,061 lei as compared to two years earlier. The dairy center sold most of the butter in the larger towns of Transylvania and in Romania itself. It established 27 agencies spread around the country, six of which were on the territory of the former kingdom. It exported as far as the United Kingdom and Palestine. In 1936 it processed 2.680,000 liters of milk, and 6.205,100 liters the following year; in 1938 it reached this amount already by August. It tied in the cooperative of the neighboring Tîrnava Mică [Kis-Küküllö] county and even of Cluj county. In 1937 it organized a special dairy center at Cristuru Secuiesc [Székelykeresztúr] for the milk cooperatives of Odorheiu county on the model of the one operating at Tîrgu Mureş.[54]

In other Székely and Hungarian areas the only possibility for economic betterment lay with the cooperatives. The Hungarian cooperatives enjoyed relatively the best treatment among all Hungarian organizations because the policies of the Romanian National Peasant Party favored the cooperative movement, as manifested in the law on cooperatives. The Hungarian consumers' cooperatives gathered in the *Hangya* (Bee) cooperative center at Aiud [Nagyenyed], whereas the producers and credit cooperatives established their center at Cluj [Kolozsvár]. These cooperatives had to rely entirely on Hungarian resources. As one of the Romanian specialists noted in 1933, they had to offer less income than the Romanian or Saxon cooperatives. This was natural, according to the Romanian author, since the Romanian and Saxon cooperatives received loans on better terms. "The Romanians received loans from the central cooperative bank, the Saxons from the Agricultural Center at Sibiu."[55] Indeed, the Romanian author put his finger on the gist of the matter. One of the greatest difficulties facing the Hungarian cooperatives was the shortage of credit, since the Romanian National Bank gave very limited loans to Hungarian agricultural institutions and eventually refrained from granting them loans altogether.

The legal status of the Hungarian cooperatives was defined by ordinance 33,000 of 1922, issued by the Cluj office of the Romanian Ministry of Justice. This directive authorized the Hungarian cooperatives to continue to operate on the basis of former Hungarian rules. Thus the autonomy of the cooperatives was preserved for the time being but, on the other hand, they could not benefit from the advantages granted to Romanian cooperatives. The law on cooperatives, promulgated on March 28, 1929, preserved the autonomy of the Hungarian cooperatives, under state supervision, until September 1, 1938.

The new law on cooperatives, promulgated on June 23, 1938, drastically altered the predicament of the Hungarian cooperatives, subordinating them to organizations representing Romanian national interests. The law dissolved the associations which until then exercised supervision over the cooperatives of minority groups and established the National Institute of Cooperatives, which became the only supervising and guiding body. This new institute was under the control of the

Romanian Minister of National Economy. The law deprived the Hungarian cooperatives of the opportunities available to them until then and put a break on their evolution. The regulatory legislation of January 20, 1939, completed the process. This regulation banned all cooperatives that were not registered with the National Institute of Cooperatives. The law also authorized the Minister, i.e. the National Institute of Cooperatives, to dissolve the board of directors or management of any cooperative without explanation, and to replace it with a board of directors consisting of seven plenipotentiary members. This entailed a complete change in the significance of the Hungarian cooperatives. The Hungarian cooperative centers were allowed to operate by the Minister of National Economy only with the proviso that half of the members on its board of directors, including the executive director, be appointed by the Minister. After this Romanianization the Hungarian cooperatives no longer could pursue activities in defense of Hungarian economic interests.[56]

It follows, therefore, that under Romanian rule the Hungarian peasants could make economic progress only for a short time. The promising beginnings of the cooperatives were thwarted by the Romanianizing and nationalizing measures of 1938. The Hungarian peasantry did not have opportunities such as those enjoyed by the Romanian peasants under Hungarian rule. Very seldom could the better-off Hungarian peasants purchase land, because various Romanian laws made it most difficult to transfer land in Greater Romania, almost to the end. Article 47 of the land reform law of Transylvania and other similar measures limited the possibility of purchasing holdings. Estates of over 50 hectares which came on the market at the beginning had to be offered to the Romanian state first. Eventually, in some areas — naturally mainly in areas with a Hungarian population — the preemptive right of the Romanian state was extended to all kinds of real estate offered for purchase. Similar limitations applied to acreage that became available as a result of the land reform. The mid-size estates that remained after the land reform could not be purchased by individuals of Hungarian background.

A new law was promulgated on March 29, 1937, limiting the transfer of real estate. According to this law the state had preemptive rights to hamlets that had been wholly or partially expropriated together with the improvements thereon. Moreover, the state had preemptive rights to all those estates, including improvements, which exceeded in part or in whole the 50 cadastral *holds*, regardless of how these estates were described at the time of expropriation, whether the area was considered cultivable or not, nor did it matter whether it was subject to expropriation at the time of the land reform or not. The conditions for the exercise of this preemptive right were to be examined at the time of purchase, and this right could not be curtailed or abrogated on the ground of the registers of titles or the nature of the expropriation order.

In connection with this law Elemér Gyárfás, a senator belonging to the Hungarian Party, intervened in the Romanian Senate when the government attempted to prevent the purchase of land Árpád Gyergyai, professor emeritus of the University of Cluj, contracted two years earlier. "One of the Counts Teleki," noted Gyárfás,

> sold his estate to a former professor of medicine for three and a half million, two years ago, and they have been running around ever since — here you can observe the implications of the law on preemption — to finalize this purchase and to find out whether the preemptive right of the state applies in this case or not. The question came up two years ago, a whole series of suits are in progress and, as far as I can see, this law was devised precisely to win the suit which otherwise they would have lost.[57]

The incident which prompted this intervention by Gyárfás was well-known both in Romanian and in Hungarian circles. It referred to the Teleki estates in the community of Luna de Jos [Kendilóna] in the county of Cluj, purchased by Gyergyai in 1935. Some Romanians also had their eyes set on the estate and, in order to prevent the purchase by Gyergyai, they mobilized their political connections, eventually leading to the adoption of what in Hungarian circles became know as the *Lex Gyergyai*.

Thus very few opportunities remained to the Hungarian peasantry in Greater Romania, economically speaking. These possibilities were not even comparable to those enjoyed by the Romanian peasantry under Hungarian rule. Under Romanian rule the Hungarian peasant could survive only by lowering his expectations considerably, and trying to engage in some secondary occupation. Often the peasants undertook artisanry. Elsewhere they hired themselves out as laborers, but most often they seized the opportunity to emigrate. Emigration was often organized by Romanian agents with contacts in high places. The process of exodus started in Hunadoara county in 1922, then spread to Arad county, and later to the German and Hungarian villages of the Banat [Bánát]. Thanks to the support of undersecretary of the Interior Richard Franasovici, an agent named Gyula Herberger launched a large-scale propaganda campaign among the Hungarians of Hunadoara county to promote emigration. As the Romanian police superintendent of Deva reported to his chief:

> The propaganda asserts that the lands of the Hungarians will be expropriated come next spring. I bring your attention to this movement, which may have harmful consequences, because the Hungarians will not fail to use this opportunity as propaganda against us.[58]

In response to the report, the chief of police received instructions by cable from the Ministry of the Interior "to take measures to ensure that his subordinates do not place obstacles in front of Herberger for the sake of personal advancement."[59]   But since not all police officers were aware of these instructions, one uninformed policeman arrested Herberger. Then, the examining judge was instructed, by cable number 56,259/924, marked strictly confidential, that Herberger be released. During the interventions in parliament, Iuliu Maniu criticized the emigration propaganda sponsored by the government, but Foreign Minister Ion G. Duca responded in a peculiar way: "I would like Mr. Maniu to answer my next question with a yes or a no: does he object to the fact that non-Romanian individuals leave the country, or doesn't he?" Maniu did not provide a definite answer. Then Duca went on to add that if individuals who had become Romanian subjects wished to take advantage of international treaties and emigrate, true Romanians could see no harm in that. Thus the Minister of the Interior easily parried the charges against him, and could calmly read out, for the sake of undermining the query a report from the chief of police in Transylvania, which included the following observation: "We are dealing here with individuals who are troublemakers; and we are glad to see them leave as soon as possible, so that their lands may be transferred to Romanian peasants."[60]

In 1924, according to official Romanian data, 811 emigrated to America from the Old Kingdom, 1,425 from Bessarabia, 2,361 from Bukovina, and 18,015 from Transylvania. Over four times as many individuals emigrated from Transylvania as from all the other provinces of Romania combined. It is obvious that most of the emigrants from Transylvania were not Romanian.[61]

During the entire period of Romanian rule the Hungarian peasant seldom enjoyed any economic progress. Those in charge of Romanian economic policies followed the basic principles advocated by Vintilă Brătianu most faithfully. The Hungarian peasants received from the pertinent Romanian agencies — the Ministry of Agriculture or other economic institutions nothing of the kind of support — the Romanian peasants had received from Hungarian agencies. If the farmers in the Hungarian villages needed machines, breeding animals, or hybrid seed, they obtained these through the cooperatives, or with the help the Transylvanian Farmers' Association. Not once did Romanian economic entities provide the Hungarian communities or farmers with free breeding animals or any other economic service. Thus the government applied the chauvinist Romanian economic policies of Brătianu even to the agricultural stratum, the least dangerous to the Romanian state.

The Hungarian Workers

In addition to the social class of peasants, the Hungarian workers also constituted a significant stratum, on account of their solidarity and their numbers. In the formerly Hungarian area the majority of the workers in heavy industry were of Hungarian ethnic background.[62] A sizable portion of the workers had gathered in trade and political organizations to struggle against capital. The first mass movement of workers under Romanian rule was the four-day railroad strike, beginning on January 20, 1919. The strike was easily put down by the Romanian military authorities. The same happened with the general strike launched on October 20, 1920. In 1923, the socialist workers of Transylvania, most of them of Hungarian background, joined the International of Amsterdam. In 1927, they united with the Socialist Democrats active in other Romanian provinces, and from then on the Hungarian workers of Transylvania operated within the Social Democratic Party under Romanian leadership. The party was aware that in the formerly Hungarian areas the majority of the workers were of Hungarian background, and therefore, included protection of minority rights on its platform. But since the leaders of the party never sent a representative with Hungarian background to parliament, the defense of minority rights was mostly for the sake of appearances, and did nothing to mitigate the discrimination suffered by workers of Hungarian background. The Social Democratic Party intervened several times on the issue of language examination for Hungarian railroad workers, or the forced dismissal of Hungarian workers from private enterprises. It was unable to obtain significant results, however, precisely because of the national sentiment of the leaders and the absence of Hungarian ethnic representatives.

Until 1930, before the economic crisis, the situation of the Hungarian workers was bearable, and even satisfactory, in most places. The Romanian government adopted from Belgium and France many measures for the protection of the workers, serving the interests of the working class. Unfortunately, when it came to applying these measures, it turned out that the interests of the workers were taken into consideration mainly if their ethnic background was Romanian. The conditions of the Hungarian working class became increasingly deplorable after 1930. Under the excuse of various language examinations the Hungarian railroad workers were released from their job one after the other. After ten or twenty years on the job, thousands of workers with families found themselves on the streets, even though they had performed outstandingly on their jobs. Yet according to the regulations, they were entitled to pension only after the age of 57. Having lost their job and left without a pension, they lived in utmost misery, awakening in them an awareness of their common Hungarian fate. Those who passed their language examination lived in constant insecurity as well because, according to the court of appeals, their knowledge of the language could be retested at any time.

Having lost their government jobs, the Hungarian workers were also forced out of private firms. The first hints of this trend can be traced back to the *Numerus Valachius* movement launched by Alexandru Vaida-Voevod who had split from the National Peasant Party. Vaida published fictitious data regarding the role played by the minorities in economic life, and demanded that in every area the "aboriginal Romanians" occupy places in appropriate numbers. Under the influence of Nazism, the extreme right-wing movements, including the Iron Guard led by Captain Corneliu Zelea Codreanu, the ranks of which were increasing at an alarming rate year after year, disseminated among large masses of Romanians ideas so dear to the nationalists, demanding the firing of the non-Romanian workers. State enterprises, or those with significant state contracts soon dismissed the greater portion of workers with Hungarian background. In any case, it was part of the program of the Liberal Party in power to support economically the Romanians in every area or, in other words, to discriminate against non-Romanians, leading to the notorious labor defense law of 1934.[63]

This law demanded that economic, industrial, commercial and other private companies employ at least 80% Romanian citizens in each of the categories defined in the law. Moreover, they were forced to select at least 50% Romanian citizens as members of their board of directors, their executive committee, or their supervising committee, including the chairperson. The categories indicated in the law were the managers, technicians, skilled workers, and laborers. In case where the ratios defined in the law were disregarded, the law prescribed penalties extending from a warning from the Ministry to closing down the firm.

The application of the law showed that the measures "in defense of the workers" were aimed at excluding blue-collar and white-collar workers of Hungarian extraction. While the law mentioned Romanian citizens, the application of the law demonstrated that this was merely to mislead the outside world, because the 80% ratio was not applied to Romanian citizens, but to ethnic Romanians. At first some companies could not carry out the inhuman regulation because they could not find a sufficient number of competent skilled workers of Romanian background to replace the Hungarians.

When the law was debated in the house and the senate, and Elemér Gyárfás intervened in the issue, the Romanian Minister of Industries and Commerce specified that the term Romanian meant Romanian citizen; in practice, however, ethnically Romanian was meant and, by June 3, 1936, the control committee in charge of the application of the law had penalized 298 enterprises, with fines totalling 24 million lei; because it could not identify a sufficient number of Romanian nationals among the employees. By August 1938 the Ministry had excluded 155 minority enterprises from public freight privileges, and 106 further enterprises a few weeks later.[64] In vain did the term Romanian mean citizen in the official interpretation of the law, if in practice the term meant a person of Romanian ethnic background. According to the instructions accompanying the law, the enterprises were required to provide yearly tables indicating among other things the ethnic background of their employees. The results were slow to manifest themselves since officially, according to the interpretation, the companies could not be forced to send away the Hungarian workers. Then, in 1937, Valériu Pop, the Minister of Industries and Commerce, summoned the companies in a confidential circular to employ ethnic Romanians in the ratio indicated in national workers' defense law. The Hungarian Party obtained a copy of Pop's confidential circular and complained to the League of Nations. After which, Pop retracted the circular.[65] The retraction, however, did not stop the damage, and companies received all kinds of penalties, including exclusion from public freight privileges, for non-compliance. These measures cut off many thousands of workers of Hungarian background from their source of income.

The Hungarians Artisans

With regards to industry, the former Hungarian territories deserve attention first of all because of the fate of the Hungarian artisans. There were hardly any Hungarian entrepreneurs in the area. The large enterprises, firms, or factories were owned primarily by Germans or Jews. During the Hungarian regime the Jews had considered themselves Hungarian. The Romanian census and practice, however, had consistently regarded them as a separate entity, and did everything to make the Jews themselves accept the consequences of discrimination. Many of them did disassociate themselves from the Hungarians, no longer feeling responsibility towards their Hungarian employees, while many others retained their Hungarian allegiance and, resisting all kinds of official pressures, continued to employ a sizable proportion of Hungarian workers at their plants. This attitude became very significant after 1934, and in some cases amounted to an act of heroism, since the firms were doubly penalized for it. Under the influence of pronounced Nazi and Iron Guard ideas, the Romanian authorities became strongly anti-Semitic and persecuted these Jewish entrepreneurs both because of their religion and because of their pro-Hungarian sentiments. In spite of this, there were several, like the executive director and owner of the well-known Dermata works (tannery) at Cluj [Kolozsvár], Mózes Farkas, who preferred to pay the fines rather than release his workers of Hungarian background.

From the Hungarian point of view artisanry was much more important than large companies. The Hungarian artisans formed a significant proportion of the population even before World War I. According to the census of 1910, 18.7% of the Hungarian population consisted of artisans. Of course, under the Romanian regime their opportunities were curtailed. They soon became the target of antagonistic measures by the Romanian authorities on account of their strong Hungarian sentiments. Within a few years they would definitely feel the crunch of the economic measures initiated against them. The first such measure was the excessive taxation to which they were subjected. According to the official bulletin of the Romanian Ministry of Finance, in old Romania the taxes of the artisans and small businessmen decreased by 11% by 1924-26, but in Transylvania they rose by 24.5%. The rise in Transylvania was most pronounced in the Székely counties. In contrast to the average, the tax on artisans and small businessmen increased by 28.6% in the county of Odorheiu [Udvarhely] 31.2% in Ciuc [Csík] county, 42% in Trei Scaune [Háromszék] county.[66]   As the years passed the pressure on

Hungarian artisans increased. Elemér Gyárfás intervened in the Romanian Senate, and Béni Szabó in the House of Delegates, to denounce the disproportionate rise in the taxes paid by Hungarian artisans. Gyárfás explained that on the basis of the sales tax promulgated on December 25, 1929, the tax assessment committee operating at the revenue office of Tîrgu Mureş (which was manned entirely by Romanians), struck the Hungarians of Reghiu [Szászrégen] with taxes four, five and even ten times as high as in the preceding year. Gyárfás presented a table upon which he had noted the extent to which the tax affecting the Hungarian artisans had increased. A person who had to pay 600 lei in taxes in 1929 was charged 1,600 lei under the same circumstances. In other instances the taxes increased from 560 to 1,540, from 134 to 1,980, from 350 to 3,850, from 203 to 2,420, from 750 to 4,400 lei, even though the rise was not warranted by any increase in sales or any other criterion. In his intervention Szabó pointed out similar manifestations on the basis of complaints he received from all over the country.[67]

As a result of the excessive taxes, the Hungarian artisans were forced to give up their licenses. At Turda [Torda], Cluj [Kolozsvár], Odorheiu-Secuiesc [Székelyudvarhely], Mircurea Ciuc [Csíkszereda] and other Hungarian towns the artisans closed down their businesses by the hundreds. They either sought some other occupation, or felt forced to emigrate. According to the Romanian census of 1930 the number of Hungarian artisans dropped by over 2%, and this decrease continued in the years following, as becomes clear from certain local censuses. According to the figures provided by the artisans' guild of Sfîntu-Gheorghe [Sepsiszentgyörgy], the number of artisans in the town decreased by 22.5% in the period from 1926 to 1936. Only 303 of 391 were able to keep their former trade. The number of apprenticeships likewise declined in the same period from 144 to 89, and the number of apprentices graduating declined from 147 to 87. Similar causes brought about similar results in Tîrgu Mureş and Odorheiu-Secuiesc. The number of artisans at Tîrgu Mureş decreased from 136 to 92 between 1920 and 1935, that of small businessmen from 107 to 39, whereas the number of artisans who did not require licenses dropped from 303 to 70. A few years later there was some improvement, but after 1937 further trade licenses were lost as a result of Romanianization.[68]

The taxes assessed on artisans were collected punctiliously. The Romanian statistical yearbook reveals that the collection of taxes was far more effective in towns with a Hungarian majority than in Romanian towns. In 1934-35 the national average for the collection of taxes was 76.1%, but the results in certain cities varied according to its dominant ethnic group. For instance, in the territory of old Romania, in the town of Drăgăşani, 52.1% of the tax assessed was collected. In Pleniţa it was 42.3%, in Focşani 60.2%, in the Romanian town of Blaj in Transylvania the rate was 47.6%, and in the purely Romanian town of Năsăud 27.7%. In contrast, the taxes collected at Odorheiu-Secuiesc, where the population consisted predominantly of Hungarian artisans, collection was 74.1%; at Miercurea Ciuc it was 79.9%; at Tîrgu Mureş 93.2%; at Sfîntu-Gheorghe 97.5%; at Petroşani [Petrozsény] 95.6%. In the following fiscal year, 1935-36, the national average was 78.5%. The rate at Drăgăşani was 45.4%, at Plenita 31.6%, at Focşani 60.9%, whereas it was 88.5% at Mircurea Ciuc, 82.8% at Odorheiu-Secuiesc, 88.5% at Sfîntu-Gheorghe, and 91.2% at Tîrgu Mureş. At Petroşani where, in addition to the artisans, there were masses of Hungarian miners, the collection rate was 99.6%.[69]

In addition to overtaxing the Hungarian artisans, Romanian economic policies were aimed at bolstering artisans of Romanian background and increasing their sources of income. The express goal of the law setting up the National Industrial Credit Institute, promulgated on June 23, 1923, was to promote Romanian industry. By Romanian industry the law meant industry in the hands of ethnic Romanians. The objective of the law regarding the Industrial Credit Institute was to provide credit to Romanian artisans. The representative of the Tranysylvanian and Eastern Hungarian region on the committee in charge of the funds of the Institute, as specified in the law, was a member of the center of Romanian artisans and businessmen of Cluj. The measure completely excluded Hungarian artisans, who constituted the large majority in those areas, from the administration of the funds. The modification to the law, adopted on May 4, 1939, added unequivocal measures favoring Romanian racist policies. According to this modification, the Institute could issue loans only to Romanian employers, and only Romanian employers were eligible to serve on the board of directors of the Institute.[70]   At the same time the government promoted legislation to close down artisan guilds catering to Hungarians. These guilds, within which the members could secure economic protection, professional training, and arbitration, united the Hungarian artisans. The Act of April 29, 1936, regarding professional training and licensing dissolved these guilds and transferred all their funds to the artisan section of the Labor Chambers established a few years earlier. From then on the artisan section within these Labor Chambers had jurisdiction in the most important matters affecting Hungarian artisans. The funds amassed by Hungarian artisans over several decades were now turned over to Romanian artisans who, of course, were in a haste to use these for Romanian purposes. The case of the Hungarian Artisans' Home of Satu Mare, followed by many similar cases, created a big stir. The artisans turned to the courts, requesting that their property rights be recognized. The court decided in their favor. In spite of this the Labor Chamber of Oradea [Nagyvárad] did not restitute the Home to its rightful owners.[71]

The anti-Hungarian intent of the 1936 Act on trades appears most clearly in that provision of the law which allowed the association of the Romanian merchants and artisans of Transylvania to continue.[72] These laws were followed by measures aimed at ensuring that apprentices of Romanian ethnic background received training at the hands of Hungarian artisans in percentages prescribed by law. As a consequence of these measures we have the peculiar situation where the Homes that were the fruit of decades of work by Hungarian guilds fell into the hands of Romanian artisans who barred Hungarian ethnic artisans from those homes. Hungarian artisans were not allowed to employ apprentices of Hungarian background, but were obliged to train Romanians. Thus economic freedom ceased to exist for the artisans as well and, in accordance with Vintilă Brătianu's chauvinist economic policies, the Romanian state ensured the economic progress of the Romanian population by means of legislation, while preventing the replacement of Hungarian artisans by another generation of Hungarians or even their use of the Homes they had built from their own earnings. After the promulgation of the minority statute, negotiations were undertaken regarding the livelihood and organization of artisans belonging to the Hungarian ethnic group. These negotiations achieved success in 1940. The Hungarian National Artisans Association, created to defend the professional interests of the Hungarian artisans, was founded at that time, but before it could begin to operate the Hungarian artisans were facing a new situation as a result of the Second Vienna Arbitration Treaty (Award).

Commerce

In the formerly Hungarian areas attached to Romania Hungarian merchants constituted but a small percentage of the business class. These Hungarians were mainly shopkeepers, since the Hungarians had never felt particularly attracted to business. A sizable proportion of the merchants were Jews who identified themselves with the Hungarian population. These experienced the same treatment as the artisans under Romanian rule. Because of their Hungarian identity they were constantly compelled to undergo extraordinary expenses. If they insisted on displaying the Hungarian version of the shop's name on their sign, they had to pay a surtax several times the normal tax. According to the Act of June 26, 1923, dealing with the assessment of community taxes and dues, taxes of 8,000 lei had to be paid to the community for any shop-sign in a foreign language.[73] According to the tabulation accompanying the Act the 8,000 lei were in lieu of the 500 lei normally paid in towns, or the 200 lei normally paid in the villages. Thus, in the villages the tax on Hungarian signs was forty times the normal amount. According to the law published in the official bulletin of April 1, 1935, those artisans and merchants who were assessed according to their bookkeeping would have to pay a surtax if their books were not in Romanian. According to the Act of 1936 on administration, if the shop-signs were displayed only in a foreign language, the owners were assessed eight times the regular tax to be paid to the community. In accordance with the law the Romanian fiscal authorities did assess the eightfold tax at Tîrgu Mureş, Cluj, and Oradea, even though by that time the Hungarian signs were merely translations underneath the Romanian name. Naturally, there were but few Hungarian businessmen who could undertake to pay the eightfold tax for a Hungarian shop-sign over an extended period of time.

The Romanianization of the employees of businesses started very early. The Romanian Governing Council of Sibiu issued a regulation in April, 1919 requiring financial institutions and other businesses to include Romanians in their management and to transfer to them a certain number of shares free of charge. In the uncertain atmosphere of the times the Hungarian banks and other businesses were worried about their survival and hastened to comply with the regulation. This was the beginning of the Romanianization of Hungarian businesses. After the Governing Council disbanded, the Romanian government of Bucharest took over the Romanianization effort. As a result of its measures the spirit of enterprise soon abated. The Romanian daily of Cluj noted regarding this period that:

> economic life in Transylvania has been agonizing for a long time.... Not only did they not introduce legality, but have trampled on the basic freedoms. Everywhere there is a reign of terror, such as we had never seen under the Hungarian regime. They treat Transylvania as if it were a colony.[74]

After 1922, when Vintilă Brătianu took over the direction of the Ministry of Finance, a renewed assault of Romanianization was directed against businesses in Transylvania. This time the ruling Liberal party intended to nationalize (i.e. Romanianize) not only the enterprises owned by the minorities, but even the Romanian enterprises belonging to the sphere of interest of the Romanian National Peasant Party, in order to bring them under the influence of banks in which the Liberals had vested interests. The authors of the French-language leaflet distributed by the Romanian opposition parties in 1924 condemned this economic activity of the Liberals in strong terms. The leaflet stated that the mining and lumber enterprises were compelled to accept:

> under the guise of nationalization, the direct influence of the banks belonging to the Liberal Party.... Under the veil of economic chauvinism we find the monstrous attempt of certain economic and political nabobs to gain hold of the economic potential of the entire country.... In order to disguise these reprehensible activities, they pin the Romanian flag over their shadiest transactions; and the most dishonorable deals come about with the help of the highest patriotism. Ad hoc laws are on the agenda. These laws would put a halt to any kind of economic enterprise and strangle all effort and initiative.[75]

This French-language protests by members of the Romanian National Peasant Party discloses some of the objectives of Romanian economic policy guided by Vintilă Brătianu. It is obvious that Brătianu himself intended to purloin the enterprises owned by non-Romanians into the hands of Romanian individuals or at least under the leadership of a Romanian majority. The economic agencies of the Liberal Party derived large profits from this "nationalization" process and their activities affected even enterprises that were already in Romanian hands. It is understandable, therefore, that the owners of such enterprises protested angrily against this side-effect of the nationalization program. As we have seen and shall see further on, they too approved of the plans for Romanizing the enterprises in minority hands and, when they came to power, Vintilă Brătianu's policies against the minorities were adopted and continued.

The legislation concerning industry, the increase in taxation and the stricter collection thereof, as well as the measures aimed at hiring Romanian personnel and excluding minority employees affected commerce along with industry. Consequently, Hungarian businesses also encountered the difficulties we have already discussed in connection with the artisans. The higher taxes assessed in towns with a Hungarian majority and the stricter auditing procedures were attempts to weaken and impoverish the Hungarian merchants along with the artisans. These tendencies of the economic policies became particularly acute after 1934.

One of the greatest difficulties confronting Hungarian commerce under Romanian rule was obtaining adequate credit; hence, credit institutions and the credit policies of the Romanian state assumed considerable importance from the Hungarian point of view. These policies provided credit to Romanian and Hungarian merchants according to the principles advocated by Vintilă Brătianu. The details of these credit policies are revealed through the issue of discounting to Hungarian banks. Naturally, until 1919 financial institutions with a Hungarian character were tied to Budapest, the country's economic hub. In fact, most of them functioned as branches of Budapest banks. When power changed hands, the connection with Budapest had to be severed. After reorganization the banks had to stand on their own feet and attempted to conduct business by adapting to the altered circumstances. As mentioned, they elected Romanians into their management, in accordance with the directive of the Governing Council of Sibiu, hoping the latter would be of assistance in securing the goodwill of those in control of credit policies.

They soon attempted to group Hungarian ethnic banks into a cooperative. The cooperative did come about under the name of Transylvanian Syndicate of Banks, but the Romanian government would not authorize it and therefore had to disband. Finally, on December 13, 1923, they succeeded in reforming at Cluj thanks to a permit obtained with great difficulty. At this time the Syndicate included 98 member institutions with a total base capital of 228 million lei.

Since the development of financial institutions is always a function of the discount credit provided by the central bank, this applied to the Hungarian banks as well; but when the direction of the Transylvanian Syndicate of Banks inquired regarding the possibility of discounting from the Romanian Banca Națională (National Bank), it turned out that the latter, dominated by the Liberal Party, was prepared to provide only very limited credit to the Hungarians banks. The Syndicate received altogether half a million lei discount credit, in spite of its base capital of 228 million. The following year the credit rose somewhat, but it was noted at the annual general meeting of June 8, 1925, that for its capital of 322 million lei provided by its 119 member institutions they received merely 19.9 million lei discount credit. At the same time the Banca Românescă, with a base capital of 380 million, received 866 million, the Banca Maramureș, with a base capital of 287 million, received 874 million, the Banca de Credit Român with a base capital of 195 million received 529 millions of discount credit.[76] The proportions did not change the following year. In 1926 the annual meeting of the Syndicate of Banks held at Oradea noted that the Syndicate had 214 members with a base capital of 398 million, yet the Banca Națională offered it merely 26 million in discount credits. Eight other minority institutions with a base capital of 125.5 million received discount credit of 10.2 million, whereas the Transylvanian Credit Bank, a prestigious old institution, received no credit at all. In the same year the Banca Maramureș, with a base capital of 125 million, received 799.9 million in discount credits.[77] In 1927, at the fourth annual meeting held at Cluj, it was noted that although the Syndicate had 214 member-institutions with a base capital of 531 million lei; it still was granted no more than 30 million in discount credit; while the Romanian banks continued to receive in the same proportions as before. The situation improved somewhat in 1928, since the 207 Hungarian member institutions with a capital of 642 million received a discount credit of 107 million, that is one sixth of their base capital. Nevertheless, the Romanian banks continued to receive three or four times their capital in discount credit. The same ratios prevailed in the following year, demonstrating all too clearly that the Romanian National Bank, within the sphere of interest of the Liberal party, faithfully applied the chauvinistic economic principles advocated by Brătianu.

For the above reasons the Hungarian banks could, of course, loan out only at higher rates of interest; basically, Hungarian business life had to make do without the so important credit support during the entire Romanian regime. The financial institutions had to rely exclusively on deposits and on each other. Nor were those banks that did not join the Syndicate any better off. All of them could survive only by paying lower interest on deposits and charging higher interest on loans. The consequence of this, in many places, was that Hungarian and other businesses preferred to turn to Romanian institutions, bypassing the minority banks. Zsigmond Szana noted in 1925 that:

> the financial institutions in the Old Kingdom paid less interest on deposits than our own institutions. But we must consider that those banks, for the most part, enjoy credits from the Banca Națională that amount to several times their base capital, whereas our own institutions receive an average of 20% of their base capital.[78]

As regards to discount credit, the Hungarian banks got into even more dire straits later on. During the world economic crisis they received practically no credit and by 1935 many Hungarian banks had to close down. After 1935, thanks to international contacts, they gained access to foreign credit, thus avoiding further cases of bankruptcy.

Hungarian institutions were discriminated against not only in the matter of discount credit, but also as a consequence of the Act regarding debts. This Act included several measures to alleviate the condition of the indebted in the villages and the towns. As a result banks throughout the country suffered great losses. Article 62 of the Act compensated the state supported Romanian financial institutions for the losses suffered as a consequence of the tax reform, but minority financial institutions received no such compensation at all. Many Hungarian banks were forced to close down as a result of discrimination and of the measures adopted to promote the principles advocated by Brătianu.[79]

These Romanian credit policies hampered considerably and at times completely paralyzed the development of Hungarian business. Since they did not have access to adequate discount credit, Hungarian banks paid less for deposits and charged more for loans than Romanian institutions. Hungarian economic life in general became subject to serious difficulties.

The Intelligentsia

The Hungarian intelligentsia consisted of several strata which had evolved at the time of the Compromise. One stratum of mid-size landowners was composed of professionals such as lawyers, doctors, etc. The Hungarian political and cultural leaders came primarily from their midst. Most of them were of the nobility, the so-called gentry. Civil servants and the employees of religious and educational institutions formed other significant strata. Professionals such as lawyers, doctors, physicians, journalists, etc., whose ranks were growing but slowly, played a relatively less-important role.

It was the mid-size and large landowners among the strata of the Hungarian intelligentsia that went broke soonest. The land reform was merciless in their regard. Indeed, according to the data from Northern Transylvania, 80.5% of the Hungarians owning estates between 100 and 500 *holds*, and 90.8% of those owning estates above 500 *holds* were expropriated.[80] The expropriation was carried out in accordance with the principles already enunciated. For instance, in the county of Turda-Arieş [Turda-Aries] 110,535 cadastral *holds* were expropriated. In this connection the best-known sociologist of the Romanians of Transylvania, Petre Suciu, noted "that the confiscated lands were mainly in

Hungarian hands before the land reform. They had estates totalling over 150,120 *holds* and retained but 39,509 *holds.*"[81] If we subtract the second figure from the first we are left with exactly 110,511 *holds*, which was the amount transferred into Romanian hands as a result of the expropriation. Thus in the county of Turda expropriation affected exclusively Hungarian landowners, even though there were quite a few Romanian landowners in the county as well.

According to the tables compiled by the Transylvanian Farmers' Union in the county of Someş [Szolnok-Doboka], only Hungarian estates were appropriated in that county as well, whereas the Romanian estates were left untouched. Of course, the class of Hungarian mid-size landowners went broke as a result. At the same time Romanian mid-size landowners were not only spared but, as we shall see below, their numbers increased. In some places even the needy of Romanian nationality were left unsatisfied because the confiscated estates were not divided up but rented out. For instance, 419 of those entitled to land in the Bánát were left landless because 1000 *holds* were rented out to a Romanian company called "Ogorul." Similarly, 10,000 *holds* were rented out in Satu Mare county to "Motocultura" Incorporated. In the community of Nojorid [Nagyürgöd] in the county of Bihor 1,000 needy peasants received no land, because the area that had been expropriated for them was handed over to an agent of the government in Oradea. The Ruthenians of Maramureş, like the Hungarians, were not given access to land. The 3,300 *hold* estate of the widow of Simion Pop, the former Romanian sheriff, was left intact. In April 1930 representatives of the landless in Maramureş [Máramaros] turned to Ion Mihalache, the Minister of Agriculture, requesting that the large estate of the Pop family be distributed among those entitled to it. Mihalache stated that he was aware of the case, but could do nothing about it.[82]

Thus the land reform had bankrupted the Hungarian mid-size owners, but spared the mid-size owners among the Romanians; in fact, more than once it even spared large estates owned by Romanians. On the basis of the provision of the land reform providing confiscated land for lots to build apartments for civil servants on the outskirts of towns, large areas in the suburbs of Hungarian towns were taken away from members of the Hungarian middle class. At Cluj, Odorheiu-Secuiesc, Tîrgu Mureş, Miercurea Ciuc and other towns the parcels of land belonging to rather poor Hungarians, members of the intelligentsia, and to artisans, were confiscated for the benefit of the Romanian middle class. Altogether 775 *holds* were confiscated at Cluj for this purpose. The confiscated area was divided into 2,672 lots, which were divided among Romanians, including: Emil Poriţiu a landlord from Cluj, who also owned a residence and an estate at Chinteni [Kajántó], and who was a member of the expropriation committee. He was awarded two lots at Cluj. Augustin Pop, a Romanian priest from Nadăş, who owned an estate at Nadăş [Nádas] and a house in Cluj, likewise received two lots. Two lots were awarded to Florea Bitichie, the Chief inspector of the Ministry of Agriculture. President Leonide Petrescu and chief inspector of roads and bridges, Eugen Tilea, a permanent resident of Braşov, also received two lots each. Ioan Lăpedatu, the director of the Romanian National Bank and former Minister of Finance, and Alexandru Lăpedatu Minister of Religious Affairs, resident of Bucharest, received a lot each. The mayor Octavian Utalea received a lot too, although he had a house at Cluj and an estate of 200 *holds* near Dej [Dés]. The prefect Septimiu Mureşan also received a lot on the grounds that he was a poor civil servant. Moreover, General Ioan Anastasiu, landlord and landowner of Suceagu [Szucsák], general of the medical corps Gheorghe Bădescu, the director of the Academy of Economics Mihail Şerban who already owned two houses at Cluj, the registrar Alessandru Pop, agrarian Judge Enea Munteanu, landlord Covrig Roşianu, university professor and bank president Leon, university professor and landlord T. Călugăreanu, professor Gheorghe Pamfil, the director of the Institute of Pharmacology who had occupied a six-room apartment as part of his appointment and had a house of his own, the pharmacist Nicolau Mantu from Turda, bank director Virgil Comşa, the executive director of the Banca Naţiunea Gheorghe Ionescu, the director of the tobacco monopoly of Bucharest Agripa Ionescu, undersecretary of finance Simionescu, the director of the coal mines of Aghireşul [Egeres] Gheorghe Manoilescu, chief superintendent Ioan Ciomac, and executive director of surveys Ioan Podariu each received one lot. Tănăsescu, former undersecretary and a resident of Bucharest, also received two lots. The agrarian judges who participated in the expropriation awarded themselves one lot each, but there were two among them who received three lots each. Among those receiving lots, there was not a single worker or lower ranking civil servant, although there were some dancers and artistes. By 1928 altogether twenty homes had been built on the 775 *holds* of terrain.[83]

Similar procedures prevailed in the towns of the Székely area. At Odorheiu-Secuiesc the lot of over one *hold* belonging to the widow Mrs. Bálint Erdős and her four children was confiscated, even though the poor woman had nothing else to rely on. The lot of Ferenc Bálint, suffered the same fate. The confiscated lots were awarded to well-paid Romanian civil servants. In Ciuc county, the Romanian middle class did increase in numbers thanks to the above procedure. In the area appropriated from the commonwealth of Borsec [Borszék], 150 lots for building villas were distributed to wealthy and distinguished Romanians among whom we find the wife of Alexandru Constantinescu, the Minister of Agriculture, Minister of Foreign Affairs I. G. Duca, Minister of Transportation, Arthur Văitoianu, county prefect Dr. Spătar, the Senator Pantelimonu Halippa, and members of parliament Iosif Blaga, Ioan Vlad, Dr. Lupaș, and E. Iorga.[84] In the counties of Trei Scauns, Mureș Turda, and all regions inhabited by Hungarians, the confiscated lands were generously distributed among members of the Romanian middle class. Some Romanian authors condemned this peculiar phenomenon, and protests by Romanians were published in some papers. The semi-official paper of the Romanian National Party of Transylvania made the following observations in 1925:

> If some time in the future the country develops on the basis of the new system of land tenure, it will become clear that the object of the expropriation was not to provide land for as many poor peasants as possible but rather to create a capitalist bourgeoisie. Only this way can we explain that in lieu of the class of rural peasants; a class of farmers came about composed of lawyers, doctors, professors, teachers, priests, civil servants, engineers, architects, wholesalers, etc. — in other words, individuals who know nothing about agriculture, village life, or animal breeding.[85]

Indeed, Romanian society evolved along these lines. The place of the Hungarian mid-size and large landowner, on the verge of bankruptcy, was taken by a class of Romanian mid-size landowners which had multiplied in numbers and assisted by all kinds of economic privileges granted by the authorities. Some of the Hungarian mid-size owners emigrated, others attempted to eke out a living on the fraction of their estates that was left to them. They were soon compelled to become involved in the political issues concerning the Hungarians of Transylvania, and assumed the leadership of Hungarian institutions in the area.

Church Personnel

As mentioned, a large number of officials, teachers, priests, professors and administrators were in the service of the Hungarian churches in Transylvania. During the Hungarian regime this personnel received a pay subsidy from the Hungarian state, much as the

Romanian personnel in comparable positions. Some institutions that were well endowed with estates were able to pay their employees from the revenue of these estates and required no state subsidies: This was the case of the Bethlen College of the Reformed Church at Nagyenyed [Aiud], for instance.

The Romanian land reform affected not only estates in private hands but also those belonging to foundations. Thus the estates of the Hungarian churches, schools and various other institutions were also confiscated. The compensation awarded for the confiscated lands was no more than one eighth, and sometimes not even 1/20 of the true value of the property, and was paid off in government bonds, several years later. Thus the Hungarian churches and cultural institutions were completely deprived of their economic foundations and, since in most cases these foundations were designed to ensure scholarships for needy students, the confiscation of the estates of the churches prevented the replacement of the Hungarian intelligentsia. Scotus Viator (R. W. Seton-Watson), the British advocate of Greater Romania, wrote to the editor of a Romanian daily in Cluj: the "land reform bankrupts not only the Hungarian landowners but, through the churches, the entire Hungarian intelligentsia, and sometimes even gives the impression of a national vendetta."[86]

In the chapter on the churches and culture we will examine in detail the situation in which the personnel of the Hungarian churches found itself as a consequence of the expropriation of the estates and the denial of state support. Suffice to mention here that the land reform affected not only the landowners but practically all of the Hungarian population, placing them into dire economic straits.

Civil Servants

The majority of the Hungarian civil servants lost their posts and their livelihood between the beginning of the Romanian occupation and the signing of the Peace Treaty of Trianon. No sooner did the Romanian military authorities assume control than they demanded that the civil servants in the area take an oath of allegiance to the Romanian state. The large majority of Hungarian civil servants refused this demand, referring to section 45 of the Hague Convention. According to that section the occupation force "may not force the population of the occupied area to take an oath of allegiance." Then the Romanian authorities declared that those civil servants who refused to take the oath would forfeit their jobs and their pension, whereas the lawyers and notaries may no longer continue to function. Indeed, once they refused to take the oath they were dismissed from their jobs without further ado.

By January 1919 the Hungarian personnel had realized that the oath of loyalty was not meant to ensure the continued employment of the Hungarian civil servants, but rather was an excuse to dismiss them. Therefore, on January 15, 1919, a delegation from Cluj came to see Iuliu Maniu declaring, in the name of the Hungarian civil servants that, in lieu of an oath, they would be willing to promise to carry out their tasks conscientiously and to abstain from all political activity. Maniu rejected this offer. During the following months thousands and tens of thousands of personnel who refused to take the oath were dismissed from their post. They soon moved to Hungary.

The other difficulty affecting the civil servants were the various measures requisitioning apartments. The Romanian civil servants and military officers streaming into the Hungarian towns requisitioned apartments everywhere. These requisitions deprived many officials of their last hope of being able to obtain a modest income by renting their apartment once they had lost their jobs. Those whose apartments were requisitioned were forced to make do with their families in a single room and, once even that room was taken away, they had to move in with friends. The matter usually ended in voluntary move to Hungary.

As vacancies were created by the dismissed Hungarian officials their place was naturally taken over by Romanians. Consequently, the personnel in Transylvania was soon replaced almost entirely. After the dissolution of the Governing Council of Sibiu, ordered in 1920, the Romanian newspapers lauded the activities of the former members of the Council. The members of the Council themselves noted:

in spite of the superficial and mistaken interpretation of military conventions, our merit is to have succeeded in taking power into our own hands and introduced a Romanian administration into every branch of government.... The attempt of the Hungarian government to maintain control until the peace treaty was signed, in accordance with the military conventions, met with our powerful and adamant resistance and was shipwrecked.

As regards the civil servants, they noted:

the rungs of the civil service, from the highest to the lowest, are occupied mostly by Romanians, and those who are not Romanian by birth, nevertheless, serve the Romanian state faithfully in accordance with Romanian principles.... We have reorganized the obsolete electoral system of the municipal and county officials and replaced it with a system of appointments.[87]

Indeed, by the time the Governing Council had functioned for a year and a half, the majority of Hungarian officials had been replaced by Romanians. The dismissed Hungarian officials continued to hope that their situation might improve. When they received the news of the signing of the Treaty of Trianon, many offered to take the oath. Most often, however, their offer was not even accepted and their situation became gradually hopeless. On June 27, 1920, that is a few weeks after the treaty had been signed, the government summoned all Hungarian officials to take the oath, in response to an open letter written by the Hungarian journalist Domokos Olajos to Prime Minister Alexandru Averescu in the *Kolozsvári Újság*. By his summons he promised that the rights acquired by taking the oath would be respected. The officials did take the oath, yet there was no favorable turn in their predicament.

Hungarian civil servants were employed, once they took the oath, in those branches of service where the experienced Hungarians could not be replaced by inexperienced Romanians: this was the case with the Hungarian postal workers, as of July 20, 1920. But most officials who did not take the oath were not rehired, even though many among the more objective Romanian experts argued that such a solution was warranted. For instance, Dr. G. Şorban, the Romanian prefect of Dej, argued in a leaflet in 1921 that even from a Romanian nationalist point of view these officials ought to be rehired.

> There are many worthy individuals among the Hungarian officials; they are honest and responsible, and we would be glad to employ them, to kill two birds with one stone: on the one hand, we would obtain the services of useful persons for the state and; on the other hand, by providing a livelihood to these persons, we would rid the country of an anti-state and dissatisfied stratum. In order to achieve these ends and win over these Hungarian officials, we must keep the spirit of all the promises we had made at Alba Iulia with regard to the entire Hungarian ethnic group of Romania.[88]

Unfortunately, these understanding words of Şorban were a cry in the wilderness. No one attempted to realize its profound truths and the predicament of those officials who did not take the oath deteriorated year after year. A collection was organized on their behalf at the beginning of 1923, but the Romanian authorities would not authorize it. The only alternatives were emigration to Hungary or suicide. While thousands of Hungarians opted for the latter solution, the majority moved to Hungary, and this was precisely the objective the Romanian authorities had in mind. As the American Unitarian Committee noted during its tour of Transylvania in 1920:

the first order of business of the Romanians was to expel from Transylvania all those Hungarians who had settled there since 1913. Their next move was against the leaders of the Hungarians, officials and teachers, who were required to take the oath of loyalty in a matter of days.... The consequence of this, as the Romanians must have foreseen, was that individuals belonging to this class left the country en masse along with their families, while the towns were flooded with civil servants hired on the spur of the moment; although there were some Transylvanian Romanians among them, most came from Bucharest. For instance, we visited Făgăras [Fogaras] in June; we estimate that of the 6,000 residents about 1,000 had been chased away one way or another; over fifty families among the latter belonged to the intelligentsia. When we arrived in Transylvania, the first wave of expulsions had already subsided; but the steady flow of emigration continued because of the living conditions under Romanian rule. On July 8 we crossed the border on a train of refugees at Baje [Püspökfürdő]. The train was composed of five freight cars filled with emigrants from Turda and their belongings. Many of the women were in tears as we crossed the border; all those departing had to take an oath that they would never return, that they are saying goodbye to Transylvania forever.

We encountered the most moving instance of exile in May, during our visit to Cluj. The Romanians had taken over an institute for the blind and deaf maintained by private charity. The Transylvanian children were let loose in the province whereas those who were born in Hungary, some fifteen of them, were given five kilos of bread, loaded onto a cattle wagon, and sent across the border. They would not even allow a physician to accompany them.[89]

Those expelled simply increased the number of those who, having lost their jobs, were intent on leaving Romania anyway. The newspaper *Luptătorul* blamed the whole Romanian government for this measure.

The Hungarian, Saxon, and Jewish employees are forced to leave their homes, while immigrants from the Old Kingdom are installed in them. If neither the Minister of the Interior nor the Minister of Defense is able to do anything about this situation, the responsibility must rest on the entire Kingdom of Romania.[90]

As a consequence of these measures by the Romanian authorities, soon over 100,000 Hungarians had left Transylvania. Most were civil servants, students, and residents of cities, members of the intelligentsia, expelled from the country. A Transylvanian writer asked:

Can we imagine, how much suffering and bitterness we are injecting into the souls of hundreds of thousands of Hungarians? Hundreds and thousands are leaving the country, wounded to the core of their being, in despair. Can we understand, can we feel what it means for someone to have to leave his birthplace, the place where she or he was raised, to which he or she is tied by relations, by memories happy and sad, by the tombs of parents and children? Can we imagine how these people curse Romanian rule and how they will exert themselves to undermine the credit and prestige of Romania? There is not a state in the world which can afford the luxury of creating relentless enemies, least of all can we, being a young country still in the process of consolidation, surrounded by enemies on all sides, whose designs and sentiments can not fill us with a feeling of self-confidence.[91]

Yet the expulsions continued. Towards the end of 1922, when Romania was once again under the administration of the Liberal Party, even the civil servants who had taken the oath were being dismissed en masse. At the instruction of the Minister of Finance Vintilă Brătianu the Hungarian employees of the Internal Revenue offices in Transylvania and the Banat were let go. The Romanian politician Caius Brediceanu observed at a popular assembly.

They chase away the old trusted employees from the internal revenue offices of Transylvania and the Banat. Two old employees of the Internal Revenue Office of Lugoj [Lugos] were thrown out. The case of the financial councillor in Satu Mare cries to the heavens. He had taken the oath of allegiance, worked loyally and diligently yet, he was put out on the street, without benefit of pension suddenly. He was told he would receive his pension, to be patient. When he declared he had nothing to live on in the meantime, they were surprised that he had been unable to collect enough funds during his tenure of office. He vegetates with his wife and eight children, and begs from the municipality. Yet we claim to be a civilized country? In this land the people had always been part of Western Civilization, but now we are coping with Balkanism.[92]

The intervention of the more understanding and humane Romanians was in vain, the dismissal of Hungarian civil servants continued. From 1919 to 1924, 197,035 Hungarian refugees left Transylvania for the rump Hungarian territory created at Trianon.[93] "In less than ten years the Hungarian population of Transylvania," noted one of the defenders of Romanian policies, "lost almost everything it had gained in 30 years." Between the censuses of 1910 and 1930 a total of 305,789 Hungarians vanished. The Romanian author noted that it was first of all "a matter of civil servants who had no roots on Transylvanian soil."[94] We have seen, however, that the civil servants would have remained gladly, but could not, on account of the measures adopted by the Romanian authorities.

The number of civil servants who stayed at their jobs diminished from year to year. The issue of their dismissal was almost constantly brought up in the Hungarian press. Most of the time the grounds for dismissal were that the person was not familiar with the official language. All Hungarian civil servants were subjected to a language test in 1924. According to the Act on the status of civil servants "those who are employed at the time of application will take an examination in 1924, as instructed by the individual ministries. Those who pass the examination will retain their post, those who fail will lose their office."[95]

The first language tests were administered generally in a spirit of comprehension and the majority of the civil servants passed. One reason for this lenience was that there were not yet sufficient numbers of Romanian intelligentsia who could have taken over the positions of the well prepared Hungarian employees without serious complications. Later, however, when as a result of the educational policies introduced by Constantin Anghelescu (Angelescu) more and more high school graduates joined the workforce, the Hungarian civil servants were subjected to further examinations, and the spirit of understanding no longer pervaded these as in 1924; hence hundreds of Hungarian employees were let go. Interventions in the House of Delegates or in the Senate were in vain, as were the protests in the press: the process could not be halted.

By 1930, there remained no more than 1,500 civil servants of Hungarian background in the formerly Hungarian areas attached to Romania.[96] Those who were dismissed from their jobs lived in misery. Receiving no pension, they could survive only if they succeeded in finding employment elsewhere. Finally in 1929, Romul Boilă, the Director of the Pension Fund, prepared the law published in number 183 of the *Monitorul Oficial*, dated August 20, 1929, which, after a protracted struggle, finally granted another extension of six months to those civil servants who had not taken the oath of allegiance before the signing of the Treaty of Trianon. This law finally settled the issue of pension for those civil servants. Of course, once again there were many abuses when it came to carrying out the provisions of the law.

After 1922, the "numerus valachius" movement initiated by Alexandru Vaida-Voevod and the dissemination of Iron Guard ideas resulted in a further decrease in the numbers of Hungarian civil servants. Soon new language tests were required in every branch of the administration. Some employees resorted to the courts to defend themselves against this requirement, since they had already passed the test in 1924 and had thus acquired tenure at their post. They insisted that the rights they had acquired be honored. The Romanian courts concluded, however, that knowledge of language could be tested at any time, and the authorities had the right to retest that aptitude even if the test had been passed. The courts would not admit proof of familiarity with the language, yet accepted the briefs filed by the agencies of the government who were party to the suits. Thus the civil servants were being let go all around, to be replaced by Romanians, as a consequence of repeated tests, or for the failure to take them.[97] Hungarian civil servants were released one after another from the postal services, the workshops of the railroads, and other state institutions. On December 10, 1934, the post office of the district of Timișoara, for instance, under ordinance number 38,865/1934 and referring to ordinance 1080/1934 of the Ministry of Transportation, declared that all auxiliary workers must be Romanian and that by April 30, 1935 at the latest, "all minority auxiliary personnel, including mailmen and assistants, be released from service." The same circular was issued at the central post office of Miercurea Ciuc, and their example was soon followed elsewhere. After the postal services, it was the turn of the railroads.

As becomes clear from the above directive of the central post office of Timișoara, the Romanian Ministry of Public Works issued orders regarding the dismissal of postal employees of Hungarian background. Most probably the other ministries issued similar confidential orders, as a consequence of which the number of Hungarian employees was reduced to almost zero. One of the most fervent apostles of Romanianization noted with pleasure, already in 1935, that "judging from the number of civil servants, with the exception of certain local offices of the administration overstaffed with minorities, the country is generally in the hands of Romanians." This statement by Mihai Manoilescu indicates how effective the recently repeated decree on language tests really was.[98]

In 1936-37, Hungarian public life became increasingly dominated by all-pervasive Romanianization. To justify the renewed assault the Romanian press argued that there was an excessive number of civil servants of Hungarian descent in government positions. Then the Hungarian papers undertook a headcount of Hungarian employees still in government service. The count indicated that in 1936 there was not a single Hungarian at the Court of Appeals — for the three Chairs of Council, the 47 judges, and the executive board of the Court were all ethnically Romanian.[99] In the county of Odorheiu, where the population, even according to the Romanian statistics, was 96% Hungarian, every single sheriff was of Romanian background. Among the twelve employees of the sheriff's office there were nine Romanians and three Hungarians. Among the 53 community and district notaries there were only 14 Hungarians until the month of March 1935; in 1936 there were only four, and by 1938 only two who did not belong to the Romanian ethnic group.[100]

It was only natural that the new appointments should conform to the same trend. Only 19 among the approximately 5,600 public shool teachers appointed in 1938 spoke Hungarian as their mother tongue, judging from their Hungarian-sounding names, although we may take it for granted that they did not admit to their Hungarian nationality.[101] In the same year, among the teachers at public secondary schools, there were but four out of 436 with a Hungarian name, whereas the 94 masters appointed to vocational schools included but one with a Hungarian name. Of the 213 postal workers and 138 civil servants granted tenure in 1938 there was not a single one with a Hungarian name, as there were none in the central offices of the administration. At the beginning of 1938 there was not a single Hungarian among the 215 engineers registered in the Association of Engineers. In the same year, in most places there were hardly any Hungarians among the provisional committee members appointed to replace the chambers of commerce and industry. There was not a single

15. Bataria's statement, in *Monitorul Official*, 1921, Numbers 69-73.

16. Venczel, *op. cit.*, p. 59.

17. *Dimineaţa*, 1927 Vol. IX (1927), Number 28.

18. The details of the process of collecting data in Northern Transsylvania are summarized in the excellent work by Venczel cited above.

19. Gábor Pál, "*A székelyföldi közbirtokok és az agrár reform*" [The Commonwealths of the Székely Region and the Land Reform], in *Magyar Kisebbség* [Hungarian Minority], Vol. 2 (1923), Numbers 1 and 2.

20. *Ibid.*, p. 226.

21. *Ibid.*, p. 226.

22. *Magyar Kisebbség* 1932, Number 11, p. 161.

23. *Ibid.*, 1936, Number 15, p. 359.

24. *Ibid.*, p. 373.

25. *Ibid.*, p. 374.

26. *Journal Officiel*, 1932, Number 1740. Quoted in Arthúr Balogh, *L'action de la Societé des Nations en matière de protection des minorités*, (Paris, 1937), p. 163.

27. *Ibid.*

28. Data from the *Enciclopedia României*, Vol. III, pp. 145-154, combined with other pertinent data from Romanian sources; Venczel, *op. cit.*, p. 56.

29. Venczel, *op. cit.*, p. 56.

30. Zoltán Szövérdi, "Milyen az erdélyi agrárreform a valóságban?" [What is the Land Reform in Transylvania Really Like?], *Magyar Szemle*, April 1928.

31. *Monitorul Oficial*, July 4, 1924, Number 143.

32. *Monitorul Oficial*, December 14, 1927, Number 276, quoted in Lajos Nagy, *A kisebbségek alkotmányjogi helyzete Nagy Romániaban* [The Constitutional Law and the Minorities in Greater Romania], (Kolozsvár, 1944), p. 159.

33. "Lege pentru creara zonelor militare," *Monitorul Oficial*, December 16, 1938, Number 293. Quoted in Nagy, p. 159.

34. *Monitorul Oficial*, Number 268, November 18, 1939. Quoted in Nagy, p. 160.

35. Ioan Fruma, *Problema Universităţii săseşti şi a instituţiei celor sapte juzi*, Sibiu, 1935, p. 105. Nagy, *op. cit.*, p. 161.

36. "Lege pentru lichidarea datoriilor agricole şi urbane," *Monitorul Oficial*, April 7, 1934, Number 83, p. 162.

37. *Monitorul Oficial*, July 1, 1924, Number 140, and November 4, 1937, Number 245. Quoted in Nagy, *op. cit.*, p. 163.

38. Quoted in András Ajtay, "A kultúrzóna," *Magyar Kisebbség*, 1924, Number 3, pp. 615-619.

39. *Transilvania, Banatul, Crisana, Maramureşul*, Vol. I (1918-1928), 313.

40. Victor Jinga, "Migraţiunile demogratice şi problema colonizărilor în România," *Analele Academiei de Înalte Studii Comerciale şi Industriale din Cluj* (Cluj, 1940), p.38.

41. "Genfi hatás a Zam-Sâncrai közbirtokosság ügyében" [The Impact of Geneva in the Affair of the Commonwealth of Zam-Sâncrai], *Magyar Kisebbség*, 1936, Number 15, pp. 339-41, Venczel, *op. cit.*, p. 132.

42. Lajos Nagy, *A kisebbségek alkotmányjogi helyzete Nagy-Romániában*. [The Constitutional Law and the Minorities in Greater Romania], (Kolozsvár, 1944), p. 161.

43. Elemér Gyárfás, "Gyárfás Elemér interpellációja," *Magyar Kisebbség*, 1936, Number 15, pp. 195-196.

44. László Fritz, "Románia egyenesadórendszere, mint a kisebbségellenes politika egyik harci eszköze" [Romania's Direct Tax System as a Weapon in its Anti-minority Policies], *Magyar Kisebbség*, 1928, Number 7, pp. 437-443.

45. *Statistica Impozitelor Directe* (Bucharest, 1926-1927), pp. 620-621. Described in Nagy, *op. cit.*, p. 203.

46. Mihály Fekete Nagy, *Carpatrost 1935, hivatalos román adatok alapján* [Carpatrost 1935, on the Basis of Official Romanian Data].

47. *Calendarul de la Blaj, pe 1938*.

48. *Az unitárius főtanács 1935-i jegyzőkönyve* [The Minutes of the Supreme Council of the Unitarian Church in 1935] (Cluj, 1935).

49. *Monitorul Oficial*, January 23, 1940. Quoted in Nagy, *op. cit.*, p. 107.

50. *Dezbatările Senatului 1924*, p. 1453.

51. *Gazeta Ciucului*, November 15, 1936.

52. Silviu Dragomir, *La Transylvanie roumaine et ses minorités ethniques*, (Bucharest, 1934), p. 58.

53. István Rugonfalvi Kiss, "Csík szék leírása" [The description of the Ciuc region], in, István Rugonfalvi Kiss, ed., *A nemes székely nemzet képe* [A portrait of the noble Székely nation], Vol. II, pp. 209-263; the above data are found in Venczel, *op. cit.*, pp. 250-252.

54. *Op. cit.*, Vol. II, pp. 158-160.

55. Gheorghe Dragoș, *Cooperaţia în Ardeal Istorie—situaţia actuală—perspective* (Bucharest, 1933), p. 188.

56. József György Oberding, "A magyar szövetkezetek jogi helyzete Romániában" [The Legal Status of Hungarian Cooperatives in Romania], *Magyar Kisebbség* 1939, p. 189; furthermore *Monitorul Oficial*, June 23, 1938, Number 141 and January 20, 1939, Number 17.

57. Elemér Gyárfás, "As ingatlan-forgalom újabb korlátozása" [Further Restriction on Real Estate Transactions], *Magyar Kisebbség*, 1937, Number 16, pp. 196-201.

58. *Dezbatările Deputaţiilor*, 1925, pp. 1383-1407; Szász, p. 106.

59. *Ibid.*

60. *Ibid.*

61. *Statistica Anuală a României*, 1924, Vol. VII; Szász, p. 51.

62. Magyar Szociáldemokrata Párt, *Az erdélyi románság küzdelme a román uralom alatt* [The Struggle of the Romanians of Transylvania under Romanian Rule], (Budapest, 1942), p. 96; Imre Mikó, "Az erdélyi magyarság sorsa a világháború után" [The Fate of Hungarians after the World War], in József Deér and László Gáldi, *Magyarok és Románok* [Hungarians and Romanians], (Budapest, 1944), Vol. II, pp. 242-244.

63. "Lege pentru utilizaera personalului romanese și interprinderi," *Monitorul Oficial*, July 16, 1934.

The Economic Livelihood of Hungarians in Greater Romania 441

64. C. Moteanu, *Oprimă etapă în politica de naţionalizare a vieţii economice* (Bucharest, no date), p. 21.

65. Nagy, *op-cit.*, p. 166.

66. *Statistica Impozitelor Directe pe anii 1925 şi 1926;* Fritz, *op. cit.*, p. 440.

67. *Magyar Kisebbség*, 1930, Number 9, pp. 412-414, 463-464.

68. Rugonfalvi Kiss, *op. cit.*, pp. 158, 205-206.

69. *Anuarul Statistic al României, 1937 şi 1938;* Nagy, *op. cit.*, p. 204.

70. "Lege pentru înfiintarea Institului Naţional de Credit al Meseriaşilor," *Monitorul Oficial*, June 23, 1923, Number 64, April 5, 1937, Number 79, May 4, 1939, Number 192; Nagy, *op. cit.*, pp. 169-170.

71. Mikó, *op. cit.*, p. 244.

72. "Lege pentru pregătirea profesională şi exersiarea meseriilor," *Monitorul Oficial*, April 30, 1936, Number 99; Nagy, *op. cit.*, p. 132.

73. *Monitorul Oficial*, June 26, 1923, Number 66; Nagy, *op. cit.*, p. 204.

74. *Patria*, December 21, 1920.

75. *La lutte contre l'absolutisme en Roumanie* (Bucharest, 1923).

76. Elmér Gyárfás, "A kisebbségi bankok és a Banca Naţională" [Minority Banks and the Banca Nationala], *Magyar Kisebbség*, 1925, pp. 530-532.

77. Elemér Gyárfás, "A pénzintézetek kínos kérdése" [The difficult issue of the financial institutions], *Magyar kisebbség*, 1927, p. 475-477.

78. *Temesvarer Zeitung*, January 1, 1925.

79. "Lege pentru lichidarea datoriilor agricole şi urbane," Article 62, *Monitorul Oficial*, April 7, 1934, Number 83; Nagy, *op. cit.*, p. 163.

80. Venczel, *op. cit.*, p. 55.

81. Petre Suciu, *Judeţul Turda. Schiţă monografică*, n.p., n.d., p. 19.

82. *Brassói Lapok*, April 10, 1930.

83. These data appear, on the basis of official Romanian statistics, in Zoltán Szövérdi, "Milyen az erdélyi agrárreform a valóságban" [What is the Transylvanian Land-reform Really Like?], *Magyar Szemle*, 1928, April, p. 345.

84. *Keleti Újság*, 1924, Number 168.

85. *Româno*, December 11, 1925.

86. *Patria*, Number 114, 1930.

87. *Ibid.*, April 15, 1920.

88. "Chronológia, 1920. jun. 27" [Chronology, June 27, 1920], in *Erdélyi Magyar Évkönyv* [Hungarian Yearbook of Transylvania], eds, István Sulyok and László Fritz (Kolozsvár, 1930), p. 241; G. Şorban, *Administraţia Ardealului*, (Dej, 1921).

89. American Unitarian Association Commission on Transylvania, *Transylvania under the Rule of Roumania; Report of the American Unitarian Commission* (Boston, 1921) p. 5, quoted by Zsombor Szász, *Erdély Romániában* [Transylvania a part of Romania] (Budapest, 1927), pp. 60-61.

90. *Luptătorul*, October 27, 1921, quoted in Szász, *op.cit.*, p. 62.

91. Dr. Ludovic Ciato, *Problema minoritară în România-Mare*, Cluj, 1926, p. 5.

92. "Erdély az erdélyieké, Bánát a bánátiaké" [Transylvania to the Transylvanians, the Banat to Those of Banat], *Brassói Lapok*, October 16, 1922.

93. Sulyok and Fritz, eds., *op. cit.*, p. 2.

442 Bíró Sándor

94. Dragomir, *op. cit.*, p. 71.
95. *Monitorul Oficial*, Number 31, 1924.
96. Mikó, *op. cit.*, p. 246, on the basis of statistics from 1930.
97. *Pandectele Române*, Vol. XV, March 1936, p. 50, quoted in Nagy, *op. cit.*, p. 188.
98. *Lumea Nouă*, March 1935.
99. *Agenda şi Anuarul magistraturii şi Baroului*, 1936, Bucharest; Nagy, *op. cit.*, p. 199.
100. Béla Ürmösi-Maurer, *Kisebbségi kérdések* [Minority Issues] (Cluj, 1937), p. 59.
101. On the basis of the 1938 volume of the *Monitorul Oficial*; Nagy, *op. cit.*, p. 194.
102. Nagy, *op. cit.*, p. 195, based on the issues of the *Monitorul Oficial* containing the appointment decrees.
103. *Ibid.*, p. 199.
104. Ürmösi-Maurer, *op. cit.*, p. 53.
105. *Ibid.*, p. 30.
106. *Enciclopedia României*, Vol. I, p. 360.
107. *Magyar Kisebbség*, 1937, p. 299.
108. *Monitorul Oficial*, March 16, 1938.
109. The information in *Calendarul Justiţiei pe anul 1937*, published in Cluj is analyzed in Arpád Kovács, "Etnikai aránytalanság a közjegyzői kamarákban" [Lack of Balance in Ethnic Representation in the Chambers of Notaries], *Magyar Kisebbség*, 1937, pp. 157-159.
110. Ürmösi-Maurer, *op. cit.*, p. 71.

Indeed, this section in no ways ensured the use of the Hungarian language. Although the language remained in oral use in those villages where there was still a notary, on the walls of most notarial offices one could read the Romanian sign: "Speak nothing but Romanian!" Hungarian could not be spoken at the councils or county assemblies, as a matter of course.

When the Romanian National Peasant Party took over the government, in 1928, under the leadership of Iuliu Maniu, the Hungarians of Transylvania expected for a long time new legislation to protect their use of the language. Unfortunately, the new Act on Administration promoted by the regime did not guarantee the right to use the mother tongue in official dealings. This Act, approved in 1929, attempted to bring about decentralization, yet it did not guarantee in any way the right to use minority languages in the community councils. Consequently the executive powers decided entirely arbitrarily regarding this right, on a case to case basis. Thus, on April 7, 1930, the president of the Romanian province of Cluj, Dr. Aurelian Dobrescu issued a directive forbidding the use of any language but Romanian. He noted in his directive that:

> since to this day there is no legislation that would allow the use of minority languages at the meetings of the county councils, county delegations and community councils, it follows that from now on the discussions at the meetings of these bodies will be held only in Romanian. Consequently, under no circumstance can it be allowed that declarations be voiced, that committee members request information or provide it, or take minutes of their meetings in anything but the official language of the state. In case some members were to disregard the rules to this effect, their declarations would be considered null and void and will not be included in the minutes.[7]

But the Act on administration sponsored by the National Peasant Party did not remain in effect in most places; for the Minister of the Interior very often dissolved the elected administrative bodies and replaced them by so-called provisional committees. Of course, in most places these provisional committees were composed exclusively of Romanians and thus the issue of resorting to the use of Hungarian became moot. It did occasionally happen that the Romanian prefect of one county or another adopted a more understanding attitude and included Hungarians among those to be appointed to the provisional committees. So it happened in the case of the appointment of the

Provisional Council of Bihor in 1931. The prefect of the county, Gheorghe Ghica, a distinguished member of the Romanian aristocracy, meaning to adopt a courteous attitude towards the county's Hungarian leaders, proposed in addition to the Romanian members recommended for appointment that Count Kálmán Tisza and Dr. Manó Markovics, the former governor, be appointed as well. Indeed, the two Hungarian members were appointed. The prefect administered them the oath and made it possible for the two members to use their mother tongue at the meetings. Ghica's attitude, however, found few followers, and was far from general.[8]

On March 27, 1936, the Romanian National Liberal Party in power once again introduced a new Act on Administration. This Act not only prohibited the use of minority languages, but prescribed severe penalties if they were used. According to its provisions the language of conducting business at community council meetings was Romanian. If the members should resort to any other language during their debates the Ministry was to dissolve the elected council and appoint a provisional committee in its place.[9] The community judge was expected to know Romanian and should someone speak up in his or her mother tongue he was to translate the contents of the intervention into Romanian immediately.

Yet another Act on Administration was adopted in 1938. The new Act repeated the stipulations of the former Act regarding the use of minority languages, but expressly authorized the members of the councils to speak in their mother tongue. In the same year, according to the diary of the ministerial council, citizens belonging to minority groups could file applications to the local authorities in their mother tongue; but this measure mentioned in the diary did not have the effect of law and was not carried out in practice.

As regards the use of language before the courts, no legislation was adopted in Romania even though by signing the Minorities Protection Treaty it had assumed the obligation that "Romanian citizens speaking a language other than Romanian should benefit from significant concessions in using their language before the courts orally or in writing." As regards practical application, the Hungarian law on nationalities could have been taken as model. Instead the courts attempted to resort to interpreters, but not everywhere. In most places the role of the interpreter was played by the attorneys themselves, or the parties to the suit. Section 22 of the so-called minorities statute issued in 1938 envisaged the possibility for citizens belonging to minority groups to use their mother tongue in front of the courts if not represented by a lawyer. But this possibility was likewise not carried out in practice.[10] Regarding formal applications, ever since 1921 the courts of Greater Romania accepted exclusively applications written in Romanian.

Everywhere in the offices, from the twenties, one could read the warning sign: "Speak nothing but Romanian!" This prohibition, of course, applied not only to oral communication, but to the language of applications as well. An interesting episode took place in 1926. The Hungarian Party entered the elections on a joint ticket with the Romanian Liberal Party at the community elections held in Transylvania. Therefore it was in the interest of the Liberal Party to attract the vote of the Hungarian majority in the towns. The mayor of Cluj, issued a directive in February 15, 1926, instructing his subordinates to accept applications in Hungarian. The directive remained in effect until the elections were over; then the directive was rescinded, a week after it had been issued.[11]

Here and there the general rulings regarding the prohibition of the use of Hungarian were occasionally applied in a more lenient manner. Hungarians often encountered more understanding Romanians in the internal revenue offices, county offices, or elsewhere who, aware of the struggle of their client would allow him or her to use the mother tongue. But this could only happen *in petto*, almost in fear, in some remote corner of the office, when the chief was absent. The Romanian military authorities considered even this to be a serious offense against the use of the official language. Therefore, on the basis of the order published in the February 11, 1938 issue of the *Monitorul Oficial*, the military commands — Romania being once again under strict state of siege — forbade the use of any language but Romanian in government offices. Point 11 of Section 1 of the order issued by the command of the VI Army Corps of Cluj, on February 23, 1938, stated clearly "that civil servants are forbidden to use any language but the official one in government offices and public institutions." Against all those who disregarded these instructions the order stipulated "jail terms extending from one month to two years" as well as the fines provided under paragraph 25 of the penal code.[12]

Applications Handled by the Authorities

As noted, in this regard the provisions of the Hungarian Law on Nationalities were applied at the beginning. From 1920 on, however, only applications in Romanian were accepted. As the American Unitarian Committee noted in 1920:

any contact with the authorities has to take place in Romanian
and when, last June, the Unitarian bishop requested permission,
in beautiful Romanian translation, under official seal, to hold the
regular consistorial meeting of the church in August, the
Romanian authorities returned the request without heeding it,
but with the comment that they will refuse to accept further
applications until the Hungarian words "Unitarian Bishop" that
appear on the circumference of the seal are replaced by
Romanian words.[13]

Until 1920 the Hungarian authorities in charge of the
denominational schools could use their mother tongue to communicate
with the educational department of the Governing Council of Sibiu.
From January 1, 1921, they had to communicate in Romanian and
Hungarian, and after January 1, 1922, exclusively in Romanian with
the Ministry.

As noted, section 14 of the statutes on minorities authorized citizens
belonging to a minority group who knew no Romanian to turn to the
community authorities with applications written in their mother tongue.
This right, however, was negated in practice by the provision that the
application must be accompanied by a certified translation. Providing
a certified translation was tantamount to asking a person who knew
Romanian to prepare the application directly in Romanian. Thus it was
possible, in theory, to address applications in the mother tongue to the
authorities, but in practice this permission was meaningless. All the
less so since, in spite of the constant requests by Hungarian members
of parliament to remove them, the signs warning that only Romanian
could be spoken in government offices were never removed.

The Use of Place Names.

A particularly painful issue was the constant interference with the
use of Hungarian place names. The Romanian authorities exhibited
great zeal in this matter from the very beginning, pushing the use of
Romanian place names to replace the Hungarian ones. Certain
interesting episodes warrant a more detailed examination of this
practice.

In its Decree Number 1 of 1919 the Governing Council stated in
unmistakable terms "that every ethnic group may resort to place names
in its own language."[14] But as soon as Romanian names were given
to localities the authorities began to pressure for their use within
Hungarian texts. As we have seen, this issue did not even come up as

regards the Romanians under Hungarian rule in the period of the Compromise; Romanians could freely resort to Romanian place names in correspondence, in the press, and in even in regard to contacts with other than Hungarian authorities. The official designation of communities, as mentioned, did not take place until around 1910 in the Romanian regions, and the Romanian names were regarded as the official ones until the end of Hungarian rule in some areas. It occurred to no agency to pressure for the use of Hungarian names in the Romanian dailies or any other Romanian publication. No Romanian complaint was recorded to this effect.

On the other hand, the authorities in charge of censoring the Hungarian papers in Romania began to prescribe the use of Romanian names in the Hungarian press after 1921. Censorship had been instituted from the beginning of the Romanian occupation in various regions of Romania, but particularly in the towns along the western borders of the country. The censors prescribed the use of Romanian place names in Hungarian texts by 1921, and with increasing frequency from then on; but since censorship was not yet universal, in some cities Hungarian reporters could continue to use Hungarian names.

Towards the end of 1933, after the assassination of Prime Minister Duca, a state of siege and prior censorship was declared once again throughout the country. The censorship was exercised by the military authorities, and they required the use of Romanian place names in the Hungarian press and in all kinds of publications that were subjected to censorship as well. By directive 155.662 of August 11, 1934, the Romanian postal services prohibited the practice of including Hungarian place names along with the Romanian names on addresses. Hungarian members of parliament objected strenuously, but to no avail; the soldiers would not listen. Even Nicolae Iorga noted in the Senate, in early 1935, "that under Hungarian rule the place names were written in Romanian, and nobody tried to prevent the Romanians from doing so." Once again, in vain, the authorities in charge of censorship stuck by their stand. From then on only Romanian place names could be used in the Hungarian press, in books, and in magazines. The science of toponymy became unfeasible. The use of Romanian names was mandated even in poetry. Hungarian writers were seized by despair. The greatest poet of the Hungarians, Sándor Reményik, expressed this bitterness in the spring of 1935, in an open letter addressed to a Romanian writer who had translated his poetry into Romanian. "I live in Cluj," he wrote to Silviu Bardeş,

but all my life I have called this city by a different name, as did
my father and grandfather. All my memories, the dreams and
loves of my youth, my wanderings among the stones of the city
and in the majestic calm of the great nature beyond the city are
all tied to that name. But then you came and decided to call it
something else. So fate decreed. And finally I said, with so
many of my companions, quoting Endre Ady, "all right, Lord,"
the regime had changed. The name of the city has changed. All
right. We have taken it calmly. Let it be so officially, it cannot
be otherwise. This is the way we see it named at the railroad
station, on every government building, and in official documents.
We did reserve for ourselves calling the city by both names in
our private correspondence. Officially and unofficially. Indeed,
I tell you Silviu Bardeş, not out of irredentism, but because it
makes one feel good to recall one's late mother and to
occasionally place a flower on her tomb. Now even that is
forbidden. But you are a poet, Silviu Bardeş. What would you
say, how would you feel if you had to write the name of your
native city in Hungarian, or Russian, or German in your poems,
yes, in your Romanian verse!

You are indeed an artist, an artist of the language. Every
true poet is such an artist. What do you think this means, this
command that I may not write the names of communities in
Hungarian in my poetry, in my short stories? What do you
think? Is the name of a place not tied to the spirit of the
language, to its innermost soul, to its mysterious rhythms, in a
manner that cannot described, with a sound that cannot be
pronounced differently? What do you think this means? Is this
not a sacrilege? The takeover of the last refuge? What do you
think, Silviu Bardeş, is this not the assassination of art, of the
soul?   This is one thing.   This is the mother tongue.
Undoubtedly sacred. Perhaps the greatest sainthood in art.[15]

The heart-gripping words of the poet were of no avail, the Romanian
authorities were adamant. Then the representatives of the Hungarian
Party attempted one more time to obtain a comforting solution. As a
result of the steps taken in the House of Delegates and at the Ministry
of the Interior, Aurelian Bentoiu, the under secretary of the Ministry,
issued circular 10.476, dated October 9, 1936, allowing the use of
Hungarian place names. The office of censorship in the capital
promised to communicate the instructions to the censorship offices in
the provinces. Unfortunately, the instructions were either not

communicated, or the provincial offices, as they claimed, did not receive them.[16] Then a member of parliament József Willer of the Hungarian Party, once again visited the Ministry of the Interior. Once again he was promised that the matter would be settled satisfactorily. Indeed, this time the promise was heeded in some provincial towns and, for a short time, the use of Hungarian place names was authorized in the press. But in most places, including Cluj, the censors continued to cross out Hungarian place names from publications; indeed, since the military authorities protested against the instructions of the Minister of the Interior, the under secretary withdrew them. In fact the situation just got worse everywhere; for instance, from the end of 1936 the use of German place names was forbidden to the Saxon newspapers of Braşov. The *Kronstädter Zeitung* of Braşov, published directive 503/1936 of the prefect in which referring to the instructions from the Ministry of the Interior, he informed the editors of the newspaper that "from December 30 on the paper may print only the official names of communities and counties. Since the instructions are most explicit we request that you do everything in order to comply, so that we may not have to resort to eventual penalties."[17]

Even Alexandru Vaida-Voevod, one of the protagonists of the anti-minorities struggle since 1933, felt the new instructions were too much. "What is the purpose of this senseless measure," he asked at one of the popular assemblies, "is it that they may call me a bad Romanian, if I should venture to criticize it?   The government expects to gain recognition for the Romanianization of names, such as not even Hungarian chauvinism had ever attempted."[18]

The provincial authorities carried out the instructions of the government even in those areas where the previous instructions issued by the under secretary of the Ministry had not required the exclusive use of the Romanian names. On February 25, 1937 the county office of Arad, prohibited the use of Hungarian geographical names by Decree Number 13:

> Throughout the county of Arad all place names, signs, and traffic or directional signals will be in Romanian. We prohibit the use of the former district, community, street, river, mountain names in the Hungarian areas. In the future only the official Romanian names may be used, whether by the authorities or by private individuals, on permanent or temporary signs and designations, as well as in publications, newspapers, periodicals, leaflets, and proclamations.

The county office would punish offenders by a fine of 1,000 lei for the first offense and, in case of repetition, by the most severe penalties.[19]

Under the rigid state of siege introduced in February 1938 the military authorities prescribed even more severe penalties for the use of Hungarian place names. These were not even tolerated in the titles of newspapers. A bunch of Hungarian dailies and periodicals had to adopt different names. Thus the *Erdélyi* (Transylvanian), *Helicon*, *Erdélyi Szemle*, *Erdélyi Múzeum*, *Erdélyi Iskola*, *Erdélyi Gazda*, *Erdélyi Fiatalok*, *Erdélyi Lapok*, *Kolozsvári Friss Újság*, *Nagyvárad* and other names were abbreviated or discarded altogether. The daily *Nagyvárad* changed its name significantly, to *Szabadság* (Liberty).

The so-called Statute on Minorities allowed some concessions in the matter of place name usage. Paragraph 18 of this statute provided that:

> in the titles of newspapers, periodicals, etc., the name of those places where these products appear may be indicated in the pertinent minority language as well. Within these serials it is permissible to use the minority language exclusively when indicating place names.[20]

In other words, as regards the titles even the statute continued to require the use of the Romanian version of the place name. In any case, the censors soon returned to their previous practice, making it impossible to use place names in the minority language even within the articles. Thus the Statute on Minorities did not bring about a solution satisfactory to the Hungarian population.

Restrictions of the Use of Hungarian in Private Life

Article 8 of the Treaty on Minorities stipulated that "no citizen of Romania may have his rights to use any language in private or business life abridged." In spite of this Romanian legislation soon included various measures prohibiting the use of Hungarian in business. In particular, it strove to force the exclusive use of Romanian on shop signs and in bookkeeping. Moreover, almost from the beginning it tried to prescribe the use of Romanian in the stores. "If only half of the effort," noted the American Unitarian Committee, "to replace Hungarian signs by Romanian ones at locations where not a soul understands Romanian, had been turned to useful administrative measures, the Hungarians would bless Providence for providing them with new rulers."[21] In several towns special translators were contracted to find the right wording for the signs. For a while the Hungarian text was allowed to appear alongside the Romanian. Later even this concession was watered down by various financial restrictions. Hungarian merchants were allowed to use a Hungarian text on their signs at the cost of having to pay manifold tax on it. The majority of shopkeepers opted to pay the higher tax rate and preserve the Hungarian text for the benefit of the Hungarian customers, but at the beginning of 1937 this too became impossible. The instructions in the application of the new Act on Administration then specified that "names and signs, including shop signs, may only be in Romanian."[22] Several shopkeepers challenged this stipulation in the courts. Indeed, the administrative courts concluded, with praiseworthy objectivity, that bilingual shop signs should be allowed.   But the Romanian authorities did not take cognizance of the court's decision and, in early 1938, required the exclusive use of Romanian on shop signs all over the country.

Cluj was the scene of interesting episodes. At the beginning of January 1938 police units visited shops and houses in Cluj and made the owners sign the following declaration as mandatory: "I, the undersigned, resolve that from February 1 on my shop sign and commercial sign will be exclusively in the official language." The summons was received by merchants, artisans, doctors, and lawyers, and the Romanian officer delivering it informed them that should they not live up to their resolution, they will be severely punished. The Hungarian vendors at the market also received a verbal command on the exclusive use of Romanian.

As the matter became common knowledge, the Cluj branch of the Hungarian Party attempted to find out who gave the instructions for the above procedure. It was unable to obtain exact information. According to the Romanian papers the initiative had come from the municipal council, but when the Hungarian Party made inquiries from Augustin Laurian, the Romanian mayor, it was told that he had no official knowledge of the matter. He had not given such orders, nor did he authorize anyone else to do so.

Then one of the reporters of the *Keleti Újság* turned to the quaestor of the Cluj police force, since the summons had been distributed around the city by police officers. The Romanian chief of police made the following statement to the reporter:

I am very surprised that journalists belonging to an ethnic minority should come to me in this matter. I am amazed that in the capital city of Transylvania there still are shop signs in Hungarian. We gave them respite until February 1; if by that time the Hungarian signs do not disappear from the market, the owners will bear the responsibility for the consequences.[23]

Towards the end of the same year the Statute on Minorities permitted the use of a minority language in addition to the compulsory use of Romanian on store signs; but because of the general insecurity no one took the trouble to convert the shop signs into a bilingual sign and thus, in this outward aspect of business life, the exclusive use of Romanian signs became the practice.

The more basic aspects of commercial life were not immune from the prescriptions requiring the use of Romanian. The Act on Cooperatives which appeared in Number 71 of the *Monitorul Oficial*, dated March 28, 1929, enjoined the cooperatives to keep their books exclusively in Romanian. The modifications to the direct tax system were published in April 1935: they prescribed that artisans and shopkeepers would have to pay a surtax if they did not keep their books exclusively in Romanian. The surtax was specified as 12%. The Act of July 16, 1934, published in issue 161 of the *Monitorul Oficial*, regarding the employment of Romanian personnel, required all firms to keep their books in Romanian. The King Carol II Commercial Code published in Number 262 of the *Monitorul Oficial*, dated November 10, 1938, specified that commercial companies could keep their books only in Romanian.[24]

Moreover, shopkeepers received constant warnings and orders to the effect that they must speak Romanian to customers visiting their store. More specifically, they were to greet everyone entering in Romanian and continue the conversation in Romanian as well, or incur severe penalties. Of course, such regulations could not be applied vis-à-vis Hungarian customers who spoke no Romanian. Yet similar measures were taken to ban the use of Hungarian from the market place. In early 1938 police agents visited the Hungarian vendors at the markets and ordered them to speak Romanian and offer their wares only in Romanian. A large delegation in Cluj attempted to obtain a more benign attitude from the chief of police on this issue, but their request was rejected. The headquarters of the Cluj Army Corps also issued an order according to which "vendors and barkers must use the Romanian language in public places; similarly, posters and advertisements may only be printed in Romanian."[25]

In the first half of 1938 all written activity in Greater Romania had to be in Romanian. Only Romanian could be spoken on railroads, at the market, on the street, or in the movies. Conductors on the trains were forbidden, by strict and reiterated orders, to provide information in anything but Romanian. Already in his order 46,481 on August 31, 1921, General Mihai Ionescu had threatened the employees of railroads with severe reprisals for disregarding the above order. "From now on we will accept no excuse from a civil servant for giving information in Hungarian." Later, in 1927, under secretary for transportation, Ionescu repeated his earlier ban on the use of Hungarian.[26] Of course, once again there were well-intentioned Romanians who were offended by such rules and did not carry them out; but the majority abided by the regulation according to which Hungarian travelers could not obtain information in their mother tongue. Later, immediately before the Second Vienna Arbitration Treaty (Award), Romanian travelers would insult Hungarian travelers who spoke Hungarian amongst themselves on the train.

Long before then the use of Hungarian had been banned from the movie-theaters. The April 30, 1936, issue of the *Monitorul Oficial*, published the regulations of the Minister of Culture regarding the control and censorship of films. According to section 48 of these regulations "all written texts must be in Romanian." The committee on films would allow the original title of the film to be shown only as a subtitle, next to the Romanian version and even this only when, in the opinion of the committee, the film was especially valuable. According to the regulations "it is forbidden to use any foreign language in the texts printed on the films." Section 49 prescribed that "the language of sound pictures that are to be shown all over Romania may only be universal cultural languages."[27]

On the basis of this regulation Hungarian was completely excluded from movie theaters. From then on the subtitles of foreign pictures could only be printed in Romanian and, furthermore, Hungarian films could no longer be projected. The regulation was carried out in spite of the indignant protests of the Hungarian speaking public and of Hungarian political leaders. Thereupon the Hungarian population organized boycotts in many towns, declaring it would no longer attend movies.

Furthermore, the Romanian postal authorities forbade the speaking of Hungarian at the post office. Those making long distance telephone calls would have their calls processed by the telephone central only if the request was made in Romanian. Fortunately problems were averted when the system of automatic connections was introduced.

The restrictions on the use of Hungarian in the schools and in church will be discussed in the chapters devoted to the situation in those institutions. Suffice to mention that the Romanian authorities did everything in their power to restrict the use of Hungarian in those areas as well.

Thus the Romanian state attempted to restrict, year after year, the use of the mother tongue by its Hungarian-speaking citizens, in spite of all its legal and valid international obligations. It succeeded in this attempt since, by the twentieth year of Romanian rule, public life had become completely Romanianized. By 1938 Hungarian could no longer be used in public without incurring the most severe penalties. Later, because of certain unfavorable developments in foreign affairs, the so-called minorities statutes included several prescriptions ensuring the use of minority languages; but, as we have seen, these prescriptions, in most cases, clashed with other measures of prohibition still in effect, hence they were not carried out in practice.

Endnotes

1. Ion Clopoțel *op. cit.*, p. 32.
2. Zoltán Baranyai, *A kisebbségi jogok védelme* [The Defense of Minority Rights] (Budapest, 1922), pp. 58-91.
3. Sulyok and Fritz, *op. cit.*, pp. 242-245.
4. Desbat Dept. 1924-25, p. 3243, quoted in Szász, *op. cit.*, pp. 76-77.
5. Institutul Social Român, *Politica externă a României: problema minorităților* (Bucharest, 1925).
6. *Adeverul*, November 13, 1925, quoted in Szász, *op. cit.*, p. 77.
7. Elemér Jakabffy, "Dobrescu nyelvrendeletéhez" [Comments on Dobrescu's Directive Regarding Language], *Magyar Kisebbség*, 1930, p. 274. Contains the integral text of the directive.
8. "A bihari új szellem" [The New Spirit from Bihar], *Magyar Kisebbség*, 1931, p. 575.
9. Paragraphs 136 and 167 of the Administrative Act of 1936.
10. Deér and Gáldi, *op. cit.*, Vol. II, 228.
11. Sulyok and Fritz, eds., *op. cit.*, p. 251.
12. Nagy, *op. cit.*, p. 112, reprints the pertinent passage from the directive of the Army Corps.
13. Szász, *op. cit.*, pp. 66-67.
14. Nagy, *op. cit.*, p. 115, point 43.
15. "Levél Silviu Bardeșhez" [Letter to Silviu Bardeș], *Ellenzék*, May 5, 1935.
16. *Magyar Kisebbség*, 1936, pp. 601-604.
17. *Ibid.*, 1937, p. 19.
18. *Ibid.*, p. 20.
19. *Magyar Kisebbség*, 1937, pp. 161-162.
20. Nagy, *op. cit.*, p. 116.
21. American Unitarian Association, *op. cit.*, p. 61; Szász, *op. cit.*, pp. 66-67.
22. "Denumirile... și firmile se fac numai în limba română," *Monitorul Oficial*, February 18, 1937, Number 40.

23. *Magyar Kisebbség*, 1938, pp. 62-63.
24. Nagy, *op. cit.*, p. 112 ff.
25. *Ibid.*, p. 115.
26. *Magyar Kisebbség*, 1927, pp. 1289-1292.
27. The decree is printed verbatim in *Magyar Kisebbség*, 1936, pp. 295-296.

Chapter III

The Religious Situation of the Hungarians
in Greater Romania

The Hungarian population which came under Romanian rule after World War I belonged to one of three great religions: The Roman Catholic, the Reformed, and the Unitarian. As regards the number of followers, the Reformed came first, followed by the Roman Catholic, then the Unitarian. According to the Romanian census of 1930, 710,706 belonged to the Reformed Church, 645,544 to the Roman Catholic, and 69,257 to the Unitarian.[1] In addition to these churches every Transylvanian denomination had Hungarian-speaking members, but the other nationalities (Romanians, Saxons) in these denominations exceeded the number of Hungarians by far, hence they could not be considered Hungarian. One exception to this statement was the Hungarian Evangelical Church, newly-formed in Greater Romania, which had about 30,000 members in 1930.

Thus more than half of the Hungarian population of Transylvania belonged to the Reformed Church. This church was undoubtedly the most significant, given the number of its faithful and the role it played in Hungarian society. Each of the Hungarian churches in Greater Romania, however, experienced the same difficulties.

Among the above churches only the Unitarian came completely under Romanian domination as a result of the Peace Treaty of Trianon. The new borders cut across the administrative units of the Roman Catholic and Reformed Churches. Only parts of the Roman Catholic bishopric of Oradea and Satu Mare, and of the Reformed District of the Bucea [Királyhágó] area fell under Romanian rule. These rump church districts had to reorganize within Romania, as did the two churches in general. Thus, the first issue confronting these churches in the Romanian state a reorganization and the definition of their legal status.

Organization and Legal Status

As soon as the Peace Treaty of Trianon came into effect and the churches could organize again, the regeneration of the administrative units left fragmentary because of the treaty lines got under way. The first to undergo this process was the reformed district of the Bucea and vicinity which was formerly part of the Reformed District east of the Tisza River. This fragment intended to form a new district, following the procedures of the church. Since the Governing Council of Sibiu, by the decree already mentioned, maintained in effect, the Hungarian canon laws, the Reformed Church availed itself of these laws. Its administration summoned an assembly of district representatives, proclaimed the formation of the Reformed District of Királyhágó [Bucea] and vicinity, elected the bishops and other officials of the district and then, still in accordance with the procedures, requested the approval of the Romanian government. The approval, however, was not forthcoming. At first the leaders of the District assumed this was because the newly-elected bishop, István Sulyok, was not to the government's liking. Then Sulyok resigned, yet the reorganization was still not sanctioned. It was only years later, in 1926, that the government ratified the election of Sulyok and accepted his oath of loyalty. Yet the diocese itself was still not recognized. They sent request upon request, delegation after delegation, to the Romanian Ministry of Religious Affairs, ecclesiastic and secular personalities acted as intermediaries with the Government, all to no avail. The official recognition of the new diocese was delayed year after year. The Hungarian Reformed clergy eventually found out that the reasons for the delay were financial; as long as the diocese was not officially recognized, it was in vain that they requested the subsidies the government awarded to other dioceses and their leaders. Indeed, this was the reason why the Reformed District of Királyhágó and vicinity received the sanction prescribed by law only in the late thirties. A royal decree of November 20, 1939 took cognizance of the requests made by the Reformed Church over the previous twenty years and officially recognized the diocese. Chapter 4 of the decree provided for state subsidies to the officials of the diocese as of April 1, 1940. Thus the long delayed issue of reorganization was finally solved and the leaders of the new unit received the state subsidies prescribed by law twenty years after the signing of the Treaty of Trianon.[2]

The Roman Catholic Church confronted more serious problems. As mentioned, the two bishoprics of the Church, that of Satu-Mare and of Oradea, fell under Romanian rule only in part. The problem of reorganization of these bishoprics took eight years to resolve. Here again the Romanian government adopted dilatory tactics. All the more so, since greater circumspection was warranted, on account of the enormous worldwide moral prestige enjoyed by the Roman Catholic church. The ecclesiastic issues confronting the Hungarian Catholics under Romanian rule could be peacefully resolved only in agreement with the Holy See, otherwise the government would expose itself to the very unpleasant charge, given the prestige of the Holy See, of being anticlerical and anti-religious. The Romanian government and the Holy See embarked upon lengthy negotiations. Rome entertained certain unrealistic hopes in the course of these negotiations. Indeed, as Netzhammer, the Romanian Catholic archbishop and former head of the Church in Transylvania observed, the Romanian members of the Uniate church elicited hopes in Rome to the effect that after the war the Orthodox Romanians would convert to Catholicism. Under the impact of such expectations:

> the first proposals for a Concordat between the Holy See and Romania were written in the euphoria of victory, the edge of which was turned against the Hungarian Catholics now under Romanian rule and aimed at the elimination of the two Hungarian bishoprics of Oradea and Satu-Mare.

According to Netzhammer, all those who entertained any doubts regarding the realization of the beautiful hopes for the conversion of the Orthodox Romanians were viewed with suspicion and antagonism in Rome.[3] Consequently the Holy See was inclined to give serious consideration to the wishes of the Romanian government and these wishes were granted, for the most part, in the Concordat signed in 1927. By this Concordat the Catholic bishoprics of Transylvania and the border regions, a thousand years old and numbering a million and a half faithful, were now subordinated to the Roman Catholic bishopric of Bucharest, consisting of merely 26 dioceses (mostly Romanianized Hungarians). The government promoted this bishop to rank of archbishop and, by the terms of the Concordat, this archbishop became a member of the Senate. Thus the over half a million Hungarian faithful backed a Hungarian representative in the Senate, the Roman Catholic church being represented by the Romanian Archbishop, Cisar. Moreover, the concordat fused the Roman Catholic bishopric of Oradea with that of Satu-Mare, and eliminated the rights and obligations of patronage. In addition, the Holy See authorized the establishment of a fifth Romanian Uniate bishopric. The Uniate and Catholic bishops formed a single episcopal council in which, in accordance with the wishes of the Romanian government the Romanian bishops were in a majority. Of course, this Romanian majority had a baneful effect on the Hungarian population. The predicament of the Hungarian Catholics became tenuous especially from a financial point of view, for the bonds

in possession of the Hungarian Catholics were now declared
"Patrimonium Sacrum", to be handled jointly by Roman Catholics and
Uniates. Consequently ecclesiastic leadership with a Romanian
majority was now in control of this purely Hungarian property, and of
course it had Romanian national interests first and foremost in mind in
all regards. Thus, the Romanian government, by means of the
Concordat, denied the Hungarian character or a Hungarian leadership
to the ecclesiastic organization of the Hungarian Catholics, in contrast
with the measures taken in former times by the Hungarian government
with regard to the Uniate Church of the Romanians.

Most Hungarian Catholics were dissatisfied with the Concordat.
Their dissatisfaction was not without reason, since the Hungarian
Catholics were subjected to serious disadvantages. Yet Romanian public
opinion was still not satisfied with the results obtained through the
Concordat. Onisifor Ghibu, a Romanian professor at the University of
Cluj, launched a vigorous movement because of some provisions of the
Concordat. The objective of the movement was the abrogation of the
ancient Roman Catholic Status and the confiscation of its goods. This
struggle sheds a sharp light, in its details, on the ecclesiastic
predicament of the Hungarian Catholics.

Ghibu launched his attacks against the Hungarian Roman Catholic
Church as early as 1923. He began to write articles in the Romanian
daily *Patria*, published in Cluj, which were later to appear in book
form.[4] Referring to historical analogies, he demanded in these articles
that some Roman Catholic churches in Cluj be turned over to the
Romanians. But the main objective of his writings was the abrogation
of the Roman Catholic Status. This Status was on ancient autonomous
setup of the Roman Catholic Archdiocese of Transylvania, with Alba
Iulia as its center, the roots of which went back to the 16th century.
The Status — the joint jurisdiction of secular leaders and the clergy
formed in the 17th century — eventually became a completely
autonomous legal entity recognized in all the ancient laws. According
to Ghibu, however, this Status was not an ecclesiastic but a Hungarian
political setup, an illegal and un-canonic institution; in other words, a
state within the state. Therefore it was the duty of the Romanian state
to dissolve it immediately and confiscate its goods.

Ghibu's articles elicited wide echoes. On February 24, 1924, Ioan
Bianu, an Orthodox senator, queried the Minister of Religious Affairs
and demanded that a thorough investigation of the Status be conducted
since, according to him, the Status was an illegal organization based on
fraud, and its operations should be considered by the Romanian state as
a provocation. Indeed, the Minister of Religious Affairs did request a

provided a detailed sketch of Ghibu's peculiar procedures which, according to him, were filled with hatred and lacked any sense of objectivity. In fact, the commission granted Ghibu in connection with the Status was now withdrawn.

Under the impact of the attacks by Ghibu, the Romanian courts refused to recognize the validity of the Roman Accord. In its ruling 51, dated July 4, 1932, the Romanian court of Cluj rejected the agreement because, it argued, it could not be valid without ratification by the Romanian parliament. The registry authorities also rejected the request of the legal representatives of the Status to modify the registration of the goods in favor of the Status. The issue of the properties continued to play the main role in the affair. The government constantly pressed for the sharing of the wealth with the Uniate Church. Further appeals to the government, and memoranda to the Holy See followed. A plan was prepared in 1937 according to which the Holy See would once again act as arbiter, on the basis of a proposal submitted by a committee of three members. The representatives of the Status sent a separate memorandum to Secretary Pacelli, pointing out that the properties were of exclusively Roman Catholic origin and that the Romanian Uniates did not even need it that much since the latter were able to retain most of their possessions at the time of the land reform, and the Romanian state even repurchased their expropriated holdings. Moreover, the Roman Catholics had to surrender many valuables to the Uniates over the past few years, including the Minorite Church and the church of Monostir. They appealed to the Holy See for support of the ancestral rights of the Hungarian Catholics of Romania.

From 1938 the situation of the Status improved somewhat. At the prompting of the Holy See the Romanian government sent a mixed committee of four members to examine the pending issues. The church was represented at the negotiations by Durcovici, the president of the archbishopric of Bucharest, and Elemér Gyárfás. After the conclusion of negotiations which lasted for months, the government finally recognized the validity of the Roman Accord, and the recognition was printed in the March 2, 1941 issue of the *Monitorul Oficial*. The Ministry of Justice also instructed the pertinent registry offices to transfer the properties of the former Status to the name of the new organization.

Thus, much as in the case of the Reformed diocese of Bucea and vicinity, the issue of the Roman Catholic Status was finally resolved only 20 years after the signing of the Peace Treaty of Trianon.

As a result of that Treaty 32 dioceses of the Evangelical Church of Hungary came under Romanian rule. These dioceses also wanted to regroup under a separate Evangelical ecclesiastic organization, as did the Reformed Dioceses of Bucea. With this objective in mind, on April 11, 1920, a conference was held at Arad where is was decided to set up an independent diocese. They elected Baron Arthur Feilitzsch as supervisor of the diocese and Dr. Gusztáv Kirschknopf, the Augustinian Evangelic minister of Cluj, as deputy bishop. The see of the diocese was to be Cluj and would consist of five parishes, each with a parish overseer and a deacon.

The new formation held its first meeting on July 6, 1921, at Cluj, where they elaborated a constitution along traditional Hungarian Protestant lines. They elected an executive committee with Feilitzsch and Kirschknopf in the lead. The Averescu regime took cognizance of the formation of the church diocese and recognized the executive committee.

The following year, however, the Liberal Party government of Ion Brătianu retracted the approval of the previous year and banned the meeting at which elections for the parish leadership were to take place. It also rejected the ecclesiastic constitution and crossed out the names of those members of the executive committee who belonged to the Evangelical Church of Cluj. The executive committee was reorganized in mid-1922 and, already at the beginning of the year, sent it for approval to the Minister of Religious Affairs of the Liberal Government.

But the Minister of Religious Affairs of the Liberal Party was still not inclined to grant recognition to the new Hungarian church unit. In 1929 the Minister of Religious Affairs (belonging to Averescu Party) declared that, in principle, he would agree to the establishment of an evangelical superintendency for the synod on the basis of a presbiter; but the superintendency was not to be considered an authority, and was only entitled to exercise the rights of ecclesiastic leadership over the faithful. Lajos Frint, the elected superintendent, was inaugurated at Arad in 1927. While the government accepted his loyalty oath to the state, it still would not recognize the superintendency from the point of view of public law. It was only at the beginning of 1940, on March 3, that the government finally granted official recognition to this Hungarian ecclesiastic organization.

We may conclude, therefore, that in the matter of the organization of Hungarian churches under Romanian rule, the government adopted a dilatory and essentially negative attitude throughout, and a satisfactory solution was reached only twenty years after the Peace Treaty of Trianon.

The situation of the Hungarian churches as regards public law was decided on the basis of principles that were completely different from the ones that obtained regarding the Romanian churches under Hungarian rule. As noted, juridically the Romanian and Hungarian churches enjoyed equal rights. In 1919 the Governing Council of Sibiu sustained the validity of the former Hungarian laws, since most of the leaders of the Council embodied the spirit of the decisions taken at Alba Iulia. One of these decisions was that "the state grants equal rights and complete denominational autonomy to all the denominations."[11] The so-called Minority Treaty of 1919 granted far lesser rights. Article 9 of the treaty granted freedom of worship and the establishment of religious organizations, whereas Article 11 granted local autonomy to the Székely communities in religious and educational matters.   But these guarantees soon went into oblivion as regards practice. A sharp differentiation prevailed between Romanian and non-Romanian churches; while the former were granted all kinds of advantages, the latter were relegated to the background in most places and in most cases.

The constitution of 1939 simply sanctioned existing practices. In Section 22 of this constitution we find the following prescriptions:

> Freedom of worship is unlimited. The state grants equal rights and equal protection to all religious denominations as long as their exercise does not conflict with public order, good morals and the administrative laws of the state. Since the Orthodox Church is the religion of the great majority of Romanians, the Orthodox Church is the ruling church in the Romanian state, whereas the Uniate Church is granted priority with regard to other denominations.... The relations between the state and the various denominations will be defined by law.

These provisions of the constitution elicited considerable anxiety in the ranks of the churches because of their vagueness. Apart from the Orthodox Church, none of the churches were satisfied with the constitutional situation thus outlined. According to Patria, a Uniate organization of Cluj, the objective of the government was to turn the Orthodox Church into a state church, all the more so, as this church had indeed been the state religion in old Romania, used and steered by all governments in accordance with their political objectives. The facts gradually confirmed that the ruling character of the Orthodox Church implied a fully privileged state church. The privileges enjoyed by the Orthodox Church granted it exceptional opportunities.   The prescriptions of the law spelled out that the members of the royal family were to be raised in the Orthodox faith, whereas the popes of the church were to be paid from the state treasury. The practice evolved according to which the feasts of the Orthodox Church were declared state holidays to be observed by members of other churches as well. Every bishop of the Orthodox Church, became members of the Senate, along with the Uniate bishops, whereas only one of the leading dignitaries of the other churches became a member, and even then only if the number of faithful attained 200,000.

These principles were embodied in the so-called Law on Religion of 1928. The law regulated in detail the relationship between the various churches. There were five groups of churches according to these regulations: 1. The ruling church (Orthodox); 2. The privileged church (Uniate); 3. Historical churches (the Latin, Ruthenian, Greek, and Armenian rites of the Catholic, Evangelical, Unitarian, Armenian, Jewish faiths, etc.); 4. A recognized church (Baptist); and 5. the non-recognized churches (Nazarenes, Adventists, etc.). This law made distinctions between religions already in its terminology, because while the two Romanian churches were referred to as "church," the others were called "cults." This law rendered the existence of the Hungarian churches most difficult because, as Sándor Makkai and others noted in parliament, the regulation prescribed what amounted to police control over every manifestation of the non-Romanian churches. According to the episcopal report of this illustrious leader of the Reformed Church in 1928:

> the distrust evident in the spirit of the law on religion, the statutory provisions for excessive controls and the right to interfere, the restrictions on church assemblies, the hindering of contributions by coreligionaires abroad, the inadequate form in which the legal person of the church is recognized, the limitations set on donations by the faithful, the diluting of sentences passed in ecclesiastic courts, the questions raised regarding the exclusive rights of religious instruction, the shaking of the prestige of the church in regard to collection of the tithe, the provisions for overseeing, by outside authorities, of internal matters pertaining to some churches — all these describe the new law on religion.[12]

The unequal legal status of the churches remained unaltered throughout Greater Romania. The discriminatory provisions were reiterated almost verbatim in the Romanian constitution of 1938. Hence the churches did not enjoy equal rights, whether on paper or in

community of Buzaháza received a lot of land from the confiscated estates, while the Romanian parish of Seuca received 47 *holds*.[15]

The Romanian government gave an evasive answer to the complaints in the report from the American committee; in part it simply denied the fact, while it did not respond at all to some others. The committee noted the facts and stated in its publication that:

> in the great debate between the minority denominations and the Romanian government the Protestant Churches of the world have a task to accomplish as long as the Romanian government does not adjust its policies in accordance with justice; the doubling of its territory increased Romania's political and international obligations twofold as well.[16]

Thus, in the opinion of the committee, the Romanian government had indeed acted unjustly in the issue of the expropriation of minority parish properties and in its attitude towards Romanian churches.

The American committee was not merely concerned with the cases pertaining to Protestant parishes; similar harm befell the Catholics. Before the land reform the parishes of the Roman Catholic diocese of Transylvania owned 4,179 *holds* of real estate. According to the quotas prescribed by the law, they should have received an additional 12,595 *holds*. In contrast only three parishes received a total of 21 *holds* whereas many other parishes had to give up even parts of their land exempted from confiscation. They surrendered 47 out of 98 *holds* at Baraolt [Barót], 76 out of 96 at Tîrgu Secuiesc [Kézdivásárhely], and 45 out of 78 at Bezidu Nou [Bozódújfalu]. The Roman Catholic parishes in the Székely area owned fewer estates than they were entitled to under the law. The only parish that retained the legal quota was Ojdula [Ozsdola].[17]

In addition to the above cases many other parishes of the Reformed and Unitarian churches lost their ecclesiastic or school estates in spite of the prescriptions of the land reform law. Thus 6 *holds* out of 22 were confiscated at Telechia [Orbaitelek], 35 out of 52 at Ilieni [Ilyefalva], 18 out of 47 at Chichiş [Kökös], 115 out of 145 at Sîncraiu [Sepsiszent-király], 4 out of 42 at Mugeni [Bögöz], and 20 out of 60 at Patakfalva.

While the Hungarian parishes suffered serious financial setbacks, the Romanian parishes received valuable estates everywhere. The procedure was most striking in the Székely areas. There was only a sparse population of Romanians in the villages with a predominantly and compactly Hungarian population, but those in charge of applying the Romanian land reform strove to provide the financial basis for the churches of the Romanians to be resettled in the area. The Uniate Romanians of Jigodiu [Zsögöd] received 10 *holds*. In the community of Vrabia [Csikverebes], where there was not a single Uniate, 9 *holds* were reserved for church purposes. The few Romanians in Tușnad Mare [Nagytusnád] received 5 *holds*, in Păuleni-Ciuc [Pálfalva] one *hold*, at Ijacobeni [Csikkászonjakabfalva] 30 *holds*. The nonexistent Romanian church at Marcoç [Márkos] received 10 *holds*, the five Romanians in Ozun [Uzon] received 10 *holds*, the 30 Romanians of Sîntionlunca [Szentivánlaborfalva] also received 10 *holds*. Similar procedures were used to set the financial foundations for the Orthodox churches as well. Thus the 34 *holds* confiscated from the Reformed parish of Reci was handed over to the Orthodox church even though there was not a single Orthodox living in Reci at the time. The 70 *holds* of forests and 10 *holds* of fields of the Reformed church of Lisnău, were transferred to the Uniate church in the community. This was generally the fate of the confiscated estates of Hungarian dioceses and parishes.

In the course of the land reform, parts of the estates of some Romanian churches were confiscated as well. The most interesting case among these was the expropriation of part of the estate of the Uniate bishopric of Blaj, some 1,600 *holds*. But on April 9, 1936, a law was printed in the *Monitorul Oficial* authorizing the Ministry of Agriculture to return the 1,600 *holds* of land confiscated from the bishopric of Blaj.[18] It is hardly necessary to mention that no Hungarian church benefitted from similar procedures.

On July 9 of the same year number 157 of the *Monitorul Oficial* printed a law which compensated the Romanian churches for the losses suffered as a result of the tax reform. There was no law dealing with the similar losses suffered by the Hungarian churches.

Another decree of 1938 provided for distributing 18,000 hectares of forests and 600 hectares of fields among the monasteries of Romanian orders. Of course, there was no such decree benefitting Hungarian monastic orders.

Another decree of 1938 placed the properties of Hungarian monastic orders of foreign origin in the hands of the Orthodox Patriarch of Bucharest. On April 2 of the same year, the *Monitorul Oficial* number 77 published the law regarding the religious foundation of Bukovina, endowing it with a distinct legal personality and declaring its officials employees of the state.

On June 5, 1939, *Monitorul Oficial* number 127 published a decree granting to the canons of the Orthodox Church and the cantors of the Orthodox and Uniate churches the benefit of a retirement age that was lower than what applied to employees of other churches.[19]

All these measures prove beyond the shadow of a doubt that the Romanian governments made every effort to increase the financial means of the Romanian national churches and to impoverish the Hungarian churches. The same purpose is clearly apparent in the determination of the amounts of subsidy awarded to priests and ministers of the various churches.

As mentioned, in former times the Hungarian government, from 1898 on, disbursed the subsidies to the priests and ministers of all churches according to the same norms, without making distinctions between nationalities. Miron (Ilie) Cristea, who was to become the Orthodox Patriarch, carried out research in the Ministry of Religious Affairs to ensure that the subsidies were disbursed even where the Uniates constituted the overwhelming majority and the number of Orthodox faithful was negligible. The Romanian church organizations found no grounds to complain about the award of the *Congrua* and its equitable distribution under Hungarian rule.

The Romanian state disbursed the *Congrua* from 1920 on. For about a decade no discrimination was felt because the amount of the *Congrua* was determined according to the prescriptions of the law, without distinction as to ethnic group. The situation changed, however, after 1930. In 1931, Nicolae Costăchescu, a minister from the National Peasant Party, raised the issue of tying the subsidy to the number of faithful. This was in conflict with the prescriptions under section 31 of the Law on Religion which, in addition to the number of faithful, also took into consideration the financial situation and actual needs of the churches in determining the amount of the subsidy. The Ministry of Religious Affairs kept an account of the faithful of only those parishes where the clergy received the subsidy. Clergy in charge of congregations numbering less than 400 or 200 faithful received no subsidy.

In 1932 the subsidy was determined according to the number of the faithful, which entailed serious consequences. According to the new system the Unitarian clergymen received subsidies amounting to 750 to 1,250 lei, the Reformed 1,150 to 1,700 lei, the Lutherans and Roman Catholics 2,050 to 3,000 lei, the Uniates 2,150 to 3,150 lei, and the Orthodox 2,150 to 3,400 lei. Thus the clergymen of purely Hungarian Unitarian and Reformed churches received about half the amount awarded to Uniate and Orthodox clergymen with the same or lesser professional training. After 1931 the subsidies received by the Hungarian churches diminished from year to year. In the two-year period from 1931 to 1933 the decreases totalled 14.815,390 lei in the case of Reformed clergymen and 2.354,350 lei in the case of the Unitarians. In the same period the subsidies to Uniate clergymen increased by 23.311,560 lei. With this measure geared to the number of faithful the government decreased the subsidies by 4.606,209 lei to the Roman Catholics, by 23.926,679 lei to the Reformed, and by 5.913,549 lei to the Unitarians.[20]

The representatives of the churches did everything possible to rectify the unjust system. In some cases a truly tragicomic situation evolved. Everyone in Transylvania was aware that the Reformed and Unitarian clergymen, most of whom had families, received in general about one third of the amount granted to the celibate Orthodox clergymen. It was also common knowledge that in a certain year the Unitarian bishop received a smaller subsidy than the doorman of parliament. In 1935 there was some improvement. Lăpedatu, the Romanian Minister of Religious Affairs earmarked 30 million lei at the beginning of 1935 in order to partially redress the balance in the award of the *Congrua* to the clergymen of various denominations. Thereby the clergymen of the Reformed and Unitarian churches received some compensation. At the same time, however, the overall amount of the *Congrua* was decreased by means of further measures. We may read the following in the administrative report prepared for the 1935 general assembly of the Reformed diocese of Transylvania:

> Although the relative amount of the *Congrua* of our clergymen increased somewhat, it is still not enough to survive on; in fact, in many places, especially in the towns, it dropped to a few hundred lei. In spite of all our efforts and struggles we have not succeeded in obtaining uniformity in the award of the *Congrua* with the majority churches.... Along with the decreases in the *Congrua* the Minister of Religious Affairs decreed that the post of clergymen that become vacant as a result of death, retirement, or resignation would not be awarded the *Congrua* the following year, i.e. that the new clergymen selected for the post would receive the *Congrua* only if he brings it with him from some other post, in which case that other post is left without it. This has also affected our diocese negatively. As of April 1, 1935 recently graduated assistant clergymen could not be appointed to posts with a *Congrua*. Petitions or personal interventions in this regard have remained without result to this day. If this measure is maintained we must count with all our clergymen being deprived of the *Congrua* in just a few years.[21]

The situation did not improve, however; two years later one of the periodicals of the Reformed Church explained that many a Reformed

continued. Since the charges placed against him proved unfounded, the authorities were obliged to release him, but made it impossible for him to continue to function at Cernatu de Sus. Finally he was expelled from Romania. Medgyaszay settled in Budapest where he tried to eke out a living in spite of hands mutilated in the course of the tortures.[25]

The persecution and physical harm to clergymen diminished in subsequent years and eventually became rather the exception. But offenses against freedom of worship became al the more frequent.

Respect for freedom of worship became the hallmark of every modern constitutional country in the 19th century. As mentioned, the Romanians under Hungarian rule had no complaints about any offense against this freedom during the period of the Compromise. Unfortunately, the Hungarians under Romanian rule had plenty of occasions to complain about offenses against their freedom during the entire period of Greater Romania. At the beginning, freedom of worship was curtailed mainly in the schools. In very many places the school authorities seemed particularly determined to force Hungarian Christian children to attend the Orthodox mass or the Uniate service. The teacher of the Romanian state school at Lisnău forced the children belonging to the Reformed church to show up at the Orthodox mass. The same happened to the Reformed children at Biuşa [Bősháza] on January 24, 1925.[26] Similar incidents occurred in 1926 and 1927. The American Committee on the Rights of Religious Minorities visiting Romania in 1927 once again noted that freedom of worship was not observed. The government, reported the committee, has restricted the autonomy of the churches. It exercises strict control over church services. One member of the Committee noticed a gendarme with fixed bayonet in one Hungarian church. Children of minority groups belonging to a different religion were sent to attend the Orthodox service. Members of Western Christian churches were forced to contribute to the construction expense of Orthodox churches. Their possessions had been confiscated, even some of their churches have been taken over. The Committee, having listed the incidents, came to the conclusion that:

> the aggressive Romanianization of the minorities and the destruction of their centuries-old schools and churches are facts, and if the Romanian state should proceed along the same road it will lose the trust of even those who have been its friends.[27]

This warning of the Committee was to no avail, the Romanian authorities continued their high-handed activities. Reports from the churches continue to mention large numbers of incidents curtailing freedom of religion. These incidents became particularly common after 1933, primarily in the purely Hungarian Székely region. We need to take a closer look at this policy of the Romanian authorities because of the peculiar causes and consequences of the persecution of the churches in the Székely region.

After 1930 the Romanian government and authorities began to Romanianize the Hungarians of the Székely land on the basis of an elaborate plan. Some Romanian scholars began to opine that many of the Székelys were of Romanian descent. At the beginning they estimated the number of Romanians who had become Székely at only a few tens of thousands, but eventually this number began to grow and a few years later reached a stage where all Székelys were declared of Romanian origin. This was the theory that served as justification for undertaking the Romanianization movement in the Székely area with all means at the government's disposal.

The most significant Romanian cultural association, the Astra, organized a cultural general assembly at Sibiu in 1930; it was at this assembly that the schedule of the Romanianization program was set. Bogdan Duica, a professor at the Romanian University of Cluj, argued that:

> today we must undertake a more aggressive national policy in Transylvania than even ten years ago. Now we must not merely defend ourselves, we must advance as well.... Our task is to carry our national language, culture and spirit to the furthest corners of our country.[28]

It became obvious from other declarations with a similar tenor that the Hungarians of the Székely area could expect the worst. The process of Romanianization got under way already the following year, although collaboration between all agencies of the government was not realized until 1934. From that time the freedom of worship of the Hungarian churches of the Székely region was annihilated. In addition to the public schools teaching in Romanian, the task of Romanianization was entrusted by the authorities to the churches founded, or soon to be founded, in the Székely region. The faithful of these churches were mainly Romanian civil servants, teachers, gendarmes, and notaries resettled in the area. From 1934 we witness the compulsory conversion of the masses of Székelys to the Romanian national religions, promoted with the cooperation of all authorities.

The crudest instances of forced conversion occurred in the so-called "Forest Region." The victims came from the ranks of the Unitarian and Reformed churches. But there were many victims of this policy in other regions as well due to the policy its advocates termed "turning back into Romanians". In Ciuc county, the Catholics were subjected to similar treatment.

The first to be affected were the faithful of the Unitarian church in the "Forest Region." The Romanian authorities intervened in 1934 in the villages along the Homorod [Homoród]. The ministers desperately called upon the leadership of the church for help, but the complaints remained entirely without effect. The leaders of the Unitarian church could not have known that the conversion work in the Székely region was undertaken as the cooperative venture of five Romanian ministries. Hence every call fell on deaf ears. There remained nothing to do but, in addition to the complaints filed with the ministry, to protest in forceful tones at Cluj meeting of the council of the church. "We are protesting, on the basis of numerous complaints," we read in the minutes, "against the authorities worrying our Unitarian faithful and interrupting the practice of our religion on the grounds of name analysis, or any other excuse."[29]

The spring of 1935 signalled the beginning of the fiercest struggles. At that time Dr. Macedon Cionca, the Romanian sheriff of Ocland [Oklánd], summoned the officials of Bățanii Mici, Bățanii Mari, Herculian [Magyarhermány], and Biborțeni [Bibarcfalva] for March 12. Most of these officials were already Romanian who had been transferred there precisely for the sake of "re-Romanization." District judge Cionca passionately called upon the officials to reconvert the "Hungarianized" Romanians, and later, addressed the Romanian officials in other areas in the same tone.

After these instructions were issued, a most interesting activity, even from a historical point of view, got under way. On March 14, Ilie Moisescu, the Romanian notary of Herculian, summoned several members of the Reformed parish to the community house and made them sign a text in Romanian. The faithful did not understand the text but preferred to go along with the insistent demand of the notary. The statement was a declaration of conversion, the content of which was communicated to the Reformed minister Ádám Rozsonday on May 8. It was from this declaration that Rozsonday found out that sixteen of his parishioners had converted to the Romanian Orthodox religion. The witnesses to the declaration were Borcoman, the secretary to the notariat, and public schoolteachers, Aurelian Savulescu and Aurelian Gândea. When Rozsonday asked the parishioners who figured in the declaration what had taken place, the latter asserted that the aforementioned witnesses were not even present at the community house when they signed the document. The faithful provided a written statement to this effect.[30]

Similar "conversions" took place in Mǎrtiniş, Biborţeni, Meresti, Vîrghiş, Kbǎţanii Mici, Filia, and Brǎdnţ. Ioan Puşcaşiu, the Romania notary at Mǎrtiniş, and the teacher, Grigor Alexandru met and, on the advice of the Uniate priest, decided that many Hungarian families were of Romanian origin. Among others the Csala, Molnár, Fodor, Jakab families, some of whom had received their title of nobility back in the 17th century, were declared to be of Romanian origin. The male members of these families were summoned to the community house where an attempt was made to persuade them to convert to the Romanian church. Persuasion did not work.

The notary resorted to more aggressive methods, but they did not frighten easily, not even when the enthusiastic representative of the state pointed a revolver at one of them in desperation. The first unsuccessful attempt was followed by softening the ground. In fact, they did manage to convert a few farmers by withholding the permit to thrash the grain, and others with the threat of withdrawing their trade license. At Meresti, the Unitarian faithful were forced to convert by fines, repeated week in and week out; some among them were sentenced to pay 2,000 lei in fines on various grounds. Others were taken to the gendarme station and beaten unconscious. These violent measures gradually shook the Székelys' determination, especially since the complaints of the churches went unheeded.

The clergymen in the parishes and dioceses under attack banded together to decide on a common defensive strategy. First of all they informed the faithful about the illegality of forced conversions and about the legal means at their disposal for reconverting. One of these means was that since the local notary refused to accept the statement of reconversion, they travelled to the seat of the district and made a declaration in front of the public notary there that they had been converted back to their church. Then the gendarme sergeant in the villages began to threaten the ministers themselves. Rozsonday was repeatedly threatened by the gendarme commander of Bǎţanii Mici and by Nicolae Munteanu, the district sergeant of Ocland; he was forbidden to instruct faithful regarding the laws on religion and the provisions governing conversions. Similar threats were directed at the Unitarian minister of Meresti, Domonkos Simén, and of Vîrghiş, István Dobay. Both were harassed in every possible way, punished, fined and soon tried on the charge of agitation against the state. It goes without

agitate against the state, was justified. Rozsonday was absolved on all three charges against him on June 3, 1937; the charges of agitation directed against Simén and other ministers were likewise dismissed. Unfortunately, the acquittal of the ministers did not prevent further aggressions which provoked astounding scenes in several places. On one occasion they wanted to bury a converted person in the Reformed cemetery at Biborţeni. When the Reformed minister refused to toll the bells, as per instruction of the assembly of the church district, the relatives of the deceased broke into the locked church with the help of the Romanian authorities and, ascending the steeple, pulled the bell ropes.[34] In other villages, the authorities attempted to convert the Reformed and Unitarian faithful by means of beatings and special punishment.

The faithful of the Catholic Church were subjected to the same acts of aggression as the Reformed and the Unitarians in all counties of the Székely region. In 1935 the notary at Lueta [Lövéte] inscribed forty Catholic families in to the Uniate Church. In the county of Ciuc this was a regular occurrence. The investigation which the authorities were forced to undertake led to no results, even though the losses affecting the Roman Catholic Church were greater than those suffered by the Reformed or Unitarian churches. In this case the Romanian Uniate priests tried to make the conversion of the Székelys easier, arguing that by transferring from the Roman Catholic to the Uniate Church, they were changing not their faith but only their rite, for the creed of the two churches was almost identical.

Other aspects of religious repression in the Székely region after 1934 were forcing the Székely children to attend mass or service at the Romanian churches and prohibiting all kinds of religious or church gatherings. The complaints to this effect become more and more common after 1934, and eventually indicate the general repression applied to the entire Székely region. In most places the teachers in the public schools forced the Reformed children to attend the Orthodox and Uniate churches. In other places they would not allow the children to attend service at the Reformed Church. This was the case in Bozies, Vulcan, Tămaşfalău, Ghindari, and Petrila [Petrilla-Lónyatelep]. In the latter two places they resorted to various devices to keep the children from participating in the Reformed service. At Căpeni [Köpec] the gendarme sergeant dissolved the meeting of the presbiter, escorted its members to the station, took their deposition and insulted them. At Aita Seacă [Szárazajta] the community notary would allow the presbiter assembly only before seven in the evening. The superintendency of schools in the county of Odorhei closed down all Sunday schools. The gendarme sergeant prevented István Kali, the minister at Păsăreni, from carrying out his work and handled him roughly. As the Presiding Council noted in its report:

> the internal missionary work has become almost completely paralyzed. There was scarcely a parish where the ladies' or men's association could function regularly. The authorities rendered the evangelizing work even more difficult by their contradictory regulations.

The bishopric requested the protection of the Ministry of Religious Affairs in vain; most of the time it did not even receive a reply to its requests. The steps taken by the authorities to curtail freedom of conscience and of worship went unchallenged, as did the hindering of the administration of confirmation, the preventing of participation at church services, and the forcing of children to attend religious instruction in Romanian. The local gendarme sergeant at Acățaria [Ákosfalva] could not put up with the sight of the Hungarian inscription on the church and had the phrase "peace be unto you," removed with an ax. The leaders of the church continued their requests unflaggingly, however hopeless they may have seemed. They pointed out the impossible situation into which they got as a result of the incredible oppression by the Romanian authorities. As noted in the report of the Presiding Council:

> there is scarcely an agency which does not usurp the right to decide in matters of church and religion. The police issue rules regarding religious gatherings, the principals of state schools arrange the nationality and religion of the pupils arbitrarily, and the gendarmes lay down the basic principles of religious instruction. Under such circumstances the building work of the clergymen and the administration of the church run into unsurmountable obstacles.[35]

In 1938 Romania experienced an internal crisis. The diplomatic situation, which did not favor Romania at the time, only made the crisis worse. King Carol II hoped to lead the country out of the crisis by dissolving all political parties and inaugurating a royal autocracy. For reasons of foreign policy, this autocracy set up an office of governorship for the minorities, and its authority was defined in the decisions of the ministerial council of August 1, 1938. The government termed these decisions "minorities statutes," although they merely amounted to the collective enumeration of the principles of former laws and directives. The immeasurable deterioration in the situation of the minorities was clearly evident in the fact that these minorities statutes, in addition to reiterating measures introduced earlier, contained various promises in response to the complaints that had been aired.

The leaders of the Hungarian churches received the statutes optimistically, expecting, in particular, an improvement in the conditions of the Székely region; but they soon had to sadly realize their mistake. As a result of the new administrative setup in the country, royal intendants were appointed to head the new provinces; these evinced various attitudes in dealing with the problems. In some provinces the local authorities resorted to even more arbitrary measures because the new provincial administration was not yet fully in operation; they were entrusted mostly to military personnel, and the latter tended to resort to the command spirit on minority issues.

One of the weightiest issues was the one regarding the long delayed solution of the problem of religious gatherings. For years the church leaders had appealed to the ministries not to hamper the meetings of the presbiters, of the women's associations, and other internal missions. Finally, as a result of the numerous memoranda, it seemed that the Minister of the Interior came up with a favorable response. The Presiding Council of the Transylvanian Reformed Church District informed the public that the Minister had authorized religious gathering by his directives of March 24 and May 26, 1938. The Presiding Council communicated the news of these directives to the royal intendants of Mureş, Someş, and Bucegi, and these in turn acknowledged the communication. Thereupon the Presiding Council published a copy of the directive in the church periodical *Református Szemle* for the benefit of the provincial ministers.

No sooner was this directive of the Minister of the Interior published than the deacons and ministers began to complain desperately once again. The Minister at Chichiş reported that he had shown the directive to the gendarmes and launched the missionary work; but two weeks later the gendarmes of Ozun prohibited all further work along those lines with the explanation that only the army corps headquarters could authorize such meetings. They took a deposition regarding the meeting in progress and forwarded it to the Romanian military courts.

János Györke, the deacon of the diocese of Bekecsalja reported on the fate of the directive. Seeking a guarantee for his evangelical work he addressed written memoranda to the prefects of Mureş and Odorhei counties requesting permission for such work throughout the church district. His reference to the directive of the Minister of the Interior was fruitless, for the prefect of Mureş did not reply to his request at all whereas the prefect of Odorheiu, referring to an order issued by the headquarters of the 5th Army Corps, rejected the deacon's request.

According to the report from the deacon's office in the church district of Gurghiu [Görgény], the Romanian authorities in that region insisted the directive of the Minister applied only to the presbiter meetings and the Te Deums.

On the basis of such complaints, the Presiding Council requested the offices of the province of Mureş to consider the directive of Ministry of the Interior regarding meetings and gatherings. This request went unheeded, while serious incidents cropped up in ever-increasing numbers. The commander of the gendarmes at Sînmiclăuş [Bethlenszentmiklós] crudely berated the church representative who handed him the official notice announcing a meeting of the presbiters and, he banned the meeting. The district notary of Şincai [Mezősámsod] banned all missionary meetings, referring to rules issued by the prefect. The head office of the province informed the Presiding Council that it had instructed the county offices to observe the directive of the Minister in a special circular. But either this did not actually happen, or the circular was ill-intentioned because, as the deacon of the church district of Mureş reported, the directive of the Minister regarding meetings was not observed by anyone in the county. The office of the province of Mureş gave an evasive reply to the request of the Presiding Council and everything remained as heretofore.[36]

The situation in the county of Odorheiu was similar. According to a report from the office of the deacon of the county, the gendarme sergeant, referring to an order from the headquarters of the 5th Army Corps, banned all religious meetings. The ministers at Mătişeni and Porumbenii Mici reported the same situation. On the advice of the gendarmerie, the minister of Atid [Etéd] requested permission for holding presbiter meetings and missionary gatherings from the county head office, but the latter refused to grant permission. Then the Presiding Council intervened, requesting the head office of the province to observe the directive issued by the Ministry of the Interior. The provincial office instructed the prefect's office to carry out the circular it had issued. All this did not help. Then the Presiding Council asked the office of the province to send a copy of the directive of the Ministry of the Interior; the latter refused.

Finally the church leadership succeeded, at the cost of several months of appealing and insisting, in procuring a copy of the aforementioned circular of the province of Mureş as well as a copy of the directive of the Ministry of Religious Affairs regarding religious meetings. Then the head office of the province of Mureș instructed the prefect of the county of Odorheiu, by order dated December 29, 1938, to go by the directive of the Ministry of the Interior in the future. According to this directive, church meetings and religious gatherings could be held freely, without prior authorization. Only the time of the gatherings must be communicated to the law enforcement offices for purposes of acknowledgement.

The Ministry of Religious Affairs sent a letter to the bishopric informing the latter about the measures it had taken to authorize religious gatherings. The Ministry of the Interior, on its part, called up the chief inspectorate of the gendarmes, as well as the executive direction of the police, telling them to take action to abide by the oft-mentioned directive of the Ministry. These law enforcement agencies were instructed not to subject religious gatherings to prior censorship or to the requirement of obtaining permission, but to be satisfied with a prior notification. In a memorandum dated November 15, 1938 it also requested the Ministry of National Defense to issue similar instructions to the pertinent military authorities.

Nevertheless, goodwill was lacking somewhere along the line because even after these repeated requests and instructions, religious gatherings were still not allowed. The Presiding Council, reporting on the above developments, concluded in a resigned tone: "There is no end to the complaints. Meetings and gatherings are still restricted. The gendarmes who show up at the meetings of presbiters object to the agendas which, according to them, are not of a religious nature."

In addition to preventing presbiter and missionary meetings, the forcing of children to attend Romanian churches was became a major grievance. Instruction for the sacrament of confirmation was forbidden at Vinţul de Sus. At Şincai, the public school teacher escorted the youngsters of Reformed religion to the Uniate church. At Aita Medie, Barolt, Tălişoara, Biborţeni, and Mureni, the children were taken either to the Orthodox or to the Uniate churches and forced to perform rituals in conflict with their faith. At Gorneşti, in order to continuously disturb the service, a physician's residence and clinic was constructed in front of the main entrance to the church, while the garage was converted into a stable. At Bicălatu, the Hungarian pupils at the state school were forbidden to pray in their mother tongue. At Cuieşd, the public school teacher punished those children who wanted to attend Sunday school. At Sîngeorgiu de Pădure and Sînpetru, the gendarmes banned instruction for the sacrament of confirmation. The teacher at the public school of Kispulyon ordered the Reformed youngsters to attend the Uniate Church on Romanian national holidays and made them sing parts of the Mass. In the diocese of Tîrnava the commanders in charge of pre-military instruction also forced the youngsters of Reformed religion to carry out the rituals of churches alien to them. The head office of the province, in its response to this complaint, asserted that according to the investigation, the Reformed youth participated in these rituals voluntarily.[37]

The most serious acts of aggression during these two years occurred once again in the Forest Region, within the realm of the already mentioned Cionca. Here the commanders of the gendarmes banned the presbiter meetings at Mureni and Biborțeni. Soon all church meetings were banned in every parish and the situation which evolved, as the deacon reported, rendered ecclesiastic administration impossible.

Having prepared an exhaustive report of the incidents, the Presiding Council requested the leadership of the Mureș head office to intervene. Most of the complaints mentioned sheriff Cionca specifically. Thereupon the head office of the province of Mureș did order an investigation of the complaints and appointed Cionca himself to head the investigation. There could be no doubt as to the final outcome. Cionca summoned the ministers of Filia, Brăduț, Bățanii Mici, Herculian, and Biborțeni and made them sign a declaration according to which Romanian authorities did not interfere with the christenings, weddings and funerals.

In its reply the Presiding Council pointed out that the sheriff, in order to obfuscate the tenor of his acts of aggression, attempted to sidetrack the issue of religious gatherings, inasmuch as no complaints had been raised regarding the christenings, weddings, or funerals. This argument did not help at all, since evidently the acts committed by Cionca were covered up by the head office of the province; hence the situation in the Forest Region remained the same.

The office of deacon reported, under number 826/1938 to the Presiding Council, that the directives brought to the attention of all heads of provinces had no effect. The authorities continued to make it impossible to hold church meetings and religious gatherings in the dioceses of Odorheiu county. What's more, the gendarmes exceeded their earlier zeal and now considered that even baptisms, marriages and funerals constituted religious gatherings and were to be announced at their headquarters. Sheriff Cionca declared that in his opinion the oft-mentioned directive from the Ministry of the Interior did not apply to meetings of the Reformed Church.

The third type of acts of aggression constituted an even more serious infraction against the freedom of worship, and it occurred with increasing frequency after 1935 in several counties. The Romanian courts preferred to schedule the sessions in suits on the greatest

ceased, yet services in Hungarian churches were still authorized, and this provided immeasurable spiritual encouragement to the faithful, which the Romanian authorities never even suspected. At times of total repression enormous spiritual comfort was derived from the phrase heard everyday in the course of the revitalized Reformed service: "God loved the world and sacrificed his only Son so that whomsoever believes in Him will not be lost but will secure life everlasting." And even the usual phase of the prayer now sounded so much more meaningful: "But deliver us from evil." The Reformed, Catholic, Unitarian, and Evangelical Hungarian believers did not have only evil Satan in mind, but also thought of the ill-will which placed them under such heavy national oppression. The Hungarian souls, excluded by external circumstances, retreated to the infinite fields of their inner spirit; in vain did the Romanian authorities persecute them, they could not reach the Hungarians in the realm of the mind, even though they tried everything in their power. After 1936 they prescribed even some of the expressions to be recited during the prayers on national holidays.

Until then the prayer for the ruler, in the Hungarian churches, was "We beg our Lord for our country's king." Onisifor Ghibu believed that on such occasions the Hungarians would secretly pray for the ruler of the Hungarian homeland. Under the impact of one of his articles the Ministry ordered that in the future the king should be mentioned by name: Carol II, the King of Romania. But this compulsion was to no avail in the world of the mind, as was the introduction ordered to the Romanian royal anthem; all this could not elicit the sincere love of the followers of the oppressed Hungarian churches towards that Romanian state which had forgotten the principle of freedom of worship to such an extent.

Endnotes

1. *Recensământul general al populaţiei României din 29 Decemvrie 1930.* (Bucharest, 1938-1941). II K. I. C. XLIII, p. 780.

2. The minutes of the special assemblies of the Reformed Church District of Oradea, Bucea and vicinity held on April 12, 1940. Oradea, 1941, pp. 6-7.

3. *Schönere Zukunft*, Vienna, April 8, 1928, quoted in Benedek Jancsó, "A katolikus egyház helyzete Romániában" [The situation of the Catholic Church in Romania], *Magyar Szemle*, Vol. 25, 1928, p. 59

4. Onisifor Ghibu, *Necesitatea revizuirii radicale a situaţiei confesiunilor din Transilvania,* (Cluj, 1923).

5. "Lege pentru regimul general ca 1 Curtelor," *Monitorul Oficial*, April 22, 1928.

6. János Scheffler, "Az 'Érdélyi Katolikus Státus' küzdelmes 20 éve" [The Turbulent Twenty Years of the Catholic Status of Transylvania], *Magyar Szemle*, May 1941. pp. 299-310. This article provides a detailed account of the campaign against the Status. Dolci's declaration found in the same place.

7. Onisifor Ghibu, *Un anachronism şi o sfidare: Statul roman-catolic ardelean*, (Cluj, 1931), p. 466.

8. The decision of the court of Cluj under 51-1932, and that of Sibiu can be found under 2065-1931. See Onisifor Ghibu, *Politica religioasă şi minoritară a României*, (Cluj, 1940), p. 1.

9. Scheffler, *op. cit.*, pp. 299-310.

10. Valér Pop, *Acordul dela Roma*, Cluj, 1934. "Egală indreptătire şi deplină libertate autonomă confesională pentru toate confesiunile din stat."

11. Article 22 of the Constitution of 1923. The Romanian text is printed in Nagy, *op. cit.*, pp. 226-28.

12. Report from the bishop of the Reformed Church District of Transylvania in 1928.

13. Sulyok and Fritz, eds., *op. cit.*, p. 72.

14. Venczel, *op. cit.*, p. 134.

15. American Unitarian Association. Commission on Transylvania *The Religious Minorities in Translyvania* (Boston, 1924); for Hungarian text, see *Magyar Kisebbség*, Vol. 4, 1925. p. 381-390.

16. *Ibid.*

17. Personal data.

18. *Monitorul Oficial*, April 9, 1936, and *Magyar Kisebbség*, 1936, pp. 258-59. Undoing the land reform in the case of the Uniate Church.

19. All these laws are listed in Nagy, *op. cit.*, p. 106.

20. Declaration by member of parliament Ferenc Laár in the *Bukaresti Magyar Tudósító* [The Hungarian Bulletin of Bucharest] in 1934. See Ürmösi-Maurer, *op. cit.*, p. 80. Moreover Laár's speech in the Romanian parliament is printed in *Magyar Kisebbség* 1934, pp. 350-51.

21. The report from the Presiding Council of the Reformed Church District of Transylvania covering the period November 1, 1933 to November 1, 1935, p. 4.

22. Report from the Presiding Council of the Reformed Church District of Transylvania, 1933-35, p. 8.

23. American Unitarian Association, *op. cit.*, p. 11.

24. Sulyok and Fritz, eds., *op. cit.*, p. 34.

25. American Unitarian Association, *Religious minorities*.

26. Report from the Presiding Council of the Reformed Church District of Transylvania, 1926, p. 72.

27. Louis C. Cornish, ed., *Romania Ten Years After* (Boston, 1929).

28. "Congresural cultural a Artei," Transylvania, 1930.

29. Report from the Main Council of the Unitarians, 1934.

30. All data originate with clergymen from the Sylvan Region who have communicated these to the author, orally or in writing, in 1938.

31. Minutes of the meeting of the general assembly of the Reformed Church District of Transylvania, in 1935. pp. 46-47.

32. All data come from the minutes of the Main Ecclesiastic Council of the Unitarians in 1935.

33. Report of the Presiding Council in 1935-37.   The case of Bogdán is discussed in detail in the minutes of the church district of the Sylvan Region as well.

34. "Hová vezetnek a kitérések?" [Where do the Conversions Lead?], *Magyar Kisebbség*, 1936, p. 395.

35. Report from the Presiding Council, 1937. Cluj, 1937.

36. Report from the Presiding Council, 1937-39. Cluj, 1939.

37. *Ibid.*

38. On the basis of data from leaders of the Reformed Church.

39. Secretarial Report in the Catholic periodical *A Nap*, July 1941.

The physician of the district visited the community at the head of a committee and determined that the classroom did not meet the health requirements, hence had to be closed down. In fact, he had the entrance sealed right away. The administration of the school and the representatives of the church all protested against the absurd decision. Then a fresh committee was dispatched, which also found much to criticize. The superintendent of schools proposed that the school be closed, although he made no mention of health hazards in his report. The head physician of the county, who came to visit the school later, determined officially that there could be no fault from a hygienic point of view. Nevertheless, the school was closed down. The officials appealed the illegal closure and the teachers began to register pupils at the beginning of the following school-year, but the gendarmes intervened, barred the teachers from the school, and the prosecutor's office initiated proceedings against the Catholic principal for having violated the seal placed on the school entrance. The Romanian court absolved the principal. The land registry authorities launched a suit against the school regarding the usufruct of the land, and requested the deletion of the right of usufruct. Before the suit came up for trial the Romanian chief county official issued an order to raze the building to the ground. Ten days later the school-building, appraised at 270,000 lei, was destroyed, the materials and the equipment sold for 10,000 lei. The local Romanian public school purchased 79 benches for its own pupils. The case was criticized at the meeting of the council of the Roman Catholic diocese by Elemér Gyárfás, member of the Senate, who added that unfortunately this was not an isolated incident. The general assembly of the diocese:

> learnt with deep sorrow and astonishment of the excesses of certain lower authorities which hurt the prestige of the church, endangered public safety and was contrary to law; the obvious aim of these excesses being the gradual elimination of denominational primary schools.[8]

In 1936 and 1937 many schools in the Székely region were closed down completely illegally, on various excuses. The Unitarian school at Maiad, in Mureş county, was closed down by directive 22,668 in 1938, simply because it exhibited "an inappropriate attitude" towards the state. This charge stemmed from an interesting incident. The school at Maiad did not have accreditation hence, at the end of the school-year, Virgil Bărbulescu, the local Romanian teacher, administered the examinations, in accordance with Romanian law. Eronim Puia, the

Romanian superintendent, witnessed these examinations. When the results were announced, it turned out that five students had failed. The leadership of the Unitarian school took cognizance of the fact. But a month and a half later the examining entities issued a fresh report according to which, contrary to their earlier determination, not five but eighteen students had failed. Everyone in the community was aware that the true purpose of this maneuver was to deprive the denominational school of students. Therefore the administration of the Unitarian School registered the students who had been flunked the second time around for the new school year, considering that the revised results were illegal. This was the incident that elicited the order to close down the school.

The above measures taken by various regimes resulted in a considerable decrease in the number of Hungarian denominational schools. Thus, of the 1104 Hungarian denominational schools operating at the end of 1920 there remained but 818 in 1928, and further decreases occurred in subsequent years. According to the reports from the deacons there were 39 schools in the purely Hungarian Odorheiu county in 1919-20, whereas there remained but 15 in 1928 — in other words, a decrease of 61.6% in eight years. The decrease in the number of schools in the Székely counties exceeded by far the decrease in other areas. In the entire Székely region as a unit, the number of Reformed schools decreased from 153 to 101 and of Catholic schools, from 128 to 92 in the 1922-37 period. Twenty-one of the 45 Unitarian Schools closed down in the same period. Roughly speaking, about 600 Hungarian denominational schools were closed under the Romanian regime.

The Students

The number of students attending Hungarian denominational schools diminished proportionately to the number of schools. This decrease was also due to the measures brought about by the educational authorities. Freedom of instruction for Hungarian children in Romania ceased as a result of the directives issued between 1922 and 1924, the Act on Primary Education in 1924, and the Act on Private Education of 1925. Pupils could be admitted to Hungarian schools only within the narrow limits set by these legal measures. Even before the law on primary education was adopted in 1924 Anghelescu obtained, by means of special measures, that the Hungarian denominational schools could admit only students who were considered to be of Hungarian background by the Romanian authorities. Paragraph 8 of the Act on Primary Education states that "those citizens of Romanian background who had lost the usage of their mother tongue must nevertheless send their children to public or private schools where the language of instruction is Romanian."[9] On the basis of these measures tens of thousands of Hungarian children were forced to attend primary schools with Romanian as the language of instruction, hence freedom of instruction ceased to exist for them. As it soon turned out, the provisions of this paragraph proved a valuable tool in the hands of adept Romanian faculty for the closing of denominational schools and forcing Hungarian children into Romanian schools, inasmuch as it lay within the purvey of the principal of the local Romanian public school to determine who was or was not of Romanian background. According to paragraph 19 of the Act, parents who wished to send their children to private schools recognized by the state were required to state their intention to this effect, in writing, to the local school authorities. In practice this requirement meant that the principal of the public school had to determine the ethnic origins of the child concerned. If the principal felt that the ethnic background of the child concerned was questionable from a Romanian point of view, he could refuse to issue the certificate that would enable the parents to register their child in a denominational school. The difficulties in obtaining this certificate, the so-called *dovadă*, often became insurmountable. Yet without it a Hungarian child could not be registered in a Hungarian school, because if the parents did that, the principal of the public school would declare the child truant and the parents would be obliged to pay a heavy fine in accordance with the stipulations of the law.

One of the greatest fears experienced by the Hungarian students during the Romanian regime was that the principal of the public school would decide that they were not of Hungarian background and then would force them to attend a public school. Indeed, the name analysis carried out by the public school authorities always took place according to the needs of the local school. If the public school did not have sufficient enrollment then, according to the confidential instructions received from the superintendent, the denominational school had to be depleted of students and the majority of Hungarian children, in spite of all proof to the contrary, would be declared of "Romanian ethnic origin." This name analysis was applied particularly in the case of Roman Catholic children but, after 1933, it was applied to children of all religions in the Székely areas. For instance, the Borbát, Farkas, Kovács, Kádár, Beke, Molnár, and other families were declared of Romanian background. The children of these families were not allowed to register at denominational schools.

For a while the parents concerned tried to ensure freedom of instruction for their children via the courts. Thus the court was called upon to determine their Hungarian ethnic background. So it happened in the case of Gergely Borcsa, Roman Catholic teacher at the high school of Miercurea Ciuc.[10] The Romanian superintendent Ghirca, barred Borcsa's daughter from the denominational school since, according to him, she was of Romanian background. Her father appealed to the Minister of Education, while at the same time challenging the ministerial measure in a suit in front of the court of appeals. In the suit he referred to his hereditary title obtained in 1700. The court of appeals took the side of Borcsa, as did the Romanian Supreme Court.[11]   But their decision, which had theoretical significance, did not entail a halt to the practice of name analysis.

When the Hungarian children could not be declared of Romanian background by any stretch of the imagination, the principals of the Romanian schools resorted to other means for barring Hungarian children from the denominational schools.   According to the prescriptions the parents had to declare their intention of sending their child to a denominational school during the period September 1 through 10. It often happened that during this selfsame period the principal of the public school was not at home, or stayed away from home until September 11. At that time, of course, he could no longer issue a certificate allowing the child to register at a denominational school. In other instances the principal was at home, but refused to issue the certificate using various excuses. For instance, he would expect, instead of oral declaration, a statement written in Romanian. Of course, the parents could not write in Romanian, so they had to leave and ask some acquaintance to help them out. But they may have forgotten to paste a stamp on the statement, while, as the Reformed Presidential Council noted, from 1934 on the Minister of Education "under directive 152.150 required that the declaration and the *dovadă* be provided with a fiscal stamp." Then the parents left again to purchase the stamp, but by the time they returned the principal had closed shop, for his office hours were over. Thus the reporting procedure sometimes required 4 or 5 days during the busiest autumn season, and it may have been to no avail because the principal refused to issue the certificate as a consequence of his analysis of family names.

The following year the parents would undertake the difficult task of securing the *dovadă* with the help of their previous experience. They took along their statement, written in Romanian and provided with the fiscal stamp. But the principal was resourceful once again. He would accept the statement in a friendly manner, but ask who was responsible for its preparation in Romanian? The parents would naively admit that the Reverend had helped them. Then the principal would reject the document and insist that they write it out anew in front of him, otherwise he would not issue the certificate. The parents often departed in irritation and had to register their children in the public school. As for the clergymen involved, often action was taken against them for having rendered such services, on the grounds of "agitation against the public school system."[12]

Hungarian church officials constantly requested that the analysis of family names be abandoned and the freedom of instruction reinstated. For a long time their requests went completely unheeded. As mentioned, the courts may have sided with the parents, but it made no difference. The Romanian authorities continued to determine the ethnic origins of the children. In 1938 and 1939 two legal measures were adopted which might have put an end to the practice of name analysis, and could have guaranteed freedom of instruction. The already-mentioned so-called Minorities Statute issued under the autocratic regime of the King included, according to paragraph 5 of the cabinet meeting minutes of August 1, 1938,

> that only those persons who were legally responsible for the child's education (father, mother, or guardian) were entitled to determine the ethnic background of the child, and they retained the right to register their children in a denominational school, a public school, or the school of any other denomination.[13]

Under the impact of the same statue the procedures for issuing the certificate were prescribed to the principals of public schools in detail. According to a directive distributed to the superintendents of education, the principals of schools were required to remain at their school office in the period September 1 through 10 in order to accept statements from parents and to issue the *dovadă*. These documents did not require franking. "The principals or their deputies may not reject the statement if these are in due form and within the prescribed period."[14]

The new law on primary schools published in the *Monitorul Oficial* number 121 of May 27, 1939, did not include the provision requiring Romanian children to attend schools with Romanian as the language of instruction. Thus, from 1939, freedom of instruction was introduced, even for Hungarian children, in theory. But in practice this freedom did not exist. In certain cases the children of parents who claimed to be Hungarian were forced to register in Romanian schools, and when the parents turned to the court for remedy, the court of Tîrgu Mureş, in its decision 12/939 of June 5, 1939 declared that forcing the child of the suitor to attend a Romanian school was legal.[15] Thus the provisions of the minority statute were in vain, especially as regards the right of the parents to determine their own ethnic belonging; the new law on primary schools omitted the provisions regarding name analysis in vain, for the practice that prevailed over a decade and a half was not abandoned, and freedom of instruction did not exist for Hungarian children even in the last few years of the regime.

Consequently, the number of pupils attending Hungarian denominational schools diminished year after year. According to the most meaningful school reports provided by the Reformed Church in 1920, out of 70,462 school-age children belonging to the Reformed Church, 43,151 or over 60% attended a Reformed school. In the period 1930-35 it was 25,633 out of 63,200, in 1934-35 it was 23,396 out of 70,218, in 1936-37 it was 22,163 out of 73,211, in 1937-38 it was 21,807 out of 73,482 and in 1938-39 it was but 21,785 out of 73,610. In 1938-39 there were 51,367 school-age children who belonged to the Catholic Church, but only 14,897 attended a Catholic denominational school.[16] In the case of the Unitarians the number of those excluded from denominational schools was even greater. In the last years of the regime only about 20 to 25% of Hungarian school-age children were able to attend Hungarian denominational schools. The remainder were forced to attend Romanian public schools.

The Predicament of Hungarian Teachers

The situation of the Hungarian teachers changed radically when Romanian troops occupied Transylvania in 1918-19. The state subsidies to teachers employed at denominational schools were not disbursed. The churches could not guarantee their pay since the foundations that served to support the schools were no longer viable, and their estates were confiscated under the guise of land-reform. Thus it became extremely difficult for the teachers to earn a living. Some felt compelled to leave and return to Hungary. Others listened to the enticing words of the Romanian authorities and entered state employ. The remainder accepted deprivation and constant harassment.

From 1922 on the regulations issued by Anghelescu made their livelihood even more difficult. Anghelescu deprived them of the privilege of half-fare on national railroads. He did not recognize their right to a pension. He also did not recognize their diplomas and insisted that they obtain certification from the Romanian government. Such a certificate was issued upon successfully passing examinations in

Romanian language, government studies, and the geography and history of Romania. Thus the Hungarian teachers had to pass an examination in Romanian already in the fourth year of the Romanian regime.

The prescription issued by Anghelescu was not applied to teachers from other ethnic groups, and this made it seem even more discriminatory. The privileges enjoyed by Saxon, Romanian, and other teachers during the Hungarian regime were retained. They continued to receive state subsidies, to enjoy half fare on the railroads, to receive pension. The Saxons were only expected to pass an examination in Romanian, there were no other restrictions on the validity of their license. But the prescription of Anghelescu that denominational schools may only employ personnel approved by the Minister applied to the Saxons as well.

The Act on Private Education, passed in December 1925, codified all these measures. This law also determined the situation of teachers. Teachers at denominational schools could practice their profession only if previously authorized by the Minister. They were not certified unless they knew Romanian. At the teacher's colleges maintained by the churches they now had to study, in addition to the Romanian language, the history, geography and government of Romania in Romanian. If the government agents sent out on inspection tours should determine, at a later date, that these graduates of the teacher's colleges did not know enough Romanian, or were not successful in teaching it, they would have to undergo a language examination, whereas their school would receive a warning, and would eventually be ordered closed.

On the basis of the law on private instruction, Hungarian teachers were subjected to the arbitrary decisions of the Romanian school authorities during the entire regime. Their situation was inferior to that of teachers at public schools. They received no state subsidies, whereas their own church authorities could provide them only with very meager salaries. Even this salary was often disbursed only in part, because the members of the diocese were poor, whereas the estates that served to support these schools had been taken away in the course of the land reform. Unlike the Hungarian state in former times, the state did not assist administratively in ensuring the collection of the salary and thus, these teachers often performed their task without pay, in rags, on a starvation diet. They had to pass an examination in Romanian already in 1924, that is only four years after the signing of the Treaty of Trianon, not only in the language, but in geography, history, and government studies as well. Further examinations followed: ten years later, in 1934, they were subjected to another language examination as a consequence of a new law promoted by Anghelescu. The Romanian language courses designed to prepare the teachers for the examination took place over several summers, depriving them of their vacation period. Moreover, the teachers were required to participate at their own expense. The examinations were administered in an entirely arbitrary manner; some committees were understanding, not expecting a perfect knowledge of the Romanian language after only four years of Romanian rule. There were other examiners, however, who subjected the candidates to tortures. If they passed the examination, this was tantamount to a recognition of the validity of their license, but did not result in any improvement in their financial condition. The government required a knowledge of Romanian, and the instruction of four subjects in the denominational schools exclusively in that language, yet did not feel obliged to provide any subsidies. It provided such assistance only in 1929 and in 1939, as a one-time measure. On the whole, during the entire regime the teachers at Hungarian denominational schools had to rely exclusively on the meager salaries they received from their diocese. This salary amounted to about one third of the salary received by public school teachers, and to about one-tenth the pay which the denominational teachers of Romanian background had at one time received from the Hungarian state by way of complementary pay. Nor did the Hungarian teachers have the right to a share of the revenue of the communities and municipalities. Although according to the law the Hungarian denominational schools were to benefit from the 14% cultural tax collected by the communities, this did not prove to be the case in practice.[17] The teachers at denominational schools did not benefit from discounts on train fares, did not receive pensions from the state and, after 1933, could only serve in the military as enlisted men, because they were not allowed to pass the officer's candidate examinations.

Thus the teachers at Hungarian denominational schools lived as paupers, in a constant state of insecurity during the Romanian regime. They did not play a significant role even in their community, because only public school teachers were appointed ex officio as members of the community council. Under the Romanian regime, especially after 1934, what had occurred in the Romanian villages under Hungarian rule — namely that the village was led by the famous triumvirate of the teacher, priest and notary belonging to the majority population of the village was not the case. After 1934 the Hungarian denominational school teachers were entirely subordinated to their colleagues at the public schools, being far inferior to them in matters of pay, but also because, over half of the denominational schools lacking accreditation, their examinations had to be administered by public school teachers as well. Thus the condition of the Hungarian denominational school teachers during the last years of the Romanian regime became completely hopeless; only after 1938, as a consequence of the Minority Statutes did their lot improve somewhat.

The Atmosphere at Hungarian Denominational Schools

Romanian educational policies attempted to influence the spirit of the Hungarian denominational schools by specific measures as early as 1920. Although Hungarian remained the language of instruction in the first years, Romanian history, geography, government studies, as well as the Romanian language had to be introduced as subjects. In the Fall of 1923 Anghelescu issued his directive 100,088/1923 regarding the denominational primary schools, in which he codified his previous directives and determined the operation of these schools until the advent of the School Act.   He prescribed that the Hungarian denominational schools could not admit children belonging to a different religion or speaking a different language, and required that the subjects in the curriculum of the public schools be taught.   Of decisive importance was his measure:

> that at all denominational schools where the language of instruction is a minority language the Romanian language (speaking, understanding, composition) be taught in Romanian in forms I and II for one period daily, whereas in forms III and IV Romanian language be taught during two periods daily (grammar, reading, interpretation, composition), along with Romanian geography and history.[18]

These subjects were to be introduced already in the academic year 1923-24, and those denominational schools whose faculty did not include teachers who could teach adequately in Romanian were required to request the delegation of public school teachers from the Ministry. Similarly, after the completion of the 6th grade, the prescribed "absolving" examination had to take place in front of a committee appointed by the district superintendency. The students had to pass the above-mentioned subjects in Romanian.

While it had taken the Hungarian government until 1879 to get around to requiring the instruction of the Hungarian language in the Romanian schools, that is twelve years after the change in sovereignty, Romanian educational policies required not only Romanian as a subject, but also three other subjects to be taught in Romanian already in the fourth year of the regime. In vain did the Hungarian school authorities request that this requirement be postponed or suspended; the Romanian authorities insisted on applying these measures. In fact, they soon prepared the famous Act on Private Education which relegated the Hungarian denominational schools into the ranks of private schools and did away with their long-standing autonomy.

The Act on Private Education was adopted in December 1925 after long debates. It was published in *Monitorul Oficial* number 283 on December 22 and, in spite of the Hungarian complaint filed in Geneva, was immediately carried out. According to this Act the public schools had primary responsibility for the instruction of children, although private schools were allowed. Private schools could be maintained by private individuals or by communities, with a permit from the Ministry. The Ministry was to supervise the private schools continuously. The language of instruction at private schools attended by children of Romanian ethnic parents would have to be Romanian. The language of instruction attended by children whose parents were of other than Romanian ethnic background would be determined by the entity in charge of the school. These schools may only admit children whose language is identical with the language of the school. In Jewish private schools the language of instruction could be either Romanian or Yiddish. The language of instruction at monastery schools would be Romanian. But whatever the language of instruction, Romanian language, as well as geography, history, and government studies in Romanian were compulsory subjects. Private schools were only authorized to issue certificates, not diplomas. Under certain conditions the Ministry could grant accreditation. Once accreditation has been obtained the private school may issue valid report cards. The pupils at unaccredited schools would be considered as private pupils who would have to undergo the prescribed year-end examination in front of public school teachers. Private students could not be admitted even to accredited private schools.

The teachers at private schools were expected to be familiar with the Romanian language, and this knowledge would be constantly tested by government authorities. Private school teachers could not exercise their profession without prior authorization from the Ministry. Their old certificate or license had to be validated by passing examinations in Romanian language and the geography, history, and government of Romania, all in Romanian. Should the government inspectors find, even upon passing the examination in Romanian language, that the teacher could not speak the language properly, they would be required to take a language course or lose their license. One of the conditions for obtaining accreditation on the part of the school was that there be at least two full-time tenured teachers.

It is clear from all this that the Hungarian denominational schools lost all their autonomy as a consequence of the Act on Private Education. By requiring that four subjects be taught in Romanian these schools now became bilingual. The hiring and employment of faculty was likewise taken away from the ecclesiastic officials in charge of the school. The teaching of the so-called four Romanian national subjects required the most effort on the part of both teachers and students and made it all the more difficult to instruct in the other subjects that could be taught in their mother tongue. The Act set a limit on the number of students that could be admitted to private schools, it required the introduction of the state curriculum, and subjected the private schools entirely to government control. The only aspect of the former autonomy that the church officials were allowed to retain was to provide the financial means for maintaining the school; for even the textbooks in use at private schools had to be authorized beforehand by the Ministry.

In addition to the Act on Private Education, the condition of the Hungarian denominational schools was also determined by the Act of 1924 dealing with public primary schools. Especially those measures of the Act which required that children of Romanian background be taught at schools where the language of instruction was exclusively Romanian, and the requirement stipulated under paragraph 161, according to which the communities were responsible for the upkeep of primary schools, had dire consequences. In practice the article was interpreted to mean that the communities were responsible for the construction and equipment of the school, as well as for its heating, light, and maintenance. Thus the residents of those communities that had a denominational school in addition to the public school had to bear the burden of maintaining two schools, which in very many places led to the closing down of the denominational school.

Article 159 of the Act on Schools was yet another heavy burden on the schools of the Hungarian areas. This article codified the directive issued earlier under number 40.771/1924 which provided privileges to Romanian teachers who moved to certain counties of the country. It provided a 50% salary increment, preferential promotions, moreover the prospect of obtaining a lot for the construction of a home. The counties concerned included Bihor, Salaj, Satu Mare, Maramureş, Odorheiu, Ciuc, Trei-Scaune, Mureş-Turda, Turda-Arieş, and Hunedoara, as well as other counties of Romania inhabited predominantly by Russians or Bulgarians. The teachers in this so-called cultural zone were obliged, according to the provisions of Article 159, to remain with some school in this zone for a minimum of four years, in exchange for the 50% pay increment, promotional preferment, and a moving allowance that was equivalent to three months pay. Those who committed themselves to settle permanently in the area would be promoted every three years, and would receive 10 hectares of land for resettlement.

The debate regarding the establishment of this cultural zone became continuous. It was interpreted in various ways by the Romanian authorities and certain specialists in educational affairs. According to the Article, the objective of the measure was "to increase the intensity of the teaching of Romanian in areas with a mixed population." When the National Hungarian party filed a complaint with the League of Nations on September 2, 1930, against this cultural zone, the official response of the Romanian government was that this zone "referred exclusively to Romanian inhabitants, and not at all to Hungarians."[19] The Romanian sector of the population in the Székely areas had been, according to the assertion of the Romanian government, kept uneducated by the Hungarians in former times, and most illiterates in the region came likewise from the ranks of the Romanians. Thus the Romanian government had established this cultural zone primarily for the sake of the Romanian masses. Proof of this was the provision that the preferential treatment accorded to teaching personnel would retain in effect for only ten years. Silviu Dragomir, university professor and leader of the minority government of 1938, noted in his French language publication, written in 1934 for the benefit of readers abroad and published at state expense, that:

> this cultural zone is designed solely to rectify the wrongs committed against the Romanian people in the past, since the Romanians in these counties had been deprived of the benefits of public education. The fact that the three counties where the Székelys live in copact masses are included in this zone does not alter the objectives of the law. Nobody wants to Romanianize the Székelys more than anyone else.[20]

Three years later August Caliani, the director of the department of private education in the Romanian Ministry of Public Education, asserted in connection with the cultural zone, in an article in the French language periodical of Astra titled *Revue de Transylvanie*, that this zone was aimed primarily at the Székelys; the Székelys who had been neglected by the Romanian governments were to acquire a deeper culture.

Thus there is contradiction even in the declarations meant for consumption abroad. But we may easily discover the reasons for the contradictions in the statements exchanged by the Romanian educational authorities and the Romanian faculty in the Székely region.

Thus Nicolae Diaconescu, a teacher from Ciumani, in the *Gazeta Ciucului*, and Iuliu Mureşan, a teacher from the county of Odorheiu, in the periodical of the Romanian teachers of that county, pointed out the real purposes of the cultural zone. It was the common opinion of the two teachers that the objective of the cultural zone was to educate the Székelys as Romanian citizens and to awaken their Romanian national consciousness. Their opinion is confirmed by Creţu, the chief inspector of Romanian administration, who uttered the following statement at the general assembly of public school teachers in the county of Ciuc on January 23, 1937: "The cultural zone was established by the Romanian educational system in order to promote the process of Romanianization even at the price of sacrifices." A great task awaits the corps of public school teachers in the Székely region. The Székely children have to be imbued with the historical fact, even on the benches of the kindergarten, that "you are not what you think you are, but rather the alienated child of a brave nation albeit for long under foreign yoke." According to Creţu only two things hampered the process of Romanianization: the lack of statistics reflecting reality, and foreign influence from abroad. The Székely and Hungarian people believe they number two million. This is deliberate distortion. "There are one million Hungarians living here, and there are no Székelys." The state regards the Székelys as a fellow-nation and will stand by their side at all cost. "This land is the sacred land of our ancestors," added Creţu. "Our ancestors lived among its rivers, mountains, and valleys, and their descendants are the Székelys. By means of the roaring waters of the Olt and Mureş rivers, we send the message that we will not abandon our work until assimilation has been completed."[21]

Indeed, both these measures of the Act on Primary Education and the Act on Private Education essentially aimed at the Romanianization of Hungarian children. This was the reason the Hungarian ecclesiastic officials objected to the laws. But even Romanian public opinion was not uniform in its assessment of the two laws. Many disapproved of the provisions of the Act on Private Education, especially as regards bilingual education and the compulsory teaching of history, geography and government in Romanian. One Romanian high school teacher objected to the law on the pages of the *Adevărul*, already at the time it was proposed. He noted that the law:

included provisions which the Romanian schools of Transylvania had not known under the old (Hungarian) regime. There are certain regulations which disregard all pedagogical considerations, and the application of which would amount to spiritual torture for children of minority groups. There are so many restrictions and prohibitions that in some places one gets the impression of reading the house-rules in a jail. Thus a new quarrel is evolving between us and the Hungarians, only this time they are the ones who are oppressed.[22]

During the parliamentary debate over the law even Iorga opposed the new measures. He noted in his speech that in this law Anghelescu:

had fused three different laws together: laws regarding private, denominational, and minority instruction. He did this because he dislikes denominational schooling and is even less attracted toward the minority schools: wherever there is a denominational school he wants to open a public school as well. My question is: for whose benefit? Not for me, not for you, but for the residents of the community in question. Then why don't they have the right, on the basis of the tax they have to pay for their school, to decide themselves what kind of school they desire?[23]

Later, when the law was adopted and the Hungarian churches filed a complaint in Geneva, at the League of Nations, because of its anti-Hungarian provisions, Iorga once again expressed his opinion against the Act on Private Education in Paris: "I was and still am against the Act on Private Education, because I am against all systems that agitate and are useless. Let me reassure you that Anghelescu's school system will never be translated into reality."[24]

As Iorga was expressing these opinions the fate of the complaint filed by Hungarian churches in Geneva was about to be decided. The specialists of Anghelescu's ministry attempted to weaken the arguments of the Hungarian churches with the same arguments they had used during the parliamentary debates. In its memorandum the Romanian government explained that the provision regarding the teaching of the country's geography and history in Romanian was included only for the sake of practicing the language. To enhance the weight and significance of this assertion the government did not hesitate, in its memorandum, to distort the former laws of Albert Apponyi. It asserted that during the Hungarian regime the Apponyi laws required that five subjects be taught in Hungarian in the primary schools sponsored by the Romanian classrooms or new school buildings were constructed in 37 communities. The construction work or remodelling cost altogether 3,813,000 lei the following year the spirit of sacrifice manifested itself even more beautifully. Between 1935 and 1937 twenty-one parishes requested a new post for teacher, whereas five parishes applied for permission to open a new school. The Ministry rejected the majority of the requests without explanation. According to the report from 1939 the attitude of the Ministry did not change. Between 1937 and 1939 they rejected 33 applications for permission to open a new school and, even as a result of the more favorable atmosphere provided by the Minorities Statute, only five new schools were authorized and 25 schools received permission to hire additional faculty. As the report states:

> the attention of our church district turned towards the denominational school in countless cases; they want new denominational schools, or additional faculty for their already existing schools. They even gladly accepted to undertake sacrifices for these purposes. The faithful at 46 Reformed communities sacrificed altogether 8,452,474 lei for the construction of new schools, the setting up of new classrooms, or for more significant remodelling, in money and in community labor. These figures are eloquent indeed! And what bitterness followed when, after the great efforts in these difficult times, the completed school was not granted permission to open.[33]

Although four subjects had to be taught in Romanian at these Hungarian denominational schools, and state entities tried to hamper the work of the schools and decrease the number of their pupils by all means at their disposal, including frequent inspections, the refusal to grant accreditation, strict examination procedures at the end of year, and the practice of name analysis, the Hungarian denominational schools continued to play an important role in most Hungarian villages. They could not harbor any kind of irredentist or anti-Romanian activity, but the pupils and the parents were conscious of being Hungarian, and devoutly so. In most villages one of the greatest fears of the students was to be left out of the denominational school since, according to the law, the school could admit only a limited number. The supernumeraries had to be sent to the public school. Of course, at the beginning of each year there was a great deal of pushing and shoving at registration time, for the first-comers were assured of a place. In a certain village in Mureş-Turda county, the heads of Reformed families spent the night in the courtyard of the school before registration to

make sure that their children would not be left out of the denominational schools as supernumeraries.[34]

We find similar examples of devotion to the denominational schools
elsewhere.   These cases provide clear proof of the fact that the
population of the Hungarian villages espoused the cause of the
denominational schools during the Romanian regime.   Most of the
estates owned by the dioceses were confiscated during the land reforms.
The Hungarian population was forced to build and maintain Romanian
churches and public schools. Yet, in spite of all this, the population
brought enormous sacrifices for the sake of Hungarian schools. In the
period 1920 to 1930 the budget for the Reformed primary schools was
an average of 18 million lei a year, whereas after 1930 the average rose
to 20 or 22 million. Our rough estimate would be that the Hungarian
population under Romanian rule spent close to one billion lei for the
expenses of primary schools. And the greater part of this enormous sum
had to come from the pennies contributed by the impoverished
Hungarian masses.[35]

During the last years of the Romanian regime (between 1934 and
1940) the development of Hungarian denominational schools came to a
total halt. Only in a few instances did the Ministry of Education grant
accreditation and issue documents authorizing the opening of a new
school. The number of students diminished steadily. The misery of the
teachers increased year by year. The amount of material to be taught
was also constantly growing. Thus all factors were unfavorable to the
Hungarian denominational schools and, in the last years of the regime,
these institutions became isolated, condemned to perdition.   Their
stagnation was closely related to the situation of the Romanian public
schools.

*The Relationship between Hungarian Denominational and
Romanian Public Schools*

When the Governing Council of Sibiu took over the administration
of schools in the formerly Hungarian areas, it defined the principles of
public instruction in its directive number 1 of January 24, 1919.
According to this directive, instruction at the public primary schools
would take place in the language of the majority of the residents of the
community, whereas parallel courses were to be set up wherever there
were sufficient pupils to employ at least one teacher. In these parallel
courses or classes the language of instruction would be the language of
the local minority group. In accordance with the basic principles
contained in the directive, Hungarian was retained as the language of

instruction in about 600 communities. In these communities the administration set up either schools with Hungarian as the language of instruction, or attached a Hungarian section to the Romanian schools. Romanian language, and the history, geography, and government of Romania were naturally taught in Romanian. At the beginning this was generally the case only where a sufficient number of Romanian ethnic teachers could be found. Since in the first years such teachers could not be found in sufficient number the state adopted some of the former Hungarian public school teachers who then took an oath of allegiance and served the state.

We can divide the history of Hungarian schools or Hungarian sections in state schools into three periods. The first period lasted until 1925, the second from 1925 to 1934, and the third from 1934 to 1940.

During the first period, from 1919 to 1924, the Hungarian schools or sections or classes attached to Romanian public schools were obviously designed to weaken the Hungarian denominational schools. By stressing Hungarian as the language of instruction, the authorities intended to entice children and parents from the Hungarian denominational schools. Therefore, in most places, the teachers in the Hungarian components of the Romanian schools did their best to have the denominational schools closed down. In many places the public school teacher of Hungarian ethnic background received employment simply on condition of being able to transfer the pupils from the Hungarian denominational schools. As mentioned, this was the cause of many of the closures. The Romanian government was not indifferent to the competition between the two school systems, especially after 1922. Unlike Hungary in former times, in Romania it never happened that the students or parents would boycott the state school which would be forced to close down on this account. Wherever there was competition between the Hungarian denominational and Romanian public school the Romanian authorities did not remain idle. The competition became unfair, because the process of name analysis and other compulsory measures were soon resorted to, as a consequence of which the Hungarian denominational school was closed down. It was mostly this process which led to the closing of hundreds of schools by the Minister of Education, Anghelescu in 1923-24.

An important process got under way in the Hungarian sections of the Romanian public schools after 1924. They began to introduce instruction exclusively in Romanian, at first in one or two places only, in city schools, then increasingly in the villages as well.[36] Often the Hungarian sections were closed down simply by order of the superintendent. The approximately 600 Hungarian sections had

decreased to 248 by 1933, and the decrease did not stop there. As one
of the Romanian chief superintendents, George Tulbure, noted in 1933,
Romanian public opinion regarded the Hungarian sections as an
anomaly.

> The objective of the school is to serve the state... We must
> strive to make Romanian language, culture, science and art into
> a force that can dominate and conquer. Dominate not only our
> souls but the souls of all citizens of the country, regardless of
> ethnic origin.[37]

Accordingly, the Hungarian sections of public school decreased to
only 112 by 1934, and to 44 by 1937, of which 17 were schools with
Hungarian as the language of instruction and 27 had Hungarian
sections; but even most of these were Hungarian on paper only, because
in reality Romanian had become the language of instruction at these
schools. Thus we can say that by 1938 instruction at all public schools
took place exclusively in Romanian.[38] The government committee on
minorities set up at this time promised, as a consequence of discussions
with the leaders of the Hungarian community of Romania, to establish
once again Hungarian sections and Hungarian schools in the villages.
Silviu Dragomir, chief government representative of minority affairs,
informed Miklós Bánffy about this commitment in the following terms:

> It is my pleasure to inform you that by its decision
> 28.427/1939 of February 14 this year the Ministry of National
> Education ordered, as a result of our intervention, in those places
> that have a significant Hungarian population, and where school-
> age children reach the number stipulated by law, the
> establishment of Hungarian sections in public primary schools or
> schools with Hungarian as the language of instruction. The
> faculty at these schools will be composed on the basis of the
> provisions of Articles 113-115 and 126 of the law. Until the
> required teaching body is trained in teachers' colleges set up for
> the purpose, the existing faculty will be responsible for
> instruction at these schools, after passing a validation
> examination.[39]

As the letter makes clear there were not enough teachers to teach
in Hungarian in the sections to be established, hence the teachers
already at the schools were expected to teach the children's mother
tongue. This commitment, however, was never realized.

The Minister, Anghelescu, required 151 villages with a Hungarian majority to build new schools. One aim of this measure was to make the Hungarian population neglect the denominational schools in their village by burdening them with the maintenance of two schools. Indeed, in many of the poorer villages the Hungarian population was unable to provide for two schools, and neglected the denominational one, leading to its closure. The measure elicited opposition even in Romanian circles. In the Romanian parliament, Ladislau Goldiş, himself, criticized the measure, which had never been applied formerly under Hungarian control. He mentioned a community where it cost 500,000 lei to erect a new school. The community, too poor, refused to assume the responsibility for the expense, but the government compelled it to do so. "What will happen," asked Goldiş, "if the peasant is unable to pay up? Will they auction away his horse and his cow in order to create the means necessary to educate his children?"[40] The instance mentioned by Goldiş happened in a Romanian village where the population was not burdened with having to maintain two schools simultaneously. We can imagine the difficulties faced in those Hungarian villages where, for a while, the population had to provide only for a denominational school until the executive order from the Minister, requiring the community to set up a public school as well.

The Hungarian population was equally burdened by the measures pertaining to the establishment of the cultural zone, and by the new public schools set up in most Székely villages after 1933. The aim of the cultural zone was the Romanianization of the Hungarians, whereas the establishment of new public schools was intended to extend the framework of the cultural zone. In most places this led to the closing or decline of the Hungarian denominational school. Between 1926 and 1936 the number of public schools in the county of Ciuc increased from 55 to 104, those in Trei-Scaune from 101 to 119, and those in Odorhei from 101 to 151. A similar or perhaps even more pronounced increase took place at the kindergarten level. The public kindergartens served the purposes of Romanianization even better; the children returning from the kindergarten had to greet their parents, who knew not a word of Romanian, in Romanian. This ulterior motive explains how come the number of kindergartens increased in Ciuc county from 5 to 58, in Trei-Scaune from 27 to 76, and in Odorhei from 18 to 40, in the period from 1926 to 1936. Anghelescu indicated the purposes of the kindergarten in his justification:

By means of the kindergarten the children of these alienated Romanians will have their national consciousness awakened, and we will win them back for Romania... By making it easier for the children to learn Romanian the kindergartens and child care centers perform Romanian cultural work.

In 1935 Anghelescu issued an order requiring the setting up of public primary schools in every village. Until then, in some villages of the Székely region and other regions with a Hungarian majority there was nothing but a denominational school, since in most of these villages there was not a soul with Romanian as a the mother tongue. Now the agencies of the Ministry of Education required the population of every village to set up a public school. This meant a great deal of worry, disadvantages and finally closure for the denominational school. For instance, at Tăureni [Bikfalva], the public school was set up in 1935 in a former dance hall. It had no students, however; then the public school teacher and the notary demanded that the Reformed minister transfer 32 of his 68 students to the public school. The clergyman refused to grant the request. Then the notary and teacher themselves selected 24 students and drove them over into the public school. A few days later the transferred students returned to their denominational school in tears. Upon hearing this, Mărgineanu, the Romanian superintendent, came to the village on December 3. He inspected the public school, where he found only six pupils. Then he left an ultimatum to the board of the denominational school, to the effect that if 32 children were not transferred to the public school within three days, it will be closed down.[41]

A public school was set up at Atia [Atyha], in Odorhei county (a Roman Catholic community), as well. Until 1935 the community had a Catholic school with three teachers and 140 students. The new Romanian public school was set up in the community house. The Romanian teacher appointed to this school taught 28 pupils for the time being. The leaders of the community were ordered to have a public school constructed comparable to the denominational school or, if unable to do so, to hand over the denominational school to the state. Thus the community was forced to construct a public school at its own expense. The residents of Lupeni [Farkaslaka] were summoned to the community house where the Romanian leaders proposed to the general assembly to hand over the Roman Catholic school, along with its lot, for the sake of a Romanian public school. Several of the self-respecting faithful at the assembly rejected the proposal, strongly protesting against the attempt to take away the Roman Catholic school. Then the gendarmes who were present intervened and dragged the protesters to the station, where they were ruthlessly beaten to the point that one of them, Dénes

Tamás, was unable to move for days. Finally a 120,000 lei surtax was assessed for the construction of the public school, and thus the school began to operate in this village as well.

Similar procedures were employed in the county of Ciuc. In 1935 at Mădăraş [Csíkmadaras] Leonte Oprea, the principal of the public school, with the help of the Romanian authorities, began to fine those parents whose children were studying at the denominational school   He continued this illegal procedure in spite of all protests, until the denominational school lost all its students. For a long time the objects placed in escrow during the fining were not returned.   Later the principal told the parents that if they agreed to sign the document he had composed, their property would be returned. The parents, knowing no Romanian, signed the document, believing it was a request for the return of their property. The document, however, was a declaration requesting that their children be transferred to the public school. Anghelescu boastfully presented the document in parliament by way of proof that the Székely population had grown tired of denominational education.   The final outcome of the fining procedure introduced at Mădăraş was that on September 15, 1936, the doors of the Roman Catholic school were closed and sealed for lack of pupils. At the same time the community was forced to set up a public school at a cost of about 2 million lei.[42]

Parents and children were repelled by public schools, not only because of Romanian as the language of instruction and the extra expense involved, but also because of the activities of the Romanian teachers sent to the so-called cultural zone in the Székely region. These teachers were not choosy as to the means employed. Unfamiliar with Hungarian they could not communicate with the children. Most of the time they resorted to corporal punishment in order to encourage the children to greater progress in learning Romanian. Elsewhere — for instance, in the kindergarten at Lupeni — the Romanian kindergarten teacher, who knew no Hungarian, tried to communicate with the children by means of an interpreter. In some places the Romanian teachers dressed the Hungarian children in Romanian national costumes, including boots and loose-sleeved shirts, demanding that they wear these on holidays.[43] They were not allowed to speak Hungarian even amongst themselves in the courtyard and classrooms of the school, and whoever forgot the rule was brutally flogged, or received strict punishment. In many cases the system to which the children were subjected became the topic of parliamentary debate. In 1934 Elemér Gyárfás queried Anghelescu on account of the activities of one Ioan Bota, a public school teacher in Corund [Korond], part of the cultural zone. In early 1934 Bota had ordered the children to bring to school two meters of linen and colored wool in order to make a Romanian flag. Some of the poorer children did not have the means to purchase the material, hence could not comply with the teacher's order. Bota then subjected them to a terrible beating. The parents turned to the Hungarian Party for remedy. Gyárfás queried the Minister on behalf of the Party, and the latter ordered an investigation on site. Anghelescu communicated the results with Gyárfás under document number 87974/1934. The investigation revealed that the complaints of the parents were justified:

> Ioan Bota applied not only disciplinary measures authorized by law but corporal punishment as well and, what is even sadder, as he admits himself and as the attached medical report proves, he exceeded all measures in applying such punishment, beating some of the students until they became incapacitated.[44]

At the conclusion of the report to Gyárfás, he mentioned the possibility of having Bota transferred from Corund. Nothing of the sort happened in 1935. Then Gyárfás renewed his query, upon which Anghelescu declared that, by his directive 786/1935 he had removed Ioan Bota from public teaching. Nevertheless, the directive was still not carried out, since the brutal teacher was still teaching at his post in 1936. We can only imagine the suffering of the children and parents who had been requesting the transfer of the brutal teacher for over three years. Finally, after renewed protests, Bota indeed departed from the scene in September 1937.

The activities of the Romanian teachers in the county of Ciuc were often similar. The "cultural zone" teacher at Racul [Csíkrákos], Ştefan Bârlea, forbade the children from using the old manner of greeting "praised be the Lord." Under number 6837/1933 the Catholic bishopric denounced Bârlea at the Ministry on this account, requesting that he be ordered to desist. Bârlea became a center of attention of the Romanians. A collaborator of the paper *Universul* asked whether the denunciation was true. "It is true," the teacher answered,

> but this does not mean I am against the form of greeting. I only object to the children's greeting in Hungarian. I would not allow the students to speak Hungarian in school or on the street. I did not come here, as a Romanian, in order to preserve the minority population's often stupid manner of thinking which, moreover, is

dangerous for the state, but rather to introduce our healthy concepts and the official language into public awareness.

An Assessment of Hungarian Primary Schooling under the Anghelescu Laws

The data of the process outlined above reveal several typical traits of the situation of primary instruction in Hungarian. Hungarian children could attend public or denominational schools. With the exception of the first couple of years, the public schools resorted increasingly to Romanian as the only language of instruction, while the denominational schools were bilingual. These two types of schools represented two cultures. In public schools, the "cultural zone" teachers tried to carry out the objectives of Romanianization by every means at their disposal, particularly once the language of instruction at these schools became entirely Romanian. Therefore, increasing number of children were herded into the public schools, thanks to the intervention of the authorities, while the numbers of Hungarian denominational schools were reduced and their situation rendered critical by means of laws governing private schooling and the primary schools. At no time did the two types of schools engage in the kind of free competition that prevailed under Hungarian rule. After 1934 the government set up public schools in every Hungarian village, and attempted to render instruction in Romanian exclusive by means of overburdening the residents of the village, name analysis, the warnings issued to denominational schools, and the closings. Romanian educational policies never provided the rural population or the children with the opportunity to choose freely the school they wished to attend. In this respect freedom of instruction never existed in Greater Romania and the government never allowed free competition between public and denominational schools. The activities of the "cultural zone" teachers elicited antagonism and increasing bitterness from the Hungarian population almost everywhere, while enhancing their devotion towards the Hungarian denominational school.

Under the bilingual system forced upon them, the Hungarian denominational schools, in a state of constant insecurity, struggled with serious handicaps. The cumbersome and mostly ill-intentioned procedures governing the granting of accreditation rendered their situation most insecure. Children and teachers were subordinated to the teachers of Romanian public schools. The parents undertook enormous sacrifices to maintain the denominational schools, since they had to bear the burden of the expenses of the public schools as well. In many places they were no longer able to cope with the double burden of maintaining schools and the persistent fines they were subjected to, hence the denominational school had to close its doors. Where the population undertook all sacrifices and exhibited unfailing devotion to its school, it usually managed to keep the denominational school going. It is true, however, that about two-thirds of these schools in 1930, and about 35% as late as the last years of the regime, were unable to obtain accreditation. As a result the parents had to bear separate expenses for year-end examinations, and the pupils at these schools were always in danger of being transferred to the public school. As for the public school teachers, they secured an income amounting to many millions from the pennies contributed by the impoverished Hungarian population for these special examinations throughout the Romanian regime. Nevertheless, the Hungarian denominational schools did manage to teach the children to read and write in their mother tongue, in spite of the bilingual system and the lack of accreditation. Moreover a profound and firm relationship evolved between the teaching corps, the churches, and their followers, which became a source of immeasurable strength for the suffering Hungarian population. It is true that the student body at the denominational schools involved no more that 25% of Hungarian school-age children, while three-fourth of them were forced into the mainly Romanian public schools. In the long run, however, studying in Romanian schools was of no benefit to them, or to the Romanian state.

This fact was noted by some of those Romanians who were more objective and better acquainted with the problems of the nationalities. As mentioned, Nicholae Iorga decidedly condemned Anghelescu's school policies on several occasions, and even the more intelligent Romanian educational leaders spoke out more than once against forced Romanianization. In the first year after the introduction of the culture zone system, the Romanian superintendent of schools in the county of Mureş-Turda noted, in his official report, that it was hopeless to send Romanian teachers who could speak not a word of Hungarian into communities with a purely Hungarian population.

> We may note after one year's experience, that these appointments were a mistake. For they sent teachers to communities where, except maybe for the notary and the gendarme, not a soul could speak Romanian, and who had never heard Hungarian in all their lives, and were even less familiar with the customs and ideas of the population among whom they came to work. Consequently these teachers, even if dedicated, struggle like fish out of water to make the children understand

a small part of the many words they pronounce. They have openly and sincerely, albeit discouragedly, declared that it is impossible to obtain any results, since the children know no Romanian. Thus the teachers are destined to remain isolated in their villages, even though they were called upon to be become the leaders of all public movements.[45]

The Romanian school superintendent stationed near the border, in the Oradea region, Dan Pompilius, condemned the aggressive Romanian educational policies in similar terms. Returning from his inspection tour in late 1926 he used harsh words to describe the impossible prescriptions of the Act on Private Education in front of a group of Hungarian journalists at Oradea:

> the requirement that third grade primary school students learn the geography of the country, as well as take 29 hours of history, in a language completely unknown to them is absurd, anti-didactic, and does not even have the excuse of ignorance. Just take a look at a school where the language of instruction is Hungarian and the struggle surrounding this unknown vocabulary. Those little ones exhibit an energy beyond their powers in the process of elaborating a whole from a mass of words they do not understand, which they naively refer to as a lesson; but that which they recite with an awful pronunciation. No Romanian or Hungarian can understand a word. This is a dizzy exercise in memorization! Is this the way we expect the child's historical and geographical notions to increase, when he cannot even say in his mother tongue what he is expected to recite in Romanian, without mistake.[46]

The teachers of Romanian background who were assigned to teach in the Hungarian villages of the borderland had to agree with these observations of the Romanian superintendent. In February 1927, at the conference of the cultural circle of Romanian teachers under the chairmanship of Ioan Bărbulescu, they declared that even from a didactic point of view it is important that the geography and history of Romanian be taught in the mother tongue.[47]

A few months later, in April 1927 the Romanian royal superintendents held their convention. At this district convention of superintendents the participants declared, on the basis of their analysis of the experiences, that the national subjects (i.e. Romanian geography, history, and government) should be taught in the mother tongue of the children in

the minority schools, both denominational and public, from the first
semester of the school-year 1927-28, on. In the following semester the
students could go over the same material in short summary sentences
in Romanian. This resolution was also approved by the chief
superintendent who was present at the convention. The Minister of
Religious Affairs and Education, Anghelescu, however, did not go along
with the resolution, and prohibited all experiments in this direction,
even if pedagogically sound.[48]

Yet the acceptance and application of this resolution would have
been all the more warranted because by then, even foreign circles had
turned against the aggressive Romanianization entailed by Romanian
educational policies. The American Committee in Defense of the Rights
of Religious Minorities, which visited Romania in 1927 under the
leadership of N. A. Atkinson, made meaningful observations regarding
its experiences in Romania. In its English-language report printed in
Boston the members of the committee noted "that the objective of
Romanian educational policies was to Romanianize the Hungarian,
German, and Russian children, and thereby the future generations."
They described in detail the attitude of the authorities oppressing the
Hungarian schools.

> Administrative pressures, the denial of accreditation,
> compulsory knowledge of Romanian, restrictions on the
> autonomy of schools, numerous interferences in the
> determination of the curriculum, the hiring of teachers and the
> admission of students, moreover the antagonistic supervision of
> the schools, the unworthy spirit in which examinations are
> conducted, all this serves to destroy the minority schools. The
> laws of 1925 regarding the minorities embody a narrow-minded
> and oppressive nationalist policies.[49]

Two years later the educational expert of the Romanian National
Peasant Party, Ghiţă Pop, member of parliament, who had been sent
abroad by his party to study minority issues, made a statement
regarding the Act on Private Education to a newspaper in Cluj.

> The present bilingual system is misguided. In my opinion the
> main purpose of instruction is to acquire knowledge, not to learn
> Romanian. I say this as a good Romanian who has not forgotten
> that we have responsibilities, as universal human beings,
> towards culture, regardless of our nationality. Undoubtedly we
> Romanians approve the idea of the minorities learning the

Chapter V

Secondary, Higher, and Extra-Mural Education
of Hungarians

At the time of the change in sovereignty in 1919 there were 62 junior high schools, 35 high-schools, 14 teacher's colleges, and nine commercial schools in operation in the Hungarian territories attached to Romania. These were all denominational schools serving the cultural aspirations of the Hungarians living in these areas. The number of public schools was less.

Since, as a result of the change in sovereignty, almost 200,000 Hungarians mostly members of the intelligentsia holding jobs as civil servants, were forced to leave the areas of Hungary attached to Romania. Most certainly some of the schools listed above had to be prepared for the loss of their student body. Indeed, the majority of these schools closed down, in a matter of a few years, mostly of their own accord. In most places, however, the Romanian government did not await this course of events, but intervened with a variety of aggressive measures to hasten the closing down of Hungarian denominational secondary schools. This process of facilitating closures characterizes the first chapter in the history of Hungarian secondary education under the Romanian regime.

Thus, partly as a result of a natural depletion of their student body and partly as a consequence of the aggressive measures introduced by Romanian educational policy, 39 Hungarian denominational junior high schools, that is 62.9% of the total, closed down in the period 1919 to 1937. During the same period seven of the 35 denominational teachers' training schools closed down. Four of the commercial schools, that is 44%, also closed down. Thus, in general over 50% of the secondary schools ceased to function.[1] These schools were as follows: the girls' Roman Catholic secondary at Dej, the girls' Roman Catholic secondary at Baraolt, the boys' Roman Catholic secondary at Braşov, the coeducational Roman Catholic secondary at Bistriţa, the coeducational Roman Catholic secondary at Frumoasa, the coeducational Roman Catholic secondary at Joseni, the coeducational Roman Catholic secondary at Haţeg, the boys' Roman Catholic secondary at Sibiu, the

boys' Roman Catholic secondary at Petrosani, the coeducational Roman
Catholic secondary at Cîrta, the coeducational Roman Catholic
secondary at Medgyes, the coeducational Roman Catholic secondary at
Sighişoara, the coeducational Roman Catholic secondary at Orăştie, the
coeducational Roman Catholic secondary at Gherla, and the
coeducational Roman Catholic secondary at Sighetul Marmaţiei.
Among the Reformed schools the following closed down: the boys'
secondary at Baraolt, the coeducational at Huedin [Bánffyhunyad], the
coeducational at Bistriţa, the coeducational at Dej, the coeducational at
Tîrnăveni, the coeducational at Făgăras, the coeducational at Tîrgu
Şecuiesc, the coeducational at Cluj, the coeducational at Ocna Mureş,
the coeducational at Cristuru Secuiesc, the girls' secondary at Odorheiu
Secuiesc, the girls at Turda, the coeducational at Zalău; moreover, the
Unitarian boys' school at Odorheiu Secuiesc, the Unitarian boys' school
at Turda, the Evangelical coeducational school at Satulung, the girls'
school at the same location, and the Evangelical girls' school at Cluj.
The following high schools had to close down: the Roman Catholic girls'
high at Arad, the Roman Catholic boys' high at Deva, the Roman
Catholic boys' high at Tîrgu Secuiesc, the Roman Catholic boys' high at
Tîrgu Mureş, the Roman Catholic boys' high at Sighetul, the Roman
Catholic boys' high at Carei, the Roman Catholic boys' high at Sibiu,
the Roman Catholic boys' high at Oradea, the Roman Catholic boys'
high at Satu Mare, the Roman Catholic girls' high at Satu Mare, the
Roman Catholic boys' high at Şimleul Silvaniei, the Roman Catholic
boys' high at Timişoara, and the Roman Catholic girls' high at the same
location. The following Reformed high schools closed down: the boys'
high at Dej, the boys' high at Făgăras, the boys' high at Sighetul
Marmaţiei, the boys' high at Orăştie, the boys' high at Odorheiu
Secuiesc, whereas the Unitarians lost the boys' high at Turda. During
the same period the Roman Catholic teachers' training school at
Şumuleu, the Roman Catholic teachers' training school at Tîrgu
Secuiesc and the teacher's training school at Cluj also closed down.
Among the Reformed teachers' training schools, the ones at Oradea,
Aiud, Sfîntu Gheorghe, and Satu Mare closed down. The following
denominational commercial schools closed down: the Roman Catholic
girls' schools at Deva and Timişoara, and the Reformed girls' school at
Braşov, the coeducational schools at Tîrnaveni and Orăştic.
     These high schools and junior high schools closed down under a
variety of circumstances. The Romanian government took over the
Roman Catholic girls' school at Sighetul Marmaţiei with the excuse that
it had been maintained by the Research Foundation, which was a state
entity, hence was inherited by the Romanian state. The Reformed

secondary school at the same location, founded in 1542, was closed down on April 19, 1921, by telegraphic order, because its principal was charged in connection with a conspiracy. A court martial acquitted the principal of the charge and its consequences.   Then the church authorities responsible for the school, assuming that the reason for closing down the schools was now moot, requested permission to reopen the school. The Romanian government, however, did not comply with the request, and the Reformed school of Sighetul Marmaţiei closed down definitely.[2] The school-building was leased, by force, to the Romanian public high school. In 1937, at the behest of the Ministry of National Education, Onisifor Ghibu, professor at the University of Cluj, transferred the deed to the building to the Romanian state without further legal proceedings.[3]

The Roman Catholic high school founded at Arad in 1845 was also taken over by the Romanian government in 1919. The excuse was that the high school had enjoyed the support of the Research Foundation. The building was turned over to a public school while the Hungarian school, with over one thousand students, had to continue to function on rented premises. The school was closed down in December 1921 because 22 of the students had been arrested on grounds of "conspiracy." The court martial found the students innocent and acquitted them of the charge. The school's accreditation, however, was denied, because its building and equipment were allegedly deficient. Within a year the Roman Catholic church had constructed a modern school building, but it applied in vain for accreditation. From then on the school was gradually depleted of students.

The Roman Catholic high school of Oradea was closed down in 1923 on the excuse that it manifested "an attitude damaging to the interests of the state." The order noted that the closure took place "on the basis of paragraph 50 of Act XXX of 1883, still in force." According to this paragraph, if a disciplinary investigation taken against the faculty of some school determines that the institution and the teaching body are engaged in unpatriotic acts and did not carry out the directives, then, after observing the steps defined in the act (warning, investigation, etc.) the school may be closed down.   But no investigation had been undertaken in the case of the Roman Catholic high school of Oradea, it had received no warning, the Minister did not explain what the unpatriotic acts had consisted of and what directives the school had not complied with; the closure resulted from a simple order from the Minister to that effect.

The Roman Catholic high school of Şimleui Silvaniei, was housed in a magnificent new structure. The Romanian municipal housing office settled residents into the building. In 1923 the school's accreditation was withdrawn on the ground that "private persons not connected with the school resided in the building." Later the authorities confiscated the entire building and transferred it into the custody of the Romanian high school. The Catholic high school continued to function for a while on rented premises but eventually the church itself closed the school down for lack of students. Octavian Prie commented on the fate of the Şimleul Silvaniei school in his article already referred to, as follows: "The case of Şimleul Silvaniei may serve as a memento to the church. If a peaceful solution cannot be found between church and state, the schools at other towns will follow."[4]

The Roman Catholic high school at Satu Mare, founded in 1835, was confiscated by the government with all its equipment. The institution transferred into a rented building, but in 1923 the government closed it down for good on the grounds that it did not have an adequate building or equipment.

Two-thirds of the students at the Roman Catholic secondary school of Carei, were excluded by order of the Minister, since they were not Catholic. Later the school was accused of irredentist ideas. All charges proved unfounded, but the extended harassment nevertheless led to the government's closing down the school and setting up a Romanian public school in its stead.

The Minister deprived the Reformed school of Zalău, the Unitarian school at Turda, and the Roman Catholic schools at Deva and Sibiu of their accreditation. Soon the Minister had the ones at Turda, Deva, and Sibiu closed down definitely. The college at Zalău could only be saved by its famous Romanian alumni, including Iuliu Maniu, from the fate suffered by the other secondary schools. The Roman Catholic high school at Miercurea Ciuc received a warning because the students sang the Catholic Church hymn about Saint Imre. The one at Cluj was warned because the students were not familiar enough with the Romanian national anthem. By directive 53.762 of June 1923, Anghelescu had the Jewish secondary schools at Oradea, Cluj, and Timişoara closed down because, according to the Minister, instruction in Romanian was for the sake of appearances only.

The most characteristic instance of the policy directed against Hungarian denominational schools was the closing of the Kocsárd Kun boarding school at Orăştie. The school had been founded in the 16th century and richly endowed in the 19th by the magnate Count Kocsárd. Many a Romanian student graduated from the school during the Hungarian regime, including Aurel Vlad and Petru Groza who was to become the famous leader of the "Plow Front." The institution had a secondary school, a boarding school, and a commercial school. In 1919 these were attended by over 500 students.

On September 20, 1922, the municipal housing office requisitioned the building of the boarding school, and the 183 resident students were forced to transfer to the building of the secondary school. At the same time, by its directive 18.997/1922 the Executive Directorate of the Minister of Education deprived the commercial school of its accreditation. Repeated requests by the officials of the church district were to no avail; finally, by order 27.438, the school received permission to operate as a private school. Further requests on the part of the church made no difference; what's more, by order 4756/1923, the Ministry of Education informed the church administration that, as of September 1, 1923, the commercial school could not even function as a private school. The general assembly of the church district "sadly noted, that the impatient policy of the government, which is not exactly in a spirit of understanding, once again sentenced one of our cultural institutions to death."[5]

After the commercial school came the turn of the secondary school itself. In its directive 84.020/1923 the Minister of Education informed the Presidential Council that it would deprive the school of Orăştie of its accreditation as of August 15, 1923. The move was justified on the grounds of irregularities such as cramped conditions, coeducation (even though this was general practice in Romania), smoking on the part of the students, sloppiness of the homework submitted by the students, etc. The general assembly received the relevant report of the Presidential Council once again "with great astonishment." The measure taken by the Minister, we read in the resolution of the assembly:

> in some of its aspects, for instance, the one referring to cramped conditions when the entire dormitory and the gymnasium had been requisitioned for the purposes of a public high school, are completely one-sided observations; the ploy to take over the entire building for the purposes of a public high school and to deprive the Hungarians scattered in the provinces from their school can clearly be perceived. The general assembly of the church district resolves that it will seek its rights through every legal forum available and will bring even to the attention of His Majesty the issue of the school deprived of its accreditation.[6]

But every effort of the church officials was in vain. At the end of the 1923-24 school-year the students at the school had to take their examination in front of a committee composed of Romanian teachers unknown to them. The committee failed 96% of the candidates and, in the following year, failed all of them. Consequently, in 1924 the famous school which once boasted of over 500 students had but 73 students left. Then the church administration decided to close the institution temporarily and to use the premises for a girls' school and an orphanage. But before it could carry out this resolution the Romanian housing office requisitioned the beautiful, modern structure, handing it over to the new Romanian Vlaicu High School which had initiated the whole process.

The administration of the Hungarian Reformed church turned to the League of Nations on account of the requisition. The Romanian government, in the clarification handed in to the League of Nations, allowed a slip of the tongue. "This Hungarian school," wrote those detailed to formulate the explanation by Anghelescu,

> was fated to perish in the midst of a great Romanian population. The church authorities, noting that the students of the institution decreased in number year after year, resolved to close it down of their own accord. While the buildings of the Reformed institution stood empty, without any specific function, the Romanian high school lacked premises. It was housed in an inadequate, rented building. Therefore the direction of the Romanian school turned to the housing office, which requisitioned the Reformed school, aware of the danger that unless it did so, it might not be able to continue to function.

The complaint filed with the League of Nations did have the result that the Romanian government decided to buy the building. Finally, the Reformed church was compelled to sell the beautiful building of the almost 400 year old college for a sum well below its true value.

As the instances enumerated above indicate, in very many places the Romanian government did not bother to await the voluntary closing of the secondary schools as a result of lack of students and of the repatriation of the masses of Hungarian intelligentsia. Where the newly formed Romanian secondary school needed it, the government closed down the Hungarian secondary school with aggressive measures and illegal procedures, to avoid dangerous competition. Most of the time the procedure's aim was to take over directly the targeted Hungarian secondary school with all its appurtenances. If this maneuver did not succeed on the first try, they nevertheless carried out their intentions in some manner or other in subsequent years. During the first phase they closed down several of the schools of Hungarian orders of monks, but did not dare take away the buildings. After 1934, however, during Anghelescu's second ministership, the government was no longer so timid. Empowered by Anghelescu, Onisifor Ghibu transferred the buildings of the Piarist high school at Timișoara, the Minorite high school at Arad, and at Șimleul Silvaniei in the name of the Romanian state; all real estate of the high schools of the Piarist order of Sighetul Marmației and the Reformed Church suffered the same fate.[7]

After the closing of schools, in the second decade of the Greater Romanian regime, the following Hungarian denominational secondary schools were still functioning: 23 junior high schools, ten high schools, seven teachers' training schools, and four commercial schools. These schools were still in operation in 1936-37 and their numbers did not change thereafter.

By location, these schools were as follows: among the Roman Catholic schools: Brașov (girls), Gheorgheni [Gyergyószentmiklós] (girls), Sibiu (girls), Reghiu (coeducational), Tîrgu Mureș (boys), Tîrgu Secuiesc (boys), Arad (girls), Lugoi (girls), Oradea (girls), Oradea Saint Vincent, (girls), Oradea Ursuline (girls), Satu Mare (girls), Șimleul Silvaniei (girls), Timișoara-Belváros (boys), Timișoara-Gyárváros. Among the Reformed schools we find: Brașov (girls), Tîrgu Mureș (girls), Oradea (girls), Sfîntu Gheorghe (girls), and Satu Mare (girls). In 1935-36 the following Hungarian denominational high schools were operating: the Roman Catholic at Arad for boys, the Roman Catholic at Brașov for boys, the boys' high schools at Miercurea Ciuc, Alba Iulia, Cluj, and Odorheiu Secuiesc, and the girls' high school at Cluj. Among the Reformed schools we find the boys' and girls' high schools at Cluj, the boys' high schools at Tîrgu Mureș, Aiud, Sfîntu Gheorghe, Satu Mare, and Zalău, moreover the Unitarian boys' high schools at Cluj and Cristuru Secuiesc. But ten high schools remained after 1936-37. In the same academic year the following teachers' training schools were functioning: the Roman Catholic colleges at Tîrgu Mureș, Oradea, and Satu Mare. The Reformed church operated the teachers training schools at Oradea, Aiud, and Odorheiu Secuiesc. Among the commercial schools still in operation in 1935-36 we find the Roman Catholic school of Cluj, the Roman Catholic girls' school at Sibiu, the Reformed boys' school at Brașov, and the Reformed girls' school at Satu Mare. In addition to these high schools there were four winter courses providing continuing education for Hungarian farmers: the courses sponsored by the Roman Catholic Church at Tîrgu Șecuiesc and Iernut, the course sponsored by the Reformed Church at Cimbrud and the course sponsored by the

Unitarians at Cristuru Secuiesc. It was only during the last years of
the regime that these schools were able to obtain accreditation.

The School Budgets

Some of the Hungarian secondary schools were maintained by the
dioceses, whereas the centuries-old high schools were maintained by the
central administration of the churches. The junior high schools required
smaller budgets, covered mostly by the occasionally remaining funds of
the dioceses or by the local parishioners. The upkeep of high schools
caused serious difficulties. Before the war each of these was maintained
mainly by contributions from the state, although there were some, such
as the Calvinist boarding school of Aiud and certain Roman Catholic
high schools, which owned enormous foundations and did not request
state support. After the war the greater part of these foundations were
expropriated as a result of the Romanian land reform. The 26,538
cadastral *holds* of estates owned by the autonomous institution
providing for the Roman Catholic secondary schools, the Status of
Transylvania, became subject to confiscation; it was able to retain a
mere 3,251 *holds*, in other words, it lost 87.74% of its estate.[8] The
Calvinist boarding schools of Cluj and Aiud suffered a similar fate. A
total of 1440 yokes *holds* of the 1,521 yokes estate of the Calvinist
boarding school of Cluj, were expropriated and 8,137 of the 10,884 hold
estate of the Calvinist boarding school of Aiud were also confiscated.[9]
The other boarding schools did not own large estates, hence they had to
rely mostly on tuition fees and state subsidies.

Since the sums paid in compensation for the expropriated estates
were insignificant (one-fifth of the actual value, and even that, only ten
years later, in government bonds at 20% of their face value), the budget
of the secondary schools represented an enormous burden on the
churches concerned. In 1920 the Romanian government did provide
some assistance, but thereafter, with the exception of the year 1929,
Greater Romania was adamant about providing help. Therefore the
secondary schools had to rely on the financial contributions of
Hungarian society and on tuition fees. It is easy to imagine the poverty
they had to endure and the meagerness of the salaries they were able
to pay their faculty. Most schools attempted to make ends meet by
selling their remaining real estate, including houses and lots of land;
but throughout the Romanian regime these schools had to cope with
utmost poverty. The officials of the churches did occasionally come up
with smaller sums to help the teachers living in misery, but since most
of the faithful also became impoverished, these occasional contributions

were rare indeed and did not amount to much. It is fair to assert that Hungarian high school and elementary school teachers formed the most impoverished stratum of Hungarian society under Romanian rule; they became typical representatives of the intellectual proletariat whose poverty had become proverbial.

The Situation of the Teachers

The situation of the teachers at Hungarian schools was determined by the provisions of the oft-mentioned Act on Private Education. Even before the law was adopted Minister of Education, Anghelescu, issued his ordinance number 100,090; which deprived the Hungarian denominational secondary schools of the autonomy granted them by erstwhile Hungarian laws. Beginning September 1, 1923 this ordinance made the curriculum of the secondary schools of old Romania, including the end of the year comprehensive examinations that had been customary in those schools, compulsory everywhere; moreover, it required that geography, history, and government be taught in Romanian. It prohibited the admission of students of a different religion or ethnic background, as well as coeducation; it subjected all students to the disciplinary measures prescribed by the Ministry. Even before the ordinance was issued the Hungarian school authorities had been notified that Hungarian denominational teachers could not travel on the railways at a discount. In vain did the chief officials of the church request that the privilege enjoyed during the Hungarian rule be reinstated; the Ministry of Education rejected the request, under number 94,041/1922, with the argument that "the faculty at denominational institutions may not enjoy privileges on Romanian railroads under any circumstances."[10] The general assembly of the church district "painfully took cognizance of the rigid decision which shows no appreciation of cultural work, and it instructed the Presidential Council to keep the issue alive and to seize every opportunity to regain the privilege." The government, however, continued to remain rigid, and the teachers at Hungarian schools remained deprived of the privilege to the end. Their complaint was all the more bitter as they were well aware that only teachers of Hungarian ethnic background were deprived of this privilege, for Romanian and Saxon denominational faculty continued to benefit from it.

Ordinance number 100,090 required that only those teachers may teach the Romanian language, history, geography, and government who have been certified to teach these subjects. Since there was no such faculty among the Hungarians the ordinances forced the Hungarian denominational schools to employ teachers of Romanian ethnic background. These received far higher pay and functioned basically as spies in the schools. The above ordinance also prescribed that all professors had to be familiar with the Romanian language and had to undergo an examination between August 15 and September 1, 1924, in Romanian language and literature, as well as in Romanian history, geography, and government. The ordinance specified that textbooks had to be approved by the Ministry and required that report cards, course catalogs, registries, schedules of classes, statistics, and yearbooks all be prepared in Romanian.

These prescriptions were fixed in the form of law by the proposals regarding private education. This Act extended the prescriptions applied to primary schools to the secondary schools as well. It decreed that the four subjects be taught in Romanian in every secondary school. It also required the so-called "absolving" (comprehensive) examination at the completion of the fourth year. It limited the rights of the entities in charge of the school in the same way as in the case of primary schools. Secondary school teachers could only be employed after obtaining a license. They had to pass the *Capacitate*, a state examination, to obtain tenure. Without this examination not a single teacher could be tenured, even if he or she had completed studies at a Romanian university and had obtained a license. The Hungarian teachers, whose salaries were meager compared to those earned by their Romanian colleagues, thus got into a deplorable situation. They received no state subsidies. If they managed to complete their studies at some Romanian university and find employment in a denominational school, they had to apply to the Ministry for permission to teach each and every year. Hence their post was not permanent, their appointment had to be renewed each year. At the beginning, a few teachers did succeed in passing the *Capacitate*, especially if they happened to know some of the professors on the examining committee from their university days. Later, however, not a single member of the teaching corps of Hungarian background was able to pass the examination, particularly in the so-called Romanian national subjects. The reason for this was the pressure exerted by the increasingly extremist and chauvinist Romanian public opinion after 1935. The Romanian organization of secondary school teachers held a congress at Timişoara in 1936. In a resolution adopted at this congress, the Romanian professors demanded the dismissal of non-Romanian instructors and the complete Romanianization of public education. A leading personality of the association of Romanian teachers, Valeriu Grecu, turned to the examining teachers in the daily

Universul on the occasion of the proclamation of the *Capacitate* examination in 1937, calling upon them not to allow a single minority professor to pass the examination. In this article he referred to the resolution adopted at Timişoara in which the professors demanded the Romanianization of education in the following terms:

> It is absolutely necessary that the task of educating future generations be entrusted only to Romanians. Similarly, it believes [i.e. the Congress] that if the children of minority groups want to stay in Romania, they have to undergo schooling by Romanian professors, in a Romanian spirit, and in Romanian language.[11]

Anghelescu himself attended the congress at Timişoara, and the importance of the resolution above is also indicated by the fact that the leading periodical in education printed its text.

The consequences of the resolution were soon to be felt. At the *Capacitate* examination organized in Iaşi in 1937, all the candidates of Hungarian background were failed even though there were some among them who had graduated only a few years earlier from a Romanian university with "magna cum laude." Those concerned were aware of the reason for the peculiar treatment. They were familiar with the resolution adopted at the congress of secondary school teachers at Timişoara and with the call for action by Valeriu Grecu. Romanian educational authorities soon banned individuals of other than Romanian ethnic background from even the possibility of presenting oneself for the *Capacitate* examination. The ordinance modifying the Act of May 15, 1928, on secondary schools was published in issue number 23 of January 29, 1938 of the Official Bulletin: "Only persons of Romanian ethnic background may present themselves for the *Capacitate* examination in Romanian language, literature, and history."[12]

Thus, as regards the national subjects, the replacement process by minority teachers became definitely impossible. They had to resign themselves to the fact that if they taught these subjects, they would never be granted tenure in their own schools.

Thus the young Hungarian teachers lived under most uncertain conditions, not only financially, but from another point of view as well. Their chairs were advertised each year, and they had to undergo the anxiety of reappointment each and every time. In addition to the state, the church authorities could also hire or fire them yearly. These procedures rendered their situation insecure and tragic. These untenured teachers were the proletarians of the profession. They could count on no sort of indemnity. Their pay was 40% less on the average, sometimes even 50% less than that of the regular teachers. The church might have granted them tenure, but this entailed certain financial risks which the Reformed and Roman Catholic Churches were unwilling to take. The Unitarian Church, which for a long time had been granting tenure as well as equal pay to its teachers, seemed the most understanding. After 1937 the general assembly of the church district granted the young teachers employed by the Reformed Church personal indemnity commensurate with their age after eight years of service, under certain conditions.

The humiliating predicament of young teachers at denominational schools did not improve during the Greater Romanian regime. At the time of the Vienna Arbitration Treaty (Award) in 1940 the change in sovereignty found teachers who had been contracted annually at the same post for ten of fifteen years without having received tenure. The insecurity of their situation had its impact on the work of Hungarian high schools, all the more so, as their state of mind differed considerably from that of teachers belonging to the older generation. In general the younger ones were more church-oriented, their social conscience more highly developed, their Hungarian outlook deeply introverted. Most of them had crossed the surf of social movements, hence the working class and the peasantry were organic parts of their concept of the Hungarian. The great intellectual triad composed of the poet Endre Ady and the novelists Dezső Szabó and Zsigmond Móricz had a determining influence on their spiritual makeup. It is clear, therefore, that only the work of these young teachers had the potential for launching a renaissance within the Hungarian schools. Unfortunately, their insecure situation, and at times their own ecclesiastic superiors who exhibited little understanding of this situation, had dire consequences. In many cases these pressures led to a neglect of punctuality and responsibility, to a certain superficiality, or even to a cynical attitude. These traits undoubtedly derived from disillusionment and, most of the time, were in stark contrast to the conscientious punctuality and thorough sense of responsibility of the older generation of Hungarian teachers.

The older generation of teachers also had their particular set of problems to confront. Most of them returned to occupy their chairs after the war, wounded in soul or body. They returned to misery and want. The position which they had attained under Hungarian rule changed radically in every respect. They had to fit in the framework of Romanian educational system. They had to pass their first examination in Romanian language in 1924. They were given a mere year to familiarize themselves with the language even though, as we have seen, the Romanian teachers had not had to take their examination until the seventeenth year of the Hungarian regime, in 1884. The language examination of 1924 was administered in a relatively humane manner. Their diplomas were recognized as valid and they were granted tenure. But soon a second, and even a third language examination followed. According to the Act on Private Education they had to take their next examination within five years, and only professors who had attained their 55th year were exempt. If in the course of an inspection the government inspectors were to conclude that a given teacher was not sufficiently familiar with the language, he could be required to take a language course. Although this ordinance prescribed merely a compulsory course, in his 1934 law on secondary education, Anghelescu ordered a further set of examinations. In spite of all protests, the teaching corps was indeed once again required to face the committee of examiners. Teachers aged 45 to 50, and even 55 were now standing in front of the examination committees. The university professors who chaired these examination committees often felt embarrassed when questioning the gray-haired candidates. According to Anghelescu's law, those who failed, had to give up their posts. Indeed, many failed. But because of vigorous protests by Hungarian leaders, Anghelescu was finally satisfied with organizing language courses, and after many an anxious moment the older teachers at the Hungarian schools were able to remain at their post which ensured them at least a meager living.

The attitudes of the older generation of Hungarian teachers could be described as identical with the antebellum *Weltanschauung* of Hungarians in general. They represented conservative Hungarian views; only exceptionally did they demonstrate a social conscience or a sociological perspective. Most were rationalists, lovers of culture, but with only slight interest in matters affecting the community. Their punctuality and sense of responsibility were exemplary. In most cases they performed their pedagogical tasks well. Their predicament also became insecure as a result of the language examinations, even though more opportunities remained to them financially speaking, than to their younger colleagues. After protracted discussion, the Romanian government finally recognized their right to a pension. They were the ones to represent the schools in teacher's organizations or ecclesiastic bodies. They were for the most part careful and reasonable individuals who, in several cases, were able to save their schools by their wise behavior, the serious difficulties that befell Hungarian institutions after the introduction of the Anghelescu laws not withstanding. Teachers of the older and younger generations both played an enormous role in preserving Hungarian general culture during the Romanian regime.

The Students

Enrollment in the secondary denominational schools varied according to the enrollment in the primary schools. Before the introduction of the Act on Private Education and the law on the graduation examination, there was no lack of students at these schools. As a result of the new laws their numbers began to decrease rapidly.

Indeed, in addition to the Act on Private Education the situation of Hungarian schools was determined by the provisions of the law on the graduation examination. Even before the promulgation of the law, ordinance 100.090 of 1923 was in effect: it prescribed that, in addition to the Romanian language, Romanian geography, history, and government also had to be taught in Romanian in every secondary school. Thus the secondary schools became bilingual, much like the primary schools. But the law on graduation examination, promulgated in 1925, increased these difficulties considerably. It forced the students at secondary schools to undergo two major examinations, the first one upon completion of the fourth year, as an entrance examination into the fifth year. This examination was also referred to as "absolving" or minor graduation examination. The subjects on this examination included the geography, history, and government of Romania, Romanian and French, as well as mathematics. If the school had accreditation, the members of the examining committee were selected from the faculty of the school, under the chairmanship of someone appointed by the Minister. The examination took place in Romanian. No student could enter the fifth year without having passed.

The graduation examination was administered after the final examinations in each subject had been passed in the eighth and last year of secondary school, in front of a committee appointed by the Minister. This committee was appointed a few weeks before the examination and consisted of teachers from the public schools. The basic principle was that the students should be examined by teachers with whom they were not acquainted. Each committee was chaired by a university professor. The examination was in two parts: oral and written. Those who failed the written part were barred from the orals. The subjects on this examination were Romanian language and literature, the history, geography and government of Romania, a modern language, and two natural sciences to be selected by the candidates from the minority schools. Apart from the last two subjects the minority candidates could not take their examination in their mother tongue, but in Romanian, in front of Romanian teachers they had never met.[13]

In spite of all the protests by those representing the interests of the Hungarians, the regime adopted the above law at the end of 1925 and carried it out immediately. The students took their examination according to the new system already in 1925. The results were truly depressing. There were 258 Roman Catholic, 200 Reformed, 71 Unitarian, 286 Evangelical, and 84 Jewish minority candidates in 1925. Of these, 28% of the Roman Catholics, 22.7% of the Reformed, 25.3% of the Unitarians, 44.4% of the Evangelicals, and 29.7% of the Jews were able to pass. On the average, 75% of the Hungarian candidates failed. The results improved somewhat in 1926, when 33% of the candidates were successful. In 1927 the results got worse again: only 8.5% of the purely Hungarian Unitarian candidates were allowed to pass, the remainder were failed by the Romanian teachers, 76% of the Roman Catholic candidates failed. At the same time 51.9% of the candidates in the old kingdom of Romania were able to pass;   clearly, the Romanian candidates taking the examination in their own language had an advantage over the Hungarian candidates who could not take their examination in their mother tongue.[14]

In 1934 Anghelescu made the law on the graduation examination and its application even stricter. Consequently Hungarian students were failing to graduate in large numbers once again. In June 1934 there were altogether 85 candidates graduating from the six Calvinist high schools, but only 13 of these were allowed to pass; in other words, the Romanian examiners flunked almost 85% of the Hungarian Calvinist candidates. For instance, not a single one of the 19 students at the high school of Tîrgu Mureş was successful, whereas only four of the 23 candidates from the Calvinist boarding school of Cluj were allowed to pass. The situation hardly improved during the Fall examinations; 87.5% of the candidates from the boarding-school Cluj and 66 and 1/3 of the candidates from the girls' high school at Cluj failed. At the same time, all the candidates from the Calvinist boarding-school at Zalău failed on the examination. The following year, 92.31% of the candidates from the boarding school of Cluj, 90.1% of the candidates from the Calvinist boarding school at Tîrgu Mureş and 90% of the candidates from the Calvinist boarding school at Sfîntu Gheorghe failed.[15]

The Hungarian school authorities concerned fought a constant struggle against the law on the graduation examination. They pointed out the absurd pedagogical notions behind the law, the practically unsurmountable difficulties the minority students had to face, the biased attitude of the state examining committees, all to no avail. Even Romanian public figures supported the Hungarian arguments. Iorga,

Ghiţă Pop and others repeatedly intervened against those provisions of the law which affected the minorities negatively, but their intervention had no more effect than the utterances by Hungarians concerned. Even the experiences gleaned from the first examination astounded the more serious Romanian experts. "What was the graduation examination like?" asked one member of the committee at Braşov, in the columns of the Romanian daily *Patria*.

> It was parody. There was one member on our committee who knew a little bit of Hungarian, and another one who knew German, and this committee was in charge of examining candidates from eight Hungarian and one German schools. When the committee found out that the students were incapable of answering in Romanian, they used a professor as interpreter to translate the questions and the answers. Can there be any doubt that such a committee is totally unfit to examine these students?[16]

The chair of this same committee, Gheorghe Popa-Lissenau, a professor at the University of Bucharest, also expressed an opinion to the effect that the examinations could only be meaningful if the candidates were examined by someone familiar with their mother tongue. "If the professor does not know the language of the candidate well, or at all, the answers cannot be correct and the judgment of the examiners cannot be accepted even if they do use an interpreter."[17]

These objective observations were in vain, for they elicited no echo. The despair of the Hungarians grew as the years passed. They demanded the use of the students' mother tongue in articles, essays, and interventions in parliament. Their demands remained without effect to the end. Even the National Peasant Party that came to power in 1928 made no change in the basic principles of the graduation examination, even though the already mentioned expert of the Party, Ghiţă Pop, consistently denounced the system. In 1929 in a statement to the *Keleti Újság*, he made a direct comparison between the former Hungarian system and the Romanian system under Anghelescu and concluded that:

> while formerly under Hungarian rule Hungarian language was taught only as a subject in the Romanian and Saxon secondary schools, all other subjects except the history of Hungarian literature were taught in the language of instruction of that school in the last two years of high school.

Then he sharply condemned the measures aiming at the imposition of the Romanian language and the law on the graduation examination as formulated by Anghelescu.

> I am in favor of the baccalauréate, of a graduation examination as advocated by Anghelescu, only we must change its application so that the candidate is enabled to take the examination in his or her own school, in front of his teachers and in the language of the school, of course, under state supervision.[18]

A few weeks later he delivered a speech in the Romanian parliament in which he demanded legislation to modify the baccalauréate system of graduation examinations. His speech once again referred to the differences between the former Hungarian system and Anghelescu's Romanian educational system.

> I too have studied under the former Hungarian regime in a Romanian high school, but I took my graduation examination in all subjects in Romanian except for Hungarian language and literature. It is inadmissible that we should grant our minority less than the rights we were allowed under the Hungarian regime.[19]

Unfortunately, these Romanian declarations led to no results. Neither the National Peasant Party regime, nor the Iorga regime which came to power in 1931 changed the law on the graduation examination. In fact the intentions of Prime Minister Iorga to change the law resulted in further restrictions of the opportunities still available to minority students. For one of the most frequent complaints in connection with the graduation examination was that even in those two subjects which the minority candidates were free to chose (natural science, chemistry, and sometimes philosophy), the examiners were Romanians asking questions in Romanian. As mentioned the more objective Romanians themselves admitted that there were tremendous obstacles when none of the members of the examining committee could speak the mother tongue of the candidates. Therefore, one of the most consistent demands of Hungarian representatives and school-supporting organizations was that members who understood Hungarian and could ask questions in Hungarian in these subjects on the graduation examination be included on examination committees.

In 1931 Iorga who, on several occasions, had condemned the graduation examination law promoted by Anghelescu, presented a proposal to the committee of parliament to the effect that the minority candidates be allowed to take their graduation examination in their mother tongue in all subjects except Romanian language and literature. The committee of the parliament not only rejected the proposal, but went so far as the to add restrictions to the measures been formulated by Anghelescu. According to their formulation, the "student may also use the language of instruction of the school" in those subjects they study in their mother tongue (natural sciences, philosophy). In practice, this meant that the use of the mother tongue was left up to the good will of the teachers concerned; and since after 1931 the ultra-nationalist and extreme right-wing Romanians increasingly dominated Romanian public opinion, fewer and fewer professors appointed to the examination committees were willing to take into consideration the difficulties experienced by the candidates in using the Romanian language. During the second ministership of Anghelescu it became impossible to use the Hungarian mother tongue on graduation examinations. From then on the young men had to be prepared for the examination in Romanian in all subjects in the minority schools and this, of course, increased the difficulties minority students had to face, almost unbearably.

These difficulties of the graduation examination were one of the principal causes of the decline of the number of students attending Hungarian secondary schools. After 1925 there was a steady decline in enrollment at all Hungarian denominational schools. According to the reports from individual high schools from the years 1919-20 and 1935-36, the number of students declined in those sixteen years as follows: from 774 to 140, at the Roman Catholic high school of Arad from 307 to 233, at the Roman Catholic girls' school high of Braşov, at Miercurea Ciuc from 400 to 212, at Alba Iulia from 468 to 248, at Cluj from 656 to 417, at the Roman Catholic girls' high school in Cluj roughly in the same proportions, at the Roman Catholic boys' high school in Odorheiu Secuiesc from 652 to 359, at Tîrgu Mureş from 508 to 382, at Aiud from 508 to 211, at Sfîntu Gheorge from 551 to 214, at Satu Mare from 1049 to 236, at Zalău from 593 to 178, at the Unitarian boarding school of Cluj from 425 to 171, at Cristuru Secuiesc from 364 to 114. The steep decline in enrollment becomes even more striking if we look at the overall numbers for the largest secondary schools of the largest Hungarian church. Enrollment in the secondary schools of the Reformed Church declined by almost 75% within 20 years. In 1920 the Reformed high schools had 8.230 registered students, in 1923 only 5838, in 1926 no more than 3139, 2,427 in 1930, 2,516 in 1934, 2635 in 1937, 2,603 in 1938, and 2,634 in 1939. The decline was almost as pronounced in the Roman Catholic secondary schools, and even more pronounced in some. Thus enrollment declined by 75% in the Hungarian denominational schools, as a whole, as a consequence of Romanian cultural policies.[20]

The decline was the result of financial restraints and aggressive intervention from the outside. Of course, the Hungarian denominational schools, deprived of their estates and lacking state subsidy, could not omit charging tuition. The discounts and rebates so common in former times could now be offered to deserving students only in very limited form. Thus many a Hungarian student was left out of high school on account of poverty. Moreover, very often certain strata of Hungarian society refrained from sending their children to Hungarian denominational schools for extraneous reasons. Those members of the Hungarian intelligentsia who were under the influence of government agencies in one way or another did not dare send their children to Hungarian schools. In many cases, government employees of Hungarian ethnic background were told directly by their supervisors to send their children to a public school with Romanian as the language of instruction. Hungarian civil servants who still retained their government jobs were jeopardizing their position by sending their children to Hungarian denominational schools, especially after 1930. Often their supervisors were content to have them transferred, at which point the Hungarian children had to be registered in a Romanian state public school of Dobrudja or Bessarabia.

The other reason for the decline in enrollment at Hungarian high schools was the well-known restrictions. As mentioned, only students of Hungarian ethnic background, and members of that denomination could enroll in a Hungarian denominational school, according to the Act on Private Education. Thus children of Jewish or other religions could not enroll in a Hungarian denominational school. Moreover, the educational inspectors resorted to the method of name analysis throughout the Greater Romanian regime. Whenever they detected names on the roster of students which they deemed to be non-Hungarian on account of their sound, they immediately decreed the transfer of said student to a school with Romanian as the language of instruction. This complete lack of freedom of instruction contributed to the decline in enrollment of the Hungarian denominational high schools and often elicited a tragic situation. The Roman Catholic high schools were particularly victimized by the process of name analysis. In vain did the parents insist that they were of Hungarian background and belonged to the Roman Catholic Church. The opinion of the Minister was "that he could not accept the principle according to which the parents themselves could decide their children's mother tongue."[21] Subsequent petitions, parliamentary interventions, dispatch of deputations were to no avail. The process of name analysis continued uninterrupted until 1938. In 1938 the Minorities Statute guaranteed the parents' right to decide their children's mother tongue and nationality, at least on paper. Unfortunately, as already mentioned, the Romanian courts found the process of name analysis and the forced transfer of Hungarian children into Romanian public schools legal, in spite of the provisions of the Minority Statute. Thus freedom of instruction did not exist after 1923, the year of the first measures introduced by Anghelescu, and throughout the regime.

How tragic were the consequences can be gathered from an article published in a Catholic weekly. The article refers to an incident at Miercurea Ciuc.

It happened at Miercurea Ciuc. A poor widow registered her talented son at the high school of Miercurea Ciuc. She intended to have her son raised as a priest who will then preach the word of Our Lord to poor and rich alike. The poor widow was also hoping that her son would be her support and keeper in old age. Since she was extremely poor, she could not come up with cost of an education. There was nothing she could do but pray with her good soul for those souls who would enable her son, by means of their donations, to embark on a career as seminarian in a Catholic institution. The name of the poor Csángo boy was György Gyüttő (Gheorghe Ghitiu). The whole village called him Gyüttő from the beginning. The Romanian registration official wrote it as Ghitiu Gyüttő on the birth certificate. Then came the inspector: on the grounds that Ghitiu is a Romanian name — as was the name of his companion Péter Kádár registered as Petru Dogar, as well as students in the 4th and 5th years whose parents claimed to be Hungarian and Roman Catholic, a claim no one had ever challenged — the inspector demanded that they be transferred immediately from the school with Hungarian as the language of instruction to a Romanian-language school. In vain did they refer to Article 35 of the Act on Private Education which explicitly permits students with Hungarian as their mother tongue to register in schools with Hungarian as the language of instruction: in vain did the parents make statements in front of two witnesses to the effect that they are Hungarian and of Roman Catholic religion; nor did the inspectors consider the official certificate issued by the Roman authorities which certified the Hungarian background and

Roman Catholic religion of all four students. The four boys had to leave. Had Minister Anghelescu and executive director Rusu been there in person, and had they witnessed the sobs and cries of the four boys, perhaps they might have relented. Not only the boys, but even the principal had to give up his position at the Hungarian school, for failing to carry out the orders of the inspector immediately and for having listened to the dictates of his conscience, of the certificates, of the law, of justice, and of his supervisors.

The doors of Catholic and Hungarian institutions may never open again to admit György Gyüttő and his companions, even though they are Catholic and Hungarian. All hope for the future dissipated for György Gyüttő. The earnest expectations of his mother turned into bitter disappointment. She went to the small church of the Csángó community, not minding the crowd gathered for the Mass, joined her hands in prayer and raising them to the skies cursed that and all those who ruined her beautifully conceived dream. And her little boy, who could never again think of becoming a priest of the Lord Jesus and step to the altar, became an apprentice cobbler. Will he ever forget all those indignities and injustices he had to suffer: the blind chauvinism which treads across all divine, natural, and human laws? But the curse of the mother has already been uttered, it floats in the air, it has penetrated as far as the throne of God of justice, and woe to him who is struck by it! Not all curses are valid, but that of the unjustly tortured mother certainly is![22]

Thousands of similar cases prove how difficult it was for many Hungarian children to be admitted to Hungarian denominational schools. It is obvious that such devices did not turn the children concerned into Romanians, but it did exclude them from Hungarian schools. And the device of name analysis, as already mentioned, never ceased throughout the whole period.

Those Hungarian children who managed, in spite of all obstacles, to become pupils at Hungarian schools, although in decreasing numbers, had to study four subjects in Romanian. Their opportunities for self-improvement were also limited since the Minister of Education had closed the study groups of Hungarian high school students. It did authorize so-called literary conferences which, however, were hardly a substitute for the study groups. The Minister also made sure that high school students would not get to read newspapers. The reading of political dailies by high school students was banned very early in the game, under severe penalties.

In the school the students were under the supervision of the teachers, and out of school by other state authorities. The police and the gendarmes were instructed to ask all students who misbehaved or got involved in some kind of protest for identification, and enter their observations in the control books in their possession.

Consequently Hungarian students had the impression of being in jail. Only within the thick walls of their school, where they were among themselves or with their teachers, could they feel at peace and protected to a certain extent. A family spirit in which the students felt very much at home prevailed at many of the Hungarian denominational schools.

The Inner Spirit of the Hungarian High Schools

Most of the Hungarian high schools represented Hungarian traditions. Roman Catholic, Calvinist and Unitarian boarding schools could trace their history back to the 16th century. The Roman Catholic boarding schools of Aiud, Odorheiu Secuiesc, and Alba Iulia could also boast of several centuries of a brilliant past, while the Romanian high schools, except for the one at Blaj, had never played a political role of nation-wide significance. While it is true that the erstwhile leaders of the Hungarians of Transylvania graduated from these schools, the schools and their faculty served primarily cultural ends and did not engage in politics. Nor did their role change under the Dual Monarchy. Many a leading politician of future Greater Romania completed his studies in Hungarian denominational high schools without being ostracized or harmed in any way on account of his nationality. There were some Romanian complaints against certain professors at the college of Orăstie after 1905, but none of an ethnic nature against the schools at Cluj or the Calvinist boarding school at Zalău.

Thus Hungarian denominational schools were no particular threat to the Romanian state. In spite of this, after 1923, Romanian educational policies placed the operations of these schools under a real yoke. We have already noted those measures limiting the financial basis of the schools and preventing their restaffing. Apart from these measures the Romanian authorities did everything within their power to ensure the advance of a Romanian spirit, while repressing Hungarian culture and values within these schools.

In 1923, with his ordinance number 100.090, Minister of Education Anghelescu introduced in addition to the study of the Romanian language, the teaching of Romanian history, geography, and government in Romanian as well. These prescriptions were preserved and reinforced in the form of legislation by the Act on Private Education and further laws affecting secondary schools, so that the four subjects had to be taught in Romanian throughout the regime.

The application of the law, along with complementary legislation was intended to ensure increasing space for the Romanian language and spirit. The concept of Anghelescu and other Romanian cultural politicians was to strengthen the patriotic education of minority children by teaching these four so-called national subjects in Romanian. In his French language publication issued in order to convince public opinion abroad, Silviu Dragomir observes, in the name of the Romanian government, that they had introduced the teaching of the four national subjects in Romanian into the minority schools because these constitute "the best means to develop a self-conscious citizenry."[23] It is hard to believe, however, that the Romanians were sincere in this regard. After all, during the Hungarian regime, they had protested for decades against the introduction of Hungarian language as a subject into the Romanian denominational schools. And it was only a matter of the Hungarian language, for in the Romanian high schools of Balázsfalva, Brassó or Naszód all subjects, apart from Hungarian, were taught in the students' Romanian mother tongue; and even the graduation examination was administered by their own teachers in their mother tongue, except for Hungarian language and literature. Hence they must have been aware that learning the language of the state does not promote a self-conscious citizenry. Most assuredly the Romanian cultural leaders had decreed the teaching of the four national subjects in Romanian in order to take up most of the time and spiritual energy of the students, and thus weaken or negate the impact of learning in their mother tongue.

The measures issued by the Ministry of Education regarding the educational policies of the minority high schools confirm this interpretation. The government decided the language of instruction, the methods of instruction, its subjects and the number of hours devoted to each. The secondary schools had to adjust to the official curriculum prescribed for public secondary schools. Each subject was taught in the same number of hours as in the public schools. Only textbooks that had been approved by the Ministry could be used. The teachers had to teach each subject in the prescribed number of hours, and it never happened that the number of contact hours in any subject taught in some Hungarian school would differ from the number of contact hours in the public school. Romanian language and literature was taught more extensively than any other subject. This subject, as well as the

Romanian "national" subjects had to be taught with the greatest
enthusiasm. The Ministry decreed that the "national subjects be
scheduled in the morning between 8 an 11 a.m., and be indicated by red
ink in the schedule of courses." The Romanian inspectors would
consider first of all the subjects underscored in red ink during their
visits.

Comments on the effectiveness of the teaching of the national
subjects was always the most important segment of the report on these
visits. Since these subjects played the most important role on the minor
graduation examination administered at the end of the fourth year as
well as on the graduation examination at the end of the eighth,
naturally the high school students devoted most of their time and
talents to learning these subjects. After 1934 the Romanian spirit
prevailed in the teaching of other subjects too. The law was modified
once again to take the administration of the first general examination
out of the hands of the teachers at minority schools. According to the
restrictions imposed by Anghelescu, a committee of teachers from other
schools, appointed by the Minister, was to decide which student could be
admitted to the fifth year of secondary school. The four national
subjects and the results obtained in them became even more important
to the students after 1934. Often a Hungarian student had to be
content with completing four years of secondary, since professors
unknown to him gave a failing grade on the minor graduation exam,
which was a prerequisite for the fifth year. The difficulties confronting
Hungarian students even exceeded those confronting other minorities
because they could not use their mother tongue in four of the five
subjects composing that examination.

Learning these subjects in Romanian rendered the work of the
minority Hungarian schools extremely difficult. The syllabi for these
courses were most extensive. The textbook for Romanian language and
literature in the lower division of the secondary schools extended over
an average of 200 to 300 pages, whereas in the upper division it was
500 to 600 pages. The textbooks for history and geography comprised
250 to 300 pages each. The contents of these textbooks, which could be
written only by ethnic Romanians, were mostly antagonistic or even
definitely anti-Hungarian. Hungarian children not only had to make
enormous efforts to learn these subjects, but underwent psychological
tortures as well. Moreover, these subjects were taught mostly by native
Romanian teachers, since the Ministry of Education seldom awarded a
license to teach these subjects to members of the Hungarian minority.
In 1929 the leaders of the Roman Catholic Status of Transylvania
requested, in a memorandum to the Maniu cabinet, that the issue be

decided fairly. "There must be an end to the abuse of denying minority teachers, graduates of Romanian universities, a license to teach the Romanian national subjects or the French language."[24] Unfortunately the request made little difference because teachers of Romanian background received a significant salary differential for teaching in Hungarian secondary schools. The Reformed Church District of Transylvania alone paid 2.4 million lei to the Romanian teachers it was compelled to hire to teach the national subjects and French in the academic year 1927-28. In some years the Hungarian schools spent up to 6.7 million lei on salaries to Romanian teachers, which sum exceeded the government subsidy authorized by the regime of the National Peasant Party.

In addition to giving enhanced importance to the national subjects, the Ministry of Education did everything to promote Romanian ideas in the teaching of other subjects as well. Every event taught during the course on world history was viewed from a Romanian perspective. Onisifor Ghibu, professor of Romanian didactics and methodology at the University of Cluj, called this perspective "Romanocentric" and felt it should be mandatory in all schools. Romanocentrism became one of the main criteria for authorizing new textbooks. Issues involving a debate between Romanians and Hungarians had to be taught in the spirit of "continuity" of the Romanian presence; the issue of Romanian uprisings was taught according to the official Romanian concepts. Latin had to be pronounced according to the rules of Romanian pronunciation.

Romanian educational policies extended to the supervision of the students at Hungarian schools even outside the classroom. In 1927 the Minister ordered "the prior censorship of the manuscript of final report cards," requested "the list of books awarded for outstanding performance on examinations, and ordered that the programs for school celebrations be submitted for prior approval," because it wanted to deprive even these occasions from serving as an opportunity for the manifestation of the Hungarian spirit. The report of the Presiding Council of the Reformed District of Transylvania, having reprinted the above orders, adds that the Romanian authorities "take the leadership of the school out of the hands of the church even as regards the most insignificant matters. Soon no right will remain us other than to provide the salaries of the faculty.[25]

Indeed, this evolution of the spirit of the Hungarian secondary schools could only come about because Romanian educational policy was bent on eliminating the former autonomy enjoyed by the Hungarian schools completely. Literally the only right remaining to those in charge of the schools was to come up with the funds for the upkeep of the schools. But even in this area the Hungarian schools did not benefit from all the opportunities that had been available to the Romanian schools under the Hungarian regime. The Ministry prohibited the use of the premises of Hungarian secondary schools — such as the auditorium and conference rooms — for any purpose other than instruction. The one time a collection was organized for the benefit of Hungarian denominational schools, the collection was forbidden.

By prescribing "national" subjects and by the strict control over the teaching of these subjects, Romanian educational policy intended to promote the education of Romanian citizens. At the same time, by its strict control over the subjects taught in Hungarian it intended to repress any possible manifestation of irredentism: in general, it was bent on eliminating any opportunity that might serve to promote the development of Hungarian national consciousness or its consolidation. The various types of educational inspectors and controllers seemed to organize get-togethers at one Hungarian school or another. "The inspector generals, the chief inspectors, the secondary inspectors, the special inspectors for the instruction of Latin, of music, etc.," we read in the above-mentioned report:

> are busy exercising the right of state control. At the final examination in one of our schools four sets of inspectors happened to meet. They take one-sided notes regarding the results of our examinations and if any of their observations require rectification, this can be done only through protracted and usual personal interventions on our part.[26]

According to the prevailing decrees the final report cards had to be in both Romanian and Hungarian. The text of the report card had to be submitted to the Romanian authorities and could only be printed upon obtention of their approval. The Romanian text always had to come first, whereas the Hungarian text had to appear on the back, as something barely tolerated. By keeping track of the books awarded to the most successful candidates, Romanian school authorities were able to force the officials at Hungarian secondary schools to present the good students with Romanian books in addition to the Hungarian ones. This of course posed no threat to the attitude of the children much because they usually abstained from reading the Romanian books, but it did occasion additional expense to the school because it felt obliged to purchase the books demanded by Romanian entities. The procurement of the Romanian flag, of the Romanian national seal, etc., also caused additional financial hardship; as mentioned, such items were provided free of charge to Romanian schools by the Hungarian authorities.

Under the circumstances Hungarian culture could manifest itself only in very moderate ways in the Hungarian secondary schools. Hungarian language was never a mandatory subject on any official examination. It did not figure as a subject at the end of the fourth year, nor on the graduation examination, albeit Romanian language and literature was one of the subjects on the graduation examination in former times. Romanian educational policy carried out what Hungarian policies had not even dreamt of, that the Ministry be in charge of preparing the curriculum even for the subjects taught in the mother tongue of the students at minority secondary schools. Hungarian language and literature could only include material mentioned in the official curriculum issued by the Ministry of Education. Some aspects of Hungarian history could be mentioned in connection with world history or Romanian history, but there was no possibility for the Hungarian students to study their true history in the Hungarian secondary schools since the establishment of Greater Romania. So-called literary conferences were authorized to study issues in literary history. These conferences included readings and recitations.

Study groups with by-laws and formal organization could not exist, as we have seen. Self-development could only take place at the cost of enormous overwork. Yet studying overtime and a more thorough approach to certain subjects was a rather frequent phenomenon in the case of the most outstanding students. Hungarian student groups, inspired by their professors, turned towards the research of Hungarian culture with increasing enthusiasm. They could see with their own eyes and experience personally in Hungarian society that in Romania, Hungarians could attain their ends only by working better and harder than the Romanians. Their professors and church leaders constantly emphasized the need for "meliorism," the predominance of quality over quantity. What is important is not how many of you there may be, they were told, but rather how you are and what inner values you represent. This emphasis on values bore visible fruit. At the religious conferences held at secondary schools the students had the opportunity to discuss individual, religious, and national problems. Thus the intellectual life of the students of Hungarian secondary schools undoubtedly reached a higher level, in their thorough approach and study of issues, than that of students before the war. The better students who attended the denominational schools benefitted from a broader and more profound education than their counterparts before the war. This applied, however, only to the small number of outstanding students. The greater majority was under constant intellectual pressure as a result of the difficulties of bilingual education and did not have the spiritual energy or the time for any deliberate tackling of serious issues. The Hungarian culture, especially its historical aspects, and Hungarian orthography of this majority were sorely lacking. Whoever was inclined to study some problem more thoroughly, for instance some issue of Hungarian history, had to do it at home, or in some library, since this was impossible at school. Consequently these students became thoroughly absorbed in Hungarian history. They viewed the various problems of Hungarian history with a fresh perspective, free of all illusions, enriched by their own social and national experiences.

The sharply anti-state irredentism that formerly characterized the Romanian secondary schools of Hungary was almost completely absent from the inner life of Hungarian secondary schools. There was not a single case where an investigation revealed legitimate grounds for charges of irredentism within Hungarian denominational secondary schools. Considering that all textbooks had to be previously authorized by the Ministry, including books on religion, irredentism in instruction could not manifest itself in any way. Nor could those in charge of the schools have allowed it, since supervision was almost continuous and any attempt at irredentism would have entailed the immediate closing down of the school. Occasionally some high school received a warning on the grounds of irredentism. For instance, the Calvinist boarding school of Cluj received a warning because its students had been singing Hungarian songs in the fields during a visit to old Kingdom of Romania, even though they had not been singing the anthem nor any other song regarded by the Romanians as irredentist such as the Kossuth song, but simple folksongs. Likewise the Roman Catholic high school of Odorheiu Secuiesc received a warning, and even lost its accreditation for a year, because its students got involved in a brawl with the students of the local Romanian high school after a soccer match, and the latter were beaten. The Calvinist high school of Aiud also received a warning because the Romanian inspector visiting during a history class received an answer to one of his questions which seemed to imply a degree of rejection of the notion of the continuity of the Romanian presence in Transylvania. Such cases, usually termed "irredentism," were the grounds for the charges brought up against Hungarian secondary denominational schools.

After 1935 the so-called Country Guard, a centrally-directed educational institution of the Romanian youths, was introduced into some Hungarian denominational schools. This institution was a large-scale experiment designed to place the youth of the entire nation under the impact of strongly nationalist and centrally directed education. The didactic principles of the Country Guard were: respect for the Romanian royal family, respect for the Romanian flag, the practice of certain half-pagan half-Christian rituals, emphasis on physical education and, above all, a unified nationalism. At the beginning of every week the Romanian national flag had to be hoisted on the flagpole in the courtyard of Hungarian schools, under ceremonial circumstances, and lowered at the end of the week in a similar manner. The ritual was punctuated by Romanian slogans, by an exhorting speech in Romanian, and by an "Our Father Who Art in Heaven" recited in Hungarian.[27] Since the recital of Our Father was the only part of the ritual that everybody liked, it was only natural that the greatest attention was devoted to it by the students, especially when the student selected to recite the prayer reached the very meaningful phrase: "and deliver us from evil."   This introduction of the Romanianizing educational institution was surely not in the interest of the Romanian state and its educational goals.

Surveying the area covered by the so-called (so-called, because there was really no purely Hungarian secondary school) Hungarian secondary instruction, we must conclude that the various secondary schools could satisfy the cultural needs of the Hungarian population only in part. It was primarily the full-fledged high schools that stood at the focus of public interest. Hungarian society should have been most interested in ensuring instruction in the Hungarian language in specialized schools, but because of their limited numbers and their inadequate funding these schools could not satisfy the expectations of the population, whereas Hungarian students were increasingly excluded from the public schools, most of which used Romanian as the language of instruction. The public commercial and vocational schools provided instruction exclusively in Romanian from the very beginning, even in towns inhabited mainly by Hungarians.   The enrollment of Hungarian students declined steadily at these schools. According to the data published in the anniversary yearbook issued by the Maniu regime Hungarian students and other non-Romanians formed 90.9% of the students at the public commercial schools in 1918-19, in the areas attached to Romania. By 1922-23 this figure had dropped to 52%, in 1925-26 to 25.8%, and in 1926-27 to 24.5% as opposed to 75.5% Romanians. In the vocational schools the decrease in the number of non-Romanian students was even more pronounced. In 1919-20 there were 39.1% Romanians as opposed to 60.9% non-Romanians, but in 1924-25 there remained but 9% non-Romanians, and in 1927-28 their proportion had dropped to 6.6% even though the ratio of the Hungarian population in these areas reached 25%, even according to the Romanian statistics. Thus Hungarian high school students were excluded not only from the Hungarian schools, but from the Romanian schools as well. In the academic year 1936-37 there were 164,603 students attending 626 public secondary schools of various types. Only 4,655 or 2.7% were Hungarian, although 13,003 would have corresponded to the ratio of the Hungarian population of the country. Thus each year there were 8,348 fewer Hungarian high school students than what the Hungarian population would have, been entitled to by their numbers. Correspondingly, as regards regular high schools, the Hungarians should have been represented by 6,455 students among the 81,714 in the country as a whole, in the year 1937-38. Instead, there were altogether 2,020 Hungarian students attending regular high school. Thus the losses to Hungarian society amounted to several thousand graduates in this area as well.

There were 132 Hungarians among the 24,877 students at state teacher's training schools in 1926-27 (0.7%); since the Hungarian minority amounted to 7.9% of the total population, the proportionate number of students would have been 1,964. Those who gained entrance to public schools were supported by the state, where 443 students received free room and board provided from funds of other institutions. The 1,837 Hungarian youths who were excluded from the teacher's training schools did not benefit from these advantages. There were 405 Hungarians among the 21,307 students attending state commercial schools in the academic year 1926-27 (i.e. 2%), although there should have been 1,683 in proportion to the Hungarian population. Thus 76% of Hungarians were excluded from the commercial schools.[28]

At the beginning there were Hungarian sections at some public schools, but these were phased out gradually. At the end the only Hungarian section still in operation was the one at the Manuit Gojdu high school in Oradea, but even there only a few subjects were taught in Hungarian.

The so-called agricultural schools played a special role among the Hungarian vocational schools. These schools were established after 1930, and they were the only type of secondary school that had not existed before World War I. The first such school was established by the Unitarians at Cristuru Secuiesc in 1930, followed in 1935 by the Roman Catholic school at Tîrgu Secuiesc and the Reformed school at Ciumbrud. The Roman Catholic school at Iernut functioned from 1933-34. The agricultural schools were open only in the winter, when the intelligent youths from the villages were registered for continuing education and trained in various agricultural pursuits. Unfortunately, the status of these schools remained in limbo for a long time; the agricultural school at Ciumbrud was granted accreditation by the Ministry of Education only in 1940.

In some areas the needs of the greatest masses of Hungarians were not satisfied in the least. The various specialized schools, including vocational, commercial, agricultural and home economics schools usually hired only teachers of Romanian background, and none of these schools had Hungarian as their language of instruction. Particularly prejudicial to the health of the Hungarian masses was the circumstance that there were no midwifery schools with Hungarian as the language of instruction anywhere, and thus the Hungarian villages remained completely without trained midwives. As mentioned, even in this area the Hungarians were far worse off than the Romanians had been under Hungarian rule where, according to the data provided by Ghibu, training in midwifery was available in Romanian.

Instruction at the Higher Level.

The fate of the Hungarian University of Cluj was undecided at the time of the change of sovereignty. For the time being the Hungarian professors remained at their post, and most of their courses were taught in the academic year 1918-19. Although the advancing Romanian troops occupied Cluj already by the end of December 1918, they did not interfere with the university for a while. Nicholae Iorga, the historian and other Romanian celebrities were of the opinion that the Hungarian population of a million and a half deserved a Hungarian university; thus some did not wish to harm the Hungarian university, but rather to organize a Romanian university alongside it.

At the prompting of Onisifor Ghibu, however, the opinion of the ruling Romanian circles soon changed, and on May 12, 1919, the Hungarian University of Cluj was taken over by force on behalf of the Romanian state and reopened in the following academic year as a Romanian state institution. The Hungarians decided to set up a Hungarian University with the combined strength of all the Hungarian churches, on the basis of the principles of the Minority Treaty and the decisions of Alba Iulia. This Hungarian university, referred to as the Interdenominational University did indeed open on October 20, 1920. Those in charge duly reported its foundation to the Ministry which, for the time being, merely acknowledged the fact without objecting. But a few months later a professor at the Romanian University of Cluj wrote an article against the Hungarian University and described its establishment as a provocation against the Romanian state. Soon the general mood was such that at the end of the 1920-21 academic year the government closed down the university forever. As Onisifor Ghibu was to admit later, the existence of the Hungarian University could not be tolerated because it would have offered too much competition to the fledgling Romanian university and, in Ghibu's opinion, the Romanians did not as yet have the wherewithal to compete.

Thus only the theological institutes and the Romanian universities remained to satisfy the needs of the Hungarians for higher institutions.

All three Hungarian denominations had their theological institutes for centuries. During the Romanian regime the Reformed and Unitarian institutes were at Cluj, the Roman Catholic theological school at Alba Iulia. In the long run the clerical career was the only one that remained for Hungarian youths where they could start to obtain a diploma without having to take an entrance examination. There were no limitations set on enrollment during most of the Romanian period, and these institutes remained available to the end to satisfy the needs of Hungarian youth.

After the signing of the Treaty of Trianon the leaders of the Hungarian churches took an oath of loyalty to the King of Romania, and the churches were recognized by the state. Soon it was possible to obtain state subsidies for the theological institutes, and their faculty received their government pay regularly throughout the Greater Romanian regime. Of course, the maintenance and repair of the buildings was the responsibility of the diocese and the Hungarian churches received no assistance specifically for this purpose. In fact, some of the buildings of the theological institutes, such as many buildings of the Reformed institute at Cluj, were requisitioned by the Romanian housing office and for over ten years became the headquarters of various government offices. Only under the Maniu regime did they finally succeed in liberating the buildings for their original purpose.

Unlike the previous Hungarian government, the Romanian government did interfere in matters of theological instruction, already in 1922. By its decree 6.046 of February 10 the Minister of Religious Affairs and education ordered the Unitarian and Calvinist theological institutes to teach Romanian language and literature, for two hours a week each, from March 1, 1922 on. History classes in Romanian were strictly mandatory and the seminarians were examined in this subject, as in various theological subjects. A religious spirit prevailed throughout at the public ceremonies of the seminarians and they avoided any item on their programs that might have offended the sensitivities of the Romanian government authorities.

The situation of Hungarian students attending Romanian universities was difficult from the beginning. For a long time they were almost unable to make headway in the antagonistic atmosphere. In the first years very few Hungarian candidates even dared register at a Romanian university. During the first decade, from 1919 to 1929, there was an average of 2,461 students attending the University of Cluj. Of these, 208 were Roman Catholic, 106 Calvinist, and 16 Unitarian Hungarians. From a comparison of the number of Romanian and Hungarian students attending other universities it becomes clear that several hundred Hungarian students were excluded from the universities as well, each year. According to the statistics on education contained in an official publication of the Ministry of Education, altogether 823 degrees in law were awarded at the four Romanian universities between 1925 and 1929. If the Hungarian population had been duly represented, Hungarian students should have earned 65 diplomas, whereas only 12 of them did. Thus the Hungarian population had 53 fewer law graduates every year. Of the 457 medical degrees awarded each year the Hungarian students should have earned 36; instead, only four did, which meant that the Hungarian population lost 32 graduates in medicine each year. Hungarian students should earned 10 of the 134 diplomas in pharmacology awarded each year, and in this field the Hungarians did earn the number of diplomas commensurate with their ratio of the population. As regards doctorates in philosophy the Hungarians should have earned 39, but obtained only six, losing 33 Ph.D.'s a year. The Hungarians should have earned 23 of the 297 degrees in science awarded each year, but obtained only three. Each year the Hungarians came up short by 102 degrees of various kinds, including 41 doctorates; hence their intellectual losses amounted to 80.3%.[29]

These data indicate that far fewer Hungarian students studied and obtained diplomas from Romanian universities than what their ratio of the total population would have entitled them to. Thus the replacement of Hungarian professionals fell short by almost three-fourths. This halting of the replacement process was not the result of natural evolution. Impoverished as it was, Hungarian society could seldom afford the many kinds of expenses involved in university studies. This was particularly true as regards students from a rural background. The funds of the ecclesiastic and social foundations which served to provide for them were lost as a consequence of the land reform, while the Romanian state provided very few scholarships to young Hungarians.

There was yet another reason for the small number of Hungarian university students: the entrance examination. After 1930 some departments would admit only students who had passed a stiff entrance examination. From 1934 on, a Hungarian student could be admitted to the School of Medicine only by way of exception, as a result of acquaintance with some distinguished professor. This amounted to open, rather than veiled "numerus clausus" as regards the Hungarian students, who found themselves excluded from the universities in even greater proportions from then on.

When Anghelescu returned to head the Ministry of Education, towards the end of 1933, this old representative of Romanian chauvinism did not delay in coming up with fresh measures against Hungarian university students. Noting from the statistics that the overwhelming majority of the students in the School of Pharmacology at the University of Cluj were of Hungarian background, he closed down that school in the Fall of 1934 and transferred it to the University of Bucharest. Thus he barred many Hungarian students from the possibility of continuing their studies, since the students from Transylvania could ill afford to complete their studies far away from home.[30] The consequence was as expected; the number of Hungarian candidates in pharmacology diminished rapidly.

Romanian educational policies not only prevented the existence of a university with Hungarian as the language of instruction but made it more difficult for Hungarian students to study at Romanian universities year after year, especially after 1930. By introducing the entrance examination in 1934 it almost completely barred candidates of other than Romanian background from the possibility of studying medicine.

Students at Romanian universities attempted to organize after the first few years. They felt that since the Romanians had been free to organize in Budapest under the Dual Monarchy and cultivate their national consciousness within the Petru Maior Student association, Hungarian students should also have the right to establish a student association on a national basis. Once again they were wrong. The university authorities barred them from organizing on a national basis by degree. There was no association of Hungarian students at any university during the interwar period.

Many enlightened Romanians did not approve of such a solution of the issue of the Hungarian student associations. In 1932 Ghiţă Pop, Undersecretary of Religious Affairs in the Maniu cabinet, openly condemned the policy of barring Hungarian student associations. He confronted Prime Minister Iorga who, in agreement with the Romanian university authorities at Cluj, rejected the application of the Hungarian students requesting permission to organize. Ghiţă Pop wrote as follows:

> I would feel it a dereliction of duty on my part if I did not point out in a few lines how mistaken is the argument propounded by the prime-minister in the Senate against the establishment of minority student associations.
>
> I find it necessary to declare from the start that this article was not inspired by a spirit of contradiction. The minorities problem is far more important and complex than to serve as a gimmick in aimless party struggles. Quite apart from all this, whatever the momentary stand taken by Professor Iorga, he can rightfully expect not to be mistaken for a streetcorner nationalist.
>
> Although it was precisely Iorga who was responsible for the theoretical and actual spread of Romanian nationalism before the war he never committed the mistake so characteristic of the loud and superficial nationalist after the war. The mistake of continuing to confront those nations with whom we had to fight, first in the political arena, then militarily, in order to win our national freedom, in the same antagonistic tone.
>
> As I assess sincerely this attitude of Iorga, I nevertheless feel bewildered by his rejection of the petition filed by Senator József Sándor recommending the authorization of minority student associations.
>
> This is not the place to argue the theory of freedom of association for national minorities. Since this right is recognized in practically all nation-states. The possibility for minority students to establish associations on a national basis also derives from this general right. If citizens belonging to minority groups who are not students at any university are free to join economic, trade, cultural, scientific, and even political associations and, indeed, they take advantage of this right, since their party participates in elections with an official slate of candidates, their candidates do get elected to parliament, it is absurd and senseless to make an exception of university students. When a few years ago the University of Cluj decreed that Hungarian university students may not organize along national lines I could hardly believe that professors who had been subjected to Hungarian oppression in Transylvania should fall into the same error. No matter how strong this term may appear, this struck me as an atrocity.

Student associations do not have and cannot have a political character; their objectives can only be cultural, educational, or comradely. The minority student cannot be forbidden from being interested in his literature and culture, or from developing himself within the framework of literary and scientific associations like the Romanian students do, for after all this is the calling of a university student. He cannot be forced to sign up with Romanian associations and live in a purely Romanian environment, unless he sincerely feels such a need. The matter becomes even more serious if what *Dimineaţa* claimed the other day is true, that the Romanian associations reject those minority students who wish to join. Is it wise and well-considered to awaken within the minority students from Transylvania or Bessarabia a feeling of persecution and deprivation of rights? And if one day we should uncover secret student organizations, should we not blame ourselves if the minority students refer to the misconception that they were forced to embark on this wayward road by our policies? Would it not be better to authorize such associations, which could be checked at any time since they would be operating legally, rather than promote some underground organization operating without controls, which could easily embark upon dangerous political tendencies?

But let us turn from theoretical debates to the realm of action. Our critics who constantly blame us for "defending" the minorities, intend to disarm us with much the same argument. They keep referring to the past, asking the academic question whether the Hungarians treated us better before the unification, and did they not persecute the Romanian language sufficiently? But their argument does not hold water because the sins committed under former Hungarian rule cannot serve to justify the sins of the new Romanian rule.

In the present instance their arguments are all the more incorrect as they are based on lack of information; for in Austria-Hungary student association could operate freely on a national basis. There were many legally established Romanian student organizations before unification, such as the "Carmen Sylva" in Graz, the "Romania Junǎ" in Vienna, the "Petru Maior" in Budapest, not to mention any number of Romanian student associations in Cernowitz. "Julia," the Romanian student association of Cluj was dissolved in 1896, as a result of false and ill-intentioned charges raised by the chauvinistic officials of the Hungarian university, if I am not mistaken...

Finally allow me to formulate the basic principle of the minority policy of the Romanian state: we must not indulge in a treatment worse than what we had been subjected to before unification in any area of the broad conglomeration of minority issues in the pertinent provinces. Secondly, we must not consider the rights granted to the oppressed Romanians in former times as the maximum that can be granted to our own minorities, but only as a minimum state of affairs and of law; let us grant them more rights rather than less than those enjoyed by ourselves in our time of servitude.

I cannot believe that Mr. Prime Minister would object to these basic principles and therefore I am confident that his loyalty and goodwill will find the means to rectify the mistake.[31]

But Ghiţă Pop's confidence in the goodwill of Iorga proved unwarranted. True, the Iorga cabinet soon fell, but its successors were in no hurry to realize the principles enunciated by Pop. The issue of Hungarian student associations remained unresolved during the entire Romanian regime. A few years later the students at the Romanian University of Cluj were discreetly informed that the officials would be willing to authorize a student association of Hungarian character under the name "Székely-land and vicinity." Yet the projected student association never materialized, because official authorization was not forthcoming. The Hungarian students by then were so wary of the intentions of the university that they did not resort to the method proposed; they feared that by stressing "Székely-land" the officials were intent on dividing the Hungarian student body. Therefore they did not push for the establishment of the association on the conditions offered.

Lacking associations catering to Hungarian students, the latter engaged in cultural and study activities through various religious associations. Thus the situation foreseen by Ghiţă Pop in his article was realized in part: Hungarian university students found room within church organizations, outside the jurisdiction of the university authorities. In fact the students were better off, for thus they avoided even the appearance of engaging in politics, which would not have been so easy within the framework of official student associations. Thus the Hungarian students did not fall into the situation the Romanian students had experienced long ago in becoming the carriers of extremist, and ultranationalist political movement within the Petru Maior and other such Romanian associations. The masses of students who joined the Iron Guard and who, after 1936, confronted official Romania with frightening power and shook the University of Cluj to its foundations, came from the ranks of these student associations. In the course of 1938 and 1939 they organized massive ultranationalist and anti-Semitic political demonstrations and attacked not only politicians but at times, their own professors. In 1939 they waylaid the Rector of the University at the corner of some street, with revolver shots. The Rector miraculously survived the attack, but the university officials surely regretted having granted Romanian university students such extensive means for political activity.[32]

Hungarian university students did not take part in such movements. They had to study in earnest in order to pass their examinations in the increasingly unfriendly atmosphere. They prepared for their calling with perseverance, if in diminishing numbers, and this was an enormous boost for the Hungarian population vegetating in untold misery.

The situation of students of Hungarian background attending Romanian universities was rendered most difficult throughout by financial deprivation, the obstacles to admission, and the ban on student organizations for Hungarians. Comparing the situation of the Hungarian university students with that of the Romanian university students attending Hungarian universities during the period of the Dual Monarchy, we note a marked decline in every respect. The financial difficulties experienced by Hungarian students were incomparably more serious. The Romanian students in former times had their tuition expenses covered for the most part by the various scholarship funds, the Gojdu and other foundations. Moreover, the various strata of Romanian society improved year after year financially, ensuring support for the students from home as well. Such financial advantages were not available to Hungarian students. The cultural foundations which might have provided the scholarships lost their resources as a consequence of the Romanian land reforms. Every class of Hungarian society grew poorer from year to year. The few remaining institutions, such as the University Student Board of Cluj, were taken over by the Romanian authorities and converted into state institutions. The Kata Bethlen association formed to assist students at Tîrgu Mureş was also closed down, whereas the Study Foundation of the county of Trei-Scaune was used for purposes other than those originally intended. Hungarian university students could count only on the pennies contributed by members of Hungarian society. Thus assistance to Hungarian students under the Romanian regime could only come from collections; the product of these, as we know, was indeed continuous and at times quite impressive.

Moreover, the situation of the Hungarian students was rendered more difficult by restrictions on admissions. They could register at Romanian universities without major obstacles until 1930, but after that it became increasingly difficult for Hungarian students to obtain diplomas from Romanian universities. They seldom dared attend foreign universities — nor did they have the financial means to do so — because the Romanian government would recognize diplomas obtained abroad only after years of processing. Thus, in this area as well, Hungarian university students were far worse off than Romanian students formerly.

Surveying the evolution of educational opportunities available to Hungarians under Romanian rule we may note that, except for the first two promising years, their situation was increasingly unfavorable year after year. In 1919 the Governing Council of Sibiu launched the direction of educational opportunities for minorities in the spirit of the decisions of Alba Iulia. From 1920, however, when the administration of Greater Romania became centered in Bucharest, the situation of schooling, for Hungarians, deteriorated continuously. The teaching of Romanian, and of the history, geography, and government of Romania was introduced from the start. After 1923 it was no longer easy for Hungarian children to study in their mother tongue. The four national subjects had to be taught in Romanian in every school, and this excessive attention to a foreign language absorbed most of the energies of the Hungarian students during the Greater Romanian period. They could study in their mother tongue only in small part, and the Hungarian denominational schools, deprived of their autonomy by the government, became bilingual throughout.

With the exception of two or three, the Hungarian denominational schools applied for state support in vain. They lost their financial foundation as a result of the Romanian land reform. The churches supporting them became impoverished for the same reason. As a consequence of government measures they lost the advantages that every denominational school had enjoyed under the former Hungarian regime. The franking privileges of the Hungarian schools were withdrawn, teachers and professors no longer received discounts on the railroads and, by depriving the schools of their accreditation, the government brought about a situation in which the Hungarian schools had to incur heavy expenses to pay the Romanian faculty who came to examine the Hungarian children. Further serious expenses were incurred by the requirement to purchase the Romanian national flag, Romanian historical pictures and Romanian books, in contrast to the

Hungarian government during the Dual Monarchy when such items were provided to the Romanian schools free of charge.

The situation of the teaching staff became incomparably worse than that of the former Romanian teaching corps on Hungarian territory. Hungarian teaching staff had to survive on minimal salaries. Hungarian teachers never enjoyed the benefits enjoyed by Romanian teachers after 1906 when Apponyi granted them salary subsidies without in the least infringing on the autonomy of Romanian schools. Only exceptionally, could Hungarian teachers teach the Romanian national subjects, and they needed ministerial authorization to be so employed. The so-called *Capacitate* examination, made the replacement of Hungarian teachers and the granting of tenure to young teachers impossible, hence the younger teachers experienced immeasurable misery.

Freedom of instruction did not exist for Hungarian students throughout the period. The right of the parents to select a school of their choice was limited by the arbitrary decisions taken by Romanian educational authorities indulging in the practice of name analysis. Enrollment at Hungarian schools decreased year after year as a result of this analysis and of the requirements regarding admissions. Students of a different religion or nationality could not attend a Hungarian school, and never during the regime could the child of Hungarian citizens attend a Hungarian school in Romania.

The autonomy of Hungarian schools ceased completely as a result of the laws sponsored by Anghelescu. The formerly public Hungarian denominational schools sank to the level of private schools and most of the preparatory schools were unable to obtain accreditation until 1940. As noted by the most significant educational report of the Hungarian churches, the only right remaining to those in charge of the schools was to find ways and means of coming up with the funds to maintain the schools. The autonomy of the Hungarian schools of Romania shrank to absolutely zero, in comparison with the autonomy enjoyed by the Romanians of Hungary during the Dual Monarchy.

In consideration of public opinion abroad, the Romanian state did not prohibit Hungarian denominational teaching, but it did set conditions which made it impossible for these schools to prosper and, in fact, forced these schools to become less and less effective.

The Romanian government explained this strict control over the Hungarian schools to international public opinion by arguing that these were nests of irredentist activities and that, in any case, in most cases these schools were superfluous, since the government, at great expense, maintained public schools with Hungarian as the language of instruction. In reality, however, the public schools with Hungarian as the language of instruction, or with Hungarian sections, gradually ceased to exist, and Hungarian was replaced by Romanian as the language of instruction. By 1938 there was not a single public school with Hungarian as the actual language of instruction, since the 44 state primary schools which theoretically had Hungarian as their language of instruction became Romanian in 1937-38. By then the public secondary schools were likewise exclusively Romanian, and Hungarian language sections were non-existent.

On the basis of the above, it may be concluded that the issue of education for the Hungarians under Romanian rule deteriorated year after year as a result of the Romanianization policies of the successive Romanian cabinets, and the Hungarians did not have the option of sending their children to schools where they could study in their mother tongue.

Hungarian Cultural Institutions Other than Schools

The cultural needs of the Hungarians under Romanian rule were satisfied by various associations, by theatrical performances, by the Hungarian press, and above all by various Hungarian literary associations. The most prestigious of these associations was the Transylvanian Museum Association (E.M.E), the Hungarian Cultural Association of Transylvania, the various casinos, women's associations, and choral and reading clubs. The Hungarians of Transylvania were served by the permanent theatrical company of Cluj and various traveling companies struggling with constant difficulties. The press was represented by dailies and various trade journals. All these organizations tried to perform their function under similar difficulties during the Romanian regime.

The Transylvanian Museum Association

Like the Romanian Astra, the Transylvanian Museum Association was established during the Austrian autocratic regime that came to power in 1849. Founded in 1959, it was always basically Hungarian because of its membership and its objectives. Naturally, it opted for Hungarian as its official language and even the representative of the Austrian autocratic regime recognized its Hungarian character without ado. Under the Austrian regime the ruler had the final word in the selection of its officials.

Eventually, as a result of the sacrifices made by its members, the association acquired a rich scientific patrimony. Its collection of minerals, its botanical collection, its enormously valuable library and other collections grew out of individual donations. When the Hungarian University of Cluj was founded in 1872, this collection of the E.M.E. was rented for purposes of university instruction. From then on the various collections, including the zoological, the botanical, the mineral, and the library itself were at the disposal of the university, and the Hungarian state in charge of the university paid a rental determined by contract. Members of the university were delegated as curators of the various collections. If the association trusted a given university professor, the latter was customarily selected as its curator. The professors were usually elected members of the association, thus eliminating any chance of friction from the start. The relationship of the association to the state was regulated by a special contract. The contract was respected by the Hungarian state which always paid punctually, the rental stipulated for the usage of the various collections of the association. The association covered its expenses from this rental charge as well as from the revenue it derived from an apartment house it owned in Cluj. The association's expenditures included its scientific and popular cultural conferences as well as the cost of various publications. During the Hungarian regime the E.M.E. entertained friendly relations with the Romanian Astra; it was represented at several general assemblies, including the anniversary meeting of Astra at Blaj, when E.M.E. expressed its good wishes in a cable signed by its secretary.

The change in sovereignty entailed a radical alteration in the situation of the E.M.E. Soon the issue of the use and ownership of the scientific collections arose, as a consequence of which the legal status of E.M.E. remained unsettled throughout the duration of the regime. It could function only at the cost of enormous efforts, of a constant defensive struggle, and under various restrictions.

The Romanian government, as we have seen, took over the Hungarian University of Cluj by force on May 12, 1919 and transformed it into a Romanian State University as of 1919-20. The officials of the Romanian University did not hesitate to use the scientific collections of the association. When, however, the E.M.E. requested the rental for the use of the collections the Romanian government refused to pay.[33]

At the same time the building owned by the Association was requisitioned by the housing office and no income was derived from it for over ten years.

Consequently, the financial situation of the E.M.E. became hopeless. At the beginning it could not hold meetings and conferences because of the state of emergency the Romanians declared in Cluj from 1918 to 1928. Thus E.M.E. became entirely inactive, not only because of its lack of a budget but also because of these external constraints. This state lasted for many years without any favorable turn in the situation of the association.

The officials of the association took the stand, from the start, that the contract between the association and the Hungarian state expired along with the Hungarian control of the territories and the closing down of the Hungarian Francis Joseph University. It offered therefore to sign a new contract with the Romanian state and to reserve the use of its collection for the Romanian university. The Romanian government did not accept this approach; regarding itself as the rightful heir of the Hungarian state, it considered the contract to be still in effect. Nevertheless, it refused to pay the yearly rental.

In 1921 the association elected new officials. These officials began to work on the legitimation of the association, but this project ran into enormous difficulties. The multitude of memoranda and deputations dispatched each year had but one result: at the recommendation of the Romanian faculty, the government began to claim the ownership of the collections of the association. But since it was forced to restrain itself, it attempted to achieve its objective in roundabout ways. One such way was to prevent the association from functioning and refuse recognition from its officials. The association, attempting to adapt to the new relations in 1924, modified its bylaws according to the prescriptions of the Romanian laws. It submitted the modified by-laws to the courts for approval and registration. But, upon a secret denunciation by Romanian professors from the University of Cluj, the modification of the bylaws was declared "forging of bylaws" and charges were placed against the officials of the association. The officials were cleared during the proceedings. Under number 4.010/612-1925 the tribunal of Cluj recognized the E.M.E. as a legal entity, but required that it operate under the bylaws adopted in 1905. These bylaws prescribed that the selection of the board of directors of the association had to be reviewed by the ruler. Prompted by the professors of the Romanian University, the government insisted on maintaining this formality even though the Romanian constitution did not require confirmation by the ruler in the case of cultural associations. The Ministry appointed Dr. Nicolae Drăganu, professor at the university, as the government's delegate to the association, in order to make sure that the bylaws of 1905 were observed.

In 1925, in order to resolve the issue of the ownership of the scientific collections that were at the core of the debate, a Romanian university professor, Dr. Alexandru Borza, came up with a clever device. He sent an application to the direction of the E.M.E. requesting the admission of 85 new Romanian members into the association. The candidates were well-known scholars in Romania. The bylaws of the association provided for rights as regards the admission of new members. The direction realized that if it admitted 85 Romanian members the association would have more Romanians than Hungarians. The Romanian majority could easily have voted for the surrender of the right of ownership over the scientific collections at a general meeting in order to hand these over to the university on a permanent basis. Indeed, this was the idea behind Borza's application, as it soon filtered out. The direction of the E.M.E. removed the issue of the admission of Romanian members from its agenda and brought about no decision.[34]

Having tried Borza's device the government returned to its former method. It declared that it would not recognize the officials of the association and would not submit their names for the king's approval. Therefore the officials of E.M.E. resigned and the association elected new officials. The government was notified regarding this new leadership and requested to submit the names for supreme confirmation. The government, however, left the memorandum unanswered for a while. Towards the end of 1926 the government finally informed the association that it had entrusted executive director Zenobie Pâclişanu from the Ministry of Religious Affairs to negotiate with the leaders of the association. These negotiations, however, did not prove fruitful, because the Romanian government demanded that the association surrender its right of ownership to its scientific collections and hand these over to the Romanian university. The association refused to comply. Its new memorandum was left unanswered and the confirmation of its officials was delayed once again.

In 1928 Professor Borza renewed his former proposal regarding membership for 87 Romanian scholars. The officials of the association declared that they would agree to decide regarding the membership applications only if the legal status of the association was cleared satisfactorily. The conditions for this clarification were as follows: the E.M.E. should award membership to the 87 Romanian scholars, should correspond with the university in Romanian, should elect a Romanian vice-president and secretary, should use no more than 10,000 lei of the sum paid for the usage of the collection for administrative purposes, while the remainder would be earmarked for the maintenance of the collections. The proposal elicited a great deal of resentment among the members of the E.M.E. since it appeared that if it was accepted the collections would be confiscated. In the course of renewed negotiations in 1929 the officials of the E.M.E. went to great lengths for the sake of reaching an understanding, but insisted on retaining the right of ownership to the collections. Since the government was bent on removing these from Hungarian custody, the negotiations once again fell through. In 1930 the government once again resorted to the old method and declared that it refused to submit the names of the officials elected in 1925 for supreme confirmation. The Romanian professors at the University of Cluj also repeated the moves they had attempted formerly and denounced the association to the court that had jurisdiction over legal persons. The denunciation proved without merit and they were unable to force the association to give up its collections. After four years of hesitations the government finally submitted the names of the officials who by then had been operating for almost ten years for the confirmation of the ruler. Thus part of the dispute was settled, but the right of ownership was still not clarified. During the entire period the university was able to use the scientific collections without paying anything.

Because of the international conjuncture in 1938 it became necessary to rectify the most blatant injustices, at least on paper. The minutes of the cabinet meeting held on August 1, 1938, included a promise to clarify the situation of the Museum Association. "The situation of the Transylvanian Museum Association is settled in a just manner in accordance with the provisions of its charter." Unfortunately no concrete measure was adopted to fulfill the promise and the legal status of the E.M.E. remained in limbo.

This protracted struggle was prejudicial to the activities of the association. The work launched in 1921 in its various sections was soon halted. The members of the association grew pessimistic and the organization of scientific conferences appeared futile to many of them. Authorization to hold conferences encountered enormous difficulties and, because of its dire financial straits, it was often unable to cover the most minimal expenses. The apartment house owned by the association provided practically no income because of the requisitions and the forced lodgings. For ten years the association did not even have sufficient funds to print the programs of the conferences, and the most basic expenses, such as postage, had to be covered by donations from members.

In 1930 the apartment building was finally released from the various requisitions and, at the same time, the legal status of the association was cleared to some extent. Another factor that contributed to the circumstances was that in 1928 a royal decree lifted prior censorship and the state of emergency that had been declared ten years earlier. With a sigh of relief the association began to reorganize its former activities. It held conferences and meetings, organized tours, and became most active in popularizing the sciences in the provincial towns. Thereafter it organized tours yearly, providing the Hungarians in the provincial towns with a great deal of satisfaction. Hungarian scholars were welcomed at Tîrgu Mureş, Aiud, Baia Mare [Nagybánya], Braşov, Sfîntu Gheorghe, Odorheiu Secuiesc, and Turda in turn, where they gave account of the latest scientific achievements under the suspicious eyes of the Romanian authorities. Unfortunately, after 1934 the difficulties kept increasing. Prior censorship was reintroduced in 1934, as was the state of siege, setting up obstacles to the authorization of tours. The speakers at a conference in Turda were harassed by the police, whereas the popularizing lectures in Cluj were banned for several months on account of a history lecture.

Nevertheless, the work of the E.M.E. was significant even under the circumstances. By the end of 1937 it had sponsored 237 conferences, 114 lectures in philosophy, philology, and history, 163 lectures in the natural sciences, and 257 in medical science. During the first twenty years of Romanian rule it published eight volumes of the periodical *Erdélyi Múzeum* [Museum of Transylvania], including 903 articles and 45 tables totalling 3,400 pages. Its series *Erdélyi Tudományos Füzetek* [Scientific Notebooks of Transylvania] printed 101 works on 2,730 pages.[35] Moreover, it published memorial volumes pertaining to five tours. On the occasion of its 75th anniversary it published an index to its scientific publications and commissioned the history of its various sections. In addition to all this it guided and kept a record of the literary and scientific activities of the Hungarian population of Transylvania, and provided the most needed services to promote these. Had it not been for the obstacles set against it by the Romanian governments it would certainly have played an even more important role. Under the circumstances, its significance and situation were nothing like what was enjoyed by Astra under Hungarian rule, during the period of the Dual Monarchy.

The Fate of the Hungarian Cultural Association of Transylvania

Before World War I the Hungarian Cultural Association of Transylvania, or E.M.K.E. by its Hungarian initials, considered the redemption of the Hungarian population scattered in predominantly Romanian areas as one of its tasks. It attempted to redeem the Hungarian children in the villages or areas subject to the Romanianization process. With the help of various foundations it established an agri-

cultural school at Geoagiu [Algyógy]. It tried to achieve this by social
and cultural means rather than pressure from the authorities. The
Romanians, however, regarded these activities as nothing less than
criminal, and the E.M.K.E. was subjected to the most vehement attacks
in the press already during that period: it was accused of forced
Hungarianization, of racism.

After the change of sovereignty it lost all its estates with the
exception of 69 *holds* of forests. The expropriation was illegal since the
law stipulated that in addition to the buildings, the yards, and orchards
the E.M.K.E. would have been entitled to 100 *holds* of fields, 200 *holds*
for its agricultural institute and 30 *holds* of land for its orphanage on
account of its status as a model estate. The association appealed the
decision of the agrarian committee in the first instance to a higher
court, on the basis of this law. It received no response for years, until
1930. Then the E.M.K.E., realizing that the *Comitetul Agrar* was
delaying the discussion of the case without justification, retracted its
appeal, as permitted by law. The *Comitetul Agrar*, however, declared
that it would not accept the retraction, inasmuch as it now intended to
reach a decision.[36] Of course, it brought about the decision in a
biased way and E.M.K.E. lost all its material possession except for those
69 *holds*.

In the meantime the Romanian owners settled on the expropriated
lands. The agricultural institute of Geoagiu was Romanianized and no
further Székely children — for whom the institute had been intended —
were allowed to enroll in it. In 1924 the tomb of Count Kocsárd Kun,
the founder of the institute, was broken into and desecrated by
"unknown culprits." The officials of the E.M.K.E. requested the
Romanian administration of the agricultural institute to restore the
crypt, but all in vain. The request was ignored; what's more, the
unknown culprits broke into the crypt a second and a third time and
scattered the bones of the great founder. The association could not
defend the memory of its former founder effectively because it had to
battle for its own survival. An investigation was launched against the
E.M.K.E. as a consequence of attacks in the Romanian press. Albeit the
first investigation cleared the association, the attacks in the press were
renewed, and a second investigation was launched. Then investigations
followed each other in quick succession, some lasting up to two years.
Finally the Romanian university professor in charge of the investigation
cleared the association, but its legal status was recognized only after
fifteen years of struggle. It could begin its work once again in 1935.
Since for fifteen years its was not recognized as a legal entity it was out
of touch with the Hungarian public to the point where it could

reorganize only slowly. In fact, it did not engage in any significant activity during the remaining years of the period.[37]

The history of the two great Hungarian associations was typical of the fate of all other cultural associations. Indeed, most Hungarian associations were closed down already in the first years of the Romanian regime. The recognition of the legal entity of those that survived came about only as a result of lengthy processes. Sometimes the documents submitted got lost, and it took years to replace them. It was extremely difficult to establish new associations and, after a while, completely impossible. A typical example is that of the Hungarian Nation's League Association of Romania. The objective of the association was to popularize the League of Nations, along the lines of similar organizations in other countries. The Hungarian representatives would have liked to establish it in Cluj, but they were unable to secure authorization to hold the organizational meeting for two years, on account of the strict measures of the state of emergency. The founding assembly met in 1927 at Odorheiu Secuiesc. The application for recognition as a legal entity was rejected by the Ministry of the Interior (under number 40.577/1927) on grounds that "legal entity cannot be granted to the Hungarian Nation's League Association of Romania."[38]

Of all the associations the choral societies enjoyed relatively better opportunities for organization. Choral societies were organized by the Hungarian Choral Association of Romania, founded on November 13, 1921. At this time there were altogether 31 choral clubs in former Hungarian areas. Thanks to the association's determined effort over the years, 356 more clubs were established, and thanks to the guidance of the association these clubs performed commendable work on behalf of Hungarian musical culture. The association organized district and national competitions, and took the initiative for the annual commemoration of the death of the great Hungarian poet, Sándor Petőfi, held every year at Sighişoara on July 31. In addition to the competitions, the association organized courses for choral directors. In the thirties the association sometimes encountered difficulties in holding the contests because the Romanian authorities viewed even these with suspicion. Therefore the leaders of the association tried to secure authorization for these competitions by requesting some member of the royal family to act as official sponsor. The request met with a favorable response on several occasions and ensured authorization for the contests.

Hungarian cultural life in general was paralyzed by prior censorship and the state of emergency which were in effect, except for five years, during the twenty-two years of the regime in most areas inhabited by Hungarians. The censors often rendered even the most innocent manifestations of Hungarian culture impossible. They hampered not only the press and theatrical performances, but limited the possibility of publishing books as well. Hence the cultural opportunities available to the Hungarian population outside of the schools were just as limited as those available within the schools.

These limitations were particularly evident when it came to the press and theatrical performances. These two important aspects of culture outside the school walls could become factors only under the most sever restrictions.

The Hungarian Press

Before World War I the Hungarian press in Transylvania was extensive, by provincial standards. Of course, this press was not of a standard to compete with that of Budapest, but it served Hungarian cultural ends well by its coverage of local issues and by providing space for literary talents. The great pioneer and master of Hungarian journalism, Miklós Bartha began his brilliant career in Cluj. There were something like fifteen to twenty dailies and innumerable weeklies and journals published in Transylvania immediately before the change in sovereignty.

The change in sovereignty placed Transylvanian journalism on an entirely new footing. The leading role of Budapest came to an end. A new Hungarian press evolved within the boundaries of the new country, mostly from Transylvanian and Hungarian papers already in existence. Placed on an independent footing the Hungarian dailies soon divested themselves of their provincial character and assumed an increasingly nationwide significance. The Hungarian population, isolated from the Hungary of Trianon and its press, and under Romanian rule, became avid readers. "One of the touching manifestations of the great collapse," wrote the famous journalist Spectator (Miklós Krenner) in this connection, "was that people began to read feverishly according to what they felt most deeply during the dire moments of chaos: pain, hesitation, unemployment, compulsion to criticize or to act."[39]

It was mainly the new Hungarian press of Transylvania that satisfied this yearning for reading materials. Most cities soon acquired their own weekly, or even daily. Dailies circulated at Arad, Timişoara, Braşov, Oradea, and Cluj, whereas elsewhere it was mostly weeklies. While before World War I Arad and Oradea had been the centers of the press of Transylvania, soon after the war Cluj became the undebatable center of the Hungarian press. It was the city with the largest Hungarian population, the Romanian Governing Council moved there from Sibiu, the most important Hungarian institutions were formed here, and the Bucharest embassies of various countries set up consulates here. All these factors contributed to making Cluj the center of the Hungarian press of Transylvania.

Two newspapers distinguished themselves among the dailies of Cluj from the beginning: the *Keleti Újság* and the *Ellenzék*. Both became recognized factors in the intellectual life of the Hungarians of Transylvania. Other dailies of nation-wide significance evolved in Brașov, *(Brassói Lapok)* and Timișoara *(Temesvári Hírlap)*, etc.

The first decade of the history of the Hungarian press in Romania was characterized by favorable financial conditions. Often the only reading material the impoverished Hungarian masses could afford was the inexpensive newspaper. Thus journalism even became good business in those years.[40] It sufficed to recruit a few writers and rent them a place by the month to launch a new paper. Quite a few Transylvanian papers got started in this way. Naturally this situation was harmful to the more serious press, since often persons without any talent or competence were hired as editors or journalists, and their activities resulted in amateur weeklies or dailies. Sometimes these papers managed to survive for quite a while by obtaining the support of the masses on account of their low cost.

It was during this period of the Hungarian press of Transylvania that the union of journalists was initiated by János Székely, the editor of the economic journal *Consum*. At first it functioned under the name of Association of Journalists of the Minorities of Transylvania and the Banat. Its objectives were to protect and represent the professional interests of newspapermen. Such an institution was needed from the start because the papers were able to pay the journalists sufficient royalties to enable them to live well as a result of their profits. Soon another organization of journalists was launched in Cluj — the so-called Journalist's Home, which maintained premises open only to journalists at the beginning. Similar clubs of journalists were formed in other cities. Unfortunately, in most places these clubs increasingly departed from their original purpose to become places of entertainment where roulette and other facilities contributed to the revenues collected.[41] These enterprises provided good income in most places to the journalists who had a share in the clubs. Its harmful effects soon became manifest because often the actual profession of the journalist became merely a second job, since the income from the club far exceeded the income they could obtain from their work as journalists. Naturally, this process led to a decrease in standards for the Hungarian press of Transylvania and served only to obtain a bad reputation for the journalist clubs. In the meantime, as economic conditions worsened and the rate of impoverishment of the Hungarians of Transylvania increased further, the publication of newspapers no longer proved profitable. Consequently many newspapers ceased publication, the journalists remained jobless or without a regular income, their only means of livelihood being their portion of the income derived from the clubs. Those journalists who had no share of the club lived in great poverty. In the thirties the publishers had to decrease the price of the issues of newspapers because of the general depression and this in turn led to decreases in the pay of the journalists, since the printing expenses could not be cut. Soon tabloids began to appear on the market, entailing a considerable decrease in the standards of the Hungarian press of Transylvania. The tabloids were issued by publishers who employed penny-journalists, which led to terrible exploitation. By then the pay of journalists sank well below the level necessary to sustain life even in the case of those employed by the more serious dailies, hence the standards dropped all across the board. Soon the editorial offices were filled by personnel without any preparation or talent who took up journalism only to try to make ends meet. Civil servants and clerical personnel who had lost their jobs, other Hungarians who lost their jobs as a result of the Romanian language examination, retired persons or students who had failed, gave each access to the editorial offices hoping to make it as journalists. But even the worst trends have their positive side: this situation led to the publication of quite a few inexpensive papers. In addition to the *Brassói Lapok* there was the *Népújság*, moreover the popular edition of the *Keleti Újság*, the *Magyar Újság*, as well as an edition of the *Ellenzék* under the title *Esti Lap*. At the end of this process there remained but four or five dailies of national significance, including the *Erdélyi Lapok* of Oradea, launched in 1932, which later assumed the title *Magyar Lapok*, dropping the name Transylvanian on account of the intervention of the censors. But even these papers of relatively large circulation had difficulty maintaining themselves.

Disregarding the impact of Romanian censorship it may be noted that the evolution of the Hungarian press faithfully reflected the predicament of the Hungarians of Transylvania. As long as the economic conditions of the Hungarian population were bearable the Hungarian press evolved normally. As the Romanian economic policies weighed more heavily on all classes of Hungarian society as a result of the depression of 1930's and of the policy of Romanianization, the development of the Hungarian press came to a halt. This situation was made worse by the well-known fact that during the fifteen years of the

Greater Romanian regime there was prior censorship which along with other symptoms accompanying the state of emergency, practically paralyzed the Hungarian press. The next chapter will describe in greater detail the issue of censorship and of freedom of the press in general.

The Hungarian press of Romania had enormous influence. In addition to the schools and the churches, Hungarian newspapers and periodicals constituted the most important factors of Hungarian culture under the Romanian regime. The journalists, much like the priests, teachers, or professors, performed heroic tasks on behalf of Hungarian culture. Their area of effectiveness was considerable, since it extended to all strata of the Hungarian society of a million and a half. This becomes clear from the circulation figures. The circulation of the leading dailies fluctuated between 6,000 and 15,000. The *Brassói Lapok* and the *Keleti Újság* attained a circulation of 15,000 at their height, while the circulation of the *Ellenzék* did not exceed 12,000. All three papers catered to various strata of the Hungarian middle class. The daily with the highest circulation was the *Jó Estét* of Cluj. This was a tabloid of a kind, but well edited, selling up to 25,000 copies. The *Népújság* of Braşov sold in even greater number of copies, reaching 50,000 at one time.[42] It was a truly well-edited daily meant primarily for the peasant masses and distributed mainly among the villages of the neighboring Székely counties. Under these circumstances, it is easy to see why the Hungarian press of Transylvania was so effective.

Inside and outside factors determined the tone and the content of the Hungarian press. The outside factors were primarily Romanian censorship and the Romanian press policies in general. As we shall see, these differed radically from the ones that prevailed under the Dual Monarchy with regard to the Romanian press of Hungary. Secondly, the tone and spirit of the Hungarian papers were determined by the value system of the editors and journalists, that is the perspective of the Hungarian middle class of Transylvania. Whoever persues the volumes of the better known dailies and weeklies would note with surprise the moderate tone of the Hungarian papers. The sharp tone of hatred, the irredentist spirit so characteristic of the former Romanian papers were lacking in the Hungarian ones. True enough, even without such a tone the simple description of facts could have a really agitating effect. The mere description of the Romanian economic, linguistic, ecclesiastic, and cultural measures could considerably whip up Hungarian public opinion, already excited on account of its personal experiences.

Under the circumstances, it is clear that the activities of the Hungarian press and the stand it took played a decisive role on many issues. Indeed, in very many cases only the press was able to bring up certain matters that could not be discussed at church meetings, in the schools, nor anywhere else. It was largely with the help of the press that the Hungarian writers and scholars concerned about their language could improve the deteriorating usage, faulty spelling habits and faulty syntax. The movement for the correct syntax of the language reached the various strata of Hungarian society by means of the press, as did a number of historical and cultural values, the latest results obtained by Hungarian science and those aspects of foreign news about which the Romanian press kept silent. When the Romanian censorship rendered every kind of criticism impossible, the Hungarian press kept the Hungarian public informed by simply reprinting the communiqués and criticisms appearing in the Romanian press. This undertaking of the Hungarian press had enormous significance. The various strata of Hungarian society became acquainted with Romanian public opinion, the most important political events and the Romanian projects threatening them, thanks to this undertaking. The popular educational role assumed by every Hungarian daily with greater or lesser competence was particularly important. The most significant weekly in this regard was undoubtedly the *Magyar Nép*, published by the Minerva press of Cluj under the editorship of Domokos Gyallay; it was read avidly by the Hungarian villagers. The weekly *Erdélyi gazda*, sponsored by the Agricultural Association of Transylvania, performed a similar task later.

Hungarian Theatrical Performances

The Hungarian theater of Transylvania had centuries-old traditions. The first permanent theater was built in Kolozsvár in 1821. This was the famous theater on Farkas Street which preceded the first theater in Pest by a decade and a half. Ever since then the Hungarian public in Transylvania had always manifested a lively interest in the theater. There were two permanent companies in Kolozsvár before World War I, while traveling companies put on shows in the provincial towns. In 1906 the theater on Farkas Street moved into the premises of the new National Theater. Its erection was made possible by the sale of the building on Farkas Street and by a loan provided by the Hungarian Commercial Bank of Pest. The Hungarian state, according to the minutes of the cabinet meetings of 1903, did not contribute at all to the expenses of construction. The director of the company was Dr. Jenő Janovics, a long time supporter of Hungarian cultural causes, who led this great Hungarian institution with competence, from its construction to the change in sovereignty of 1919. Janovics had a summer theater constructed near the permanent building along the promenade; lighter plays, musicals, and ballets were performed here from spring until fall. This building was called the "Szinkör." The site of this building was donated by the city of Kolozsvár "for Hungarian theatrical purposes, in perpetuity" whereas the costs of construction were assumed by the director without any support from the state or the municipality. The construction of this second theater was particularly fortunate for Hungarian drama in Kolozsvár and Transylvania, which soon was entirely relegated to these premises soon after 1919.[43]

A year-and-a-half after the arrival of the Romanian troops in December 1918, the secretary of state of the Romanian government, the oft-mentioned Onisifor Ghibu, took over the National Theater on János Hunyadi Square, by force, for the Romanian theater. The document of transfer was signed by the director, Jenő Janovics, Lajos Parlagi, and Kálmán Geréb on the Hungarian side, and by Onisifor Ghibu, Vasile Hossu, and Constantin Pavel on the Romanian side. In this document Dr. Ghibu states that he is assuming control of the National Theater on behalf of the state, although Janovics was allowed to remain in charge for the time being.

Since it was obvious that the theater would soon be completely removed from Hungarian control, it occurred to Janovics to try to obtain the former theater building on Farkas Street, still in fair condition, for the Hungarian company. Therefore he requested the Romanian Governing Council of Sibiu to give him access to the theater on Farkas Street, and grant him the right to operate it for thirty years so that he might remodel it at his own expense, while his company would move out of the National Theater. The Governing Council replied to this proposal on September 16. The reply indicated that the former Hungarian National Theater was now a Romanian National Theater, whereas the Szinkör on the mall would remain available for Hungarian performances. Unless the performances at the Szinkör were initiated by the beginning of October all the members of the Hungarian company would be expelled from the country. Hence the Hungarian company had to leave the Hungarian National Theater by the end of October.

The last performance of the Hungarian National Theater was held on September 30: it was Shakespeare's *Hamlet.* The enormous house was sold out to the anxious and inwardly weeping Hungarian public. Even the foyers of the theater were filled to the brim. Endless applause greeted the great artists, István Szentgyörgyi, Lili Poór, Aranka Laczkó, and Janovics. The Romanian censorship had been in operation for already nine months, carefully perusing every play before its performance. It authorized only the first line of the great monologue of Hamlet. But even this line was enough, because the actor, instead of reciting the line in despair, recited those immortal words in a tone fired by the passion to survive: "To be or not to be, that is the question." One could hear the muffled or not so muffled response from the jam-packed audience: "We want to be and to live." The mood became more intense from minute to minute; the spectators listened to every moment of the performance with increasing passion, enthusiasm and determination. When the last words had sounded the audience stood up and staged a demonstration along with the sobbing actors. The detectives and agents penetrating into the hall soon herded the sobbing Hungarians out of the beautiful hall of the no longer Hungarian theater building. With this last great adventure the Hungarian language activity of the National Theater of Cluj came to an end.

By October 2 the entire Hungarian company was already at the Szinkör, where a performance was held on the 4th. They had to start once again from scratch. The entire equipment of the National Theater was left behind for the Romanians. Decors and costumes had to be secured anew, the equipment had to be expanded. But the Hungarian public supported the theater with great devotion and each performance was sold out to full houses.

In the Spring of 1921 the Romanian government tried to ban Hungarian theater. Then director Janovics sent an open letter to Octavian Goga, then Minister of Cultural Affairs. As one of the active representatives of Hungarian intellectual life in Transylvania, he requested Goga, to allow the 128 years old Hungarian company from Transylvania to continue to function. The Romanian and the Hungarian press commented on the letter in detail and, prompted by public opinion, Goga agreed to meet Janovics. As a result of the meeting the issue regarding the functioning of the theater as well as the request of the provincial company for authorization to perform were handled favorably. In accordance with Goga's directive in Arad, Oradea, Timişoara, Satu Mare, Deva, and the capital cities of the Székely counties received permission to become the sites of per-formances by traveling companies in addition to the permanent company in Cluj. Altogether nine Hungarian companies performed in Transylvania. The loyalty of the audiences ensured the performances by the companies for years; the heyday of the theater in Transylvania was reborn. The Hungarian population, which had to retreat on every front, remained touchingly loyal to the Hungarian theater. Those employed by the companies were able to make a decent living. Of course, the company of Cluj was at an advantage; it catered to sizable crowds since it was permanent, and represented the old traditions of the largest Hungarian city. Among the actors we find the well-known Ferenc Táray, Margit Dajka, and two who were to become popular in Budapest as well: (Pufi) Sándor Tompa and Manyi Kiss.

After the progress of the first few years a decline set in, caused primarily by external factors. On March 17, 1926 the Romanian House of Deputies passed a law which set the sales tax on tickets at Hungarian theaters at 25% as opposed to 13% for the Romanian theaters. This soon resulted in a decline of the Hungarian theater. The impoverishment of the Hungarian population contributed to the decline, as did the general crisis of the economy and of the theater, which soon became manifest all over the world. The Hungarian companies folded up one after the other. The better actors left the country whereas those who had stayed behind in Transylvania thanks to a visa, also left once their visa expired and they could not renew it. The crisis of the theater was felt equally and increasingly in Cluj and in the provinces. The support of the Hungarian press was all in vain, as were the many enthusiastic proposals for reconstruction: the process of decline caused by internal and external factors could not be halted. The authorities also exerted increasing pressure on the Hungarian actors and banned quite a few performances. The economic crisis was made worse by the fact that the government, under the guise of liberalism, put an end to the territorial restrictions set on the performances by directors. From then on directors and their agents engaged in cut-throat competition to secure the audiences of provincial towns. House to house pandering and other well-known marks of the misery surrounding Bohemian life became regular features once again. Complete financial bankruptcy soon made it impossible for most provincial companies to function.

Only the permanent company of Cluj remained. In 1928-29 it accepted responsibility for the direction of the theater at Oradea as well and organized a separate company for performances there. The following year Timişoara requested the same service. In 1930 the companies organized by Janovics put on 407 shows in Cluj, 397 at Oradea, as well as a large number of shows at Timişoara, Satu Mare and Baia Mare.

After 1930 the theater of Cluj was also experiencing dire difficulties as a consequence of the Depression. The Association of the Supporters of the Theater was formed; later it was Janovics and Company, a stockholders' corporation dealing in subscriptions for the theater and the movies, that tried to ensure the survival of the Hungarian theater. In 1933 Janovics retired from the theater and from its direction. The

Thalia corporation, established that same year, took over the fund-raising campaign. This corporation placed Imre Kádár at the head of the theater company. The company at Cluj became stronger as a consequence of Kádár's competent leadership and of the gradual recovery from the Great Depression. The series of performances it put on at Tîrgu Mureş, Oradea, Timişoara, and Braşov, in addition to Cluj itself, were evidence of this recovery.

The Hungarian theater was able to survive the Depression only by adapting entirely to the taste of its audience, since it could count on no other source of revenue. This adjustment, however, led to a decline of standards. The more serious Hungarian theatergoers witnessed with anxiety the loose and immoral plays that figured on the program. A struggle was soon launched to restore more serious theater. Within the framework of the Association of Supporters the best known representatives of Hungarian public life did everything to raise the standards, with support from the press; indeed, the Hungarian theaters soon turned to more serious theater and its popularization. Consequently the premiers of the valuable drama of József Nyírő, Károly Kós, Áron Tamási, and István Nagy helped to make their names household words. The drama contests sponsored each year by the Theater at Cluj and the Art Guild of Transylvania also resulted in the production of valuable plays. Another innovation by the Theater was its open-air productions. These were held in the enormous courtyard of the Calvinist boarding-school adjoining the 400 year-old Reformed Church in the old town. The Hungarian audiences in Cluj and, soon thereafter, in the provinces, received these outdoor performances with a great deal of pleasure and appreciation.

The problem of replacement for the theater companies caused headaches. The company attempted to resolve this issue by organizing a course under the direction of Elemér Hetényi. The course occasionally revealed individuals with great talent. Among these we find Alíz Fényes, Sándor Tompa, György Kovács, and István Nagy, who were to endow the company in Cluj with an aura of fame.

The Hungarian theater ensured the continuity of Hungarian dramatic arts in Transylvania under Romanian rule. It had enormous national significance, especially if we consider that these theaters were the only place besides the churches whence Hungarian speech could be heard by large audiences. Once the titles or subtitles of films could only be read in Romanian or some foreign language the Hungarian public relied even more heavily on the theater. This was also the period when Hungarian drama met its true calling and the enrichment of its programs. Performances were often banned; nevertheless Hungarian classics were usually authorized, thanks to the intervention of some understanding artistic supervisors such as Emil Isac. Performances of *Bánk Bán, Bizánc*, and other plays prompted the Hungarian audiences to serious self-examination and thorough analysis of issues. There were times, however, when even the best known plays became banned. After 1937 the performance of *János Vitéz* was banned, and even *Az ember tragédiája* [The Tragedy of Man] — especially its revolutionary scene — could only be performed by emendating significant portions of the play.

While Hungarian theater continued in Cluj relatively undisturbed, the activities of amateur groups that had replaced the theater companies encountered increasing difficulties in the provinces. Authorization for amateur performances became much like a sea serpent, without beginning or end. Authorization was tied to conditions which made it impossible to know in advance whether the play rehearsed for months could be presented or not. Consequently these amateur performances, so significant for promoting the solidarity of the peasant population and their education outside of the classroom, encountered the greatest difficulties throughout the regime. For instance, after 1934 it became impossible to obtain permission for any kind of amateur program in certain areas. Because of this insecurity healthy initiatives for the uniform direction of amateur productions could not take place. Several attempts were made to settle the issue of authorization in a uniform manner: these were unsuccessful during the Romanian regime because of the suspicious attitude of the authorities.

The Hungarian public would have liked to greet artists or companies from Budapest, who could have revitalized the programs of theater in Transylvania by their visiting performance. Unfortunately, such visits ran into great difficulties. Not once during the 22 years of the Romanian regime was there a visit by the National Theater of Budapest — unlike what occurred during the Hungarian regime, when similar visits were authorized every year for the benefit of the Romanians. Conscious of the negative attitude of the authorities, Hungarian cultural leaders in Transylvania did not even think of it after one or two feeble attempts. Thus the Hungarian public could not experience what the Romanian public had been able to experience under Hungarian rule. Likewise the Romanian authorities did not show much understanding in the matter of facilitating performances by touring companies. Least of all, they had no understanding regarding amateur performances by the Hungarian peasantry.

The Hungarian population built cultural centers in some of the larger villages and often tried to use these premises for shows. The most interesting attempt of this kind took place at Sînmartin. On the initiative of clergyman Vilmos Bálint, the Catholic League of Nations put on a series of performances repeated each year. With the help of smallholders, the cultural center was equipped with seating, a stage, and electric power. The local actors undertook the performance of increasingly ambitious plays, year after year, and the people were extremely interested. By 1932 they were putting on comedies by Molière. Unfortunately the Romanian authorities made the continuation of this most interesting initiative impossible after 1934. Unitarian and Calvinist Church organizations made similar attempts. These attempts proved that everywhere the curiosity of the people could easily be aroused. But the Romanian authorities were most suspicious in this area, rendering the education of the peasantry outside of the schools virtually impossible after 1934.

Surveying the cultural life of the Hungarians under Romanian rule we may note that when the Romanian authorities did not intervene to hamper its progress, there were rather healthy initiatives and encouraging results. The theater, the press, the cultural organizations relied equally on support from the Hungarian population and blended increasingly with it. This was their only chance of survival; for these institutions did not receive, nor could they expect to receive any assistance from the Romanian state. As we have seen, the Romanian Astra had received government subsidies for decades in former times, and the Hungarian public as well as the provincial authorities attempted to help it by their courteous attitude during its general assembly meetings. Hungarian cultural associations did not encounter similar sympathy in Romania. Every Hungarian cultural organization had to face most severe difficulties, since their property had been taken away during the land reform, or by some other Romanian measure, whereas their work in the Hungarian environment, which might have enabled them to recoup their financial basis, was constantly hampered by the authorities. The state of siege, the censorship that lasted for fifteen years, the often contradictory official measures, the arbitrariness of the provincial authorities reduced Hungarian cultural activities to a minimum, or halted these completely. We shall see in the chapter on basic freedoms that Romanian cultural policies always viewed the issue of Hungarian culture from an ultra-nationalist point of view and subjected all cultural associations to strict political controls. This process often required heroic perseverance on the part of those who led and guided Hungarian cultural affairs.

The Romanian policies that prevailed with regard to the issue of Hungarian culture were all the more painful as Romanian associations received all kinds of support from the authorities. After 1919 the Astra became practically a government institution receiving millions in assistance from various ministries. While the Hungarian churches and Hungarian cultural associations very seldom benefitted from the confiscation of Hungarian estates during the land reform, Astra received plots of land in almost every village in the Székely area for the placing of various cultural centers. It acquired lots and buildings from the Private Properties of Ciuc county, and huge sums from the budgets of counties and municipalities earmarked for the subvention of Romanianizing activities in the Székely area. In 1928 Astra received 600,000 lei from the Ministry of Education, 2,085,750 lei from the Ministry of Culture, 200,000 lei from the Ministry of Agriculture, and 300,000 lei from the Ministry of Health. In the same year the county, municipal, and community treasuries contributed 1,031,164 lei to the branches of Astra. The Act of 1926 on the Romanian theater also ensured an income from the tax on movie tickets for the purposes of Astra. In 1928 the Association received an income of 1,249,418 lei from this source, and estimated this source of revenue to increase to 3,500,000 lei. As a consequence of this enormous financial subvention Astra was able to build almost one hundred cultural centers in the purely or overwhelmingly Hungarian Székely land, mostly with the help of forced labor obtained from local Hungarians.

As mentioned, the E.M.K.E. in the meantime was deprived of all financial support; for fifteen years, during which it was subjected to investigations, it fought a life and death struggle, while the E.M.E., also deprived of its financial base, became so impoverished that it could not even afford to print the programs of its conferences. Most likely the objective was the same as the one which guided Romanian cultural policies. Hungarian culture had to fight for its rights throughout the regime because, according to the Romanian concept, only culture in Romanian language should benefit from the freedom to develop and enjoy the goodwill of the authorities. It was simply the touching affection manifested by the Hungarian population towards its culture that made it possible for Hungarian culture to survive with rather impressive results.

Hungarian Literature in Transylvania

During those twenty-two years the Hungarian literature of Transylvania could come about, literally, only from the fire of the Hungarian soul, from a love towards the Hungarian language that overcame all obstacles, and from the sacrifices and work of the true, talented writers. At the time of the collapse the writers had no reserves to rely on. They had but one periodical, the *Erdélyi Szemle*, founded by S. László Nagy in 1916. Only the most optimistic could expect support from the large masses of readers. Printing companies operating along altruistic principles were a thing of the future when the first devotees of Hungarian literature in Transylvania started out on the fertile soil of the literary planters of Transylvania.

Nevertheless we may note a favorable conjuncture of several factors in the cradle of Hungarian literature in Transylvania. One of these factors was the barely surviving tradition of Transylvanian autonomy. During the Dual Monarchy most Transylvanian talents left for Budapest, and the uniformity obtained at the state, or some other level, hardly favored special perspectives or particular local traditions.

Still, Transylvania was just being discovered immediately after the war. Both the special economic and artistic questions of the Transylvanian situation found their students. István Bethlen and others examined the economic importance; Károly Kós pointed out and voiced the artistic and cultural significance of Transylvania. First, Károly Kós demonstrated the unique aspects and values of Transylvanian culture, which could not be found in the rest of Hungary. It is not by chance, therefore, that Károly Kós was the greatest representative of the so-called Transylvanism, which stressed the uniqueness of post war Transylvanian literature.

It was only a few steps that led from the recognition of the Transylvanian questions and values to the voicing of the possibilities for an independent Transylvanian literature. The doors were closed toward the Hungarian state when the Romanian troops occupied Transylvania and part of southeastern Hungary, and when most of these gains were confirmed in the Peace Treaty of Trianon. The Hungarian writers under Romanian rule had to respond to the question: is it possible to have a separate Transylvanian literature? They soon answered this question in the affirmative, though little did they know each other, and at first only in the previously mentioned *Erdélyi Szemle* could they publish their works. They had to get to know each other: they needed funds for publications, they needed printing presses, and publishers, but most of all they needed readers who could support them materially and with love. Thus, work started to complete assignments and within a few years everything developed that was needed for a new Transylvanian literature: periodicals, publishing companies, and a reading public. A decisive point was the meeting of the writers and the public, which could be achieved after years of heroic work. This era is justly called the heroic age of Transylvanian literature.

The great writers of this era grouped around *Erdélyi Szemle*. Soon there appeared poets like Sándor Reményik, Lajos Áprily and László Tompa, whose poems are still valued as outstanding examples of Transylvanian poetry. Sándor Makkai also became known in this journal along with most of those writers who became known as representatives of Transylvanian literature. The periodical printed poems, short stories and essays. Its monopoly was soon lost, as already in 1919 there were start-up attempts in Tîrgu Mureş and in Oradea. In Tîrgu Mureş, Ernő Osvát started the periodical *Zord Idő*, while in Oradea, Géza Tabéry took a similar initiative. A firmly grounded literary center developed, however, only in Cluj. This largest city of Transylvania was permeated with Hungarian intellectual traditions. It was in this city in 1921 that *Pásztortűz* was founded, which is the most recognized periodical of Transylvanian Hungarian literature to this day.

All of these initiatives and attempts, however, did not have an impact on a wide segment of the masses. The organization of the reading public was a problem that had yet to be resolved. This assignment was based on the need to awaken interest in Transylvanian literature and for this task the writers had to unite in order to publish books that attracted the interest of the masses. The means for this difficult undertaking formed the most beautiful chapter of the heroic age of Transylvanian literature. The writers hit the road like ancient balladeers to search out and win over the audience.

They appeared in a town or a village that constituted a regional center by train, on foot, sometimes by cart to proclaim in living words the rights and beauties of the reborn Hungarian literature of Transylvania. Among them we find Sándor Reményik, Jenő Szentimrei, Mária Berde, Lajos Szini and, most of all, the grey-haired Elek Benedek, who had returned from Budapest and who carried on his pilgrimage through the Hungarian villages of Transylvania at the head of a group of Székelys with a vigor that belied his age. The negative attitude of all kinds of officials, the suspicious interest on the part of the police, the difficulties in obtaining permission for holding soirées and conferences did not deter the participants from these heroic ventures. They carried on their work of rallying audiences with the enthusiasm and fanaticism of prophets fired by their calling. The results were not long in waiting. By 1924 the stratum of the Hungarian public that appreciated literature was emotionally ready to appreciate and support a literature peculiar to Transylvania. A decisive step was taken that year to organize the writers and to ensure institutionally that their works would be published.

In 1924 Imre Kádár, Károly Kós, Ernő Ligeti, József Nyírő, Árpád Paál, and István Zágoni established the Art Guild of Transylvania, the publishing house of the Hungarian writers of Transylvania. Although the Minerva literary and printing corporation was in existence since 1921, the writers needed in addition, an institution devoted exclusively to the artistic publication of literary works and its financial benefits. This new organization provided a definite guarantee that the new Hungarian literature of Transylvania and the reading public would find each other. This fortunate event closed the heroic era of the Hungarian literature of Transylvania in which poetry and the short story played the major role. The great poets — Reményik, Áprily, Tompa, Mária Berde, Domokos Sipos and others — were followed by the promising prose writers: Károly Kós, Domokos Gyallay, Sándor Makkai, József Nyírő, Jenő Szentimrei, Benő Karácsony, Ernő Ligeti, György Szántó, Áron Tamási, Endre Balogh, etc. The authors of the most famous works the best known novels and plays of Transylvanian literature, would come from among their rank.

Indeed, the best known products of the Hungarian literature of Transylvania were novels and plays. Their publication was made possible by the establishment of the Art Guild of Transylvania. The Guild recruited subscribers and undertook literary publicity to guarantee the appreciation of the writers' works even financially. In order to achieve this, however, it was necessary to smooth out the contradictions between the writers and to establish a writers' cooperative. Both these tasks were accomplished, thanks to diplomatic skills of Aladár Kuncz, and a cooperative of Hungarian writers of Transylvania was formed at the palace of Baron János Kemény at Brîncoveneşti Mur [Marosvécs]. From then on it became a tradition for the members of the Helikon of Transylvania, the name adopted by this writers' cooperative, to meet each year at the palace. Soon everyone who made a valuable contribution to Hungarian literature was invited to join the cooperative. It was these writers, enjoying the hospitality of the Baron, who brought up and discussed the more important issues affecting Hungarian literature in Transylvania and intellectual life in general. Two years later, in 1928, the cooperative acquired an official organ and a publication voicing its literary policies. The writers assembled in Helikon were guided by the principle of art for art's sake. Each kept their own ideology, but it was understood that they would exclude all tendencies from their writing, and express eternal human principles above all ideologies, "to sound out loud the melody of man." In addition to this humanism, the intellectual attitude of most members of the Helikon of Transylvania was marked by the so-called Transylvanianism.

According to Károly Kós, Transylvanianism meant the special way of thinking and perceiving existence that characterized the population of Transylvania. Its basis was Transylvania which, by its isolated unity, created spiritual forces bringing together the peculiarities of the various nationalities of the area into a harmonic whole. During its thousand-year-long history no nationality was able to or even wanted to transform the other nationalities into its own image. Forces from the outside may have attempted to do this, but failed. The particular culture of each of the three ethnic groups include certain traits which signified the common Transylvanian color. The ethnic groups of Transylvania differed both physically and mentally from their brothers beyond the borders of the country. Thus the Hungarians of Transylvania differed from those of Hungary, the Saxons differed from the Germans of Germany, and the Transylvanian Romanians differed from those of Romania. Each ethnic group preserved its own individuality, however, since the Romanian had remained Romanian, the Hungarian and the Székely have remained Hungarian, and the Saxon had remained German, yet each had something in common, which is particularly obvious in their mental makeup, and this common nature was derived from their common history and from the memories of the struggles fought in common. This common trait was the Transylvanian mentality, in other words Transylvanianism, which none of the brothers living beyond the borders of Transylvania have been able to understand and appreciate.

It was this Transylvanian spirit that found expression in the various genres of Hungarian literature in Transylvania, but mostly in its poetry, its novels, and its essays. Of course, Transylvanianism was the result of a mentality held in common, and almost every writer added concepts to it. It was expressed in the guise of a program in the first issue of the *Erdélyi Helikon*, above the signature of nine writers. There can be no doubt that the most talented representatives of Hungarian literature in Transylvania, with one or two exceptions, were Transylvanianists. Of course, they were subjected to various attacks on the part of writers representing different ideologies. Neither left-wing nor right-wing writers were Transylvanianist, and attacked the latter regularly. The latest attack came from Ferenc Szemlér, in the name of the young writers; Károly Kós defended the movement, rejecting the assertions of the Szemlér in unmistakable terms.

Novels and plays were the best known genres of the Hungarian literature of Transylvania within Hungarian intellectual life in general, and even within world literature by means of one or two creations. The *Fekete kolostor* [Black Monastery] of Aladár Kuncz, and certain works of József Nyírő were translated into several foreign languages and obtained world-wide success. The historical novels and novels with a Székely theme that created the greatest stir within Hungarian intellectual life. The best known among the historical novels were *Vaskenyéren* [On Iron Bread] by Domokos Gyallay, *Fekete vőlegények* [Black Grooms] by Irén Gulácsy, *Sibói bölény* [The Bison from Sibó] by József Nyírő, *Az országépítő* [The Country Builder] and *Varjú nemzetség* [Nation of Crows] by Károly Kós, *Ördögszekér* [The Devil's Cart], *Táltos király* [Shaman King], and *Sárga vihar* [Yellow Storm] by Sándor Makkai, etc. The two Székely writers, Nyírő and Tamási depicted the way of life, peculiarities and struggles of the Székely nation in their great works. They brought freshness and vigor into literature by their language, their original and new topics, their rendering of Székely traits. Their writings conquered the public of Trianon Hungary.

The writers of Transylvania made bold attempts at innovation in the dramatic genre as well. The plays of the Hungarian writers from Transylvania can be considered successful efforts, in several respects, towards establishing a new form of drama after the Hungarian and world-wide crisis experienced by the genre. Literary history will surely designate the rightful place earned by such works as the *Budai Nagy Antal* of Károly Kós, the *Énekes madár* [Songbird] and *Vitéz lélek* [Hero's Soul] of Áron Tamási, and the *Jézusfaragó ember* [The Jesus Carving Man] by József Nyírő, which scored success in both Transylvania and Hungary.

If we consider the relationship between the Hungarian literature of Transylvania and the Hungarian population, there, we must note first of all, that most writers did fulfill the role traditionally ascribed to Hungarian writers in general: to proclaim the truths most significant to the life of a nation while guiding that nation. Whether we look at the work of poets or prose writers we keep encountering principles and concepts awaiting realization for the sake of improving the fate of the Hungarian population of Transylvania. In many respects, Reményik, Áprily, Tompa, Makkai, Kós, Tamási, to mention but the best known, were intellectual leaders, guardians to point out the means of defense and survival in the face of the increasingly dangerous blows suffered under foreign rule. Unfortunately, the most characteristic trait of the Hungarians of Transylvania relegated to the fate of a minority — the sad situation of Transylvania itself — was reflected in their works only in part. True, it was not possible to provide a faithful description of the situation because of outside obstacles, the censorship, and the state of emergency. But many of these writers did not seem to experience the bloody realities of Hungarian life and preferred to write poems about individual moods, or work on foreign topics. Nevertheless the minority situation and the most important issues of Hungarian fate in Transylvania are fairly well reflected in the works of some writers. Poems, stories, novels and plays testified to the suffering of Hungarians under Romanian rule. Many of these writers expressed this situation seeking answers to the questions that arose. Most famous from this point of view were Reményik, Áprily, Makkai, Nyírő, Tamási, Sándor Kacsó, Ferenc Balázs and, in the last years of his life, Jenő Dsida.

The poetry of Reményik is a wonderful mirror which reflects clearly, besides the individual fate of the poet, the life of the Hungarians as a minority population. The so-called "Poems from the Frontier Fortress" describe the dark episodes of the period of Romanian occupation. In his later poems we find questions and answers regarding the greatest issues confronting the Hungarians in Transylvania. He was able to express the situation of the Hungarians with great power in some of his poems. Censorship and state of siege had paralyzed all manifestations of community life: we can struggle against it only in spirit, making fist, in silence, "whenever possible." To defend Hungarian life which took refuge in the church and the denominational school, it was necessary to remind all Hungarians of the significance of the two bastions. And the poem, soon recited all over Transylvania, came into being: "Do not give up the church, the church, the schools!" Hungarian life was thus reflected in the poems of Áprily, in the essays and novels of Makkai, in the works of Nyírő, Tamási, Kacsó, and Ferenc Balázs. In his book, *A magunk reviziója* [A Revision of Ourselves], Makkai points to the factors of the inner spiritual renaissance of the Hungarians as prerequisites for survival in a state of minority. The colorful forms and events of Székely life find expression in the novels of József Nyírő, whereas Áron Tamási uses his brilliant pen to express the sense of humor and the wily nature of the people, a closed book to strangers. In his work *Szülőföldem* [The Land of My Birth] he provides a picture of the mood of the years 1938-1939 and of the Székely region subjected to Romanianizing, in a style and form of incomparable beauty. The issues confronting the Hungarians of Transylvania are so much part of the works of Sándor Kacsó and Ferenc Balázs that the value of their work is determined mainly by this relevant information and the national policies they reflect. The spiritual vicissitudes of the period of oppression from 1933 through 1937 are best immortalized in Jenő Dsida's famous *Psalmus Hungaricus*, distributed in manuscript form. In the refrain of the six great sections of the poem, the poet curses himself, hence all Hungarian writers, in harsh language should they ever forget their people:

> Let the water I swallow turn to bile/ If I forget you! / Let them drive/ A red-hot nail of iron through my tongue/ If I do not mention you!/ Let the light of my two eyes be extinguished/ If they do not look upon you,/ My people, you saint, your cursed, yet first-come!

The Hungarian literature of Transylvania thus reflected the situation and attitudes of the Hungarians under Romanian rule. In addition to expressing community life, the writers raised issues of national policy and fought for the survival of the Hungarian population. This activity of theirs usually took place on the pages of newspapers and periodicals. They were harassed by police and the courts mainly because of their writings in the papers. Since the writers refrained from expressing irredentist sentiments in their works, or even of describing Romanian oppression in too realistic terms, the Romanian government harassed the Hungarian writers of Transylvania relatively little. Lóránd Daday was sentenced to jail for six months for his book published in Hungary. The writings of Nyírő and of others were condemned by court orders in the first and second instances on various spurious charges. Domokos Gyallay was harassed and fined for publishing readers for small children. In the years 1936 to 1939 many a poem, short story and other works fell victim to censors. László Tompa tried to publish a volume of poetry in the last years of the regime. The censor banned 96 of the hundred poems at first reading. Only after an extended process could some of the poems finally appear.

All in all, Romanian oppression, which functioned so effectively against various cultural manifestations, was less efficient when it came to literature. Nor is this surprising. The Romanian censors, clever as they may have been, had difficulty in tracing the hidden thoughts of the Hungarian writers in the realm of ideas. This literature was able to influence the life of the Hungarian community in Transylvania enormously. It was precisely the Hungarian literature of Transylvania that was largely responsible for keeping up and bolstering the sentiments, self-respect and identity of the Hungarians in Transylvania. The fact that about 25% of the 6,000 books published during the 22 years of the regime were works of literature, is some indication of literary production. Hungarians of Transylvania viewed the new Transylvanian literature with proud satisfaction and received the news of the successes obtained by Hungarian writers with much pleasure. In addition to the recognition obtained in Budapest, favorable reception in England or France was particularly appreciated. When Aladár Kuncz's *Black Monastery* was translated into English and French, and the news of the great success obtained by these versions reached Romania, the Hungarian public of Transylvania pondered with satisfaction the ancient truth of *sub pondere crescit palma*. This pride was some compensation at a time when the Romanian government strove to weaken Hungarian cultural life and hamper the progress of Hungarian science in Transylvania.

Endnotes

1. These data were, collected by Endre Barabás, deceased in 1945, the true expert on the issue of Hungarian schools in Romania, on the basis of Hungarian school yearbooks: "A magyar iskolaügy helyzete Romániában 1918-1940" [The Issue of Hungarian Schools in Romania from 1918 to 1940], in, *Kisebbségi Körlevél* [Minority Circular], Vol. I (1939), Numbers 5 and 6.

2. This fact and the following information regarding secondary schools is taken from issues 14 and 17 of *Magyar Kisebbség*, 1924; moreover, from the enclosures to the Mémoire supplémentai re submitted to the League of Nations in 1925.

3. Onisifor Ghibu, *Politica religioasă și minoritară a României* (Cluj: 1940), p. 832.

4. Prie, *op. cit.*

5. Minutes of the general assembly of the Reformed Church District of Transylvania in 1923, p. 122.

6. *Ibid.*, p. 123.

7. Ghibu, *Politica religioasă*, p. 832.

8. Section on the churches of the minorities and on the land reform in Transylvania in Sulyok and Fritz, eds., *op. cit.*, p. 72.

9. Report of the Governing Council of the Reformed Diocese of Transylvania from November 1, 1933 to November 1, 1935, pp. 24-25.

10. Minutes of the general assembly of the Reformed Diocese of Transylvania, in 1923, p. 70.

11. *Universul*, December 5, 1936.

12. *Monitorul Oficial*, January 29, 1938.

13. *Monitorul Oficial*, March 8, 1925.

14. A. Dima, *Școala secundară în lumina bacalaureatului*, Bucharest, 1928.

15. The report of the Governing Council of the Reformed Diocese of Transylvania, 1933-35, p. 60.

16. *Patria*, August 2, 1925.

17. *Revista Generală a Învățământului*, September 1925, p. 445.

18. *Keleti Újság*, February 1, 1929.

19. *Brassói Lapok*, February 22, 1929.

20. The data are taken from the official church reports.

21. Barabás, *A romániai magyar nyelvű oktatás*.
22. *Erdélyi Tudósító*, a social weekly of the Catholic Church, Braşov, December 9, 1928. Reprinted in Barabás, *A romániai magyar nyelvű oktatás*, pp. 62-73.
23. Dragomir, *op. cit.*, "elles ont été introduites comme le meilleur moyen de former la conscience civique," p. 183.
24. *Erdélyi Tudósító*, January 27, 1929.
25. The 1928 report of the Governing Council of the Reformed Diocese of Transylvania, 1928, pp. 20-21.
26. *Ibid.*
27. *Magyar Szemle*, August 1939.
28. Barabás, *op. cit.*, p. 29.
29. Barabás, *op. cit.*
30. *Magyar Kisebbség*, 1934, pp. 255-56.
31. "Student associations and minority rights," *Adevărul*, March 15, 1932. A Hungarian translation of the article printed in Ürmösi-Maurer, *op. cit.*, pp. 102-115.
32. For a short summary of the work of the Romanian University of Cluj, see Sándor Bíró, "A kolozsvári egyetem a román uralom alatt" [The University of Cluj under Romanian Rule]. In, *Erdély Magyar Egyeteme* [Transylvania's Hungarian University]. Eds., György Bisztray, Attila T. Szabó, and Lajos Tamás, (Kolozsvár, 1941), pp. 305,-332.
33. Lajos Kántor, "Az Erdélyi Múzeum-Egyesület utolsó 10 esztendeje" [The Last Ten Years of the E.M.E.]. In: Sulyok and Fritz, eds., *op. cit.*, p. 216 ff.
34. *Ibid.*
35. Attila T. Szabó, "Az erdélyi tudományos élet húsz éve" [Twenty Years of Scholarly Life in Transylvania], *Keleti Újság*, December 25, 1938.
36. Oberding, *op. cit.*, p. 71.
37. *Magyar Kisebbség*, 1923, pp. 705-11, and 1935, p. 644.
38. *Ibid.*, 1930, p. 627.
39. *Magyar Kisebbség*, 1923, p. 665.
40. Géza Berey, *Néhány szó az újságírásról* [A Few Words about Journalism] (Satu Mare, 1936), p. 53.
41. *Ibid.*
42. According to the data collected by Ernő Ligeti.
43. Iván Dávid, "Az erdélyi magyar színészet két évtizedes útja" [Two Decades of Hungarian Theater in Transylvania], *Keleti Újság*, December 25, 1938.

Chapter VI

Rights and Freedoms of the Hungarians in Romania

The experience of the Hungarian population that came under Romanian rule naturally warranted a determined defensive stand. The Romanian governments did their best to repress the Hungarian population and gradually restrict all opportunities to use their language, attend their churches, and tend to their cultural needs. The leaders of the Hungarians had to take up the cudgels to defend against such attempts. Their defense invariably assumed legal forms, available itself of the opportunities afforded by law. In the course of this struggle they learned that human rights and other freedoms guaranteed in the constitution and in other codes could seldom be put into practice, and even their to a very limited extent. In most areas under Romanian control, the less well known restrictions in force during the Hungarian regime before World War I, continued to be applied almost to the end.

1. *Freedom of the Individual*

By the provisions of the Treaty on Minorities, Romania agreed to guarantee complete protection of life and freedom for its minority residents. Individual freedoms were defined in identical ways in the Constitution of 1923 and 1938. In paragraph 11 of the Constitution of 1923, and in paragraph 12 of the Royal Constitution of 1938, we read that "individual freedoms are guaranteed."[1]

The concept of individual freedom usually includes the inviolability of residence and personal freedoms. The constitution provided that it could not be suspended and a state of emergency could be declared only by special act of parliament. In spite of this, a state of emergency and prior censorship were in fact applied in the areas inhabited by the Hungarian population for fifteen out of the twenty-two years of the regime. The state of emergency was lifted only during the years 1928 to 1933.

The special measures accompanying the state of emergency limited individual rights thoroughly or eliminated them altogether. The state of emergency was declared immediately after the beginning of the occupation, and the Romanian state, legitimized by the peace treaties,

severely restricted both the inviolability of residence and individual
freedoms. House searches and requisitions of lodging became the order
of the day. The minorities, particularly the Hungarians, were regarded
with suspicion anyway, and Romanian security groups tried to check
Hungarians under suspicion by means of arbitrary house searches.
"Individual freedom, what a travesty it has become," noted the first
Romanian governor of the county of Someş, George Şorban, in his
already-quoted leaflet. "The state security police, the gendarmes, or the
office in charge of quartering troops wake us from our deepest slumber,
insisting that we identify ourselves, contribute food, or move out of our
house within 24 hours." This statement faithfully reflected the
prevailing situation. As we have seen in Chapter I, in the Hungarian
towns of Transylvania, the Romanian authorities did everything in their
power to evict Hungarian civil servants, harassing them with particular
relish, with the help of various measures for the requisition of lodgings.
The apartments of Hungarians were requisitioned by civil servants
relocated from the old kingdom of Romania; the rents offered were
minimal, and even these often were not paid. The officials would have
been able to find lodging without resort to force, by a modicum of
goodwill, because Hungarians who lost their jobs and were deprived of
other economic opportunities would have been more than happy to rent
homes if they could realize a decent rent for them. However, this never
occurred to the Romanian authorities, even though as high-ranking
officials, they earned good salaries.

The requisition of lodgings was usually carried out by a Romanian
plenipotentiary, who committed all kinds of abuses. His decisions
brooked no appeal. More than once, the more decent Romanians
themselves objected to the heartless measures. For instance, the daily
Dacia of Bucharest received an interesting communication from its
correspondent in Cluj, in the spring of 1920. The correspondent noted
that while the attempts on the part of the political leaders to
Romanianize the towns of Transylvania was praiseworthy, it was legal
only within certain bounds.

I have been in this city for a few months, and have witnessed
some deplorable incidents. I have seen furniture and bundles
hurled onto the street in the rain, on the order of the housing
office. On Friday, April 27, I witnessed an incident such as I had
never seen before. S. Abraham, the owner of one of the shops on
Main Square, received an order to vacate his premises within 24
hours and hand over his keys to the Romanian merchant Ion
Pop, who, not satisfied with his own premises, was able to obtain

the requisition by means of a bribe. Upon receiving the order, Abraham lost his mind and had to be taken to a mental asylum. His shop, however, was vacated and handed over to Ioan Pop.[2]

These requisitions, lasting for years, terror and uncertainty everywhere. In his leaflet already cited, Şorban demanded goodwill on the part of the Romanian authorities and the re-establishment of civil rights.

> Without individual freedom there in no labor, no trust, no gaiety, no spirit of enterprise, no progress, and no healing. Let them abolish therefore everything that curtails this freedom; let them abolish the state security agency and forbid the army to interfere in matters that do not concern it.... The issue of quartering of troops must be justly resolved. If this issue remains unresolved two cardinal rights of the citizens are affected — their right to own property as well as their right to individual freedom. These measures also contributed, to a large extent, to a lack of enterprise on the part of our businessmen.[3]

Unfortunately the warning by the Romanian governor went unheeded, as were warnings issued in subsequent years. Hungarians and Romanians both pointed out the grave consequences of the state of emergency and of the special measures taken by military and gendarme authorities, as well as of the reckless abuse of citizens' and human rights. But the state emergency was not lifted. The French-language leaflet of protest issued by the opposition parties in 1923 is filled with expressions of indignation over the repression of civil rights:

> Individual liberties have been suspended. The state of emergency has been officially declared even in the Romanian areas of Transylvania where the aggressive attitude of the Hungarians were used as an excuse to suspend all the liberties of the population, which in turn is no longer able to contain its resentment and rebellion.... The population is bitterly resentful everywhere of the abuses committed by the administration — abuses which increase by the day. The authorities even resort to the power of the army to repress the most basic rights of the citizenry.[4]

The state of emergency and the concomitant special measures remained in effect in Transylvania until 1928; and the requisitions of apartments did not cease even after that. On February 17, 1929, landlords and owners of homes held a national congress in Cluj, at which they protested against the requisitions which had been going on for eleven years.[5] By then, the situation had improved somewhat; as a result of the lifting of the state of emergency, the dreaded requisitions now took place within certain guidelines, and if these guidelines were disregarded, it was possible to appeal to the courts. On several occasions, the courts did restore citizens rights, and the owners of illegally expropriated apartments could recover their homes? For instance, the home of the greatest Hungarian poet of Romania, Sándor Reményik, was finally relinquished in 1934, after fifteen years of forced quartering. In his case, the solution was delayed by the fact that the person lodged in his house and paying minimal rent was a Romanian court martial judge.

The state of emergency was restored after 1933, and was in affect until 1940. This renewed state of emergency was far more severe than the preceding one in its infringements on civil rights. After 1935, a simple trip taken by Hungarian residents could result in serious harassment by the authorities in some places. The reign of terror of the gendarmes was especially evident in the Hungarian villages of the Székely areas. Individuals returning to visit their parents from other towns had to report to the gendarmerie within 24 hours; the gendarmes suspected irredentist agents among Hungarians they did not personally know. House searches and routine checking of personal identification were the order of the day. Travellers staying with Hungarian priests were closely watched; in general, contacts between the Hungarian villagers and any outsider was hampered or prevented by the most extreme means.

Individual freedom was restricted not only outside the home, but even within the walls of one's own house. On national holidays, the Romanian police inspected all houses, checking to see whether the national flag was openly displayed. This practice was initiated already in the first years of the Romanian regime and never abandoned, even though some Romanian leaders in Transylvania were offended by it. Alexandru Vaida-Voevod spoke out against it at the Grand Assembly of the Romanian National Party of Transylvania at Timişoara, in 1923: "During the Hungarian regime we were not allowed to display the Romanian flag, but no one was forced to display the Hungarian one."[6] In spite of this warning, however, Hungarians were still forced to display the Romanian flag on their own houses.

The house searches and illegal arrests created insecurity and a complete suspension of individual rights throughout the long period of the state of emergency. As Nicoale Ghiulea, a professor of sociology at the Romanian university of Cluj noted in 1926:

> There is no country in the world where the citizens are beaten and tortured more cruelly than in our own; it's done to the point where the moral pain and humiliation exceeds the physical abuse. There is no country in the world where citizens are deprived of their individual freedoms to the extent they are in our country. Anyone can arrest anyone, under any pretext, in fact, even without one.

Then Ghiulea pointed out that these arrests victimized innocent people more often than they did the guilty. He added:

> In civilized countries culprits can be punished only if their guilt has been verified in court, and no one can be caned or tortured if caning and torture are not among the permissible forms of punishment. We are talking about abuses, about beating the innocent, about jailing honorable people, about trampling underfoot the freedom and honor of peaceful citizens, about mistreated citizens who seek only to defend their rights as guaranteed in the constitution and in other statutes.[7]

These statements confirm the sad facts listed by Costa Foru, the famous Romanian journalist, in his book on the abuses committed by the state security agency. "The abuses of the law enforcement agencies," he wrote in his introduction,

> whose members hail from the most unsavory strata of the population, have no bounds... they arrest persons and keep them in jail for weeks and months without the slightest knowledge of the authorities. They whip and cane them, and the victim has no recourse whatever to medical or legal assistance. In addition to these illegal arrests, the members of the police force and of the gendarmerie commit innumerable acts that are in flagrant violation of the law.[8]

These abuses of a cruder type became less frequent with the state of emergency in 1928, and finally occurred only in isolated instances. Until 1930-32, the entire Hungarian press and, more particularly, the public in Ciuc were incensed by the Szakáli case. István Szakáli, a Székely farmer from Tomeşti [Csíkszenttamás] was arrested by the police in response to a denunciation by a person under investigation on charges of theft. After a four-day interrogation, the chief of the forces at Cîrta [Csíkkarcfalva] summoned the judge from Tomeşti and ordered him to remove the corpse of Szakáli from police headquarters at Cîrţa and to return it surreptitiously to the village. The judge refused to carry out this order. Szakáli's corpse was eventually removed to Tomeşti by the police. According to the autopsy, death was caused by drowning. The police, on the other hand, claimed that Szakáli was the victim of a heart attack, but later modified their account stating that Szakáli had hanged himself in an unguarded moment. József Willer, a deputy in the Romanian House of Deputies, turned to the Ministers of the Interior and of Justice at the December 3, 1931 session, and he requested an investigation.[9] The inquiry dragged on for a long time and was inconclusive.

After 1933, the abuses against personal freedom again multiplied. The so-called "Re-Romanianizing" activity entailed large numbers of arrests, house-searches and tortures among the Hungarians of the Székely region. As we have seen in our chapter on religious affairs, the investigations of abuses by the authorities were usually fruitless and did not help prevent further abuses. We may note that the notion of "habeas corpus," common since 1789 and since 1673 in England, existed in Greater Romania only to a very limited extent. The complaints about, and protests against, confiscations usually went unheeded.

Property Rights

As we have noted in the chapter on economic conditions, the beginnings of Romanian rule in Hungarian areas newly attached to Romania coincided with all kinds of confiscations of property. Thus, property rights became illusory from the very beginning and, in later years, were severely limited both by the constitution and other laws. Land, fields, meadows, forests, houses, and even churches were subject to expropriation if this was deemed necessary from the Romanian point of view. As long as these expropriation affected only Hungarian properties, the Romanians of Transylvania, being the primary beneficiaries, hardly complained against the limits set on property rights. But when their own property was in jeopardy here and there, especially in the case of mineral rights, they protested loudly against the confiscations. These protests found expression in the already cited French-language leaflet distributed for consumption abroad. In connection with the constitution forced on the country by the Liberal

Party dominated regime in 1923, it noted that this constitution served to eradicate the old guarantees of property rights:

> Economically speaking, the adoption of the constitution drafted by the Liberal Party gives the Party priority rights by the blows it metes out to private property. Under the old constitution private property was sacred. In the new version, private property is merely guaranteed.... They have opened the way to every kind of arbitrary confiscation, and all mineral rights, all the treasures of the sub-soil suddenly became the property of the state.[10]

The protests, of course, were to no avail; the regime of the Liberal Party, and later the protesters themselves, continued the policy of expropriation, usually targeting properties of non-Romanians. The case of the expropriation of the Reformed Church of Sîntimbru became particularly notorious. Erected in the 15th century in commemoration of the battle fought by János Hunyadi against the Turks at Marosszentimre [Sîntimbru], this church was one of the most beautiful historical monuments in all of Transylvania. Twenty-eight *holds* of fields and 2 *holds* of gardens constituted part of the property. Coveting the property, the local Romanian Uniates, turned to the Agrarian committee to obtain the church on the grounds that the Reformed diocese had become depopulated. Two days later, the Committee expropriated the church and the surrounding lands by its directive 48/1923 of March 29, 1923. It turned the church over to the Uniate clergy and ceded the lands to the Romanian peasants, since, as it stated in its decision, "there remained not a single Reformed person at Sântimrea, and the Reformed parish no longer exists." The representatives of the Reformed Church pointed out in their appeal that the church had 95 members, hence the decision of the Agrarian committee was unwarranted. The appeals agency, however, confirmed the original decision on different grounds:

> Since it is not known whether the church was erected by the religious authorities or by the state, it is the Minister of Religious Affairs and of the Arts who has to decide whether the church is a historical monument and it is for the Minister to say what should become of it, which denomination should be entrusted with its upkeep.

The central leadership of the Uniate Church did not approve of the expropriation. The official paper of the diocese of Blaj expresses this negative attitude:

We do not know what our church authorities intend to do with the church at Sîntimbru. But we do know that there is no legal basis for expropriating church buildings. Therefore we are against this expropriation and, if it were up to us, this church could become Uniate only with the agreement of the pertinent Reformed ecclesiastic authorities. In other words, who can assure us that other churches would not be expropriated in the same manner.

This protest by the Uniate press pointed to the dangers inherent in the situation: as soon as this kind of expropriation became possible, no property right of any kind remained safe. Consequently, the Uniate Church did not accept the church building, and it was solely due to its influence that the building did in the end remain in the hands of the Reformed Church.[11] The protests by the Reformed clergyman concerned had no effect whatever. They sent deputations and memoranda, they pleaded and begged, they intervened in parliament, all in vain. But because the Archbishop of Blaj perceived that expropriation was involved, he did not allow the Uniate diocese of Sîntimbru to take over the illegally confiscated Reformed Church building.

In the chapter on economic affairs, we have seen the endless series of illegal expropriations or confiscations affecting the Hungarians on Romanian soil. We may note without the slightest exaggeration that neither individuals nor institutions were safe as regards their property rights. We have seen the arguments used to deprive Székelys of their private property in Ciuc county, we have also seen the subsequent measures leading to limitations on properties owned by Hungarians. Lands, estates, and claims resulting from defaults on bank loans were seized in the name of various laws whenever these were in the interest of Romanian nationalists. After 1933, as mentioned, these measures always were taken on the basis of ethnic discrimination. Romanian ethnic churches and banks were exempted from financial damage resulting from the tax reform, the so-called "conversion law", while Hungarian churches and banks were not.

The properties of Hungarian artisans' associations were entrusted to Romanian organizations, whereas those of the Romanian artisans of Cluj were allowed to remain in their hands. The lands derived from later expropriations along the borders were distributed exclusively among ethnic Romanians.

For a long time it seemed as if homes were exempt from the possibility of expropriation; but we have seen that the property rights of homeowners was also limited for almost a decade and a half by the practice of quartering troops. After 1932 Hungarian Roman Catholics were forced to admit that even the right to own their homes was not immune to confiscation by Romanians.

Indeed, Onisifor Ghibu, the oft-mentioned and oft-quoted university professor and member of the Romanian Academy, embarked from 1931 on activities directed at the confiscation of the remaining properties of the Roman Catholic Status of Transylvania as well as those of certain orders. After the first wave of expropriations, the 26,538 *holds* of lands of the Status had been reduced to a mere 3,251 *holds*. Moreover, it had owned several nice apartment buildings in Cluj, which enabled it to cover the strictly cultural expenses of the church.   Ghibu and the Romanian public raised doubts about their right to the remaining property as well; with the help of various official trusts Ghibu embarked on action to take away these properties.   As a consequence of the struggle already described, and of certain biased verdicts by the Romanian courts at Sibiu and in Cluj, nearly 300,000,000 lei worth of real estate (houses, lands, etc.) belonging to the Status were transferred to the Romanian state. At the same time the buildings belonging to the Piarist high school at Timişoara, the Minorite high schools at Arad and Şimleul Silvaniei, and the Piarist and Reformed high schools at Sighetul Marmaţiei were also transferred by Ghibu to the state. In each case, the excuse given was that these institutions had been created at one time by the Hungarian state, hence their properties were actually Hungarian state properties to which the Romanian state was now entitled by right of inheritance. As a consequence of this intervention by Ghibu, the Hungarian Roman Catholic Church was deprived of properties worth almost 600 million lei.[12] The news of his activities spread far and wide, and one of the most prestigious components of the francophone press in Geneva concluded what the Hungarians had known for a long time: "The slyness involved, and the transgressions against the laws in effect demonstrate that in Romania they will stop at nothing in order to impoverish the Hungarian minority."[13]

Indeed, because of these manifold limitations set on the right private property, the Hungarians who came under Romanian rule suffered enormous financial losses. One of the experts on the issue estimated the losses suffered by the Hungarians by 1930 at 41,660,837,490 lei — that is the equivalent of 40 million English pounds sterling or 200 million

U.S. dollars.[14] The losses resulting from later confiscations and expropriations — the expropriations for the military purposes, the financial disadvantages resulting from the economic laws passed in 1937-39 — amounted, according to very rough estimates, to 15 billion additional lei. All in all, therefore, the various social strata among the Hungarian population lost about 56 billion lei worth of properties, which is exactly the amount of reparations that Hungary was forced to pay as a result of the cease-fire of 1945.

We may conclude that this most important human right proclaimed during the French Revolution, the right to private property remained nothing but an illusion to the Hungarian population throughout the Romanian regime. The property of Hungarians was restricted on the most varied excuses, as a consequence of which the population lost the equivalent of close to 300 million dollars (1945 equivalent). As we have seen, the large scale impoverishment of the Hungarian population was the consequence of the financial losses it suffered.

Freedom of the Press

Since the French Revolution, every modern nation-state has recognized the immeasurable significance of freedom of the press. The Constitution of 1923, expressly guaranteed this freedom. According to paragraph 25 of the constitution "no censorship can be instituted, nor any measure restricting publications, or the sale and distribution of these."

By the time this provision of the constitution came into effect, prior censorship in the formerly Hungarian areas attached Romania had been in effect for four years, since the beginning of the occupation. As long as this occupation could be considered a temporary measure, the state of emergency and censorship could be justified according to the terms of the Peace Treaty. These measures were understandable in view of the possible disturbances resulting from the change in sovereignty. But with the signing and proclamation of the Peace Treaty in 1920, this period of uncertainty came to an end. The retention of the state of emergency and of censorship was not justified by any actual disturbance. In spite of this both measures remained in effect unchanged, curtailing to a large extent the activities of the Hungarian press.

Prior censorship and a state emergency were declared along the border by directive 2939 of July 1920, and extended to the entire country by directive 4209 of October 1920 and directive 853 of March 1921 to the borders themselves. Directive 32 of January 1922, abolished censorship in all areas except those under military control and in areas where the state of emergency had been specially declared. Directive 246 issued at the end of January in the same year, abolished prior censorship during elections for the constitutional assembly. But directive 131 published in the *Monitorul Oficial* of January 23, 1923, proclaimed the state of emergency and prior censorship along the Hungarian border, including a line extending to the towns of Sighetul Marmaţiei, Dej, Apahida, Aiud, Lunca Mureşului, Teiuş, Alba Iulia, and Petroşani. Consequently all the larger Hungarian towns, including Cluj, Oradea, Timişoara, and Arad — all centers of Hungarian intellectual life — fell within the purview of the censorship measure. In other, mainly Romanian areas, the Romanian papers were no longer subjected to censorship.[15]

The Romanians of Transylvania themselves noted the strangeness of this situation more than once and protested against it with praiseworthy objectivity. Everyone was curious to see whether the government would abolish censorship after the adoption of the constitution. After all, the paragraph of the constitution already cited did not authorize any form of prior censorship. In spite of this, censorship continued in the larger towns inhabited by the minorities, and protests by Hungarians were in vain. Then the expert on minorities of the Romanian National Party of Transylvania, Ghiţă Pop, intervened in the matter at the May 30, 1923 session of parliament. He objected to the retention of censorship and pointed to the freedom of the press that had prevailed within the former Hungarian state which made do without censorship. "Suffice to note that from 1867 until the war broke out, there was neither state of emergency nor censorship in Transylvania. During those 42 years no newspaper appeared with columns in blank, not even Romanian papers. We protest against these sins of the government in the name of national diplomacy and of the decisions adopted at Alba Iulia.[16]

Pop's intervention, however, remained without serious repercussions; the situation changed not a bit and Hungarian papers were still subject to censorship. As we shall see, the activities of the censors elicited most peculiar and hair-raising scenes. In their private contacts and on other occasions the Hungarians did not fail to complain to their Romanian acquaintances about this curtailment of the freedom of the press, which applied mainly to Hungarian papers. Towards the end of 1923, the Bucharest daily of the Romanian National Party of Transylvania tried to bring up once again the subject of restrictions on the freedom of the press. The author of the article demanded in harsh words that the freedom of the press guaranteed in the constitution translated into reality:

> Five years after the cease-fire in Transylvania censorship still stands. The minority papers, the primary victims of censorship, are published with columns in blank even today. What may be printed in the Romanian dailies of Bucharest may not appear in the minority newspapers of Timişoara, Arad, Oradea, Satu Mare, etc. In some cities, the minorities publications are subjected to threefold censorship: by the military, the civilian administration, and the prosecutor's office.

The article condemned censorship in harsh words and demanded freedom of the press.[17]

However, neither Romanian nor Hungarian interventions led to any result. Romanians did enjoy freedom of the press, but the Hungarian papers within the areas under state of emergency did not. Prior censorship was retained by the Liberal government and by the Averescu regime which followed it. Finally, in 1928, the National Peasant Party regime presided by Iuliu Maniu satisfied the demands made over the years. Decree 2489 published in number 260 of the official paper on November 21, 1928, put a halt to censorship of the press throughout the country.[18]

Finally freedom of the press was extended to the Hungarian press as well. From 1928 to 1933, there was no prior censorship. During this five-year period, the Hungarian press was able to progress and write more freely. Soon, however, restriction were set once again on; prior censorship was reinstated by decrees of February 5, 1933 and December 30, 1933 throughout the country. From then on, until the end of the regime in 1940, censorship remained in force. Of course, it affected primarily the Hungarian press, since it was much more lenient when it came to newspapers published in Romanian.

The Hungarian Press in the Shadow of the Censors

In general censorship strangled all criticism in the Hungarian press. Prior controls as practiced by the military authorities were always aimed against description of the reality and manifestations of critical analysis.

Whatever the censors objected to was crossed out in red pencil in the submitted manuscript. Often even prior censorship did not protect the other papers from further harassment. This should come as no surprise because, in the realm of ideas, it becomes all the easier to express certain things by means of similes and hidden meaning when the censors are uneducated. They took revenge against issues of the papers after censorship for any manifestations of the critical spirit in even greater rage. Then the papers were banned one after another. There was scarcely a year when some Hungarian paper or other was not banned. The police banned the *Temesvári Napló* on June 24, 1920. On December 29 of the same year, the *Rendkívüli Újság* of Timişoara suffered the same fate. The *Nagyváradi Napló* was banned the same day. On January 15, 1921, the *Brassói Lapok* lost its right of distribution by mail. On March 5, 1921, Ioan Meteş, the mayor of Cluj, banned all Hungarian papers in the city since, in his opinion, they were too critical of the measures adopted by the Romanian authorities. For ten days not a single Hungarian paper appeared on the streets.[19]

In February 1922, the *Ellenzék* of Cluj printed a report on conditions prevailing at the clinics of the city. The article described in satirical tones the varied treatments to which the patients were subjected and certain other manifestations, without blaming the dominant Romanian population in any way. The morning after the article was published, the editors of the *Ellenzék* were warned by telephone three times that no one should remain on the premises in the evening, because the patriotic Romanian students were preparing a demonstration. The editors immediately called police headquarters and requested protection. The chief of police refused police protection on the grounds that he had no reason to dispatch troops on the basis of mere rumors. On February 6, in accordance with the warning received over the telephone, a huge crowd attacked the paper's editorial office and vandalized the presses. Chairs and tables were smashed, windows shattered, the copies of the papers torn to pieces and the premises ransacked. Nor did they stop at that. On March 1, 1922, the postal services withdrew the right of distribution by mail from the *Ellenzék* for a period of six months.

On January 22, 1924, the *Esti Lap* of Oradea was banned. The weekly *Székely Szó* published at Gherogheni soon suffered the same fate. On January 12, 1925, the Minister of the Interior banned the *Friss Újság* of Oradea for three months. On April 7 of the same year, the weekly *Katolikus Élet* of Satu Mare suffered the same fate. In 1926, it was the turn of the *Magyar Újság* of Arad and the *Székely Napló* of Tîrgu Mureş to be banned. All this happened during the period of censorship when the articles printed in these papers had already been subjected to previous press controls. But the closing down of newspapers and aggressive demonstrations occurred even in the period of freedom of the press, when there was no censorship. Thus, on March 19, 1931, a group of Romanian student protestors broke into the editorial offices of the daily *Magyar Szó* at Oradea, smashed the furniture and scattered the records. Later they smashed the windows of the offices of the paper *Nagyvárad.*[20]

At the beginning, it was the practice of the censors to cross out the objectionable parts of the text of a given article, while the remaining words could be printed. Thus the papers were printed with parts left in blank or with asterisks in lieu of the deleted words. The January 13, 1921, issue of the *Bihari Újság* reprinted a censored article which appeared in a Transylvanian paper on December 25, 1920:

> How can we move when in Transylvania once again***. How can we move when we are exposed to that terrible misunderstanding***. Today we may say so outright, as well as the fact that we cannot extend a hand covered with kid-gloves to the one who ***. Today we awakened to the holiday of love, but we are not even asking for love. We are sober enough to know that ***. We are requesting dignified conditions from those in power and guarantees regarding the Hungarian population *** let it begin the renewal of its economic and cultural work. ***[21]

Soon the Romanian authorities realized that this manner of censorship was too obvious, revealing the workings of administrative aggression. The editors of the papers, therefore, received orders to the effect that they may not leave blank spaces in lieu of the deleted parts and that the sentences rendered absurd by deletions should be replaced by short connecting sentences that made sense. Indeed, after this directive was put into practice, the intervention of the censors became less obvious. But the editorial offices continued to worry about the possible consequences of some misunderstood metaphore. The temporary or permanent ban placed upon a given newspaper, could occur without any apparent reason in the period of regular censorship. The permanent ban placed upon the *Rendkívüli Újság* of Arad provides a classic illustration of this procedure.

The *Rendkívüli Újság* was launched as a weekly in 1920. Each of its articles was authorized by previous censorship. Yet, censorship proved no protection and the paper was banned on account of one the censored articles. In consideration of the affection and loyalty of its reading public, the owner of the paper wanted to transform the weekly into a daily, but could not realize his project for a long time because of objections on the part of government officials. The Romanian authorities justified their ban on the grounds that there was no paper.

Then the owner, in order to disprove this explanation, purchased a quantity of paper sufficient to print the newspaper for six months. Thus, the first issue of his converted daily could finally appear on October 1. This limited freedom did not last long though. On Christmas Eve, as the special issue was already coming off the presses, Romanian soldiers and detectives entered the editorial offices carrying an order issued by the military command banning the paper for a period of three months, without explanation. The Hungarian delegation that visited the police prefect to inquire about the ban received no explanation or justification regarding the procedure of the military. An investigation, was launched, beginning with the arrest of the editor-in-chief of the paper on Christmas night. He was released a few days later, but the reasons for his arrest or his release were not communicated to him. Later, the case was adjourned indefinitely without further discussion, and the paper could appear once again, but only after the three-month period had expired. The owner and editor-in-chief never found out what caused the ban or the arrest of the editor. Before Easter of 1921, the police appeared in the printing shop once again, confiscated the articles passed by the censor, and arrested the editor-in-chief along with the responsible director. Two days later, the editor-in-chief was released without interrogation, and the responsible editor released upon signing a deposition. The charge of irredentism mentioned in the deposition by way of justification for the arrest, proved so ridiculous, that no further investigation or discussion was undertaken in the matter. On June 30, the military commander at Arad summoned the responsible editor to inform him that were no objection to the continued publication of the paper, and the officials of the paper got ready for the publication of further issues. They formulated an appeal to subscribers. When the text of the appeal was submitted to the censorship office in accordance with the laws, the chief censor refused to read the text. He referred to the order of the prefect according to which any new periodical could appear only with the consent of the prefect. The prefect, however, was not at home. When he returned, he responded to the inquiry as follows: "In consideration of the tendency of the paper, I feel that it is not needed." The advocates of the paper then turned to Petru Groza, the Minister of Transylvania, whose good intentions and democratic attitude were well known. Groza wrote the prefect a letter, as a consequence of which the prefect authorized the paper in October 1921. But now it was the chief of police who intervened, banning the paper for good on January 3, 1922. When the journalist Endre Andor inquired regarding the reasons for the ban, the chief of police, Ovidius Gritta made the following declaration: "I have banned it, period. If I do something, I don't have to provide a justification. And if the Minister himself authorizes it a hundred times, I will ban it a hundred times."[22]

As becomes clear from this history of the banning of the *Rendkívüli Újság* of Arad, censorship did not protect the papers and the journalists from further consequences. Nor did it protect them from press trials. These press trials were common practice during the period of censorship, as well as during the period of freedom of the press in 1928-33. The slightest hint, the mildest criticism were sufficient grounds to launch a press trial. Perusing the records of these press trials and the volumes of the *Magyar Kisebbség* [Hungarian Minority] which published the sentences brought in these trials, we do not find a single case even approaching in severity the expressions or intentions contained in the articles published in the *Tribuna* and other Romanian papers in the period of the Dual Monarchy, under Hungarian rule. The Hungarian papers, aware of Romanian censorship and the severity of Romanian authorities, wrote far more mildly and in a more subdued way than had the Romanian papers in former times. The editor-in-chief carried out internal censorship before sending any article to the censors and rewrote or blunted any portion that might be subject to censorship. Nevertheless, in most cases the censors still found objectionable parts.

The attitude of the Romanian courts during these press trials was quite interesting. Their procedures were designed to exhaust the journalists by means of repeated harassment, innumerable summonses and fines. They usually refrained from sentencing anyone to extensive jail terms, hardly warranted by the mild expressions used by the authors. Nevertheless, many Hungarian journalists spent time in jail, and practically no journalist of any significance had been spared a couple of dozen press trials. Endre Szász, the editor-in-chief of the *Keleti Újság*, underwent 75 press trials. Domokos Olajos had nearly 50, Miklós Krenner (Spectator) had 25, whereas Jenő Szentimrei, József Végh, János Botos, Gyula Walter, József Nyírő, János Mátrai, and István Zágoni had to defend themselves in court against press trial in from ten to fifteen instances. The following Hungarian journalists received jail sentences as a result of press trials held in Cluj: István Ványolos (three months), János Zomora (three months), Tibor Rajnai (a month and a half), Aladár Bakos (one month), Domokos Olajos (a month and a half). At Tîrgu Mureş the following spent time in jail: Zoltán Finta (two months), Zsigmond Gyulai (three months), László Sebestyén (three months). At Oradea: László Béltelki (six months), Árpád Árvay (two months). Albert Figus sat for one month at Satu Mare. Later, Béla Hekszner sat for three months, and János Pap, a Uniate of

Romanian descent, sat for one month at Cluj. Many other journalists had been sentenced, but benefitted from an amnesty. Among these we find: Miklós Krenner, Jenő Szentimrei, György Perédi, Lajos Pap, Sándor Hegedűs, Sándor Dénes, László Baradlay, etc. Many a journalist was severely fined for some courageous piece of writing, among them Béla Demeter, János Botos, and József Nyírő. The Romanian authorities were aware of the touchy situation created by the numerous press trials and therefore extended the occasional amnesties to press trials as well. 1,200 press trials benefitted from an amnesty during the Greater Romanian regime. A rough estimate of the amounts involved in fines levied against Hungarian journalists, in the area of Cluj alone, would be a half a million lei.[23]

In the first days of December 1932, a Romanian crowd returning from an "anti-revisionist" rally entered Cornești [Sînfalva], a community of Turda-Arieş county, destroyed the homes of the Hungarian population, and seriously battered several Hungarians. When the Hungarian papers gave a faithful description of these events, it was not the Romanians who were punished for the demonstration, the destruction of property or for the assault on human beings, but the Hungarian journalist who reported it. The Romanian courts did not consider the anti-Hungarian agitation by Romanians a punishable offense, even though the Hungarian criminal code remained in effect until 1936. Its Article V of 1878, protected the national sentiments of the nationalities by declaring agitation against nationalities a punishable offense. As mentioned, before 1918, in a specific instance, a Hungarian court had found József Imre, an official from Hunyad [Hunedoara] county, guilty of disturbing peaceful relations between the nationalities by an article he had written about the Romanian intelligentsia. Not a single Romanian journalist was sentenced for agitation against Hungarians during the Romanian regime. In 1936, the editor Octavian Dobrota published an article in the November 12 issue of the weekly *Glas Românesc în Regiunea Secuizată* that surpassed all previous incitements at hatred. In this article the editor threatened the Hungarians with the organization of a Saint Bartholomew night among them, referred to the Hungarians as vipers, and demanded that they be sent to the stake. The leaders of the Hungarians of the county of Odorheiu, denounced Oktavian Dobrota on the basis of Article 172 of Law V of 1878 still in effect, but the prosecutor's office of Odorheiu Secuiesc responded with the argument that it could not proceed, for want of a crime committed.[24]

In the chapter on language, we have seen the struggle of the Hungarian publishers and the parliamentary representatives of the

Hungarians to preserve the use of Hungarian place names. One of the greatest regrets of the Hungarian papers was that after 1933, they could not print place names in Hungarian for the benefit of the Hungarian readers in their papers.

Censorship extended not merely to newspapers and periodicals, but to all publications. Scientific, literary and artistic productions had to be submitted to the censors just like the drafts of articles meant for the papers. Thus, freedom of thought suffered the same limitations as freedom of the press. Any book that was not to the censors' liking could not be published. Books that had passed censorship and had been printed were often subjected to confiscation. In 1922, Elemér Jakabffy, one of the best prepared intellectual and political leaders of the Hungarian minority of Transylvania, published extensive statistics under the title *The Statistics of Transylvania*. In the introduction to his work he responded to the distortions contained in the official publication, *Dicţionarul Transilvaniei*, published in 1921 by the heads of the provincial office of the Bureau of Statistics in Cluj, G. Martinovici and N. Istrati. In this work, the Romanian authors simply exchanged the Hungarian population of many a community with Romanians, and in many places they purported to count several hundred Romanians, where in 1910 there had been not even a dozen. Instead of responding with scientific arguments to Jakabffy's challenge, the Romanian authors turned to the court-martial authorities, which proceeded to confiscate all the copies of Jakabffy's publication and launched court-martial against the author for his publication.

The censorship of books and other publications followed the same line as the censorship of newspapers. The objectionable parts had to be omitted. The fate of the reading primer published by the Minerva publishing house of Cluj in 1935, created a great stir. The primer was written by Domokos Gyallay, the editor of the weekly *Magyar Nép*, which was most popular and had a wide circulation. It was designed for those Hungarians who could not learn to read and write in their mother tongue on account of the cultural and educational policies promoted by the government. The material of the book had been examined and approved beforehand by the censorship bureau of Cluj. Then the book was printed and distributed. Hungarian priests who learned about the publication through advertisements in the papers brought it to the attention of their flock, and the primer soon became very popular among the population eager to receive an education. It sold close to 40,000 copies within a matter of a few years. It was appreciated by the people because it taught the illiterate adults and youngsters who remained illiterate through no fault of their own, to read easily with the help of the most modern educational devices.   But the Romanian teachers of the "cultural zone" soon realized the danger this book represented to their effort to Romanianize, and sent their denunciations or their requests to have the book banned one after the other to the Ministry of Education. The Minister of Education, Anghelescu, well-known for his anti-Hungarian sentiments, discussed the matter with his colleague the Minister of the Interior, who banned the primer through a directive published in the bulletin of the gendarmerie. The directive ordered the gendarmes to confiscate the primer wherever it was found, since the Minister of the Interior had banned its distribution. The Hungarian press and population, however, was not familiar with the official bulletin of the gendarmes, hence could not have known about the ban. It could not have imagined that the Romanian authorities would consider this primer, the contents of which were entirely innocuous and which had already been approved by the censors, as a threat. Great was their consternation when official court proceedings were launched against almost 50 priests, accused of disseminating the forbidden publication. All the priests were found guilty and had to pay a heavy fine because of the struggle against illiteracy among the Hungarian population.

The author of the primer, Domokos Gyallay, was also summoned to appear at the court of Tîrgu Mureş. He was charged with spreading what according to the Romanian interpretation constituted an "irredentist spirit in the primer." The specifics of the accusation were interesting. Objections were raised to a poem by Károly Kisfaludy written at least eighty years before the advent of Romanian rule and titled "Szülőföldem szép határa" [The Beautiful Horizons of my Village]. The Romanian prosecutor was convinced this poem contained veiled irredentism. Objection was raised against the few sentences of the primer in which the author discussed the numerical ranking of the countries of Europe and pointed out that the Hungarians were in twelfth place. The conclusion was that the Hungarian nation was not among the smallest. The prosecutor perceived this as an attempt to arouse Hungarian racial pride. A third objection purported to detect irredentist intentions in the sentence the author used to illustrate the pronunciation of the letter "sz:" "szép város Szeged" [Szeged is a beautiful city]. The last and most serious objection was that the author included in his primer an illustration representing the poet Petőfi clad in ceremonial Hungarian dress. On the basis of all this, the Romanian attorneys came to the conclusion that the author of the primer was an incorrigible irredentist, whose intention was to incite peaceloving peasants otherwise, satisfied with the Romanian regime against the

Romanian state, by publishing such a primer. The court had better sense and refrained from sentencing the author.

We may summarize the principles guiding the Romanian censors on the basis of examples culled from Hungarian papers and publications:

1. The censors consistently intervened to prevent the promotion of ethnic solidarity among the various strata of the Hungarian population through the Hungarian press. No article aimed at enhancing ethnic solidarity or organizing boycotts could appear in print. As can be seen from the censored issue of the *Bihari Újság*, where the article mentioned that one could not extend a kid glove when it came to social conflicts, the censor erased the remainder of the sentence. Obviously, he intended to prevent the spread of the principle of a Hungarian boycott against those who abandoned the Hungarians to their fate. As we have seen, the Romanian press of Hungary in the period of the Dual Monarchy enjoyed the broadest possible freedom in the matter of proclaiming and organizing ethnic boycotts, and Hungarian prosecutors never initiated proceedings for articles advocating such action. The Romanian censorship offices received instructions to that effect precisely because the Romanians of Transylvania were well aware of the tremendous impact of boycotts and expressions of solidarity, popularized in wide circles by the Romanian press. The Romanian censors never allowed articles attacking renegade Hungarians for fraternizing with the Romanians to appear in the Hungarian press. Nor would they allow articles designed to organize social resistance against measures oppressing the Hungarian population. Hungarian papers did not even attempt to do what constituted one of the points of the program presented by the *Libertatea* of Orăştie, namely to train the Romanian people to perform acts of terrorism against the authorities.

2. Another principle of the censors was to intervene at all times to prevent the publication of positive statements describing the Hungarian ethnic group, in other words, any article that might serve to foster Hungarian national consciousness. As mentioned, they even objected to such manifestations in a primer, and called the author an irredentist for merely mentioning statistics on the population of Hungary. They were afraid that the readers of the primer would feel their pride enhanced once they found out that the Hungarian nation was not so small or so negligible an entity

as the Romanians made them out to be.   The bureaus of
censorship consistently attempted to prevent the publication of
any communication that might serve to enhance Hungarian
national consciousness of anything along those lines.

3. The Romanian bureaus of censorship consistently and
deliberately prevented the Hungarian press from criticizing the
Romanian state, Romanian national sentiment, or Romanian
historical figures.   Criticism directed against the state or the
leading nation in the state of the type and tone practiced by the
Romanian papers under Hungarian rule remained impossible
throughout the Romanian regime.   Expressions resorted to by the
Romanian press without any risk, such as those in connection
with the millennial celebrations (the ceremony was "a great
steal," the occupation of the fatherland "an act of turpitude"),
could not be used by the Hungarian papers.   Hungarian
journalists, irritated by the extensive harassment against them,
overcame this prohibition by simply reprinting articles published
in Romanian opposition papers.   Of course, Romanian journalists
could resort to the sharpest critical tones and when censorship
prevented Hungarian papers from resorting to criticism, the
Hungarian papers simply repeated the descriptions and criticisms
printed in the Romanian press.   This method became particularly
common after 1934, when every Hungarian paper sported a
column title "What do we read in the Romanian press?"   The
censors did not delete these clippings or quotes, hence the
Hungarian public was able to become aware of conditions in the
country.

4. It was a basic principle of the Romanian censors not to allow
the printing of any news that might reflect favorably on
Hungary in the eyes of the Hungarian readers.   The most
innocuous message from Budapest was ruthlessly deleted.   In
1937, the censors deleted an article from the periodical *Kiáltó
Szó* published in Cluj, which presented doctrines taught by the
Reformed Church in connection with the Eucharistic Congress
taking place in Budapest.   All the censor noted was that the
article mentioned a congress in Budapest, and this was enough
for him to intervene.   Calendars and books could not print any
photographs relating to Hungary.   In vain do we search the
Hungarian calendars for communications such as used to fill the
Romanian calendars of yore printed in Hungary.   All the copies

of the *Kalotaszegi Naptár* printed at Huedin in 1936 were
confiscated because the calendar included a portrait of the
Hungarian prime minister, allowed by the censor. It also
happened that the censor was not sufficiently conversant in
intellectual matters, and raised the most absurd objections. Even
high-ranking Romanian officials made such mistakes
occasionally. In connection with an eviction trial, in Cluj, a
lawyer named Horváth described an apartment, which "rather
resembled Gorki's *The Lower Depths* than the apartment of a
respectable person." The judge then summoned Maxim Gorki to
make a statement regarding his shelter. At Christmas in 1921,
the Hungarian women of Satu Mare organized a collection for
underprivileged children. The donation of a Catholic priest,
József Csáki, was registered under the name "Saint Anthony" on
the roster of donors. The police, however, suspected irredentist
motives behind the collection and ordered an immediate
investigation. All the donors, including "Saint Anthony," were
summoned for the investigation.

In 1938, the material for the Reformed calendar to be
published in Cluj was submitted to the censor. Included was a
report on a book, titled *Kősziklán épült ház ostroma* [The Siege
of a House Built on Rock] by Bálint Kocsi-Csergő, a Reformed
clergyman from the 17th century. This report presented the
ecclesiastic and political conditions of the time, as described in
the book, without any hint of the present. Nevertheless, the
censorship office deleted the entire report and banned its
publication.

5. The censors did not merely ban items from appearing in the
Hungarian press, but also prescribed what was to be published.
Such cases occurred even before 1937, but these were not so
general, and constituted abuses of authority more than anything
else. Such was the case of the weekly *Székely Nép* of Sfîntu
Gheorghe in 1936. In October of that year Bidu, the prefect of
the county of Trei-Scaune, delivered a speech in which he made
inappropriate statements with regard to the Hungarians. He
sent the text of his speech to the editors of the weekly, enjoining
them to publish it in its entirety. The editors did not comply
with this illegal order. The censor, who wished to abide by the
laws as well, censored the paper as usual and gave permission
for printing. Bidu, however, banned the publication of the
Székely Nép for failure to comply with his orders. The editors

then turned to the attorney general's office, which lifted the ban and authorized publication. The issues of the paper were distributed to the subscribers. Then the prefect, disregarding the authorization of the attorney general, issued orders to have the paper confiscated. His agents went all around town and removed all unsold copies of the paper from the newsstands.[25]

From 1938, the censors regularly prescribed the material to be published in the Hungarian papers . The articles prepared in the censorship bureau were sent over to the editorial offices of Hungarian papers with an order to publish at such and such a place within the paper. Soon all Hungarian newspapers were printing articles written in the censorship office and serving Romanian ends. Some of these articles attacked the internal enemies of the government, while others served the ends of defense. For a year and a half all the papers of Cluj were required to print on the front page an appeal by the colonel serving as prefect of Cluj county for donations on behalf of the Romanian army. Soon they were required to publish articles in which the readers of these Hungarian papers could find insults directed against Hungary and sharp condemnations of actions taken by the Hungarian Government. Thus, in this last period of the regime, the censors were no longer content to prevent the publication of items that might prove harmful to Romanians, but obliged the Hungarian papers to print articles prepared in advance and serving Romanian purposes at a specific location in the paper. Thus not even the faintest shadow of freedom remained to the Hungarian press.

Freedom of Assembly and Association

Freedom of assembly and association, the most significant right besides the freedom of the press, was restricted in the same manner throughout the period of Romanian rule. Each of the Romanian constitutions explicitly guaranteed freedom of assembly. According to Article 28 of the Constitution of 1923, "Romanians have the right to assemble peacefully and unarmed in order to discuss all problems without distinction as to race, language, or religion, while observing the laws which regulate the exercise of this right. Prior authorization is not required for such activity." In spite of this provision of the Constitution, the Romanian executive placed strict restrictions of the exercise of this right during the fifteen years of the state of emergency and, in several places, made the exercise of this right altogether impossible. Since, as we have seen, the state of emergency was applied primarily in the areas inhabited by Hungarians, particularly before 1928, the restrictions also hampered primarily the Hungarians right to assemble.

From the beginning of the occupation to 1928, that is during the first ten years of Romanian rule, it was primarily the military authorities, while later it was the civilian and police authorities that placed restrictions of the right of assembly. The process was never uniform. In some places, meetings could only be authorized by the military, elsewhere it was the police, and in some areas three authorities had to concur. There was no preferential treatment of any kind as regards the purpose and character of the meeting; prior authorization was required indiscriminately, whether the meeting was of a religious, cultural, or political nature. In most places, however, the military played the primary role as a result of the nature of the state of emergency. In general, the military authorities intervened in all matters, in a decisive way. It was they who decided whether a meeting should or should not be authorized. As Şorban noted in his leaflet already cited: "High-ranking officers from the Old Kingdom now played a role in politics, in administration, in transportation, in the press, and even in literature and the arts. They hit upon a new concept of esthetic beauty: "What I say is beautiful is beautiful, because it is beautiful, otherwise I cut you down!" Then Şorban comments: "But is it really necessary that Transylvania remain under a military caretaker even today?"[26] This military caretaking government lasted until 1928, and from 1918 to 1940 along the borders; in other areas of the country it resumed from 1933 to 1940.

If a Hungarian cultural association or diocese planned to organize a meeting, a cultural event, or some religious assembly, it had to request prior approval. In the villages, the authorization came from the notary or the sheriff, whereas in the towns it was the superintendent of police, the governor of the county and the military command. As mentioned, in most cities authorization had to be granted by all three entities. This procedure hampered the orderly existence of Hungarian cultural associations, religious gatherings and disrupted to a considerable extent. There were times when the E. M. E. was unable to function at all because of the difficulties in securing permissions for meetings. As an expert on the history of the E. M. E. reported in one of his articles, the state of emergency signified that it took six to eight days to secure authorization for conferences or meetings, provided one took the applications everywhere in person and was lucky enough to get them approved on the first try. Therefore, they usually turned to some clever younger man to run these errands, since the procedure required a great deal of perseverance and physical effort. At the beginning of 1928, the association hired a new young secretary. Since he was not familiar with the difficulties involved in securing authorizations, Baron Sándor Mansberg, the vice-president, sent him special written instructions containing detailed information. The instructions ran as follows:

The application is to be addressed to the command of the Army Corps, in three original copies; the first of these requires an eight lei stamp, the others one lei each. Copy one goes to the *Siguranţa*, by the railroad, Str. Basarab, corner house, first floor. Secondly, after the *Siguranţa* peruses the application, it goes to the police superintendent (two-lei application, an eight lei stamp, Room 2 on the first floor, through the lobby, to the room opening on the street. Thirdly, if the superintendent signs it, the application is to be carried to the county office, ground floor, on the right hand side (one copy of the application remains here). It is to be registered, and a pertinent dossier is prepared in the next room. On the first floor, the secretary takes the original copy, to be signed by the prefect (it is registered on that floor as well). Fourthly, once the *Siguranţa*, the police and the county office have signed the application, it goes to the army corps headquarters (Str. Regală 19, V, 21) where it is to be submitted with an eight lei stamp, and whence it would be sent to Major Gutean at the barracks on C. Dorobanţilor. The latter will "elaborate" it and submit it to the General for his signature (the General signs on Wednesdays and Saturdays). Then it is returned to the barracks, where they make out a transmittal slip and send it to the police. The following day the authorization may be retrieved from the office of the Police Superintendent (with a five lei stamp).

The entire process pertained to a cultural event against which no Romanian authority had ever raised a serious objection on grounds of national security. These were the circumstances under which the E. M. E. was forced to struggle in Kolozsvár, the center of intellectual life in Transylvania, for an entire decade, from 1918 to 1928. The officials of the association sent various memoranda requesting that the lengthy procedures be simplified, in consideration of the cultural function of the association, but these requests went unheeded.

The state of emergency was lifted from 1928 to 1933, except for the strip along the borders. During this period, freedom of assembly should not have been curtailed in any way, in accordance with the provisions of the constitution. But the Romanian authorities still paid no heed to

the right of assembly guaranteed by the constitution. As mentioned, the
text of the constitution specified that prior authorization for the exercise
of this right was unnecessary; in spite of this, prior police authorization
was required by the police for any meeting or assembly to be held in
areas inhabited by the Hungarians. The prefect of the county of
Odorhei issued a directive in September 1932, requiring application for
holding any public meeting. This circular made the securing of prior
authorization mandatory throughout the county. These applications had
to be submitted to the county office at least ten days in advance along
with the recommendation of the local police of sheriff.[27] Similar
restrictions prevailed in other areas inhabited by Hungarians.

According to a directive issued on December 30, 1933, the military
authorities were once again authorized to forbid or dissolve any
gathering regardless of the number of participants or of the venue if, in
their estimation, such gatherings or meetings would cause a
disturbance.[28] These provisions were rendered even stricter by the
Act of February 11, 1938. They were also rendered simpler, however,
by specifying that military authorization was the only one required for
holding meetings. General Cristea Vasilescu, the commander of Army
Corps IV of Cluj, prescribed the following in his directive number 1 of
February 23, 1938:

Under the state of emergency, in the district of the IV Army
Corps, any meetings and gatherings that have not been
authorized by the Army Corps are forbidden in Cluj or without
the permission of the local command in those areas where
military units are stationed, or without the permission of the
local county authorities in other areas of district. Permission
issued by the police headquarters in the towns and by the county
office in the communities is required for betrothals, weddings,
baptisms, village bals, conferences, soirées and cultural events.
Permission has to be requested ahead of time, indicating the
objective, venue, and exact time of the gathering in the
application. If these prescriptions are not observed, the
organizers as well as the participants are considered in
contravention of the order.... All those contravening the order
will be subject to court-martial and, in accordance with
paragraph 5 of royal decree 856/1938, will be sentenced to
imprisonment for a period of one month to two years and to the
payment of a fine as stipulated in paragraph 25 of the law code.

These provisions completely paralyzed the life of associations in most places. Once again, a meeting of even two of three individuals became a danger; after all, even for a christening held in someone's private home, permission had to be requested from the army corps headquarters. We have seen the situation resulting from this directive in the religious and ecclesiastic life of the Székely area. It completely halted the Bible-reading circles, the presbyters, as well as this sort of religious or ecclesiastic meeting, at times rendering the very administration of the churches an impossibility. This terrible nightmare lasted all way to the Vienna Arbitration Treaty (Award) of August 30, 1940, and continued in southern Transylvania for years thereafter.

In most places, the masses of Hungarians were completely deprived of the right of association and meeting as a result of the state of emergency, in effect for fifteen years. Enormous patience and perseverance were needed to secure the prescribed permission under the circumstances. Innumerable times some meeting would be announced in the press weeks in advance, and the participants would appear at the usual place and at the announced time only to be informed in a few lines tacked to the door that the meeting has been postponed because the authorities had not granted the permission requested.

There was no time to publish this information in the press because no one knew until the last moment whether or not permission would be forthcoming. The result of the process was exactly as the Romanian authorities expected: fostering disinterest on the part of members in the activities of their association. Hungarian papers and the reports of associations are filled with invitations such as this one: "If the members of the association do not meet the prescribed quorum three times in a row the meeting will be held regardless of a quorum." Thus the official restrictions achieved their objective: in most cases lack of participation prevented the associations from fulfilling their true purpose and performing their task.

It also happened quite frequently that the authorized general assembly was dissolved by the Romanian authorities while the deliberations were already under way. There were notorious cases when some meeting of a sizable congregation was rendered impossible. In the 1934 report by the bishop of the Hungarian Unitarian Church we read:

As regards this past year I feel as if the Lord had been addressing me: do not look back, lest you turn into a pillar of salt! Whichever way I look I see but darkness, smoke rising to the skies, and destruction.... Should I mention the shameful, humiliating treatment which disrupted, with a crudeness reminiscent of a state of war, our synod of consecration and foundation at Cristur?[29]

These cases make it clear to what extent the Romanian citizens of Hungarian nationality were deprived of the freedom of assembly guaranteed in the constitution. As regards to the freedom of association, the constitution contained guarantees similar to those for the freedom of assembly. In spite of this, when it came to applying the law regarding legal persons, the Romanian courts and authorities questioned the legal personality of former Hungarian associations, or failed to recognize them altogether, placing these associations in a position of utmost insecurity. Recognition of the Transylvanian Museum Association, of the Székely National Museum of Sfîntu Gheorghe, of the Teleki Library, as well as of Hungarian Cultural Association of Transylvania was delayed for the duration of the regime, excepting the last one. This recognition was still not granted in spite of the promises contained in the Minority Statute of 1938. The courts granted recognition to legal persons on the basis of a recommendation from the pertinent ministry, but this recommendation was delayed indefinitely. In our chapter on culture we have described the difficulties experienced by new associations in gaining authorization, that is legal recognition. Thus, the right of association of Romanian citizens of Hungarian background was extremely restricted throughout the regime, and the legal personality of the most significant and oldest Hungarian associations and foundations was not recognized. The recognition of the Hungarian Farmers' Association of Transylvania took almost ten years, the Ministry requesting even more documentation, the documentation getting misplaced, etc., until finally their quest was crowned with success in 1929. Thus, the Romanian state leadership restricted the rights of Hungarians in a manner similar to the one employed in other areas.

Freedom of Worship

As we have seen in the chapter on churches, freedom of religion was limited to a single right in Romania: the right to hold service. Indeed, as regards to this freedom there were no restrictions throughout the duration of the regime. Divine services were authorized in all parts of the country, regardless of the language spoken. In some cases, however, even the services were restricted: when held by those churches which were defined as "sects" according to the Romanian ideology. For instance, strong official pressures were placed on the Baptist Church in Transylvania, as well as in the old Kingdom, in an attempt to deprive it of its followers. In 1936, the repression of the Baptists attained such proportions that they invited a retired British general to visit Romania to help settle their problem. The British general visited all the pertinent Romanian ministers, requesting freedom of religion for the Baptist Church. Indeed, the ministers promised this to him orally, and he invariably recorded these promises and discussions in writing to inform his coreligionists. But oral permission and assurances on the part of the ministers did not suffice to grant actual freedom of religion to the Baptists. The general was still on his tour, when the Baptist Churches and prayer-houses were once again closed down; in fact, some of them were even destroyed on the orders of the local authorities. Romanian ecclesiastic and legal thinking always regarded the Baptist Church as an anti-Romanian and anti-state cell of foreign agents, hence freedom of worship was never extended to them in practice.

Thus, there was freedom to hold services in most areas throughout Greater Romania, with the exception of the Baptist Church. When it came to national holidays, however, the authorities intervened as regards to the order of service, its form, its timing and, after 1936, even as regards to the text of the prayers to be recited. The gendarmes in the villages, the police or military authorities in the towns prescribed when religious services must be held in the different churches to celebrate the Romanian national holiday. The state officials, often uninformed as regards to ecclesiastic matters, included principles unacceptable to the Protestant Churches. For instance, they ordered the recital of Te Deums, although such a service was not customary in Protestant Churches. The gendarmes and police came with fixed bayonets on several occasions at such services, and it even happened in some villages that the commander of the local gendarmerie entered the church accompanied by his police dog. We have seen in the chapter on the churches how consistently the authorities disregarded the freedom of conscience of the Hungarian population. There were plenty of cases, each and every year, where the local authorities, particularly the teachers, would drag Reformed, Unitarian, or Roman Catholic children to the Romanian national churches and compel them to participate in a service that was alien to them. We have seen to what extent it had become impossible in the Székely areas to hold religious or presbyterian meetings after 1935, and how often Hungarians were forced to perform labor on public projects on Hungarian Christian holidays. The same process was employed to force Hungarians to participate in the erection of Romanian churches. The Romanian church-buildings erected in the Székely areas after 1935 were built mostly by Hungarian residents belonging to other churches. Thus freedom of worship, in spite of the pertinent provisions of the constitution and of the laws on religion, was trampled underfoot in these regards throughout the duration of the regime. The Hungarian churches had to fight practically hand to hand combat in order to maintain the continuity of ecclesiastic life and to enhance the faith of the congregation, especially after 1934.

The Use of National Symbols

As we have seen, during the first thirty years of the Hungarian regime, the Romanian population could use their national symbols undisturbed, and later under certain restrictions, on the basis of court decisions and authorization granted by the Prime Minister. The Romanian colors were integrated into their folk costumes, which they could wear in the Hungarian House of Parliament or elsewhere undisturbed; the colors could also be used in their folk art, whereas the anti-Hungarian anthem of the Romanians of Transylvania could be intoned freely, in the opinion of the Hungarian courts. The same freedom prevailed in the cult of Romanian historical figures, including the organization of the worship of Abraham Iancu. The Hungarians who came under Romanian rule expected similar opportunities from the authorities.

Once again, the chauvinist principles applied by the Romanian authorities in other areas extended to these issues as well. Presuming anti-Romanian attitudes in the use of Hungarian national colors, the singing of the Hungarian anthem, the statues of Hungarian historical figures from the first moment of the occupation, they banned these ruthlessly.

The successive Romanian cabinets adopted a uniformly negative attitude with regard to the use of Hungarian national colors. Hungarian flags could not be displayed, not even ribbons with the national colors, and those who disregarded these directives were severely punished. Where such attempts were made the courts passed sentences and the gendarmes committed atrocities. In 1926, before the Averescu cabinet came to power, the Hungarians of Transylvania reached an agreement with Averescu's party to support the government at the polls. In order to ensure success the Minister of the Interior, Octavian Goga, had authorized the voters in some of the Székely counties to march to the polling places under the Hungarian flag. This authorization had a lot to do with the fact that the Averescu government obtained such large numbers of votes in the areas inhabited by Hungarians. After the fall of the Averescu government there were no prospects for any similar authorization. Hungarian colors were persecuted, whether in folk costumes, in folk art, in Székely decorative entrances or fancy wood-carvings,[30] as were those who combined red, white and green [the Hungarian colors] with other colors in bunches of flowers or other displays. The Romanian courts and other authorities sentenced large numbers of Hungarians for infractions against these orders. In many places, the issue did not even reach the courts because local authorities determined and executed penalties on their own: usually a terrible beating administered to the suspect. Of course, in spite of these risks it was not possible to abolish the love of the Hungarian population for their national colors, and this love continued to live in their souls throughout the regime.

At the beginning, the singing of the national anthem did not always elicit bans from the Romanian authorities, but soon the issue resulted in solutions unfavorable to the Hungarian population as well. Of course, the singing of the anthem was forbidden in public places or at meetings from the start. When the French general Henri Berthelot visited Cluj in 1919, the masses of Hungarians gathered in front of his hotel to express their wishes. This crowd of several thousand intoned the national anthem. The Romanian military intervened before they could even finish; their commander ordered fire and the last chords of the anthem intermingled with the last sighs of those wounded to death. From then on the anthem could never by sung outdoors under Romanian rule.

In the first two years, the anthem was occasionally sung at religious services. In most places, the Romanian authorities seriously harmed the clergymen involved, but there was no general prohibition. At the beginning of 1923, however, the Minister of Religious Affairs and Education issued a directive banning the singing of the anthem in all churches. In his directive addressed to the bishop of the Reformed Church (number 14.005/1923) we may read the following:

> Since we found out that the Hungarian anthem is sung in the Reformed Churches of the country it is my honor to request that you take measures that those hymns which may offend the patriotic sentiments of the Romanian people be omitted from the religious services, in order to avoid conflicts between members of different denominations.[31]

The Governing Council responded to this directive that Psalm 36 of the Psalm book (i.e. Ferenc Kölcsey's anthem) was never officially declared the Hungarian anthem, and even its text is but a brief excerpt from the whole poem. The Governing Council added that prior to this directive, the Ministry had addressed circular 56.222/1922 to the civilian authorities, informing them that in the future "those hymns which may offend the sentiments of the Romanian people may not be sung in church." Thus, the Romanian Minister had first turned to the civilian authorities, and only afterwards did he turn to the central direction of the church, insisting that the objectionable parts be omitted from the service. Upon the response of the Governing council, the Minister emphasized once again that the Hungarian national anthem may not be included under any guise in the divine service of the Reformed Church of the Romanian state.[32] This second, even more peremptory order closed the issue and the singing of the anthem was definitely banned in Greater Romania.

Even though the text of the anthem contains no derogatory statement regarding any other nation — after all it consists of a prayer and supplication — without any revolutionary trait that might incite anyone, unlike the "Awake from your Dreams" of the Romanians, or the French *Marseillaise,* nevertheless the Romanian authorities banned the singing of the anthem. Their justification that the singing of the anthem "may offend the patriotic sentiments of the Romanian people was entirely fictitious, because in those areas where the Hungarians lived in compact masses, as for instance in the Székely areas, there simply was no Romanian resident who could have been scandalized by this song. It is obvious, therefore, that by banning the anthem the Romanian authorities were bent on weakening the national consciousness of the Hungarians and on providing satisfaction to chauvinistic Romanians.

The Romanian authorities and public opinion were equally intolerant with regard to Hungarian historical figures. There was hardly any room for respecting Hungarian heroes in Greater Romania. From the very beginning Hungarian monuments were knocked down and removed. By this deplorable destruction of monuments, the Romanians attempted to prevent the Hungarians under their rule from harboring respect and appreciation towards Hungarian historical figures. The first statue knocked down was that of the poet Petőfi at Tîrgu Mureş, on May 13, 1919; it was then removed to the courtyard of city-hall. On August 18, 1920, the statue of Lajos Kossuth at Salonta [Nagyszalonta] suffered the same fate. The excitement over these destructive acts had hardly died down when, on the following May 7, the bust of István Széchenyi above the well on Széchenyi square in Cluj was knocked over. A few years later, his memorial tablet near the Iron Gate, on the banks of the Danube, was also removed. At the same time, the bust honoring the militia of 1848 at Sighetul Marmaţiei was destroyed. On April 21, 1923, the Romanian municipal council at Arad had the memorial tablets removed from the Palace of Culture. On April 24, the stained glass windows representing István Bocskai, Gábor Bethlen, Lajos Kossuth, and Ferenc Deák were removed from the Palace of Culture at Tîrgu Mureş. On July 4, the statue of Saint László was removed from its site at Oradea and transferred to the courtyard of the bishopric. On January 7, 1924, the statue of Bocskai at Miercurea Nirajului [Nyárádszereda] was knocked down. On July 2, 1925, the monuments of the thirteen martyrs of Arad, and the statues of Kossuth, were removed on orders from the Ministry. On August 8, the "Iron Székely" monument of Odorheiu Secuiesc suffered the same fate.[33] By then there as hardly any statue left in Transylvania representing a Hungarian historical figure. After an interruption that lasted a few years, the destruction of Hungarian statues recommenced under the impact of renewed Romanian nationalism. Several Romanian papers raised the issue of the beautiful creation of János Fadrusz, the Mátyás Hunyadi statue at Cluj. For the time being, however, the statue was saved by the Romanian perception that Mátyás was a heroic representative of the Romanian race. The name of Mátyás was not inscribed as Matei Corvinul on the statue in Romanian, and this masterpiece survived for the time being. Only for a short while, however, because soon voices were heard once again demanding the removal of the statue. At the end of 1932, one group of students from the Romanian university of Cluj marched to the statue and placed a bronze plague on it, with the words of Nicholas Iorga, the Romanian historian: "You were victorious everywhere, but your own nation defeated you when you attempted to conquer invincible Moldavia."[34] Under the protection of this plaque, in Romanian, the statue adorned the main square without further attacks until 1937. Then Octavian Prie, former under-secretary of education, published an article about the statue in a Romanian newspaper of Cluj. In this article he explained, that the Romanians were deceiving themselves in considering Mátyás a Romanian. Mátyás was a renegade who bore no relationship to the Romanian people; hence the Romanians are not obligated to tolerate his statue in the capital city of Transylvania. Nevertheless, Prie's article had no repercussions, for whatever reason, and the statue of Mátyás remained.

The other masterpiece of Fadrusz, the Miklós Wesselényi statue at Zalău, was accorded the same treatment as most Hungarian statues. It was removed in 1936 and transferred to an unknown destination. Statues were removed from Hungarian towns once again towards the end of 1936. Between 2 and 3 a.m. on September 26, fifteen to twenty Romanian youths surrounded the Main Square at Satu Mare, particularly the Roman Catholic Church. The streetlights were put out and guards were placed at all streets approaching the square. The Romanian police posted here was enticed away. Then they took out the ropes they brought along and looped these around the necks of the statues of Saint László and Saint István placed in niches on the facade of the church. The two statues were finally yanked down and smashed to pieces, except for the heads. The heads were then carted away. A message on the pedestal said "We shall meet again in heaven." The Hungarian residents of Satu Mare found out about the events the following morning with great indignation. Prompted by this sentiment the police launched a pretend investigation, which ended unsuccessfully, as usual.[35]

In the final analysis, the Romanian authorities would allow respect for only one Hungarian figure. The annual Petőfi festival organized by the Hungarian choral association at Sighișoara was not hampered. Often the reason for this was that the leaders of the choral association placed the festival under the protection of some member of the royal family.

Contacts with Hungarians Beyond the Borders

As discussed, Romanians living under Hungarian rule were in constant touch with the Romanians of the Romanian kingdom. These contacts were easy in both directions because border restrictions introduced after World War I did not yet exist. Passports were issued without much difficulty to the Romanian residents, and Romanians visiting Hungary from Romania were not prevented from entering the country. Scholars, journalists, officers of the army, members of the Romanian royal family, could cross the borders whenever and wherever they liked. They participated in Romanian festivals in Hungary and at assemblies, delivering speeches and encouraging the Romanians to persevere.

The Hungarians who came under Romanian rule enjoyed no such opportunities. In the first year only those who emigrated permanently from Romania and promised never to return to Transylvania were allowed to cross the border. Later it was possible to secure a passport only if the applicant had ample funds, it could not be obtained through normal channels on account of the ambiguous formalities involved. Money, however, could always procure a passport. Of course, not many persons could afford to take that route, hence poor persons, students, and others could visit Hungary only with great difficulty. Of course, it was even more difficult to obtain a passport during the state of emergency. The documents needed to secure a passport were often quite impossible to obtain, especially when it came to military documents. These documents could be secured with relative ease in the period 1928 to 1933, but the difficulties were reintroduced after that. During the last years of the regime, after 1937, a Hungarian could obtain a passport only by resorting to contacts in high places. The military documents needed by the male population had to be issued by the general staff in Bucharest where no application was handled without some special contact. On the other hand, the old Greek proverb, that there is no wall high enough that a mule loaded with gold could not jump, remained true throughout the regime.

After 1930, opportunity arose even for Hungarians living under modest circumstances to visit their relatives in Hungary from time to time. This opportunity was group travel referred to as "sport trains" or "penny trains." So-called collective passports covering four to five hundred persons could be secured at relatively little cost and under rather simplified procedures. On such occasions, one could remain in Hungary for six to eight days, but everyone had to return on the same train at the appointed time, otherwise they would not be allowed across the border.

Contacts in the other direction were even more difficult. The Romanian consulate of Budapest kept close track of those Hungarians whose travel to Romania would not be in the best interests of Romania. They were never granted visas to enter the country. Famous Hungarian scholars or public figures could under no circumstances visit relatives under Romanian rule. As mentioned, Nicholas Iorga's visit to Hungary under the former regime encountered no difficulty, even though the Hungarian authorities were well aware of his anti-Hungarian irredentist attitude. The Hungarians under Romanian rule could experience nothing of the sort. In vain did distinguished Hungarian intellectuals such as Gyula Szekfű or Elek Benedek apply for visas to visit Romania. Certain writers or poets were granted visas to Romania thanks to their acquaintances, but their steps were carefully watched. Dezső Kosztolányi received a visa thanks to his old Romanian acquaintance, art supervisor Emil Isac, but his Romanian acquaintance or some agent was constantly at his side from the moment of his arrival in order to "assist" him as a matter of "respect." In other words, while Kosztolányi was able to visit Cluj, he could not meet with the Hungarian leaders there without the presence of some Romanian witness. It was out of the question for Hungarians from Hungary to participate at some meeting to give a speech, to comment publicly. Such intervention would prompt immediate reprisals against the organizers. During the entire regime, the Hungarians under Romanian rule and those on the other side of the border could come into contact only under great difficulties, hence Hungarians on different sides of the border knew little about one another. International solidarity or national unity could exist only for a narrow stratum, while large masses of the Hungarians of Transylvania knew hardly anything about life beyond the borders.

The Political Rights of the Hungarians

The political life of the Hungarians under Romanian rule started with the signing of the Treaty of Trianon on June 4, 1920. During the period of occupation, until the treaty, the Hungarian population could not participate in elections, that is could not field candidates. One reason for this was that the Hungarian leaders were disoriented by the entirely unfamiliar circumstances; another reason was that their constitutional status was not clear. Even the issue of the boundary lines was unresolved until the treaty was signed, and there was no way of knowing how the representatives of the great powers meeting in Paris would resolve the issue.

Political orientation got underway soon after the treaty was signed. The first sign of this was the publication of the famous pamphlet "Kiáltó Szó" [Shouting word] by three outstanding leaders: Károly Kós, Árpád Pál, and István Zágoni. The three authors wrote an essay, each regarding the opportunities and tasks facing the Hungarians under the new constitutional situation. Soon the first Hungarian organization, the Hungarian Association, was founded in Cluj on July 6, 1921. The basic principle of the association was that the Minorities Treaty created minority civil rights, hence these minorities had the right to form public organizations on the basis of national sentiment. The Romanian government, however, did not accept this interpretation and dissolved the Hungarian Association permanently in October 1922.

Soon after the dissolution of the Hungarian Association, on December 28, 1922, the National Hungarian Party was founded. It came about as the merger of two political organizations, the Hungarian People's Party and the Hungarian National Party. The first chairman of the National Hungarian Party was Baron Sámuel Jósika, its executive director was Dr. Gusztáv Haller, and its secretary Dr. István Naláczy. The Hungarian Party was established after participation in the first national elections. These elections were announced for March 6, 1922, by the cabinet under the prime minister of the Liberal Party leader, Ionel Brătianu. Voting took place between March 6 and 10. The large majority of the Hungarians of Transylvania had been deliberately omitted from the voters' lists long before the elections.

The Hungarian population was consoled by the fact that it was able to elect its own candidates in the purely Hungarian areas anyway. It did not count on what was to happen, even though it should have had no illusions had it paid closer attention to the last two elections. The Romanian authorities had interfered with the manifestation of the voters' will to such an extent during the elections of 1919 and 1920, that even the Romanians of Transylvania, so used to complaining about Hungarian electoral abuses in former times, were caught unprepared. At the end of the second elections in 1920, the best known newspaper of the Romanians of Transylvania noted sadly: "We have demonstrated many times, with the help of data, names, and documents, that the interference of the Romanian authorities went further than the interference of former Hungarian governments."

The Hungarian population did not pay much attention to the Romanian electoral frauds, hence it was completely unprepared to cope with the devices used against it. The government instructed the local authorities to hamper the work of all opposition parties, and the Hungarian parties first of all. Thirty-four of the thirty-eight candidates presented by the Hungarian Party were declared ineligible on a variety of clever pretexts. While about one-third of the candidates presented by the Romanian parties were rejected, nine-tenths of the Hungarians suffered that fate. The Hungarian candidates were rejected "not individually but as a group," noted a Romanian paper.[36] According to the provisions of the law, representatives had to be nominated by fifty voters and senators by at least twenty-five. The recommendation had to be forwarded to the president of the board of elections by at least ten voters; the president was expected to verify the identity of the voters. In case of rejection, the president had to communicate the reason for the rejection in writing. The law provided that every fifty-thousand voters could elect a representative, and every one hundred thousand could chose a senator. If the provisions of the law had been observed, the Hungarian population would have been represented by at least 25 to 30 delegates and 12 to 15 senators. But the intentions of the government were revealed already at the time of the nomination. As mentioned, 34 of the 38 candidates were rejected under various excuses. The nomination of József Sándor at Huedin was rejected on the grounds that the signatures were illegible. The nomination of József Willer at Oradea was rejected because the date appeared at the bottom rather than at the top. That of Imre Pécsy at Zalău was rejected because two different kinds of ink were used for the signatures. Albert Nagy was arrested on the day of the nomination, and when he was set free in the afternoon he was informed that he had been hired as a deputy chairman of elections, which made his ineligible to become a representative.

The nomination of Elemér Gyárfás at Miercurea Ciuc was rejected in the midst of scenes that were deserving of slapstick comedy. His advisors paid a call to the chairman of the elections and were prepared for all kinds of tricks; but reality, and the resourcefulness of the men of the Liberal Party, exceeded all expectations. First, the chairman rejected the nomination on the grounds that it has not been demonstrated that the candidate was sane. Then those who brought the nomination were able to prove that, the chairman asked them to prove that he was not the owner of a whorehouse. This too was demonstrated. The third objection was that they had not proven that the candidate did not have a criminal record. But those who brought the nomination were once again prepared. Then Ciurea, the chairman of the committee was about to accept the nomination, since he could not think of any more excuses. But the prefect who was present stepped forward and pulled a document from his pocket removing Ciurea from his post as chairman and appointing another in his place. The new chairman rejected the nomination of Gyárfás definitively on the grounds that it appeared, from the similarity of the handwritings, that all signatures were by a single hand.

The elections took place after the nomination had been rejected. As regards to the excesses and unlawful acts committed, these elections exceeded the worst forebodings of both Hungarian and Romanian voters. The Hungarian population, numbering a million and a half, were able to elect but one representative: György Bernády. The Romaniar National Party of Transylvania also came out with ruffled feathers from the electoral campaign. Iuliu Maniu protested against, the high-handed actions of the government in a cable to the king. In this cable he noted that:

> the government intimidated the electors by the most incredible means. The chairmen of the elections boards rejected nominations. They also interrupted the voting and stole the

ballots from the urns in the middle of the night. The elections were the result of the wildest corruption, bribery, arrests, agitations, capture, and detention of candidates, etc. Consequently the day of polling became, in Transylvania, a day of mourning and dejection, drowned in national disgrace and scandal for all Europe to see.

The Romanian papers expressed their concern over the abuses committed against the Hungarians. One of them mentioned that what the Romanians were doing to one another was just business as usual; but what is done to the minorities was most deplorable: "That there should be a government, in the fourth year of coexistence with the minorities, that will exclude them from public life by means of all kinds of lowly acts — this is no longer a purely domestic issue, but may even harm our reputation abroad."[37] The newspaper of the conservatives wrote as follows:

As a consequence of the unification of Transylvania with Romania, two million Hungarians became Romanian subjects — two million residents of foreign extraction, all law-abiding subjects, who undoubtedly form a distinct ethnic group. The electoral campaign of Mr. Brătianu ended with the dangerous precedent of depriving these two million residents of even a single representative. The land of the Székelys is at the heart of the plateau of Transylvania, and the Romanians do not even constitute 1% of the population of this area; yet the Székelys were not allowed to send their representative to the Romanian parliament. In order to obtain such a result, Mr. Brătianu had to resort to means and excuses that are unworthy of a civilized state.[38]

The government itself became aware that it had exceeded the limit with regard to the Hungarians, hence it relented its terror during the partial elections that followed. Thus, József Sándor and Tibor Zima became members of the Romanian parliament.

The only consolation of the Hungarians after the elections and makeup elections was that some representatives of the Romanian National Party of Transylvania had themselves come to the conclusion that the election process was better under the former Hungarian regime. Among others, Alexandru Vaida-Voevod, former representative in the Hungarian House of Parliament and erstwhile Prime Minister of Greater Romania, made a statement to that effect. During the by-elections at Ighiu [Igen] in 1923, Vaida-Voevod was subjected to some sorry experiences. The Romanians of Transylvania nominated Professor Silviu Dragomir to run in the district of Igen. Vaida-Voevod had some beloved acquaintances among the voters in the district from the Hungarian period, when they elected him with great enthusiasm as their representative against the official candidate put up by the Hungarian government party. Now, in an effort to be of assistance, he accompanied Dragomir on his campaign tour and spoke to the voters wherever he could. But seldom was he allowed to deliver a speech, because the government had sent confidential instructions before the campaign to all the gendarme stations in the district. In this circular, the gendarmes were instructed, "to accuse the representatives of the opposition of rebellion, disorderly conduct, disturbance of the peace." All propaganda inimical to the Government must elicit the charge that there has been rebellion, peace and public safety have been disturbed."[39] The gendarmes carried on the instructions contained in the circular. They arrested Vaida-Voevod and Dragomir several times and made them trek long distances. According to the description in one Romanian paper, the gendarmes occupied entire villages, dispersing groups of voters with bayonet charges, and expelled the observers placed by the opposition parties at the urns during the night. They even shot at the supports of Dragomir and missed no opportunity to tamper with the results of the elections. Vaida-Voevod, bitterly disappointed, exposed the actions of the government in harsh words wherever he could. He referred to the Romanian parliament as "a house of thieves," and at the same time told the Romanian voters that "it was better under the Hungarians."[40] He exploded when facing the peasants of the community of Circău [Krakkó]: "Is it not true, brothers, that it was better under the Hungarians than it is today?" Some of the peasants responded: "Maybe it was better, but maybe things will improve in Greater Romania." Grigore N. Filipescu was so scandalized by these words that he immediately left the election meeting.[41]

Naturally, the election results favored the government. After his defeat Dragomir provided the following account of the electoral campaign in one of the Romanian newspapers: "Whoever reflects that all these happenings — the arrests, the bayonet attacks — were carried out by the gendarmes in a most brutal manner, may assess the terrible condition into which respect for the most basic rights guaranteed in the Constitution had fallen for every citizen of the country...." Then he added: "I have filled many pages with the centuries-old struggles and sufferings of my Transylvanian brothers. But none is as painful and shameful than the murder of the general elections held at Ighiu."[42]

Vaida-Voevod repeated his report of the experiences at Ighiu at the March 16, 1923 meeting of the Romanian Parliament; in fact, excerpts from that speech were printed in the French-language leaflet of the opposition parties for the benefit of readers abroad. Vaida-Voevod declared in parliament that he would not recognize the legitimacy of that parliament, because it was born of a *coup d'état* of cheating, and theft.

Deeply hurt in my feelings as citizen as a lover of justice and of national freedom which I have defended all through my life, I have decided that I would not enter these halls again because the base procedures resorted to by the present government against the voters are such as even the notorious Tisza and Andrássy cabinets had never dared commit against the Romanian nation.... It has happened to me personally that I was surrounded by bayonets and rudely chased out of the villages in the district of Ighiu, where I had once, under Hungarian rule, been able to organize and carry out the political struggles of the Romanian National Party. You may imagine, therefore, how they deal with the masses: they become the victims of the abuses of the armed authorities and the objects of persecution by an anarchical administration, while they are also exposed to the system of justice adjusted to the intentions of the government party.[43]

Indeed, these observations of Vaida-Voevod did conform to reality. But if such were the procedures employed against candidates of Romanian background, one may imagine the treatment accorded to voters of Hungarian ethnic background. As mentioned, Hungarian candidates were rejected in far greater proportion than those of Romanian background. The later elections held under the auspices of the Liberal Party took place in the midst of similar abuses. The voters received no compensation for the mistreatment they suffered on these occasions. The validity of the elections was decided by parliament itself, which naturally rejected the complaints voiced. Since the courts were subordinated to the power of the Government, they seldom dared to reach decisions which might have harmed the interests of the ruling party. Cicio-Pop, the elderly leader of the Romanians of Transylvania during the Hungarian regime, noted sadly at the time of the validation of the results obtained during the elections of 1927 under the auspices of the Liberal Party: "Under the Hungarian regime we marched to the polls between the bayonets of the gendarmes but could vote openly for the Romanian National Party. Now entire villages were barred from marching to the polling stations, and the Romanian captain in charge of the police forces told his troops, in front of our observers, to shoot down those who approached the station. During the Hungarian regime, if a policeman beat a Romanian voter, we denounced him to the authorities. The Hungarian judge sentenced the man to three years in jail. Nowadays — and I recite these facts with great regret Romanian judges falsify the results of the voting because they have been assured of amnesty: "A country such as ours where the military is involved in politics and the judges forge the votes is a lost country." After the same elections, a Romanian daily observed that "the elections just completed constitute one of the saddest chapters in the political history of Transylvania. In the county of Odorhei, the minority voters were kept away from the polling places en masse. The agents of the Liberal Party voted with identification cards confiscated from the voters. The elections in the counties of Ciuc and Trei-Saune were no different."[44]

Indeed, the elections of 1927, entailed abuses no less than those omitted in 1922. Because of the considerable terror the Hungarian population, albeit much more politically conscious by then, was able to elect only 8 delegates and one senator. The relatively cleanest election campaign was organized by the Maniu cabinet in 1928, when the supporters of the Hungarian Party were able to elect 16 Hungarian delegates and six senators. Later, elections took place once again in the midst of considerable intimidation. The pressure of the authorities was especially heavy during the general elections of 1933 and 1937. Both elections took place under the auspices of the Liberal Party. In 1937, a hitherto unheard of event took place: the gendarmes fired volleys at the supporters of the Hungarian party to prevent them from approaching the polling station. There were several dead and some seriously wounded.

Thus, the number of Hungarian representative varied considerably during the Greater Romanian regime. They had to struggle against most unfavorable conditions in the House of Delegates and the Senate. They attempted to fulfill their difficult calling in the midst of physical insults, constant spiteful interruptions, mockery, slander in words and in writing in the press. They achieved little in this atmosphere of antagonistic chauvinism. They struggled outside the parliament as well, intervening at the ministries and defending the Hungarian plaintiffs in front of the authorities against the abuses they suffered. The best known among them were oft mentioned in the Romanian press as well: József Willer, Elemér Gyárfás, József Sándor, Ferenc Laár, Nándor Hegedűs, Elemér Jakabffy, were often signaled out by the

Romanian journalists and presented in a consistently negative light to the Romanian readers. The editor-in-chief of the Romanian daily *Curentul* delivered an attack against Nándor Hegedűs in a lead article, because Hegedűs had sent an open letter requesting him to let up on the campaign of hatred against the Hungarian population. Thus, the Hungarian representatives had to deal with the most unpleasant environment in both the Parliament and the Romanian press, which further limited their already meager opportunities.

The political weight of the Hungarian population, however, was not determined by the number of their representatives in parliament. The material conditions of the population, its political consciousness, as well as world public opinion were far more significant. The Hungarian representatives lived under far less favorable material conditions than had their Romanian counterparts under the Hungarian regime. As a consequence of the deliberate policies of impoverishment all strata of Hungarian society had to suffer financially and, of course, this affected the results of the political struggles as well. Domestically, the Hungarian population hardly had any influence. It had to thank foreign public opinion for its political clout and for most of the results achieved in its defensive struggle. Every Romanian cabinet was wary of creating a negative impression abroad. As long as the prestige of the League of Nations was relatively unscathed, that is until 1934, the complaints filed with this body occasionally bore fruit. The government sacrificed enormous sums to obtain favorable echoes from the public opinion abroad and on some more difficult issues it spared no expense to make its anti-Hungarian measures appear in a favorable light. We have seen how the government was able to mislead the League of Nations in 1924, by presenting a fake version of the Apponyi laws, at later on it resorted to similar devices to win over public opinion abroad. They did not always succeed, even though Romania availed itself of far more favorable opportunities than Hungary had during the Dual Monarchy. Before World War I, the writers and scientists of Europe had a much higher regard for truth than for the sympathy of the government of some state.

Therefore, in a given case, they might support without hesitation the side of what they deemed to be the absolute truth without regard to any other consideration, and denounce injustice without regard for the opinion of the government concerned. This explains in part the stand taken by Björnstjerne Björnson, Lev Tolstoy, and others on the side of the Romanians of Hungary. Moreover, these great writers could receive information from the Romanians of Hungary without the least obstacle or adverse consequence, even though this information was altogether one-sided. The situation changed after the war. Most of the Western powers were interested in maintaining the status quo brought about by the peace treaties signed in the Paris region, and therefore, strove to weaken all the complaints which reached them from the minority groups within the successor states. Romania had close diplomatic ties with France, and managed to maintain excellent relations with official and semi-official circles in Great Britain as well. Therefore, there were few independent-thinking individuals in these countries who might have raised their voice against the injustices committed in the successor states, especially in Romania. Between the two wars, some intellectuals adopted an attitude which the French writer Julien Benda described as "the betrayal of the intellectuals" in his world-famous book of the same title. Benda noted that writers, members of the intelligentsia, had betrayed their calling by not taking a stand on the side of absolute justice merely because of problems of daily life and difficulties in making ends meet. The validity of Julien Benda's statement was apparent in the issue of the oppressed minorities living under foreign rule. Those who spoke out in the cause of truth, without regard for the antagonism of their own government or the government of Romania, were few and far between. Nevertheless, there were one or two well-known intellectuals who did. There were Frenchmen such as Henri Barbusse, Victor Margueritte, and Romain Rolland, as well as Englishmen such as Harold Sidney Harmsworth Rothermere or Carlile Aylmer Macartney. Their intervention improved the opportunities available to Hungarians considerably, as did the intervention of various international organizations of minorities and similar organizations.

By 1934, however, Romania had made itself largely independent of public opinion abroad, especially in the West. The most oppressive measures against the Hungarian minority were adopted between 1934 and 1938, when the impoverishment and repression of the Hungarians assumed even greater proportions than earlier. By late 1937, however, Romania no longer dared undertake the most serious injustices. Thus, it happened that the outcome of the steps taken by Onisifor Ghibu, to transfer the properties of the Order of Premontre and other religious orders to the credit of the state was not ultimately supported by the government, on account of the manifestations of public opinion abroad and of the firm stand adopted by the Holy See. The change of regime brought about in 1938, by the international conjuncture resulted in some degree of improvement but, as mentioned, the situation remained unchanged as regards to the more basic issues.

Local self-government had very little significance in the political life of the Hungarian population. Local autonomy was eliminated already during the first years of the Romanian regime. The Romanians of Transylvania realized themselves what a big mistake this had been, and demanded on several occasions that administrative autonomy be restored. The Liberal Party, however, was not favorably inclined, even though many a Romanian newspaper launched a press campaign for the sake of maintaining or restoring autonomy. In 1923, *Lupta* pointed to the decline in Transylvania resulting from the elimination of autonomy. It called attention to all the difficulties resulting from centralization in Bucharest. "All matters takes months to resolve, because Bucharest has to be consulted even on the least weighty decisions. It would be the obligation of Romanian governments, the paper noted, to render it impossible for the population of Transylvania to make unfavorable comparisons with the former regime:

> We should have preserved the good things about the old system, rather then destroy them. Instead, they preserved only the Hungarian laws of Transylvania, while dismantling many good institutions, including autonomy at the community and county levels which was living reality in former times, providing the population with the opportunity to become directly involved in the government of towns and counties and contributing to the education of the residents of Transylvania in matters of citizenship.[45]

Unfortunately, neither this warning of the Romanian paper, nor the interventions by Romanians and Hungarians of Transylvania made any difference. Until 1925, there was no autonomy of any kind. Although the Act on Administration passed by the Liberal Party regime in 1925 did bring about a weak version of local autonomy but, as already mentioned, the modifications brought about by frequent laws on administration, as well as the system of interim committees appointed from above, which became endemic in Romania "rendered the autonomy provided by law, weak in any case, completely useless." Except for one or two years, the Hungarian communities and townships with a Hungarian majority were led by appointed councils, the so-called *interimar* committees throughout the regime, and only by accident — did these committees ever include Hungarians.

Equality Before the Law

It is obvious from our arguments that the Hungarian population in Greater Romania, very seldom enjoyed equal rights with the

Romanians. Because of the institutional advantages accruing to the Romanian state-creating population in political, economic, cultural, and other areas, equal rights suffered very serious setbacks. Occasionally, the Romanian courts made praiseworthy efforts to interpret the laws in a balanced manner. But the courts were never entirely independent. They were compelled to carry out the instructions received from the government in electoral and other matters. In matters of national interest, as defined by the government, they abided by instructions from the government. In those cases, where the courts supported Hungarian claims against Romanians — for instance in matters of expropriation of land judgements in favor of, the Hungarians from Deva, from Sîncrai from Cîrta, etc. — Romanian authorities would not allow the legal decisions to go into effect. Thus, the Hungarians, even if the Romanian courts brought just verdicts, could never know whether these legal decisions could be enforced vis-à-vis the Romanians. Thus, they seldom felt the protection of the laws, and the nowadays oft-mentioned "freedom from fear" feeling was unknown to them in Greater Romania. If conflicts arose among Hungarians, the courts usually brought just decisions. The Romanian Supreme Court, the Court of Appeals, was the last hope for many a Hungarian. But when it was a matter of providing justice to a Hungarian party vis-à-vis, a Romanian or vis-à-vis the state, the courts usually avoided the issue or passed a sentence in favor of the Romanian party or the Romanian state. As we have seen, a Romanian court hastened to recognize the illegal arguments propounded by Onisifor Ghibu in 1932, transferring the properties of the Hungarian Catholic Status to the name of the Romanian state in the land registry.

In 1938, the judges ceased to be unremovable. From then on, even the faint hopes placed in the impartiality of judges dissipated. In the last two years of the Greater Romanian regime, during the period of government by decree, the courts were entirely at the service of the government.

In the final analysis, Hungarians under Romanian rule, very seldom enjoyed equality before the law in Greater Romania, and in the political field, very often were handed unfavorable sentences by the Romanian courts. Hence Hungarians harbored very little trust in Romanian judges.

Endnotes

1. Şorban, *op. cit.*
2. *Dacia,* May 18, 1920.
3. Şorban, *op. cit.,* pp. 96-98.
4. *La lutte contre l'absolutisme,* pp. 13-15.

5. Entries for February 17, 1929, in Sulyok and Fritz, eds., *op. cit.*, p. 2.

6. "Az erdélyi románok temesvári nagygyűlése" [The Grand Assembly of the Romanians of Transylvania at Temesvár], *Krassó-Szörényi Lapok*, April 26, 1923.

7. In: Nicolae Ghiulea, "Apărarea națională," *Societatea de Mâine*, June 18, 1926, p. 510, quoted by Szász, *op. cit.*, pp. 127-128.

8. C. G. Costa-Foru, *Abuzurile și crimele siguranței generale ale statului* (Bucharest, 1925) p. 4. Szász, *op. cit.*, pp. 124-125.

9. The intervention by József Willer was printed in *Magyar Kisebbség*, 1931, pp. 888-892.

10. *La lutte contre l'absolutisme en Roumanie* (Bucharest, 1923), p. 16.

11. Oberding, *op. cit.*, p. 67; Szász, *op. cit.*, pp. 173-174.

12. Onisifor Ghibu, *Politica religioasă*, p. 832.

13. *Courier de Genève*, March 5, 1937, printed in Ghibu, *ibid.*, pp. 321-324. Later, as a result of pressure by foreign public opinion, the government returned the Felix spa to the Premontre Order.

14. Oberding, *op. cit.*, p. 96.

15. On the basis of the official bulletin, *Monitorul Oficial*, Nagy, *op. cit.*, pp. 88-94, gives a detailed account of the Romanian measures introducing the state of emergency and censorship.

16. "Verekedés a parlamentben" [Brawl in the Parliament], *Új Kelet*, June 1, 1923.

17. *România*, November 11, 1923.

18. *Monitorul Oficial*, November 21, 1928, Number 260; Nagy, *op. cit.*, p. 90.

19. Consult the chronology in Sulyok and Fritz, eds., *op. cit.*

20. *Magyar Kisebbség*, 1931, p. 319.

21. "Illusztráció a kisebbségek védelmében" [Illustration in defense of the minorities], *Bihari Újság*, January 13, 1921.

22. *Magyar Kisebbség*, 1923, p. 132.

23. These data were kindly provided by Gyula Walter.

24. *Magyar Kisebbség*, 1936, p. 270; Imre Mikó, *Huszonkét év. Az erdélyi magyarság politikai története 1918 december 1-től 1940 augusztus 30-ig* [Twenty-two Years. The Political History of the Hungarians of Transylvania from December 1, 1918, to August 30, 1940] (Budapest, 1941), pp. 169-170.

25. These data were kindly provided by Domokos Gyallay.

26. Șorban, *op. cit.*, p. 81.

27. László Fritz, "Újabb kisebbségi jogsérelmek" [Further Minority Grievances], *Magyar Kisebbség*, 1931, p. 783.

28. The complete text of the decree is printed in the February 25, 1938, issue of the *Keleti Újság* published in Cluj. The decree was communicated to the Hungarian residents by means of posters in Romanian.

29. The minutes of the Main Council of the Unitarian Church, Cluj, 1935.

30. "Csendőrök fenyegetik Udvarhely megyében a székely népművészetet" [In Odorhei County the Gendarmes are Threatening Székely Folk Art], *Keleti Újság*, June 8, 1934.

31. The 1923 report of the Governing Council of the Reformed Church of Transylvania.

32. *Ibid.*

666 Bíró Sándor

33. The chronological appendix, Sulyok and Fritz, eds., *op. cit.*
34. Personal collection.
35. *Magyar Kisebbség*, 1936, p. 538.
36. *Gazeta Ardealului*, February 28, 1922.
37. *Epoca*, March 8, 1922.
38. *Le Progrès*, March 13, 1922.
39. *Lupta*, February 27, 1923.
40. "Contractul dela Alba Iulia" *Înfrăţirea*, March 3, 1923.
41. Ion Rusu Abrudeanu, *Păcatele Ardealului faţă de sufletul vechiului regat* (Bucharest, 1930), p. 524.
42. "După alegeruea dela Ighiu...," *Adevărul*, March 4, 1923.
43. *La lutte contre l'absolutisme*, pp. 56-58.
44. *Dimineaţa*, July 9, 1927.
45. "Împiedicaţi decadenţa oraşelor ardeleneşti," *Lupta*, May 3, 1923.

List of Maps

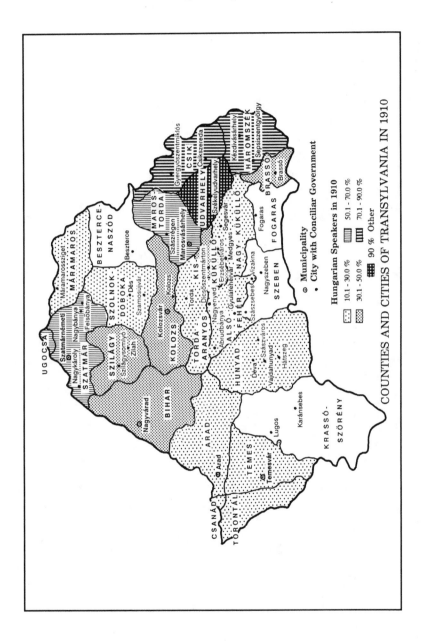

COUNTIES AND CITIES OF TRANSYLVANIA IN 1910

⊙ Municipality
• City with Conciliar Government

Hungarian Speakers in 1910

10.1 - 30.0 %   50.1 - 70.0 %
30.1 - 50.0 %   70.1 - 90.0 %
                       90 % Other

COUNTIES AND CITIES OF TRANSYLVANIA IN 1930

⊙ Municipality
• Other Type of City

Bibliography

Newspapers and Periodicals

Adevărul. Bucharest.
Anuarul Liceului Ortodox Român "Andrei Şaguna" din Braşov. Braşov.
Anuarul Pedagogic. Sibiu.
Anuarul Statistic al României. Bucharest.
Aurora. Bucharest.
Biruinţa. Cluj.
Brassói Lapok. Brassó.
Biserica Ortodoxă Română. Bucharest.
Biserica şi Şcoala. Arad.
Bihari Újság. Nagyvárad.
Bukaresti Magyar Tudósító. Bucharest.
Calendarul dela Blaj. Blaj.
Cerculariu către clerul şi poporul ortodox român din arhidieceza Transilvaniei. Sibiu.
Cultura Creştină. Blaj.
Courrier de Genève. Geneva.
Călindarul poporului. Budapest, Sibiu.
Cuvântul. Bucharest.
Dacia. Bucharest.
Dezbatările Deputaţilor. Bucharest.
Deşteptarea. Cernauţi.
Dimineaţa. Bucharest.
Drapelul. Lugoj.
Dezbatările Senatului. Bucharest.
Erdélyi Kalendárium. Torda.
Ellenzék. Kolozsvár.
Erdélyi Magyar Évkönyv 1918-1929, eds. István Sulyok . and László Fritz. Kolozsvár, 1930.
Epoca. Bucharest.
Erdélyi Tudósító. Brassó.
Foaia Poporului. Sibiu.
Gazeta Ardealului. Cluj.
Gazeta Ciucului. Miercurea-Ciuc.
Gazeta Transilvaniei. Braşov.

Gazeta Țăranilor. Curtea de Agres.
Generația Unirii. Bucharest.
Înfrățirea. Cluj.
Journal Officiel. League of Nations, London.
Kelet. Kolozsvár.
Képviselőházi Iromdnyok. Budapest.
Krassó-Szörényi Lapok. Lugos.
Képviselőházi Napló. Budapest.
Keleti Újság. Kolozsvár.
Libertatea. Orăştie.
Lumea Nouă. Bucharest.
Lupta. Bucharest.
Luceafărul. Sibiu.
Luptătorul. Bucharest.
Magyar Kisebbség. Lugos.
Magyar Statisztikai Közlemények. Budapest.
Magyar Törvénytár. Budapest.
Monitorul Oficial. Bucharest.
A Nap. Arad.
Nagyvárad. Nagyvárad.
Neamul Românesc. Bucharest, Văleni de Munte. Iaşi.
Observatorul Social-Economic. Cluj.
Protocolul Congresului Național Bisericesc din Sibiu.
    Sibiu.
Pesti Hírlap. Pest.
Le progrès. Bucharest.
Patria. Cluj.
Revista Economică. Sibiu.
Revista Generală a Învățământului. Bucharest.
Românul. Arad.
România. Bucharest.
Revista Orăştiei. Orăştie.
Revista Bistriței. Bistrița.
Statistica Anuală a României. Bucharest.
Statistica Impozitelor Directe. Bucharest.
Statisztikai Közlemények. Budapest.
Şezătarea Săteanului. Bucharest.
Tribuna. Sibiu.
Tribuna Poporului, 1897-1905. Arad.
Transilvania, Banatul, Crişana şi Maramureşul, 1918-1928, eds.
    Dimitrie Gusti and Emanoil Bucuţa, I-II. Bucharest, 1929.
Timpul. Bucharest.

Telegraful Român. Sibiu.

Temesvarer Zeitung. Temesvár.

Ţara. Timişoara.

Ţara Bârsei. Braşov.

Tara Noastră. Cluj.

Universul. Bucharest.

Unirea. Blaj.

Új Kelet. Kolozsvár.

Viitorul. Bucharest.

Books and Essays

Abrudeanu, Ion Rusu. *Păcatele Ardealului faţă de sufletul vechiului regat.* Bucharest, 1930.

Albrecht, Dezső. "A román diákmozgalom története" [The History of the Romanian Student Movement]. *Magyar Kisebbség*, Vol. 8 (1929), pp. 52-59, 97-100.

Ajtay, András. "A kultúrzóna," [The Cultural Zone]. *Magyar Kisebbség*, Vol. 3 (1924), pp. 615-619.

Albani, Tiron. *Leul dela Siseşti. De ce s'a prăbuşit Monarchia Austro-Ungară.* Oradea, 1936.

American Unitarian Association. Commission on Transylvania, *The Religious Minorities in Transylvania.* Boston, 1924.

American Unitarian Association. Commission on Transylvania, *Transylvania under the Rule of Roumania; Report of the American Unitarian Commission.* Boston, 1921.

Andor, Endre. "Sajtónk küzdelmeihez," [Regarding the Struggles of Our Press]. *Magyar Kisebbség*, Vol. 2 (1923), pp. 128-132.

"A Nemzeti Nevelésügyi Minisztérium rendelete az iskolai beiratkozásokról," [The Directive of the Ministry of Education Regarding Registration in Schools] *Magyar Kisebbség*, Vol. 17, (1938), pp. 447-448.

"A romániai kisebbségi magyar nemzet politikai, kulturális és közgazdasági helyzetképe a genfi kongresszus előtt," [A Description of the Political, Cultural, and Economic Situation of the Hungarian Minority of Romania Presented to the Congress of Geneva]. *Magyar Kisebbség* Vol. 9 (1930), pp. 608-648.

Az Athenaeum nagy képes naptára [The Great Illustrated Calendar of the Athenaeum]. Budapest, 1892.

Băilă, Ion. "Trecutul Ardealului," *Adevărul.* March 16, 1929.

676 Sándor Bíró

Balogh, Arthur. *L'action de la Société des Nations en matière de protection des minorités*. Paris, 1937.

Balogh, Pál. *A népfajok Magyarországon* [Ethnic Groups in Hungary]. Budapest, 1902.

Barabás, Endre. "A magyar iskolaügy helyzete Romániában 1918-1940" [The School Issue of the Hungarians in Romania, 1918-40]. *Kisebbségi Körlevél*, Vol. 1, 1939.

Barabás, Endre. *A romániai magyar nyelvű oktatás első tíz éve. 1918-1928.* [The First Decade of Instruction in the Hungarian Language in Romania]. Lugoj, 1929.

Barabás, Endre. "Az Apponyi-féle törvény, a Népszövetség és a Romániai Magyar Kisebbség" [The Apponyi Laws, the League of Nations and the Hungarian Minority of Romania]. *Külügyi Szemle*, Vol. 8 (1931).

Barabás, Endre. *Az erdélyi és magyarországi román egyházak és iskolák élete és szervezete a világháború előtt* [The Activities and Organization of the Romanian Churches and Schools of Transyvania and Hungary before the World War]. Lugos, n.d.

Baranyai, Zoltán. *A kisebbségi jogok védelme* [The Defense of Minority Rights]. Budapest, 1922.

Bărbat, A. *Politica economică ungurească și dezvoltarea burgheziei române în Ardeal.* Cluj, 1936.

Barna [Barabás], Endre. *Magyar tanulságok a bukaresti kiállításról* [Lessons for Hungarians to be Learnt from the Bucharest Fair]. Kolozsvár, 1906.

Barna [Barabás], Endre. *Románia nemzetiségi politikája és az oláh ajkú magyar polgárok* [Romania's Nationalities Policies and Hungarian Citizens of Romanian Background]. Kolozsvár, 1908.

Bârseanu, Andrei. *Istoria școalelor centrale române gr.-or. din Brașov.* Brașov, 1902.

Berey, Géza. *Néhány szó az újságírókról* [A Few Words about Journalists]. Szatmár, 1936.

Bethlen, István. *Az oláhok birtokvásárlásai Magyarországon az utolsó öt év folyamán* [Purchases of Estates by Romanians in Hungary in the Last Five Years]. Budapest, 1912.

Bíró, Sándor [Sándor Enyedi]. "A román 'országőr'" [The Romanian "Guardian of the Nation"]. *Magyar Szemle*, Vol. 36 (1939), pp. 356-366.

Bíró, Sándor. "A kolozsvári egyetem a román uralom alatt" [The University of Cluj under Romanian rule]. In *Erdély Magyar Egyeteme* [Transylvania's Hungarian University]. Eds. György Bisztray, Attila T. Szabó, and Lajos Tamás. Kolozsvár, 1941, pp. 305-332.

Bíró, Sándor. *A Tribuna és a magyarországi román közvélemény* [The *Tribuna* and Romanian Public Opinion in Hungary]. Kolozsvár, 1942.

Bölöni, Miklós and Ürmösi, Károly. "A 14%-os iskolai segély és a magyar felekezeti iskolák" [The 14 percent subvention to schools and the Hungarian denominational schools]. *Kisebbségi Jogélet*, 1937.

Brătianu, Vintilă I. C. *Viața și opera lui Vintilă I. C. Bratianu*. Bucharest, 1936.

Breazu, Ion. "Literatura Tribunei." *Dacoromania*, Vol. 8 (1934/35), pp. 1-111.

Breazu, Ion. "Matei Millo în Transilvania și Banat (1870)." *Fraților Alexandru și Ion I. Lăpedatu, la împlinirea vârstei de 60 ani.* Bucharest, 1936, pp. 193-207.

Cărtile săteanului român. Păcatele noastre de Petre Suciu. Cluj-Gherla, 1903.

Ciato, Ludovic. *Problema minoritară în România-Mare.* Cluj, 1926.

Ciorogariu, Roman. *Zile trăite.* Oradea, 1926.

Clopoțel, Ion. *Revoluția din 1918 și unirea Ardealului cu România.* Cluj, 1926.

Colan, I. *Casina română din Brașov 1835-1935.* Brașov, 1935.

Colescu, Leonida. *Recensământul general al populațiunei Romăniei.* Bucharest, 1905.

Cornish, Louis C., ed. *Roumania Ten Years After* Boston, 1929.

Costa-Foru, C. G. *Abuzurile și crimele siguranței generale ale statului.* Bucharest, 1925.

Dare de seamă asupra învățământului primar din judeţul Mureș-Turda pe anul școlar 1924-1925. Tîrgu Mureș, 1926.

Dariu, Ion. *Arion, sau culegere de cânturi naționale spre întrebuinţarea tinerimei de ambe sexe.* Brașov, 1881.

Dariu, Ion. *Carte de cântece pentru tinerimea școlară.* Brașov, 1900.

Dávid, Iván. "Az erdélyi magyar színészet két évtizedes útja" [Two Decades of Hungarian Theater in Transylvania]. *Keleti Újság,* December 25, 1938.

Deér, József and Gáldi, László, eds. *Magyarok és románok* [Hungarians and Romanians], Vols. I-II, Budapest, 1943-44.

Dima, A. *Şcoala secundară în lumina bacalaureatului.* Bucharest, 1928.

678   Sándor Bíró

"Dokumentumok" [Documents]. *Magyar Kisebbség*, Vol. 10 (1931), pp. 305-320.

"Dokumentumok" [Documents]. *Magyar Kisebbség*, Vol. 13 (1934), pp. 350-359, 468-471.

Dragomir, Silviu. *La Transylvanie roumaine et ses minorités ethniques.* Bucharest, 1924.

Dragos, Gheorghe. *Cooperatia in Ardeal. Istorie — situatia actuala — perspective.* Bucharest, 1933.

Eisenmann, Louis. *Le compromis austro-hongrois de 1867.* Paris, 1904.

"Emlékirat a Ciuc-i Magánjavak ügyében" [Memorandum Regarding the Private Properties of Ciuc]. *Magyar Kisebbség*, Vol. 15 (1936), pp. 373-374.

Enciclopedia Romaniei. Vols. I-IV, Bucharest, 1938-43.

Enescu, Ion and Enescu, Iuliu. *Ardealul, Banatul, Crisana si Maramuresul din punct de vedere agricol, cultural si economic.* Bucharest, 1920.

"Események" [Events]. *Magyar Kisebbség*, Vol. 14 (1935), pp. 646-47.

"Események" [Events]. *Magyar Kisebbség*, Vol. 15 (1936), pp. 195-196, 258-59, 360, 394-395, 537-538, 601-604.

"Események" [Events]. *Magyar Kisebbség*, Vol. 16 (1937) pp. 18-19, 161-162, 298-299.

"Események" [Events]. *Magyar Kisebbség*, Vol. 17 (1938), pp. 62-66.

Fritz, László. "Az erdélyi román kultúrzóna ügye a Népszövetség előtt" [The Issue of the Romanian Cultural Zone of Transylvania in Front of the League of Nations]. *Magyar Kisebbség*, Vol. 11 (1932), pp. 348-352.

Fritz, László. "Románia egyenesadórendszere, mint a kisebbségellenes politika egyik harci eszköze," [Romania's Direct Tax System as a Weapon in its Anti-minorities Policies]. *Magyar Kisebbség*, Vol. 7 (1928), pp. 437-443.

Fritz, László. "Újabb kisebbségi jogsérelmek" [Further Minority Grievances]. *Magyar Kisebbség*, Vol. 10 (1931), pp. 783-785.

Fruma, Ioan. *Problema universității săsești și a instituției celor șapte juzi.* Sibiu, 1935.

Gál, Kelemen. "Az elemi iskolai rendelet román főpapok és államférfiak megvilágításában" [The Ordinance Regarding Primary Schools According to Romanian Ecclesiastics and Statemen]. *Magyar Kisebbség*, Vol. 3 (1924), pp. 2-17.

Garoflid, Constantin. *Chestia agraria în România.* n.p., n.d.

Garoflid, Constantin. "Regimul agrar în România." *Enciclopedia Romaniei*, Vol. I, pp. 577-585.

"Genfi hatás a Zam-Sancrai-i közbirtokosság ügyében" [The Impact of Geneva in the Affair of the Commonwealth of Zam-Sancrai]. *Magyar Kisebbség*, Vol. 15 (1936), pp. 339-342.

Ghibu, Onisifor. *Necesitatea revizuirii radicale a situaţiei confesiunilor din Transilvania*. Cluj, 1923.

Ghibu, Onisifor. *Politica religioasă şi minoritară a României. Fapte şi documente carii impun o nouă orientare*. Cluj, 1940.

Ghibu, Onisifor. *Şcoala românească din Transilvania şi Ungaria*. Bucharest, 1915.

Ghibu, Onisifor. *Un anachronism şi o sfidare: Statul roman-catolic ardelean*. Cluj, 1931.

Ghibu, Onisifor. *Viaţa şi organizatia bisericească şi şcolară in Transilvania şi Ungaria*. Bucharest, 1915.

Ghiulea, Nicolae. "Apărarea naţională." *Societatea de Mâine*, Vol. 3 (1926), pp. 509-510.

Gyárfás, Elemér. "A kisebbségi bankok és a Banca Naţională [Minority Banks and the Banca Naţională]. *Magyar Kisebbség*, Vol. 4 (1925) pp. 530-532.

Gyárfás, Elemér. "A pénzintézetek kínos kérdése" [The Difficult Issue of Financial Institutions]. *Magyar Kisebbség*, Vol. 6 (1927), pp. 475-477.

Gyárfás, Elemér. "Az ingatlan forgalom újabb korlátozása" [Further Restrictions on Real Estate Transactions]. *Magyar Kisebbség*, Vol. 16 (1937), pp. 196-201.

Gyárfás, Elemér. Felszólalása [His Intervention]. *Magyar Kisebbség*, Vol. 6 (1927), pp. 189-192.

Gyárfás, Elemér. Interpellációja [His Intervention]. *Magyar Kisebbség*, Vol. 9 (1930), pp. 412-414.

Gyárfás, Elemér. Interpellációja [His Intervention]. *Magyar Kisebbség*, Vol. 15 (1936), pp. 195-196.

Haret, Spiru C. *"Ale tale dintru ale tale." La implinirea celor ani*. Bucharest, 1911.

"Hogyan folytak a Népszövetségnek beígért egyezkedési tárgyalások a román kormány és a 'Csíki Magánjavak' megbizottai között?" [The Negotiations promised to the League of Nations between the Romanian Government and the Representatives of the Private Properties of Csík?]. *Magyar Kisebbség*, Vol. 11 (1932), pp. 161-167.

Iorga, Nicolae. *Histoire des roumains de la péninsule des Balkans*. Bucharest, 1919.

Iorga, Nicolae. *Istoria românilor*. Vols. I - X, Bucharest, 1936-39.

Iorga, Nicolae. *Les hongrois et la nationalité roumaine en 1909*. Vălenii de Munte, 1909.

680   Sándor Bíró

Iorga, Nicolae. *Pagini despre Besarabia de astăzi.* Vălenii de Munte, 1911.

Institutul Social Roman. *Politica externa a României.* Bucharest, 1925.

"Itéletek" [Judgments]. *Magyar Kisebbség,* Vol. 13 (1934), pp. 310-312; Vol. 14 (1935), pp. 475-479.

Iuga, A. *Cu privire la Vasile Lucaciu. Acte, documente, procese.* Baia Mare, n.d.

Jakabffy, Elemér. *Adatok a románság történetéhez a magyar uralom alatt* [Data to the History of the Romanians under Hungarian Rule]. Lugos, 1931.

Jakabffy, Elemér. "Astra és EMKE" [The Astra and the EMKE]. *Magyar Kisebbség,* Vol. 2 (1923), pp. 705-711.

Jakabffy, Elemér. *A románok hazánkban és a román királyságban* [The Romanians in Our Country and in the Kingdom of Romania]. Budapest, 1918.

Jakabffy, Elemér. "Dobrescu rendeletéhez" [Comments on Dobrescu's Directive]. *Magyar Kisebbség,* Vol. 9 (1930), pp. 273-275.

Jancsó, Benedek. "A katolikus egyház helyzete Romániában" [The Situation of the Catholic Church in Romania]. *Magyar Szemle,* Vol. 25 (1928), p. 59.

Jinga, Victor. "Migraţiunile demografice şi problema colonizărilor în România." *Analele Academiei de Înalte Studii Comerciale şi Indurstiale din Cluj.* Cluj, 1940.

Kántor, Lajos. "Az Erdélyi Múzeum-Egyesület története 1924-től napjainkig" [The History of the Transylvanian Museum Association from 1924 to the Present]. *Erdélyi Múzeum,* Vol. 35 (1930).

Kenéz, Béla. *Nép és föld* [The People and the Land]. Budapest, 1917.

Kiss, Árpád. "Az állami magyar tannyelvű elemi iskolák és magyar tagozatok" [State Primary Schools with Hungarian as the Language of Instruction and Hungarian Sections]. *Magyar Kisebbség,* Vol. 15 (1936), pp. 205-209, 547-564; Vol. 16 (1937), pp. 419-425.

Kniezsa, István. "Keletmagyarország helynevei" [Place Names in Eastern Hungary]. In *Magyarok és románok* [Hungarians and Romanians]. Vol. I, eds. József Deér and László Gáldi. Budapest, 1943, pp. 111-313.

Kovács, Árpád. "Etnikai aránytalanság a közjegyzői kamarákban" [Ethnic Disproportion in the Chambers of Notaries]. *Magyar Kisebbség,* Vol. 16 (1937), pp. 158-160.

Közigazgatási nemzeti kalendárium; hivatali és irodai használatra az 1914. évre [National Administrative Calendar for Official Use, for the Year 1914]. Budapest, n.d.

"L'Alsace-Lorraine, et l'Empire Germanique," *Revue des Deux Mondes* Vol. 38 (1880), pp. 721-757; Vol. 40 (1880), pp. 241-291.

La lutte contre l'absolutisme en Roumanie. Bucharest, 1923.

Lucaciu, Vasile. *Biserica Sfîntei Uniri a tuturor Românilor.* Baia Mare, 1892.

Lupaş, Ion. *Istoria bisericească a Românilor ardeleni.* Sibiu, 1918.

Lupaş, Ion. *Conţributiuni la istoria ziaristicei româneşti ardelene.* Sibiu, 1926.

Magyar Királyi Belügyminisztérium tiszti névtára [The List of Officials of the Royal Hungarian Ministry of the Interior]. Budapest, 1873.

Magyari, Piroska. *A magyarországi románok iskolaügye* [The issue of the Education of the Romanians of Hungary]. Szeged, 1936.

Magyar Szociáldemokrata Párt, *Az erdélyi románság küzdelme a román uralom alatt* [The Struggle of the Romanians of Transylvania under Romanian Rule]. Budapest, 1942.

Maneguţiu, N. *Alamanachul Sfîntului Nicolae.* Sibiu, 1902.

Memoriei prea fericitului Patriarh Miron. Caransebeş, 1939.

Mikó, Imre. "Az erdélyi magyarság sorsa a világháború után" [The Fate of the Hungarians of Transylvania after the World War]. In *Magyarok és románok,* II, eds., József Deér and László Gáldi. Budapest, 1943, pp. 208-250.

Mikó, Imre. *Huszonkét év. Az erdélyi magyarság politikai története 1918 december 1-töl 1940 augusztus 30-ig* [Twenty-two Years. The Political History of the Hungarians of Transylvania from December 1, 1918, to August 30, 1940]. Budapest, 1941.

Mikó, Imre. *Nemzetiségi jog és nemzetiségi politika* [The Rights of Nationalities and the Nationalities Policies]. Kolozsvár, 1944.

Ministerul Agricultură i şi Domeniilor. *L'agriculture en Roumanie: album statistique, publié à l'occasion du XIVᵉ Congrès International d'Agriculture.* Bucharest, 1929.

Moldovan, Silvestru. *Ţara noastră.* Sibiu, 1894.

Moldovan, Silvestru. *Zărandul şi Munţii Apuseni ai Transilvaniei.* Sibiu, 1898.

Moldovan, Silvestru and Togan, Nicolae. *Dicţionarul numirilor de localităţi cu poporaţiune română din Ungaria.* Sibiu, 1909.

Moteanu, C. *O primă etapă în politica de naţionalizare a vieţii economice.* Bucharest, n.d.

Nagy, Lajos. *A kisebbségek alkotmányjogi helyzete Nagy-Romániában.* [The Constitution Law and the Minorities in Greater Romania]. Kolozsvár, 1944.

Nicoale, H. Petre. *Băncile româneşti din Ardeal şi Banat.* Sibiu, 1936.

682   Sándor Bíró

Oberding, József György. "A magyar szövetkezetek jogi helyzete Romániában" [The Legal Status of the Hungarian Cooperatives in Romania]. *Magyar Kisebbség*, Vol. 18 (1939), pp. 189-196.

Păcăţian, V. Teodor. *Cartea de aur sau luptele politice-naţionale ale românilor de sub coroana ungară*. Vols. I-VIII, Sibiu, 1902-1915.

Pál, Gábor. "A székelyföldi közbirtokok és az agrárreform" [Commonwealths of the Székely Region and the Land Reform]. *Magyar Kisebbség*, Vol. 2 (1923), pp. 4-15 and 46-57.

Panaitescu, P. P. "Planurile lui Ioan Câmpineanu pentru unitatea naţională a românilor. *Anuarul Institutului de Istorie Naţională, Cluj*, Vol. 3 (1924/25), pp. 63-106.

Papp, József. "Epizódok a románság történetéből a magyar uralom alatt" [Episodes from the History of the Romanians under Hungarian Rule]. *Magyar Kisebbség*, Vol. 10 (1931), Vol. II (1932).

Pesti, Alfréd. *Magyarország orvosainak évkönyve és címtára*. [Yearbook and Register of Physicians in Hungary]. Budapest, 1914.

Petrescu, P. *Monografia institutului de credit şi de economii "Albina"*. N.p., n.d.

Pop, Valer. *Accordul dela Roma*. Cluj, 1934.

Posch, Mihály, ed. *Községi és közjegyzők zsebnaptára* [Pocket Diary for Community and District Notaries], Budapest, 1912-1914.

Poslușnicu, M. *Istoria muzicii la români*. Bucharest, 1900.

Prie, Octavian. "Prea multe şcoli ungureşti în Ardeal." *Ţara Noastră* (1923), pp. 1174-1176.

Procesul de presă al ziarului "Foia Poporului". Sibiu, 1894.

Program'a gimnasiului Sup. Gr. Cat. din Blasiu pe anul şcolar 1868-69. Blasiu, 1869.

Puşcariu, Ioan Cavaler de. *Notiţe despre întâmplările contemporane*. Sibiu, 1913.

Puşcariu, Sextil. *Răsunetul războiului pentru independenţa în Ardeal*. Bucharest, 1927.

Recensământul general al populaţiei României din 29 Decemvrie 1930. Vol. II, Bucharest, 1938-1941.

"Románok rólunk," [Romanians About Us]. *Magyar Kisebbség*, Vol. 13 (1934), pp. 255-256; Vol. 16 (1937), pp. 107-108.

Roşca, Eusebiu. *Monografia Institutului seminalial teologic-pedagogic "Andreian."* Sibiu, 1911.

Roşca, Eusebiu. *Monografia mitropoliei ortodoxe române a Ardealului*. Sibiu, 1937.

Rugonfalvi Kiss, István. *A nemes székely nemzet képe* [A Portrait of the Noble Székely Nation]. Vols. I-III, Debrecen, 1939.

Scheffler, János. "Az Erdélyi Katolikus Status küzdelmes húsz éve"
[The Twenty-year Struggle of the Catholic Status of Transylvania].
Magyar Szemle, Vol. 38 (1941).
Sebess, Dénes. *Adatok a magyar agrárpolitikához a jobbágyság
felszabadítása után* [Contribution to the Study of Hungarian Land
Policies since the Emancipation of the Serfs]. Budapest, 1908.
*Şematismul Veneratului Cler at Arhidiecezei Metropolitane gr.- cat.
române de Alba Iulia şi Făgăraş pe anul Domnului 1900.* Blaj, 1909.
Serbările dela Blaj. Blaj, 1911.
Silasi, Gregoriu. "Apologie. Discusiuni filologice şi istorice maghiare
privitoare la români, învederite şi rectificate de—. I. Paul Hunfalvy
despre Cronica lui George Gav. Şincai." *Tribuna*, 1884, Nos. 15-17.
Sirianu, Mircea. *La question de Transylvanie et l'unité politique
roumaine.* Paris, 1916.
Slavici, Ion. *Amintiri.* Bucharest, 1924.
Slavici, Ion. *Închisorile mele.* Bucharest, 1921.
Slavici, Ion. *Lumea prin care am trecut.* Bucharest, 1930.
Slavici, Ion. *Politica naţională română.* Bucharest, 1915.
Slavici, Ion. *Românii din Ardeal.* Bucharest, 1910.
Şorban, George. *Administraţia Ardealului.* Dej, 1921.
Spectator (Miklós Krenner). "A tétova sajtó" [The Hesitant Press].
Magyar Kisebbség, Vol. 2 (1923), pp. 665-677.
Statisztikai, Hivatal. A Magyar Korona Országainak Mezőgazdasági
Statisztikája [Agricultural Statistics Pertaining to the Lands of the
Hungarian Crown], Vols. I-V. Budapest, 1897-1900.
Suciu, Petre. *Clasele noastre sociale în Ardeal.* Turda, 1930.
Suciu, Petre. *Judeţul Turda. Schiţă monografică.* N.p., n.d.
Suciu, Petre. "Problema oraşelor ardelene," *Societatea de Mâine.* Vol.
I. (1924), pp. 512-513.
Suciu, Petre. *Probleme ardelene.* Cluj, 1924.
Suciu, Petre. *Proprietatea agrară in Ardeal.* Cluj, 1931.
Szabó, Jenő. *A görög-katolikus magyarság utolsó kálvária útja* [The Last
Calvary of the Uniate Hungarians]. N.p., n.d.
Szabó, T. Attila. "Az erdélyi tudományos élet húsz éve" [Twenty Years
of Scientific Life in Transylvania]. *Keleti Újság*, December 25, 1938.
Szász, Zsombor. *Erdély Romániában. Népkisebbségi tanulmány.*
[Transylvania as Part of Romania. A Study in Ethnic Minorities].
Budapest, 1927.
Szövérdi, Zoltán. "Milyen az erdélyi agrárreform a valóságban" [What
the Transylvanian Land-reform is Really Like] *Magyar Szemle*, Vol.
25 (1928).
Tokaji, László. *Eladó ország* [A Country for Sale]. Kolozsvár, 1913.

Tóth, Zoltán. Az "Astra" románosító tevékenysége a Székelyföldön [The Rumanianizing Activities of Astra in the Székely Region]. Kolozsvár, 1942.

Triteanu, Lazăr. Şcoala noastră 1850-1916. Zona culturală. Sibiu, 1919.

Tulbure, George. "Aspecte din politica şcolară," Ţara Bârsei revista literara, 1933.

Ürmösi-Maurer, Béla. Kisebbségi kérdések. [Minority Issues], Cluj-Kolozsvár, 1937.

Vágó, Ferenc. "A Magyarországi községi és közjegyzők évkönyve az 1884-85 évekre" [Yearbook of the Community and District Notaries of Hungary, for the Years 1884-85]. Nagyvárad, 1885.

Venczel, József. Az erdélyi román földbirtokreform [The Romanian Land-reform in Transylvania]. Kolozsvár, 1942.

Name Index for Part I

686 Sándor Bíró

Barkóczi 122
Barlovan, Petru 66
Bărnuţiu, Simion 251-252, 287
Bârsan, Zacarias 294
Bârseanu, Andrei 250
Bartha 267
Bartoc 122
Bartók 122
Béla Jankovich 177
Benedek, Artúr 52, 267
Beöthy, Andor 259
Berdean, Florea 317
Besanu 49
Bethlen, Gábor 263
Bethlen, Count István 73
Bíró, Sándor ix
Birtolon, Emilia 267
Bismarck, Otto von 114
Björnson, Björnstjerne 353
Blaga, Iosif 172, 265
Bob, Ilieş 63
Boeriu, George 48
Bogdan, M. 204, 265
Bogdan-Duica, Gheorghe 255
Bogyi, Traian 57
Bohatielu, Alexandru 47, 48
Bőhm, Lajos 52
Bohoczel, Alexandru 62
Bordan, Octavian 63
Bordia, Alexandru 65
Borgovan, Vasile 259
Borlea, Sigmund 48, 51
Botta, Emil 63
Bousznera, Guido 51
Brabat, Alexandru 57
Brâncovan, Bibescu 287
Branişte, Valeriu 110, 350
Brătescu, I. 216
Brătianu, Ion C. (1821-1891) xvi, 95, 292, 331
Bredean, Athanaz 65
Brediceanu, Coriolan 63, 102, 103
Bretter, Gizella 267

Name Index for Part II

Costăchescu, Nicolae 479
Crăciunescu 467
Creţu 527
Cristea, Miron (Ilie) 479
Csáki, József 640
Csala family 488
Czeglédi, Miklós 436
Daday, Lóránd 615
Dajka, Margit 604
Dávid, Ferenc 502
Deák, Ferenc 446, 633
Demeter, Béla 635
Demetrescu 467
Dénes, Sándor 635
Diaconescu, Nicolae 527
Dobay, István 488
Dobrescu, Aurelian 447
Dobrota, Oktavian 635
Dogar, Petru (Péter Kádár) 568
Dolci 465
Drăganu, Nicolae 591
Dragomir, Silviu 526, 536, 571, 640
Dsida, Jenő 614
Duca, Ion G. 411, 426, 451
Duica, Bogdan 486
Durcovici 469
Erdős, Bálint Mrs. 425
Fadrusz, János 633, 634
Farkas 517
Farkas family 415
Farkas, Mózes 415
Feilitzsch, Baron Arthur 470
Fényes, Alíz 605, 606
Figus, Albert 634
Filipescu, Grigore N. 640
Fodor family 488
Foru, Costa G. 623
Franasovici, Richard 410
Francis Joseph, Emperor and King 384, 388
Frint, Lajos 470
Gálffy, Lőrinc 483
Gândea, Aurelian 487

Geographic Index for Part I

Balázsfalva [Blaj] 21, 35, 49, 52, 65, 84, 95, 108, 129, 158, 167, 172,
    194, 243, 245, 246, 248, 251-255, 257, 261, 263, 264, 266, 267-273,
    279, 288, 291, 295, 331, 334, 337, 339, 342, 343, 362
Bâle [Basel] 113
Balkan peninsula 158
Balkan 214, 216, 300, 323, 363, 372, 373
Balomir [Balomirul de Cîmp] 152
Bánát [Bánság, Banat] 8, 32, 44, 54, 198, 214
Bánffyhunyad [Huedin] 62
Banica [Băniţa] 18
Bărăbant [Borbánd] 115
Barátos [Brăteşti, Brateş] 121
Bărnuţiu 252
Báródbeznye [Bezneaca] 121
Barosság [Barcaság, Ţara Bîrsei] 10
Barót [Baraolt] 7
Basel [Bâle] 113
Béganyiresd [Breazova] 173
Belényes [Beiuş] 40, 49, 65, 245-247, 253, 255, 258-261, 267, 268
Belfast 364
Belgrade 179
Belső-Szolnok [Szolnok Doboka] county 47, 86
Bendorf [Beneşti] 174
Berekszó [Bîrsău] 174
Berlin 254, 287
Bern ix
Bernád [Bernadea] 173
Besenyő [Viişoara] 70
Bessarabia xiii, xv, 10, 29, 33, 56, 74, 119, 182, 214-216, 297-299,
    360-362, 372, 373
Beszterce [Bistriţa] county xv, 6, 7, 24, 25, 35, 63, 167, 170, 108, 330,
    204, 205
Beszterce-Naszód [Bistriţa-Năsăud] county 3, 10, 14, 17, 23, 25, 38, 50,
    53, 68, 96, 98, 99, 103, 104, 116, 175, 228
Beszterce-Aranyos River Basin 5
Bethlen [Beclean] 7, 66, 333
Bezneaca [Báródbeznye] 121
Bichiş [Bükkös] 114
Bihar [Bihor] county xiv, 23, 38, 68, 92, 159, 259, 296, 321
Birda [Birola] 173
Blaj [Balázsfalva] 267, 292
Boholc [Boholţ] 174

716 Sándor Bíró

Gyergyószentmiklós [Gheorgheni] 7, 62
Gyergyótölgyes [Tulgheş] 65
Gyulafehérvár [Alba Iulia] 58, 61, 62, 87, 94, 129, 162, 163, 168, 183,
    263, 334, 335
Gyulavidék 41
Hajdúdorog 156, 157
Halumány 173
Hari [Hariş] 114
Háromszék [Trei Scaune] county xiv, 10, 14, 50, 72
Határszög 116
Hátszeg [Haţeg] 35, 62, 66
Hegyeslak [Hăzeşti] 174
Herepe [Herepeia] 114
Hétfalu [Şapte Sate] 10
Honoros [Honoriei] 23
Hortobágyfalva [Cornăţel] 174
Hungary ix, xi, xii, xiii, xvii, xviii, xix, 1, 4, 5, 8, 12, 14, 15, 26, 27, 29,
    31-35, 37, 41-42, 44, 46-47, 50, 52, 55, 56, 59, 69, 70, 72, 81, 82, 84,
    85, 106, 107, 114, 117-120, 122, 123, 128, 132, 136, 139, 141, 142,
    147, 153, 158-160, 170, 178, 179-181, 183, 189, 190, 196, 205,
    208-210, 212-218, 221, 222, 227, 231, 232, 236, 246, 247, 250-254,
    256, 265-268, 272-274, 276, 277, 278, 282-298, 300-302, 276, 309-314,
    322, 326-332, 335-337, 339-344, 346-348, 352, 353, 354, 355, 358-360,
    362-364, 370-373
Hunyad [Hunedoara] county 14, 19, 38, 45, 50, 53, 63, 67-69, 86, 87, 96,
    98-100, 103-106, 202, 221, 240, 241, 245, 268, 319
Huszár 23
Ialomiţa county 27
Iaşi county 27, 28, 60, 121, 287, 298
Igen [Ighiu] 114, 359
Ilfov county 27
Illenbák [Ilimbav] 174
Ilva [Lunca Bradului] 8, 65
Northern Ireland 363
Isacova 299
Istvánlak 173
Italy 190
Iuliu Maniu 43
Izgár [Izgar] 173
Izmail 181
Jakabfalva [Iacobeni] 174
Jánosda [Ianoşda] 174

Geographic Index for Part II

727